GENERAL MOTORS | CAMARO 1982-92 REPAIR MANUAL

CHILTON'S

Covers all U.S. and Canadian models of Chevrolet Camaro

by **Don Schnell**, A.S.E., S.A.E.

CHILTON *Automotive Books*

PUBLISHED BY **HAYNES NORTH AMERICA**, Inc.

Haynes®

AUTOMOTIVE PARTS & ACCESSORIES ASSOCIATION MEMBER

Manufactured in USA
© 1992 Haynes North America, Inc.
ISBN 0-8019-8260-X
Library of Congress Catalog Card No. 91-058869
13 14 15 16 17 9876543210

Haynes Publishing Group
Sparkford Nr Yeovil
Somerset BA22 7JJ England

Haynes North America, Inc
861 Lawrence Drive
Newbury Park
California 91320 USA

ABCDE
FGHIJ
KLMNO
PQRS 2

4F2

Contents

Contents

SAFETY NOTICE

Proper service and repair procedures are vital to the safe, reliable operation of all motor vehicles, as well as the personal safety of those performing repairs. This manual outlines procedures for servicing and repairing vehicles using safe, effective methods. The procedures contain many NOTES, CAUTIONS and WARNINGS which should be followed, along with standard procedures to eliminate the possibility of personal injury or improper service which could damage the vehicle or compromise its safety.

It is important to note that repair procedures and techniques, tools and parts for servicing motor vehicles, as well as the skill and experience of the individual performing the work vary widely. It is not possible to anticipate all of the conceivable ways or conditions under which vehicles may be serviced, or to provide cautions as to all possible hazards that may result. Standard and accepted safety precautions and equipment should be used when handling toxic or flammable fluids, and safety goggles or other protection should be used during cutting, grinding, chiseling, prying, or any other process that can cause material removal or projectiles.

Some procedures require the use of tools specially designed for a specific purpose. Before substituting another tool or procedure, you must be completely satisfied that neither your personal safety, nor the performance of the vehicle will be endangered.

Although information in this manual is based on industry sources and is complete as possible at the time of publication, the possibility exists that some car manufacturers made later changes which could not be included here. While striving for total accuracy, the authors or publishers cannot assume responsibility for any errors, changes or omissions that may occur in the compilation of this data.

PART NUMBERS

Part numbers listed in this reference are not recommendations by Haynes North America, Inc. for any product brand name. They are references that can be used with interchange manuals and aftermarket supplier catalogs to locate each brand supplier's discrete part number.

SPECIAL TOOLS

Special tools are recommended by the vehicle manufacturer to perform their specific job. Use has been kept to a minimum, but where absolutely necessary, they are referred to in the text by the part number of the tool manufacturer. These tools can be purchased, under the appropriate part number, from your local dealer or regional distributor, or an equivalent tool can be purchased locally from a tool supplier or parts outlet. Before substituting any tool for the one recommended, read the SAFETY NOTICE at the top of this page.

ACKNOWLEDGMENTS

This publication contains material that is reproduced and distributed under a license from Ford Motor Company. No further reproduction or distribution of the Ford Motor Company material is allowed without the express written permission from Ford Motor Company.

Portions of materials contained herein have been reprinted with the permission of General Motors Corporation, Service Technology Group.

1

GENERAL
INFORMATION
AND
MAINTENANCE

HOW TO USE THIS BOOK

This Chilton's Total Car Care manual is intended to help you learn more about the inner workings of your Camaro while saving you money on its upkeep and operation.

The beginning of the book will likely be referred to the most, since that is where you will find information for maintenance and tune-up. The other sections deal with the more complex systems of your vehicle. Systems (from engine through brakes) are covered to the extent that the average do-it-yourselfer can attempt. This book will not explain such things as rebuilding a differential because the expertise required and the special tools necessary make this uneconomical. It will, however, give you detailed instructions to help you change your own brake pads and shoes, replace spark plugs, and perform many more jobs that can save you money and help avoid expensive problems.

A secondary purpose of this book is a reference for owners who want to understand their vehicle and/or their mechanics better.

Where to Begin

Before removing any bolts, read through the entire procedure. This will give you the overall view of what tools and supplies will be required. So read ahead and plan ahead. Each operation should be approached logically and all procedures thoroughly understood before attempting any work.

If repair of a component is not considered practical, we tell you how to remove the part and then how to install the new or rebuilt replacement. In this way, you at least save labor costs.

Avoiding Trouble

Many procedures in this book require you to "label and disconnect . . . "a group of lines, hoses or wires. Don't be think you can remember where everything goes—you won't. If you hook up vacuum or fuel lines incorrectly, the vehicle may run poorly, if at all. If you hook up electrical wiring incorrectly, you may instantly learn a very expensive lesson.

You don't need to know the proper name for each hose or line. A piece of masking tape on the hose and a piece on its fitting will allow you to assign your own label. As long as you remember your own code, the lines can be reconnected by matching your tags. Remember that tape will dissolve in gasoline or solvents; if a part is to be washed or cleaned, use another method of identification. A permanent felt-tipped marker or a metal scribe can be very handy for marking metal parts. Remove any tape or paper labels after assembly.

Maintenance or Repair?

Maintenance includes routine inspections, adjustments, and replacement of parts which show signs of normal wear. Maintenance compensates for wear or deterioration. Repair implies that something has broken or is not working. A need for a repair is often caused by lack of maintenance. for example: draining and refilling automatic transmission fluid is maintenance recommended at specific intervals. Failure to do this can shorten the life of the transmission/transaxle, requiring very expensive repairs. While no maintenance program can prevent items from eventually breaking or wearing out, a general rule is true: MAINTENANCE IS CHEAPER THAN REPAIR.

Two basic mechanic's rules should be mentioned here. First, whenever the left side of the vehicle or engine is referred to, it means the driver's side. Conversely, the right side of the vehicle means the passenger's side. Second, screws and bolts are removed by turning counterclockwise, and tightened by turning clockwise unless specifically noted.

Safety is always the most important rule. Constantly be aware of the dangers involved in working on an automobile and take the proper precautions. Please refer to the information in this section regarding SERVICING YOUR VEHICLE SAFELY and the SAFETY NOTICE on the acknowledgment page.

Avoiding the Most Common Mistakes

Pay attention to the instructions provided. There are 3 common mistakes in mechanical work:

1. Incorrect order of assembly, disassembly or adjustment. When taking something apart or putting it together, performing steps in the wrong order usually just costs you extra time; however, it CAN break something. Read the entire procedure before beginning. Perform everything in the order in which the instructions say you should, even if you can't see a reason for it. When you're taking apart something that is very intricate, you might want to draw a picture of how it looks when assembled in order to make sure you get everything back in its proper position. When making adjustments, perform them in the proper order. One adjustment possibly will affect another.

2. Overtorquing (or undertorquing). While it is more common for overtorquing to cause damage, undertorquing may allow a fastener to vibrate loose causing serious damage. Especially when dealing with aluminum parts, pay attention to torque specifications and utilize a torque wrench in assembly. If a torque figure is not available, remember that if you are using the right tool to perform the job, you will probably not have to strain yourself to get a fastener tight enough. The pitch of most threads is so slight that the tension you put on the wrench will be multiplied many times in actual force on what you are tightening.

There are many commercial products available for ensuring that fasteners won't come loose, even if they are not torqued just right (a very common brand is Loctite®). If you're worried about getting something together tight enough to hold, but loose enough to avoid mechanical damage during assembly, one of these products might offer substantial insurance. Before choosing a threadlocking compound, read the label on the package and make sure the product is compatible with the materials, fluids, etc. involved.

3. Crossthreading. This occurs when a part such as a bolt is screwed into a nut or casting at the wrong angle and forced. Crossthreading is more likely to occur if access is difficult. It helps to clean and then lubricate fasteners, then to start threading the bolt, spark plug, etc. with your fingers. If you encounter resistance, unscrew the part and start over again at a different angle until it can be inserted and turned several times without much effort. Keep in mind that many parts have tapered threads, so that gentle turning will automatically bring the part you're threading to the proper angle. Don't put a wrench on the part until it's been tightened a couple of turns by hand. If you suddenly encounter resistance, and the part has not seated fully, don't force it. Pull it back out to make sure it's clean and threading properly.

Be sure to take your time and be patient, and always plan ahead. Allow yourself ample time to perform repairs and maintenance.

TOOLS AND EQUIPMENT

▶ **See Figures 1 thru 15**

Without the proper tools and equipment it is impossible to properly service your vehicle. It would be virtually impossible to catalog every tool that you would need to perform all of the operations in this book. It would be unwise for the amateur to rush out and buy an expensive set of tools on the theory that he/she may need one or more of them at some time.

The best approach is to proceed slowly, gathering a good quality set of those tools that are used most frequently. Don't be misled by the low cost of bargain tools. It is far better to spend a little more for better quality. Forged wrenches, 6 or 12-point sockets and fine tooth ratchets are by far preferable to their less expensive counterparts. As any good mechanic can tell you, there are few worse experiences than trying to work on a vehicle with bad tools. Your monetary savings will be far outweighed by frustration and mangled knuckles.

Begin accumulating those tools that are used most frequently: those associated with routine maintenance and tune-up. In addition to the normal assortment of screwdrivers and pliers, you should have the following tools:

• Wrenches/sockets and combination open end/box end wrenches in sizes ⅛–¾ in. and/or 3mm–19mm 13⁄16 in. or ⅝ in. spark plug socket (depending on plug type).

➡**If possible, buy various length socket drive extensions. Universal-joint and wobble extensions can be extremely useful, but be careful when using them, as they can change the amount of torque applied to the socket.**

• Jackstands for support.
• Oil filter wrench.

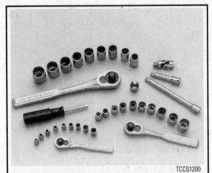

Fig. 1 All but the most basic procedures will require an assortment of ratchets and sockets

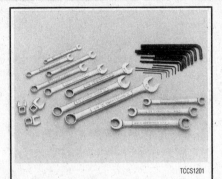

Fig. 2 In addition to ratchets, a good set of wrenches and hex keys will be necessary

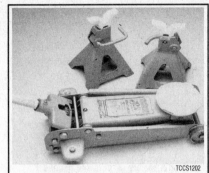

Fig. 3 A hydraulic floor jack and a set of jackstands are essential for lifting and supporting the vehicle

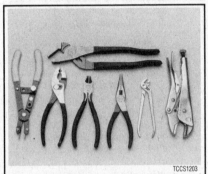

Fig. 4 An assortment of pliers, grippers and cutters will be handy for old rusted parts and stripped bolt heads

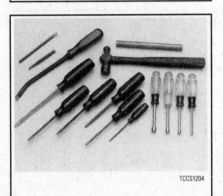

Fig. 5 Various drivers, chisels and prybars are great tools to have in your toolbox

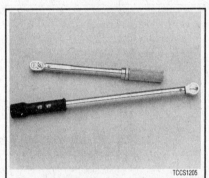

Fig. 6 Many repairs will require the use of a torque wrench to assure the components are properly fastened

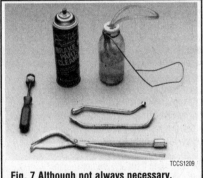

Fig. 7 Although not always necessary, using specialized brake tools will save time

Fig. 8 A few inexpensive lubrication tools will make maintenance easier

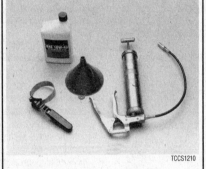

Fig. 9 Various pullers, clamps and separator tools are needed for many larger, more complicated repairs

- Spout or funnel for pouring fluids.
- Grease gun for chassis lubrication (unless your vehicle is not equipped with any grease fittings)
- Hydrometer for checking the battery (unless equipped with a sealed, maintenance-free battery).
- A container for draining oil and other fluids.
- Rags for wiping up the inevitable mess.

In addition to the above items there are several others that are not absolutely necessary, but handy to have around. These include an equivalent oil absorbent gravel, like cat litter, and the usual supply of lubricants, antifreeze and fluids. This is a basic list for routine maintenance, but only your personal needs and desire can accurately determine your list of tools.

After performing a few projects on the vehicle, you'll be amazed at the other tools and non-tools on your workbench. Some useful household items are: a large turkey baster or siphon, empty coffee cans and ice trays (to store parts), a ball of twine, electrical tape for wiring, small rolls of colored tape for tagging lines or hoses, markers and pens, a note pad, golf tees (for plugging vacuum lines), metal coat hangers or a roll of mechanic's wire (to hold things out of the way), dental pick or similar long, pointed probe, a strong magnet, and a small mirror (to see into recesses and under manifolds).

A more advanced set of tools, suitable for tune-up work, can be drawn up easily. While the tools are slightly more sophisticated, they need not be outrageously expensive. There are several inexpensive tach/dwell meters on the market that are every bit as good for the average mechanic as a professional model. Just be sure that it goes to a least 1200–1500 rpm on the tach scale and that it works on 4, 6 and 8-cylinder engines. The key to these purchases is to make them with an eye towards adaptability and wide range. A basic list of tune-up tools could include:

- Tach/dwell meter.
- Spark plug wrench and gapping tool.
- Feeler gauges for valve adjustment.
- Timing light.

The choice of a timing light should be made carefully. A light which works on the DC current supplied by the vehicle's battery is the best choice; it should

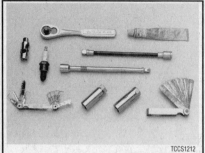

Fig. 10 A variety of tools and gauges should be used for spark plug gapping and installation

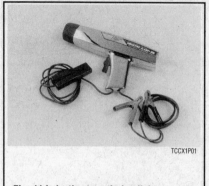

Fig. 11 Inductive type timing light

Fig. 12 A screw-in type compression gauge is recommended for compression testing

Fig. 13 A vacuum/pressure tester is necessary for many testing procedures

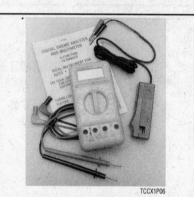

Fig. 14 Most modern automotive multimeters incorporate many helpful features

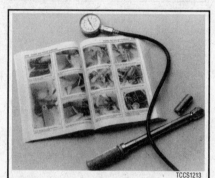

Fig. 15 Proper information is vital, so always have a Chilton Total Car Care manual handy

have a xenon tube for brightness. On any vehicle with an electronic ignition system, a timing light with an inductive pickup that clamps around the No. 1 spark plug cable is preferred.

In addition to these basic tools, there are several other tools and gauges you may find useful. These include:

• Compression gauge. The screw-in type is slower to use, but eliminates the possibility of a faulty reading due to escaping pressure.

• Manifold vacuum gauge.

• 12V test light.

• A combination volt/ohmmeter

• Induction Ammeter. This is used for determining whether or not there is current in a wire. These are handy for use if a wire is broken somewhere in a wiring harness.

As a final note, you will probably find a torque wrench necessary for all but the most basic work. The beam type models are perfectly adequate, although the newer click types (breakaway) are easier to use. The click type torque wrenches tend to be more expensive. Also keep in mind that all types of torque wrenches should be periodically checked and/or recalibrated. You will have to decide for yourself which better fits your pocketbook, and purpose.

Special Tools

Normally, the use of special factory tools is avoided for repair procedures, since these are not readily available for the do-it-yourself mechanic. When it is possible to perform the job with more commonly available tools, it will be pointed out, but occasionally, a special tool was designed to perform a specific function and should be used. Before substituting another tool, you should be convinced that neither your safety nor the performance of the vehicle will be compromised.

Special tools can usually be purchased from an automotive parts store or from your dealer. In some cases special tools may be available directly from the tool manufacturer.

SERVICING YOUR VEHICLE SAFELY

▶ **See Figures 16, 17 and 18**

It is virtually impossible to anticipate all of the hazards involved with automotive maintenance and service, but care and common sense will prevent most accidents.

The rules of safety for mechanics range from "don't smoke around gasoline," to "use the proper tool(s) for the job." The trick to avoiding injuries is to develop safe work habits and to take every possible precaution.

Do's

• Do keep a fire extinguisher and first aid kit handy.

• Do wear safety glasses or goggles when cutting, drilling, grinding or prying, even if you have 20–20 vision. If you wear glasses for the sake of vision, wear safety goggles over your regular glasses.

• Do shield your eyes whenever you work around the battery. Batteries contain sulfuric acid. In case of contact with, flush the area with water or a mixture of water and baking soda, then seek immediate medical attention.

• Do use safety stands (jackstands) for any undervehicle service. Jacks are for raising vehicles; jackstands are for making sure the vehicle stays raised until you want it to come down.

• Do use adequate ventilation when working with any chemicals or hazardous materials. Like carbon monoxide, the asbestos dust resulting from some brake lining wear can be hazardous in sufficient quantities.

• Do disconnect the negative battery cable when working on the electrical system. The secondary ignition system contains EXTREMELY HIGH VOLTAGE. In some cases it can even exceed 50,000 volts.

• Do follow manufacturer's directions whenever working with potentially hazardous materials. Most chemicals and fluids are poisonous.

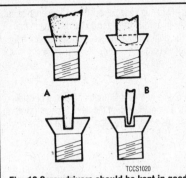

Fig. 16 Screwdrivers should be kept in good condition to prevent injury or damage which could result if the blade slips from the screw

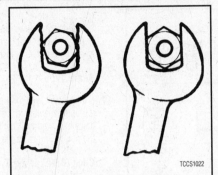

Fig. 17 Using the correct size wrench will help prevent the possibility of rounding off a nut

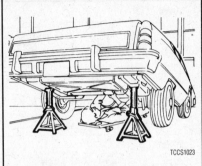

Fig. 18 NEVER work under a vehicle unless it is supported using safety stands (jackstands)

• Do properly maintain your tools. Loose hammerheads, mushroomed punches and chisels, frayed or poorly grounded electrical cords, excessively worn screwdrivers, spread wrenches (open end), cracked sockets, slipping ratchets, or faulty droplight sockets can cause accidents.

• Likewise, keep your tools clean; a greasy wrench can slip off a bolt head, ruining the bolt and often harming your knuckles in the process.

• Do use the proper size and type of tool for the job at hand. Do select a wrench or socket that fits the nut or bolt. The wrench or socket should sit straight, not cocked.

• Do, when possible, pull on a wrench handle rather than push on it, and adjust your stance to prevent a fall.

• Do be sure that adjustable wrenches are tightly closed on the nut or bolt and pulled so that the force is on the side of the fixed jaw.

• Do strike squarely with a hammer; avoid glancing blows.

• Do set the parking brake and block the drive wheels if the work requires a running engine.

Don'ts

• Don't run the engine in a garage or anywhere else without proper ventilation—EVER! Carbon monoxide is poisonous; it takes a long time to leave the human body and you can build up a deadly supply of it in your system by simply breathing in a little at a time. You may not realize you are slowly poisoning yourself. Always use power vents, windows, fans and/or open the garage door.

• Don't work around moving parts while wearing loose clothing. Short sleeves are much safer than long, loose sleeves. Hard-toed shoes with neoprene soles protect your toes and give a better grip on slippery surfaces. Watches and jewelry is not safe working around a vehicle. Long hair should be tied back under a hat or cap.

• Don't use pockets for toolboxes. A fall or bump can drive a screwdriver deep into your body. Even a rag hanging from your back pocket can wrap around a spinning shaft or fan.

• Don't smoke when working around gasoline, cleaning solvent or other flammable material.

• Don't smoke when working around the battery. When the battery is being charged, it gives off explosive hydrogen gas.

• Don't use gasoline to wash your hands; there are excellent soaps available. Gasoline contains dangerous additives which can enter the body through a cut or through your pores. Gasoline also removes all the natural oils from the skin so that bone dry hands will suck up oil and grease.

• Don't service the air conditioning system unless you are equipped with the necessary tools and training. When liquid or compressed gas refrigerant is released to atmospheric pressure it will absorb heat from whatever it contacts. This will chill or freeze anything it touches.

• Don't use screwdrivers for anything other than driving screws! A screwdriver used as an prying tool can snap when you least expect it, causing injuries. At the very least, you'll ruin a good screwdriver.

• Don't use an emergency jack (that little ratchet, scissors, or pantograph jack supplied with the vehicle) for anything other than changing a flat! These jacks are only intended for emergency use out on the road; they are NOT designed as a maintenance tool. If you are serious about maintaining your vehicle yourself, invest in a hydraulic floor jack of at least a 1½ ton capacity, and at least two sturdy jackstands.

FASTENERS, MEASUREMENTS AND CONVERSIONS

Bolts, Nuts and Other Threaded Retainers

▶ See Figures 19 and 20

Although there are a great variety of fasteners found in the modern car or truck, the most commonly used retainer is the threaded fastener (nuts, bolts, screws, studs, etc.). Most threaded retainers may be reused, provided that they are not damaged in use or during the repair. Some retainers (such as stretch bolts or torque prevailing nuts) are designed to deform when tightened or in use and should not be reinstalled.

Whenever possible, we will note any special retainers which should be replaced during a procedure. But you should always inspect the condition of a retainer when it is removed and replace any that show signs of damage. Check all threads for rust or corrosion which can increase the torque necessary to achieve the desired clamp load for which that fastener was originally selected. Additionally, be sure that the driver surface of the fastener has not been compromised by rounding or other damage. In some cases a driver surface may become only partially rounded, allowing the driver to catch in only one direction. In many of these occurrences, a fastener may be installed and tightened, but the driver would not be able to grip and loosen the fastener again.

If you must replace a fastener, whether due to design or damage, you must ALWAYS be sure to use the proper replacement. In all cases, a retainer of the same design, material and strength should be used. Markings on the heads of most bolts will help determine the proper strength of the fastener. The same material, thread and pitch must be selected to assure proper installation and safe operation of the vehicle afterwards.

Thread gauges are available to help measure a bolt or stud's thread. Most automotive and hardware stores keep gauges available to help you select the proper size. In a pinch, you can use another nut or bolt for a thread gauge. If the bolt you are replacing is not too badly damaged, you can select a match by finding another bolt which will thread in its place. If you find a nut which threads properly onto the damaged bolt, then use that nut to help select the replacement bolt.

❉❉ WARNING

Be aware that when you find a bolt with damaged threads, you may also find the nut or drilled hole it was threaded into has also been damaged. If this is the case, you may have to drill and tap the hole, replace the nut or otherwise repair the threads. NEVER try to force a replacement bolt to fit into the damaged threads.

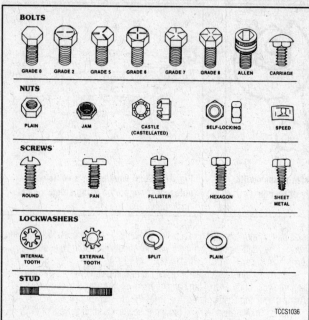

Fig. 19 There are many different types of threaded retainers found on vehicles

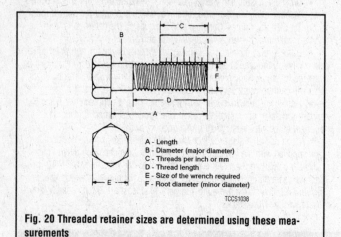

A - Length
B - Diameter (major diameter)
C - Threads per inch or mm
D - Thread length
E - Size of the wrench required
F - Root diameter (minor diameter)

TCCS1038

Fig. 20 Threaded retainer sizes are determined using these measurements

Torque

Torque is defined as the measurement of resistance to turning or rotating. It tends to twist a body about an axis of rotation. A common example of this would be tightening a threaded retainer such as a nut, bolt or screw. Measuring torque is one of the most common ways to help assure that a threaded retainer has been properly fastened.

When tightening a threaded fastener, torque is applied in three distinct areas, the head, the bearing surface and the clamp load. About 50 percent of the measured torque is used in overcoming bearing friction. This is the friction between the bearing surface of the bolt head, screw head or nut face and the base material or washer (the surface on which the fastener is rotating). Approximately 40 percent of the applied torque is used in overcoming thread friction. This leaves only about 10 percent of the applied torque to develop a useful clamp load (the force which holds a joint together). This means that friction can account for as much as 90 percent of the applied torque on a fastener.

TORQUE WRENCHES

♦ See Figure 21

In most applications, a torque wrench can be used to assure proper installation of a fastener. Torque wrenches come in various designs and most automo-

tive supply stores will carry a variety to suit your needs. A torque wrench should be used any time we supply a specific torque value for a fastener. Again, the general rule of "if you are using the right tool for the job, you should not have to strain to tighten a fastener" applies here.

Beam Type

The beam type torque wrench is one of the most popular types. It consists of a pointer attached to the head that runs the length of the flexible beam (shaft) to a scale located near the handle. As the wrench is pulled, the beam bends and the pointer indicates the torque using the scale.

Click (Breakaway) Type

Another popular design of torque wrench is the click type. To use the click type wrench you pre-adjust it to a torque setting. Once the torque is reached, the wrench has a reflex signaling feature that causes a momentary breakaway of the torque wrench body, sending an impulse to the operator's hand.

Pivot Head Type

♦ See Figure 22

Some torque wrenches (usually of the click type) may be equipped with a pivot head which can allow it to be used in areas of limited access. BUT, it must be used properly. To hold a pivot head wrench, grasp the handle lightly, and as you pull on the handle, it should be floated on the pivot point. If the handle comes in contact with the yoke extension during the process of pulling, there is a very good chance the torque readings will be inaccurate because this could alter the wrench loading point. The design of the handle is usually such as to make it inconvenient to deliberately misuse the wrench.

➡ It should be mentioned that the use of any U-joint, wobble or extension will have an effect on the torque readings, no matter what type of wrench you are using. For the most accurate readings, install the socket directly on the wrench driver. If necessary, straight extensions (which hold a socket directly under the wrench driver) will have the least effect on the torque reading. Avoid any extension that alters the length of the wrench from the handle to the head/driving point (such as a crow's foot). U-joint or wobble extensions can greatly affect the readings; avoid their use at all times.

Rigid Case (Direct Reading)

A rigid case or direct reading torque wrench is equipped with a dial indicator to show torque values. One advantage of these wrenches is that they can be held at any position on the wrench without affecting accuracy. These wrenches are often preferred because they tend to be compact, easy to read and have a great degree of accuracy.

TORQUE ANGLE METERS

Because the frictional characteristics of each fastener or threaded hole will vary, clamp loads which are based strictly on torque will vary as well. In most applications, this variance is not significant enough to cause worry. But, in certain applications, a manufacturer's engineers may determine that more precise clamp loads are necessary (such as is the case with many aluminum cylinder heads). In these cases, a torque angle method of installation would be specified. When installing fasteners which are torque angle tightened, a predetermined seating torque and standard torque wrench are usually used first to remove any compliance from the joint. The fastener is then tightened the specified additional portion of a turn measured in degrees. A torque angle gauge (mechanical protractor) is used for these applications.

Standard and Metric Measurements

♦ See Figure 23

Throughout this manual, specifications are given to help you determine the condition of various components on your vehicle, or to assist you in their installation. Some of the most common measurements include length (in. or cm/mm), torque (ft. lbs., inch lbs. or Nm) and pressure (psi, in. Hg, kPa or mm

CONVERSION FACTORS

LENGTH-DISTANCE

Inches (in.)	x 25.4	= Millimeters (mm)	x .0394	= Inches
Feet (ft.)	x .305	= Meters (m)	x 3.281	= Feet
Miles	x 1.609	= Kilometers (km)	x .0621	= Miles

VOLUME

Cubic Inches (in3)	x 16.387	= Cubic Centimeters	x .061	= in3
IMP Pints (IMP pt.)	x .568	= Liters (L)	x 1.76	= IMP pt.
IMP Quarts (IMP qt.)	x 1.137	= Liters (L)	x .88	= IMP qt.
IMP Gallons (IMP gal.)	x 4.546	= Liters (L)	x .22	= IMP gal.
IMP Quarts (IMP qt.)	x 1.201	= US Quarts (US qt.)	x .833	= IMP qt.
IMP Gallons (IMP gal.)	x 1.201	= US Gallons (US gal.)	x .833	= IMP gal.
Fl. Ounces	x 29.573	= Milliliters	x .034	= Ounces
US Pints (US pt.)	x .473	= Liters (L)	x 2.113	= Pints
US Quarts (US qt.)	x .946	= Liters (L)	x 1.057	= Quarts
US Gallons (US gal.)	x 3.785	= Liters (L)	x .264	= Gallons

MASS-WEIGHT

Ounces (oz.)	x 28.35	= Grams (g)	x .035	= Ounces
Pounds (lb.)	x .454	= Kilograms (kg)	x 2.205	= Pounds

PRESSURE

Pounds Per Sq. In. (psi)	x 6.895	= Kilopascals (kPa)	x .145	= psi
Inches of Mercury (Hg)	x .4912	= psi	x 2.036	= Hg
Inches of Mercury (Hg)	x 3.377	= Kilopascals (kPa)	x .2961	= Hg
Inches of Water (H_2O)	x .07355	= Inches of Mercury	x 13.783	= H_2O
Inches of Water (H_2O)	x .03613	= psi	x 27.684	= H_2O
Inches of Water (H_2O)	x .248	= Kilopascals (kPa)	x 4.026	= H_2O

TORQUE

Pounds-Force Inches (in-lb)	x .113	= Newton Meters (N·m)	x 8.85	= in-lb
Pounds-Force Feet (ft-lb)	x 1.356	= Newton Meters (N·m)	x .738	= ft-lb

VELOCITY

Miles Per Hour (MPH)	x 1.609	= Kilometers Per Hour (KPH)	x .621	= MPH

POWER

Horsepower (Hp)	x .745	= Kilowatts	x 1.34	= Horsepower

FUEL CONSUMPTION*

Miles Per Gallon IMP (MPG)	x .354	= Kilometers Per Liter (Km/L)	
Kilometers Per Liter (Km/L)	x 2.352	= IMP MPG	
Miles Per Gallon US (MPG)	x .425	= Kilometers Per Liter (Km/L)	
Kilometers Per Liter (Km/L)	x 2.352	= US MPG	

*It is common to covert from miles per gallon (mpg) to liters/100 kilometers (1/100 km), where mpg (IMP) x 1/100 km = 282 and mpg (US) x 1/100 km = 235.

TEMPERATURE

Degree Fahrenheit (°F) = (°C x 1.8) + 32
Degree Celsius (°C) = (°F − 32) x .56

Fig. 23 Standard and metric conversion factors chart

TCCS1044

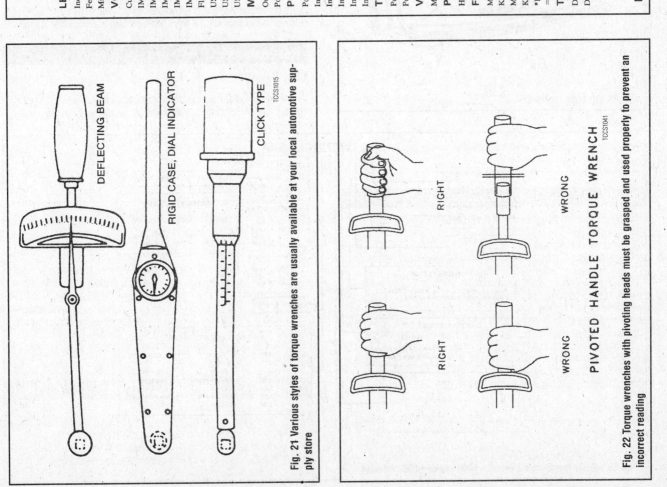

DEFLECTING BEAM

RIGID CASE, DIAL INDICATOR

CLICK TYPE

TCCS1015

Fig. 21 Various styles of torque wrenches are usually available at your local automotive supply store

RIGHT

RIGHT

WRONG

RIGHT

WRONG

PIVOTED HANDLE TORQUE WRENCH

TCCS1041

Fig. 22 Torque wrenches with pivoting heads must be grasped and used properly to prevent an incorrect reading

Hg). In most cases, we strive to provide the proper measurement as determined by the manufacturer's engineers.

Though, in some cases, that value may not be conveniently measured with what is available in your toolbox. Luckily, many of the measuring devices which are available today will have two scales so the Standard or Metric measurements may easily be taken. If any of the various measuring tools which are available to you do not contain the same scale as listed in the specifications, use the accompanying conversion factors to determine the proper value.

The conversion factor chart is used by taking the given specification and multiplying it by the necessary conversion factor. For instance, looking at the first line, if you have a measurement in inches such as "free-play should be 2 in." but your ruler reads only in millimeters, multiply 2 in. by the conversion factor of 25.4 to get the metric equivalent of 50.8mm. Likewise, if the specification was given only in a Metric measurement, for example in Newton Meters (Nm), then look at the center column first. If the measurement is 100 Nm, multiply it by the conversion factor of 0.738 to get 73.8 ft. lbs.

SERIAL NUMBER IDENTIFICATION

Vehicle

▶ See Figures 24, 25, 26, 27 and 28

The Vehicle Identification Number (VIN) is stamped on a plate located on the top left hand side (driver's side) of the instrument panel so that it can be seen by looking through the windshield.

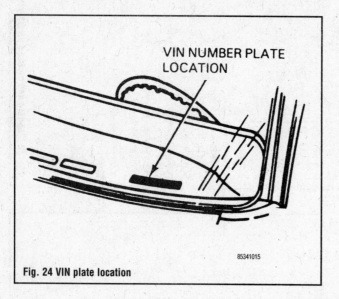

Fig. 24 VIN plate location

Engine

The 4-cylinder engine VIN code is stamped on the left side transmission mounting flange of the engine, directly above the starter.

The V6 VIN code for 1982–83 Camaros is stamped at the top center of the engine block, behind the water pump. An optional engine VIN code is location in front of the engine block, right side, below the cylinder head.

The V6 VIN code for 1984–88 Camaros is stamped on the left side transmission mounting flange of the engine. An optional engine VIN code location is also on the transmission mounting flange, directly above the main VIN code number.

The V8 engine VIN codes are normally on the front of the engine block, directly below the right cylinder head. The stamping contains nine positions, and are broken down as follows:

- Position 1—GM car division identifier
- Position 2—Model year code
- Position 3—Car assembly plant code
- Position 4 through 9—Assembly plant sequential number of vehicle

Transmission

▶ See Figures 29 and 30

A transmission VIN number is stamped on each transmission. The location of the transmission serial number on each transmission is shown in the illustrations.

Rear Axle

▶ See Figures 31

Rear axle ratio, differential type, manufacturer and build date are stamped on the right axle tube on the forward side and on a metal tag attached to the axle cover.

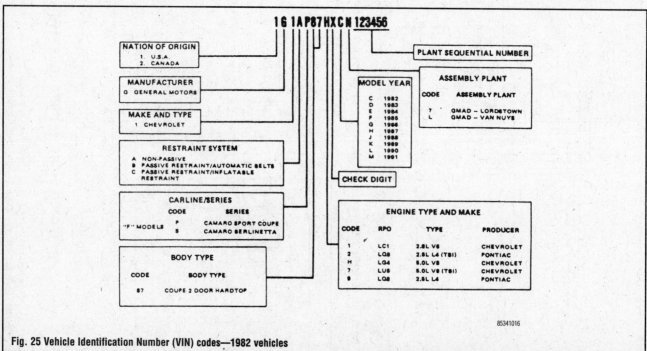

Fig. 25 Vehicle Identification Number (VIN) codes—1982 vehicles

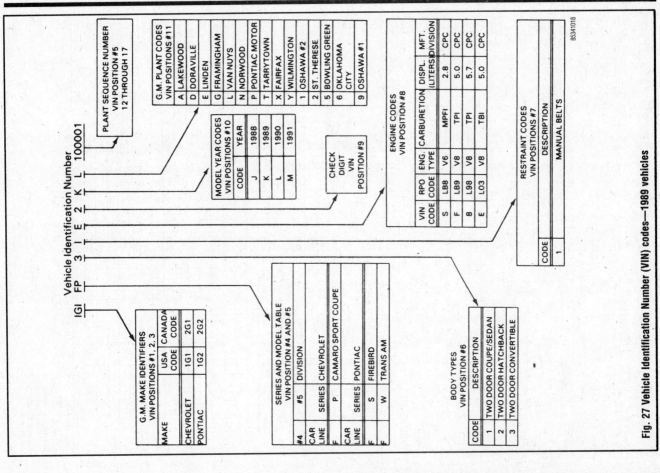

Fig. 27 Vehicle Identification Number (VIN) codes—1989 vehicles

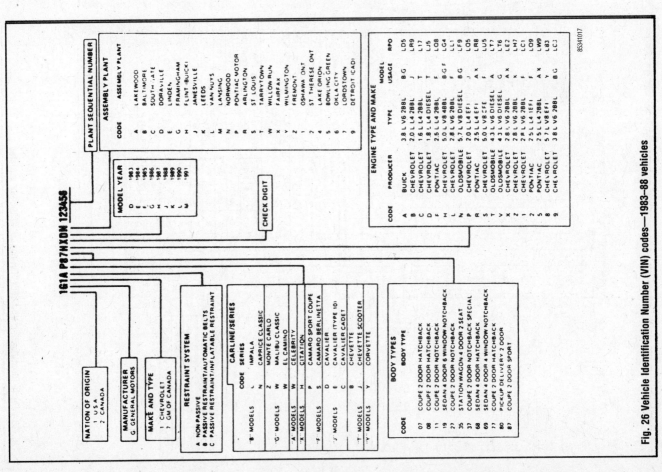

Fig. 26 Vehicle Identification Number (VIN) codes—1983–88 vehicles

ENGINE APPLICATION

Year	Engine Code	No. Cyl.	Actual Displacement			Type	Fuel System	Built By
			cu. in.	cc	Liters			
1982	2	4	151	2474	2.5	L4	TBI	Pontiac
	1	6	173	2835	2.8	V6	Carb	Chevrolet
	H	8	305	4998	5.0	V8	Carb	Chevrolet
	7	8	305	4998	5.0	V8	CFI	Chevrolet
1983	2	4	151	2474	2.5	L4	TBI	Pontiac
	1	6	173	2835	2.8	V6	Carb	Chevrolet
	H	8	305	4998	5.0	V8	Carb	Chevrolet
	S	8	305	4998	5.0	V8	CFI	Chevrolet
1984	2	4	151	2474	2.5	L4	TBI	Pontiac
	1	6	173	2835	2.8	V6	Carb	Chevrolet
	H	8	305	4998	5.0	V8	Carb	Chevrolet
	G	8	305	4998	5.0	V8	Carb	Chevrolet
1985	2	4	151	2474	2.5	L4	TBI	Pontiac
	S	6	173	2835	2.8	V6	MPI	Chevrolet
	H	8	305	4998	5.0	V8	Carb	Chevrolet
	G	8	305	4998	5.0	V8	Carb	Chevrolet
	F	8	305	4998	5.0	V8	TPI	Chevrolet
1986	2	4	151	2474	2.5	L4	TBI	Pontiac
	S	6	173	2835	2.8	V6	MPI	Chevrolet
	H	8	305	4998	5.0	V8	Carb	Chevrolet
	G	8	305	4998	5.0	V8	Carb	Chevrolet
	F	8	305	4998	5.0	V8	TPI	Chevrolet
1987	S	6	173	2835	2.8	V6	MPI	Chevrolet
	H	8	305	4998	5.0	V8	Carb	Chevrolet
	F	8	305	4998	5.0	V8	TPI	Chevrolet
	8	8	350	5735	5.7	V8	TPI	Chevrolet
1988	S	6	173	2835	2.8	V6	MPI	Chevrolet
	E	8	305	4998	5.0	V8	TPI	Chevrolet
	F	8	305	4998	5.0	V8	TPI	Chevrolet
	8	8	350	5735	5.7	V8	TPI	Chevrolet
1989	S	6	173	2835	2.8	V6	MPI	Chevrolet
	E	8	305	4998	5.0	V8	EFI	Chevrolet
	F	8	305	4998	5.0	V8	TPI	Chevrolet
	8	8	350	5735	5.7	V8	TPI	Chevrolet
1990	T	6	191	3130	3.1	V6	MPI	Chevrolet
	E	8	305	4998	5.0	V8	EFI	Chevrolet
	F	8	305	4998	5.0	V8	TPI	Chevrolet
	8	8	350	5735	5.7	V8	TPI	Chevrolet
1991	T	6	191	3130	3.1	V6	MPI	Chevrolet
	E	8	305	4998	5.0	V8	EFI	Chevrolet
	F	8	305	4998	5.0	V8	TPI	Chevrolet
	8	8	350	5735	5.7	V8	TPI	Chevrolet
1992	T	6	191	3130	3.1	V6	MPI	Chevrolet
	E	8	305	4998	5.0	V8	EFI	Chevrolet
	F	8	305	4998	5.0	V8	TPI	Chevrolet
	8	8	350	5735	5.7	V8	TPI	Chevrolet

Carb—Carbureted
CFI—Cross Fire Injection
EFI—Electronic Fuel Injection
MPI—Multi-Port Injection
TBI—Throttle Body Injection
TPI—Tuned Port Injection

82601C34

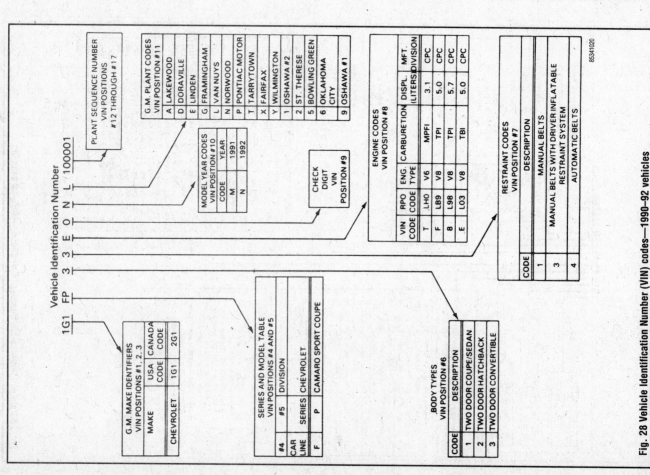

Fig. 28 Vehicle Identification Number (VIN) codes—1990–92 vehicles

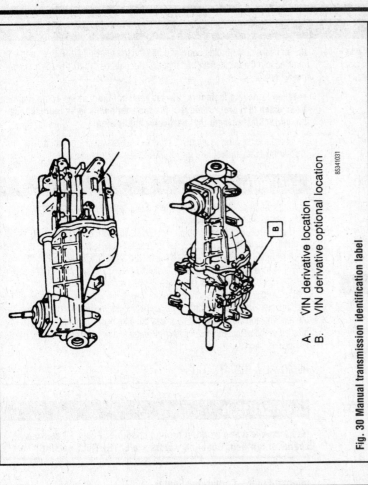

A. VIN derivative location
B. VIN derivative optional location

Fig. 30 Manual transmission identification label

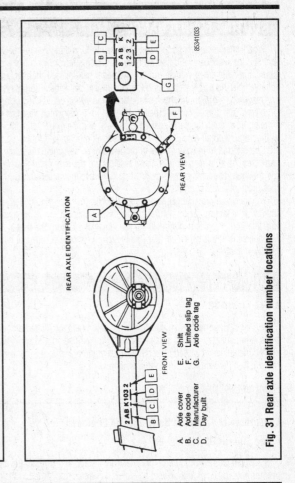

REAR AXLE IDENTIFICATION

REAR VIEW

FRONT VIEW

A. Axle cover   E. Shift
B. Axle code   F. Limited slip tag
C. Manufacturer   G. Axle code tag
D. Day built

Fig. 31 Rear axle identification number locations

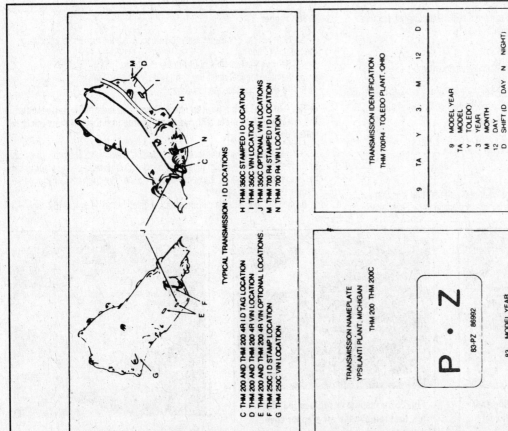

TYPICAL TRANSMISSION - I D LOCATIONS

C THM 200 AND THM 200 4R I D TAG LOCATION   H THM 350C STAMPED I D LOCATION
D THM 200 AND THM 200 4R VIN LOCATION   J THM 350C VIN LOCATION
E THM 200 AND THM 200 4R VIN OPTIONAL LOCATIONS J THM 350C OPTIONAL VIN LOCATIONS
F THM 250C I D STAMP LOCATION   M THM 700 R4 STAMPED I D LOCATION
G THM 250C VIN LOCATION   N THM 700 R4 VIN LOCATION

TRANSMISSION IDENTIFICATION
THM 700R4 · TOLEDO PLANT. OHIO

9   TA   Y   3.   M   12   D

9   MODEL YEAR
TA   MODEL
Y   TOLEDO
3   YEAR
M   MONTH
12   DAY
D   SHIFT ID   DAY   N   NIGHT)

TRANSMISSION NAMEPLATE
YPSILANTI PLANT. MICHIGAN
THM 200 THM 200C

83-PZ 86992

P · Z

83   MODEL YEAR
PZ   MODEL
86992   SERIAL NO

Fig. 29 Typical automatic transmission VIN location locations

ROUTINE MAINTENANCE

Proper maintenance and tune-up is the key to long and trouble-free vehicle life, and the work can yield its own rewards. Studies have shown that a properly tuned and maintained vehicle can achieve better gas mileage than an out-of-tune vehicle. As a conscientious owner and driver, set aside a Saturday morning, say once a month, to check or replace items which could cause major problems later. Keep your own personal log to jot down which services you performed, how much the parts cost you, the date, and the exact odometer reading at the time. Keep all receipts for such items as engine oil and filters, so that they may be referred to in case of related problems or to determine operating expenses. As a do-it-yourselfer, these receipts are the only proof you have that the required maintenance was performed. In the event of a warranty problem, these receipts will be invaluable.

The literature provided with your vehicle when it was originally delivered includes the factory recommended maintenance schedule. If you no longer have this literature, replacement copies are usually available from the dealer. A maintenance schedule is provided later in this section, in case you do not have the factory literature.

Air Cleaner

▶ See Figure 32

The air cleaner has a dual purpose. It not only filters the ducted air entering the engine, but also acts as a flame arrester if the engine should backfire. If an engine maintenance procedure requires the temporary removal of the air cleaner, remove it; otherwise, never run the engine without it.

REMOVAL & INSTALLATION

Carbureted and Throttle Body Injected Engines

▶ See Figures 33, 34 and 35

1. Clean the dirt and foreign material from the top and sides of the air cleaner housing. This will prevent any foreign material from entering the engine, via the intake manifold.
2. Remove the nut(s) or screw clamp at the top of the air cleaner. Remove the air cleaner from the top of the assembly.
3. Remove the air filter.
To install:
4. Clean the inside of the air cleaner housing using a damp cloth.
5. Install the air filter into the housing.
6. Install the top of the air cleaner assembly, making sure it is seated properly.
7. Secure the cover using the clamp fasteners, bolt and/or wing nut(s).

Port Fuel Injected Engines

1985–1992 VEHICLES

▶ See Figure 36

The air cleaner assembly on Camaros equipped with port fuel injection is mounted remotely near the radiator. The air enters the engine by flowing through the air intake duct, throttle body, and into the intake manifold. The air is then directed into the intake manifold runners, through the cylinder heads and into the cylinders.

➡**When removing fasteners, always reinstall them at the same location from which they were removed. If a fastener needs to be replaced, use the correct fastener for that particular application.**

To replace the filter assembly, simply remove the retainers from the air cleaner housing, and remove the air filter assembly from the unit.

Fuel Filter

There are three different types of fuel filters that may be used on these vehicles: internal filter, in-line filter and in-tank filter.

The internal filter is used on all carburetors and is located in the inlet fitting. A spring is installed behind the filter to hold the filter outward, sealing it against the inlet fitting. A check valve is also built into the fuel filter element.

The in-line fuel filter is just that, installed in the fuel tank-to-engine fuel line, usually mounted on the rear crossmember of the Camaro.

The in-tank fuel filter is located on the lower end of the fuel pickup tube in the fuel tank. The filter is made of woven plastic and prevents dirt from entering the fuel line and also stops water, unless the filter becomes completely submerged in the water. This filter is self-cleaning and normally requires no maintenance.

REMOVAL & INSTALLATION

✳✳ CAUTION

Never smoke when working around gasoline! Avoid all sources of sparks or ignition. Gasoline vapors are EXTREMELY volatile!

Internal Filter—Carbureted Engine

▶ See Figure 37

1. Remove the air cleaner assembly. Disconnect the fuel line connection at the fuel inlet filter nut.
2. Remove the fuel inlet nut from the carburetor.
3. Remove the fuel filter and spring.
4. To install, replace the fuel filter.

➡**The fuel filter has a built in check valve; and must be installed with the check valve to meet with safety standards in the event the vehicle is rolled over.**

5. Install the fuel inlet filter spring, filter and check valve assembly in carburetor. The check valve end of filter should faces toward the fuel line. The ribs on the closed end of the filter element will prevent the filter from being installed incorrectly unless it is forced.
6. Install the nut in the carburetor and tighten nut to 46 ft. lbs. (62 Nm).

Fig. 32 View of the air intake ducting and filter housing—Carbureted and TBI vehicles

Fig. 33 To inspect or replace the air filter, first remove the air cleaner cover retainer . . .

Fig. 34 . . . then lift off the cover

Fig. 35 Remove the air filter from the housing

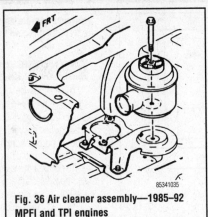

Fig. 36 Air cleaner assembly—1985–92 MPFI and TPI engines

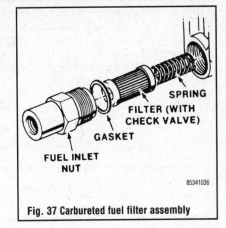

Fig. 37 Carbureted fuel filter assembly

7. Install the fuel line and tighten the connection.
8. Start the engine and check for leaks. Install the air cleaner assembly.

In-line Filter—Fuel Injected Vehicles

▶ See Figures 38 and 39

✲✲ CAUTION

To reduce the risk of fire and personal injury, it is necessary to relieve the fuel pressure before servicing the fuel system.

1. Release the fuel system pressure as follows:
   a. Remove the fuel pump fuse from the fuse block.
   b. Start the engine. Allow it to run out of fuel.
   c. Engage starter to make sure it is out of fuel.
   d. Turn the car off. Replace the fuse.
2. Using two wrenches, hold the wrench on the fuel filter stationary while loosening the fuel line nut with the other wrench.
3. Repeat Step 2 on the other side of the fuel filter.
4. Loosen the fuel filter bracket screw and remove the fuel filter and O-rings.
5. To install, make sure that the O-rings are good. If not, replace them.
6. Slide the fuel filter into the bracket making sure of the filter fuel flow direction is correct.
7. Install O-rings and the fuel lines.
8. Using two wrenches, torque the fittings to 22 ft. lbs. (30 Nm).
9. Turn the ignition switch ON to prime the fuel system and check for leaks.

Positive Crankcase Ventilation (PCV) System

▶ See Figures 40, 41 and 42

The Positive Crankcase Ventilation (PCV) system must be operating correctly to provide complete removal of the crankcase vapors. Fresh air is supplied to the crankcase from the air filter, mixed with the internal exhaust gases, passed through the PCV valve and into the intake manifold.

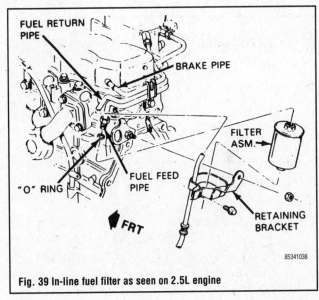

Fig. 39 In-line fuel filter as seen on 2.5L engine

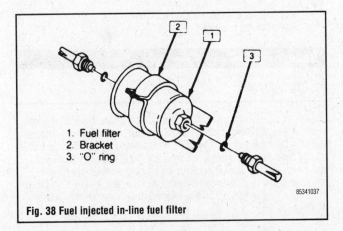

1. Fuel filter
2. Bracket
3. "O" ring

Fig. 38 Fuel injected in-line fuel filter

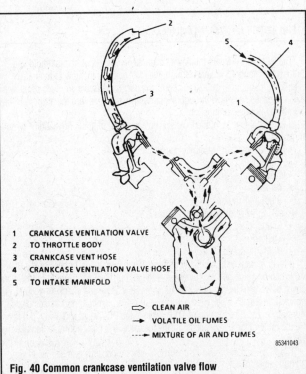

1 CRANKCASE VENTILATION VALVE
2 TO THROTTLE BODY
3 CRANKCASE VENT HOSE
4 CRANKCASE VENTILATION VALVE HOSE
5 TO INTAKE MANIFOLD

⇨ CLEAN AIR
➡ VOLATILE OIL FUMES
--- ➤ MIXTURE OF AIR AND FUMES

Fig. 40 Common crankcase ventilation valve flow

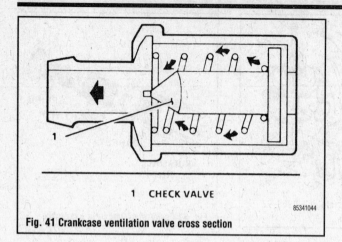

1 CHECK VALVE

85341044

Fig. 41 Crankcase ventilation valve cross section

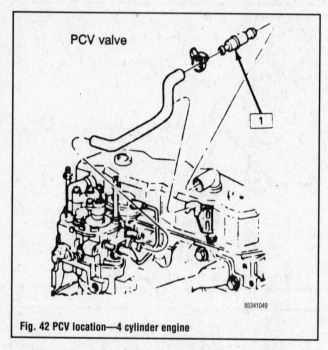

PCV valve

85341049

Fig. 42 PCV location—4 cylinder engine

The PCV valve meters the flow at a rate depending upon the manifold vacuum. If the manifold vacuum is high, the PCV restricts the flow to the intake manifold. If abnormal operating conditions occur, excessive amounts of internal exhaust gases back flow through the crankcase vent tube into the air filter to be burned by normal combustion.

Incorrect operation of the PCV system can cause multiple driveability symptoms.

A plugged valve or hose may cause:
• Rough idle
• Stalling or slow idle speed
• Oil leaks
• Sludge in engine
A leaking valve or hose would cause:
• Rough idle
• Stalling
• High idle speed
If the engine is exhibiting any of these conditions, a quick check of the PCV valve can be made. While the engine is idling, pull the PCV valve from the valve cover, place your thumb over the end of the PCV valve and check for vacuum. If no vacuum exists, check for a plugged PCV valve, manifold port, hoses or deteriorated hoses. Turn the engine **OFF**, remove the PCV valve and shake it. Listen for the rattle of the check needle inside the valve. If it does not rattle, replace the valve.

The PCV system should be checked at every oil change and serviced every 30,000 miles.

➡Never operate an engine without a PCV valve or a ventilation system, except as directed by this test procedure, for it can become damaged.

Evaporative Emission (EVAP) Control System

The Evaporative Emission (EVAP) control system used on all vehicles is the charcoal canister storage method. This method transfers fuel vapor from the fuel tank to an activated carbon (charcoal) storage device (canister) to hold the vapors when the vehicle is not operating. When the engine is running, the fuel vapor is purged from the carbon element by intake air flow and consumed in the normal combustion process.

Removal of the vapors from the canister is accomplished by a solenoid operated bowl vent or vacuum operated purge valve mounted on the canister. In addition to the fuel system vents and canister, the fuel tank requires a non-vented gas cap. The domed fuel tank positions a vent high enough above the fuel to keep the vent pipe in the vapor at all times. The single vent pipe is routed directly to the canister.

These systems commonly use an in-line EVAP pressure control valve as a pressure relief valve. When vapor pressure in the tank exceeds approximately 0.7 psi, the diaphragm valve opens, allowing vapors to vent to the canister. Once the in tank pressure drops below 0.7 psi, the valve closes causing vapors to be help in the tank.

If the EVAP system is not functioning properly, any one of the following conditions may be as result:
1. Poor idle, stalling, and poor driveability can be caused by:
• Inoperative purge solenoid valve
• Damaged canister
• Hoses split, cracked or not connected to the proper tubes
2. Evidence of fuel loss or fuel vapor odor can be caused by:
• Liquid fuel leaking from the fuel lines
• Cracked or damaged canister
• Inoperative canister control valve
• Disconnected, misrouted, kinked, deteriorated or damaged vapor hoses or control hoses.

If the solenoid valve is open, or is not receiving power, the canister can purge to the intake manifold at the incorrect time. This can allow extra fuel during warm-up, which can cause rough or unstable idle.

REMOVAL & INSTALLATION

EVAP Canister

▶ **See Figure 43**

The EVAP control system uses a 1500cc charcoal canister to absorb fuel vapors from the fuel tank. Under certain operating conditions, the purge solenoid valve will open, allowing stored vapor to flow into the intake manifold for combustion.

1. Tag and disconnect all hoses connected to the charcoal canister.
2. Loosen the retaining clamps and then lift out the canister.

➡**Some models do not have replaceable filters.**

3. If equipped, grasp the filter in the bottom of the canister with your fingers and pull it out. Replace it with a new one.
4. Install canister and tighten retaining clamps.
5. Install all hoses to canister.

Battery

PRECAUTIONS

Always use caution when working on or near the battery. Never allow a tool to bridge the gap between the negative and positive battery terminals. Also, be careful not to allow a tool to provide a ground between the positive cable/terminal and any metal component on the vehicle. Either of these conditions will cause a short circuit, leading to sparks and possible personal injury.

Do not smoke or all open flames/sparks near a battery; the gases contained in the battery are very explosive and, if ignited, could cause severe injury or death.

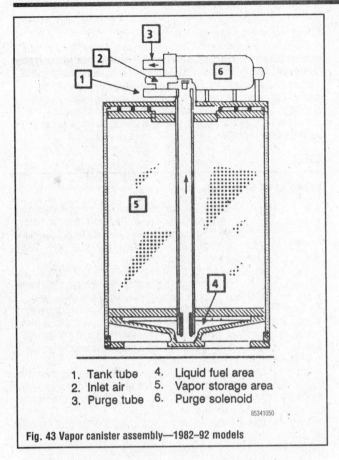

1. Tank tube
2. Inlet air
3. Purge tube
4. Liquid fuel area
5. Vapor storage area
6. Purge solenoid

85341050

Fig. 43 Vapor canister assembly—1982–92 models

All batteries, regardless of type, should be carefully secured by a battery hold-down device. If not, the terminals or casing may crack from stress during vehicle operation. A battery which is not secured may allow acid to leak, making it discharge faster. The acid can also eat away at components under the hood.

Always inspect the battery case for cracks, leakage and corrosion. A white corrosive substance on the battery case or on nearby components would indicate a leaking or cracked battery. If the battery is cracked, it should be replaced immediately.

GENERAL MAINTENANCE

Always keep the battery cables and terminals free of corrosion. Check and clean these components about once a year.

Keep the top of the battery clean, as a film of dirt can help discharge a battery that is not used for long periods. A solution of baking soda and water may be used for cleaning, but be careful to flush this off with clear water. DO NOT let any of the solution into the filler holes. Baking soda neutralizes battery acid and will de-activate a battery cell.

Batteries in vehicles which are not operated on a regular basis can fall victim to parasitic loads (small current drains which are constantly drawing current from the battery). Normal parasitic loads may drain a battery on a vehicle that is in storage and not used for 6–8 weeks. Vehicles that have additional accessories such as a phone or an alarm system may discharge a battery sooner. If the vehicle is to be stored for longer periods in a secure area and the alarm system is not necessary, the negative battery cable should be disconnected to protect the battery.

Remember that constantly deep cycling a battery (completely discharging and recharging it) will shorten battery life.

BATTERY FLUID

▶ See Figure 44

Check the battery electrolyte level at least once a month, or more often in hot weather or during periods of extended vehicle operation. On non-sealed batteries, the level can be checked either through the case (if translucent) or by removing the cell caps. The electrolyte level in each cell should be kept filled to the split ring inside each cell, or the line marked on the outside of the case.

If the level is low, add only distilled water through the opening until the level is correct. Each cell must be checked and filled individually. Distilled water should be used, because the chemicals and minerals found in most drinking water are harmful to the battery and could significantly shorten its life.

If water is added in freezing weather, the vehicle should be driven several miles to allow the water to mix with the electrolyte. Otherwise, the battery could freeze.

Although some maintenance-free batteries have removable cell caps, the electrolyte condition and level on all sealed maintenance-free batteries must be checked using the built-in hydrometer "eye." The exact type of eye will vary. But, most battery manufacturers, apply a sticker to the battery itself explaining the readings.

➡ **Although the readings from built-in hydrometers will vary, a green eye usually indicates a properly charged battery with sufficient fluid level. A dark eye is normally an indicator of a battery with sufficient fluid, but which is low in charge. A light or yellow eye usually indicates that electrolyte has dropped below the necessary level. In this last case, sealed batteries with an insufficient electrolyte must usually be discarded.**

Checking the Specific Gravity

▶ See Figures 45, 46 and 47

A hydrometer is required to check the specific gravity on all batteries that are not maintenance-free. On batteries that are maintenance-free, the specific gravity is checked by observing the built-in hydrometer "eye" on the top of the battery case.

✳✳ CAUTION

Battery electrolyte contains sulfuric acid. If you should splash any on your skin or in your eyes, flush the affected area with plenty of clear water. If it lands in your eyes, get medical help immediately.

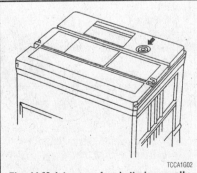

TCCA1G02

Fig. 44 Maintenance-free batteries usually contain a built-in hydrometer to check fluid level

TCCA1P07

Fig. 45 On non-sealed batteries, the fluid level can be checked by removing the cell caps

TCCA1P08

Fig. 46 If the fluid level is low, add only distilled water until the level is correct

Fig. 47 Check the specific gravity of the battery's electrolyte with a hydrometer

The fluid (sulfuric acid solution) contained in the battery cells will tell you many things about the condition of the battery. Because the cell plates must be kept submerged below the fluid level in order to operate, the fluid level is extremely important. And, because the specific gravity of the acid is an indication of electrical charge, testing the fluid can be an aid in determining if the battery must be replaced. A battery in a vehicle with a properly operating charging system should require little maintenance, but careful, periodic inspection should reveal problems before they leave you stranded.

At least once a year, check the specific gravity of the battery. It should be between 1.20 and 1.26 on the gravity scale. Most auto stores carry a variety of inexpensive battery hydrometers. These can be used on any non-sealed battery to test the specific gravity in each cell.

The battery testing hydrometer has a squeeze bulb at one end and a nozzle at the other. Battery electrolyte is sucked into the hydrometer until the float is lifted from its seat. The specific gravity is then read by noting the position of the float. If gravity is low in one or more cells, the battery should be slowly charged and checked again to see if the gravity has come up. Generally, if after charging, the specific gravity between any two cells varies more than 50 points (0.50), the battery should be replaced, as it can no longer produce sufficient voltage to guarantee proper operation.

CABLES

▶ **See Figures 48 thru 53**

Once a year (or as necessary), the battery terminals and the cable clamps should be cleaned. Loosen the clamps and remove the cables, negative cable first. On top post batteries, the use of a puller specially made for this purpose is recommended. These are inexpensive and available in most parts stores. Side terminal battery cables are secured with a small bolt.

Clean the cable clamps and the battery terminal with a wire brush, until all corrosion, grease, etc., is removed and the metal is shiny. It is especially important to clean the inside of the clamp thoroughly (an old knife is useful here), since a small deposit of oxidation there will prevent a sound connection and inhibit starting or charging. Special tools are available for cleaning these parts, one type for conventional top post batteries and another type for side terminal batteries. It is also a good idea to apply some dielectric grease to the terminal, as this will aid in the prevention of corrosion.

After the clamps and terminals are clean, reinstall the cables, negative cable last; DO NOT hammer the clamps onto battery posts. Tighten the clamps securely, but do not distort them. Give the clamps and terminals a thin external coating of grease after installation, to retard corrosion.

Check the cables at the same time that the terminals are cleaned. If the cable insulation is cracked or broken, or if the ends are frayed, the cable should be replaced with a new cable of the same length and gauge.

Fig. 48 Loosen the battery cable retaining nut . . .

Fig. 49 . . . then disconnect the cable from the battery

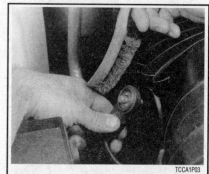

Fig. 50 A wire brush may be used to clean any corrosion or foreign material from the cable

Fig. 51 The wire brush can also be used to remove any corrosion or dirt from the battery terminal

Fig. 52 The battery terminal can also be cleaned using a solution of baking soda and water

Fig. 53 Before connecting the cables, it's a good idea to coat the terminals with a small amount of dielectric grease

CHARGING

A battery should be charged at a slow rate to keep the plates inside from getting too hot. However, if some maintenance-free batteries are allowed to discharge until they are almost "dead," they may have to be charged at a high rate to bring them back to "life." Always follow the charger manufacturer's instructions on charging the battery.

REPLACEMENT

When it becomes necessary to replace the battery, select one with an amperage rating equal to or greater than the battery originally installed. Deterioration and just plain aging of the battery cables, starter motor, and associated wires makes the battery's job harder in successive years. This makes it prudent to install a new battery with a greater capacity than the old.

Early Fuel Evaporation (EFE) System

⬥ **See Figures 54 and 55**

The EFE system is used on some engines to provide a source of quick heat to the engine induction system during cold driveway. There are two types of EFE systems: the vacuum servo type (located in the exhaust manifold) and the electric grid type (located under the carburetor).

The vacuum servo type consists of a valve in the exhaust manifold and a EFE control solenoid valve which is controlled by the ECM.

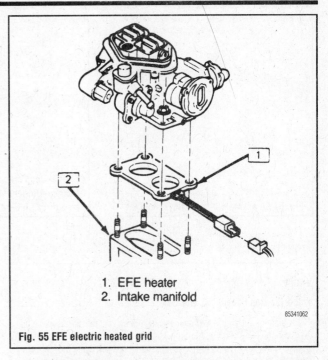

1. EFE heater
2. Intake manifold

Fig. 55 EFE electric heated grid

The electrical type consists of an electrical grid plate, mounted directly under the carburetor. The ECM controls the grid plate voltage by way of an EFE relay.

Both types are designed to produce rapid heating of the intake manifold, providing quick fuel evaporation and a more even distribution of fuel to aid in cold engine operation.

Every 30,000 miles, check the EFE valve (make sure it is free, not sticking) and the hoses for cracking or deterioration. If necessary, replace or lubricate. Check the electrically heated grid for meltdown and replace as necessary.

Belts

INSPECTION

⬥ **See Figures 56, 57, 58, 59 and 60**

Inspect the belts for signs of glazing or cracking. A glazed belt will be perfectly smooth from slippage, while a good belt will have a slight texture of fabric visible. Cracks will usually start at the inner edge of the belt and run outward. All worn or damaged drive belts should be replaced immediately. It is best to replace all drive belts at one time, as a preventive maintenance measure, during this service operation.

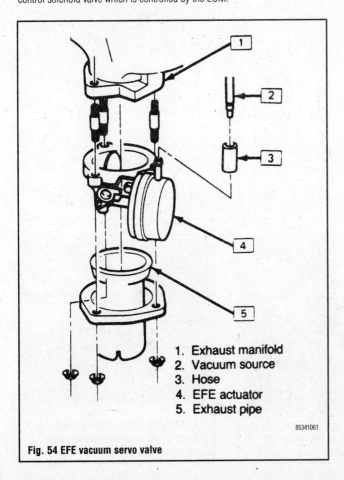

1. Exhaust manifold
2. Vacuum source
3. Hose
4. EFE actuator
5. Exhaust pipe

Fig. 54 EFE vacuum servo valve

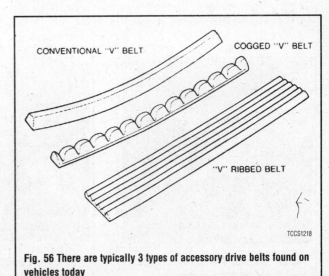

Fig. 56 There are typically 3 types of accessory drive belts found on vehicles today

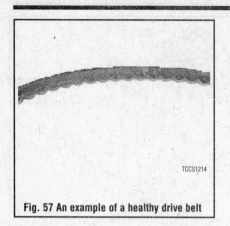

Fig. 57 An example of a healthy drive belt

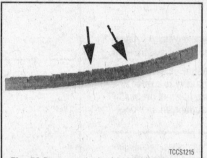

Fig. 58 Deep cracks in this belt will cause flex, building up heat that will eventually lead to belt failure

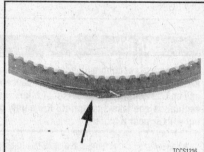

Fig. 59 The cover of this belt is worn, exposing the critical reinforcing cords to excessive wear

ADJUSTING

V-Belts

▶ See Figures 61, 62, 63 and 64

Belts are normally adjusted by loosening the bolts of the accessory being driven and moving that accessory on its pivot points until the proper tension is applied to the belt. The accessory is held in this position while the bolts are tightened. To determine proper belt tension, you can purchase a belt tension gauge or simply use the deflection method. To determine deflection, press inward on the belt at the mid-point of its longest straight run. The belt should deflect (move inward) ⅜–½ in. (10–13mm). A general rule for alternator belt tension is that the pulley should not be capable of being turned with hand pressure.

Serpentine Belt

On most newer vehicles, a single belt is used to drive all of the engine accessories formerly driven by multiple V-belts. The single belt is referred to as a serpentine belt. All the belt driven accessories are rigidly mounted with belt tension maintained by a spring loaded tensioner. Because of the belt tensioner, no adjustment is necessary.

REMOVAL & INSTALLATION

V-Belt

▶ See Figures 65, 66, 67 and 68

To remove a V-style drive belt, simply loosen the accessory being driven and move it on its pivot point to free the belt. Then, remove the belt.

It is important to note that on engines with many driven accessories, several or all of the belts may have to be removed to get at the one to be replaced.

Fig. 60 Installing too wide a belt can result in serious belt wear and/or breakage

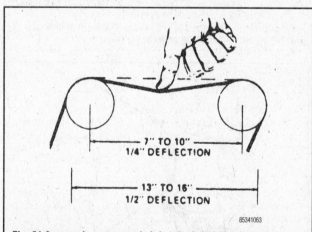

Fig. 61 A gauge is recommended, but the belt deflection may be checked using light thumb pressure

Fig. 62 Loosening alternator pivot/adjustment bolt in order to tighten the belt

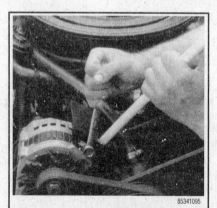

Fig. 63 Apply tension to the belt being careful not to damage the case

Fig. 64 Using a ½ in. ratchet, apply tension to the air conditioning belt while tightening the pivot bolt

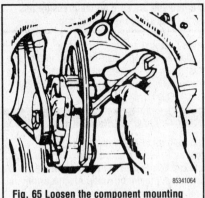

Fig. 65 Loosen the component mounting and adjusting bolts slightly

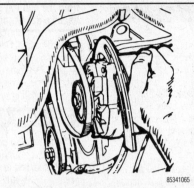

Fig. 66 Remove the belt by pushing the component toward the engine

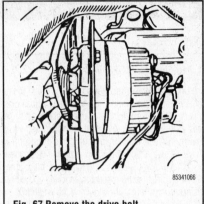

Fig. 67 Remove the drive belt

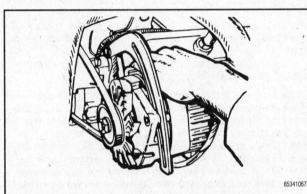

Fig. 68 To tighten the belt, pull the component away from the engine and tighten the mounting bolts to specifications

Serpentine Belt

▸ **See Figures 69 and 70**

A belt tensioner is used on these models, to maintain proper belt tension. To relieve belt tension, rotate the belt tensioner (using a 15mm socket) to relieve pressure on the belt. With tension relieved, the belt may then be removed from the engine. It is important to note the belt location at each pulley, to assure correct installation, and proper operation of the engine cooling system. A diagram may be helpful in denoting belt positioning.

→ **Take care not to bend the tensioner when applying torque. Damage to the tensioner will occur. Maximum torque to load belt should not exceed 30 ft. lbs. (41 Nm).**

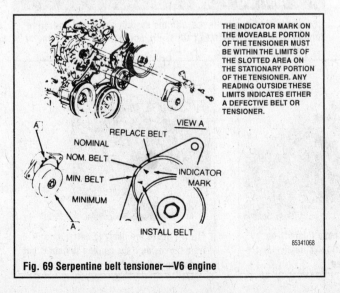

THE INDICATOR MARK ON THE MOVEABLE PORTION OF THE TENSIONER MUST BE WITHIN THE LIMITS OF THE SLOTTED AREA ON THE STATIONARY PORTION OF THE TENSIONER. ANY READING OUTSIDE THESE LIMITS INDICATES EITHER A DEFECTIVE BELT OR TENSIONER.

Fig. 69 Serpentine belt tensioner—V6 engine

1. Used belt acceptable wear range
2. New belt range
3. Arm
4. Spindle
5. Fixed belt length indicator
6. With new belt installed, fixed pointer must fall within this range
7. Minimum length—new belt
8. Nominal length—new belt
9. Maximum length—new belt
10. Replace belt position

Fig. 70 Serpentine belt tensioner—V8 engine

Hoses

INSPECTION

▶ See Figures 71, 72, 73 and 74

Upper and lower radiator hoses along with the heater hoses should be checked for deterioration, leaks and loose hose clamps at least every 15,000 miles (24,000 km). It is also wise to check the hoses periodically in early spring and at the beginning of the fall or winter when you are performing other maintenance. A quick visual inspection could discover a weakened hose which might have left you stranded if it had remained unrepaired.

Whenever you are checking the hoses, make sure the engine and cooling system are cold. Visually inspect for cracking, rotting or collapsed hoses, and replace as necessary. Run your hand along the length of the hose. If a weak or swollen spot is noted when squeezing the hose wall, the hose should be replaced.

REMOVAL & INSTALLATION

1. Remove the radiator pressure cap.

✱✱ CAUTION

Never remove the pressure cap while the engine is running, or personal injury from scalding hot coolant or steam may result. If possible, wait until the engine has cooled to remove the pressure cap. If this is not possible, wrap a thick cloth around the pressure cap and turn it slowly to the stop. Step back while the pressure is released

TCCS1219

Fig. 71 The cracks developing along this hose are a result of age-related hardening

from the cooling system. When you are sure all the pressure has been released, use the cloth to turn and remove the cap.

2. Position a clean container under the radiator and/or engine draincock or plug, then open the drain and allow the cooling system to drain to an appropriate level. For some upper hoses, only a little coolant must be drained. To remove hoses positioned lower on the engine, such as a lower radiator hose, the entire cooling system must be emptied.

✱✱ CAUTION

When draining coolant, keep in mind that cats and dogs are attracted by ethylene glycol antifreeze, and are quite likely to drink any that is left in an uncovered container or in puddles on the ground. This will prove fatal in sufficient quantity. Always drain coolant into a sealable container. Coolant may be reused unless it is contaminated or several years old.

3. Loosen the hose clamps at each end of the hose requiring replacement. Clamps are usually either of the spring tension type (which require pliers to squeeze the tabs and loosen) or of the screw tension type (which require screw or hex drivers to loosen). Pull the clamps back on the hose away from the connection.

4. Twist, pull and slide the hose off the fitting, taking care not to damage the neck of the component from which the hose is being removed.

➡ If the hose is stuck at the connection, do not try to insert a screwdriver or other sharp tool under the hose end in an effort to free it, as the connection and/or hose may become damaged. Heater connections especially may be easily damaged by such a procedure. If the hose is to be replaced, use a single-edged razor blade to make a slice along the portion of the hose which is stuck on the connection, perpendicular to the end of the hose. Do not cut deep so as to prevent damaging the connection. The hose can then be peeled from the connection and discarded.

5. Clean both hose mounting connections. Inspect the condition of the hose clamps and replace them, if necessary.

To install:

6. Dip the ends of the new hose into clean engine coolant to ease installation.

7. Slide the clamps over the replacement hose, then slide the hose ends over the connections into position.

8. Position and secure the clamps at least ¼ in. (6.35mm) from the ends of the hose. Make sure they are located beyond the raised bead of the connector.

9. Close the radiator or engine drains and properly refill the cooling system with the clean drained engine coolant or a suitable mixture of ethylene glycol coolant and water.

10. If available, install a pressure tester and check for leaks. If a pressure tester is not available, run the engine until normal operating temperature is reached (allowing the system to naturally pressurize), then check for leaks.

✱✱ CAUTION

If you are checking for leaks with the system at normal operating temperature, BE EXTREMELY CAREFUL not to touch any moving or

TCCS1220

Fig. 72 A hose clamp that is too tight can cause older hoses to separate and tear on either side of the clamp

TCCS1221

Fig. 73 A soft spongy hose (identifiable by the swollen section) will eventually burst and should be replaced

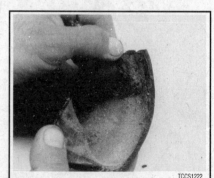

TCCS1222

Fig. 74 Hoses are likely to deteriorate from the inside if the cooling system is not periodically flushed

hot engine parts. Once temperature has been reached, shut the engine OFF, and check for leaks around the hose fittings and connections which were removed earlier.

Air Conditioning System

SYSTEM SERVICE & REPAIR

➡**It is recommended that the A/C system be serviced by an EPA Section 609 certified automotive technician utilizing a refrigerant recovery/recycling machine.**

The do-it-yourselfer should not service his/her own vehicle's A/C system for many reasons, including legal concerns, personal injury, environmental damage and cost.

According to the U.S. Clean Air Act, it is a federal crime to service or repair (involving the refrigerant) a Motor Vehicle Air Conditioning (MVAC) system for money without being EPA certified. It is also illegal to vent R-12 and R-134a refrigerants into the atmosphere. State and/or local laws may be more strict than the federal regulations, so be sure to check with your state and/or local authorities for further information.

➡**Federal law dictates that a fine of up to $25,000 may be levied on people convicted of venting refrigerant into the atmosphere.**

When servicing an A/C system you run the risk of handling or coming in contact with refrigerant, which may result in skin or eye irritation or frostbite. Although low in toxicity (due to chemical stability), inhalation of concentrated refrigerant fumes is dangerous and can result in death; cases of fatal cardiac arrhythmia have been reported in people accidentally subjected to high levels of refrigerant. Some early symptoms include loss of concentration and drowsiness.

➡**Generally, the limit for exposure is lower for R-134a than it is for R-12. Exceptional care must be practiced when handling R-134a.**

Also, some refrigerants can decompose at high temperatures (near gas heaters or open flame), which may result in hydrofluoric acid, hydrochloric acid and phosgene (a fatal nerve gas).

It is usually more economically feasible to have a certified MVAC automotive technician perform A/C system service on your vehicle.

R-12 Refrigerant Conversion

If your vehicle still uses R-12 refrigerant, one way to save A/C system costs down the road is to investigate the possibility of having your system converted to R-134a. The older R-12 systems can be easily converted to R-134a refrigerant by a certified automotive technician by installing a few new components and changing the system oil.

The cost of R-12 is steadily rising and will continue to increase, because it is no longer imported or manufactured in the United States. Therefore, it is often possible to have an R-12 system converted to R-134a and recharged for less than it would cost to just charge the system with R-12.

If you are interested in having your system converted, contact local automotive service stations for more details and information.

PREVENTIVE MAINTENANCE

Although the A/C system should not be serviced by the do-it-yourselfer, preventive maintenance should be practiced to help maintain the efficiency of the vehicle's A/C system. Be sure to perform the following:

• The easiest and most important preventive maintenance for your A/C system is to be sure that it is used on a regular basis. Running the system for five minutes each month (no matter what the season) will help ensure that the seals and all internal components remain lubricated.

➡**Some vehicles automatically operate the A/C system compressor whenever the windshield defroster is activated. Therefore, the A/C system would not need to be operated each month if the defroster was used.**

• In order to prevent heater core freeze-up during A/C operation, it is necessary to maintain proper antifreeze protection. Be sure to properly maintain the engine cooling system.

• Any obstruction of or damage to the condenser configuration will restrict air flow which is essential to its efficient operation. Keep this unit clean and in proper physical shape.

➡**Bug screens which are mounted in front of the condenser (unless they are original equipment) are regarded as obstructions.**

• The condensation drain tube expels any water which accumulates on the bottom of the evaporator housing into the engine compartment. If this tube is obstructed, the air conditioning performance can be restricted and condensation buildup can spill over onto the vehicle's floor.

SYSTEM INSPECTION

Although the A/C system should not be serviced by the do-it-yourselfer, system inspections should be performed to help maintain the efficiency of the vehicle's A/C system. Be sure to perform the following:

The easiest and often most important check for the air conditioning system consists of a visual inspection of the system components. Visually inspect the system for refrigerant leaks, damaged compressor clutch, abnormal compressor drive belt tension and/or condition, plugged evaporator drain tube, blocked condenser fins, disconnected or broken wires, blown fuses, corroded connections and poor insulation.

A refrigerant leak will usually appear as an oily residue at the leakage point in the system. The oily residue soon picks up dust or dirt particles from the surrounding air and appears greasy. Through time, this will build up and appear to be a heavy dirt impregnated grease.

For a thorough visual and operational inspection, check the following:

• Check the surface of the radiator and condenser for dirt, leaves or other material which might block air flow.

• Check for kinks in hoses and lines. Check the system for leaks.

• Make sure the drive belt is properly tensioned. During operation, make sure the belt is free of noise or slippage.

• Make sure the blower motor operates at all appropriate positions, then check for distribution of the air from all outlets.

➡**Remember that in high humidity, air discharged from the vents may not feel as cold as expected, even if the system is working properly. This is because moisture in humid air retains heat more effectively than dry air, thereby making humid air more difficult to cool.**

Windshield Wipers

ELEMENT (REFILL) CARE & REPLACEMENT

▶ **See Figures 75, 76 and 77**

For maximum effectiveness and longest element life, the windshield and wiper blades should be kept clean. Dirt, tree sap, road tar and so on will cause streaking, smearing and blade deterioration if left on the glass. It is advisable to wash the windshield carefully with a commercial glass cleaner at least once a month. Wipe off the rubber blades with the wet rag afterwards. Do not attempt to move wipers across the windshield by hand; damage to the motor and drive mechanism will result.

To inspect and/or replace the wiper blade elements, place the wiper switch in the **LOW** speed position and the ignition switch in the **ACC** position. When the wiper blades are approximately vertical on the windshield, turn the ignition switch to **OFF**.

Examine the wiper blade elements. If they are found to be cracked, broken or torn, they should be replaced immediately. Replacement intervals will vary with usage, although ozone deterioration usually limits element life to about one year. If the wiper pattern is smeared or streaked, or if the blade chatters across the glass, the elements should be replaced. It is easiest and most sensible to replace the elements in pairs.

If your vehicle is equipped with aftermarket blades, there are several different types of refills and your vehicle might have any kind. Aftermarket blades and arms rarely use the exact same type blade or refill as the original equipment.

Regardless of the type of refill used, be sure to follow the part manufacturer's instructions closely. Make sure that all of the frame jaws are engaged as the refill is pushed into place and locked. If the metal blade holder and frame are allowed to touch the glass during wiper operation, the glass will be scratched.

Fig. 75 Most aftermarket blades are available with multiple adapters to fit different vehicles

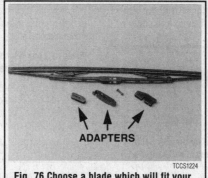

Fig. 76 Choose a blade which will fit your vehicle, and that will be readily available next time you need blades

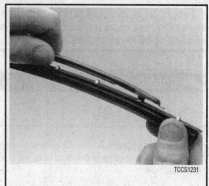

Fig. 77 When installed, be certain the blade is fully inserted into the backing

Tires and Wheels

Common sense and good driving habits will afford maximum tire life. Make sure that you don't overload the vehicle or run with incorrect pressure in the tires. Either of these will increase tread wear. Fast starts, sudden stops and sharp cornering are hard on tires and will shorten their useful life span.

➡ **For optimum tire life, keep the tires properly inflated, rotate them often and have the wheel alignment checked periodically.**

Inspect your tires frequently. Be especially careful to watch for bubbles in the tread or sidewall, deep cuts or underinflation. Replace any tires with bubbles in the sidewall. If cuts are so deep that they penetrate to the cords, discard the tire. Any cut in the sidewall of a radial tire renders it unsafe. Also look for uneven tread wear patterns that may indicate the front end is out of alignment or that the tires are out of balance.

TIRE ROTATION

♦ **See Figure 78**

Tires must be rotated periodically to equalize wear patterns that vary with a tire's position on the vehicle. Tires will also wear in an uneven way as the front steering/suspension system wears to the point where the alignment should be reset.

Rotating the tires will ensure maximum life for the tires as a set, so you will not have to discard a tire early due to wear on only part of the tread. Regular rotation is required to equalize wear.

When rotating "unidirectional tires," make sure that they always roll in the same direction. This means that a tire used on the left side of the vehicle must not be switched to the right side and vice-versa. Such tires should only be rotated front-to-rear or rear-to-front, while always remaining on the same side of the vehicle. These tires are marked on the sidewall as to the direction of rotation; observe the marks when reinstalling the tire(s).

Some styled or "mag" wheels may have different offsets front to rear. In these cases, the rear wheels must not be used up front and vice-versa. Furthermore, if these wheels are equipped with unidirectional tires, they cannot be rotated unless the tire is remounted for the proper direction of rotation.

➡ **The compact or space-saver spare is strictly for emergency use. It must never be included in the tire rotation or placed on the vehicle for everyday use.**

TIRE DESIGN

♦ **See Figure 79**

For maximum satisfaction, tires should be used in sets of four. Mixing of different brands or types (radial, bias-belted, fiberglass belted) should be avoided. In most cases, the vehicle manufacturer has designated a type of tire on which the vehicle will perform best. Your first choice when replacing tires should be to use the same type of tire that the manufacturer recommends.

When radial tires are used, tire sizes and wheel diameters should be selected to maintain ground clearance and tire load capacity equivalent to the original specified tire. Radial tires should always be used in sets of four.

✳✳ CAUTION

Radial tires should never be used on only the front axle.

When selecting tires, pay attention to the original size as marked on the tire. Most tires are described using an industry size code sometimes referred to as P-Metric. This allows the exact identification of the tire specifications, regardless of the manufacturer. If selecting a different tire size or brand, remember to check the installed tire for any sign of interference with the body or suspension while the vehicle is stopping, turning sharply or heavily loaded.

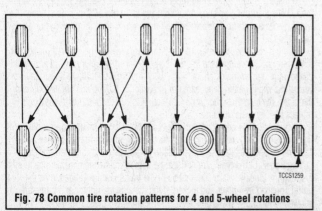

Fig. 78 Common tire rotation patterns for 4 and 5-wheel rotations

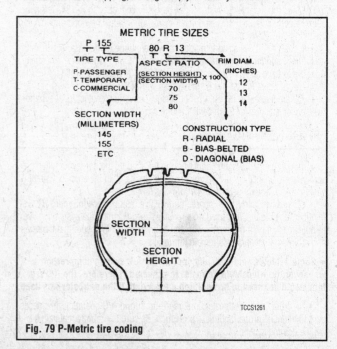

Fig. 79 P-Metric tire coding

Snow Tires

Good radial tires can produce a big advantage in slippery weather, but in snow, a street radial tire does not have sufficient tread to provide traction and control. The small grooves of a street tire quickly pack with snow and the tire behaves like a billiard ball on a marble floor. The more open, chunky tread of a snow tire will self-clean as the tire turns, providing much better grip on snowy surfaces.

To satisfy municipalities requiring snow tires during weather emergencies, most snow tires carry either an M + S designation after the tire size stamped on the sidewall, or the designation "all-season." In general, no change in tire size is necessary when buying snow tires.

Most manufacturers strongly recommend the use of 4 snow tires on their vehicles for reasons of stability. If snow tires are fitted only to the drive wheels, the opposite end of the vehicle may become very unstable when braking or turning on slippery surfaces. This instability can lead to unpleasant endings if the driver can't counteract the slide in time.

Note that snow tires, whether 2 or 4, will affect vehicle handling in all non-snow situations. The stiffer, heavier snow tires will noticeably change the turning and braking characteristics of the vehicle. Once the snow tires are installed, you must re-learn the behavior of the vehicle and drive accordingly.

➡**Consider buying extra wheels on which to mount the snow tires. Once done, the "snow wheels" can be installed and removed as needed. This eliminates the potential damage to tires or wheels from seasonal removal and installation. Even if your vehicle has styled wheels, see if inexpensive steel wheels are available. Although the look of the vehicle will change, the expensive wheels will be protected from salt, curb hits and pothole damage.**

TIRE STORAGE

If they are mounted on wheels, store the tires at proper inflation pressure. All tires should be kept in a cool, dry place. If they are stored in the garage or basement, do not let them stand on a concrete floor; set them on strips of wood, a mat or a large stack of newspaper. Keeping them away from direct moisture is of paramount importance. Tires should not be stored upright, but in a flat position.

INFLATION & INSPECTION

◗ **See Figures 80 thru 85**

The importance of proper tire inflation cannot be overemphasized. A tire employs air as part of its structure. It is designed around the supporting strength of the air at a specified pressure. For this reason, improper inflation drastically reduces the tire's ability to perform as intended. A tire will lose some air in day-to-day use; having to add a few pounds of air periodically is not necessarily a sign of a leaking tire.

TCCS1095

Fig. 80 Tires with deep cuts, or cuts which bulge, should be replaced immediately

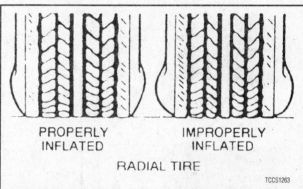

PROPERLY INFLATED   IMPROPERLY INFLATED

RADIAL TIRE

TCCS1263

Fig. 81 Radial tires have a characteristic sidewall bulge; don't try to measure pressure by looking at the tire. Use a quality air pressure gauge

CONDITION	RAPID WEAR AT SHOULDERS	RAPID WEAR AT CENTER	CRACKED TREADS	WEAR ON ONE SIDE	FEATHERED EDGE	BALD SPOTS	SCALLOPED WEAR
EFFECT							
CAUSE	UNDER-INFLATION OR LACK OF ROTATION	OVER-INFLATION OR LACK OF ROTATION	UNDER-INFLATION OR EXCESSIVE SPEED*	EXCESSIVE CAMBER	INCORRECT TOE	UNBALANCED WHEEL OR TIRE DEFECT*	LACK OF ROTATION OF TIRES OR WORN OR OUT-OF-ALIGNMENT SUSPENSION.
CORRECTION	ADJUST PRESSURE TO SPECIFICATIONS WHEN TIRES ARE COOL ROTATE TIRES			ADJUST CAMBER TO SPECIFICATIONS	ADJUST TOE-IN TO SPECIFICATIONS	DYNAMIC OR STATIC BALANCE WHEELS	ROTATE TIRES AND INSPECT SUSPENSION

*HAVE TIRE INSPECTED FOR FURTHER USE.

TCCS1267

Fig. 82 Common tire wear patterns and causes

Two items should be a permanent fixture in every glove compartment: an accurate tire pressure gauge and a tread depth gauge. Check the tire pressure (including the spare) regularly with a pocket type gauge. Too often, the gauge on the end of the air hose at your corner garage is not accurate because it suffers too much abuse. Always check tire pressure when the tires are cold, as pressure increases with temperature. If you must move the vehicle to check the tire inflation, do not drive more than a mile before checking. A cold tire is generally one that has not been driven for more than three hours.

A plate or sticker is normally provided somewhere in the vehicle (door post, hood, tailgate or trunk lid) which shows the proper pressure for the tires. Never counteract excessive pressure build-up by bleeding off air pressure (letting some air out). This will cause the tire to run hotter and wear quicker.

❊❊ CAUTION

Never exceed the maximum tire pressure embossed on the tire! This is the pressure to be used when the tire is at maximum loading, but it is rarely the correct pressure for everyday driving. Consult the owner's manual or the tire pressure sticker for the correct tire pressure.

Once you've maintained the correct tire pressures for several weeks, you'll be familiar with the vehicle's braking and handling personality. Slight adjustments in tire pressures can fine-tune these characteristics, but never change the cold pressure specification by more than 2 psi. A slightly softer tire pressure will give a softer ride but also yield lower fuel mileage. A slightly harder tire will give crisper dry road handling but can cause skidding on wet surfaces. Unless you're fully attuned to the vehicle, stick to the recommended inflation pressures.

All automotive tires have built-in tread wear indicator bars that show up as ½ in. (13mm) wide smooth bands across the tire when 1/16 in. (1.5mm) of tread remains. The appearance of tread wear indicators means that the tires should be replaced. In fact, many states have laws prohibiting the use of tires with less than this amount of tread.

You can check your own tread depth with an inexpensive gauge or by using a Lincoln head penny. Slip the Lincoln penny (with Lincoln's head upside-down) into several tread grooves. If you can see the top of Lincoln's head in 2 adjacent grooves, the tire has less than 1/16 in. (1.5mm) tread left and should be replaced. You can measure snow tires in the same manner by using the "tails" side of the Lincoln penny. If you can see the top of the Lincoln memorial, it's time to replace the snow tire(s).

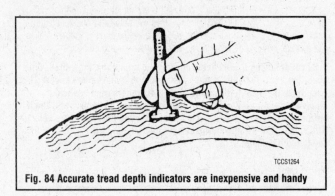

TCCS1264

Fig. 84 Accurate tread depth indicators are inexpensive and handy

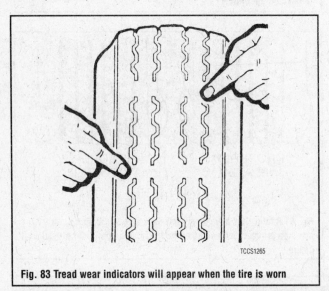

TCCS1265

Fig. 83 Tread wear indicators will appear when the tire is worn

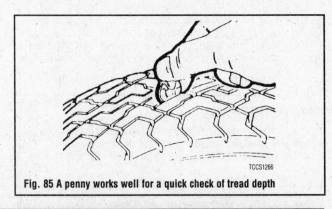

TCCS1266

Fig. 85 A penny works well for a quick check of tread depth

FLUIDS AND LUBRICANTS

Fluid Disposal

Used fluids such as engine oil, transmission fluid, antifreeze and brake fluid are hazardous wastes and must be disposed of properly. Before draining any fluids, consult with your local authorities; in many areas waste oil, etc. is being accepted as a part of recycling programs. A number of service stations and auto parts stores are also accepting waste fluids for recycling.

Be sure of the recycling center's policies before draining any fluids, as many will not accept different fluids that have been mixed together.

Fuel Recommendations

The engine is designed to operate on unleaded gasoline ONLY and is essential for the proper operation of the emission control system. The use of unleaded fuel will reduce spark plug fouling, exhaust system corrosion and engine oil deterioration.

In most parts of the United States, fuel with an octane rating of 87 should be used; in high altitude areas, fuel with an octane rating as low as 85 may be used.

In some areas, fuel consisting of a blend of alcohol may be used; this blend of gasoline and alcohol is known as gasohol. When using gasohol, never use blends exceeding 10% ethanol (ethyl or grain alcohol) or 5% methanol (methyl or wood alcohol).

➡**The use of fuel with excessive amounts of alcohol may jeopardize the new car and emission control system warranties.**

Engine Oil Recommendations

▶ **See Figure 86 and 87**

Use only oil which has the API (American Petroleum Institute) designation **SG**, **CC**, **CD**, **SG/CC** or **SG/CD**.

Since fuel economy is effected by the viscosity (thickness) of the engine oil, it is recommended to select an oil with reference to the outside temperature. For satisfactory lubrication, use a lower viscosity oil for colder temperatures and a higher viscosity oil for warmer temperatures.

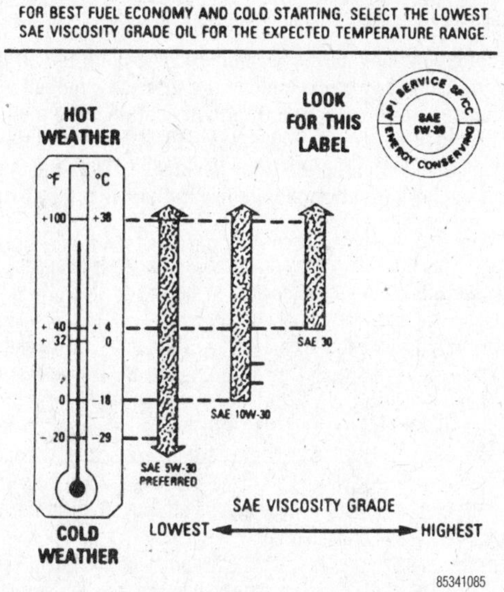

Fig. 86 Recommended SAE viscosity grade engine oil

Engine

OIL LEVEL CHECK

◗ See Figures 88, 89, 90 and 91

Your engine oil should be checked at regular intervals (such as every fuel stop). Check the engine oil as follows:

1. Make sure the car is parked on level ground.

2. When checking the oil level it is best for the engine to be at normal operating temperature, although checking the oil immediately after stopping will lead to a false reading. Wait a few minutes after turning off the engine to allow the oil to drain back into the crankcase.

3. Open the hood and locate the dipstick which should be on either the passenger's side for the V8 engine or driver's side for the L4 and V6 engines. Pull the dipstick from its tube, wipe it clean and then reinsert it.

4. Pull the dipstick out again and, holding it horizontally, read the oil level. The oil should be between the **FULL** and **ADD** marks on the dipstick. If the oil is below the **ADD** mark, add oil of the proper viscosity through the capped opening in the top of the cylinder head cover.

5. Replace the dipstick and check the oil level again after adding any oil. Be careful not to overfill the crankcase. Approximately 1 quart (0.9L) of oil will raise the level from the **ADD** mark to the **FULL** mark. Excess oil will generally be consumed at an accelerated rate.

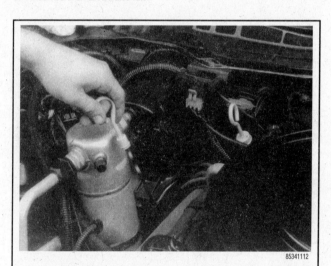

Fig. 88 Wipe the dipstick clean and insert it into the dipstick tube, making sure it is fully inserted

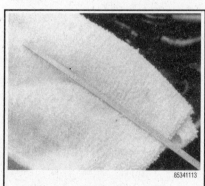

Fig. 87 Look for the API oil identification label when choosing your engine oil

Fig. 89 While holding the dipstick level, read the oil mark on the stick

Fig. 90 Remove the oil filler cap from the valve cover. Most filler caps are marked with the proper type of fluid

Fig. 91 Add clean oil to the engine to achieve the correct level, indicated on dipstick. Do not overfill

ENGINE OIL AND FILTER CHANGE

▶ **See Figures 92, 93 and 94**

Under normal operating conditions, the oil is to be changed every 7,500 miles (12,000km) or 12 months, whichever occurs first.

➡**Although the manufacturer recommends changing the filter at the first oil change and then at every other oil change, (unless 12 months pass between changes), Chilton recommends changing the filter with each service. It is a small price to pay for extra protection.**

When driving conditions frequently include dusty or polluted areas, trailer towing, idling for long periods of time, or low speed operation, or when operating at temperatures below freezing or driving short distances (under 4 miles or 6.4km), change the oil and filter more frequently. Under these circumstances, oil has a greater chance of building up sludge and contaminants which could damage your engine. If your vehicle use fits into one or more of these categories, (as it does for most vehicles), it is suggested that the oil and filter be changed every 3,000 miles (1361km) or 3 months, whichever comes first.

The oil should be disposed of properly after it is drained from the vehicle. Store the oil in a suitable container and take the container to an official oil recycling station. Most gas stations or oil and lube facilities will take the used oil at little or no expense to you.

Oil should always be changed after the engine has been running long enough to bring it up to normal operating temperature. Hot oil will flow more easily and will carry more contaminants than will cold oil. The oil drain plug is located on the bottom of the oil pan (bottom of the engine, underneath the car). The oil filter is located on the left side of most engines covered by this manual. To change the oil and filter:

1. Run the engine until it reaches normal operating temperature.
2. Raise the front of the vehicle and support it safely using a suitable pair of jackstands.
3. Slide a drain pan of a least 6 quarts capacity under the oil pan. Wipe the drain plug and surrounding area clean using an old rag.

✳✳ **CAUTION**

The EPA warns that prolonged contact with used engine oil may cause a number of skin disorders, including cancer! You should make every effort to minimize your exposure to used engine oil. Protective gloves should be worn when changing the oil. Wash your hands and any other exposed skin areas as soon as possible after exposure to used engine oil. Soap and water, or waterless hand cleaner should be used.

4. Loosen the drain plug using a ratchet, short extension and socket or a box-wrench. Turn the plug out by hand, using a rag to shield your fingers from the hot oil. By keeping an inward pressure on the plug as you unscrew it, oil won't escape past the threads and you can remove it without being burned by hot oil.

➡**If the drain plug is equipped with a removable washer or gasket, check its condition and replace, if necessary, to provide a leakproof seal.**

5. Quickly withdraw the plug and move your hands out of the way. Allow the oil to drain completely into the pan, then install and carefully tighten the drain plug. Be careful not to overtighten the drain plug, otherwise you'll be buying a new pan or a replacement plug for stripped threads.

➡**Although some manufacturers recommend changing the oil filter every other oil change, we recommend the filter be changed each time you change your oil. The old filter will contain up to a quart of dirty oil, which will contaminate the clean oil. Also, the benefit of clean oil is quickly lost if the old filter is clogged. The added protection for your engine far outweighs the few dollars saved by using an old filter.**

6. Move the drain pan under the oil filter. Use a strap-type or cap-type filter wrench to loosen and remove the oil filter from the engine block. Keep in mind that it's holding about one quart of hot, dirty oil.
7. Empty the old filter into the drain pan and properly dispose of the filter.
8. Using a clean rag, wipe off the filter adapter on the engine block. Be sure that the rag doesn't leave any lint which could clog an oil passage.
9. Coat the rubber gasket on the filter with fresh oil, then spin it onto the engine by hand; when the gasket touches the adapter surface, give it another 1/3–1/2 turn, (but no more, or you'll squash the gasket and it will leak).
10. Refill the engine with the correct amount of fresh oil. Please refer to the Capacities chart at the end of this section.
11. Check the oil level on the dipstick. It is normal for the level to be a bit above the full mark. Start the engine and allow it to idle for a few minutes.

✳✳ **CAUTION**

Do not run the engine above idle speed until it has built up oil pressure, as indicated when the oil light goes out.

12. Shut off the engine and allow the oil to flow back to the crankcase for a minute, then recheck the oil level. Check around the filter and drain plug for any leaks, and correct as necessary.

Manual Transmissions

FLUID RECOMMENDATIONS

- 1982–85 4-speed manual transmissions—SAE 80W/90 GL-5 gear lubricant
- 1986–87 4–speed manual transmission—Dexron®II automatic transmission fluid
- 1982–84 5-speed manual transmissions—use SAE 80W/90 GL-5 gear lubricant (SAE 80W GL-5 in Canada)
- 1985–92 5-speed manual transmissions—Dexron®II automatic transmission fluid

LEVEL CHECK

The oil in the manual transmission should be checked every 12 months or 15,000 miles.
1. Raise the car and support on jackstands as close to level as possible.
2. Remove the filler plug from the side of the transmission housing.

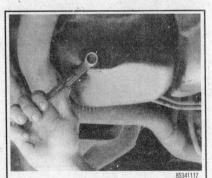
Fig. 92 Use a wrench or a socket to loosen the oil pan drain plug, but use care, the engine oil may be very hot

Fig. 93 Use an oil filter wrench to loosen, but not to install a filter

Fig. 94 Before installing a new oil filter, lightly coat the rubber gasket with clean oil

3. If lubricant begins to trickle out of the hole, there is enough and you need not go any further. Otherwise, carefully insert your finger (watch out for sharp threads) and check to see if the oil is up to the edge of the hole.

4. If not, add oil through the hole until the level is at the edge of the hole. Most lubricants come in a plastic squeeze bottle with a nozzle; making additions simple.

5. Install and tighten the filler plug.

DRAIN AND REFILL

The fluid in the manual transmission does not require changing. If you do choose to change the transmission fluid, the fluid can be drained out through the lower drain plug hole on the side of the transmission. Fill the transmission with the recommended lubricant to the bottom of the filler plug hole and install the filler plug.

Automatic Transmission

FLUID RECOMMENDATIONS

Use only Dexron®II Automatic Transmission Fluid.

LEVEL CHECK

▶ See Figure 95

Check the automatic transmission fluid level at each oil change. Driving with too much or too little transmission fluid can damage the transmission. The dipstick can be found in the rear of the engine compartment. The fluid level should be checked only when the transmission is at normal operating temperature. If your Camaro has been driven at highway speeds for a long time, in city traffic in hot weather, or pulling a trailer, wait for about 30 minutes for the fluid to cool down so a correct reading can be read.

1. Park the car on a level surface, with the parking brake on. Start the engine and let it idle for about 15 minutes. Move the transmission through all the gears and then back to **P**.

2. Remove the dipstick and carefully touch the wet end of the dipstick to see if the fluid is cool, warm, or hot. Wipe it clean and then reinsert it firmly. Be sure that it has been pushed all the way in. Remove the dipstick again and check the fluid level while holding it horizontally.

    a. If fluid is cool (room temperature), the level should be about ⅛–⅜ in. (3–10mm) below the ADD mark.

    b. If fluid is warm, the level should be close to the **ADD** mark, either above or below.

    c. If fluid is too hot to touch, the level should be at the **FULL** mark.

3. If the fluid level is low, add Dexron®II automatic transmission fluid (ATF) through the dipstick tube. This is easily done with the aid of a funnel. Check the level often as you are filling the transmission. Be extremely careful not to overfill it. Overfilling will cause slippage, seal damage and overheating.

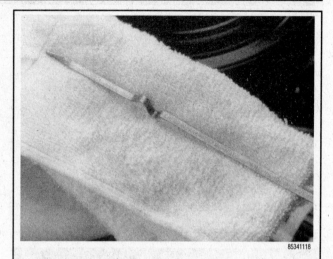

Fig. 95 Read automatic transmission fluid level on dipstick and add, as required

Approximately 1 pint (0.473L) of ATF will raise the fluid level from one notch/line to the other.

➡ **If the fluid on the dipstick appears discolored (brown or black), or smells burnt, serious transmission troubles, probably due to overheating, should be suspected. The transmission should be inspected by a qualified technician to locate the cause of the burnt fluid.**

DRAIN AND REFILL

Please refer to the "PAN AND FILTER SERVICE" procedure listed in this section.

PAN AND FILTER SERVICE

▶ See Figures 96 thru 104

The automatic transmission fluid and filter should be changed every 15,000 miles (24,000km) if your Camaro is driven in heavy city traffic in hot weather, in hilly or mountainous terrain, frequent trailer pulling, or uses such as found in taxi, police car or delivery service. If your Camaro is driven under other than listed above conditions, change the fluid and filter every 30,000 miles (48,300km).

1. Raise and support the car on jackstands. Place an oil catch pan under the transmission.

2. Remove the oil pan bolts from the front and sides only.

3. Loosen rear oil pan bolts approximately 4 turns.

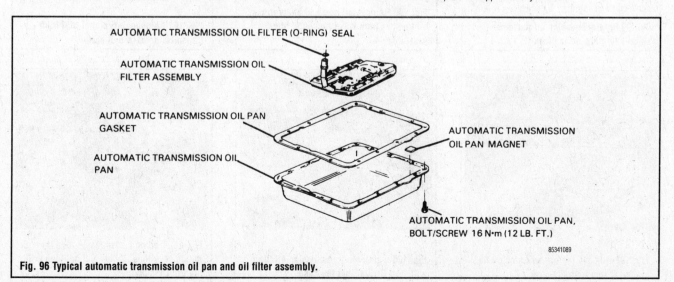

Fig. 96 Typical automatic transmission oil pan and oil filter assembly.

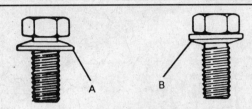

A AUTOMATIC TRANSMISSION OIL PAN BOLT/SCREW
  AND CONICAL WASHER ASSEMBLY IS REUSABLE
B AUTOMATIC TRANSMISSION OIL PAN BOLT/SCREW
  AND CONICAL WASHER ASSEMBLY IS NOT REUSABLE

Fig. 97 Automatic transmission oil pan bolt and conical washer assembly

✳✳ WARNING

Do not damage the transmission case or oil pan sealing surfaces.

  4. Lightly tap the oil pan with a rubber mallet or gently pry it downward to allow fluid to drain.
  5. Remove the remaining oil pan bolts, then remove the oil pan and pan gasket.
  6. Remove the filter and seal.
  7. Clean the transmission case and oil pan gasket surfaces with suitable solvent and air dry. Make sure to remove all traces of the old gasket.

To install:
  8. Coat the seal with a small amount of Transjel®.
  9. Install the new seal onto the filter.
  10. Install the new filter into the case.
  11. Install the oil pan and new gasket.

➥On 1991 and later vehicles, inspect the oil pan screws and washer assemblies. The screws must not be used if the conical washer is reversed. Failure to replace the screw and washer assembly may result in improper fastening of system components.

  12. Install the oil pan bolts and tighten them to 12 ft. lbs. (16 Nm).
  13. Lower the car.
  14. Fill the transmission to proper level with Dexron®II fluid.
  15. Check cold fluid level reading for initial fill. Do not overfill the transmission.
  16. Follow the fluid level check procedure described before.
  17. Check the oil pan gasket for leaks.

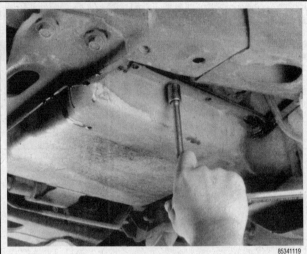

Fig. 98 Removing side transmission oil pan bolts

Fig. 99 Pry transmission oil pan down slightly to allow oil to drain

Fig. 100 Remove oil pan and allow excess oil to drain from valve body and filter assembly

Fig. 101 Remove gasket material from transmission case and pan

Fig. 102 Remove the transmission oil filter and O-ring from the case

Fig. 103 Install the transmission oil filter with new O-ring, into the case

Fig. 104 Adding transmission fluid through the dipstick tube. Be careful not to overfill the transmission.

Drive Axle

FLUID RECOMMENDATIONS

On standard differential rear axle assemblies, use SAE 80W-90 GL-5 (SAE 80W GL-5 in Canada) gear lubricant. On limited slip differential rear axle assemblies, use 4 fl. oz. of limited slip differential additive lubricant and SAE 80W-90 GL-5 gear lubricant.

LEVEL CHECK

▶ **See Figure 105**

The gear lubricant in the drive axle should be checked every 12 months or 15,000 miles (24,000km).
1. Raise the car and support on jackstands as close to level as possible.
2. Remove the filler plug from the side of the drive axle housing.
3. If lubricant begins to trickle out of the hole, there is enough and you need not go any further. Otherwise, carefully insert your finger (watch out for sharp threads) and check to see if the lubricant is up to the edge of the hole.
4. If not, add oil through the hole until the level is at the edge of the hole. Most gear lubricants come in a plastic squeeze bottle with a nozzle; making additions simple.
5. Install and tighten the filler plug.

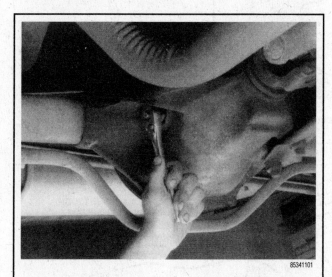

Fig. 105 Removing filler plug to check rear axle lubricant

DRAIN AND REFILL

The rear axle should have the gear lubricant changed every 7,500 miles (12,000km). If equipped with a limited slip differential, be sure to add 4 oz. (118mL) of GM limited slip additive part No. 1052358.
1. Raise the car and support on jackstands. Place a container under the differential to catch the fluid.
2. Remove the bolts retaining the parking brake cable guides and position aside.
3. Clean all dirt from the area around the cover. Remove the bolts retaining the cover to the housing. Pry the cover from the differential housing and allow the fluid to drain into the catch pan.
To install:
4. With the cover and housing washed free of oil and gasket material, apply sealer to the mating surfaces.
5. Using a new gasket, install the cover and torque the bolts to 20 ft. lbs. (27 Nm) in a clockwise pattern to insure uniform draw on the gasket. Fill the differential with fluid through the fill plug and add limited slip additive, as required.
6. Install the parking brake cable guides, if removed.

7. The fluid level should reached a level within ⅜ in. (10mm) of the filler plug hole. Replace the filler plug. Lower the car and inspect for leaks.

Cooling System

❈❈ CAUTION

When draining the coolant, keep in mind that cats and dogs are attracted by the ethylene glycol antifreeze, and are quite likely to drink any that is left in an uncovered container or in puddles on the ground. This will prove fatal in sufficient quantity. Always drain the coolant into a sealable container. Coolant should be reused unless it is contaminated or several years old (in which case it should be taken to a recycling facility such as a service station).

FLUID RECOMMENDATIONS

When adding or changing the fluid in the system, create a 50/50 mixture of high quality ethylene glycol antifreeze and water.

LEVEL CHECK

▶ **See Figure 106**

The fluid level may be checked by observing the fluid level marks of the recovery tank. The level should be between the **FULL HOT** and **FULL COLD** mark when the system is at normal operating temperature. When the engine is cold, the fluid level should be above the **FULL COLD** mark on the reservoir. At normal operating temperatures, the level should be between the **ADD** and the **FULL** marks. Only add coolant to bring the level to the **FULL** mark.

❈❈ CAUTION

Should it be necessary to remove the radiator cap, make sure that the system has had time to cool, reducing the internal pressure. If the system is opened while the engine is still hot, scalding fluid and steam may be blown out under pressure.

DRAINING AND REFILLING

▶ **See Figures 107 thru 112**

❈❈ CAUTION

Do not remove a radiator cap while the engine and radiator are still hot. Danger of burns by scalding fluid and steam under pressure may result!

1. With a cool engine, slowly rotate the radiator cap counterclockwise to the detent without pressing down on the cap.
2. Wait until any remaining pressure is relieved by listening for a hissing sound.
3. After all the pressure is relieved, press down on the cap and continue to rotate the radiator cap counterclockwise.
4. With a suitable container to catch the fluid under the radiator, open the radiator drain cock.
5. If equipped, remove the engine block drain plugs and the knock sensor, located on either side of the engine block. This will help to drain the coolant from the block.
6. Loosen or slide the recovery tank hose clamp at the radiator filler neck overflow tube and remove the hose. Holding the hose down to the drain pan, allow the recovery tank to empty. Attach the hose to the filler neck overflow and tighten the clamp.
7. Close the radiator drain cock and install the engine block drain plug and knock sensor. Tighten the knock sensor to 14 ft. lbs. (19 Nm), the engine block drain plug to 15 ft. lbs. (21 Nm), and the drain cock to 13 inch lbs. (1.5 Nm).
8. Add enough coolant mixture to fill the system to a level just below the radiator neck. Fill the reservoir assembly to the "FULL COLD" mark.

Fig. 106 Fluid level marks on the coolant recovery tank. With a warm system, coolant level should be just below the FULL HOT mark on tank

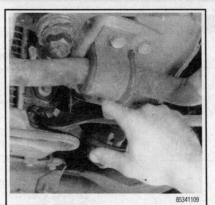

Fig. 107 Open radiator drain cock to drain coolant from the system

Fig. 108 Adding coolant to the recovery tank to fill to the proper level

Fig. 109 Be sure the rubber gasket on the radiator cap has a tight seal

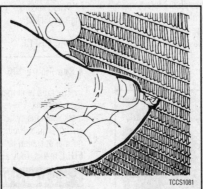

Fig. 110 Periodically remove all debris from the radiator fins

Fig. 111 Cooling systems should be pressure tested for leaks periodically

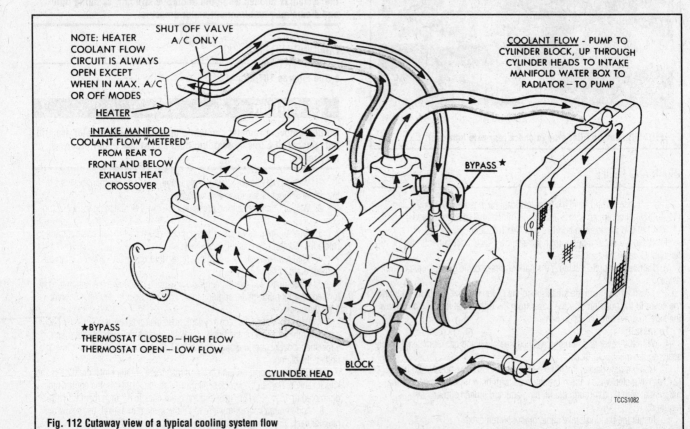

Fig. 112 Cutaway view of a typical cooling system flow

➡️Fill the cooling system with a 50/50 mixture of water and Ethylene Glycol antifreeze. Freezing protection should be appropriate for temperatures of -34°F (-37°C). When filling the coolant system, add two cooling system sealer pellets (GM part no. 3634621 or equivalent).

9. Firmly set the parking brake. Run the engine with the radiator cap OFF, until normal operating temperature is reached.

✳✳ CAUTION

Under some conditions, ethylene glycol is flammable. To avoid being burned when adding engine coolant, do not spill it on the exhaust system or on hot engine parts.

10. With the engine idling, add engine coolant to the radiator until the level reaches the bottom of the radiator fill neck. Install the cap assembly. When installing the cap, make sure that the arrows on the cap line up with the overflow tube.

➡️**Never add cold water to an overheated engine.**

11. Add coolant to the recovery tank, as necessary.
12. After filling the radiator and recovery tank, run the engine until it reaches normal operating temperature, to make sure that the thermostat has opened and all the air is bled from the system.

FLUSHING AND CLEANING THE SYSTEM

◆ See Figure 113

The cooling system should be drained, thoroughly flushed and refilled at least every 30,000 miles or 24 months. This operation should be done with the engine cold.
1. Drain the cooling system as described earlier in this section.
2. Fill the cooling system with warm water and start the engine. Run the engine until normal operating temperature is reached.
3. At this point, turn the engine off and again drain the cooling system.
4. Repeat this procedure until the fluid draining from the system is nearly colorless.
5. Remove, empty and reinstall the coolant recovery reservoir assembly.
6. Fill the cooling system with a 50/50 mixture of ethylene glycol antifreeze, as outlined in the previous procedure.

Brake Master Cylinder

FLUID RECOMMENDATIONS

When adding or replacing the brake fluid, always use a top quality fluid, such as Delco Supreme II or equivalent DOT-3 fluid. DO NOT allow the master cylinder reservoir to remain open for long periods of time; brake fluid absorbs moisture from the air, reducing its effectiveness and causing corrosion in the lines.

➡️**Avoid spilling brake fluid on any of the vehicle's painted surfaces, wiring cables or electrical connections. Brake fluid will damage paint and electrical connections. If any fluid is spilled on the vehicle, flush with water to lessen damage.**

LEVEL CHECK

◆ See Figures 114, 115 and 116

The master cylinder is located in the left rear section of the engine compartment. The brake master cylinder consists of an aluminum body and a translucent nylon reservoir with minimum fill indicators.
1. Check the master cylinder body for cracks. Inspect the area around the master cylinder for brake fluid. Leaks are indicated if there is at least a drop of fluid. A damp condition is not normal.
2. Inspect the level of the brake fluid to assure it is at the correct height. Clean the top of the reservoir cap so that all dirt is removed. Remove the cap(s) or reservoir cover and the reservoir diaphragm.
3. Inspect the brake fluid level. Add clean DOT-3 brake fluid as required to bring the fluid level to the line located inside the neck of the reservoir fill opening.
4. Install the reservoir cap.

✳✳ WARNING

Any sudden decrease in the fluid level indicates a possible leak in the system and should be checked out immediately. Do not allow brake fluid to spill on the vehicle's finish; it will remove the paint. In case of a spill, flush the area with water and mild soap.

Hydraulic Clutch System

FLUID RECOMMENDATIONS

- 1982–1991—Delco Supreme II Brake fluid or an equivalent fluid that meets DOT-3 specifications
- 1992—Hydraulic clutch fluid, GM part number 12345347 or equivalent

LEVEL CHECK

The clutch master cylinder is normally located below the brake master cylinder. The reservoir for it is located right beside the brake master cylinder and is made of translucent nylon. The fluid level of the reservoir should be kept near the top of the observation window. Before removing the cap to the reservoir, clean all dirt from the area. This will prevent system contamination due to particles falling into the reservoir when the caps are removed.

Fig. 113 Flush system until the fluid drained is nearly colorless

Fig. 114 Check master cylinder fluid level against indicator on side of reservoir. Fluid level should not be below MIN marking on reservoir

Fig. 115 Remove the reservoir cover, inspect condition of brake fluid and reservoir diaphragm

Fig. 116 Add clean brake fluid meeting DOT-3 requirements to fill reservoir to the proper level

Fig. 117 Common power steering pump location

Fig. 118 Power steering pump reservoir cap with fluid level indicator attached

Power Steering Pump

FLUID RECOMMENDATIONS

- GM power steering fluid, or equivalent.

LEVEL CHECK

▶ See Figures 117, 118 and 119

Power steering fluid level should be checked at least twice a year. To prevent possible overfilling, check the fluid level only when the fluid has warmed to operating temperatures and the wheels are turned straight ahead. If the level is low, fill the pump reservoir until the fluid level measures between the COLD and HOT marks on the reservoir dipstick. Low fluid level usually produces a moaning sound as the wheels are turned (especially when standing still or parking) and increases steering wheel effort.

Steering Gear

FLUID RECOMMENDATIONS

The 1982–92 vehicles are equipped with a power steering gear. All vehicles use GM power steering fluid, or equivalent.

Chassis Greasing

Chassis lubrication can be performed with a pressurized grease gun or by using a hand-operated grease gun. Wipe the grease fittings clean before greasing in order to prevent the possibility of forcing any dirt into the component.

Body Lubrication

HOOD LATCH AND HINGES

Clean the latch surfaces and apply clean engine oil to the latch pilot bolts and the spring anchor. Use the engine oil to lubricate the hood hinges as well. Use a chassis grease to lubricate all the pivot points in the latch release mechanism.

DOOR HINGES

The gas tank filler door, car door, and rear hatch or trunk lid hinges should be wiped clean and lubricated with clean engine oil. Silicone spray also works well on seals, but must be applied more often. Use engine oil to lubricate the trunk or hatch lock mechanism and the lock bolt and striker. The door lock cylinders can be lubricated easily with a shot of silicone spray or one of the many dry penetrating lubricants commercially available.

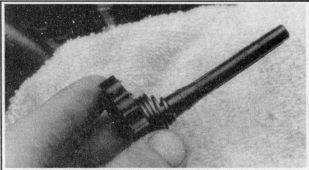

Fig. 119 Note location of power steering fluid on indicator. Do not overfill power steering pump when adding fluid

PARKING BRAKE LINKAGE

Use chassis grease on the parking brake cable where it contacts the guides, links, levers, and pulleys. The grease should be water resistant for durability.

ACCELERATOR LINKAGE

Lubricate the throttle lever, and the accelerator pedal lever at the support inside the car with clean engine oil.

TRANSMISSION SHIFT LINKAGE

Lubricate the shift linkage with water resistant chassis grease which meets GM Specification 6031M or its equal.

Front Wheel Bearings

Once every 30,000 miles, clean and repack wheel bearings with a wheel bearing packer. Remove any excess grease from the exposed surface of the hub and seal.

REMOVAL, REPACKING, INSTALLATION AND ADJUSTMENT

▶ See Figures 120 thru 133

✵✵ WARNING

It is important that wheel bearings be properly adjusted after installation. Improperly adjusted wheel bearings can cause steering instability, front end shimmy and wander, and increased tire wear.

Fig. 120 Pry the dust cap from the hub, taking care not to distort or damage its flange

Fig. 121 Once the ends are cut, grasp the cotter pin and pull or pry it free of the spindle

Fig. 122 If difficulty is encountered, gently tap on the pliers with a hammer to help free the cotter pin

Fig. 123 Loosen and remove the castellated nut from the spindle

Fig. 124 Remove the washer from the spindle

Fig. 125 With the nut and washer out of the way, the outer bearings may be removed from the hub

Fig. 126 Pull the hub and inner bearing assembly from the spindle

Fig. 127 Use a small prytool to remove the old inner bearing seal

Fig. 128 With the seal removed, the inner bearing may be withdrawn from the hub

Fig. 129 Thoroughly pack the bearing with fresh, high temperature wheel bearing grease before installation

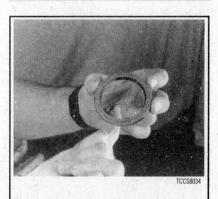

Fig. 130 Apply a thin coat of fresh grease to the new inner bearing seal lip

TCCS8035

Fig. 131 Use a suitably sized driver to install the inner bearing seal to the hub

TCCS8036

Fig. 132 With new or freshly packed bearings, tighten the nut to 12 ft. lbs. (16 Nm) while gently spinning the wheel, then adjust the bearings

TCCS8037

Fig. 133 After the bearings are adjusted, install the dust cap by gently tapping on the flange—DO NOT damage the cap by hammering on the center

1. Raise the car and support it at the lower arm. Remove the tire and wheel assembly.
2. Remove the brake caliper and support it on a wire.
3. Remove the dust cap, cotter pin, castle nut, thrust washer and outside wheel bearing.
4. Pull the disc/hub assembly from the steering knuckle.
5. Pry out the inner seal and remove the inner bearing.
6. Wipe out the grease from inside the hub.
7. Clean the wheel bearings thoroughly with solvent and check their condition before installation. After cleaning, check parts for excessive wear and replace damaged parts.

❊❊ WARNING

Do not allow the bearing to spin when blowing dry with compressed air, as this would allow the bearing to turn without lubrication.

8. Apply a sizable amount of lubricant to the palm of one hand. Using your other hand, work the bearing into the lubricant so that the grease is pushed through the rollers and out the other side. Keep rotating the bearing while continuing to push the lubricant through it.
9. Apply grease to the inside of the hub and install the inner bearing in the hub. Install a new grease seal, be careful not to damage the seal.
10. Install the disc/hub assembly onto the steering knuckle. Install the outer bearing, thrust washer and castle nut. Torque the nut to 12 ft. lbs. (16 Nm) while turning the wheel.
11. Back the nut off and retighten it by hand until nearest slot aligns with the cotter pin hole.
12. Insert a new cotter pin.
13. Mount a dial indicator onto the vehicle so that any end-play in the hub can be measured. Measure the end-play and record the value. End-play should be between 0.001–0.005 in. (0.025–0.127mm). If play exceeds this tolerance, the wheel bearings should be replaced.

JUMP STARTING A DEAD BATTERY

♦ **See Figure 134**

Whenever a vehicle is jump started, precautions must be followed in order to prevent the possibility of personal injury. Remember that batteries contain a small amount of explosive hydrogen gas which is a by-product of battery charging. Sparks should always be avoided when working around batteries, especially when attaching jumper cables. To minimize the possibility of accidental sparks, follow the procedure carefully.

❊❊ CAUTION

NEVER hook the batteries up in a series circuit or the entire electrical system will go up in smoke, including the starter!

Vehicles equipped with a diesel engine may utilize two 12 volt batteries. If so, the batteries are connected in a parallel circuit (positive terminal to positive terminal, negative terminal to negative terminal). Hooking the batteries up in parallel circuit increases battery cranking power without increasing total battery voltage output. Output remains at 12 volts. On the other hand, hooking two 12 volt batteries up in a series circuit (positive terminal to negative terminal, positive terminal to negative terminal) increases total battery output to 24 volts (12 volts plus 12 volts).

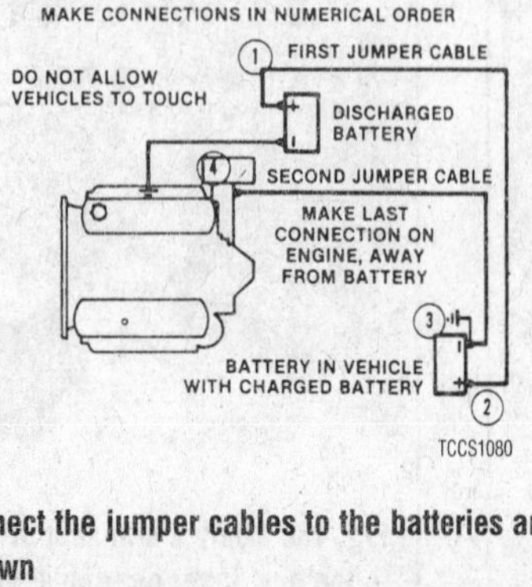

Jump Starting Precautions

- Be sure that both batteries are of the same voltage. Vehicles covered by this manual and most vehicles on the road today utilize a 12 volt charging system.
- Be sure that both batteries are of the same polarity (have the same terminal, in most cases NEGATIVE grounded).
- Be sure that the vehicles are not touching or a short could occur.
- On serviceable batteries, be sure the vent cap holes are not obstructed.
- Do not smoke or allow sparks anywhere near the batteries.
- In cold weather, make sure the battery electrolyte is not frozen. This can occur more readily in a battery that has been in a state of discharge.
- Do not allow electrolyte to contact your skin or clothing.

Jump Starting Procedure

1. Make sure that the voltages of the 2 batteries are the same. Most batteries and charging systems are of the 12 volt variety.
2. Pull the jumping vehicle (with the good battery) into a position so the jumper cables can reach the dead battery and that vehicle's engine. Make sure that the vehicles do NOT touch.
3. Place the transmissions of both vehicles in **Neutral** (MT) or **P** (AT), as applicable, then firmly set their parking brakes.

➡ **If necessary for safety reasons, the hazard lights on both vehicles may be operated throughout the entire procedure without significantly increasing the difficulty of jumping the dead battery.**

MAKE CONNECTIONS IN NUMERICAL ORDER

① FIRST JUMPER CABLE

DO NOT ALLOW VEHICLES TO TOUCH

DISCHARGED BATTERY

SECOND JUMPER CABLE

MAKE LAST CONNECTION ON ENGINE, AWAY FROM BATTERY

BATTERY IN VEHICLE WITH CHARGED BATTERY

TCCS1080

Fig. 134 Connect the jumper cables to the batteries and engine in the order shown

4. Turn all lights and accessories OFF on both vehicles. Make sure the ignition switches on both vehicles are turned to the **OFF** position.

5. Cover the battery cell caps with a rag, but do not cover the terminals.

6. Make sure the terminals on both batteries are clean and free of corrosion or proper electrical connection will be impeded. If necessary, clean the battery terminals before proceeding.

7. Identify the positive (+) and negative (−) terminals on both batteries.

8. Connect the first jumper cable to the positive (+) terminal of the dead battery, then connect the other end of that cable to the positive (+) terminal of the booster (good) battery.

9. Connect one end of the other jumper cable to the negative (−) terminal on the booster battery and the final cable clamp to an engine bolt head, alternator bracket or other solid, metallic point on the engine with the dead battery. Try to pick a ground on the engine that is positioned away from the battery in order to minimize the possibility of the 2 clamps touching should one loosen during the procedure. DO NOT connect this clamp to the negative (−) terminal of the bad battery.

✳✳ CAUTION

Be very careful to keep the jumper cables away from moving parts (cooling fan, belts, etc.) on both engines.

10. Check to make sure that the cables are routed away from any moving parts, then start the donor vehicle's engine. Run the engine at moderate speed for several minutes to allow the dead battery a chance to receive some initial charge.

11. With the donor vehicle's engine still running slightly above idle, try to start the vehicle with the dead battery. Crank the engine for no more than 10 seconds at a time and let the starter cool for at least 20 seconds between tries. If the vehicle does not start in 3 tries, it is likely that something else is also wrong or that the battery needs additional time to charge.

12. Once the vehicle is started, allow it to run at idle for a few seconds to make sure that it is operating properly.

13. Turn ON the headlights, heater blower and, if equipped, the rear defroster of both vehicles in order to reduce the severity of voltage spikes and subsequent risk of damage to the vehicles' electrical systems when the cables are disconnected. This step is especially important to any vehicle equipped with computer control modules.

14. Carefully disconnect the cables in the reverse order of connection. Start with the negative cable that is attached to the engine ground, then the negative cable on the donor battery. Disconnect the positive cable from the donor battery and finally, disconnect the positive cable from the formerly dead battery. Be careful when disconnecting the cables from the positive terminals not to allow the alligator clips to touch any metal on either vehicle or a short and sparks will occur.

JACKING

▶ **See Figure 135**

Your vehicle was supplied with a jack for emergency road repairs. This jack is fine for changing a flat tire or other short term procedures not requiring you to go beneath the vehicle. If it is used in an emergency situation, carefully follow the instructions provided either with the jack or in your owner's manual. Do not attempt to use the jack on any portions of the vehicle other than specified by the vehicle manufacturer. Always block the diagonally opposite wheel when using a jack.

A more convenient way of jacking is the use of a garage or floor jack. You may use the floor jack to raise the vehicle in the areas shown in the illustration .

Never place the jack under the radiator, engine or transmission components. Severe and expensive damage will result when the jack is raised. Additionally, never jack under the floorpan or bodywork; the metal will deform.

Whenever you plan to work under the vehicle, you must support it on jackstands or ramps. Never use cinder blocks or stacks of wood to support the vehicle, even if you're only going to be under it for a few minutes. Never crawl under the vehicle when it is supported only by the tire-changing jack or other floor jack.

➥ **Always position a block of wood or small rubber pad on top of the jack or jackstand to protect the lifting point's finish when lifting or supporting the vehicle.**

Small hydraulic, screw, or scissors jacks are satisfactory for raising the vehicle. Drive-on trestles or ramps are also a handy and safe way to both raise and support the vehicle. Be careful though, some ramps may be too steep to drive your vehicle onto without scraping the front bottom panels. Never support the vehicle on any suspension member (unless specifically instructed to do so by a repair manual) or by an underbody panel.

Jacking Precautions

The following safety points cannot be overemphasized:
• Always block the opposite wheel or wheels to keep the vehicle from rolling off the jack.
• When raising the front of the vehicle, firmly apply the parking brake.
• When the drive wheels are to remain on the ground, leave the vehicle in gear to help prevent it from rolling.
• Always use jackstands to support the vehicle when you are working underneath. Place the stands beneath the vehicle's jacking brackets. Before climbing underneath, rock the vehicle a bit to make sure it is firmly supported.

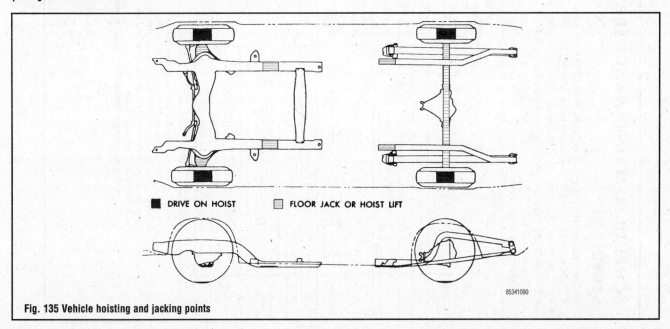

DRIVE ON HOIST   FLOOR JACK OR HOIST LIFT

85341090

Fig. 135 Vehicle hoisting and jacking points

SCHEDULED MAINTENANCE SERVICES

SCHEDULE I

Follow Schedule I if your vehicle is MAINLY driven under one or more of the following conditions:
- When most trips are less than 6 kilometers (4 miles).
- When most trips are less than 16 kilometers (10 miles) and outside temperatures remain below freezing.
- When most trips include extended idling and/or frequent low-speed operation as in stop-and-go traffic. †
- Towing a trailer. **
- Operating in dusty areas.

The services shown in this schedule up to 80 000 km (48,000 miles) are to be performed after 80 000 km (48,000 miles) at the same intervals.

ITEM NO.	TO BE SERVICED	WHEN TO PERFORM — Kilometers (Miles) or Months, Whichever Occurs First	KILOMETERS (000) 5 / MILES 3	10 / 6	15 / 9	20 / 12	25 / 15	30 / 18	35 / 21	40 / 24	45 / 27	50 / 30	55 / 33	60 / 36	65 / 39	70 / 42	75 / 45	80 / 48
1.	Engine Oil & Oil Filter Change*	Every 5 000 km (3,000 mi.) or 3 mos.	•	•	•	•	•	•	•	•	•	•	•	•	•	•	•	•
2.	Chassis Lubrication	Every other oil change		•		•		•		•		•		•		•		•
3.	Throttle Body Mounting Bolt Torque (some models)*	At 10 000 km (6,000 mi.) only		•														
4.	Tire & Wheel Inspection & Rotation	At 10 000 km (6,000 mi.) and then every 25 000 km (15,000 mi.)		•					•					•				
5.	Engine Accessory Drive Belt Inspection											•						
6.	Cooling System Service*	Every 50 000 km (30,000 mi.) or 24 mos.										•						
7.	Front Wheel Bearing Repack	See explanation for service interval																
8.	Transmission Service																	
9.	Spark Plug Replacement*											•						
10.	Spark Plug Wire Inspection (some models)* ‡											•						
11.	PCV Valve Inspection (some models)* ‡											•						
12.	EGR System Inspection (some models)* ‡	Every 50 000 km (30,000 mi.)										•						
13.	Air Cleaner & PCV Filter Replacement*											•						
14.	Engine Timing Check (some models)*											•						
15.	Fuel Tank, Cap & Lines Inspection* ‡											•						

† Note: Schedule I should also be followed if the vehicle is used for delivery service, police, taxi or other commercial applications.

‡ The U.S. Environmental Protection Agency has determined that the failure to perform this maintenance item will not nullify the emission warranty or limit recall liability prior to the completion of vehicle useful life. General Motors, however, urges that all recommended maintenance services be performed at the indicated intervals and the maintenance be recorded in section E of the owner's maintenance schedule.

* An Emission Control Service

** Trailering is not recommended for some models. See your Owner's Manual for details.

85341091

SCHEDULED MAINTENANCE SERVICES

SCHEDULE II

Follow Schedule II ONLY if none of the driving conditions specified in Schedule I apply.

WHEN TO PERFORM — Kilometers (Miles) or Months, Whichever Occurs First

The services shown in this schedule up to 75 000 km (45,000 miles) are to be performed after 75 000 km (45,000 miles) at the same intervals.

ITEM NO.	TO BE SERVICED	WHEN TO PERFORM	KILOMETERS (000) 12.5 / MILES (000) 7.5	25 / 15	37.5 / 22.5	50 / 30	62.5 / 37.5	75 / 45
1.	Engine Oil Change*	Every 12 500 km (7,500 mi.) or 12 mos.	●	●	●	●	●	●
	Oil Filter Change*	At first and then every other oil change	●		●		●	
2.	Chassis Lubrication	Every 12 500 km (7,500 mi.) or 12 mos.	●	●	●	●	●	●
3.	Throttle Body Mounting Bolt Torque (some models)*	At 12 500 km (7,500 mi.) only	●					
4.	Tire & Wheel Inspection & Rotation	At 12 500 km (7,500 mi.) and then every 25 000 km (15,000 mi.)	●		●		●	
5.	Engine Accessory Drive Belt Inspection	Every 50 000 km (30,000 mi.) or 24 mos.				●		
6.	Cooling System Service*	Every 50 000 km (30,000 mi.)				●		
7.	Front Wheel Bearing Repack	Every 50 000 km (30,000 mi.)				●		
8.	Transmission Service	See explanation for service interval.						
9.	Spark Plug Replacement*	Every 50 000 km (30,000 mi.)				●		
10.	Spark Plug Wire Inspection (some models)*‡					●		
11.	PCV Valve Inspection (some models)*‡					●		
12.	EGR System Inspection (some models)*‡					●		
13.	Air Cleaner & PCV Filter Replacement*					●		
14.	Engine Timing Check (some models)*					●		
15.	Fuel Tank, Cap & Lines Inspection*‡					●		

‡ The U.S. Environmental Protection Agency has determined that the failure to perform this maintenance item will not nullify the emission warranty or limit recall liability prior to the completion of vehicle useful life. General Motors, however, urges that all recommended maintenance services be performed at the indicated intervals and the maintenance be recorded in section E of the owner's maintenance schedule.

* An Emission Control Service

8534109Z

CAPACITIES

Year	VIN	Engine No. Cyl. Liters	Crankcase Includes Filter (qts.)	Transmission (pts.) 4-Sp	5-Sp	Auto.	Drive Axle (pts.)	Fuel Tank (gal.)	Cooling System (qt.) w/AC	wo/AC
1982	2	4-2.5L	3	3.5	—	7	3.5	16	9.1	8.8
	1	6-2.8L	4	3.5	—	7	3.5	16	9.1	8.8
	H	8-5.0L	5	3.5	—	7	3.5	16	9.1	8.8
	7	8-5.0L	5	3.5	—	7	3.5	16	9.1	8.8
1983	2	4-2.5L	3	3.5	3.5	7	3.5	16	9.1	8.8
	1	6-2.8L	4	3.5	3.5	7	3.5	16	9.1	8.8
	H	8-5.0L	5	3.5	3.5	7	3.5	16	9.1	8.8
	7	8-5.0L	5	3.5	3.5	7	3.5	16	9.1	8.8
1984	2	4-2.5L	3	3.5	3.5	7	3.5	16	9.1	8.8
	1	6-2.8L	4	3.5	3.5	7	3.5	16	9.1	8.8
	H	8-5.0L	5	3.5	3.5	7	3.5	16	9.1	8.8
	G	8-5.0L	5	3.5	3.5	7	3.5	16	9.1	8.8
1985	2	4-2.5L	3	—	4.0	10	3.5	15.5	13.0	12.75
	S	6-2.8L	4	—	4.0	10	3.5	15.5	12.5	12.5
	H	8-5.0L	5	—	4.0	10	3.5	16.2	17.0	15.5
	G	8-5.0L	5	—	4.0	10	3.5	16.2	17.0	17.0
	F	8-5.0L	5	—	4.0	10	3.5	15.5	17.0	17.0
1986	2	4-2.5L	3	—	6.6	10	3.5	15.5	9.8	9.8
	S	6-2.8L	4	—	6.6	10	3.5	15.5	12.5	12.5
	H	8-5.0L	5	—	6.6	10	3.5	16.2	15.6	15.3
	G	8-5.0L	5	—	6.6	10	3.5	16.2	17.0	17.0
	F	8-5.0L	5	—	6.6	10	3.5	15.5	17.0	17.0
	8	8-5.7L	5	—	6.6	10	3.5	15.5	17.0	17.0
1987	S	6-2.8L	4	—	6.6	10	3.5	15.5	12.5	12.5
	H	8-5.0L	5	—	6.6	10	3.5	16.2	15.6	15.3
	F	8-5.0L	5	—	6.6	10	3.5	15.5	17.0	17.0
	8	8-5.7L	5	—	6.6	10	3.5	15.5	17.0	17.0
1988	S	6-2.8L	4	—	5.8	10	3.5	15.9	12.5	12.5
	E	8-5.0L	5	—	5.8	10	3.5	15.9	15.6	15.3
	F	8-5.0L	5	—	5.8	10	3.5	15.9	17.0	17.0
	8	8-5.7L	5	—	5.8	10	3.5	15.9	17.0	17.0
1989	S	6-2.8L	4	—	5.9	10	3.5	15.5	12.4	12.4
	E	8-5.0L	5	—	5.9	10	3.5	15.5	15.6	15.6
	F	8-5.0L	5	—	5.9	10	3.5	15.5	17.0	17.0
	8	8-5.7L	5	—	5.9	10	3.5	15.5	17.0	17.0
1990	T	6-3.1L	4	—	5.9	10	4.0	15.5	14.5	14.5
	E	8-5.0L	5	—	5.9	10	4.0	15.5	18.0	17.5
	F	8-5.0L	5	—	5.9	10	4.0	15.5	17.4	17.3
	8	8-5.7L	5	—	5.9	10	4.0	15.5	16.3	16.1
1991	T	6-3.1L	4	—	5.9	10	4.0	15.5	14.8	14.7
	E	8-5.0L	5	—	5.9	10	4.0	15.5	18.0	17.4
	F	8-5.0L	5	—	5.9	10	4.0	15.5	18.0	17.9
	8	8-5.7L	5	—	5.9	10	4.0	15.5	16.7	16.6
1992	T	6-3.1L	4	—	5.9	10	4.0	15.5	14.7	14.7
	E	8-5.0L	5	—	5.9	6.3	4.0	15.5	18.0	17.3
	F	8-5.0L	5	—	5.9	10	4.0	15.5	17.3	17.1
	8	8-5.7L	5	—	5.9	10	4.0	15.5	16.4	16.4

82601C12

ENGLISH TO METRIC CONVERSION: MASS (WEIGHT)

Current mass measurement is expressed in pounds and ounces (lbs. & ozs.). The metric unit of mass (or weight) is the kilogram (kg). Even although this table does not show conversion of masses (weights) larger than 15 lbs, it is easy to calculate larger units by following the data immediately below.

To convert ounces (oz.) to grams (g): multiply th number of ozs. by 28
To convert grams (g) to ounces (oz.): multiply the number of grams by .035

To convert pounds (lbs.) to kilograms (kg): multiply the number of lbs. by .45
To convert kilograms (kg) to pounds (lbs.): multiply the number of kilograms by 2.2

lbs	kg	lbs	kg	oz	kg	oz	kg
0.1	0.04	0.9	0.41	0.1	0.003	0.9	0.024
0.2	0.09	1	0.4	0.2	0.005	1	0.03
0.3	0.14	2	0.9	0.3	0.008	2	0.06
0.4	0.18	3	1.4	0.4	0.011	3	0.08
0.5	0.23	4	1.8	0.5	0.014	4	0.11
0.6	0.27	5	2.3	0.6	0.017	5	0.14
0.7	0.32	10	4.5	0.7	0.020	10	0.28
0.8	0.36	15	6.8	0.8	0.023	15	0.42

ENGLISH TO METRIC CONVERSION: TEMPERATURE

To convert Fahrenheit (°F) to Celsius (°C): take number of °F and subtract 32; multiply result by 5; divide result by 9

To convert Celsius (°C) to Fahrenheit (°F): take number of °C and multiply by 9; divide result by 5; add 32 to total

Fahrenheit (F)		Celsius (C)		Fahrenheit (F)		Celsius (C)		Fahrenheit (F)		Celsius (C)	
°F	°C	°C	°F	°F	°C	°C	°F	°F	°C	°C	°F
−40	−40	−38	−36.4	80	26.7	18	64.4	215	101.7	80	176
−35	−37.2	−36	−32.8	85	29.4	20	68	220	104.4	85	185
−30	−34.4	−34	−29.2	90	32.2	22	71.6	225	107.2	90	194
−25	−31.7	−32	−25.6	95	35.0	24	75.2	230	110.0	95	202
−20	−28.9	−30	−22	100	37.8	26	78.8	235	112.8	100	212
−15	−26.1	−28	−18.4	105	40.6	28	82.4	240	115.6	105	221
−10	−23.3	−26	−14.8	110	43.3	30	86	245	118.3	110	230
−5	−20.6	−24	−11.2	115	46.1	32	89.6	250	121.1	115	239
0	−17.8	−22	−7.6	120	48.9	34	93.2	255	123.9	120	248
1	−17.2	−20	−4	125	51.7	36	96.8	260	126.6	125	257
2	−16.7	−18	−0.4	130	54.4	38	100.4	265	129.4	130	266
3	−16.1	−16	3.2	135	57.2	40	104	270	132.2	135	275
4	−15.6	−14	6.8	140	60.0	42	107.6	275	135.0	140	284
5	−15.0	−12	10.4	145	62.8	44	112.2	280	137.8	145	293
10	−12.2	−10	14	150	65.6	46	114.8	285	140.6	150	302
15	−9.4	−8	17.6	155	68.3	48	118.4	290	143.3	155	311
20	−6.7	−6	21.2	160	71.1	50	122	295	146.1	160	320
25	−3.9	−4	24.8	165	73.9	52	125.6	300	148.9	165	329
30	−1.1	−2	28.4	170	76.7	54	129.2	305	151.7	170	338
35	1.7	0	32	175	79.4	56	132.8	310	154.4	175	347
40	4.4	2	35.6	180	82.2	58	136.4	315	157.2	180	356
45	7.2	4	39.2	185	85.0	60	140	320	160.0	185	365
50	10.0	6	42.8	190	87.8	62	143.6	325	162.8	190	374
55	12.8	8	46.4	195	90.6	64	147.2	330	165.6	195	383
60	15.6	10	50	200	93.3	66	150.8	335	168.3	200	392
65	18.3	12	53.6	205	96.1	68	154.4	340	171.1	205	401
70	21.1	14	57.2	210	98.9	70	158	345	173.9	210	410
75	23.9	16	60.8	212	100.0	75	167	350	176.7	215	414

TCCS1C01

ENGLISH TO METRIC CONVERSION: LENGTH

To convert inches (ins.) to millimeters (mm): multiply number of inches by 25.4

To convert millimeters (mm) to inches (ins.): multiply number of millimeters by .04

Inches	Decimals	Milli-meters	Inches to millimeters inches	mm	Inches	Decimals	Milli-meters	Inches to millimeters inches	mm
1/64	0.051625	0.3969	0.0001	0.00254	33/64	0.515625	13.0969	0.6	15.24
1/32	0.03125	0.7937	0.0002	0.00508	17/32	0.53125	13.4937	0.7	17.78
3/64	0.046875	1.1906	0.0003	0.00762	35/64	0.546875	13.8906	0.8	20.32
1/16	0.0625	1.5875	0.0004	0.01016	9/16	0.5625	14.2875	0.9	22.86
5/64	0.078125	1.9844	0.0005	0.01270	37/64	0.578125	14.6844	1	25.4
3/32	0.09375	2.3812	0.0006	0.01524	19/32	0.59375	15.0812	2	50.8
7/64	0.109375	2.7781	0.0007	0.01778	39/64	0.609375	15.4781	3	76.2
1/8	0.125	3.1750	0.0008	0.02032	5/8	0.625	15.8750	4	101.6
9/64	0.140625	3.5719	0.0009	0.02286	41/64	0.640625	16.2719	5	127.0
5/32	0.15625	3.9687	0.001	0.0254	21/32	0.65625	16.6687	6	152.4
11/64	0.171875	4.3656	0.002	0.0508	43/64	0.671875	17.0656	7	177.8
3/16	0.1875	4.7625	0.003	0.0762	11/16	0.6875	17.4625	8	203.2
13/64	0.203125	5.1594	0.004	0.1016	45/64	0.703125	17.8594	9	228.6
7/32	0.21875	5.5562	0.005	0.1270	23/32	0.71875	18.2562	10	254.0
15/64	0.234375	5.9531	0.006	0.1524	47/64	0.734375	18.6531	11	279.4
1/4	0.25	6.3500	0.007	0.1778	3/4	0.75	19.0500	12	304.8
17/64	0.265625	6.7469	0.008	0.2032	49/64	0.765625	19.4469	13	330.2
9/32	0.28125	7.1437	0.009	0.2286	25/32	0.78125	19.8437	14	355.6
19/64	0.296875	7.5406	0.01	0.254	51/64	0.796875	20.2406	15	381.0
5/16	0.3125	7.9375	0.02	0.508	13/16	0.8125	20.6375	16	406.4
21/64	0.328125	8.3344	0.03	0.762	53/64	0.828125	21.0344	17	431.8
11/32	0.34375	8.7312	0.04	1.016	27/32	0.84375	21.4312	18	457.2
23/64	0.359375	9.1281	0.05	1.270	55/64	0.859375	21.8281	19	482.6
3/8	0.375	9.5250	0.06	1.524	7/8	0.875	22.2250	20	508.0
25/64	0.390625	9.9219	0.07	1.778	57/64	0.890625	22.6219	21	533.4
13/32	0.40625	10.3187	0.08	2.032	29/32	0.90625	23.0187	22	558.8
27/64	0.421875	10.7156	0.09	2.286	59/64	0.921875	23.4156	23	584.2
7/16	0.4375	11.1125	0.1	2.54	15/16	0.9375	23.8125	24	609.6
29/64	0.453125	11.5094	0.2	5.08	61/64	0.953125	24.2094	25	635.0
15/32	0.46875	11.9062	0.3	7.62	31/32	0.96875	24.6062	26	660.4
31/64	0.484375	12.3031	0.4	10.16	63/64	0.984375	25.0031	27	690.6
1/2	0.5	12.7000	0.5	12.70					

ENGLISH TO METRIC CONVERSION: TORQUE

To convert foot-pounds (ft. lbs.) to Newton-meters: multiply the number of ft. lbs. by 1.3

To convert inch-pounds (in. lbs.) to Newton-meters: multiply the number of in. lbs. by .11

in lbs	N-m	in lbs	N-m	in lbs	N-m	in lbs	N-m	in lbs	N-m
0.1	0.01	1	0.11	10	1.13	19	2.15	28	3.16
0.2	0.02	2	0.23	11	1.24	20	2.26	29	3.28
0.3	0.03	3	0.34	12	1.36	21	2.37	30	3.39
0.4	0.04	4	0.45	13	1.47	22	2.49	31	3.50
0.5	0.06	5	0.56	14	1.58	23	2.60	32	3.62
0.6	0.07	6	0.68	15	1.70	24	2.71	33	3.73
0.7	0.08	7	0.78	16	1.81	25	2.82	34	3.84
0.8	0.09	8	0.90	17	1.92	26	2.94	35	3.95
0.9	0.10	9	1.02	18	2.03	27	3.05	36	4.0

TCCS1C02

ENGLISH TO METRIC CONVERSION: TORQUE

Torque is now expressed as either foot-pounds (ft./lbs.) or inch-pounds (in./lbs.). The metric measurement unit for torque is the Newton-meter (Nm). This unit—the Nm—will be used for all SI metric torque references, both the present ft./lbs. and in./lbs.

ft lbs	N-m	ft lbs	N-m	ft lbs	N-m	ft lbs	N-m
0.1	0.1	33	44.7	74	100.3	115	155.9
0.2	0.3	34	46.1	75	101.7	116	157.3
0.3	0.4	35	47.4	76	103.0	117	158.6
0.4	0.5	36	48.8	77	104.4	118	160.0
0.5	0.7	37	50.7	78	105.8	119	161.3
0.6	0.8	38	51.5	79	107.1	120	162.7
0.7	1.0	39	52.9	80	108.5	121	164.0
0.8	1.1	40	54.2	81	109.8	122	165.4
0.9	1.2	41	55.6	82	111.2	123	166.8
1	1.3	42	56.9	83	112.5	124	168.1
2	2.7	43	58.3	84	113.9	125	169.5
3	4.1	44	59.7	85	115.2	126	170.8
4	5.4	45	61.0	86	116.6	127	172.2
5	6.8	46	62.4	87	118.0	128	173.5
6	8.1	47	63.7	88	119.3	129	174.9
7	9.5	48	65.1	89	120.7	130	176.2
8	10.8	49	66.4	90	122.0	131	177.6
9	12.2	50	67.8	91	123.4	132	179.0
10	13.6	51	69.2	92	124.7	133	180.3
11	14.9	52	70.5	93	126.1	134	181.7
12	16.3	53	71.9	94	127.4	135	183.0
13	17.6	54	73.2	95	128.8	136	184.4
14	18.9	55	74.6	96	130.2	137	185.7
15	20.3	56	75.9	97	131.5	138	187.1
16	21.7	57	77.3	98	132.9	139	188.5
17	23.0	58	78.6	99	134.2	140	189.8
18	24.4	59	80.0	100	135.6	141	191.2
19	25.8	60	81.4	101	136.9	142	192.5
20	27.1	61	82.7	102	138.3	143	193.9
21	28.5	62	84.1	103	139.6	144	195.2
22	29.8	63	85.4	104	141.0	145	196.6
23	31.2	64	86.8	105	142.4	146	198.0
24	32.5	65	88.1	106	143.7	147	199.3
25	33.9	66	89.5	107	145.1	148	200.7
26	35.2	67	90.8	108	146.4	149	202.0
27	36.6	68	92.2	109	147.8	150	203.4
28	38.0	69	93.6	110	149.1	151	204.7
29	39.3	70	94.9	111	150.5	152	206.1
30	40.7	71	96.3	112	151.8	153	207.4
31	42.0	72	97.6	113	153.2	154	208.8
32	43.4	73	99.0	114	154.6	155	210.2

TCCS1C03

ENGLISH TO METRIC CONVERSION: FORCE

Force is presently measured in pounds (lbs.). This type of measurement is used to measure spring pressure, specifically how many pounds it takes to compress a spring. Our present force unit (the pound) will be replaced in SI metric measurements by the Newton (N). This term will eventually see use in specifications for electric motor brush spring pressures, valve spring pressures, etc.

To convert pounds (lbs.) to Newton (N): multiply the number of lbs. by 4.45

lbs	N	lbs	N	lbs	N	oz	N
0.01	0.04	21	93.4	59	262.4	1	0.3
0.02	0.09	22	97.9	60	266.9	2	0.6
0.03	0.13	23	102.3	61	271.3	3	0.8
0.04	0.18	24	106.8	62	275.8	4	1.1
0.05	0.22	25	111.2	63	280.2	5	1.4
0.06	0.27	26	115.6	64	284.6	6	1.7
0.07	0.31	27	120.1	65	289.1	7	2.0
0.08	0.36	28	124.6	66	293.6	8	2.2
0.09	0.40	29	129.0	67	298.0	9	2.5
0.1	0.4	30	133.4	68	302.5	10	2.8
0.2	0.9	31	137.9	69	306.9	11	3.1
0.3	1.3	32	142.3	70	311.4	12	3.3
0.4	1.8	33	146.8	71	315.8	13	3.6
0.5	2.2	34	151.2	72	320.3	14	3.9
0.6	2.7	35	155.7	73	324.7	15	4.2
0.7	3.1	36	160.1	74	329.2	16	4.4
0.8	3.6	37	164.6	75	333.6	17	4.7
0.9	4.0	38	169.0	76	338.1	18	5.0
1	4.4	39	173.5	77	342.5	19	5.3
2	8.9	40	177.9	78	347.0	20	5.6
3	13.4	41	182.4	79	351.4	21	5.8
4	17.8	42	186.8	80	355.9	22	6.1
5	22.2	43	191.3	81	360.3	23	6.4
6	26.7	44	195.7	82	364.8	24	6.7
7	31.1	45	200.2	83	369.2	25	7.0
8	35.6	46	204.6	84	373.6	26	7.2
9	40.0	47	209.1	85	378.1	27	7.5
10	44.5	48	213.5	86	382.6	28	7.8
11	48.9	49	218.0	87	387.0	29	8.1
12	53.4	50	224.4	88	391.4	30	8.3
13	57.8	51	226.9	89	395.9	31	8.6
14	62.3	52	231.3	90	400.3	32	8.9
15	66.7	53	235.8	91	404.8	33	9.2
16	71.2	54	240.2	92	409.2	34	9.4
17	75.6	55	244.6	93	413.7	35	9.7
18	80.1	56	249.1	94	418.1	36	10.0
19	84.5	57	253.6	95	422.6	37	10.3
20	89.0	58	258.0	96	427.0	38	10.6

TCCS1C04

ENGLISH TO METRIC CONVERSION: LIQUID CAPACITY

Liquid or fluid capacity is presently expressed as pints, quarts or gallons, or a combination of all of these. In the metric system the liter (l) will become the basic unit. Fractions of a liter would be expressed as deciliters, centiliters, or most frequently (and commonly) as milliliters.

To convert pints (pts.) to liters (l): multiply the number of pints by .47
To convert liters (l) to pints (pts.): multiply the number of liters by 2.1
To convert quarts (qts.) to liters (l): multiply the number of quarts by .95

To convert liters (l) to quarts (qts.): multiply the number of liters by 1.06
To convert gallons (gals.) to liters (l): multiply the number of gallons by 3.8
To convert liters (l) to gallons (gals.): multiply the number of liters by .26

gals	liters	qts	liters	pts	liters
0.1	0.38	0.1	0.10	0.1	0.05
0.2	0.76	0.2	0.19	0.2	0.10
0.3	1.1	0.3	0.28	0.3	0.14
0.4	1.5	0.4	0.38	0.4	0.19
0.5	1.9	0.5	0.47	0.5	0.24
0.6	2.3	0.6	0.57	0.6	0.28
0.7	2.6	0.7	0.66	0.7	0.33
0.8	3.0	0.8	0.76	0.8	0.38
0.9	3.4	0.9	0.85	0.9	0.43
1	3.8	1	1.0	1	0.5
2	7.6	2	1.9	2	1.0
3	11.4	3	2.8	3	1.4
4	15.1	4	3.8	4	1.9
5	18.9	5	4.7	5	2.4
6	22.7	6	5.7	6	2.8
7	26.5	7	6.6	7	3.3
8	30.3	8	7.6	8	3.8
9	34.1	9	8.5	9	4.3
10	37.8	10	9.5	10	4.7
11	41.6	11	10.4	11	5.2
12	45.4	12	11.4	12	5.7
13	49.2	13	12.3	13	6.2
14	53.0	14	13.2	14	6.6
15	56.8	15	14.2	15	7.1
16	60.6	16	15.1	16	7.6
17	64.3	17	16.1	17	8.0
18	68.1	18	17.0	18	8.5
19	71.9	19	18.0	19	9.0
20	75.7	20	18.9	20	9.5
21	79.5	21	19.9	21	9.9
22	83.2	22	20.8	22	10.4
23	87.0	23	21.8	23	10.9
24	90.8	24	22.7	24	11.4
25	94.6	25	23.6	25	11.8
26	98.4	26	24.6	26	12.3
27	102.2	27	25.5	27	12.8
28	106.0	28	26.5	28	13.2
29	110.0	29	27.4	29	13.7
30	113.5	30	28.4	30	14.2

TCCS1C05

ENGLISH TO METRIC CONVERSION: PRESSURE

The basic unit of pressure measurement used today is expressed as pounds per square inch (psi). The metric unit for psi will be the kilopascal (kPa). This will apply to either fluid pressure or air pressure, and will be frequently seen in tire pressure readings, oil pressure specifications, fuel pump pressure, etc.

To convert pounds per square inch (psi) to kilopascals (kPa): multiply the number of psi by 6.89

Psi	kPa	Psi	kPa	Psi	kPa	Psi	kPa
0.1	0.7	37	255.1	82	565.4	127	875.6
0.2	1.4	38	262.0	83	572.3	128	882.5
0.3	2.1	39	268.9	84	579.2	129	889.4
0.4	2.8	40	275.8	85	586.0	130	896.3
0.5	3.4	41	282.7	86	592.9	131	903.2
0.6	4.1	42	289.6	87	599.8	132	910.1
0.7	4.8	43	296.5	88	606.7	133	917.0
0.8	5.5	44	303.4	89	613.6	134	923.9
0.9	6.2	45	310.3	90	620.5	135	930.8
1	6.9	46	317.2	91	627.4	136	937.7
2	13.8	47	324.0	92	634.3	137	944.6
3	20.7	48	331.0	93	641.2	138	951.5
4	27.6	49	337.8	94	648.1	139	958.4
5	34.5	50	344.7	95	655.0	140	965.2
6	41.4	51	351.6	96	661.9	141	972.2
7	48.3	52	358.5	97	668.8	142	979.0
8	55.2	53	365.4	98	675.7	143	985.9
9	62.1	54	372.3	99	682.6	144	992.8
10	69.0	55	379.2	100	689.5	145	999.7
11	75.8	56	386.1	101	696.4	146	1006.6
12	82.7	57	393.0	102	703.3	147	1013.5
13	89.6	58	399.9	103	710.2	148	1020.4
14	96.5	59	406.8	104	717.0	149	1027.3
15	103.4	60	413.7	105	723.9	150	1034.2
16	110.3	61	420.6	106	730.8	151	1041.1
17	117.2	62	427.5	107	737.7	152	1048.0
18	124.1	63	434.4	108	744.6	153	1054.9
19	131.0	64	441.3	109	751.5	154	1061.8
20	137.9	65	448.2	110	758.4	155	1068.7
21	144.8	66	455.0	111	765.3	156	1075.6
22	151.7	67	461.9	112	772.2	157	1082.5
23	158.6	68	468.8	113	779.1	158	1089.4
24	165.5	69	475.7	114	786.0	159	1096.3
25	172.4	70	482.6	115	792.9	160	1103.2
26	179.3	71	489.5	116	799.8	161	1110.0
27	186.2	72	496.4	117	806.7	162	1116.9
28	193.0	73	503.3	118	813.6	163	1123.8
29	200.0	74	510.2	119	820.5	164	1130.7
30	206.8	75	517.1	120	827.4	165	1137.6
31	213.7	76	524.0	121	834.3	166	1144.5
32	220.6	77	530.9	122	841.2	167	1151.4
33	227.5	78	537.8	123	848.0	168	1158.3
34	234.4	79	544.7	124	854.9	169	1165.2
35	241.3	80	551.6	125	861.8	170	1172.1
36	248.2	81	558.5	126	868.7	171	1179.0

2

ENGINE PERFORMANCE AND TUNE-UP

TUNE-UP PROCEDURES

In order to extract the full measure of performance and economy from your engine it is essential that it is properly tuned at regular intervals. A regular tune-up will keep your Camaro's engine running smoothly and will prevent the annoying breakdowns and poor performance associated with an untuned engine.

A complete tune-up should be performed every 30,000 miles (48,000 km). This interval should be halved if the car is operated under severe conditions such as trailer towing, prolonged idling, start-and-stop driving, or if starting or running problems are noticed. It is assumed that the routine maintenance described in Section 1 has been kept up, as this will have a decided effect on the results of a tune-up. All of the applicable steps of a tune-up should be followed in order, as the result is a cumulative one.

If the specifications on the underhood tune-up sticker in the engine compartment of your car disagree with the "Tune-Up Specifications" chart in this Section, the figures on the sticker must be used. The sticker often reflects changes made during the production run.

Spark Plugs

▶ See Figures 1 and 2

A typical spark plug consists of a metal shell surrounding a ceramic insulator. A metal electrode extends downward through the center of the insulator and protrudes a small distance. Located at the end of the plug and attached to the side of the outer metal shell is the side electrode. The side electrode bends in at a 90¯ angle so that its tip is just past and parallel to the tip of the center electrode. The distance between these two electrodes (measured in thousandths of an inch or hundredths of a millimeter) is called the spark plug gap.

The spark plug does not produce a spark, but instead provides a gap across which the current can arc. The coil produces anywhere from 20,000 to 50,000 volts (depending on the type and application) which travels through the wires to the spark plugs. The current passes along the center electrode and jumps the gap to the side electrode, and in doing so, ignites the air/fuel mixture in the combustion chamber.

SPARK PLUG HEAT RANGE

▶ See Figure 3

Spark plug heat range is the ability of the plug to dissipate heat. The longer the insulator (or the farther it extends into the engine), the hotter the plug will operate; the shorter the insulator (the closer the electrode is to the block's cooling passages) the cooler it will operate. A plug that absorbs little heat and remains too cool will quickly accumulate deposits of oil and carbon since it is not hot enough to burn them off. This leads to plug fouling and consequently to

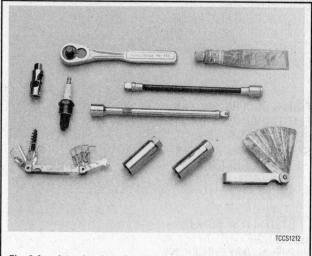

Fig. 2 A variety of tools and gauges are needed for spark plug service

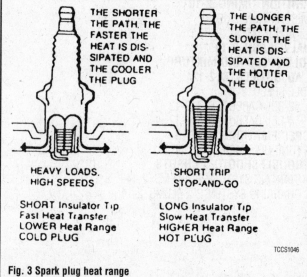

THE SHORTER THE PATH, THE FASTER THE HEAT IS DISSIPATED AND THE COOLER THE PLUG

THE LONGER THE PATH, THE SLOWER THE HEAT IS DISSIPATED AND THE HOTTER THE PLUG

HEAVY LOADS, HIGH SPEEDS

SHORT Insulator Tip
Fast Heat Transfer
LOWER Heat Range
COLD PLUG

SHORT TRIP STOP-AND-GO

LONG Insulator Tip
Slow Heat Transfer
HIGHER Heat Range
HOT PLUG

Fig. 3 Spark plug heat range

misfiring. A plug that absorbs too much heat will have no deposits but, due to the excessive heat, the electrodes will burn away quickly and might possibly lead to preignition or other ignition problems. Preignition takes place when plug tips get so hot that they glow sufficiently to ignite the air/fuel mixture before the actual spark occurs. This early ignition will usually cause a pinging during low speeds and heavy loads.

The general rule of thumb for choosing the correct heat range when picking a spark plug is: if most of your driving is long distance, high speed travel, use a colder plug; if most of your driving is stop and go, use a hotter plug. Original equipment plugs are generally a good compromise between the 2 styles and most people never have the need to change their plugs from the factory-recommended heat range.

REMOVAL & INSTALLATION

A set of spark plugs usually requires replacement after about 20,000–30,000 miles (32,000–48,000 km), depending on your style of driving. In normal operation plug gap increases about 0.001 in. (0.025mm) for every 2500 miles (4000 km). As the gap increases, the plug's voltage requirement also increases. It requires a greater voltage to jump the wider gap and about two to three times as

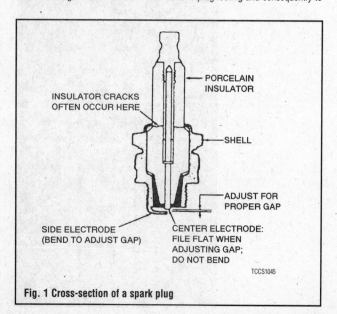

PORCELAIN INSULATOR

INSULATOR CRACKS OFTEN OCCUR HERE

SHELL

ADJUST FOR PROPER GAP

SIDE ELECTRODE (BEND TO ADJUST GAP)

CENTER ELECTRODE: FILE FLAT WHEN ADJUSTING GAP; DO NOT BEND

Fig. 1 Cross-section of a spark plug

much voltage to fire the plug at high speeds than at idle. The improved air/fuel ratio control of modern fuel injection combined with the higher voltage output of modern ignition systems will often allow an engine to run significantly longer on a set of standard spark plugs, but keep in mind that efficiency will drop as the gap widens (along with fuel economy and power).

When you're removing spark plugs, work on one at a time. Don't start by removing the plug wires all at once, because, unless you number them, they may become mixed up. Take a minute before you begin and number the wires with tape.

1. Disconnect the negative battery cable, and if the vehicle has been run recently, allow the engine to thoroughly cool.

2. Carefully twist the spark plug wire boot to loosen it, then pull upward and remove the boot from the plug. Be sure to pull on the boot and not on the wire, otherwise the connector located inside the boot may become separated.

3. Using compressed air, blow any water or debris from the spark plug well to assure that no harmful contaminants are allowed to enter the combustion chamber when the spark plug is removed. If compressed air is not available, use a rag or a brush to clean the area.

➡ Remove the spark plugs when the engine is cold, if possible, to prevent damage to the threads. If removal of the plugs is difficult, apply a few drops of penetrating oil or silicone spray to the area around the base of the plug, and allow it a few minutes to work.

4. Using a spark plug socket that is equipped with a rubber insert to properly hold the plug, turn the spark plug counterclockwise to loosen and remove the spark plug from the bore.

✳✳ WARNING

Be sure not to use a flexible extension on the socket. Use of a flexible extension may allow a shear force to be applied to the plug. A shear force could break the plug off in the cylinder head, leading to costly and frustrating repairs.

To install:

5. Inspect the spark plug boot for tears or damage. If a damaged boot is found, the spark plug wire must be replaced.

6. Using a wire feeler gauge, check and adjust the spark plug gap. When using a gauge, the proper size should pass between the electrodes with a slight drag. The next larger size should not be able to pass while the next smaller size should pass freely.

7. Carefully thread the plug into the bore by hand. If resistance is felt before the plug is almost completely threaded, back the plug out and begin threading again. In small, hard to reach areas, an old spark plug wire and boot could be used as a threading tool. The boot will hold the plug while you twist the end of the wire and the wire is supple enough to twist before it would allow the plug to crossthread.

✳✳ WARNING

Do not use the spark plug socket to thread the plugs. Always carefully thread the plug by hand or using an old plug wire to prevent the possibility of crossthreading and damaging the cylinder head bore.

8. Carefully tighten the spark plug. If the plug you are installing is equipped with a crush washer, seat the plug, then tighten about ¼ turn to crush the washer. If you are installing a tapered seat plug, tighten the plug to specifications provided by the vehicle or plug manufacturer.

9. Apply a small amount of silicone dielectric compound to the end of the spark plug lead or inside the spark plug boot to prevent sticking, then install the boot to the spark plug and push until it clicks into place. The click may be felt or heard, then gently pull back on the boot to assure proper contact.

INSPECTION & GAPPING

◆ **See Figures 4, 5, 6 and 7**

Check the plugs for deposits and wear. If they are not going to be replaced, clean the plugs thoroughly. Remember that any kind of deposit will decrease the efficiency of the plug. Plugs can be cleaned on a spark plug cleaning machine, which can sometimes be found in service stations, or you can do an acceptable job of cleaning with a stiff brush. If the plugs are cleaned, the electrodes must be filed flat. Use an ignition points file, not an emery board or the like, which will leave deposits. The electrodes must be filed perfectly flat with sharp edges; rounded edges reduce the spark plug voltage by as much as 50%.

Check spark plug gap before installation. The ground electrode (the L-shaped one connected to the body of the plug) must be parallel to the center electrode and the specified size wire gauge (please refer to the Tune-Up Specifications chart for details) must pass between the electrodes with a slight drag.

➡**NEVER adjust the gap on a used platinum type spark plug.**

Always check the gap on new plugs as they are not always set correctly at the factory. Do not use a flat feeler gauge when measuring the gap on a used plug, because the reading may be inaccurate. A round-wire type gapping tool is the best way to check the gap. The correct gauge should pass through the electrode gap with a slight drag. If you're in doubt, try one size smaller and one larger. The smaller gauge should go through easily, while the larger one shouldn't go through at all. Wire gapping tools usually have a bending tool attached. Use that to adjust the side electrode until the proper distance is obtained. Absolutely never attempt to bend the center electrode. Also, be careful not to bend the side electrode too far or too often as it may weaken and break off within the engine, requiring removal of the cylinder head to retrieve it.

Spark Plug Wires

TESTING, REMOVAL & INSTALLATION

◆ **See Figures 8 and 9**

Every 15,000 miles (24,000 km), inspect the spark plug wires for burns, cuts, or breaks in the insulation. Check the boots and the nipples on the distributor cap. Replace any damaged wiring.

Every 45,000 miles (72,000 km) or so, the resistance of the wires should be checked with an ohmmeter. Wires with excessive resistance will cause misfiring, and may make the engine difficult to start in damp weather. Generally, the useful life of the cables is 45,000–60,000 miles (72,000–96,000 km).

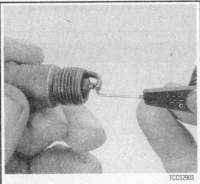

TCCS2903

Fig. 4 Checking the spark plug gap with a feeler gauge

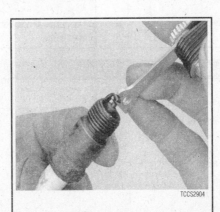

TCCS2904

Fig. 5 Adjusting the spark plug gap

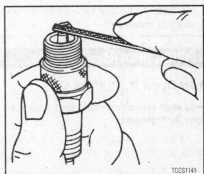

TCCS1141

Fig. 6 If the standard plug is in good condition, the electrode may be filed flat—WARNING: do not file platinum plugs

A normally worn spark plug should have light tan or gray deposits on the firing tip.

A physically damaged spark plug may be evidence of severe detonation in that cylinder. Watch that cylinder carefully between services, as a continued detonation will not only damage the plug, but could also damage the engine.

An oil fouled spark plug indicates an engine with worn poston rings and/or bad valve seals allowing excessive oil to enter the chamber.

This spark plug has been left in the engine too long, as evidenced by the extreme gap. Plugs with such an extreme gap can cause misfiring and stumbling accompanied by a noticeable lack of power.

A carbon fouled plug, identified by soft, sooty, black deposits, may indicate an improperly tuned vehicle. Check the air cleaner, ignition components and engine control system.

A bridged or almost bridged spark plug, identified by a build-up between the electrodes caused by excessive carbon or oil build-up on the plug.

TCCA1P40

Fig. 7 Inspect the spark plug to determine engine running conditions

85342304

Fig. 8 Number the distributor cap towers to denote correct spark plug wire installation

It should be remembered that resistance is also a function of length; the longer the wire, the greater the resistance. Thus, if the wires on your car are longer than the factory originals, resistance will be higher, quite possibly outside these limits.

When installing new wires, replace them one at a time to avoid mix-ups. If it becomes necessary to remove all of the wires from the distributor cap or coil packs at one time, take the time to label the distributor cap/coil pack towers to denote the cylinder number of the wire for that position. When this is done, incorrect positioning of wires can more easily be avoided. Start by replacing the longest one first. Route the wire over the same path as the original and secure in place.

HEI Plug Wire Resistance Chart

Wire Length	Minimum	Maximum
0–15 inches	3000 ohms	10,000 ohms
15–25 inches	4000 ohms	15,000 ohms
25–35 inches	6000 ohms	20,000 ohms
Over 35 inches		25,000 ohms

853420C1

Fig. 9 Use the spark plug wire length to determine the appropriate resistance

FIRING ORDERS

▶ See Figures 10, 11, 12 and 13

➡ To avoid confusion, remove and tag the spark plug wires one at a time, for replacement.

If a distributor is not keyed for installation with only one orientation, it could have been removed previously and rewired. The resultant wiring would hold the correct firing order, but could change the relative placement of the plug towers in relation to the engine. For this reason it is imperative that you label all wires before disconnecting any of them. Also, before removal, compare the current wiring with the accompanying illustrations. If the current wiring does not match, make notes in your book to reflect how your engine is wired.

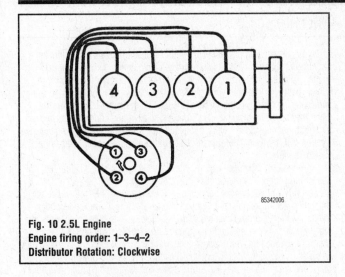

Fig. 10 2.5L Engine
Engine firing order: 1–3–4–2
Distributor Rotation: Clockwise

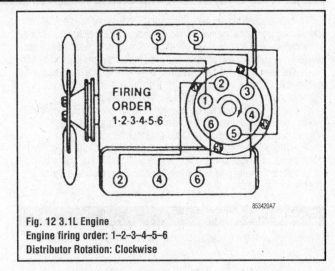

Fig. 12 3.1L Engine
Engine firing order: 1–2–3–4–5–6
Distributor Rotation: Clockwise

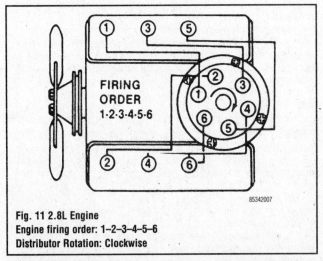

Fig. 11 2.8L Engine
Engine firing order: 1–2–3–4–5–6
Distributor Rotation: Clockwise

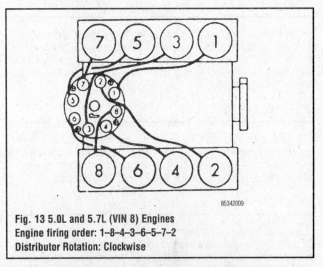

Fig. 13 5.0L and 5.7L (VIN 8) Engines
Engine firing order: 1–8–4–3–6–5–7–2
Distributor Rotation: Clockwise

ELECTRONIC IGNITION SYSTEM

General Information

♦ See Figure 14

The High Energy Ignition (HEI) system controls the fuel combustion by providing a spark to ignite the compressed air/fuel mixture at the correct time. To provide improved engine performance, fuel economy, and control of exhaust emissions, the engine control module (ECM) controls distributor spark advance (timing) with an ignition control system.

The distributor may have an internal, or external ignition coil. To be certain of the type coil used for your vehicle, visually inspect the ignition system. If the ignition coil is inside the distributor cap, it connects through a resistance brush to the rotor. If your vehicle is equipped with an external ignition coil, it connects to the rotor through a high tension wire.

The distributor contains the ignition control module, and the magnetic triggering device. The magnetic pickup assembly contains a permanent magnet, a pole piece with internal "teeth", and a pickup coil (not to be confused with the ignition coil).

All spark timing changes are done electronically by the engine control module (ECM) which monitors information from various engine sensors. The ECM computes the desired spark timing and then signals the distributor ignition module to change the timing accordingly. No vacuum or mechanical advance systems are used.

In the HEI system, as in other electronic ignition systems, the breaker points have been replaced with an electronic switch — a transistor — which is located within the ignition module. This switching transistor performs the same function

the points did in a conventional ignition system; it simply turns the coil's primary current on and off at the correct time. Essentially, electronic and conventional ignition systems operate on the same principle.

Fig. 14 Distributor with exterior ignition coil—1987 vehicle shown

The module which houses the switching transistor is controlled (turned on and off) by a magnetically generated impulse induced in the pickup coil. When the teeth of the rotating timer align with the teeth of the pole piece, the induced voltage in the pickup coil signals the electronic module to open the coil primary circuit. The primary current then decreases, and a high voltage is induced in the ignition coil secondary windings, which is then directed through the rotor and high voltage leads (spark plug wires) to fire the spark plugs.

In essence, the pickup coil module system simply replaces the conventional breaker points and condenser. The condenser found within the distributor is for radio suppression purposes only and has nothing to do with the ignition process. The ignition module automatically controls the dwell period, increasing it with increasing engine speed. Since dwell is controlled in this manner, it cannot be adjusted. The module itself is non-adjustable/non-repairable and must be replaced if found defective.

System Precautions

Before proceeding with troubleshooting, take note of the following precautions:

TIMING LIGHT USE

Care should be exercised when connecting a timing light or other pick-up equipment. Do not force anything between the boots and wiring, or through the silicone jacket. Connections should be made in parallel using an adapter. Inductive pickup timing lights are the best kind to use with the ignition systems covered by this manual.

SPARK PLUG WIRES

The plug wires used with these systems are of a different construction than conventional wires. When replacing them, make sure you get the correct wires, since conventional wires will not carry the voltage. Also, handle the wires carefully to avoid cracking or splitting them, and NEVER pierce the wires.

TACHOMETER USE

Not all tachometers will operate or indicate correctly when used on an HEI or C³I system. While some tachometers may give a reading, this does not necessarily mean the reading is correct. In addition, some tachometers hook up differently from others. If you cannot figure out whether or not your tachometer will work on your car, check with the tachometer manufacturer.

➡**The tachometer terminal should never be allowed to touch ground, as damage to the computer control module and/or ignition coil assembly can result.**

CONNECTORS

When disengaging connectors, do not use a screwdriver or other tool to release the locking tab, as this might break the connector.

SYSTEM TESTERS

Instruments designed specifically for testing HEI or C³I systems are available from several tool manufacturers. Some of these will even test the module itself. However, the tests given in the following section will require only an ohmmeter and a voltmeter.

Testing

The symptoms of a defective component within the HEI or C$SS3I system are exactly the same as those you would encounter in a conventional system. Some of these symptoms are:

- Hard or no starting
- Rough Idle
- Poor fuel economy
- Engine misses under load or while accelerating

PRELIMINARY CHECKS

If you suspect a problem in your ignition system, there are certain preliminary checks which you should carry out before you begin to check the electronic portions of the system. First, it is extremely important to make sure the vehicle battery is in a good state of charge. A defective or poorly charged battery will cause the various components of the ignition system to read incorrectly when they are being tested. Second, make sure all wiring connections are clean and tight, not only at the battery, but also at the distributor cap (if so equipped), ignition coil, camshaft and/or crankshaft sensors (if so equipped) and at the control module.

Since the only difference between these ignition systems lies before the spark plug wiring, it is important to check the secondary ignition circuit first. If the secondary circuit checks out properly (there is spark), then the engine condition is probably not the fault of the ignition system. To check the secondary ignition system, perform a simple spark test. Remove one of the plug wires and insert some sort of extension in the plug socket. An old spark plug with the ground electrode removed makes a good extension. Hold the wire and extension using an insulated tool (NOT BY HAND) about ¼ in. (6mm) away from the block and crank the engine. If a normal spark occurs, then the problem is most likely not in the ignition system. Check for fuel system problems, or fouled spark plugs.

If, however, there is no spark or a weak spark, then further ignition system testing will have to be done. Troubleshooting techniques fall into various categories, depending on the nature of the problem and the system being tested. Categories will include symptoms such as the engine cranks, but will not start or the engine runs rough.

HEI SYSTEM

When testing the HEI system, there are 2 major categories of problems, (1) Engine cranks, but will not start or (2) Engine runs, but runs rough or cuts out.

If the engine will not start, perform a spark test as described earlier. This will narrow the problem area down considerably. If no spark occurs, check for the presence of normal battery voltage at the battery (**BAT**) terminal on the ignition coil. The ignition switch must be in the **ON** position for this test. Either a voltmeter or a test light wire may be used for this test. Connect the test light wire to ground and the probe end to the **BAT** terminal at the coil. If the light comes on, you have voltage to the distributor and/or spark plug wires. If the light fails to come on, this indicates an open circuit in the ignition primary wiring leading to the distributor. In this case, you will have to check wiring continuity back to the ignition switch using a test light. If there is battery voltage at the BAT terminal, but no spark at the plugs, then the problem probably lies within the distributor assembly.

If, on the other hand, the engine starts, but runs roughly or cuts out, make sure the plug wires are in good shape first. There should be no obvious cracks or breaks. You can check the plug wires with an ohmmeter, but do not pierce the wires with a probe. Check the chart for the correct plug wire resistance. If the plug wires are OK, remove the cap assembly and check for moisture, cracks, chips, or carbon tracks, or any other high voltage leads or failures. Replace the cap if any defects are found. Make sure the timer wheel rotates when the engine is cranked.

If the trouble has been narrowed down to the units within the distributor, the following tests can help pinpoint the defective component. An ohmmeter with both high and low ranges should be used. These tests are made with the cap assembly removed and the battery wire disconnected. If a tachometer is connected to the **TACH** terminal, disconnect it before making these tests.

Ignition Coil

EXTERNALLY MOUNTED

◗ **See Figure 15**

1. Disconnect the coil wires and set the ohmmeter on the high scale.
2. Connect the ohmmeter to the ignition coil as illustrated in Step 1 of the accompanying figure.
3. The ohmmeter should read near infinite or very high.
4. Next, set the ohmmeter to the low scale and connect test leads as illustrated in Step 2 of the accompanying figure.
5. The reading should be very low or zero.

TESTING IGNITION COIL

OHMMETER   OHMMETER   OHMMETER

**CHECK IGNITION COIL WITH OHMMETER FOR
OPENS AND GROUNDS:**
  STEP 1. — USE HIGH SCALE. SHOULD READ VERY
HIGH (INFINITE). IF NOT, REPLACE COIL.
  STEP 2. — USE LOW SCALE. SHOULD READ VERY
LOW OR ZERO. IF NOT, REPLACE COIL.
  STEP 3. — USE HIGH SCALE. SHOULD NOT READ
INFINITE. IF IT DOES, REPLACE COIL.

85342043

Fig. 15 Testing external ignition coil

6. Now set the ohmmeter on the high scale and connect test leads as illustrated in Step 3 of the accompanying figure. The ohmmeter should not read infinity.

7. If any results of the 3 tests listed above do not agree with the desired readings, replace the ignition coil.

INTERNALLY MOUNTED

▶ **See Figure 16**

1. Connect an ohmmeter between the **TACH** and **BAT** terminals on the ignition coil. The primary coil resistance should be zero or nearly zero ohms.

2. To check the coil secondary resistance, connect an ohmmeter between the high tension terminal and the **BAT** terminal. Note the reading. Connect the ohmmeter between the high tension terminal and the **TACH** terminal. Note the reading. The resistance in both cases should be 6,000–30,000Ω. Be sure to test between the high tension terminal and both the **BAT** and **TACH** terminals.

3. Replace the coil only if the readings in Step 1 and Step 2 are infinite.

➡These resistance checks will not disclose shorted coil windings. This condition can only be detected with scope analysis or a suitably designed coil tester. If these instruments are unavailable, replace the coil with a known good coil as a final coil test.

Pickup Coil

▶ **See Figure 17**

1. To test the pickup coil, first disconnect the white and green module leads. Set the ohmmeter on the high scale and connect it between a ground and either the white or green lead. Any resistance measurement less than infinity requires replacement of the pickup coil.

2. Pickup coil continuity is tested using an ohmmeter (on low range) between the white and green leads. Normal resistance is 500–1,500Ω. If a vac-

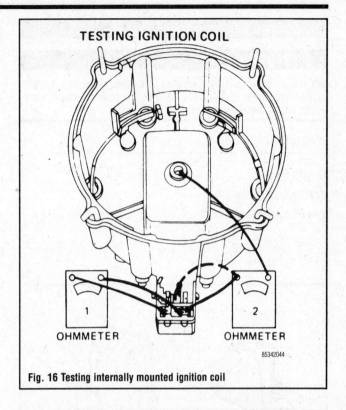

TESTING IGNITION COIL

1 OHMMETER   2 OHMMETER

85342044

Fig. 16 Testing internally mounted ignition coil

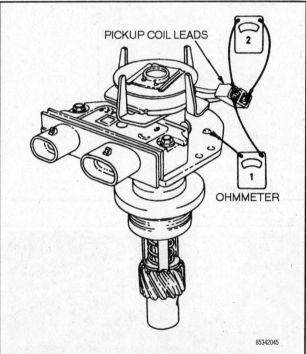

PICKUP COIL LEADS

OHMMETER

85342045

Fig. 17 Testing Pickup coil—Test 1 should read infinite at all times. Test 2 should read a steady value of 500–1500 ohms.

uum unit is used, move the vacuum advance arm while performing this test. This will detect any break in coil continuity. Such a condition can cause intermittent misfiring. Replace the pickup coil if the reading is outside the specified limits.

3. If no defects have been found at this time, and you still have a problem, then the module will have to be checked. If you do not have access to a module tester, the only possible alternative is a substitution test. If the module fails the substitution test, replace it.

Component Replacement

❈❈❈ CAUTION

When handling secondary spark plug leads with the engine running or starting, insulated pliers must be used and care exercised to prevent a possible electrical shock.

HEI SYSTEM

Ignition Coil

EXTERNALLY MOUNTED

▶ See Figures 18, 19 and 20

1. Disconnect the negative battery cable.
2. Disconnect the ignition coil wire from the coil. Do so by pulling on the boot of the wire while twisting it.

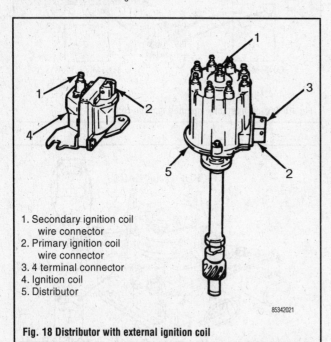

1. Secondary ignition coil wire connector
2. Primary ignition coil wire connector
3. 4 terminal connector
4. Ignition coil
5. Distributor

Fig. 18 Distributor with external ignition coil

Fig. 19 Release the locking tab and remove the harness connector from the coil

Fig. 20 With the mounting screw(s) removed, lift the coil from the engine compartment

3. Disconnect the harness connector from the ignition coil.
4. Remove the coil mounting screws and the ignition coil. If necessary, drill out and remove the rivets holding the coil to the bracket.
   To install:
5. Place the ignition coil in position on the mounting bracket and install the mounting screws.
6. Reconnect the harness connectors to the ignition coil. Confirm that the harness connectors are firmly attached to the coil.
7. Install the secondary coil wire to the coil tower.
8. Connect the negative battery cable.

INTERNALLY MOUNTED

▶ See Figure 21

1. Disconnect the negative battery cable.
2. Remove the cover and wire retainer.
3. Disconnect the battery feed wire and coil connections from the cap.
4. Remove the coil cover attaching screws and cover.
5. Remove the coil attaching screws and lift the coil assembly from the distributor cap.

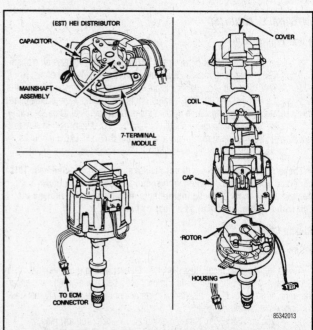

Fig. 21 Distributor and related components with internal ignition coil

To install:

6. Position the ignition coil and the leads into the cap. Be certain that the resistor brush, ground lead and seal are properly positioned.

7. Install the mounting screws.

8. Install the coil cover and retainers. Reconnect the feed wires and coil connections to the cap.

9. Install the cover and wire retainer. Reconnect the negative battery cable.

Distributor Cap

♦ See Figures 22 and 23

1. If removing the ignition wires at the cap, take a moment to label the spark plug wire positioning for each cylinder, at each tower. This will avoid improper wire placement during assembly.

2. Disconnect the ignition switch wire from the distributor cap. Also disconnect the tachometer wire, if so equipped.

3. Release the coil connectors from the cap.

4. Remove the distributor cap by turning the four latches (the L4 distributor has 2 latches) counterclockwise.

5. Remove the cap. Installation is the reverse of removal. Be sure you get the ignition and tachometer wires connected to the correct terminals.

3. Remove the 2 module attaching screws and lift the module up. Remove the leads from the module, observing the colors on each lead. These leads can not be interchanged.

➡If the module is to be reused, do not wipe the grease from the module or the distributor base. If a new module is to be installed, a package of silicone grease will be included with it. Spread the grease on the metal face of the module and on the distributor base where the module seats. This grease is necessary for module cooling.

To install:

4. Install the module, tighten the retaining screws and connect the wiring.

5. Install the distributor rotor and distributor cap.

6. Connect the negative battery cable.

Pickup Coil

♦ See Figure 25

1. Disconnect the negative battery cable.

2. Remove the distributor cap and then the rotor.

3. Remove 3 screws from the magnetic shield. Remove the magnetic shield and C-washer. Remove the magnet, pole piece and pickup coil.

4. Installation is the reverse of the removal procedure.

Fig. 22 Release the retainers on the distributor cap by turning them counterclockwise

Fig. 23 Removing the distributor cap. Notice that all towers on cap are labeled with the corresponding engine cylinder number

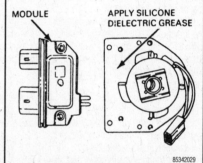

Fig. 24 Ignition coil module mounting— always coat the base with silicone dielectric grease

Rotor

1. Disconnect the negative battery cable.

2. Remove the distributor cap.

3. Unscrew the two rotor attaching screws and then lift off the rotor.

4. For installation, make sure the rotor is positioned in the correct direction and tighten the retaining screws.

Capacitor

The capacitor, if equipped, is part of the ignition coil wire harness assembly. Since the capacitor is used only for radio noise suppression, it will seldom need replacement.

1. Disconnect the negative battery cable.

2. Remove the distributor cap and rotor.

3. Remove the capacitor attaching screws and unplug the connector from the module. Remove the module.

To install:

4. Plug the connector into the capacitor. Install the capacitor and secure in place using the mounting screws. Be sure the ground lead is under the screw.

5. Install the rotor and distributor cap.

6. Connect the negative battery cable.

Module

♦ See Figure 24

➡It is not necessary to remove the distributor from the vehicle.

1. Disconnect the negative battery cable.

2. Remove the distributor cap, rotor and pickup coil.

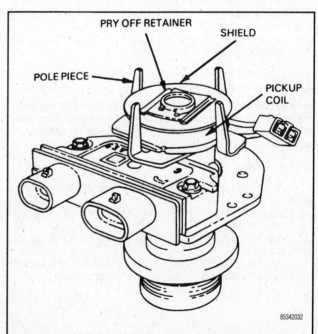

Fig. 25 Pickup coil and related components—distributor with external coil

IGNITION TIMING

Description

Ignition timing is the measurement, in degrees of crankshaft rotation, of the point at which the spark plugs fire in each of the cylinders. It is measured in degrees before or after Top Dead Center (TDC) of the compression stroke.

Because it takes a fraction of a second for the spark plug to ignite the mixture in the cylinder, the spark plug must fire a little before the piston reaches TDC. Otherwise, the mixture will not be completely ignited as the piston passes TDC and the full power of the explosion will not be used by the engine.

The timing measurement is given in degrees of crankshaft rotation before the piston reaches TDC (BTDC). If the setting for the ignition timing is 5° BTDC, the spark plug must fire 5° before each piston reaches TDC. This only holds true, however, when the engine is at idle speed.

As the engine speed increases, the pistons go faster. The spark plugs have to ignite the fuel even sooner if it is to be completely ignited when the piston reaches TDC.

If the ignition is set too far advanced (BTDC), the ignition and expansion of the fuel in the cylinder will occur too soon and try to force the piston down while it is still traveling up. This causes engine ping. If the ignition spark is set too far retarded, after TDC (ATDC), the piston will have already passed TDC and started on its way down when the fuel is ignited. This will cause the piston to be forced down for only a portion of its travel, resulting in poor engine performance and lack of power.

When timing the engine, the Number 1 plug wire should be used to trigger the timing light. On engines where timing is adjustable, the notch for the No. 1 cylinder is usually scribed across all three edges of the double sheaf pulley. Another notch located 180° away from the No. 1 cylinder notch is scribed only across the center section of the pulley to make it distinguishable from the No. 1 cylinder notch.

There are two basic types of timing lights available. The first type of light operates from the car's battery. Two alligator clips connect to the battery terminals, while a third wire connects to the spark plug with an adapter or to the spark plug wire with an inductive pickup. This type of light is more expensive, but the xenon bulb provides a nice bright flash which can even be seen in sunlight. The second type replaces the battery source with 110-volt house current. Some timing lights have other functions built into them, such as dwell meters, tachometers, or remote starting switches. These are convenient, in that they reduce the tangle of wires under the hood, but may duplicate the functions of tools you already have.

Because this car uses electronic ignition, you should use a timing light with an inductive pickup. This pickup simply clamps around the Number 1 spark plug wire (in this case, the coil wire), eliminating the adapter. It is not susceptible to crossfiring or false triggering, which may occur with a conventional light due to the greater voltages produced by these systems.

ADJUSTMENT

➡When adjusting the timing, refer to the instructions on the emission control sticker inside the engine compartment. If the instructions on the label disagree with the procedure listed below, follow the instructions on the label.

1982–87 Vehicles

1. Locate the timing marks on the crankshaft pulley and the front of the engine.
2. Clean off the marks and coat them with white paint or chalk, if necessary, so that they may be seen.
3. Run the engine until it reaches normal operating temperature, then shut off the engine.
4. With the ignition OFF, connect a tachometer to the distributor, and a timing light with an inductive pickup lead to the No. 1 spark plug wire.

✳✳ WARNING

Never pierce a secondary ignition wire in order to connect a timing light. A pierced wire may lead to engine misfiring and driveability problems.

5. To properly set the ignition timing, the EST must be placed in the bypass mode.
   a. On the 2.5L engine, refer to the emission control label for the procedure.

➡If the label is missing or unreadable, contact your Chevrolet dealer for a replacement.

   b. On 2.8L and 5.0L carbureted engines, disconnect the 4-wire EST connector at the distributor. (Fault code 42 may be set in ECM memory, and must be cleared once the procedure is completed). Proceed to Step 7.
   c. On 2.8L, 5.0L and 5.7L fuel injected engines, with the engine RUNNING and all accessories off, use a jumper wire to connect diagnostic terminal B and ground terminal A of the 12-terminal Assembly Line Diagnostic Link (ALDL) usually located under the left side of the instrument panel. DO NOT disconnect the 4-wire EST connector at the distributor. Aim the timing light at the timing mark; the line on the balancer or pulley will line up with the timing mark. Increase engine speed and check for timing advance. If the timing still advances with engine speed, perform Step 6. If timing does not advance with engine speed, proceed to Step 7.

➡If timing advances with engine speed, it will be necessary to disconnect the single-wire Set Timing connector. (Fault code 42 may be set in ECM memory, and must be cleared once the procedure is completed).

6. Remove the jumper wire from the ALDL, and shut off the ignition. Disconnect the Set Timing connector, usually located under the plastic cover above the heater unit, in the engine compartment. (The wire in this connector is normally Tan/Black.)
7. With the engine running and all accessories off, aim the light at the timing mark. The line on the balancer or pulley will line up with the timing mark. If a change in timing is necessary, loosen the hold-down clamp bolt at the base of the distributor. While observing the timing mark, rotate the distributor slightly until the line indicates the correct timing. Use the timing specification on the emission control label in the engine compartment. If this label is missing or damaged, refer to the Tune-Up Specifications chart in this Section.
8. Once the timing is set to specification, tighten the distributor hold-down clamp. Recheck the timing to make sure it did not change while the bolt was being tightened.
9. Remove the jumper wire from the ALDL connector, if applicable, with the engine still running. (Usually, if this is performed before the engine is shut off, no trouble codes will be stored.)
10. Turn the engine OFF, then remove the timing light and tachometer. Reconnect the number 1 spark plug wire, if disconnected.
11. Attach the 4-wire EST connector at the distributor, or reconnect the Set Timing connector, if applicable.
12. Check for fault code 42, and clear, if necessary, by disconnecting the negative battery cable for at least 30 seconds.

➡To prevent ECM damage, the key must be in the OFF position when disconnecting or reconnecting battery cables.

1988–90 Vehicles

▶ See Figure 26

➡When adjusting the timing, refer to the instructions on the emission control sticker inside the engine compartment. If the instructions on the label disagree with the procedure listed below, follow the instructions on the label.

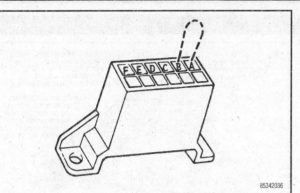

Fig. 26 Grounding the diagnostic terminal in order to set ignition timing

1. Locate the timing marks on the crankshaft pulley and the front of the engine.

2. Clean off the marks and coat them with white paint or chalk, so that they may be easily seen.

3. Run the engine until it reaches normal operating temperature, then shut off the engine.

4. With the ignition OFF, connect a tachometer to the distributor, and a timing light with an inductive pickup lead to the No. 1 spark plug wire.

✳✳ WARNING

Never pierce a secondary ignition wire in order to connect a timing light. A pierced wire may lead to engine misfiring and driveability problems.

5. Start the engine. With the engine running and all accessories off, use a jumper wire to connect diagnostic terminal **B** and ground terminal **A** of the 12-terminal Assembly Line Diagnostic Link (ALDL), located under the instrument panel.

➡ **If jumping the ALDL terminals does not prevent timing advance, the EST bypass wire will have to be disconnected instead.**

6. Aim the timing light at the timing mark. The line on the balancer or pulley will line up with the timing mark. If a change in timing is necessary, loosen the hold-down clamp bolt at the base of the distributor. While observing the timing mark, rotate the distributor slightly until the line indicates the correct timing. Use the timing specification on the emission control label in the engine compartment. If this label is missing or damaged, refer to the Tune-Up Specifications chart in this Section.

7. Once the timing is set to specification, tighten the distributor hold-down clamp. Recheck the timing to make sure it did not change while the bolt was being tightened.

8. With the engine still running, unground the diagnostic terminal. (Ungrounding the diagnostic terminal while the engine is still running will usually prevent trouble codes from being stored.)

9. Turn the engine OFF and remove the timing light and tachometer. Reconnect the number 1 spark plug wire, if disconnected.

1991–92 Vehicles

▸ See Figure 27

➡ **When adjusting the timing, refer to the instructions on the emission control sticker inside the engine compartment. If the instructions on the**

label disagree with the procedure listed below, follow the instructions on the label.

1. Locate the timing marks on the crankshaft pulley and the front of the engine.

2. Clean off the marks and coat them with white paint or chalk, if necessary, so that they may be seen.

3. Run the engine until it reaches normal operating temperature, then shut off the engine.

4. With the ignition **OFF**, connect a tachometer to the distributor, and the pickup lead of an inductive timing light to the No. 1 spark plug wire. Connect the timing light power leads according to the manufacturer's instructions.

✳✳ WARNING

Never pierce a secondary ignition wire in order to connect a timing light. A pierced wire may lead to engine misfiring and driveability problems.

5. Start the engine. With the engine running at normal operating temperature and all accessories OFF, disconnect the EST bypass connector.

➡ **An ECM code will be set when the EST bypass connector is disconnected.**

6. Aim the timing light at the timing mark. The line on the balancer or pulley will line up with the timing mark. If a change in timing is necessary, loosen the hold-down clamp bolt at the base of the distributor. While observing the timing mark, rotate the distributor slightly until the line indicates the correct timing. Use the timing specification on the emission control label in the engine compartment. If this label is missing or damaged, refer to the Tune-Up Specifications chart in this Section.

7. Tighten the distributor hold-down bolt and recheck the ignition timing to make sure the distributor was not moved when the bolt was tightened.

8. Turn the engine OFF and remove the timing light and tachometer. Reconnect the number 1 spark plug wire, if disconnected.

9. Connect the EST bypass connector, then check for and clear the ECM code by disconnecting the negative battery cable for at least 30 seconds.

➡ **To prevent ECM damage, the key must be in the OFF position when disconnecting or reconnecting battery cables.**

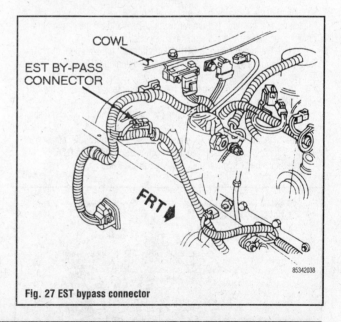

Fig. 27 EST bypass connector

VALVE LASH

All models utilize a hydraulic valve lifter system to obtain zero lash. No periodic adjustment is necessary. An initial adjustment is required anytime that the lifters are removed or the valve train is disturbed. This procedure is covered in Section 3.

IDLE SPEED AND MIXTURE ADJUSTMENTS

➨Mixture adjustments are factory set and sealed; no adjustment attempt should be made, except by an authorized GM dealer or reputable shop equipped with the necessary equipment.

Idle Speed

2-BBL CARBURETOR

Without Air Conditioning

▶ See Figure 28

➨The engine must be running in "Closed Loop" mode (engine fully warmed) when making all idle speed adjustments. In this mode, the oxygen sensor affects control of the fuel delivery.

1. Refer to the emission label on the vehicle and prepare the engine for adjustments (set the timing). Remove the air cleaner and set the parking brake. Connect a tachometer to the distributor connector.
2. Place the transmission in **DRIVE** for automatic transmission, or **NEUTRAL** for manual transmission; make sure that the solenoid is energized.
3. Open the throttle slightly to allow the solenoid plunger to extend. Adjust the curb idle speed to the specified rpm by turning the solenoid screw.
4. De-energize the solenoid by disconnecting the electrical lead.
5. Set the basic idle speed rpm by turning the idle speed screw. After adjustment, reconnect the solenoid electrical lead.
6. Remove the tachometer and install the air cleaner.

With Air Conditioning

▶ See Figure 29

➨The engine must be running in "Closed Loop" mode (engine fully warmed) when making all idle speed adjustments. In this mode, the oxygen sensor affects control of the fuel delivery.

1. Refer to the emission label on the vehicle and prepare the engine for adjustments (set the timing). Remove the air cleaner and set the parking brake. Connect a tachometer to the distributor connector.
2. Place the transmission in **DRIVE** for automatic transmission, or **NEUTRAL** for manual transmission. Turn the air conditioning **OFF** and set the curb idle speed by turning the idle speed screw.
3. Disconnect the electrical lead at the A/C compressor, then turn the A/C switch **ON**.
4. With the solenoid energized, open the throttle slightly to allow the solenoid plunger to extend.
5. Turn the solenoid screw to adjust to the specified rpm. After adjustment, reconnect the A/C compressor lead and turn the air conditioning **OFF**.
6. Remove the tachometer and install the air cleaner.

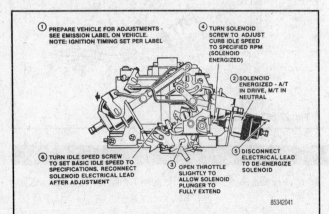

Fig. 28 Idle speed adjustments—2-bbl carburetor (without air conditioning)

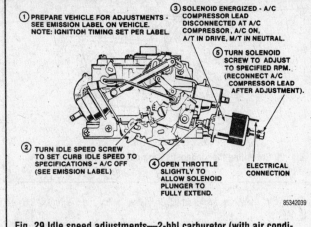

Fig. 29 Idle speed adjustments—2-bbl carburetor (with air conditioning)

4-BBL CARBURETOR

Without Air Conditioning

▶ See Figure 30

➨The engine must be running in "Closed Loop" mode (engine fully warmed) when making all idle speed adjustments. In this mode, the oxygen sensor affects control of the fuel delivery.

1. Refer to the emission label on the vehicle and prepare the engine for adjustments (set the timing). Set the parking brake. Connect a tachometer to the distributor connector.
2. Place the transmission in **DRIVE** for automatic transmission, or **NEUTRAL** for manual transmission.
3. De-energize the idle speed solenoid by disconnecting the electrical lead.
4. Set the basic idle speed rpm by turning the idle speed screw.
5. Connect a jumper wire from a 12-volt power supply to the solenoid.
6. Open the throttle partially to ensure that the solenoid plunger is fully extended, and allow the throttle lever to close on the plunger.
7. Turn the solenoid plunger to adjust to the specified rpm. After adjustment, disconnect the jumper wire and reconnect the solenoid electrical lead.
8. Remove the tachometer and install the air cleaner.

With Air Conditioning

▶ See Figure 30

➨The engine must be running in "Closed Loop" mode (engine fully warmed) when making all idle speed adjustments. In this mode, the oxygen sensor affects control of the fuel delivery.

1. Refer to the emission label on the vehicle and prepare the engine for adjustments (set the timing). Set the parking brake. Connect a tachometer to the distributor connector.
2. Place the transmission in **DRIVE** for automatic transmission, or **NEUTRAL** for manual transmission. Turn the air conditioning **OFF**.
3. De-energize the idle speed solenoid by disconnecting the electrical lead.
4. Set the basic idle speed rpm by turning the idle speed screw. After adjustment, reconnect the solenoid electrical lead.
5. Disconnect the electrical lead from the A/C compressor and turn the A/C switch **ON**.
6. Open the throttle partially to ensure that the solenoid plunger is fully extended, and allow the throttle lever to close on the plunger.
7. Turn the solenoid plunger to adjust to the specified rpm. After adjustment, reconnect the A/C compressor lead and turn the air conditioning **OFF**.
8. Remove the tachometer and install the air cleaner.

GASOLINE ENGINE TUNE-UP SPECIFICATIONS

Year	Engine ID/VIN	Engine Displacement Liters (cc)	Spark Plugs Gap (in.)	Ignition Timing (deg.) MT	Ignition Timing (deg.) AT	Fuel Pump (psi)	Idle Speed (rpm) MT	Idle Speed (rpm) AT	Valve Clearance In.	Valve Clearance Ex.
1982	2	2.5 (2475)	0.060	8B	8B	9–13	775	500	Hyd.	Hyd.
	1	2.8 (2835)	0.045	10B	10B	4–6.5	850	700	Hyd.	Hyd.
	7	5.0 (5011)	0.045	—	6B	9–13	—	500	Hyd.	Hyd.
	H	5.0 (5011)	0.045	6B	6B	4–6.5	750	575	Hyd.	Hyd.
1983	2	2.5 (2475)	0.060	8B	8B	9–13	775	500	Hyd.	Hyd.
	1	2.8 (2835)	0.045	10B	10B	4–6.5	850	700	Hyd.	Hyd.
	7	5.0 (5011)	0.045	—	6B	9–13	—	500	Hyd.	Hyd.
	H	5.0 (5011)	0.045	6B	6B	4–6.5	750	575	Hyd.	Hyd.
1984	2	2.5 (2475)	0.060	8B	8B	9–13	775	500	Hyd.	Hyd.
	1	2.8 (2835)	0.045	10B	10B	4–6.5	850	700	Hyd.	Hyd.
	H	5.0 (5011)	0.045	6B	6B	4–6.5	750	575	Hyd.	Hyd.
	G	5.0 (5011)	0.045	6B	6B	4–6.5	750	550	Hyd.	Hyd.
1985	2	2.5 (2475)	0.060	8B	8B	9–13	775	500	Hyd.	Hyd.
	S	2.8 (2835)	0.045	10B	10B	6–8	600	500	Hyd.	Hyd.
	G	5.0 (5011)	0.045	6B	6B	9–13	750	550	Hyd.	Hyd.
	H	5.0 (5011)	0.045	6B	6B	9–13	750	550	Hyd.	Hyd.
	F	5.0 (5011)	0.045	—	6B	9–13	—	500	Hyd.	Hyd.
1986	2	2.5 (2475)	0.060	8B	8B	9–13	775	500	Hyd.	Hyd.
	S	2.8 (2835)	0.045	10B	10B	40–47	600	500	Hyd.	Hyd.
	G	5.0 (4999)	0.045	6B	6B	9–13	750	550	Hyd.	Hyd.
	H	5.0 (4999)	0.045	6B	6B	9–13	750	550	Hyd.	Hyd.
	F	5.0 (4999)	0.045	—	6B	40–47	—	500	Hyd.	Hyd.
1987	S	2.8 (2835)	0.045	10B	10B	40–47	700	700	Hyd.	Hyd.
	H	5.0 (4999)	0.035	6B	6B	9–13	500	500	Hyd.	Hyd.
	F	5.0 (4999)	0.035	6B	6B	41–47	500	500	Hyd.	Hyd.
	8	5.7 (5737)	0.035	6B	6B	41–47	450	400	Hyd.	Hyd.
1988	S	2.8 (2835)	0.045	10B	10B	40–47	700	700	Hyd.	Hyd.
	F	5.0 (5011)	0.035	6B	6B	40–47	700	700	Hyd.	Hyd.
	E	5.0 (5011)	0.035	6B	6B	9–13	700	700	Hyd.	Hyd.
	8	5.7 (5733)	0.035	6B	6B	40–47	700	700	Hyd.	Hyd.
1989	S	2.8 (2835)	0.045	10B	10B	41–47	700	700	Hyd.	Hyd.
	7	3.8 (3786)	0.035	—	①	34–40	—	①	Hyd.	Hyd.
	F	5.0 (5011)	0.035	6B	6B	41–47	700	700	Hyd.	Hyd.
	E	5.0 (5011)	0.035	6B	6B	9–13	700	700	Hyd.	Hyd.
	8	5.7 (5733)	0.035	6B	6B	41–47	700	700	Hyd.	Hyd.
1990	T	3.1 (3136)	0.045	10B	10B	41–47	①	①	Hyd.	Hyd.
	F	5.0 (5011)	0.035	6B	6B	41–47	600	600	Hyd.	Hyd.
	E	5.0 (5011)	0.035	—	—	9–13	600	600	Hyd.	Hyd.
	8	5.7 (5733)	0.035	6B	6B	41–47	600	600	Hyd.	Hyd.

85342B30

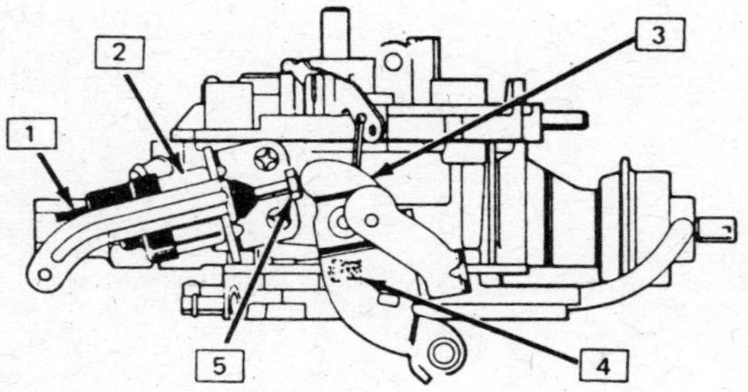

1
2
3
4
5
1 ELECTRICAL CONNECTOR
2 IDLE SPEED SOLENOID
3 THROTTLE LEVER
4 IDLE SPEED SCREW
5 PLUNGER
85342042

Fig. 30 Idle speed adjustments—4-bbl carburetor

GASOLINE ENGINE TUNE-UP SPECIFICATIONS

Year	Engine ID/VIN	Engine Displacement Liters (cc)	Spark Plugs Gap (in.)	Ignition Timing (deg.) MT	Ignition Timing (deg.) AT	Fuel Pump (psi)	Idle Speed (rpm) MT	Idle Speed (rpm) AT	Valve Clearance In.	Valve Clearance Ex.
1991	T	3.1 (3136)	0.045	10B	10B	41–47	675	675	Hyd.	Hyd.
	F	5.0 (5011)	0.035	—	—	41–47	600	600	Hyd.	Hyd.
	E	5.0 (5011)	0.035	6B	6B	9–13	600	600	Hyd.	Hyd.
	8	5.7 (5733)	0.035	6B	6B	41–47	600	600	Hyd.	Hyd.
1992	T	3.1 (3136)	0.045	10B	10B	9–13	675	675	Hyd.	Hyd.
	F	5.0 (5011)	0.035	—	—	41–47	600	600	Hyd.	Hyd.
	E	5.0 (5011)	0.035	6B	6B	9–13	600	600	Hyd.	Hyd.
	8	5.7 (5733)	0.035	6B	6B	41–47	600	600	Hyd.	Hyd.
1993	S	3.4 (3350)	0.045	①	①	41–47	750	750	Hyd.	Hyd.
	P	5.7 (5733)	0.050	①	①	41–47	①	①	Hyd.	Hyd.
1994	S	3.4 (3350)	0.045	①	①	41–47	750	750	Hyd.	Hyd.
	P	5.7 (5733)	0.050	①	①	41–47	①	①	Hyd.	Hyd.

NOTE: The Vehicle Emission Control Information label often reflects specification changes made during production. The label figures must be used if they differ from those in this chart.
B—Before Top Dead Center
Hyd.—Hydraulic
① Refer to Vehicle Emission Control Information label

85342C3A

Troubleshooting Basic Starting System Problems

Problem	Cause	Solution
Starter motor rotates engine slowly	• Battery charge low or battery defective • Defective circuit between battery and starter motor • Low load current • High load current	• Charge or replace battery • Clean and tighten, or replace cables • Bench-test starter motor. Inspect for worn brushes and weak brush springs. • Bench-test starter motor. Check engine for friction, drag or coolant in cylinders. Check ring gear-to-pinion gear clearance.
Starter motor will not rotate engine	• Battery charge low or battery defective • Faulty solenoid • Damaged drive pinion gear or ring gear • Starter motor engagement weak • Starter motor rotates slowly with high load current • Engine seized	• Charge or replace battery • Check solenoid ground. Repair or replace as necessary. • Replace damaged gear(s) • Bench-test starter motor • Inspect drive yoke pull-down and point gap, check for worn end bushings, check ring gear clearance • Repair engine
Starter motor drive will not engage (solenoid known to be good)	• Defective contact point assembly • Inadequate contact point assembly ground • Defective hold-in coil	• Repair or replace contact point assembly • Repair connection at ground screw • Replace field winding assembly
Starter motor drive will not disengage	• Starter motor loose on flywheel housing • Worn drive end busing • Damaged ring gear teeth • Drive yoke return spring broken or missing	• Tighten mounting bolts • Replace bushing • Replace ring gear or driveplate • Replace spring
Starter motor drive disengages prematurely	• Weak drive assembly thrust spring • Hold-in coil defective	• Replace drive mechanism • Replace field winding assembly
Low load current	• Worn brushes • Weak brush springs	• Replace brushes • Replace springs

TCCS2C01

Troubleshooting Basic Charging System Problems

Problem	Cause	Solution
Noisy alternator	• Loose mountings • Loose drive pulley • Worn bearings • Brush noise • Internal circuits shorted (High pitched whine)	• Tighten mounting bolts • Tighten pulley • Replace alternator • Replace alternator • Replace alternator
Squeal when starting engine or accelerating	• Glazed or loose belt	• Replace or adjust belt
Indicator light remains on or ammeter indicates discharge (engine running)	• Broken belt • Broken or disconnected wires • Internal alternator problems • Defective voltage regulator	• Install belt • Repair or connect wiring • Replace alternator • Replace voltage regulator/alternator
Car light bulbs continually burn out— battery needs water continually	• Alternator/regulator overcharging	• Replace voltage regulator/alternator
Car lights flare on acceleration	• Battery low • Internal alternator/regulator problems	• Charge or replace battery • Replace alternator/regulator
Low voltage output (alternator light flickers continually or ammeter needle wanders)	• Loose or worn belt • Dirty or corroded connections • Internal alternator/regulator problems	• Replace or adjust belt • Clean or replace connections • Replace alternator/regulator

TCCS2C02

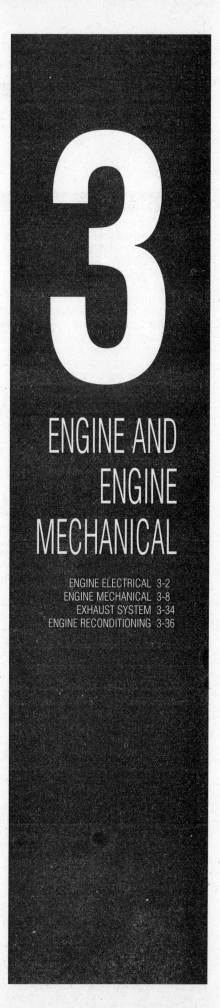

3

ENGINE AND ENGINE MECHANICAL

ENGINE ELECTRICAL

The engine electrical system can be broken down into three inter-related, but distinct systems:

1. The starting system.
2. The charging system.
3. The ignition system.

Battery and Starting System

The battery is the first link in the chain of mechanisms which work together to provide cranking of the automobile engine. In most modern cars, the battery is a lead-acid electrochemical device consisting of six two-volt (2V) subsections connected in series so the unit is capable of producing approximately 12V of electrical pressure. Each subsection, or cell, consists of a series of positive and negative plates held a short distance apart in a solution of sulfuric acid and water. The two types of plates are of dissimilar metals. This causes a chemical reaction to be set up, and it is this reaction which produces current flow from the battery when its positive and negative terminals are connected to an electrical appliance such as a lamp or motor.

The continued transfer of electrons would eventually convert the sulfuric acid in the electrolyte to water and make the two plates identical in chemical composition. As electrical energy is removed from the battery, its voltage output tends to drop. Thus, measuring battery voltage and battery electrolyte composition are two ways of checking the ability of the unit to supply power. During the starting of the engine, electrical energy is removed from the battery. However, if the charging circuit is in good condition and the operating conditions are normal, the power removed from the battery will be replaced by the generator (or alternator) which will force electrons back through the battery, reversing the normal flow, and restoring the battery to its original chemical state.

The battery and starting motor are linked by very heavy electrical cables designed to minimize resistance to the flow of current. Generally, the major power supply cable that leaves the battery goes directly to the starter, while other electrical system needs are supplied by a smaller cable. During the starter operation, power flows from the battery to the starter and is grounded through the car's frame and the battery's negative ground strap.

The starting motor is a specially designed, direct current electric motor capable of producing a very great amount of power for its size. One thing that allows the motor to produce a great deal of power is its tremendous rotating speed. It drives the engine through a tiny pinion gear (attached to the starter's armature), which drives the very large flywheel ring gear at a greatly reduced speed. Another factor allowing it to produce so much power is that only intermittent operation is required of it. Thus, little allowance for air circulation is required, and the windings can be built into a very small space.

The starter solenoid is a magnetic device which employs the small current supplied by the starting switch circuit of the ignition switch. This magnetic action moves a plunger which mechanically engages the starter and electrically closes the heavy switch which connects it to the battery. The starting switch circuit consists of the starting switch contained within the ignition switch, a transmission neutral safety switch or clutch pedal switch, and the wiring necessary to connect these with the starter solenoid or relay.

A pinion, which is a small gear, is mounted to a one-way drive clutch. This clutch is splined to the starter armature shaft. When the ignition switch is moved to the **start** position, the solenoid plunger slides the pinion toward the flywheel ring gear via a collar and spring. If the teeth on the pinion and flywheel match properly, the pinion will engage the flywheel immediately. If the gear teeth butt one another, the spring will be compressed and will force the gears to mesh as soon as the starter turns far enough to allow them to do so. As the solenoid plunger reaches the end of its travel, it closes the contacts that connect the battery and starter and then the engine is cranked.

As soon as the engine starts, the flywheel ring gear begins turning fast enough to drive the pinion at an extremely high rate of speed. At this point, the one-way clutch begins allowing the pinion to spin faster than the starter shaft so that the starter will not operate at excessive speed. When the ignition switch is released from the starter position, the solenoid is de-energized, and a spring contained within the solenoid assembly pulls the gear out of mesh and interrupts the current flow to the starter.

Some starters employ a separate relay, mounted away from the starter, to switch the motor and solenoid current on and off. The relay thus replaces the solenoid electrical switch, but does not eliminate the need for a solenoid mounted on the starter used to mechanically engage the starter drive gears. The relay is used to reduce the amount of current the starting switch must carry.

The Charging System

The automobile charging system provides electrical power for operation of the vehicle's ignition and starting systems and all the electrical accessories. The battery serves as an electrical surge or storage tank, storing (in chemical form) the energy originally produced by the engine driven generator. The system also provides a means of regulating alternator output to protect the battery from being overcharged and to avoid excessive voltage to the accessories.

The storage battery is a chemical device incorporating parallel lead plates in a tank containing a sulfuric acid-water solution. Adjacent plates are slightly dissimilar, and the chemical reaction of the two dissimilar plates produces electrical energy when the battery is connected to a load such as the starter motor. The chemical reaction is reversible, so that when the generator is producing a voltage (electrical pressure) greater than that produced by the battery, electricity is forced into the battery, and the battery is returned to its fully charged state.

Alternators are used on the modern automobiles for they are lighter, more efficient, can rotate at higher speeds and have fewer brush problems. In an alternator, the field rotates while all the current produced passes only through the stators windings. The brushes bear against continuous slip rings rather than a commutator. This causes the current produced to periodically reverse the direction of its flow. Diodes (electrical one-way switches) block the flow of current from traveling in the wrong direction. A series of diodes is wired together to permit the alternating flow of the stator to be converted to a pulsating, but unidirectional flow at the alternator output. The alternator's field is wired in series with the voltage regulator.

➡**Please refer to Section 2 for ignition system testing procedures.**

Ignition Coil

REMOVAL & INSTALLATION

Internally Mounted Coil

1. Disconnect and label the wires from cap.
2. Remove the distributor cap from the distributor.
3. On the distributor cap, remove the coil cover attaching screws and the cover.
4. Remove the ignition coil attaching screws and lift the coil from the cap.
To install:
5. Position the coil and secure it with the attaching screws. Be sure to install the carbon button and rubber disc first.
6. Install the coil cover and attaching screws.
7. Install the distributor cap.
8. Connect the wires to the cap.

Externally Mounted Coil

1. Label and disconnect the wires from the coil.
2. Remove the ignition coil mounting bolts and the coil.
To install:
3. To install, position the coil into place and secure it with the mounting bolts.
4. Connect the wires to the coil.

Ignition Module

REMOVAL & INSTALLATION

1. Disconnect the wires from the cap.
2. Remove the distributor cap.
3. Remove the two module attaching screws and capacitor attaching screw. Lift module, capacitor and harness assembly from base.

4. Disconnect wiring harness.

To install:

5. Apply silicone grease underneath the module. This grease is necessary for ignition module cooling.

6. Connect the wiring harness.

7. Install the module and attaching screws.

8. Install the distributor cap and wires.

Distributor

REMOVAL & INSTALLATION

▶ **See Figures 1, 2, 3, 4 and 5**

1. Disconnect the negative battery cable.

2. Remove the air cleaner assembly.

3. Unplug and label the electrical connections from the distributor.

4. Remove the distributor cover and wire retainer, if equipped. Turn the retaining screws counterclockwise and remove the cap.

5. Mark the relationship of the rotor to the distributor housing and the housing relationship to the engine.

6. Remove the distributor retaining bolt and hold-down clamp.

7. Pull the distributor up until the rotor just stops turning counterclockwise and again note the position of the rotor.

8. Remove the distributor from the engine.

To install:

9. Insert the distributor into the engine, with the rotor aligned to the last mark made, then slowly install the distributor the rest of the way until all marks previously made are aligned.

10. Install the distributor hold-down clamp and retaining bolt.

11. If removed, install the wiring harness retainer and secondary wires.

12. Install the distributor cap.

13. Engage the wire connections on the distributor. Make certain the connectors are fully seated and latched.

14. Reconnect the negative battery cable.

➡ **If the engine was accidentally cranked after the distributor was removed, the following procedure can be used during installation.**

15. Remove the No. 1 spark plug.

16. Place a finger over the spark plug hole. Have a helper turn the engine slowly using a wrench on the crankshaft bolt until compression is felt.

17. Align the timing mark on the pulley to **0** on the engine timing indicator.

18. Turn the rotor to point to the No. 1 spark plug tower on the distributor cap.

19. Install the distributor assembly in the engine and ensure the rotor is pointing toward the No. 1 spark plug tower.

20. Install the cap and spark plug wires.

21. Check and adjust engine timing.

Alternator

DESCRIPTION

An alternator differs from a DC shunt generator in that the armature is stationary, and is called the stator, while the field rotates and is called the rotor. The higher current values in the alternator's stator are conducted to the external circuit through fixed leads and connections, rather than through a rotating commutator and brushes as in a DC generator. This eliminates a major point of maintenance.

Fig. 1 Matchmarking the rotor

85343001

Fig. 2 Unplugging the connector

85343002

Fig. 3 Loosening the hold-down bolt

85343003

Fig. 4 Removing the hold-down bolt and clamp

85343004

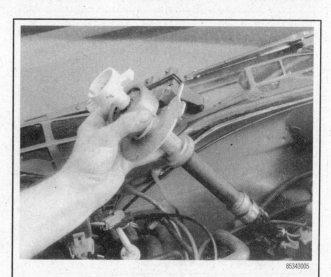

Fig. 5 Removing the distributor

85343005

The rotor assembly is supported in the drive end frame by a ball bearing and at the other end by a roller bearing. These bearings are lubricated during assembly and require no maintenance. There are six diodes in the end frame assembly. These diodes are electrical check valves that also change the alternating current developed within the stator windings to a direct (DC) current at the output (BAT) terminal. Three of these diodes are negative and are mounted flush with the end frame while the other three are positive and are mounted into a strip called a heat sink. The positive diodes are easily identified as the ones within small cavities or depressions.

The alternator charging system is a negative (–) ground system which consists of an alternator, a regulator, a charge indicator, a storage battery and wiring connecting the components, and fuse link wire.

The alternator is belt-driven from the engine. Energy is supplied from the alternator/regulator system to the rotating field through two brushes to two slip-rings. The slip-rings are mounted on the rotor shaft and are connected to the field coil. This energy supplied to the rotating field from the battery is called excitation current and is used to initially energize the field to begin the generation of electricity. Once the alternator starts to generate electricity, the excitation current comes from its own output rather than the battery.

The alternator produces power in the form of alternating current. The alternating current is rectified by 6 diodes into direct current. The direct current is used to charge the battery and power the rest of the electrical system.

When the ignition key is turned ON, current flows from the battery, through the charging system indicator light on the instrument panel, to the voltage regulator, and to the alternator. Since the alternator is not producing any current, the alternator warning light comes on. When the engine is started, the alternator begins to produce current and turns the alternator light off. As the alternator turns and produces current, the current is divided in two ways: part to the battery(to charge the battery and power the electrical components of the vehicle), and part is returned to the alternator (to enable it to increase its output). In this situation, the alternator is receiving current from the battery and from itself. A voltage regulator is wired into the current supply to the alternator to prevent it from receiving too much current which would cause it to put out too much current. Conversely, if the voltage regulator does not allow the alternator to receive enough current, the battery will not be fully charged and will eventually go dead.

The battery is connected to the alternator at all times, whether the ignition key is turned ON or not. If the battery were shorted to ground, the alternator would also be shorted. This would damage the alternator. To prevent this, a fuse link is installed in the wiring between the battery and the alternator. If the battery is shorted, the fuse link melts, protecting the alternator.

An alternator is better that a conventional, DC shunt generator because it is lighter and more compact, because it is designed to supply the battery and accessory circuits through a wide range of engine speeds, and because it eliminates the necessary maintenance of replacing brushes and servicing commutators.

PRECAUTIONS

To prevent serious damage to the alternator and the rest of the charging system, the following precautions must be observed:
- Never reverse the battery connections.

- Booster batteries for starting must be connected properly: positive-to-positive and negative-to-ground.
- Disconnect the battery cables before using a fast charger; the charger has a tendency to force current through the diodes in the opposite direction for which they were designed. This burns out the diodes.
- Never use a fast charger as a booster for starting the vehicle.
- Never disconnect the voltage regulator while the engine is running.
- Avoid long soldering times when replacing diodes or transistors. Prolonged heat is damaging to AC alternators.
- Do not use test lamps of more than 12 volts (V) for checking diode continuity.
- Do not short across or ground any of the terminals on the AC alternator.
- The polarity of the battery, alternator, and regulator must be matched and considered before making any electrical connections within the system.
- Never operate the alternator on an open circuit. make sure that all connections within the circuit are clean and tight.
- Disconnect the battery terminals when performing any service on the electrical system. This will eliminate the possibility of accidental reversal of polarity.
- Disconnect the battery ground cable if arc welding is to be done on any part of the car.

CHARGING SYSTEM TROUBLESHOOTING

There are many possible ways in which the charging system can malfunction. Often the source of a problem is difficult to diagnose, requiring special equipment and a good deal of experience. However, when the charging system fails completely and causes the dash board warning light to come on or the battery to become dead the following items may be checked:
1. The battery is known to be good and fully charged.
2. The alternator belt is in good condition and adjusted to the proper tension.
3. All connections in the system are clean and tight.

REMOVAL & INSTALLATION

▶ **See Figures 6, 7 and 8**

While internal alternator repairs are possible, they require specialized tools and training. Therefore, it is advisable to replace a defective alternator as an assembly, or have it repaired by a qualified shop.
1. Disconnect the battery ground cable.
2. Tag and disconnect the alternator wiring.
3. Remove any drive belt(s) which may interfere with alternator removal.
4. Support the alternator and remove the mount bolt(s). Remove the unit from the vehicle.

To install:
5. Position the alternator into place and install the mount bolt(s) loosely.
6. Install the drive belt(s). On V-belts, tighten the belt enough to allow approximately ½ in. (13mm) of play on the longest run between pulleys.
7. Connect the alternator wiring.
8. Connect the battery ground cable.

Fig. 6 Loosening the wire connector bolt

Fig. 7 Removing the through-bolt

Fig. 8 Unplugging the harness

Voltage Regulator

REMOVAL & INSTALLATION

♦ **See Figures 9 and 10**

➥This procedure is to be performed with the alternator removed from the vehicle. The new style CS alternators on 1987–92 vehicles are non-serviceable and must be replaced as an assembly.

1. Make scribe marks on the end frames to make reassembly easier.
2. Remove the 4 through-bolts and separate the drive end frame assembly from the rectifier end frame assembly.
3. Remove the 3 diode trio attaching nuts and the 3 regulator attaching screws.
4. Remove the diode trio and the regulator from the end frame.

To install:

5. Push the brushes into the brush holder and install a brush retainer or a tooth pick to hold the brushes in place.
6. Install the regulator into the alternator.

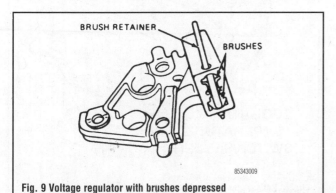

Fig. 9 Voltage regulator with brushes depressed

7. Install the diode trio.
8. Install the halves of the alternator and secure the halves with the 4 through-bolts. After the alternator is assembled, remove the brush retainer.

Starter

REMOVAL & INSTALLATION

♦ **See Figures 11, 12, 13, 14 and 15**

1. Disconnect the negative battery cable.
2. Raise and safely support the vehicle.
3. Disconnect all wiring from the starter solenoid. Replace each nut as the connector is removed (as thread sizes differ from connector to connector). Note or tag the wiring positions for installation.
4. Remove the bracket from the starter and the two mounting bolts. On engines with a solenoid heat shield, remove the front bracket upper bolt and detach the bracket from the starter.
5. Remove the front bracket bolt or nut. Lower the starter front end first, and then remove the unit from the car.

To install:

6. Position the starter into place and secure it with the front bracket bolt and nut. Torque the two mounting bolts to 25–35 ft. lbs.

❈❈ CAUTION

If shims were removed, they must be replaced to ensure proper pinion-to-flywheel engagement.

7. On engines with a solenoid heat shield, attach the bracket to the starter. Install the bracket to the starter and the two mounting bolts. Install the front bracket upper bolt.
8. Connect all wiring to the starter solenoid and tighten the nuts.
9. Lower the vehicle.
10. Connect the negative battery cable.

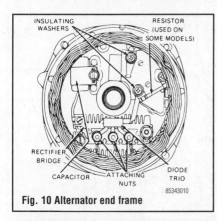

Fig. 10 Alternator end frame

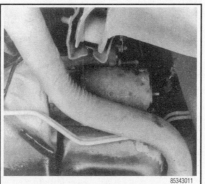

Fig. 11 View of the starter on a V8

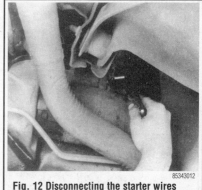

Fig. 12 Disconnecting the starter wires

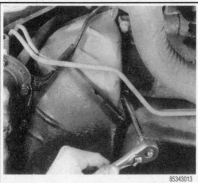

Fig. 13 Loosening the starter mounting bolts

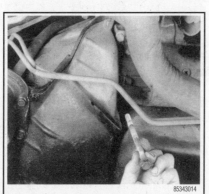

Fig. 14 Removing the starter mounting bolts

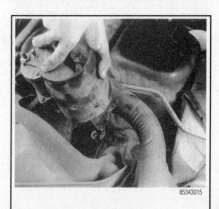

Fig. 15 Removing the starter

SOLENOID REPLACEMENT

1. Remove the screw and washer from the motor connector strap terminal.
2. Remove the two solenoid retaining screws.
3. Twist the solenoid housing clockwise to remove the flange key from the keyway in the housing. Then remove the housing.
4. To re-install the unit, place the return spring on the plunger and place the solenoid body on the drive housing. Turn counterclockwise to engage the flange key. Place the two retaining screws in position and install the screw and washer which secures the strap terminal. Install the unit on the starter.

Sending Units and Sensors

➡ **For additional information on engine sensors, refer to Sections 2 and 4 of this manual.**

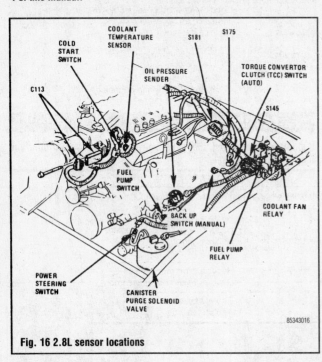

Fig. 16 2.8L sensor locations

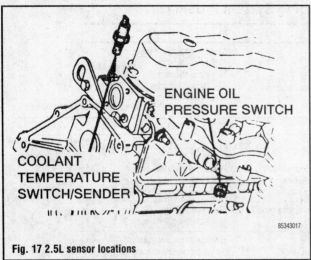

Fig. 17 2.5L sensor locations

REMOVAL & INSTALLATION

Sensors

◗ **See Figures 16, 17, 18 and 19**

Oil Pressure Sending Unit

Replace the sending unit by disconnecting the electrical connector and using a special socket to remove it.

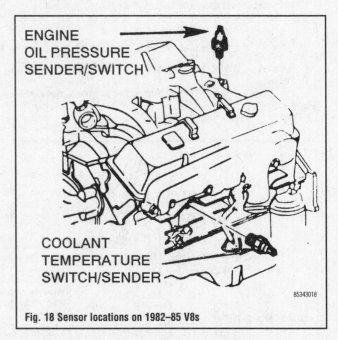

Fig. 18 Sensor locations on 1982–85 V8s

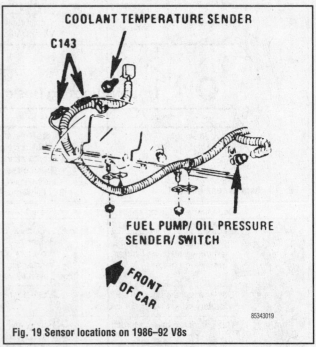

Fig. 19 Sensor locations on 1986–92 V8s

Troubleshooting Basic Starting System Problems

Problem	Cause	Solution
Starter motor rotates engine slowly	· Battery charge low or battery defective	· Charge or replace battery
	· Defective circuit between battery and starter motor	· Clean and tighten, or replace cables
	· Low load current	· Bench-test starter motor. Inspect for worn brushes and weak brush springs.
	· High load current	· Bench-test starter motor. Check engine for friction, drag or coolant in cylinders. Check ring gear-to-pinion gear clearance.
Starter motor will not rotate engine	· Battery charge low or battery defective	· Charge or replace battery
	· Faulty solenoid	· Check solenoid ground. Repair or replace as necessary.
	· Damaged drive pinion gear or ring gear	· Replace damaged gear(s)
	· Starter motor engagement weak	· Bench-test starter motor
	· Starter motor rotates slowly with high load current	· Inspect drive yoke pull-down and point gap, check for worn end bushings, check ring gear clearance
	· Engine seized	· Repair engine
Starter motor drive will not engage (solenoid known to be good)	· Defective contact point assembly	· Repair or replace contact point assembly
	· Inadequate contact point assembly ground	· Repair connection at ground screw
	· Defective hold-in coil	· Replace field winding assembly
Starter motor drive will not disengage	· Starter motor loose on flywheel housing	· Tighten mounting bolts
	· Worn drive end busing	· Replace bushing
	· Damaged ring gear teeth	· Replace ring gear or driveplate
	· Drive yoke return spring broken or missing	· Replace spring
Starter motor drive disengages prematurely	· Weak drive assembly thrust spring	· Replace drive mechanism
	· Hold-in coil defective	· Replace field winding assembly
Low load current	· Worn brushes	· Replace brushes
	· Weak brush springs	· Replace springs

TCCS2C01

Troubleshooting Basic Charging System Problems

Problem	Cause	Solution
Noisy alternator	· Loose mountings	· Tighten mounting bolts
	· Loose drive pulley	· Tighten pulley
	· Worn bearings	· Replace alternator
	· Brush noise	· Replace alternator
	· Internal circuits shorted (High pitched whine)	· Replace alternator
Squeal when starting engine or accelerating	· Glazed or loose belt	· Replace or adjust belt
Indicator light remains on or ammeter indicates discharge (engine running)	· Broken belt	· Install belt
	· Broken or disconnected wires	· Repair or connect wiring
	· Internal alternator problems	· Replace alternator
	· Defective voltage regulator	· Replace voltage regulator/alternator
Car light bulbs continually burn out— battery needs water continually	· Alternator/regulator overcharging	· Replace voltage regulator/alternator
Car lights flare on acceleration	· Battery low	· Charge or replace battery
	· Internal alternator/regulator problems	· Replace alternator/regulator
Low voltage output (alternator light flickers continually or ammeter needle wanders)	· Loose or worn belt	· Replace or adjust belt
	· Dirty or corroded connections	· Clean or replace connections
	· Internal alternator/regulator problems	· Replace alternator/regulator

TCCS2C02

ENGINE MECHANICAL

Engine

REMOVAL & INSTALLATION

In the process of removing the engine, you will come across a number of steps which call for the removal of a separate component or system, such as "disconnect the exhaust system" or "remove the radiator." In most instances, a detailed removal procedure can be found elsewhere in this manual.

It is virtually impossible to list each individual wire and hose which must be disconnected, simply because so many different model and engine combinations have been manufactured. Careful observation and common sense are the best possible approaches to any repair procedure.

Removal and installation of the engine can be made easier if you follow these basic points:

- If you have to drain any of the fluids, use a suitable container.
- Always tag any wires or hoses and, if possible, the components they came from before disconnecting them.
- Because there are so many bolts and fasteners involved, store and label the retainers from components separately in muffin pans, jars or coffee cans. This will prevent confusion during installation.
- After unbolting the transmission or transaxle, always make sure it is properly supported.
- If it is necessary to disconnect the air conditioning system, have this service performed by a qualified technician using a recovery/recycling station. If the system does not have to be disconnected, unbolt the compressor and set it aside.
- When unbolting the engine mounts, always make sure the engine is properly supported. When removing the engine, make sure that any lifting devices are properly attached to the engine. It is recommended that if your engine is supplied with lifting hooks, your lifting apparatus be attached to them.
- Lift the engine from its compartment slowly, checking that no hoses, wires or other components are still connected.
- After the engine is clear of the compartment, place it on an engine stand or workbench.
- After the engine has been removed, you can perform a partial or full teardown of the engine using the procedures outlined in this manual.

2.5L Engine

▶ See Figure 20

1. Disconnect the negative battery cable.
2. Remove the air cleaner duct.
3. Mark the hood location on the hood supports and remove the hood.
4. Remove the water pump drive belt.
5. Drain the radiator and remove the radiator hoses. Disconnect the heater hoses and the transmission cooler lines.
6. Remove the upper half of the radiator shroud, if equipped with a manual transmission. Remove the radiator and fan shroud assembly, if equipped with an automatic transmission.
7. Disconnect the throttle linkage, including the cruise control detent cable.
8. Remove the air conditioning compressor and lay aside.

➡Do not disconnect the air conditioning lines.

9. Disconnect the power steering pump and drain the fluid into a suitable container. Remove the vacuum brake booster line.
10. Remove the distributor cap and spark plug wires.
11. Disconnect the engine electrical connection at the bulkhead connection and disconnect any necessary vacuum hoses.
12. Working inside the vehicle, remove the right-hand hush panel and disconnect the ECM harness at the ECM. Raise and safely support the vehicle. Remove the right fenderwell splash shield and feed the harness through the fenderwell.
13. Disconnect the exhaust pipes at the exhaust manifolds and remove exhaust system from the vehicle.
14. Remove the flywheel cover and remove the converter bolts, if equipped with automatic transmission.
15. Disconnect the transmission and starter wire connections.

16. Remove the bellhousing and the motor mount through-bolts.
17. Disconnect the clutch fork return spring, if equipped with a manual transmission. Lower the vehicle.
18. Relieve the fuel system pressure. Disconnect the fuel lines.
19. Support the transmission with a suitable jack. Attach an engine lifting device.
20. Remove the engine assembly.

To install:

21. Position the engine assembly in the vehicle.
22. Attach the motor mount to engine brackets and lower the engine in place. Remove the engine lifting device and the transmission jack.
23. Raise and support the vehicle safely.
24. Install the motor mount through-bolts and tighten the nuts to specification. Install the bellhousing bolts and tighten to 35 ft. lbs. (47 Nm).
25. On vehicles with automatic transmission, install the converter to flywheel attaching bolts to 46 ft. lbs. (63 Nm).
26. Install the flywheel splash shield and tighten to 89 inch lbs. (10 Nm). Install the clutch return spring, if equipped with manual transmission.
27. Connect the starter wires and the fuel lines.
28. Install the exhaust system.
29. Lower the vehicle.
30. Install the power steering pump and the air conditioning compressor.
31. Connect the bulkhead harness connector, wires and hoses. Reroute the ECM harness in its original location. Install the hush panel and fenderwell splash panel.
32. Install the radiator, fan and fan shroud. Connect the radiator and heater hoses, along with the transmission cooler lines.
33. Connect the vacuum brake booster line, the throttle linkage and cruise control cable. Install the distributor cap.
34. Fill the cooling system with the proper type and amount of coolant and the crankcase with the proper type of oil to the correct level.
35. Install the water pump drive belt, the air cleaner duct and the hood.
36. Connect the negative battery cable, start the engine and check for leaks.

2.8L and 3.1L Engines

▶ See Figure 21

1. Disconnect the negative battery cable.
2. Remove the air cleaner duct.
3. Mark the hood location on the hood supports and remove the hood.
4. Remove the water pump drive belt.
5. Drain the radiator and remove the radiator hoses. Disconnect the heater hoses and the transmission cooler lines.
6. Remove the fan shroud, fan and radiator.
7. Disconnect the throttle linkage, including the cruise control detent cable.
8. Remove the air conditioning compressor and lay aside. Remove the power steering pump and lay aside.

➡Do not disconnect the air conditioning or power steering lines.

9. Remove the vacuum brake booster line.
10. Remove the distributor cap and spark plug wires.
11. Disconnect the necessary electrical connections and hoses.
12. Raise and safely support the vehicle.
13. Disconnect the exhaust pipes at the exhaust manifolds.
14. Remove the flywheel cover and remove the converter bolts.
15. Disconnect the starter wire connections.
16. Remove the bellhousing and the motor mount through-bolts.
17. Lower the vehicle.
18. Relieve the fuel system pressure. Disconnect the fuel lines.
19. Support the transmission with a suitable jack. Attach an engine lifting device.
20. Remove the engine assembly.

To install:

21. Position the engine assembly in the vehicle.
22. Attach the motor mount to engine brackets and lower the engine in place. Remove the engine lifting device and the transmission jack.
23. Raise and support the vehicle safely.
24. Install the motor mount through-bolts and tighten the nuts to 50 ft. lbs. (68 Nm). Install the bellhousing bolts and tighten to 35 ft. lbs. (47 Nm).

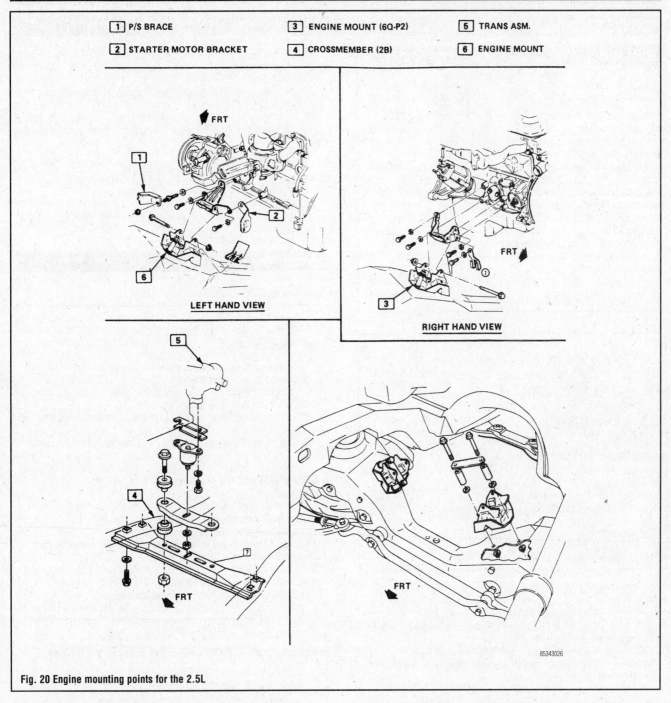

1	P/S BRACE	3	ENGINE MOUNT (6Q-P2)	5	TRANS ASM.
2	STARTER MOTOR BRACKET	4	CROSSMEMBER (2B)	6	ENGINE MOUNT

LEFT HAND VIEW

RIGHT HAND VIEW

85343026

Fig. 20 Engine mounting points for the 2.5L

25. On vehicles with automatic transmission, install the converter to flywheel attaching bolts to 46 ft. lbs. (63 Nm).

26. Install the flywheel splash shield and tighten to 89 inch lbs. (10 Nm).

27. Connect the starter wires and the fuel lines.

28. Install the exhaust pipe on the exhaust manifold.

29. Lower the vehicle.

30. Install the power steering pump and the air conditioning compressor.

31. Connect the necessary wires and hoses.

32. Install the radiator, fan and fan shroud. Connect the radiator and heater hoses and the transmission cooler lines.

33. Connect the vacuum brake booster line, the throttle linkage and cruise control cable. Install the distributor cap.

34. Fill the cooling system with the proper type and amount of coolant and the crankcase with the proper type of oil to the correct level.

35. Install the water pump drive belt, the air cleaner duct and the hood.

36. Connect the negative battery cable, start the engine and check for leaks.

5.0L and 5.7L Engines

▶ **See Figure 22**

1. Disconnect the negative battery cable.

2. Mark the location of the hood on the hood hinges and remove the hood.

3. Remove the air cleaner.

4. Drain the cooling system.

5. Remove the radiator hoses.

6. Disconnect the transmission cooler lines, the electrical connectors and retaining clips at the fan and remove the fan and shroud.

7. Remove the radiator.

8. Remove the accessory drive belt.

9. Disconnect the throttle cable.

10. Remove the plenum extension screws and the plenum extension, if equipped.

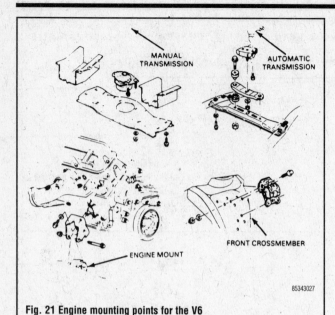

Fig. 21 Engine mounting points for the V6

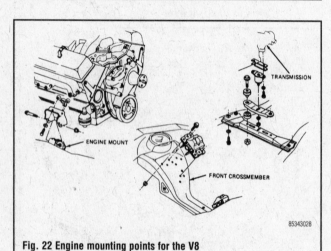

Fig. 22 Engine mounting points for the V8

11. Disconnect the spark plug wires at the distributor and remove the distributor.

12. Disconnect the necessary vacuum hoses and wiring.

13. Disconnect the power steering and air conditioning compressors from their respective brackets and lay them aside.

14. Properly relieve the fuel system pressure. Disconnect the fuel lines.

15. Disconnect the negative battery cable at the engine block.

16. Raise and safely support the vehicle.

17. Remove the exhaust pipes at the exhaust manifolds.

18. Remove the flywheel cover and remove the converter to flywheel bolts.

19. Disconnect the starter wires.

20. Remove the bellhousing bolts and the motor mount through-bolts.

21. Lower the vehicle.

22. Support the transmission with a suitable jack.

23. Remove the AIR/converter bracket and ground wires from the rear of the cylinder head.

24. Attach a suitable lifting device and remove the engine assembly.

To install:

25. Position the engine assembly in the vehicle.

26. Attach the motor mount to engine brackets and lower the engine into place.

27. Remove the engine lifting device and the transmission jack.

28. Raise and safely support the vehicle.

29. Install the motor mount through-bolts and tighten to 50 ft. lbs. (68 Nm).

30. Install the bellhousing bolts and tighten to 35 ft. lbs. (47 Nm).

31. On vehicles with automatic transmission, install the converter to flywheel bolts. Tighten the bolts to 46 ft. lbs. (63 Nm). Install the flywheel cover.

32. Connect the starter wires and the fuel lines.

33. Connect the exhaust pipe at the exhaust manifold.

34. Lower the vehicle.

35. Connect the necessary wires and hoses.

36. Install the power steering pump and air conditioning compressor in their respective brackets.

37. Install the radiator, fan and fan shroud, radiator hoses and heater hoses.

38. Connect the transmission cooler lines and cooling fan electrical connectors.

39. Install the distributor.

40. Install the plenum extension, if equipped.

41. Fill the cooling system with the proper type and quantity of coolant and the crankcase with the proper type of oil to the correct level.

42. Install the air cleaner and the hood.

43. Connect the negative battery cable, start the engine, check for leaks and check timing.

Rocker Arm Cover

REMOVAL & INSTALLATION

2.5L Engine

▶ See Figure 23

1. Disconnect the negative battery cable.

2. Remove the air cleaner assembly.

3. Disconnect the throttle cable at the throttle body.

4. Remove the PCV valve from the cover.

5. Remove the spark plug wires from the clips. Remove the clips from the valve cover.

6. Remove the EGR valve. Loosen the throttle body to gain clearance, as required.

7. Remove the valve cover retaining bolts and remove the cover. Tap on the valve cover with the palm of your hand or use a soft mallet to loosen.

To install:

8. Clean the sealing surface on cylinder head and intake manifold of all old RTV or gasket. Make sure no oil or old gasket is present when applying new RTV or gasket.

9. Place a 1/16 in. (5mm) bead of RTV sealant all around the rocker arm sealing surface or use a cork style gasket. (When going around the attaching bolt holes, always flow the RTV on the inboard side of the holes).

10. Install cover and torque bolts to 8 ft. lbs. (11 Nm).

11. Finish installation by reversing removal procedure.

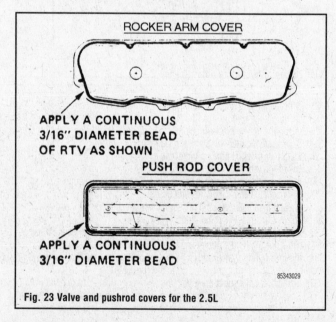

Fig. 23 Valve and pushrod covers for the 2.5L

2.8L and 3.1L Engines

▶ See Figure 24

1. Disconnect the negative battery cable.
2. For the left side valve cover removal, proceed as follows:
    a. Remove the accessory drive belt.
    b. Remove the transmission dipstick, if required.
    c. Remove the air management hose and air conditioning bracket, if equipped.
    d. Remove the intake plenum and throttle body assembly, on fuel injected engines.
    e. Remove the valve cover reinforcements and nuts.
3. For the right side valve cover removal, proceed as follows:
    a. Remove the EGR valve adapter with the EGR valve and shield from the exhaust manifold.
    b. Remove the coil and coil mounting bracket from the cylinder head.
    c. Disconnect the crankcase vent pipe.
    d. Remove the intake plenum and throttle body assembly.
    e. Remove the valve cover reinforcements and nuts.
4. Remove cover. If cover adheres to cylinder head, shear off by bumping end of rocker arm cover with palm of hand or rubber mallet. If cover still will not come loose, CAREFULLY pry until loose. DO NOT DISTORT THE SEALING FLANGE.

To install:

5. Clean the sealing surface on cylinder head and intake manifold of all old RTV or gasket. Make sure no oil or old gasket is present when applying new RTV or gasket.

6. Place a ⅛ in. (3mm) bead of RTV sealant all around the rocker arm sealing surface or use a cork style gasket. (When going around the attaching bolt holes, always flow the RTV on the inboard side of the holes).
7. Install cover and torque bolts to 8 ft. lbs. (10 Nm).
8. Finish installation by reversing removal procedure.

5.0L and 5.7L Engines

▶ See Figures 25, 26, 27 and 28

1. Disconnect the negative battery cable.
2. Remove the air cleaner, if necessary.
3. To remove the right side valve cover, perform the following:
    a. Through 1988: Disconnect the EGR solenoid transfer tube from the plenum. Remove the coil and mounting bracket from the cylinder head. Remove the plenum, runners and throttle body assembly on tuned port

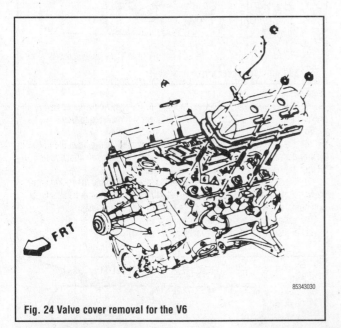

Fig. 24 Valve cover removal for the V6

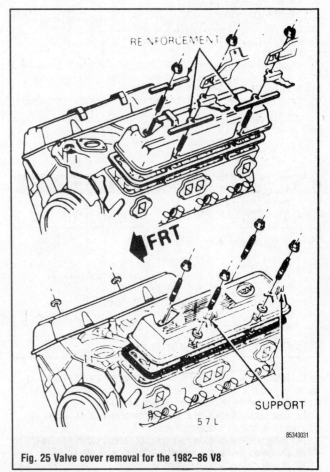

Fig. 25 Valve cover removal for the 1982–86 V8

Fig. 26 Valve cover bolt removal for 1987–92 V8

Fig. 27 Valve cover removal for 1987–92 V8

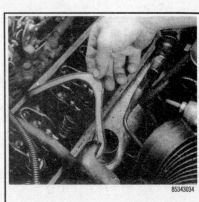

Fig. 28 Removing the valve cover gasket

injected models. Remove the valve cover retainers and nuts. Remove the valve cover.

b. 1989–1992 vehicles: Remove the EGR pipe assembly, if necessary. Unplug the electrical connections and wiring harnesses as necessary. Label and disconnect the spark plug wires from the distributor. Remove the crankcase vent hoses and valves. Remove the coil. Remove the AIR control valve, check valve, pipes and hoses. Remove the valve cover bolts and remove the cover.

4. To remove the left side valve cover, perform the following:

a. Through 1988: Remove the air management hose, if equipped. Remove the plenum and throttle body assembly on tuned port injected models. Remove the air conditioning bracket. Remove the valve cover reinforcements and nuts. Remove the valve cover.

b. 1989–1992 vehicles: Unplug the electrical connections and the wiring harnesses, as necessary. Remove the alternator and disconnect the crankcase hoses and the PCV valve. Remove the valve cover bolts and remove the valve cover.

5. If cover adheres to cylinder head, shear off by bumping end of rocker arm cover with palm of hand or rubber mallet. If cover still will not come loose, CAREFULLY pry until loose. DO NOT DISTORT THE SEALING FLANGE.

To install:

6. Clean the sealing surface of cylinder head and intake manifold of all old RTV or gasket. Make sure no oil or old gasket is present when applying new RTV or gasket.

7. Place a ⅛ in. (3mm) bead of RTV sealant all around the rocker arm sealing surface or use a cork style gasket. (When going around the attaching bolt holes, always flow the RTV on the inboard side of the holes).

8. Install cover and torque bolts to 8 ft. lbs. (11 Nm).

9. Finish installation by reversing removal procedure.

Pushrod Side Cover

REMOVAL & INSTALLATION

2.5L Engine

▶ See Figure 23

1. Disconnect the negative battery cable.
2. Mark and remove the distributor assembly.
3. Remove the ignition coil and bracket.
4. Remove the side cover retaining nuts and remove the cover.

To install:

5. Clean the cover sealing surfaces of all RTV or gasket material.

6. Place a ¹⁄₁₆ in. (5mm) bead of RTV sealant all around the rocker arm sealing surface or use a cork style gasket. (When going around the attaching bolt holes, always flow the RTV on the inboard side of the holes).

7. Install cover and torque bolts to 89 inch lbs. (10 Nm).

8. Finish installation by reversing removal procedure.

Rocker Arms

REMOVAL & INSTALLATION

▶ See Figures 29, 30, 31 and 32

Be sure to keep all the components in the exact order of removal so they may be installed in there original location; adjust the valve lash after replacing the rocker arms. Coat the replacement rocker arm and ball with engine oil before installation.

Rocker arms studs that have damaged threads or are loose in the cylinder heads may be replaced by reaming the bore and installing oversize studs. Oversizes available are 0.003 in. (0.076mm) and 0.013 in (0.33mm). The bore may also be tapped and screw-in studs installed. Several aftermarket companies produce complete rocker arm stud kits with installation tools.

➡The 2.5L engine use bolts instead of studs, 2.8L and 3.1L engines use threaded studs, the 3.4L, 5.0L and 5.7L engines use press fit studs.

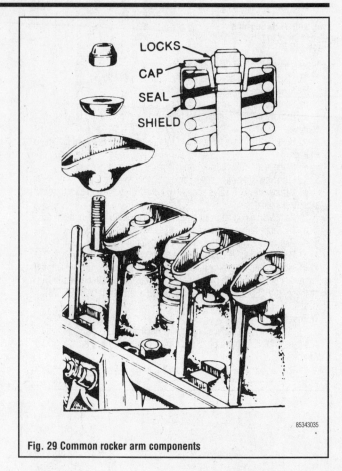

Fig. 29 Common rocker arm components

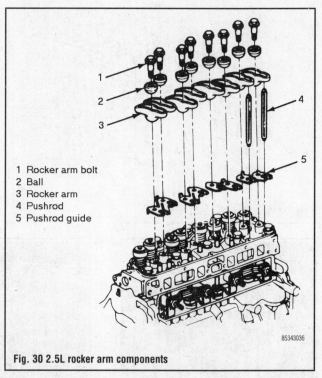

1 Rocker arm bolt
2 Ball
3 Rocker arm
4 Pushrod
5 Pushrod guide

Fig. 30 2.5L rocker arm components

Except 2.5L Engines

1. Disconnect the negative (–) battery cable.
2. Remove the rocker arm cover as outlined in this section

3. Remove the rocker arm nuts, balls and rocker arms. Place components in a rack so they can be reinstalled in the same location.

To install:

4. Coat the bearings surfaces with a thin coating of Molykote® or its equivalent.

Fig. 31 Remove the rocker arm retaining nut

Fig. 32 Then remove the rocker arm pivot

5. Install the pushrods and make sure the rod is in the lifter seat.

6. Install the rocker arm, balls and nut. Tighten the nut until all lash is eliminated.

7. The engine must be on the No. 1 firing position before proceeding. This may be determined by placing your fingers on the No. 1 rocker arms as the mark crankshaft damper is rotated towards the "0" on the timing tab. If the arms did not move, it is in the No. 1 firing position. If they did move, turn the crankshaft one full revolution to reach the No. 1 position. Remember, the mark on the crankshaft balancer must be aligned with the "0" on the timing tab.

8. Adjust the valves as follows:

V6 ENGINES

With the engine on the number 1 firing position, exhaust valves 1, 2 and 3 and intake valves 1, 5 and 6 may be adjusted. Back out the adjusting nut until lash is felt at the pushrod. Tighten the adjusting nut until all lash is removed, then tighten the nut an additional 1½ turns to center the lifter plunger. Turn the engine one revolution until the "0" timing mark is once again aligned. Exhaust valves 4, 5 and 6 and intake valves 2, 3 and 4 may be adjusted.

V8 ENGINES

With the engine on the number 1 firing position, exhaust valves 1, 3, 4 and 8, intake valves 1, 2, 5 and 7 may be adjusted. Back out the adjusting nut until lash is felt at the pushrod. Tighten the adjusting nut until all lash is removed, then tighten an additional 1 turn to center the lifter plunger. Turn the engine one revolution until the 0 timing mark is once again aligned. Exhaust valves 2, 5, 6 and 7, intake valves 3, 4, 6 and 8 may be adjusted.

9. Install the rocker arm cover.

2.5L Engine

1. Disconnect the negative battery cable.
2. Remove the valve cover.
3. Remove the rocker arm bolt, ball and rocker arm.
4. Remove the pushrods, if necessary. Place components in a rack so they can be reinstalled in the same location.

To install:

5. Coat the bearings surfaces with a thin coating of Molykote® or its equivalent.

6. Install the pushrod, if removed, through the cylinder head and into the lifter seat.

7. Install the rocker arm, ball and bolt. Torque to 22 ft lbs. (30 Nm).

8. Install the valve cover.

Thermostat

REMOVAL & INSTALLATION

▶ **See Figures 33, 34 and 35**

✳✳ CAUTION

When draining the coolant, keep in mind that cats and dogs are attracted by the ethylene glycol antifreeze, and are quite likely to drink any that is left in an uncovered container or in puddles on the

Fig. 33 Removing the thermostat housing bolts

Fig. 34 Removing the thermostat housing

Fig. 35 Removing the thermostat

ground. This will prove fatal in sufficient quantity. Always drain the coolant into a sealable container. Coolant should be reused unless it is contaminated or several years old.

1. Disconnect the negative battery cable.
2. Remove any components necessary to gain access to the thermostat.
3. Drain the cooling system to below the level of the thermostat.

➡It is not necessary to remove the radiator hose from the thermostat housing.

4. Remove the two retaining bolts from the thermostat housing and remove the thermostat.

To install:
5. Using a new gasket, install the thermostat and housing.
6. Tighten the bolts to 21 ft lbs. (28 Nm).
7. Fill and bleed the cooling system.

Intake Manifold

REMOVAL & INSTALLATION

➡When servicing all vehicles, be absolutely sure to mark vacuum hoses and wiring so that these items may be properly reconnected during installation. Also, when disconnecting fitting lines (fuel lines, power brake vacuum lines, transmission and engine cooler lines, etc.), always use two flare nut (or line) wrenches. Hold the wrench on the large fitting with pressure on the wrench as if you were tightening the fitting (clockwise), THEN loosen and disconnect the smaller fitting from the larger fitting. If this is not done, damage to the line will result. Always relieve fuel system pressure before disconnecting lines.

❋❋ CAUTION

When draining the coolant, keep in mind that cats and dogs are attracted by the ethylene glycol antifreeze, and are quite likely to drink any that is left in an uncovered container or in puddles on the ground. This will prove fatal in sufficient quantity. Always drain the coolant into a sealable container. Coolant should be reused unless it is contaminated or several years old.

2.5L Engine

▶ **See Figure 36**

1. Disconnect the negative battery cable at the battery.
2. Remove the air cleaner assembly.

3. Remove the PCV valve and hose.
4. Drain the cooling system.
5. Disconnect the fuel lines from the Throttle Body Injection (TBI) unit.
6. Mark and disconnect the vacuum lines and the electrical connections from the TBI unit.
7. Disconnect the linkage from the TBI unit (throttle, downshift, and/or cruise control, as applicable).
8. Disconnect the coolant inlet and outlet hoses from the intake manifold.
9. Remove the air conditioning compressor support brackets and the compressor. DO NOT disconnect the refrigerant lines from the compressor. Lay the compressor aside.
10. Remove the manifold attaching bolts and remove the manifold.

To install:
11. Position the manifold into place and install manifold attaching bolts. Torque manifold bolts to
  specification (see illustration for tightening sequence and torque specifications).
12. Install the air conditioning compressor and compressor support brackets, if so equipped.
13. Connect the coolant inlet and outlet hoses to the intake manifold.
14. Connect the linkage to the TBI unit (throttle, downshift, and/or cruise control, as applicable).
15. Connect the vacuum lines and the electrical connections to the TBI unit.
16. Connect the fuel lines to the Throttle Body Injection (TBI) unit.
17. Install the PCV valve and hose.
18. Install the air cleaner assembly.
19. Connect the negative battery cable at the battery.
20. Fill the cooling system.

2.8L and 5.0L Carbureted Engines

▶ **See Figures 37, 38, 39, 40 and 41**

1. Remove the air cleaner.
2. Drain the radiator.
3. Disconnect:
  a. Battery cables at the battery.
  b. Upper radiator and heater hoses at the manifold.
  c. Crankcase ventilation hoses as required.
  d. Fuel line at the carburetor.
  e. Accelerator linkage.
  f. Vacuum hose at the distributor, if equipped.
  g. Power brake hose at the carburetor base or manifold, if applicable.
  h. Temperature sending switch wires.
4. Remove the distributor cap and scribe the rotor position relative to the distributor body, and engine.
5. Remove the distributor.
6. If applicable, remove the alternator upper bracket. As required, remove the air cleaner bracket, and accelerator bellcrank.

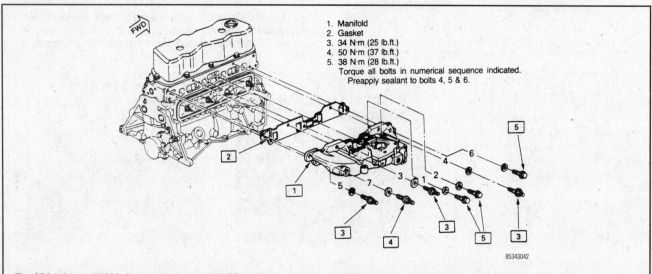

1. Manifold
2. Gasket
3. 34 N·m (25 lb.ft.)
4. 50 N·m (37 lb.ft.)
5. 38 N·m (28 lb.ft.)
Torque all bolts in numerical sequence indicated. Preapply sealant to bolts 4, 5 & 6.

85343042

Fig. 36 Intake manifold bolt torque sequence for 2.5L engine

Fig. 37 Intake manifold bolt removal

Fig. 38 Prying loose the manifold

Fig. 39 Lifting off the manifold

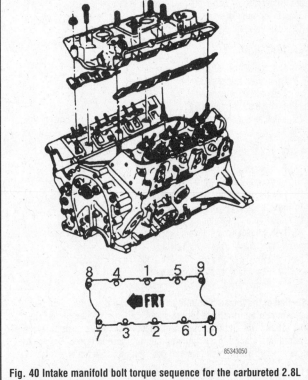
Fig. 40 Intake manifold bolt torque sequence for the carbureted 2.8L

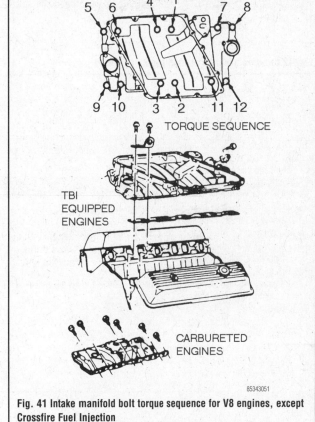
Fig. 41 Intake manifold bolt torque sequence for V8 engines, except Crossfire Fuel Injection

7. Remove the manifold-to-head attaching bolts, then remove the manifold and carburetor as an assembly.

8. Mark and disconnect all emission related items (e.g.: wiring, vacuum hoses, etc.) which are connected to manifold mounted items.

9. If the manifold is to be replaced, transfer the carburetor (and mounting studs), water outlet and thermostat (use a new gasket) heater hose adapter, EGR valve (use new gasket) and, if applicable, TVS switch(s) and the choke coil.

To install:

10. Before installing the manifold, thoroughly clean the gasket and sealing surfaces of the cylinder heads and manifold.

11. Install the manifold end seals, folding the tabs if applicable, and the manifold/head gaskets, using a sealing compound around the water passages.

➡ **Make sure that the new manifold gaskets match the old ones EXACTLY.**

12. When installing the manifold, care should be taken not to dislocate the end seals. It is helpful to use a pilot in the distributor opening. Tighten the manifold bolts to 30 ft. lbs. (40 Nm) for 5.0L or 20–25 ft. lbs. (27–34 Nm) for 2.8L in the sequence illustrated.

13. Install the distributor with the rotor in its original location as indicated by the scribe line. If the engine has been disturbed, refer to the previous Distributor Removal and Installation procedure.

14. If applicable, install the alternator upper bracket and adjust the belt tension.

15. Connect all disconnected components at their original locations.

16. Fill the cooling system, start the engine, check for leaks and adjust the ignition timing and carburetor idle speed and mixture.

TBI Equipped 5.0L Engine

1982–1983 CROSSFIRE FUEL INJECTION MODELS

▶ **See Figures 42 and 43**

1. Disconnect the negative battery cable at the battery.
2. Remove the air cleaner assembly.
3. Drain the cooling system.
4. Disconnect the fuel inlet line.
5. Remove the exhaust gas recirculation (EGR) solenoid.
6. Disconnect the wiring from the idle air motors, injectors, and the throttle position sensor (TPS).

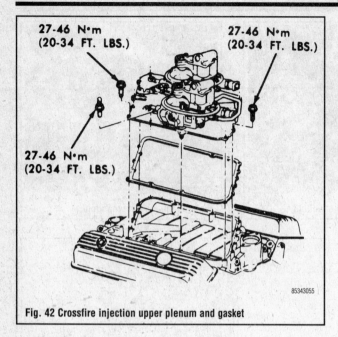

27-46 N•m
(20-34 FT. LBS.)

27-46 N•m
(20-34 FT. LBS.)

27-46 N•m
(20-34 FT. LBS.)

85343055

Fig. 42 Crossfire injection upper plenum and gasket

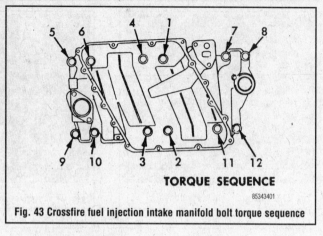

TORQUE SEQUENCE

85343401

Fig. 43 Crossfire fuel injection intake manifold bolt torque sequence

7. Disconnect the fuel return line at the rear TBI unit.

8. Remove the power brake booster line.

9. Disconnect the accelerator and cruise control cables, unbolt the cable bracket from the manifold and tie the cable and bracket assembly out of the way.

10. Disconnect the positive crankcase ventilation valve hose at the manifold and move the hose aside.

11. Mark and disconnect any vacuum hoses which will interfere with removal of the manifold.

12. If you plan on removing the TBI units from the upper manifold plate, remove the fuel balance tube (connecting the units) at this time.

13. Remove the bolts which attach the upper manifold plate (or TBI plate) to the intake manifold. Lift the TBI and plate assembly off of the intake manifold.

14. Remove the distributor as previously outlined.

15. Disconnect the upper radiator hose from the thermostat housing.

16. Disconnect the heater hose from the intake manifold.

17. Remove the intake manifold-to-cylinder head bolts and lift the intake manifold assembly off of the engine.

To install:

18. Clean the sealing surfaces.

19. Install the gaskets and apply a ¾₁₆ in. (5mm) bead of RTV sealant on the front and rear ridge of the cylinder case.

20. Hold the gaskets in place by extending the RTV bead up onto the gasket ends. Use sealer at the water passages.

21. Position the intake manifold assembly onto the engine and install the intake manifold-to-cylinder head bolts. Torque bolts in sequence to 25–45 ft. lbs. (34–61 Nm).

22. Connect the heater hose to the intake manifold.

23. Connect the upper radiator hose to the thermostat housing.

24. Install the distributor.

25. Position the TBI and plate assembly on the intake manifold with a new gasket. Install the bolts which attach the upper manifold plate (or TBI plate) to the intake manifold and torque to specification.

26. If the TBI units on CFI engines were removed, install the fuel balance tube (connecting the units).

27. Connect vacuum hoses which were disconnected for removal of the manifold.

28. Connect the positive crankcase ventilation valve hose.

29. Install the cable bracket to the manifold and connect the accelerator and cruise control cables.

30. Install the power brake booster line.

31. Connect the fuel return line at the TBI unit.

32. Connect the wiring to the idle air motors, injectors, and the throttle position sensor (TPS).

33. Install the exhaust gas recirculation (EGR) solenoid.

34. Connect the fuel inlet line to the TBI unit.

35. Install the air cleaner assembly.

36. Connect the negative battery cable at the battery.

37. Fill the cooling system.

38. Start the engine and check for leaks.

1988–1992 MODELS

1. Disconnect the negative battery cable.

2. Drain the cooling system.

3. Remove the air cleaner.

4. Remove the throttle body.

5. Label and unplug all vacuum hose and electrical connections on the manifold.

6. Disconnect the upper radiator hose from the manifold.

7. Mark the distributor position and remove it.

8. Remove the EGR valve, if necessary.

9. Remove the intake manifold bolts and studs.

10. Remove the manifold and discard the gaskets.

To install:

11. Make sure the sealing surfaces are clean.

12. Install the gaskets and apply a ¾₁₆ in. (5mm) bead of RTV sealant on the front and rear ridge of the cylinder block.

13. Hold the gaskets in place by extending the RTV bead up onto the gasket ends. Use sealer at the water passages.

14. Install the intake manifold.

➡Sealing of the intake manifold to the "V" of the engine is obtained by employing an intermediate torque specification to all the attaching bolts, alternately, in the proper sequence. This step is used to rock the manifold into place before applying the final torque figure. Failure to follow this two-step procedure can result in possible leaks.

15. Install the intake manifold attaching bolts. Tighten them, using the proper sequence, to 89 in lbs. (10 Nm).

16. Final torque the bolts, using the proper sequence, to 35 ft lbs. (47 Nm).

17. Install the EGR valve.

18. Install the distributor.

19. Connect the upper radiator hose to the thermostat housing.

20. Install the throttle body.

21. Engage all electrical and hose connections.

22. Fill the cooling system.

23. Connect the negative battery cable.

24. Install the air cleaner.

1985–1992 MFI Engines

2.8L AND 3.1L ENGINES

♦ See Figure 44

1. Disconnect the negative battery cable.

2. Drain the coolant.

3. Remove the air inlet duct at the throttle body and the crankcase vent pipe.

4. Unplug the vacuum harness from the throttle body.

5. Remove the throttle body.

6. Remove the EGR transfer tube. Discard the gasket.

7. Remove the A/C compressor-to-plenum bracket attaching hardware and bracket.

8. Remove the plenum attaching bolts and plenum. Discard the gaskets.

9. Remove the fuel rail.

10. Label and unplug the wires from the spark plugs.

11. Label and unplug the wires at the coil.

12. Remove the distributor cap and spark plug wires.

13. Mark the distributor position and remove it.

14. Label and disconnect the emission canister hoses.

15. Remove the valve covers.

16. Remove the upper radiator hose at the manifold.

17. Unplug the coolant switch and sensor.

18. Remove the heater inlet pipe from the manifold.

19. Remove the center intake manifold bolts.

20. Remove the center intake manifold and gasket. Discard the gasket.

21. Remove the transmission dipstick.

22. Remove the manifold bolts.

23. Remove the manifold. Discard the gaskets and remove the RTV sealant from the front and rear ridges of the block.

To install:

24. Apply a ³⁄₁₆ in. (5mm) bead of RTV sealant on the front and rear ridges of the block. Make sure the surfaces are clean.

25. Install the new gaskets on the cylinder heads. Hold the gaskets in place by extending the RTV bead up onto the gasket ends. Certain GM intake gaskets will have to be cut to be install behind the pushrods. Cut these gaskets as required and only where necessary.

26. Install the intake manifold along with the intake manifold bolts. Torque bolts in sequence to 13–25 ft. lbs. (18–34 Nm) on 2.8L engines and 19 ft lbs. (26 Nm) on 3.1L engines.

27. Install the center intake manifold with a new gasket. Tighten the bolts to 15 ft lbs. (21 Nm).

28. Connect the coolant switches.

29. Install the upper radiator hose.

30. Install the valve covers.

31. Install the heater inlet pipe.

32. Connect the emission canister hoses.

33. Install the distributor to the matchmarks, hold down bolt, spark plug wires and distributor cap.

34. Install the spark plug wires to the spark plugs and connect the wires at the coil.

35. Install the fuel rail.

36. Install the plenum with new gaskets. Tighten the bolts to 18 ft lbs. (25 Nm) on 2.8L engines or 15 ft lbs. (21 Nm) on 3.1L engines.

37. Install the A/C compressor-to-plenum bracket and attaching hardware.

38. Install the EGR transfer tube with a new gasket. Tighten the bolts to 19 ft lbs. (26 Nm).

39. Install the throttle body.

40. Connect the vacuum harness and air inlet duct to the throttle body.

41. Install the transmission dipstick.

42. Connect and other remaining hoses or wires.

43. Fill the cooling system.

44. Start the engine and check for proper operation.

5.0L AND 5.7L ENGINES

▶ See Figure 45

1. Disconnect the negative battery cable.

2. Remove the air intake duct.

3. Drain the cooling system.

4. Disconnect the control cables from the throttle body.

5. Label and unplug all wiring connectors and hoses from the throttle body and plenum.

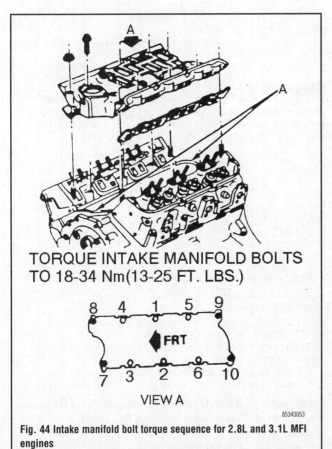

Fig. 44 Intake manifold bolt torque sequence for 2.8L and 3.1L MFI engines

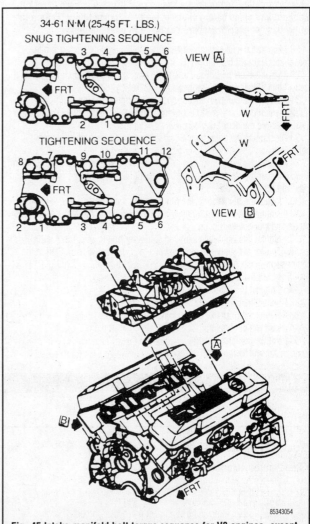

Fig. 45 Intake manifold bolt torque sequence for V8 engines, except Crossfire Fuel Injection

6. Disconnect the AIR hoses from the air management valve.
7. Disconnect the fuel lines.
8. Label and unplug the spark plug wires at the cap.
9. Mark the distributor position and remove it.
10. Unplug the injector wiring harness.
11. Remove the left side runner-to-plenum bolts.
12. Remove the left side runner-to-manifold bolts.
13. Remove the right side runner-to-plenum bolts.
14. Remove the right side runner-to-manifold bolts.
15. Remove the EGR solenoid, if necessary.
16. Remove the right side manifold-to-runner bolt.
17. Remove the plenum, right side runners and gaskets. Discard the gaskets.
18. Remove the left side manifold-to-runner bolt.
19. Remove the left side runners and gaskets. Discard the gaskets.
20. Disconnect the upper radiator hose from the thermostat housing.
21. Remove the EGR valve, if necessary.
22. Unplug any other electrical or hose connections, as necessary.
23. Remove the intake manifold bolts.
24. Remove the intake manifold and gaskets. Discard the gaskets.

To install:

25. Apply a ³⁄₁₆ in. (5mm) bead of RTV sealant on the front and rear ridges of the block. Make sure the surfaces are clean.
26. Install the new gaskets on the cylinder heads. Hold the gaskets in place by extending the RTV bead up onto the gasket ends.
27. Install the intake manifold.

➡Sealing of the intake manifold to the "V" of the engine is obtained by employing an intermediate torque specification to all the attaching bolts, alternately, in the proper sequence. This step is used to rock the manifold into place before applying the final torque figure. Failure to follow this two-step procedure can result in possible leaks.

28. Install the intake manifold attaching bolts. Tighten them, using the proper sequence, to 89 in lbs. (10 Nm).
29. Final torque the bolts, using the proper sequence, to 35 ft lbs. (47 Nm).
30. Install the EGR valve using a new gasket.
31. Connect the upper radiator hose to the thermostat housing.
32. Install new gaskets on the runners and intake manifold. Make sure the gasket sealing surfaces are clean.
33. Install the left side runners and finger-tighten the runner-to-manifold bolts.
34. Install the left side manifold-to-runner bolt. Torque to 25 ft lbs. (34 Nm).
35. Install the right side runners. Finger-tighten the runner-to-manifold and manifold-to-runner bolts.
36. Install the plenum and the runner-to-plenum bolts.
37. Tighten the runner-to-manifold bolts to 25 ft lbs. (34 Nm). Start in the center and work outwards.
38. Tighten the right side manifold-to-runner bolt to 25 ft lbs. (34 Nm).
39. Tighten the runner to plenum bolts to 25 ft lbs. (34 Nm). Start in the center and work outwards.
40. Install the distributor.
41. Connect the fuel lines.
42. Install the EGR valve solenoid.
43. Connect the control cables to the throttle body.
44. Connect all remaining hose and wiring connections.
45. Fill the cooling system.
46. Connect the negative battery cable.

Exhaust Manifold

REMOVAL & INSTALLATION

Except 2.5L Engines

▶ See Figures 46 thru 51

1. Disconnect the negative battery cable.
2. Remove the air cleaner on carbureted engines.
3. If applicable, remove the air cleaner pre-heater shroud.
4. Disconnect the air injection reaction pipes, if equipped.
5. Unplug the oxygen sensor connector.

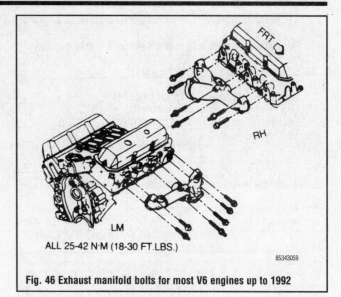

ALL 25-42 N·M (18-30 FT.LBS.)

85343059

Fig. 46 Exhaust manifold bolts for most V6 engines up to 1992

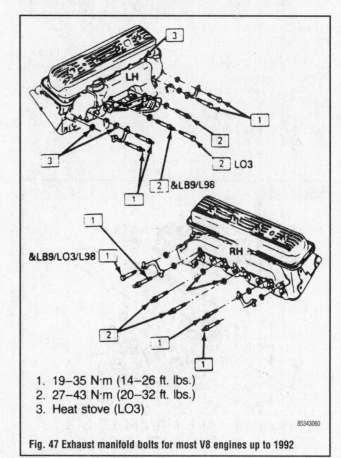

1. 19–35 N·m (14–26 ft. lbs.)
2. 27–43 N·m (20–32 ft. lbs.)
3. Heat stove (LO3)

85343060

Fig. 47 Exhaust manifold bolts for most V8 engines up to 1992

6. Label and unplug the spark plug wires.
7. Remove the spark plug wire heat shields, if equipped.
8. Remove any components which may interfere with removal.
9. Disconnect the exhaust pipe from the manifold and hang it from the frame out of the way.
10. On some engines, it will be necessary to bend the locktabs from the bolt. Remove the end bolts, then the center bolts. Remove the manifold.

➡A thin wall 6-point socket, sharpened at the leading edge and tapped onto the head of the bolt, simplifies bending the locktabs.

To install:
11. Make sure the mating surfaces are clean.

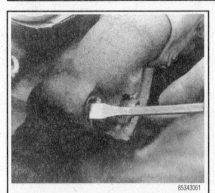

Fig. 48 On some engines, the bolts are held by lock tabs

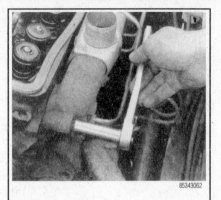

Fig. 49 Removing the attaching bolts

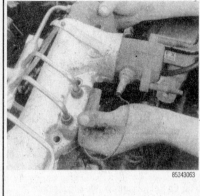

Fig. 50 Disconnecting the oxygen sensor

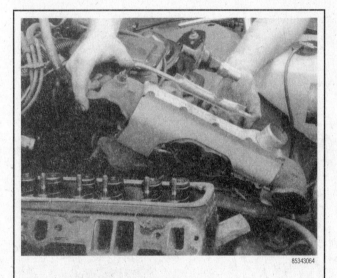

Fig. 51 Removing the exhaust manifold

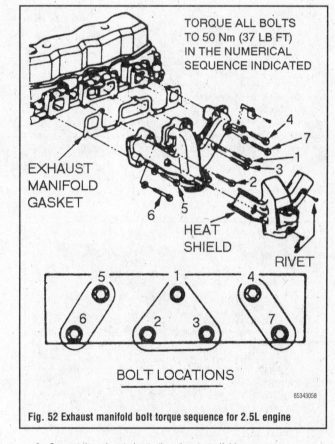

Fig. 52 Exhaust manifold bolt torque sequence for 2.5L engine

12. Install a new gasket, if applicable.
13. Position the exhaust manifold onto the engine. Torque the attaching bolts to:
   - 1982–1992 V6 engines: 25 ft lbs. (34 Nm)
   - 1982–1992 V8 engines: 26 ft lbs. (35 Nm)
14. Bend the locktabs over the bolts.
15. Connect the exhaust pipe to the manifold.
16. Install all components removed.
17. Connect the oxygen sensor.
18. Install the spark plug wire heat shields.
19. Connect the spark plug wires.
20. If equipped, install the air cleaner pre-heater shroud.
21. If equipped, connect the air injection reaction pipes.
22. Connect the battery.

2.5L Engine

▸ See Figure 52

1. Disconnect the negative battery cable at the battery.
2. Remove the air cleaner assembly, be sure to mark any disconnected hoses for proper reinstallation.
3. Unplug the oxygen sensor and disconnect the exhaust pipe from the exhaust manifold.
4. Remove the engine oil level dipstick and tube.
5. Remove the exhaust manifold attaching bolts and remove the manifold.

To install:

6. Position the exhaust manifold onto the engine with a new gasket. Torque the bolts, following the correct sequence, to 44 ft lbs. (60 Nm).
7. Install the engine oil level dipstick tube and dipstick.

8. Connect the exhaust pipe to the exhaust manifold.
9. Engage the oxygen sensor connector.
10. Install the air cleaner assembly and connecting hoses.
11. Connect the negative battery cable at the battery.

Radiator

REMOVAL & INSTALLATION

▸ See Figures 53 thru 60

1. Disconnect the negative battery cable.
2. Drain the cooling system.

❋❋ CAUTION

When draining the coolant, keep in mind that cats and dogs are attracted by the ethylene glycol antifreeze, and are quite likely to

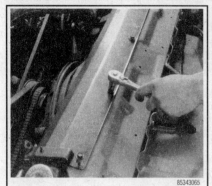

Fig. 53 Removing radiator upper shield bolts

Fig. 54 Removing radiator upper shield

Fig. 55 Unplugging the fan connector

Fig. 56 Removing the electric fan

Fig. 57 Disconnecting the overflow hose

Fig. 58 Disconnecting the upper hose

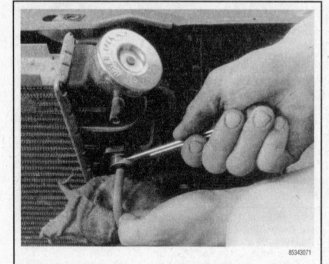

Fig. 59 Disconnecting the transmission cooler lines

Fig. 60 Lifting out the radiator

drink any that is left in an uncovered container or in puddles on the ground. This will prove fatal in sufficient quantity. Always drain the coolant into a sealable container. Coolant should be reused unless it is contaminated or several years old.

3. Remove the air inlet ducts and air cleaner, if necessary.
4. Remove the electric cooling fan, if equipped.
5. Disconnect the coolant overflow tank hose.
6. Disconnect upper and lower radiator hoses.
7. On vehicles equipped with automatic transmission, disconnect and plug the transmission fluid cooler lines.
8. Disconnect and plug the engine oil cooler lines, if equipped.

9. Remove fan shroud assembly, if applicable.
10. Remove the upper radiator mount screws.
11. Remove the radiator assembly by lifting straight up.

➡The radiator assembly is held at the bottom by two cradles secured to the radiator support.

12. If installing a new radiator, transfer the fittings from the old radiator to the new radiator.
13. Replace the radiator assembly by reversing the above steps. Check that radiator lower cradles are located properly in radiator recess.
14. Refill the cooling system. Check the engine oil and transmission fluid levels, if necessary. Run engine for a short period of time and check for leaks.

Engine Oil Cooler

The engine oil cooler consists of an adapter, bolted to the engine block, to which the oil filter is screwed onto. The adapter has 2 hoses which attach to the oil cooler and the radiator, these hoses are the inlet and return lines.

REMOVAL & INSTALLATION

1. Disconnect the negative battery cable. Drain the cooling system into a suitable container.

❉❉ CAUTION

When draining the coolant, keep in mind that cats and dogs are attracted by the ethylene glycol antifreeze, and are quite likely to drink any that is left in an uncovered container or in puddles on the ground. This will prove fatal in sufficient quantity. Always drain the coolant into a sealable container. Coolant should be reused unless it is contaminated or several years old.

2. Remove the radiator, if the oil cooler is to be repaired or replaced, otherwise remove the engine oil cooler from the radiator as necessary.
3. Remove the oil filter.
4. Remove the hoses from the oil cooler adapter.
5. Unscrew the oil cooler adapter retainer and remove the assembly. Discard the gasket.
6. Installation is the reverse of the removal procedure. Use new gaskets.

Electric Cooling Fan

REMOVAL & INSTALLATION

1. Disconnect the battery ground cable.
2. Remove the air cleaner and ducts, if necessary.
3. Unplug the fan harness connector.
4. Remove the fan frame to radiator support mounting bolts and remove the fan assembly. Some models are retained by clips. Remove these, then slide the fan assembly from the radiator.
5. Install the cooling fan frame to the radiator support bolt. Reconnect the wiring harness, the negative battery cable and check fan operation.

Belt-Driven Cooling Fan

REMOVAL & INSTALLATION

1. Disconnect the negative battery cable.
2. Remove the fan shroud, as required.
3. Remove the fan-to-water pump attaching bolts or nuts.
4. Remove the fan belts.
5. Remove the cooling fan and clutch assembly. Separate the clutch assembly from the fan.

➡Store the clutch in an upright position to prevent seal leakage.

6. Installation is the reverse of the removal procedure.

Water Pump

REMOVAL & INSTALLATION

❉❉ CAUTION

When draining the coolant, keep in mind that cats and dogs are attracted by the ethylene glycol antifreeze, and are quite likely to drink any that is left in an uncovered container or in puddles on the ground. This will prove fatal in sufficient quantity. Always drain the coolant into a sealable container. Coolant should be reused unless it is contaminated or several years old.

2.5L Engine

⬥ See Figure 61

1. Drain the cooling system.
2. Remove the accessory drive belts.
3. Remove the fan and pump pulley.
4. Remove the heater hose and lower radiator hose from the water pump.
5. Remove the pump from the block.

To install:

6. Coat the new gasket with RTV sealer. Install the pump and torque bolts to 25 ft lbs. (34 Nm).
7. Install the hose and lower radiator hose to the water pump.
8. Install the pump pulley and fan.
9. Install the accessory drive belts.
10. Fill the cooling system, start the engine and check for leaks.

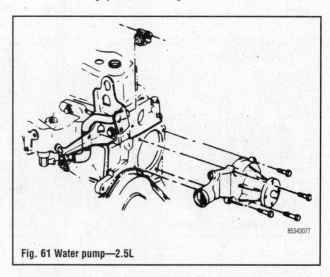

Fig. 61 Water pump—2.5L

85343077

V6 Engines

1. Disconnect the negative battery cable.
2. Drain the cooling system.
3. Remove the air intake duct and air cleaner, if necessary.
4. Remove the drive belt.
5. Disconnect the heater and radiator hoses from the water pump.
6. Remove the power steering pump bracket and swing aside.
7. Remove the water pump bolts. Mark the bolts to their corresponding locations for proper installation.

To install:

8. Clean the gasket surface.
9. Install the water pump with a new gasket. Apply sealer to the bolt threads.
10. Tighten the large bolts to 25 ft lbs. (34 Nm), medium bolts to 15 ft lbs. (21 Nm) and the small bolts to 88 inch lbs. (10 Nm).
11. Install the power steering pump bracket.
12. Connect the heater and radiator hoses.
13. Install the drive belt.
14. Install the air cleaner and duct.
15. Fill the cooling system. Start the engine and check for leaks.

V8 Engines

⬥ See Figures 62, 63, 64 and 65

1. Disconnect the negative battery cable.
2. Drain the cooling system.
3. Remove the air intake duct and air cleaner, if necessary.
4. Remove the drive belt(s) and the water pump pulley.
5. Disconnect the heater and radiator hoses from the water pump.
6. Remove the water pump attaching bolts, then remove the pump. Mark the bolts to their corresponding locations for proper installation.

To install:

7. Clean the gasket mating surfaces.
8. Install the water pump with a new gasket.

Fig. 62 Removing the heater hoses

Fig. 63 Removing the attaching bolts

Fig. 64 Removing the water pump from the engine

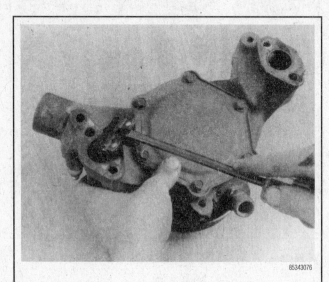

Fig. 65 Scraping off the old gasket material

9. Install the coolant pump and bolts to the front cover using the dowel pins as a guide.
10. Tighten the bolts to 30 ft lbs. (41 Nm).
11. Connect the heater and radiator hoses to the water pump.
12. Install the water pump pulley and the drive belt(s).
13. Fill the cooling system. Start the engine and check for leaks.

Cylinder Head

REMOVAL & INSTALLATION

✳✳ CAUTION

Properly relieve the fuel system pressure before disconnecting any lines.

➡When servicing the engine, be absolutely sure to mark vacuum hoses and wiring so that these items may be properly reconnected during installation. Also, when disconnecting fittings of metal lines (fuel, power brake vacuum), always use two flare nut (or line) wrenches. Hold the wrench on the large fitting with pressure on the wrench as if you were tightening the fitting (clockwise), THEN loosen and disconnect the smaller fitting from the larger fitting. If this is not done, damage to the line will result.

✳✳ CAUTION

When draining the coolant, keep in mind that cats and dogs are attracted by the ethylene glycol antifreeze, and are quite likely to

drink any that is left in an uncovered container or in puddles on the ground. This will prove fatal in sufficient quantity. Always drain the coolant into a sealable container. Coolant should be reused unless it is contaminated or several years old.

2.5L Engine

◆ See Figure 66

1. Disconnect the negative battery cable.
2. Drain the engine block and radiator of coolant.
3. Raise and safely support the vehicle. Remove the exhaust pipe and lower the vehicle.
4. Remove the oil level indicator tube.
5. Remove the air cleaner.
6. Unplug the electrical and vacuum connections and disconnect the linkage from the TBI unit.
7. Disconnect the fuel lines.
8. Remove the EGR valve.
9. Disconnect the heater hoses from the intake manifold.
10. Remove the ignition coil.
11. Disconnect all electrical connections from the intake manifold and cylinder head.
12. If the vehicle has air conditioning, remove the compressor and position it out of the way. Do not disconnect the refrigerant lines.
13. Remove the alternator and lay the unit aside. If necessary, remove the alternator brackets.
14. Remove any other brackets or components mounted on the cylinder head.
15. Remove the upper radiator hose.

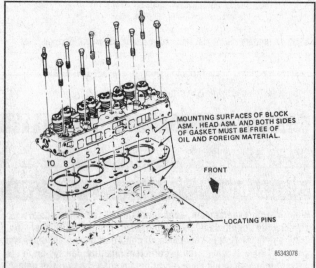

Fig. 66 Cylinder head bolt torque sequence for 2.5L engine

16. Remove the rocker arm cover and back off the rocker arm nuts/bolts and pivot the rocker arms out of the way so that the pushrods can be removed. Identify the pushrods so that they can be reinstalled in their original locations.

17. Remove the cylinder head bolts and cylinder head. Remove the intake and exhaust manifolds, as required.

To install:

18. Thoroughly clean all mating surfaces of oil, grease and old gasket material. Clean the head bolts and cylinder block threads, otherwise an accurate torque specification will not be attained.

19. Install a new gasket on the block mating surface. Position the cylinder head on the block.

➡ **Clean the bolt threads, apply sealing compound and install the bolts finger-tight.**

20. Tighten the head bolts a little at a time using the correct sequence and torque to 92 ft lbs. (125 Nm).

21. Install the pushrods and rocker arms. Refer to the procedures described earlier in this section.

22. Refill the cooling system and check for leaks. The remaining installation is the reverse of the removal procedure.

2.8L and 3.1L Engines

▶ **See Figure 67**

1. Disconnect the negative battery cable.
2. Relieve the fuel system pressure and drain the engine coolant from the radiator into a suitable container.
3. Remove the intake manifold and the spark plugs.
4. Remove the dipstick tube and bracket. Raise and support the vehicle safely. Drain the oil and remove the oil filter. Lower the vehicle.
5. Remove the exhaust manifolds.
6. Remove the drive belt(s).
7. Remove the air conditioning compressor and bracket, reposition it aside. Do not disconnect the lines.
8. Remove the power steering pump and bracket, reposition it aside.
9. Remove the alternator and bracket, reposition it aside.

10. Remove the ground cable from the rear of the cylinder head and remove the engine lift bracket.

11. Remove the rocker arm covers.
12. Loosen the rocker arms until the pushrods can be removed.
13. Remove the cylinder head bolts and remove the cylinder heads.

To install:

14. Clean the gasket mating surfaces of all components. Be careful not to nick or scratch any surfaces as this will allow leak paths. Clean the bolt threads in the cylinder block and on the head bolts. Dirt will affect bolt torque.

15. Place the head gaskets in position over the dowel pins.
16. Install the cylinder heads.
17. Coat the cylinder head bolts threads with GM sealer 1052080 or equivalent, and install the bolts. Tighten the bolts in the proper sequence to:
   - 1982–1987 engines: 70 ft lbs. (90 Nm)
   - 1988–1992 engines: 1st step: 40 ft lbs. (55 Nm); 2nd step: tighten an additional ¼ (90 degree) turn

18. Install the pushrods and loosely retain them with the rocker arms. Make sure the lower ends of the pushrods are in the lifter seats. Refer to the rocker arm procedures outlined earlier in this section.

19. Install the power steering pump bracket and pump. Do the same for the air conditioning compressor bracket and compressor.

20. Install the ground cable to the rear of the cylinder head.
21. Install the exhaust manifolds.
22. Install the dipstick tube and bracket.
23. Install the intake manifold.
24. Install the alternator bracket and alternator.
25. Install the drive belt(s).
26. Install the spark plugs.
27. Fill the cooling system with the proper type and quantity of coolant. Install a new oil filter and fill the crankcase with the proper type and quantity of oil.
28. Connect the negative battery cable, start the vehicle and check for leaks.

5.0L and 5.7L Engines

▶ **See Figures 68 thru 76**

1. Disconnect the negative battery cable. Drain the cooling system and relieve the fuel system pressure.
2. Raise and support the vehicle safely. Drain the engine oil and remove the oil filter. Lower the vehicle.
3. Remove the drive belt(s) and remove the intake manifold.
4. Remove the power steering pump, alternator bracket or the air conditioning compressor mounting bracket and position aside. Do not disconnect the lines from the air conditioning compressor.
5. Remove the exhaust manifolds and the valve covers.
6. Remove the rocker arms and pushrods.
7. Remove the cylinder head bolts and the cylinder head.

To install:

8. Clean the gasket mating surfaces of all components. Be careful not to nick or scratch any surfaces as this will allow leak paths. Clean the bolt threads in the cylinder block and on the head bolts. Dirt will affect bolt torque.

➡ **When using a steel gasket, coat both sides of the new gasket with a thin even coat of sealer. If using a composition gasket, do not use any sealer.**

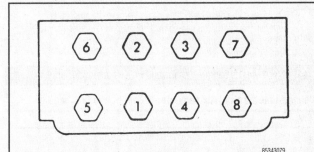

85343079

Fig. 67 Cylinder head bolt torque sequence for all V6 engines

85343080

Fig. 68 Pushrod removal—V8 engines

85343081

Fig. 69 Removing the AIR tube clamp—V8 engines

85343082

Fig. 70 AIR hose removal—V8 engines

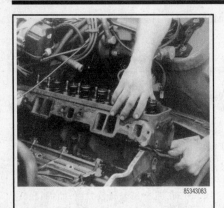

Fig. 71 Prying loose the head; V8 engines

Fig. 72 Lifting off the head—V8 engines

Fig. 73 Scraping off the old gasket material—V8 engines

Fig. 74 Torquing the upper head bolts—V8 engines

Fig. 75 Torquing the lower head bolts—V8 engines

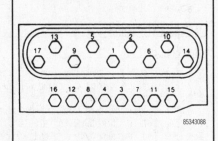

Fig. 76 Cylinder head bolt torque sequence—V8 engines

9. Position the head gasket over the dowel pins with the bead up. Install the cylinder head over the dowel pins and gasket.

10. Coat the threads of the head bolts with GM 1052080 thread sealer or equivalent. Install the head bolts and tighten in sequence, in three passes, to 65 ft lbs. (92 Nm).

11. Install the exhaust manifolds.

12. Install the pushrods and rocker arms, refer to the procedures outlined earlier in this section. Install the valve covers.

13. Install the power steering pump and alternator bracket or air conditioning compressor mounting bracket, as necessary.

14. Install the intake manifold.

15. Install the accessory drive belt(s).

16. Fill the cooling system with the proper type and amount of coolant. Connect the negative battery cable.

17. Raise and support the vehicle safely. Install a new oil filter, lower the vehicle. Fill the crankcase with the proper type and quantity of engine oil.

18. Start the engine, check for leaks and check the ignition timing.

Oil Pan

REMOVAL & INSTALLATION

✳✳ CAUTION

The EPA warns that prolonged contact with used engine oil may cause a number of skin disorders, including cancer! You should make every effort to minimize your exposure to used engine oil. Protective gloves should be worn when changing the oil. Wash your hands and any other exposed skin areas as soon as possible after exposure to used engine oil. Soap and water, or waterless hand cleaner should be used.

Except 2.5L Engine

▶ **See Figures 77 thru 83**

1. Disconnect the negative battery cable. Remove the air cleaner.
2. Remove the distributor cap. Remove the fan shroud assembly.
3. Raise the vehicle and support it safely with jackstands.
4. Drain the engine oil.

✳✳ CAUTION

Be sure that the catalytic converter is cool before proceeding.

5. Remove the air injection pipe at the catalytic converter, if applicable.
6. Remove the catalytic converter hanger bolts. Disconnect the exhaust pipe at the manifold.
7. Remove the starter bolts, loosen the starter brace, then lay the starter aside.
8. Remove the front engine mount through-bolts.
9. Raise the engine enough to provide sufficient clearance for oil pan removal.
10. Remove the oil pan bolts.

➡ **If the front crankshaft throw prohibits removal of the pan, turn the crankshaft to position the throw horizontally.**

11. Remove the oil pan from the vehicle.
12. Remove the old RTV sealant or gasket from the oil pan and engine block.

To install:

13. Run a ⅛ in. (3mm) bead of RTV around the oil pan sealing surface or install a new gasket. Remember to keep the RTV on the INSIDE of the bolt holes.

14. Install the pan and pan bolts. Torque the pan bolts to:
- 2.8L & 3.1L V6 (M6 x 1 X 16.0 bolts): 6–9 ft. lbs. (8–12 Nm)
- 2.8L & 3.1L V6 (M8 x 1.25 x 14.0 bolts): 15–22 ft. lbs. (20–30 Nm)
- 1982–84 V8 engine (⁵⁄₁₆–18 bolts): 165 inch lbs. (10 Nm)
- 1982–84 V8 engine (¼–20 bolts): 80 inch lbs. (8 Nm)

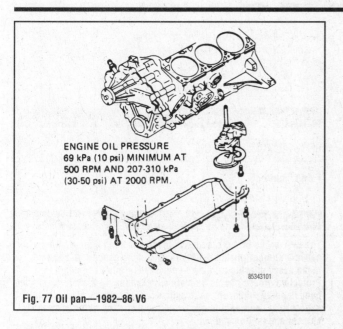

ENGINE OIL PRESSURE
69 kPa (10 psi) MINIMUM AT
500 RPM AND 207-310 kPa
(30-50 psi) AT 2000 RPM.

85343101

Fig. 77 Oil pan—1982–86 V6

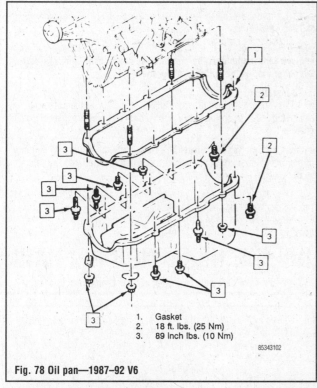

1. Gasket
2. 18 ft. lbs. (25 Nm)
3. 89 inch lbs. (10 Nm)

85343102

Fig. 78 Oil pan—1987–92 V6

- 1985 V8 engine
- 1985 V8 engine
- 1985 V8 en
- 1985 V8
Nm)
- 1986
- 1986–92
- 1986–92 V8
Nm)
15. Lower the engine and
Torque bolts to 48 ft. lbs. (65 Nm

16. Install the starter a
17. Connect the exha
hanger bolts.
18. Install the air
19. Lower the v
20. Connect the
21. Install the
22. Fill the
23. Start

2.5L Eng

◆ See

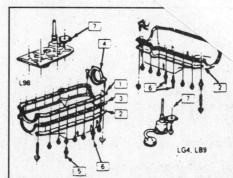

1. Gasket
2. Reinforcement
3. Oil pan
4. Retainer
5. Stud (LB9, L98)
6. Stud (L98)
7. Oil pump

ENGINE OIL PRESSURE 10 LBS MINIMUM AT 500 RPM AND 30-55 LBS AT 2000 RPM
OIL FILTER BY-PASS VALVE OPERATES AT 9 TO 11 LBS PRESSURE

85343103

Fig. 79 Oil pan—V8

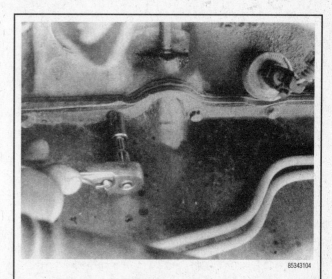

85343104

Fig. 80 Removing the oil pan bolts

85343105

Fig. 81 Prying loose the oil pan

85343106

Fig. 82 Removing the pan

85343107

Fig. 83 Removing the pan gasket

nd starter brace, then secure using starter bolts.
ust pipe at the manifold. Install the catalytic converter

njection pipe at the catalytic converter.
hicle.
an shroud assembly. Install the distributor cap.
the negative battery cable at the battery and air cleaner.
engine with engine oil.
e engine and check for leaks.

ne

Figure 84

1. Disconnect the negative battery cable at the battery.
2. Raise the vehicle and support it safely with jackstands.
3. Drain the engine oil.
4. Disconnect the exhaust pipe at the manifold.
5. Loosen the exhaust pipe hanger bracket.
6. Remove the starter assembly.
7. Remove the flywheel dust cover.
8. Remove the front engine mount through-bolts.
9. Carefully raise the engine enough to provide sufficient clearance to lower the oil pan.
10. Remove the oil pan retaining bolts and remove the oil pan.

To install:
11. Clean all old RTV from the mating surfaces.
12. Install the rear gasket into the rear main bearing cap and apply a small amount of RTV where the gasket engages into the engine block.
13. Install the front gasket.
14. Install the side gaskets, using grease as a retainer. Apply a small amount of RTV where the side gaskets meet the front gasket.
15. Install the oil pan.

➡ **Install the oil pan-to-timing cover bolts last, as these holes will not align until the other pan bolts are snug.**

16. Torque the pan bolts to 53 inch lbs. (6 Nm) for 1982–1985 models and 90 inch lbs. (10 Nm) for 1986 models.
17. Lower the engine and install the front mount through-bolts. Torque bolts to 48 ft lbs. (65 Nm).
18. Install the flywheel dust cover.

19. Install the starter assembly.
20. Connect the exhaust pipe at the manifold.
21. Tighten the exhaust pipe hanger bracket.
22. Lower the vehicle.
23. Connect the negative battery cable at the battery.
24. Fill the engine with engine oil and start engine. Check for leaks.

Oil Pump

REMOVAL & INSTALLATION

▶ **See Figure 85**

1. Drain and remove the oil pan.

✳ CAUTION

The EPA warns that prolonged contact with used engine oil may cause a number of skin disorders, including cancer! You should make every effort to minimize your exposure to used engine oil. Protective gloves should be worn when changing the oil. Wash your hands and any other exposed skin areas as soon as possible after exposure to used engine oil. Soap and water, or waterless hand cleaner should be used.

2. Remove the oil pump-to-rear main bearing cap bolt. Remove the pump and the extension shaft.
3. Remove the cotter pin, spring and pressure regulator valve.

➡ **Place your thumb over the pressure regulators bore before removing the cotter pin, as the spring is under pressure.**

To install:
4. Assemble pump and extension shaft to rear main bearing cap, aligning slot on top end of extension shaft with drive tang on lower end of distributor driveshaft.

➡ **When assembling the driveshaft extension to the driveshaft, the end of the extension nearest the washers must be inserted into the driveshaft.**

5. Insert the driveshaft extension through the opening in the main bearing cap and block until the shaft mates into the distributor drive gear.
6. Install the pump onto the rear main bearing cap and install the attaching bolts. Torque the bolts to specifications:
   - L4 engines: 22 ft lbs. (30 Nm)
   - V6 engines: 25–35 ft lbs. (35–47 Nm)
   - V8 engines: 65 ft lbs. (88 Nm)
7. Install the oil pan and fill the crankcase with engine oil.

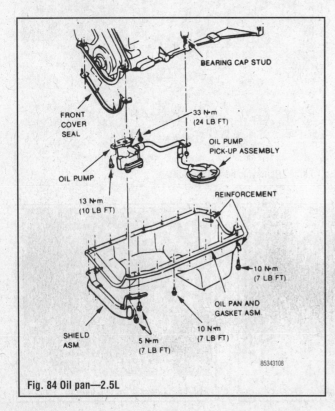

Fig. 84 Oil pan—2.5L

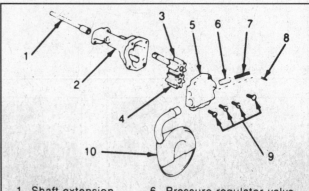

1. Shaft extension
2. Pump body
3. Drive gear and shaft
4. Idler gear
5. Pump cover
6. Pressure regulator valve
7. Pressure regulator spring
8. Retaining pin
9. Screws
10. Pickup screen and pipe

Fig. 85 Oil pump—V8

Fig. 86 Removing the pulley

Fig. 87 Removing the damper

Fig. 88 Removing the timing cover bolts

Crankshaft Damper

REMOVAL & INSTALLATION

♦ See Figures 86 and 87

1. Disconnect the negative battery cable.
2. Remove the fan and shroud, if necessary.
3. Remove the drive belt(s), then remove the crankshaft pulley bolts.
4. Remove the damper center bolt. Install a suitable damper removing tool, then remove the damper from the crankshaft.

If the damper is to be replaced, new balance weights of the same size must be installed on the new balancer assembly in the same hole locations as the old assembly.

5. Installation is the reverse of removal.

Timing Chain and Gear Cover

REMOVAL & INSTALLATION

Except 2.5L Engine

♦ See Figures 88 and 89

1. Disconnect the battery ground cable. Drain the cooling system.
2. Remove the fan shroud or the upper radiator support and drive belts. Remove the fan and pulley from the water pump.
3. Remove the alternator upper and lower brackets, air brace with brackets, and power steering lower bracket (move it aside).
4. Remove the radiator lower hose and the heater hose from the water pump. Remove the water pump bolts and the water pump.
5. If A/C equipped, remove the compressor and move aside. Remove the compressor mounting bracket.
6. Remove the damper pulley retaining bolt and the damper pulley.
7. Remove the timing gear cover bolts and the timing gear cover.

➡With the timing gear cover removed, use a large screwdriver to pry the oil seal from the cover. To install the new oil seal, lubricate it with engine oil and drive it into place.

To install:

8. Prepare the mating surfaces for reinstallation of the timing gear cover. Coat the new gasket with RTV sealer.
9. Install the timing gear cover and timing gear cover bolts. Torque the cover bolts to specifications:
- V6 engines (M8 x 1.25 bolts): 13–22 ft. lbs. (18–30 Nm)
- V6 engines (M10 x 1.5 bolts): 20–35 ft. lbs. (27–48 Nm)
- V8 engines (all bolts): 69–130 inch lbs. (8–14 Nm)
10. Install the damper pulley by pulling the damper onto the crankshaft. Use tool J-23523 or equivalent. Install the damper pulley retaining bolt and torque bolts to 67–85 ft. lbs. (90–110 Nm).
11. If A/C equipped, install the compressor mounting bracket and compressor.
12. Install the water pump and the water pump bolts.
13. Install the radiator lower hose and the heater hose to the water pump.

14. Install the alternator upper and lower brackets, air brace with brackets and the power steering lower bracket.
15. Install the fan and pulley to the water pump. Install the fan shroud or the upper radiator support and drive belts and adjust.
16. Connect the battery ground cable.
17. Fill the cooling system, start the engine and check for leaks.

2.5L Engine

♦ See Figures 90 and 91

1. Remove the drive belts. Remove the hub center bolt, then slide the hub and pulleys from the crankshaft.

➡If only removing the oil seal, simply pry the oil seal from the front cover using a large screwdriver. Be careful not to distort the sheet metal timing gear cover.

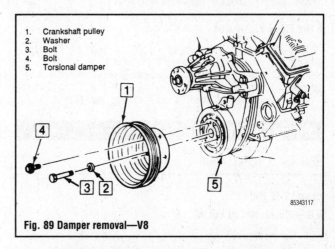

1. Crankshaft pulley
2. Washer
3. Bolt
4. Bolt
5. Torsional damper

Fig. 89 Damper removal—V8

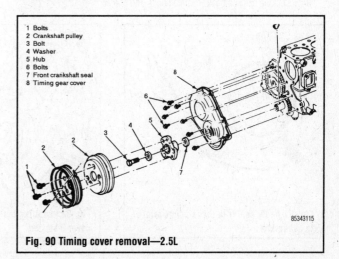

1 Bolts
2 Crankshaft pulley
3 Bolt
4 Washer
5 Hub
6 Bolts
7 Front crankshaft seal
8 Timing gear cover

Fig. 90 Timing cover removal—2.5L

2. Remove the oil pan-to-front cover screws and the front cover-to-block screws. Pull the cover forward enough to permit the cutting of the oil pan front seal. Using a sharp knife, cut the seal close to the block at both corners.

3. Remove the front cover and clean any portion of old gasket from the sealing surfaces. Clean portions of the old gasket from the block.

To install:

4. Use a new front oil pan gasket, cut the tabs from the gasket. Replace the crankshaft oil seal.

5. Place RTV sealer in the corners of the new oil pan gasket and the new timing gear cover gasket.

6. Install the front cover and install the oil pan-to-front cover screws and the front cover-to-block screws. Torque screws to 90 inch lbs. (10 Nm).

7. Install the hub and pulleys onto the crankshaft. Install the hub center bolt and torque to 162 ft lbs. (220 Nm).

8. Install the drive belts and adjust.

TIMING GEAR COVER OIL SEAL REPLACEMENT

▶ See Figures 92 and 93

1. After removing the gear cover, pry or drive the oil seal out of the cover with a small prybar or an oil seal removal tool.

2. Install a new lip seal with the lip (open side of seal) inside and drive or press the seal into place.

3. Lightly coat seal with engine oil before installing cover on block.

Timing Chain Or Gear

REMOVAL & INSTALLATION

Except 2.5L Engine

▶ See Figures 94, 95 and 96

1. Remove the timing gear cover.

2. With the timing gear cover removed, rotate the engine as follows:
   a. Place the #1 piston at T.D.C with the marks on the camshaft sprocket at 6 O'clock and the crankshaft sprocket at 12 O:clock.
   b. Make sure the #1 cylinder is on the compression stroke with both valves closed.

3. Remove the bolts holding the camshaft sprocket to the camshaft. Pull the camshaft sprocket forward.

4. If the camshaft sprocket will not move, give the sprocket a light blow with a plastic mallet, on the lower edge. Remove the sprocket and timing chain.

5. Remove the crankshaft gear using a gear puller. Make sure the keyway does not fall into the oil pan.

To install:

6. Install the crankshaft gear about ½ inch from the crankshaft stop.

7. Position the chain onto the cam gear, then slide the chain and cam gear onto the crank gear and camshaft, keeping the timing marks aligned at all times.

8. Install the camshaft gear retaining bolts and tighten.

9. Turn the crankshaft over two revolutions with the crankshaft bolt to check to see if the timing marks are perfectly aligned. If not, remove the cam gear and realign.

2.5L Engine

▶ See Figure 97

The 4-cylinder engine uses a gear driven camshaft. To remove the timing gear, refer to the camshaft removal section. The camshaft must be removed from the engine so that the timing gear may be pressed from the shaft.

✳ WARNING

The thrust plate must be positioned so that the woodruff key in the shaft does not damage it when the shaft is pressed out of the gear. Properly support the hub of the gear or the gear will be seriously damaged. The crankshaft gear may be removed with a gear puller while in place in the block.

Crankshaft Sprocket

REMOVAL & INSTALLATION

1. Remove the front cover and timing chain.

2. To remove the crankshaft sprocket, it may be necessary to remove the radiator to gain sufficient clearance.

3. Using a puller, remove the crankshaft sprocket.

4. To install, pay attention to the position of the woodruff key. Slide the sprocket onto the crankshaft.

5. To complete the installation, reverse the removal procedures.

Camshaft and Bearings

REMOVAL & INSTALLATION

▶ See Figures 98 thru 106

✳ CAUTION

When draining the coolant, keep in mind that cats and dogs are attracted by the ethylene glycol antifreeze, and are quite likely to drink any that is left in an uncovered container or in puddles on the ground. This will prove fatal in sufficient quantity. Always drain the coolant into a sealable container. Coolant should be reused unless it is contaminated or several years old.

4-Cylinder Engines

There are two ways to go about this task: either remove the engine from the car, or remove the radiator, grill and any other supports which are directly in

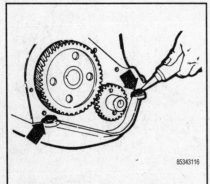

Fig. 91 Apply sealer to these points prior to assembly

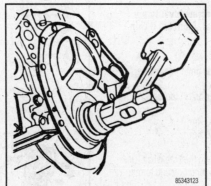

Fig. 92 Installing the oil seal with the cover installed

Fig. 93 Installing the oil seal with the cover removed

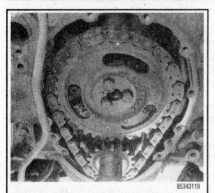

Fig. 94 Timing marks aligned with No.1 piston at TDC

Fig. 95 Timing marks aligned with No.4 (V6) or No.6 (V8) piston at TDC

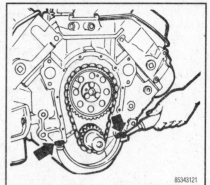

Fig. 96 Apply sealer to these points prior to assembly

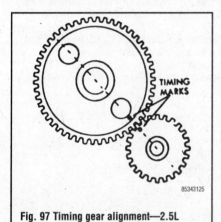

Fig. 97 Timing gear alignment—2.5L

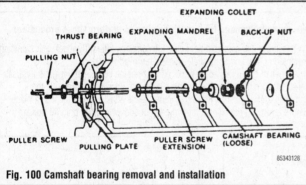

Fig. 98 Using bolts to aid in camshaft removal and installation

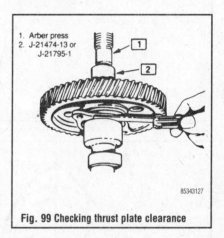

Fig. 99 Checking thrust plate clearance

Fig. 100 Camshaft bearing removal and installation

front of the engine. If the second alternative is chosen, you may have to disconnect the motor mounts, and raise the front of the engine. This will give you the necessary clearance to remove the camshaft from the engine.

1. Drain the engine oil and the cooling system. Remove the radiator.
2. Remove the fan, drive belts and water pump pulley. Remove the valve cover. Loosen the rocker arms and pivot them, then remove the pushrods.
3. Remove the oil pump driveshaft and gear assembly. This is located under a small plate secured by two bolts near the oil filter. Remove the spark plugs.
4. Mark the position of the distributor rotor, housing, and engine block. Remove the distributor.
5. Remove the valve lifters. They are located behind the pushrod cover.
6. Remove the timing gear cover.
7. Insert a screwdriver through the holes in the timing gear and remove the 2 camshaft thrust plate screws.
8. Pull the camshaft and gear assembly out through the front of the engine block.

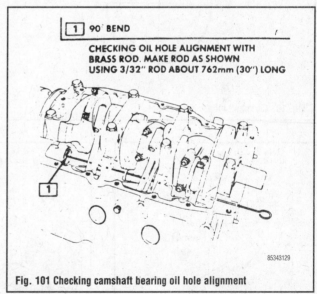

Fig. 101 Checking camshaft bearing oil hole alignment

➡When removing the camshaft, be careful not to damage the camshaft bearings.

9. If the camshaft is to be removed from the timing gear, place the assembly in an arbor press and separate.

❊❊ CAUTION

When removing the timing gear from the camshaft, the thrust plate must be positioned so that the woodruff key does not damage it.

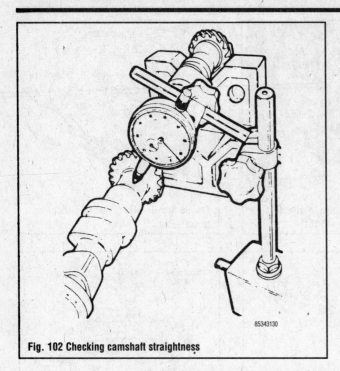

Fig. 102 Checking camshaft straightness

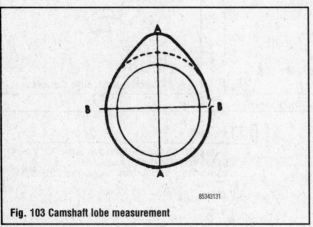

Fig. 103 Camshaft lobe measurement

To install:

10. To install the timing gear to the camshaft, press the assembly together and measure the end clearance. There should be 0.0015–0.0050 in. (0.038–0.127mm) between the thrust plate and the camshaft.

➡**If the clearance is less than 0.0015 in. (0.038mm), replace the spacer ring; if more than 0.0050 in. (0.127mm), replace the thrust ring.**

11. Lubricate the camshaft, bearings, and lifters. Slide the camshaft assembly into the engine and align the timing marks of the camshaft gear and crankshaft gear.

12. Complete the installation by reversing the removal procedure.

V6 and V8 Engines

1. Remove the engine from the vehicle or remove all components from the front of the engine (radiator, grille, etc.).
2. Remove the timing gear cover and chain.
3. Mark the distributor rotor, housing and engine block, then remove the distributor. Remove the fuel pump and fuel pump pushrod on carbureted engines.
4. Remove the intake manifold and valve covers. Loosen the rocker arms and pivot out of way. Remove the pushrods and valve lifters.
5. Remove the oil pump drive.
6. Slide the camshaft toward the front of the engine (be careful not to damage the camshaft bearings).

To install:

7. Lubricate all parts. Slide the camshaft onto the camshaft bearings.
8. Install the fuel pump and fuel pump pushrod.
9. Install the distributor and align all matchmarks.
10. Install the oil pump drive.
11. Install the valve lifters, pushrods and rocker arms.
12. Install the intake manifold and valve covers.
13. Install the timing and timing chain cover.
14. Install the radiator.
15. Fill the cooling system, start the engine and check for leaks.

BEARING REMOVAL & INSTALLATION

➡**It is recommended for a machine shop to perform these procedures.**

To remove the camshaft bearings, the camshaft lifters, flywheel, rear camshaft expansion plug, and crankshaft must be removed.

Camshaft bearings can be replaced with engine completely or partially disassembled. To replace bearings without complete disassembly remove the camshaft and crankshaft leaving cylinder heads attached and pistons in place. Before removing crankshaft, tape threads of connecting rod bolts to prevent

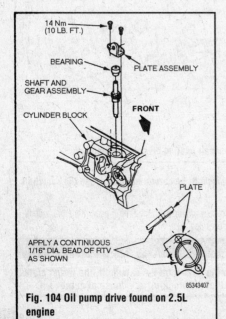

Fig. 104 Oil pump drive found on 2.5L engine

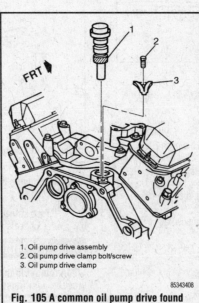

1. Oil pump drive assembly
2. Oil pump drive clamp bolt/screw
3. Oil pump drive clamp

Fig. 105 A common oil pump drive found on V6 engines

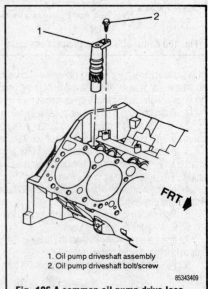

1. Oil pump driveshaft assembly
2. Oil pump driveshaft bolt/screw

Fig. 106 A common oil pump drive location on V8 engines

damage to crankshaft. Fasten connecting rods against sides of engine so they will not be in the way while replacing camshaft bearings.

If excessive wear is indicated, or if the engine is being completely rebuilt, camshaft bearings should be replaced as follows: Drive the camshaft rear plug from the block. Assemble the removal puller with its shoulder on the bearing to be removed. Gradually tighten the puller nut until bearing is removed. Remove remaining bearings, leaving the front and rear for last. To remove front and rear bearings, reverse position of the tool, so as to pull the bearings in toward the center of the block. Leave the tool in this position, pilot the new front and rear bearings on the installer, and pull them into position as follows:

- 4 cylinder engines: Ensure oil holes are properly aligned.
- V6 engines: Ensure the rear and intermediate bearing oil holes are aligned between the 2 and 3 o'clock positions and the front bearing oil holes are at 1:00 and between 2 and 3 o'clock positions.
- V8 engines: Ensure the No. 1 (front) camshaft bearing holes are an equal distance from the 6 o'clock position. The No. 2 through 4 inner bearing holes must be positioned at the 5 o'clock position towards the left side (drivers) of the engine, even with the bottom of the cylinder bore. The No. 5 bearing oil holes must be positioned at 12 o'clock.

Return the tool to its original position and pull remaining bearings into position.

➡Ensure that oil holes are properly aligned. Replace camshaft rear plug, and stake it into position to aid retention.

INSPECTION

Camshaft Lobe Lift

Check the lift of each lobe in consecutive order and make a note of the reading.

1. Remove the fresh air inlet tube and the air cleaner. Remove the heater hose and crankcase ventilation hoses. Remove valve rocker arm cover(s).
2. Remove the rocker arm stud nut or fulcrum bolts, fulcrum seat and rocker arm.
3. Make sure the pushrod is in the valve tappet socket. Install a dial indicator so that the actuating point of the indicator is in the pushrod socket (or the indicator ball socket adapter tool is on the end of the pushrod) and in the same plane as the pushrod movement.
4. Disable the ignition and fuel systems.
5. Install a remote starter switch. Crank the engine with the ignition and fuel system disabled. Turn the crankshaft over until the tappet is on the base circle of the camshaft lobe. At this position, the pushrod will be in its lowest position.
6. Zero the dial indicator. Continue to rotate the crankshaft slowly until the pushrod is in the fully raised position.
7. Compare the total lift recorded on the dial indicator with the specification shown on the Camshaft Specification chart.

To check the accuracy of the original indicator reading, continue to rotate the crankshaft until the indicator reads zero. If the lift on any lobe is below specified wear limits listed, the camshaft and the valve tappet operating on the worn lobe(s) must be replaced.

8. Install the rocker arm, fulcrum seat and stud nut or fulcrum bolts. Adjust the valves, if required (refer to the valves procedure in this section).
9. Install the valve rocker arm cover(s) and the air cleaner.

Camshaft End Play

➡On all gasoline V8 engines, prying against the aluminum-nylon camshaft sprocket, with the valve train load on the camshaft, can break or damage the sprocket. Therefore, the rocker arm adjusting nuts must be backed off, or the rocker arm and shaft assembly must be loosened sufficiently to free the camshaft. After checking the camshaft end play, check the valve clearance. Adjust if required (refer to procedure in this section).

1. Push the camshaft toward the rear of the engine. Install a dial indicator or equivalent so that the indicator point is on the camshaft sprocket attaching screw.
2. Zero the dial indicator. Position a prybar between the camshaft gear and the block. Pull the camshaft forward and release it. Compare the dial indicator reading with the specifications.
3. If the end play is excessive, check the spacer for correct installation before it is removed. If the spacer is correctly installed, replace the thrust plate.
4. Remove the dial indicator.

Valve Lifters

REMOVAL & INSTALLATION

▶ See Figures 107 thru 113

1. Remove the intake manifold, valve cover and pushrod cover (4-cylinder). Disassemble the rocker arms and remove the pushrods.
2. Remove the lifters. If they are coated with varnish, clean with carburetor cleaning solvent.
3. If installing new lifters or you have disassembled the lifters, they must be primed before installation. Submerge the lifters in SAE 10 oil and carefully push down on the plunger with a ⅛ in. (3mm) drift. Hold the plunger down (DO NOT pump), then release the plunger slowly. The lifter is now primed.
4. Coat the bottoms of the lifters with Molykote® before installation. Install the lifters and pushrods into the engine in their original position.
5. Install the rocker arms and adjust the valves. Complete the installation by reversing the removal procedure.

Freeze Plugs

REMOVAL & INSTALLATION

✳✳ CAUTION

When draining the coolant, keep in mind that cats and dogs are attracted by the ethylene glycol antifreeze, and are quite likely to drink any that is left in an uncovered container or in puddles on the ground. This will prove fatal in sufficient quantity. Always drain the coolant into a sealable container. Coolant should be reused unless it is contaminated or several years old.

Fig. 107 View of the intake removed

Fig. 108 Removing the lifter retainer hold-down bolts—roller cam models

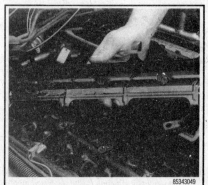

Fig. 109 Removing the lifter retainer hold-down—roller cam models

Fig. 110 Removing the lifter retainers—roller cam models

Fig. 111 Removing a lifter

Fig. 112 This is a roller-type lifter—V8 engines

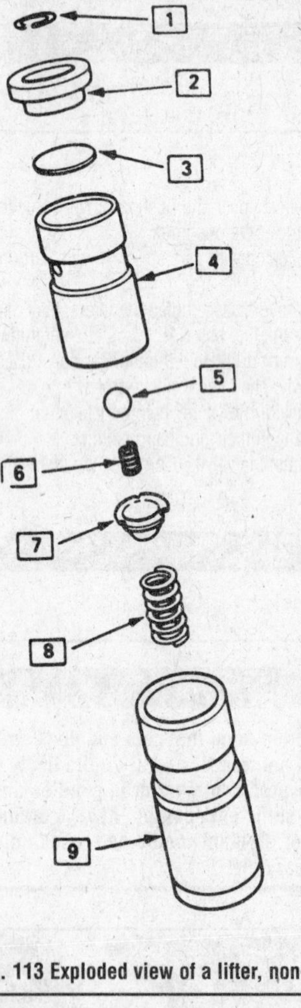

1. Retainer spring
2. Push rod seat
3. Rocker feed metering valve
4. Plunger
5. Ball check valve
6. Ball check valve spring (high ball lifter only)
7. Ball check valve retainer
8. Plunger spring
9. Lifter body

Fig. 113 Exploded view of a lifter, non-roller type

1. Disconnect the negative battery cable.
2. Drain the cooling system.
3. Raise and support the vehicle safely.
4. Remove the coolant drain plug on the side of the block, if equipped. If not you can use a punch to put a small hole in the center of the freeze plug that is being replaced.
5. Remove all components in order to gain access to the freeze plug(s).
6. Using a punch, tap the bottom corner of the freeze plug to cock it in the bore. Remove the plug using pliers.
7. Clean the freeze plug hole and coat the new plug with sealer.
8. Using a suitable tool, install the freeze plug into the block.
9. Connect the negative battery cable, fill the cooling system, start the engine and check for leaks.

Rear Main Oil Seal

REMOVAL & INSTALLATION

✳✳ CAUTION

The EPA warns that prolonged contact with used engine oil may cause a number of skin disorders, including cancer! You should make every effort to minimize your exposure to used engine oil. Protective gloves should be worn when changing the oil. Wash your hands and any other exposed skin areas as soon as possible after exposure to used engine oil. Soap and water, or waterless hand cleaner should be used.

1-Piece Neoprene Seal

♦ See Figures 114, 115 and 116

➡ The rear main seal is a one piece unit. It can be removed or installed without removing the oil pan or crankshaft.

1. Jack up your vehicle and support it with jackstands.
2. Remove the transmission.
3. If equipped with a manual transmission, remove the clutch and pressure plate.
4. Remove the flywheel assembly.
5. Using a suitable tool, pry the old seal out.
6. Inspect the crankshaft for nicks or burrs, correct as required.

ONE PIECE REAR MAIN OIL SEAL

Fig. 114 The one-piece seal

To install:

7. Clean the area and coat the seal with engine oil. Install the seal onto tool J–34686 or equivalent. Install the seal into the engine.

8. Install the flywheel and torque to specification.

9. Install the transmission. (If equipped with a manual transmission, install the clutch and pressure plate first.)

10. Check the fluid levels, start the engine and check for leaks.

2-Piece Neoprene Seal

♦ **See Figures 117, 118, 119 and 120**

Both halves of the rear main oil seal can be replaced without removing the crankshaft. Always replace the upper and lower seal together. The lip should face the front of the engine. Be very careful that you do not break the sealing bead in the channel on the outside portion of the seal while installing it. An installation tool can be fabricated to protect the seal bead.

1. Remove the oil pan, oil pump and rear main bearing cap.

2. Remove the oil seal from the bearing cap by prying it out.

3. Remove the upper half of the seal with a small punch. Drive it around far enough to be gripped with pliers.

4. Clean the crankshaft and bearing cap.

5. Coat the lips and bead of the seal with light engine oil, keeping oil from the ends of the seal.

6. Position the fabricated tool between the crankshaft and seal seat.

7. Position the seal between the crankshaft and tip of the tool so that the seal bead contacts the tip of the tool. The oil seal lip should face the FRONT of the engine.

8. Roll the seal around the crankshaft using the tool to protect the seal bead from the sharp corners of the crankcase.

9. The installation tool should be left installed until the seal is properly positioned with both ends flush with the block.

10. Remove the tool.

11. Install the other half of the seal in the bearing cap using the tool in the same manner as before. Light thumb pressure should install the seal.

12. Install the bearing cap with sealant applied to the mating areas of the cap and block. Keep sealant from the ends of the seal.

13. Torque the rear main bearing cap to specifications.

14. Install the oil pump and oil pan.

15. Fill the engine with engine oil, start the engine and check for leaks.

Rope Seal

♦ **See Figures 121, 122 and 123**

➡ **The following procedure is only to be used as an oil seal repair while the engine is in the vehicle. Whenever possible the crankshaft should be removed and a new complete rope seal installed.**

1. Disconnect the negative battery cable.

2. Drain the engine oil and remove the oil pan.

3. Remove the rear main bearing cap.

4. Insert packing tool J–29114–2 or equivalent, against 1 end of the seal in the cylinder block. Drive the old seal gently into the groove until it is packed tight. This will vary from ¼ in. (6mm) to ¾ in. (19mm) depending on the amount of pack required.

5. Repeat the procedure on the other end of the seal.

6. Measure the amount the seal was driven up on one side and add ¹⁄₁₆ in. (1.6mm). Using a suitable cutting tool, cut that length from the old seal removed from the rear main bearing cap. Repeat the procedure for the other side. Use the rear main bearing cap as a holding fixture when cutting the seal.

7. Install guide tool J–29114–1 or equivalent, onto the cylinder block.

8. Using the packing tool, work the short pieces cut in Step 6 into the guide tool and then pack into the cylinder block. The guide tool and packing tool are machined to provide a built in stop. Use this procedure for both sides. It may help to use oil on the short pieces of the rope seal when packing them into the cylinder block.

9. Remove the guide tool.

10. Apply Loctite 414 or equivalent, to the seal groove in the rear main bearing cap. Within 1 minute, insert a new seal into the groove and push into place with tool J–29590 until the seal is flush with the block. Cut the excess seal material with a sharp cutting tool at the bearing cap parting line.

11. Apply a thin film of chassis grease to the rope seal. Apply a thin film of RTV sealant on the bearing cap mating surface around the seal groove. Use the sealer sparingly.

12. Plastigage® the rear main bearing cap as outlined in MEASURING REAR MAIN CLEARANCE in this section and check with specification. If out of specification, check for frying of the rope seal which may be causing the cap to not seat properly.

13. Install all remaining components and inspect for leaks.

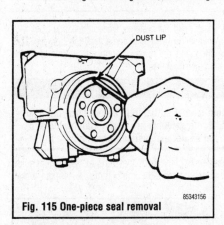

Fig. 115 One-piece seal removal

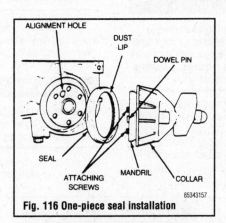

Fig. 116 One-piece seal installation

Fig. 117 Two-piece seal lower half removal

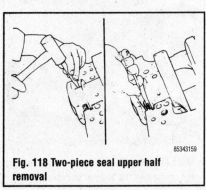

Fig. 118 Two-piece seal upper half removal

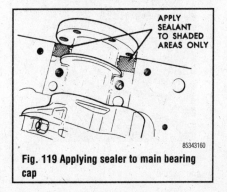

Fig. 119 Applying sealer to main bearing cap

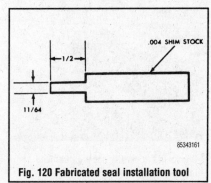

Fig. 120 Fabricated seal installation tool

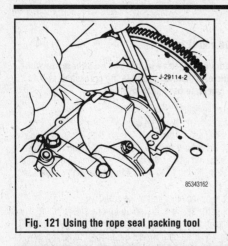

Fig. 121 Using the rope seal packing tool

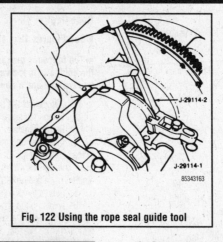

Fig. 122 Using the rope seal guide tool

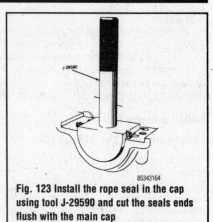

Fig. 123 Install the rope seal in the cap using tool J-29590 and cut the seals ends flush with the main cap

Flywheel and Ring Gear

REMOVAL & INSTALLATION

The ring gear is an integral part of the flywheel and is not replaceable.

1. Remove the transmission.

2. Remove the six bolts attaching the flywheel to the crankshaft flange. Remove the flywheel.

3. Inspect the flywheel for cracks, and inspect the ring gear for burrs or worn teeth. Replace the flywheel if any damage is apparent. Remove burrs with a mill file.

4. Install the flywheel. The flywheel will only attach to the crankshaft in one position, as the bolt holes are unevenly spaced. Install the bolts and torque to specification. Tighten bolts in crisscross pattern.

EXHAUST SYSTEM

♦ **See Figures 124 and 125**

Inspection

➡**Safety glasses should be worn at all times when working on or near the exhaust system. Older exhaust systems will almost always be covered with loose rust particles which will shower you when disturbed. These particles are more than a nuisance and could injure your eye.**

☀ CAUTION

Do NOT perform exhaust repairs or inspection with the engine or exhaust hot. Allow the system to cool completely before attempting any work. Exhaust systems are noted for sharp edges, flaking metal and rusted bolts. Gloves and eye protection are required. A healthy supply of penetrating oil and rags is highly recommended.

Your vehicle must be raised and supported safely to inspect the exhaust system properly. By placing 4 safety stands under the vehicle for support should provide enough room for you to slide under the vehicle and inspect the system completely. Start the inspection at the exhaust manifold where the header pipe is attached and work your way to the back of the vehicle. On dual exhaust systems, remember to inspect both sides of the vehicle. Check the complete exhaust system for open seams, holes loose connections, or other deterioration which could permit exhaust fumes to seep into the passenger compartment. Inspect all mounting brackets and hangers for deterioration, some models may have rubber O-rings that can be overstretched and non-supportive. These components will need to be replaced if found. It has always been a practice to use a pointed tool to poke up into the exhaust system where the deterioration spots are to see whether or not they crumble. Some models may have heat shield covering certain parts of the exhaust system , it will be necessary to remove these shields to have the exhaust visible for inspection also.

REPLACEMENT

There are basically two types of exhaust systems. One is the flange type where the component ends are attached with bolts and a gasket in-between. The other exhaust system is the slip joint type. These components slip into one another using clamps to retain them together.

☀ CAUTION

Allow the exhaust system to cool sufficiently before spraying a solvent exhaust fasteners. Some solvents are highly flammable and could ignite when sprayed on hot exhaust components.

Before removing any component of the exhaust system, ALWAYS squirt a liquid rust dissolving agent onto the fasteners for ease of removal. A lot of knuckle

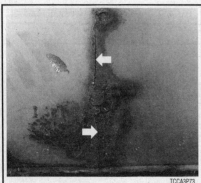

Cracks in the muffler are a guaranteed leak

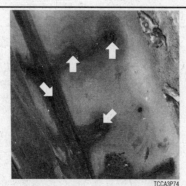

Check the muffler for rotted spot welds and seams

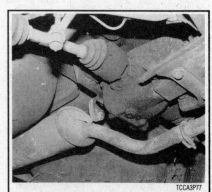

Make sure the exhaust components are not contacting the body or suspension

skin will be saved by following this rule. It may even be wise to spray the fasteners and allow them to sit overnight.

Flange Type

Before removing any component on a flange type system, ALWAYS squirt a liquid rust dissolving agent onto the fasteners for ease of removal. Start by unbolting the exhaust piece at both ends (if required). When unbolting the headpipe from the manifold, make sure that the bolts are free before trying to remove them. if you snap a stud in the exhaust manifold, the stud will have to be removed with a bolt extractor, which often means removal of the manifold itself. Next, disconnect the component from the mounting; slight twisting and turning may be required to remove the component completely from the vehicle. You may need to tap on the component with a rubber mallet to loosen the component. If all else fails, use a hacksaw to separate the parts. An oxy-acetylene cutting torch may be faster but the sparks are DANGEROUS near the fuel tank, and at the very least, accidents could happen, resulting in damage to the undercar parts, not to mention yourself.

Slip Joint Type

Before removing any component on the slip joint type exhaust system, ALWAYS squirt a liquid rust dissolving agent onto the fasteners for ease of removal. Start by unbolting the exhaust piece at both ends (if required). When unbolting the headpipe from the manifold, make sure that the bolts are free

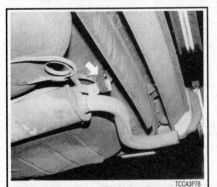

TCCA3P78

Check for overstretched or torn exhaust hangers

TCCA3P75

Example of a badly deteriorated exhaust pipe

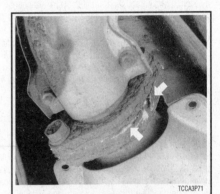

TCCA3P71

Inspect flanges for gaskets that have deteriorated and need replacement

TCCA3P76

Some systems, like this one, use large O-rings (donuts) in between the flanges

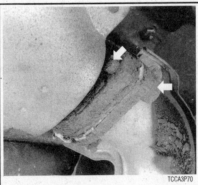

TCCA3P70

Nuts and bolts will be extremely difficult to remove when deteriorated with rust

TCCA3P72

Example of a flange type exhaust system joint

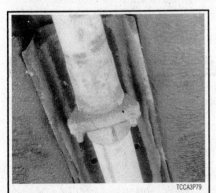

TCCA3P79

Example of a common slip joint type system

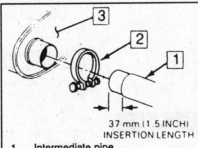

37 mm (1.5 INCH)
INSERTION LENGTH

1. Intermediate pipe
2. Clamp
3. Muffler

85343171

Fig. 124 Intermediate pipe attachment at muffler

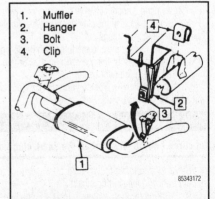

1. Muffler
2. Hanger
3. Bolt
4. Clip

85343172

Fig. 125 Muffler hanger attachment

before trying to remove them. if you snap a stud in the exhaust manifold, the stud will have to be removed with a bolt extractor, which often means removal of the manifold itself. Next, remove the mounting U-bolts from around the exhaust pipe you are extracting from the vehicle. Don't be surprised if the U-bolts break while removing the nuts. Loosen the exhaust pipe from any mounting brackets retaining it to the floor pan and separate the components.

ENGINE RECONDITIONING

Determining Engine Condition

Anything that generates heat and/or friction will eventually burn or wear out (i.e. a light bulb generates heat, therefore its life span is limited). With this in mind, a running engine generates tremendous amounts of both; friction is encountered by the moving and rotating parts inside the engine and heat is created by friction and combustion of the fuel. However, the engine has systems designed to help reduce the effects of heat and friction and provide added longevity. The oiling system reduces the amount of friction encountered by the moving parts inside the engine, while the cooling system reduces heat created by friction and combustion. If either system is not maintained, a break-down will be inevitable. Therefore, you can see how regular maintenance can affect the service life of your vehicle. If you do not drain, flush and refill your cooling system at the proper intervals, deposits will begin to accumulate in the radiator, thereby reducing the amount of heat it can extract from the coolant. The same applies to your oil and filter; if it is not changed often enough it becomes laden with contaminates and is unable to properly lubricate the engine. This increases friction and wear.

There are a number of methods for evaluating the condition of your engine. A compression test can reveal the condition of your pistons, piston rings, cylinder bores, head gasket(s), valves and valve seats. An oil pressure test can warn you of possible engine bearing, or oil pump failures. Excessive oil consumption, evidence of oil in the engine air intake area and/or bluish smoke from the tail pipe may indicate worn piston rings, worn valve guides and/or valve seals. As a general rule, an engine that uses no more than one quart of oil every 1000 miles is in good condition. Engines that use one quart of oil or more in less than 1000 miles should first be checked for oil leaks. If any oil leaks are present, have them fixed before determining how much oil is consumed by the engine, especially if blue smoke is not visible at the tail pipe.

COMPRESSION TEST

▶ **See Figure 126**

A noticeable lack of engine power, excessive oil consumption and/or poor fuel mileage measured over an extended period are all indicators of internal engine wear. Worn piston rings, scored or worn cylinder bores, blown head gaskets, sticking or burnt valves, and worn valve seats are all possible culprits. A check of each cylinder's compression will help locate the problem.

➡**A screw-in type compression gauge is more accurate than the type you simply hold against the spark plug hole. Although it takes slightly longer to use, it's worth the effort to obtain a more accurate reading.**

1. Make sure that the proper amount and viscosity of engine oil is in the crankcase, then ensure the battery is fully charged.
2. Warm-up the engine to normal operating temperature, then shut the engine **OFF**.
3. Disable the ignition system.
4. Label and disconnect all of the spark plug wires from the plugs.
5. Thoroughly clean the cylinder head area around the spark plug ports, then remove the spark plugs.
6. Set the throttle plate to the fully open (wide-open throttle) position. You can block the accelerator linkage open for this, or you can have an assistant fully depress the accelerator pedal.
7. Install a screw-in type compression gauge into the No. 1 spark plug hole until the fitting is snug.

✴✴ WARNING

Be careful not to crossthread the spark plug hole.

8. According to the tool manufacturer's instructions, connect a remote starting switch to the starting circuit.
9. With the ignition switch in the **OFF** position, use the remote starting switch to crank the engine through at least five compression strokes (approximately 5 seconds of cranking) and record the highest reading on the gauge.
10. Repeat the test on each cylinder, cranking the engine approximately the same number of compression strokes and/or time as the first.
11. Compare the highest readings from each cylinder to that of the others. The indicated compression pressures are considered within specifications if the lowest reading cylinder is within 75 percent of the pressure recorded for the highest reading cylinder. For example, if your highest reading cylinder pressure was 150 psi (1034 kPa), then 75 percent of that would be 113 psi (779 kPa). So the lowest reading cylinder should be no less than 113 psi (779 kPa).
12. If a cylinder exhibits an unusually low compression reading, pour a tablespoon of clean engine oil into the cylinder through the spark plug hole and repeat the compression test. If the compression rises after adding oil, it means that the cylinder's piston rings and/or cylinder bore are damaged or worn. If the pressure remains low, the valves may not be seating properly (a valve job is needed), or the head gasket may be blown near that cylinder. If compression in any two adjacent cylinders is low, and if the addition of oil doesn't help raise compression, there is leakage past the head gasket. Oil and coolant in the combustion chamber, combined with blue or constant white smoke from the tail pipe, are symptoms of this problem. However, don't be alarmed by the normal white smoke emitted from the tail pipe during engine warm-up or from cold weather driving. There may be evidence of water droplets on the engine dipstick and/or oil droplets in the cooling system if a head gasket is blown.

OIL PRESSURE TEST

Check for proper oil pressure at the sending unit passage with an externally mounted mechanical oil pressure gauge (as opposed to relying on a factory installed dash-mounted gauge). A tachometer may also be needed, as some specifications may require running the engine at a specific rpm.

1. With the engine cold, locate and remove the oil pressure sending unit.
2. Following the manufacturer's instructions, connect a mechanical oil pressure gauge and, if necessary, a tachometer to the engine.
3. Start the engine and allow it to idle.
4. Check the oil pressure reading when cold and record the number. You may need to run the engine at a specified rpm, so check the specifications chart located earlier in this section.
5. Run the engine until normal operating temperature is reached (upper radiator hose will feel warm).
6. Check the oil pressure reading again with the engine hot and record the number. Turn the engine **OFF**.
7. Compare your hot oil pressure reading to that given in the chart. If the reading is low, check the cold pressure reading against the chart. If the cold pressure is well above the specification, and the hot reading was lower than the specification, you may have the wrong viscosity oil in the engine. Change the oil, making sure to use the proper grade and quantity, then repeat the test.

Low oil pressure readings could be attributed to internal component wear, pump related problems, a low oil level, or oil viscosity that is too low. High oil pressure readings could be caused by an overfilled crankcase, too high of an oil viscosity or a faulty pressure relief valve.

Buy or Rebuild?

Now that you have determined that your engine is worn out, you must make some decisions. The question of whether or not an engine is worth rebuilding is largely a subjective matter and one of personal worth. Is the engine a popular one, or is it an obsolete model? Are parts available? Will it get acceptable gas mileage once it is rebuilt? Is the car it's being put into worth keeping? Would it be less expensive to buy a new engine, have your engine rebuilt by a pro, rebuild it yourself or buy a used engine from a salvage yard? Or would it be simpler and less expensive to buy another car? If you have considered all these matters and more, and have still decided to rebuild the engine, then it is time to decide how you will rebuild it.

➡The editors at Chilton feel that most engine machining should be performed by a professional machine shop. Don't think of it as wasting money, rather, as an assurance that the job has been done right the first time. There are many expensive and specialized tools required to perform such tasks as boring and honing an engine block or having a valve job done on a cylinder head. Even inspecting the parts requires expensive micrometers and gauges to properly measure wear and clearances. Also, a machine shop can deliver to you clean, and ready to assemble parts, saving you time and aggravation. Your maximum savings will come from performing the removal, disassembly, assembly and installation of the engine and purchasing or renting only the tools required to perform the above tasks. Depending on the particular circumstances, you may save 40 to 60 percent of the cost doing these yourself.

A complete rebuild or overhaul of an engine involves replacing all of the moving parts (pistons, rods, crankshaft, camshaft, etc.) with new ones and machining the non-moving wearing surfaces of the block and heads. Unfortunately, this may not be cost effective. For instance, your crankshaft may have been damaged or worn, but it can be machined undersize for a minimal fee.

So, as you can see, you can replace everything inside the engine, but, it is wiser to replace only those parts which are really needed, and, if possible, repair the more expensive ones. Later in this section, we will break the engine down into its two main components: the cylinder head and the engine block. We will discuss each component, and the recommended parts to replace during a rebuild on each.

Engine Overhaul Tips

Most engine overhaul procedures are fairly standard. In addition to specific parts replacement procedures and specifications for your individual engine, this section is also a guide to acceptable rebuilding procedures. Examples of standard rebuilding practice are given and should be used along with specific details concerning your particular engine.

Competent and accurate machine shop services will ensure maximum performance, reliability and engine life. In most instances it is more profitable for the do-it-yourself mechanic to remove, clean and inspect the component, buy the necessary parts and deliver these to a shop for actual machine work.

Much of the assembly work (crankshaft, bearings, piston rods, and other components) is well within the scope of the do-it-yourself mechanic's tools and abilities. You will have to decide for yourself the depth of involvement you desire in an engine repair or rebuild.

TOOLS

The tools required for an engine overhaul or parts replacement will depend on the depth of your involvement. With a few exceptions, they will be the tools found in a mechanic's tool kit (see Section 1 of this manual). More in-depth work will require some or all of the following:
- A dial indicator (reading in thousandths) mounted on a universal base
- Micrometers and telescope gauges
- Jaw and screw-type pullers
- Scraper
- Valve spring compressor
- Ring groove cleaner
- Piston ring expander and compressor
- Ridge reamer
- Cylinder hone or glaze breaker
- Plastigage®
- Engine stand

The use of most of these tools is illustrated in this section. Many can be rented for a one-time use from a local parts jobber or tool supply house specializing in automotive work.

Occasionally, the use of special tools is called for. See the information on Special Tools and the Safety Notice in the front of this book before substituting another tool.

OVERHAUL TIPS

Aluminum has become extremely popular for use in engines, due to its low weight. Observe the following precautions when handling aluminum parts:
- Never hot tank aluminum parts (the caustic hot tank solution will eat the aluminum.
- Remove all aluminum parts (identification tag, etc.) from engine parts prior to the tanking.
- Always coat threads lightly with engine oil or anti-seize compounds before installation, to prevent seizure.
- Never overtighten bolts or spark plugs especially in aluminum threads.

When assembling the engine, any parts that will be exposed to frictional contact must be prelubed to provide lubrication at initial start-up. Any product specifically formulated for this purpose can be used, but engine oil is not recommended as a prelube in most cases.

When semi-permanent (locked, but removable) installation of bolts or nuts is desired, threads should be cleaned and coated with Loctite, or another similar, commercial non-hardening sealant.

CLEANING

♦ See Figures 127, 128, 129 and 130

Before the engine and its components are inspected, they must be thoroughly cleaned. You will need to remove any engine varnish, oil sludge and/or carbon deposits from all of the components to insure an accurate inspection. A crack in the engine block or cylinder head can easily become overlooked if hidden by a layer of sludge or carbon.

Most of the cleaning process can be carried out with common hand tools and readily available solvents or solutions. Carbon deposits can be chipped away using a hammer and a hard wooden chisel. Old gasket material and varnish or sludge can usually be removed using a scraper and/or cleaning solvent. Extremely stubborn deposits may require the use of a power drill with a wire brush. If using a wire brush, use extreme care around any critical machined surfaces (such as the gasket surfaces, bearing saddles, cylinder bores, etc.). USE OF A WIRE BRUSH IS NOT RECOMMENDED ON ANY ALUMINUM COMPONENTS. Always follow any safety recommendations given by the manufacturer of the tool and/or solvent. You should always wear eye protection during any cleaning process involving scraping, chipping or spraying of solvents.

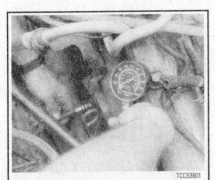
TCCS3801
Fig. 126 A screw-in type compression gauge is more accurate and easier to use without an assistant

TCCS3132
Fig. 127 Use a gasket scraper to remove the old gasket material from the mating surfaces

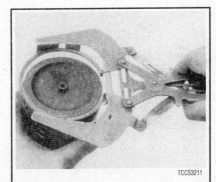
TCCS3211
Fig. 128 Use a ring expander tool to remove the piston rings

An alternative to the mess and hassle of cleaning the parts yourself is to drop them off at a local garage or machine shop. They will, more than likely, have the necessary equipment to properly clean all of the parts for a nominal fee.

✺✺ CAUTION

Always wear eye protection during any cleaning process involving scraping, chipping or spraying of solvents.

Remove any oil galley plugs, freeze plugs and/or pressed-in bearings and carefully wash and degrease all of the engine components including the fasteners and bolts. Small parts such as the valves, springs, etc., should be placed in a metal basket and allowed to soak. Use pipe cleaner type brushes, and clean all passageways in the components. Use a ring expander and remove the rings from the pistons. Clean the piston ring grooves with a special tool or a piece of broken ring. Scrape the carbon off of the top of the piston. You should never use a wire brush on the pistons. After preparing all of the piston assemblies in this manner, wash and degrease them again.

✺✺ WARNING

Use extreme care when cleaning around the cylinder head valve seats. A mistake or slip may cost you a new seat.

When cleaning the cylinder head, remove carbon from the combustion chamber with the valves installed. This will avoid damaging the valve seats.

REPAIRING DAMAGED THREADS

▶ **See Figures 131, 132, 133, 134 and 135**

Several methods of repairing damaged threads are available. Heli-Coil (shown here), Keenserts, and Microdot are among the most widely used. All involve basically the same principle—drilling out stripped threads, tapping the hole and installing a prewound insert—making welding, plugging and oversize fasteners unnecessary.

Two types of thread repair inserts are usually supplied: a standard type for most inch coarse, inch fine, metric course and metric fine thread sizes and a spark lug type to fit most spark plug port sizes. Consult the individual tool manufacturer's catalog to determine exact applications. Typical thread repair kits will contain a selection of prewound threaded inserts, a tap (corresponding to the outside diameter threads of the insert) and an installation tool. Spark plug inserts usually differ because they require a tap equipped with pilot threads and a combined reamer/tap section. Most manufacturers also supply blister-packed thread repair inserts separately in addition to a master kit containing a variety of taps and inserts plus installation tools.

Before attempting to repair a threaded hole, remove any snapped, broken or damaged bolts or studs. Penetrating oil can be used to free frozen threads. The offending item can usually be removed with locking pliers or using a screw/stud extractor. After the hole is clear, the thread can be repaired, as shown in the series of accompanying illustrations and in the kit manufacturer's instructions.

Engine Preparation

To properly rebuild an engine, you must first remove it from the vehicle, then disassemble and diagnose it. Ideally you should place your engine on an engine stand. This affords you the best access to the engine components. Follow the manufacturer's directions for using the stand with your particular engine. Remove the flywheel or flexplate before installing the engine to the stand.

Now that you have the engine on a stand, and assuming that you have drained the oil and coolant from the engine, it's time to strip it of all but the necessary components. Before you start disassembling the engine, you may want to take a moment to draw some pictures, or fabricate some labels or containers to mark the locations of various components and the bolts and/or studs which fasten them. Modern day engines use a lot of little brackets and clips which hold wiring harnesses and such, and these holders are often mounted on studs and/or bolts that can be easily mixed up. The manufacturer spent a lot of time and money

Fig. 129 Clean the piston ring grooves using a ring groove cleaner tool, or . . .

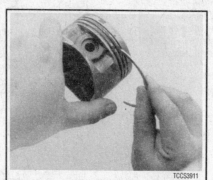

Fig. 130 . . . use a piece of an old ring to clean the grooves. Be careful, the ring can be quite sharp

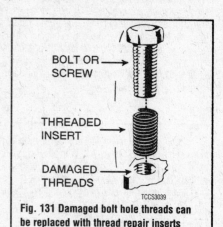

Fig. 131 Damaged bolt hole threads can be replaced with thread repair inserts

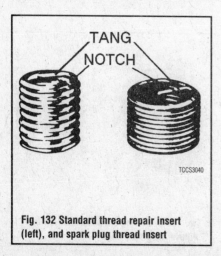

Fig. 132 Standard thread repair insert (left), and spark plug thread insert

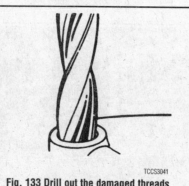

Fig. 133 Drill out the damaged threads with the specified size bit. Be sure to drill completely through the hole or to the bottom of a blind hole

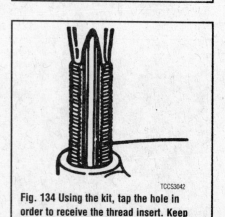

Fig. 134 Using the kit, tap the hole in order to receive the thread insert. Keep the tap well oiled and back it out frequently to avoid clogging the threads

designing your vehicle, and they wouldn't have wasted any of it by haphazardly placing brackets, clips or fasteners on the vehicle. If it's present when you disassemble it, put it back when you assemble, you will regret not remembering that little bracket which holds a wire harness out of the path of a rotating part.

You should begin by unbolting any accessories still attached to the engine, such as the water pump, power steering pump, alternator, etc. Then, unfasten any manifolds (intake or exhaust) which were not removed during the engine removal procedure. Finally, remove any covers remaining on the engine such as the rocker arm, front or timing cover and oil pan. Some front covers may require the vibration damper and/or crank pulley to be removed beforehand. The idea is to reduce the engine to the bare necessities (cylinder head(s), valve train, engine block, crankshaft, pistons and connecting rods), plus any other 'in block' components such as oil pumps, balance shafts and auxiliary shafts.

Finally, remove the cylinder head(s) from the engine block and carefully place on a bench. Disassembly instructions for each component follow later in this section.

Cylinder Head

There are two basic types of cylinder heads used on today's automobiles: the Overhead Valve (OHV) and the Overhead Camshaft (OHC). The latter can also be broken down into two subgroups: the Single Overhead Camshaft (SOHC) and the Dual Overhead Camshaft (DOHC). Generally, if there is only a single camshaft on a head, it is just referred to as an OHC head. Also, an engine with a OHV cylinder head is also known as a pushrod engine.

Most cylinder heads these days are made of an aluminum alloy due to its light weight, durability and heat transfer qualities. However, cast iron was the material of choice in the past, and is still used on many vehicles today. Whether made from aluminum or iron, all cylinder heads have valves and seats. Some use two valves per cylinder, while the more hi-tech engines will utilize a multi-valve configuration using 3, 4 and even 5 valves per cylinder. When the valve contacts the seat, it does so on precision machined surfaces, which seals the combustion chamber. All cylinder heads have a valve guide for each valve. The guide centers the valve to the seat and allows it to move up and down within it. The clearance between the valve and guide can be critical. Too much clearance and the engine may consume oil, lose vacuum and/or damage the seat. Too little, and the valve can stick in the guide causing the engine to run poorly if at all, and possibly causing severe damage. The last component all cylinder heads have are valve springs. The spring holds the valve against its seat. It also returns the valve to this position when the valve has been opened by the valve train or camshaft. The spring is fastened to the valve by a retainer and valve locks (sometimes called keepers). Aluminum heads will also have a valve spring shim to keep the spring from wearing away the aluminum.

An ideal method of rebuilding the cylinder head would involve replacing all of the valves, guides, seats, springs, etc. with new ones. However, depending on how the engine was maintained, often this is not necessary. A major cause of valve, guide and seat wear is an improperly tuned engine. An engine that is running too rich, will often wash the lubricating oil out of the guide with gasoline, causing it to wear rapidly. Conversely, an engine which is running too lean will place higher combustion temperatures on the valves and seats allowing them to wear or even burn. Springs fall victim to the driving habits of the individual. A driver who often runs the engine rpm to the redline will wear out or break the springs faster then one that stays well below it. Unfortunately, mileage takes it toll on all of the parts. Generally, the valves, guides, springs and seats in a cylinder head can be machined and re-used, saving you money. However, if a valve is burnt, it may be wise to replace all of the valves, since they were all operating in the same environment. The same goes for any other component on the cylinder head. Think of it as an insurance policy against future problems related to that component.

Unfortunately, the only way to find out which components need replacing, is to disassemble and carefully check each piece. After the cylinder head(s) are disassembled, thoroughly clean all of the components.

DISASSEMBLY

♦ **See Figures 136 thru 141**

Before disassembling the cylinder head, you may want to fabricate some containers to hold the various parts, as some of them can be quite small (such as keepers) and easily lost. Also keeping yourself and the components organized will aid in assembly and reduce confusion. Where possible, try to maintain a components original location; this is especially important if there is not going to be any machine work performed on the components.

1. If you haven't already removed the rocker arms and/or shafts, do so now.
2. Position the head so that the springs are easily accessed.
3. Use a valve spring compressor tool, and relieve spring tension from the retainer.

➡ **Due to engine varnish, the retainer may stick to the valve locks. A gentle tap with a hammer may help to break it loose.**

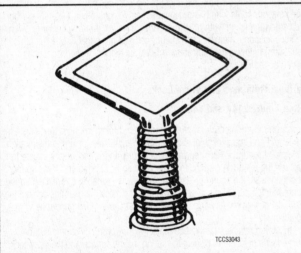

TCCS3043

Fig. 135 Screw the insert onto the installer tool until the tang engages the slot. Thread the insert into the hole until it is ¼–½ turn below the top surface, then remove the tool and break off the tang using a punch

TCCS3137

Fig. 136 When removing an OHV valve spring, use a compressor tool to relieve the tension from the retainer

TCCS3138

Fig. 137 A small magnet will help in removal of the valve locks

TCCS3139

Fig. 138 Be careful not to lose the small valve locks (keepers)

Fig. 139 Remove the valve seal from the valve stem—O-ring type seal shown

Fig. 140 Removing an umbrella/positive type seal

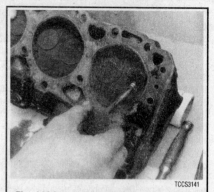

Fig. 141 Invert the cylinder head and withdraw the valve from the valve guide bore

4. Remove the valve locks from the valve tip and/or retainer. A small magnet may help in removing the locks.

5. Lift the valve spring, tool and all, off of the valve stem.

6. If equipped, remove the valve seal. If the seal is difficult to remove with the valve in place, try removing the valve first, then the seal. Follow the steps below for valve removal.

7. Position the head to allow access for withdrawing the valve.

➡Cylinder heads that have seen a lot of miles and/or abuse may have mushroomed the valve lock grove and/or tip, causing difficulty in removal of the valve. If this has happened, use a metal file to carefully remove the high spots around the lock grooves and/or tip. Only file it enough to allow removal.

8. Remove the valve from the cylinder head.

9. If equipped, remove the valve spring shim. A small magnetic tool or screwdriver will aid in removal.

10. Repeat Steps 3 though 9 until all of the valves have been removed.

INSPECTION

Now that all of the cylinder head components are clean, it's time to inspect them for wear and/or damage. To accurately inspect them, you will need some specialized tools:

- A 0–1 inch micrometer for the valves
- A dial indicator or inside diameter gauge for the valve guides
- A spring pressure test gauge

If you do not have access to the proper tools, you may want to bring the components to a shop that does.

Valves

▶ See Figures 142 and 143

The first thing to inspect are the valve heads. Look closely at the head, margin and face for any cracks, excessive wear or burning. The margin is the best place to look for burning. It should have a squared edge with an even width all around the diameter. When a valve burns, the margin will look melted and the edges rounded. Also inspect the valve head for any signs of tulipping. This will show as a lifting of the edges or dishing in the center of the head and will usually not occur to all of the valves. All of the heads should look the same, any that seem dished more than others are probably bad. Next, inspect the valve lock grooves and valve tips. Check for any burrs around the lock grooves, especially if you had to file them to remove the valve. Valve tips should appear flat, although slight rounding with high mileage engines is normal. Slightly worn valve tips will need to be machined flat. Last, measure the valve stem diameter with the micrometer. Measure the area that rides within the guide, especially towards the tip where most of the wear occurs. Take several measurements along its length and compare them to each other. Wear should be even along the length with little to no taper. If no minimum diameter is given in the specifications, then the stem should not read more than 0.001 in. (0.025mm) below the specification. Any valves that fail these inspections should be replaced.

Springs, Retainers and Valve Locks

▶ See Figures 144 and 145

The first thing to check is the most obvious, broken springs. Next check the free length and squareness of each spring. If applicable, insure to distinguish between intake and exhaust springs. Use a ruler and/or carpenters square to measure the length. A carpenters square should be used to check the springs for squareness. If a spring pressure test gauge is available, check each springs rating and compare to the specifications chart. Check the readings against the specifications given. Any springs that fail these inspections should be replaced.

The spring retainers rarely need replacing, however they should still be checked as a precaution. Inspect the spring mating surface and the valve lock retention area for any signs of excessive wear. Also check for any signs of cracking. Replace any retainers that are questionable.

Valve locks should be inspected for excessive wear on the outside contact area as well as on the inner notched surface. Any locks which appear worn or broken and its respective valve should be replaced.

Fig. 142 Valve stems may be rolled on a flat surface to check for bends

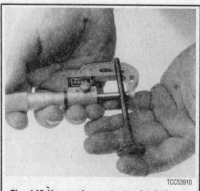

Fig. 143 Use a micrometer to check the valve stem diameter

Fig. 144 Use a caliper to check the valve spring free-length

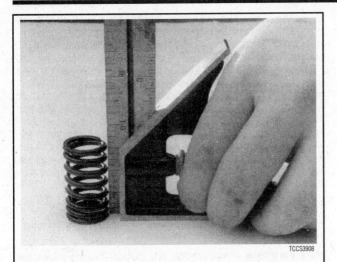

Fig. 145 Check the valve spring for squareness on a flat surface; a carpenter's square can be used

Cylinder Head

There are several things to check on the cylinder head: valve guides, seats, cylinder head surface flatness, cracks and physical damage.

VALVE GUIDES

▶ See Figure 146

Now that you know the valves are good, you can use them to check the guides, although a new valve, if available, is preferred. Before you measure anything, look at the guides carefully and inspect them for any cracks, chips or breakage. Also if the guide is a removable style (as in most aluminum heads), check them for any looseness or evidence of movement. All of the guides should appear to be at the same height from the spring seat. If any seem lower (or higher) from another, the guide has moved. Mount a dial indicator onto the spring side of the cylinder head. Lightly oil the valve stem and insert it into the cylinder head. Position the dial indicator against the valve stem near the tip and zero the gauge. Grasp the valve stem and wiggle towards and away from the dial indicator and observe the readings. Mount the dial indicator 90 degrees from the initial point and zero the gauge and again take a reading. Compare the two readings for a out of round condition. Check the readings against the specifications given. An Inside Diameter (I.D.) gauge designed for valve guides will give you an accurate valve guide bore measurement. If the I.D. gauge is used, compare the readings with the specifications given. Any guides that fail these inspections should be replaced or machined.

VALVE SEATS

A visual inspection of the valve seats should show a slightly worn and pitted surface where the valve face contacts the seat. Inspect the seat carefully for severe pitting or cracks. Also, a seat that is badly worn will be recessed into the cylinder head. A severely worn or recessed seat may need to be replaced. All cracked seats must be replaced. A seat concentricity gauge, it available, should be used to check the seat run-out. If run-out exceeds specifications the seat must be machined (if no specification is given use 0.002 in. or 0.051mm).

CYLINDER HEAD SURFACE FLATNESS

▶ See Figures 147 and 148

After you have cleaned the gasket surface of the cylinder head of any old gasket material, check the head for flatness.

Place a straightedge across the gasket surface. Using feeler gauges, determine the clearance at the center of the straightedge and across the cylinder head at several points. Check along the centerline and diagonally on the head surface. If the warpage exceeds 0.003 in. (0.076mm) within a 6.0 in. (15.2cm) span, or 0.006 in. (0.152mm) over the total length of the head, the cylinder head must be resurfaced. After resurfacing the heads of a V-type engine, the intake manifold flange surface should be checked, and if necessary, milled proportionally to allow for the change in its mounting position.

CRACKS AND PHYSICAL DAMAGE

Generally, cracks are limited to the combustion chamber, however, it is not uncommon for the head to crack in a spark plug hole, port, outside of the head or in the valve spring/rocker arm area. The first area to inspect is always the hottest: the exhaust seat/port area.

A visual inspection should be performed, but just because you don't see a crack does not mean it is not there. Some more reliable methods for inspecting for cracks include Magnaflux®, a magnetic process or Zyglo®, a dye penetrant. Magnaflux® is used only on ferrous metal (cast iron) heads. Zyglo® uses a spray on fluorescent mixture along with a black light to reveal the cracks. It is strongly recommended to have your cylinder head checked professionally for cracks, especially if the engine was known to have overheated and/or leaked or consumed coolant. Contact a local shop for availability and pricing of these services.

Physical damage is usually very evident. For example, a broken mounting ear from dropping the head or a bent or broken stud and/or bolt. All of these defects should be fixed or, if irrepairable, the head should be replaced.

REFINISHING & REPAIRING

Many of the procedures given for refinishing and repairing the cylinder head components must be performed by a machine shop. Certain steps, if the inspected part is not worn, can be performed yourself inexpensively. However, you spent a lot of time and effort so far, why risk trying to save a couple bucks if you might have to do it all over again?

Valves

Any valves that were not replaced should be refaced and the tips ground flat. Unless you have access to a valve grinding machine, this should be done by a machine shop. If the valves are in extremely good condition, as well as the valve seats and guides, they may be lapped in without performing machine work.

It is a recommended practice to lap the valves even after machine work has been performed and/or new valves have been purchased. This insures a positive seal between the valve and seat.

Fig. 146 A dial gauge may be used to check valve stem-to-guide clearance; read the gauge while moving the valve stem

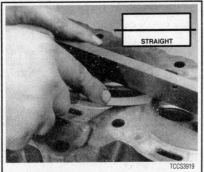

Fig. 147 Check the head for flatness across the center of the head surface using a straightedge and feeler gauge

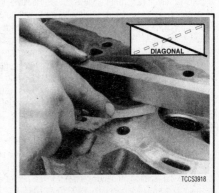

Fig. 148 Checks should also be made along both diagonals of the head surface

LAPPING THE VALVES

➡Before lapping the valves to the seats, read the rest of the cylinder head section to insure that any related parts are in acceptable enough condition to continue.

➡Before any valve seat machining and/or lapping can be performed, the guides must be within factory recommended specifications.

1. Invert the cylinder head.
2. Lightly lubricate the valve stems and insert them into the cylinder head in their numbered order.
3. Raise the valve from the seat and apply a small amount of fine lapping compound to the seat.
4. Moisten the suction head of a hand-lapping tool and attach it to the head of the valve.
5. Rotate the tool between the palms of both hands, changing the position of the valve on the valve seat and lifting the tool often to prevent grooving.
6. Lap the valve until a smooth, polished circle is evident on the valve and seat.
7. Remove the tool and the valve. Wipe away all traces of the grinding compound and store the valve to maintain its lapped location.

✳ WARNING

Do not get the valves out of order after they have been lapped. They must be put back with the same valve seat they were lapped with.

Springs, Retainers and Valve Locks

There is no repair or refinishing possible with the springs, retainers and valve locks. If they are found to be worn or defective, they must be replaced with new (or known good) parts.

Cylinder Head

Most refinishing procedures dealing with the cylinder head must be performed by a machine shop. Read the sections below and review your inspection data to determine whether or not machining is necessary.

VALVE GUIDE

➡If any machining or replacements are made to the valve guides, the seats must be machined.

Unless the valve guides need machining or replacing, the only service to perform is to thoroughly clean them of any dirt or oil residue.

There are only two types of valve guides used on automobile engines: the replaceable-type (all aluminum heads) and the cast-in integral-type (most cast iron heads). There are four recommended methods for repairing worn guides.

- Knurling
- Inserts
- Reaming oversize
- Replacing

Knurling is a process in which metal is displaced and raised, thereby reducing clearance, giving a true center, and providing oil control. It is the least expensive way of repairing the valve guides. However, it is not necessarily the best; and in some cases, a knurled valve guide will not stand up for more than a short time. It requires a special knurler and precision reaming tools to obtain proper clearances. It would not be cost effective to purchase these tools, unless you plan on rebuilding several of the same cylinder head.

Installing a guide insert involves machining the guide to accept a bronze insert. One style is the coil-type which is installed into a threaded guide. Another is the thin-walled insert where the guide is reamed oversize to accept a split-sleeve insert. After the insert is installed, a special tool is then run through the guide to expand the insert, locking it to the guide. The insert is then reamed to the standard size for proper valve clearance.

Reaming for oversize valves restores normal clearances and provides a true valve seat. Most cast-in type guides can be reamed to accept an valve with an oversize stem. The cost factor for this can become quite high as you will need to purchase the reamer and new, oversize stem valves for all guides which were reamed. Oversizes are generally 0.003 to 0.030 in. (0.076 to 0.762mm), with 0.015 in. (0.381mm) being the most common.

To replace cast-in type valve guides, they must be drilled out, then reamed to accept replacement guides. This must be done on a fixture which will allow centering and leveling off of the original valve seat or guide, otherwise a serious guide-to-seat misalignment may occur making it impossible to properly machine the seat.

Replaceable-type guides are pressed into the cylinder head. A hammer and a stepped drift or punch may be used to install and remove the guides. Before removing the guides, measure the protrusion on the spring side of the head and record it for installation. Use the stepped drift to hammer out the old guide from the combustion chamber side of the head. When installing, determine whether or not the guide also seals a water jacket in the head, and if it does, use the recommended sealing agent. If there is no water jacket, grease the valve guide and its bore. Use the stepped drift, and hammer the new guide into the cylinder head from the spring side of the cylinder head. A stack of washers the same thickness as the measured protrusion may help the installation process.

VALVE SEATS

➡Before any valve seat machining can be performed, the guides must be within factory recommended specifications.

➡If any machining or replacements were made to the valve guides, the seats must be machined.

If the seats are in good condition, the valves can be lapped to the seats, and the cylinder head assembled. See the valves section for instructions on lapping.

If the valve seats are worn, cracked or damaged, they must be serviced by a machine shop. The valve seat must be perfectly centered to the valve guide, which requires very accurate machining.

CYLINDER HEAD SURFACE

If the cylinder head is warped, it must be machined flat. If the warpage is extremely severe, the head may need to be replaced. In some instances, it may be possible to straighten a warped head enough to allow machining. In either case, contact a professional machine shop for service.

CRACKS AND PHYSICAL DAMAGE

Certain cracks can be repaired in both cast iron and aluminum heads. For cast iron, a tapered threaded insert is installed along the length of the crack. Aluminum can also use the tapered inserts, however welding is the preferred method. Some physical damage can be repaired through brazing or welding. Contact a machine shop to get expert advice for your particular dilemma.

ASSEMBLY

The first step for any assembly job is to have a clean area in which to work. Next, thoroughly clean all of the parts and components that are to be assembled. Finally, place all of the components onto a suitable work space and, if necessary, arrange the parts to their respective positions.

1. Lightly lubricate the valve stems and insert all of the valves into the cylinder head. If possible, maintain their original locations.
2. If equipped, install any valve spring shims which were removed.
3. If equipped, install the new valve seals, keeping the following in mind:
- If the valve seal presses over the guide, lightly lubricate the outer guide surfaces.
- If the seal is an O-ring type, it is installed just after compressing the spring but before the valve locks.
4. Place the valve spring and retainer over the stem.
5. Position the spring compressor tool and compress the spring.
6. Assemble the valve locks to the stem.
7. Relieve the spring pressure slowly and insure that neither valve lock becomes dislodged by the retainer.
8. Remove the spring compressor tool.
9. Repeat Steps 2 through 8 until all of the springs have been installed.

Engine Block

GENERAL INFORMATION

A thorough overhaul or rebuild of an engine block would include replacing the pistons, rings, bearings, timing belt/chain assembly and oil pump. For OHV engines also include a new camshaft and lifters. The block would then have the cylinders bored and honed oversize (or if using removable cylinder sleeves, new sleeves installed) and the crankshaft would be cut undersize to provide new wearing surfaces and perfect clearances. However, your particular engine may not have everything worn out. What if only the piston rings have worn out and the clearances on everything else are still within factory specifications? Well, you could just replace the rings and put it back together, but this would be a very rare example. Chances are, if one component in your engine is worn, other components are sure to follow, and soon. At the very least, you should always replace the rings, bearings and oil pump. This is what is commonly called a "freshen up".

Cylinder Ridge Removal

Because the top piston ring does not travel to the very top of the cylinder, a ridge is built up between the end of the travel and the top of the cylinder bore.

Pushing the piston and connecting rod assembly past the ridge can be difficult, and damage to the piston ring lands could occur. If the ridge is not removed before installing a new piston or not removed at all, piston ring breakage and piston damage may occur.

➡It is always recommended that you remove any cylinder ridges before removing the piston and connecting rod assemblies. If you know that new pistons are going to be installed and the engine block will be bored oversize, you may be able to forego this step. However, some ridges may actually prevent the assemblies from being removed, necessitating its removal.

There are several different types of ridge reamers on the market, none of which are inexpensive. Unless a great deal of engine rebuilding is anticipated, borrow or rent a reamer.

1. Turn the crankshaft until the piston is at the bottom of its travel.
2. Cover the head of the piston with a rag.
3. Follow the tool manufacturers instructions and cut away the ridge, exercising extreme care to avoid cutting too deeply.
4. Remove the ridge reamer, the rag and as many of the cuttings as possible. Continue until all of the cylinder ridges have been removed.

DISASSEMBLY

▶ **See Figures 149 and 150**

The engine disassembly instructions following assume that you have the engine mounted on an engine stand. If not, it is easiest to disassemble the engine on a bench or the floor with it resting on the bellhousing or transmission mounting surface. You must be able to access the connecting rod fasteners and turn the crankshaft during disassembly. Also, all engine covers (timing, front, side, oil pan, whatever) should have already been removed. Engines which are seized or locked up may not be able to be completely disassembled, and a core (salvage yard) engine should be purchased.

If not done during the cylinder head removal, remove the pushrods and lifters, keeping them in order for assembly. Remove the timing gears and/or timing chain assembly, then remove the oil pump drive assembly and withdraw the camshaft from the engine block. Remove the oil pick-up and pump assembly. If equipped, remove any balance or auxiliary shafts. If necessary, remove the cylinder ridge from the top of the bore. See the cylinder ridge removal procedure earlier in this section.

Rotate the engine over so that the crankshaft is exposed. Use a number punch or scribe and mark each connecting rod with its respective cylinder number. The cylinder closest to the front of the engine is always number 1. However, depending on the engine placement, the front of the engine could either be the flywheel or damper/pulley end. Generally the front of the engine faces the front of the vehicle. Use a number punch or scribe and also mark the main bearing caps from front to rear with the front most cap being number 1 (if there are five caps, mark them 1 through 5, front to rear).

✷ WARNING

Take special care when pushing the connecting rod up from the crankshaft because the sharp threads of the rod bolts/studs will score the crankshaft journal. Insure that special plastic caps are installed over them, or cut two pieces of rubber hose to do the same.

Fig. 149 Place rubber hose over the connecting rod studs to protect the crankshaft and cylinder bores from damage

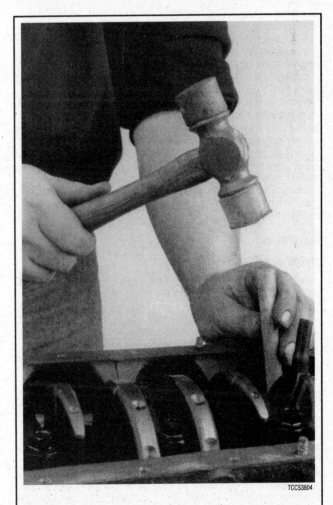

Fig. 150 Carefully tap the piston out of the bore using a wooden dowel

Again, rotate the engine, this time to position the number one cylinder bore (head surface) up. Turn the crankshaft until the number one piston is at the bottom of its travel, this should allow the maximum access to its connecting rod. Remove the number one connecting rods fasteners and cap and place two lengths of rubber hose over the rod bolts/studs to protect the crankshaft from damage. Using a sturdy wooden dowel and a hammer, push the connecting rod up about 1 in. (25mm) from the crankshaft and remove the upper bearing insert. Continue pushing or tapping the connecting rod up until the piston rings are out of the cylinder bore. Remove the piston and rod by hand, put the upper half of the bearing insert back into the rod, install the cap with its bearing insert installed, and hand-tighten the cap fasteners. If the parts are kept in order in this manner, they will not get lost and you will be able to tell which bearings came form what cylinder if any problems are discovered and diagnosis is necessary. Remove all the other piston assemblies in the same manner. On V-style engines, remove all of the pistons from one bank, then reposition the engine with the other cylinder bank head surface up, and remove that banks piston assemblies.

The only remaining component in the engine block should now be the crankshaft. Loosen the main bearing caps evenly until the fasteners can be turned by hand, then remove them and the caps. Remove the crankshaft from the engine block. Thoroughly clean all of the components.

INSPECTION

Now that the engine block and all of its components are clean, it's time to inspect them for wear and/or damage. To accurately inspect them, you will need some specialized tools:
- Two or three separate micrometers to measure the pistons and crankshaft journals
- A dial indicator
- Telescoping gauges for the cylinder bores
- A rod alignment fixture to check for bent connecting rods

If you do not have access to the proper tools, you may want to bring the components to a shop that does.

Generally, you shouldn't expect cracks in the engine block or its components unless it was known to leak, consume or mix engine fluids, it was severely overheated, or there was evidence of bad bearings and/or crankshaft damage. A visual inspection should be performed on all of the components, but just because you don't see a crack does not mean it is not there. Some more reliable methods for inspecting for cracks include Magnaflux®, a magnetic process or Zyglo®, a dye penetrant. Magnaflux® is used only on ferrous metal (cast iron). Zyglo® uses a spray on fluorescent mixture along with a black light to reveal the cracks. It is strongly recommended to have your engine block checked professionally for cracks, especially if the engine was known to have overheated and/or leaked or consumed coolant. Contact a local shop for availability and pricing of these services.

Engine Block

ENGINE BLOCK BEARING ALIGNMENT

Remove the main bearing caps and, if still installed, the main bearing inserts. Inspect all of the main bearing saddles and caps for damage, burrs or high spots. If damage is found, and it is caused from a spun main bearing, the block will need to be align-bored or, if severe enough, replacement. Any burrs or high spots should be carefully removed with a metal file.

Place a straightedge on the bearing saddles, in the engine block, along the centerline of the crankshaft. If any clearance exists between the straightedge and the saddles, the block must be align-bored.

Align-boring consists of machining the main bearing saddles and caps by means of a flycutter that runs through the bearing saddles.

DECK FLATNESS

The top of the engine block where the cylinder head mounts is called the deck. Insure that the deck surface is clean of dirt, carbon deposits and old gasket material. Place a straightedge across the surface of the deck along its centerline and, using feeler gauges, check the clearance along several points. Repeat the checking procedure with the straightedge placed along both diagonals of the deck surface. If the reading exceeds 0.003 in. (0.076mm) within a 6.0 in. (15.2cm) span, or 0.006 in. (0.152mm) over the total length of the deck, it must be machined.

CYLINDER BORES

♦ See Figure 151

The cylinder bores house the pistons and are slightly larger than the pistons themselves. A common piston-to-bore clearance is 0.0015–0.0025 in. (0.0381mm–0.0635mm). Inspect and measure the cylinder bores. The bore

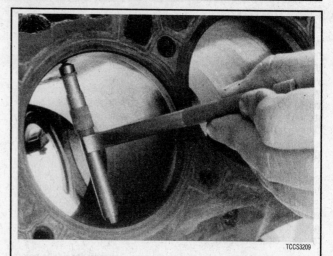

TCCS3209

Fig. 151 Use a telescoping gauge to measure the cylinder bore diameter—take several readings within the same bore

should be checked for out-of-roundness, taper and size. The results of this inspection will determine whether the cylinder can be used in its existing size and condition, or a rebore to the next oversize is required (or in the case of removable sleeves, have replacements installed).

The amount of cylinder wall wear is always greater at the top of the cylinder than at the bottom. This wear is known as taper. Any cylinder that has a taper of 0.0012 in. (0.305mm) or more, must be rebored. Measurements are taken at a number of positions in each cylinder: at the top, middle and bottom and at two points at each position; that is, at a point 90 degrees from the crankshaft center-line, as well as a point parallel to the crankshaft centerline. The measurements are made with either a special dial indicator or a telescopic gauge and micrometer. If the necessary precision tools to check the bore are not available, take the block to a machine shop and have them mike it. Also if you don't have the tools to check the cylinder bores, chances are you will not have the necessary devices to check the pistons, connecting rods and crankshaft. Take these components with you and save yourself an extra trip.

For our procedures, we will use a telescopic gauge and a micrometer. You will need one of each, with a measuring range which covers your cylinder bore size.

1. Position the telescopic gauge in the cylinder bore, loosen the gauges lock and allow it to expand.

➡ **Your first two readings will be at the top of the cylinder bore, then proceed to the middle and finally the bottom, making a total of six measurements.**

2. Hold the gauge square in the bore, 90 degrees from the crankshaft centerline, and gently tighten the lock. Tilt the gauge back to remove it from the bore.
3. Measure the gauge with the micrometer and record the reading.
4. Again, hold the gauge square in the bore, this time parallel to the crankshaft centerline, and gently tighten the lock. Again, you will tilt the gauge back to remove it from the bore.
5. Measure the gauge with the micrometer and record this reading. The difference between these two readings is the out-of-round measurement of the cylinder.
6. Repeat steps 1 through 5, each time going to the next lower position, until you reach the bottom of the cylinder. Then go to the next cylinder, and continue until all of the cylinders have been measured.

The difference between these measurements will tell you all about the wear in your cylinders. The measurements which were taken 90 degrees from the crankshaft centerline will always reflect the most wear. That is because at this position is where the engine power presses the piston against the cylinder bore the hardest. This is known as thrust wear. Take your top, 90 degree measurement and compare it to your bottom, 90 degree measurement. The difference between them is the taper. When you measure your pistons, you will compare these readings to your piston sizes and determine piston-to-wall clearance.

Crankshaft

Inspect the crankshaft for visible signs of wear or damage. All of the journals should be perfectly round and smooth. Slight scores are normal for a used crankshaft, but you should hardly feel them with your fingernail. When measuring the crankshaft with a micrometer, you will take readings at the front and rear of each journal, then turn the micrometer 90 degrees and take two more readings, front and rear. The difference between the front-to-rear readings is the journal taper and the first-to-90 degree reading is the out-of-round measurement. Generally, there should be no taper or out-of-roundness found, however, up to 0.0005 in. (0.0127mm) for either can be overlooked. Also, the readings should fall within the factory specifications for journal diameters.

If the crankshaft journals fall within specifications, it is recommended that it be polished before being returned to service. Polishing the crankshaft insures that any minor burrs or high spots are smoothed, thereby reducing the chance of scoring the new bearings.

Pistons and Connecting Rods

PISTONS

♦ See Figure 152

The piston should be visually inspected for any signs of cracking or burning (caused by hot spots or detonation), and scuffing or excessive wear on the skirts. The wristpin attaches the piston to the connecting rod. The piston should move freely on the wrist pin, both sliding and pivoting. Grasp the connecting rod securely, or mount it in a vise, and try to rock the piston back and forth along the centerline of the wristpin. There should not be any excessive play evident between the piston and the pin. If there are C-clips retaining the pin in the piston then you have wrist pin bushings in the rods. There should not be any excessive play between the wrist pin and the rod bushing. Normal clearance for the wrist pin is approx. 0.001–0.002 in. (0.025mm–0.051mm).

Use a micrometer and measure the diameter of the piston, perpendicular to the wrist pin, on the skirt. Compare the reading to its original cylinder measurement obtained earlier. The difference between the two readings is the piston-to-wall clearance. If the clearance is within specifications, the piston may be used as is. If the piston is out of specification, but the bore is not, you will need a new piston. If both are out of specification, you will need the cylinder rebored and oversize pistons installed. Generally if two or more pistons/bores are out of specification, it is best to rebore the entire block and purchase a complete set of oversize pistons.

CONNECTING ROD

You should have the connecting rod checked for straightness at a machine shop. If the connecting rod is bent, it will unevenly wear the bearing and piston, as well as place greater stress on these components. Any bent or twisted connecting rods must be replaced. If the rods are straight and the wrist pin clearance is within specifications, then only the bearing end of the rod need be checked. Place the connecting rod into a vice, with the bearing inserts in place, install the cap to the rod and torque the fasteners to specifications. Use a telescoping gauge and carefully measure the inside diameter of the bearings. Compare this reading to the rods original crankshaft journal diameter measurement. The difference is the oil clearance. If the oil clearance is not within specifica-

tions, install new bearings in the rod and take another measurement. If the clearance is still out of specifications, and the crankshaft is not, the rod will need to be reconditioned by a machine shop.

➡You can also use Plastigage® to check the bearing clearances. The assembling section has complete instructions on its use.

Camshaft

Inspect the camshaft and lifters/followers as described earlier in this section.

Bearings

All of the engine bearings should be visually inspected for wear and/or damage. The bearing should look evenly worn all around with no deep scores or pits. If the bearing is severely worn, scored, pitted or heat blued, then the bearing, and the components that use it, should be brought to a machine shop for inspection. Full-circle bearings (used on most camshafts, auxiliary shafts, balance shafts, etc.) require specialized tools for removal and installation, and should be brought to a machine shop for service.

Oil Pump

➡The oil pump is responsible for providing constant lubrication to the whole engine and so it is recommended that a new oil pump be installed when rebuilding the engine.

Completely disassemble the oil pump and thoroughly clean all of the components. Inspect the oil pump gears and housing for wear and/or damage. Insure that the pressure relief valve operates properly and there is no binding or sticking due to varnish or debris. If all of the parts are in proper working condition, lubricate the gears and relief valve, and assemble the pump.

REFINISHING

♦ See Figure 153

Almost all engine block refinishing must be performed by a machine shop. If the cylinders are not to be rebored, then the cylinder glaze can be removed with a ball hone. When removing cylinder glaze with a ball hone, use a light or penetrating type oil to lubricate the hone. Do not allow the hone to run dry as this may cause excessive scoring of the cylinder bores and wear on the hone. If new pistons are required, they will need to be installed to the connecting rods. This should be performed by a machine shop as the pistons must be installed in the correct relationship to the rod or engine damage can occur.

Pistons and Connecting Rods

♦ See Figure 154

Only pistons with the wrist pin retained by C-clips are serviceable by the home-mechanic. Press fit pistons require special presses and/or heaters to remove/install the connecting rod and should only be performed by a machine shop.

All pistons will have a mark indicating the direction to the front of the engine and the must be installed into the engine in that manner. Usually it is a notch or arrow on the top of the piston, or it may be the letter F cast or stamped into the piston.

Fig. 152 Measure the piston's outer diameter, perpendicular to the wrist pin, with a micrometer

Fig. 153 Use a ball type cylinder hone to remove any glaze and provide a new surface for seating the piston rings

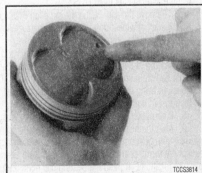

Fig. 154 Most pistons are marked to indicate positioning in the engine (usually a mark means the side facing the front)

C-CLIP TYPE PISTONS

1. Note the location of the forward mark on the piston and mark the connecting rod in relation.
2. Remove the C-clips from the piston and withdraw the wrist pin.

➡ **Varnish build-up or C-clip groove burrs may increase the difficulty of removing the wrist pin. If necessary, use a punch or drift to carefully tap the wrist pin out.**

3. Insure that the wrist pin bushing in the connecting rod is usable, and lubricate it with assembly lube.
4. Remove the wrist pin from the new piston and lubricate the pin bores on the piston.
5. Align the forward marks on the piston and the connecting rod and install the wrist pin.
6. The new C-clips will have a flat and a rounded side to them. Install both C-clips with the flat side facing out.
7. Repeat all of the steps for each piston being replaced.

ASSEMBLY

Before you begin assembling the engine, first give yourself a clean, dirt free work area. Next, clean every engine component again. The key to a good assembly is cleanliness.

Mount the engine block into the engine stand and wash it one last time using water and detergent (dishwashing detergent works well). While washing it, scrub the cylinder bores with a soft bristle brush and thoroughly clean all of the oil passages. Completely dry the engine and spray the entire assembly down with an anti-rust solution such as WD-40® or similar product. Take a clean lint-free rag and wipe up any excess anti-rust solution from the bores, bearing saddles, etc. Repeat the final cleaning process on the crankshaft. Replace any freeze or oil galley plugs which were removed during disassembly.

Crankshaft

♦ **See Figures 155, 156, 157 and 158**

1. Remove the main bearing inserts from the block and bearing caps.
2. If the crankshaft main bearing journals have been refinished to a definite undersize, install the correct undersize bearing. Be sure that the bearing inserts and bearing bores are clean. Foreign material under inserts will distort bearing and cause failure.
3. Place the upper main bearing inserts in bores with tang in slot.

➡ **The oil holes in the bearing inserts must be aligned with the oil holes in the cylinder block.**

4. Install the lower main bearing inserts in bearing caps.
5. Clean the mating surfaces of block and rear main bearing cap.
6. Carefully lower the crankshaft into place. Be careful not to damage bearing surfaces.
7. Check the clearance of each main bearing by using the following procedure:
    a. Place a piece of Plastigage® or its equivalent, on bearing surface across full width of bearing cap and about ¼ in. off center.
    b. Install cap and tighten bolts to specifications. Do not turn crankshaft while Plastigage® is in place.
    c. Remove the cap. Using the supplied Plastigage® scale, check width of Plastigage® at widest point to get maximum clearance. Difference between readings is taper of journal.
    d. If clearance exceeds specified limits, try a 0.001 in. or 0.002 in. undersize bearing in combination with the standard bearing. Bearing clearance must be within specified limits. If standard and 0.002 in. undersize bearing does not bring clearance within desired limits, refinish crankshaft journal, then install undersize bearings.
8. If equipped with a rope or two-piece rear main seal, Install it now.
9. After the bearings have been fitted, apply a light coat of engine oil to the journals and bearings. Install the rear main bearing cap. Install all bearing caps except the thrust bearing cap. Be sure that main bearing caps are installed in original locations. Tighten the bearing cap bolts to specifications.
10. Install the thrust bearing cap with bolts finger-tight.
11. Pry the crankshaft forward against the thrust surface of upper half of bearing.

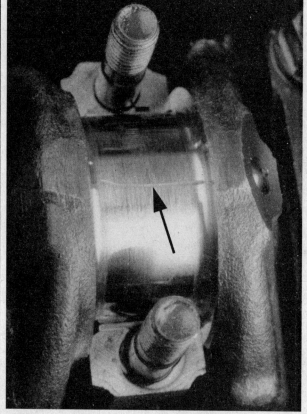

TCCS3243

Fig. 155 Apply a strip of gauging material to the bearing journal, then install and torque the cap

12. Hold the crankshaft forward and pry the thrust bearing cap to the rear. This aligns the thrust surfaces of both halves of the bearing.
13. Retain the forward pressure on the crankshaft. Tighten the cap bolts to specifications.
14. Measure the crankshaft end-play as follows:
    a. Mount a dial gauge to the engine block and position the tip of the gauge to read from the crankshaft end.
    b. Carefully pry the crankshaft toward the rear of the engine and hold it there while you zero the gauge.
    c. Carefully pry the crankshaft toward the front of the engine and read the gauge.
    d. Confirm that the reading is within specifications. If not, install a new thrust bearing and repeat the procedure. If the reading is still out of specifications with a new bearing, have a machine shop inspect the thrust surfaces of the crankshaft, and if possible, repair it.
15. If equipped with a one-piece rear main seal, install it now.
16. Rotate the crankshaft so as to position the first rod journal to the bottom of its stroke.

Pistons and Connecting Rods

♦ **See Figures 159 thru 164**

1. Before installing the piston/connecting rod assembly, oil the pistons, piston rings and the cylinder walls with light engine oil. Install connecting rod bolt protectors or rubber hose onto the connecting rod bolts/studs. Also perform the following:
    a. Select the proper ring set for the size cylinder bore.
    b. Position the ring in the bore in which it is going to be used.
    c. Push the ring down into the bore area where normal ring wear is not encountered.
    d. Use the head of the piston to position the ring in the bore so that the ring is square with the cylinder wall. Use caution to avoid damage to the ring or cylinder bore.

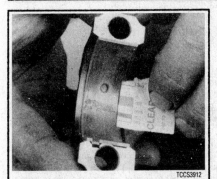

Fig. 156 After the cap is removed again, use the scale supplied with the gauging material to check the clearance

Fig. 157 A dial gauge may be used to check crankshaft end-play

Fig. 158 Carefully pry the crankshaft back and forth while reading the dial gauge for end-play

Fig. 159 Install the pistons with the notch facing forward and the oil bearing tang slots facing the opposite side of the camshaft

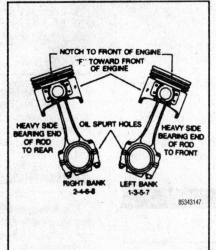

Fig. 160 Piston-to-rod relationship; V6 & V8 engines

Fig. 161 Checking the piston ring-to-ring groove side clearance using the ring and a feeler gauge

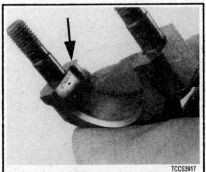

Fig. 162 The notch on the side of the bearing cap matches the tang on the bearing insert

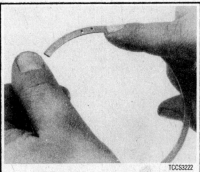

Fig. 163 Most rings are marked to show which side of the ring should face up when installed to the piston

Fig. 164 Install the piston and rod assembly into the block using a ring compressor and the handle of a hammer

e. Measure the gap between the ends of the ring with a feeler gauge. Ring gap in a worn cylinder is normally greater than specification. If the ring gap is greater than the specified limits, try an oversize ring set.

f. Check the ring side clearance of the compression rings with a feeler gauge inserted between the ring and its lower land according to specification. The gauge should slide freely around the entire ring circumference without binding. Any wear that occurs will form a step at the inner portion of the lower land. If the lower lands have high steps, the piston should be replaced.

2. Unless new pistons are installed, be sure to install the pistons in the cylinders from which they were removed. The numbers on the connecting rod and bearing cap must be on the same side when installed in the cylinder bore. If a connecting rod is ever transposed from one engine or cylinder to another, new bearings should be fitted and the connecting rod should be numbered to correspond with the new cylinder number. The notch on the piston head goes toward the front of the engine.

3. Install all of the rod bearing inserts into the rods and caps.

4. Install the rings to the pistons. Install the oil control ring first, then the second compression ring and finally the top compression ring. Use a piston ring expander tool to aid in installation and to help reduce the chance of breakage.

5. Make sure the ring gaps are properly spaced around the circumference of the piston. Fit a piston ring compressor around the piston and slide the piston and connecting rod assembly down into the cylinder bore, pushing it in with

the wooden hammer handle. Push the piston down until it is only slightly below the top of the cylinder bore. Guide the connecting rod onto the crankshaft bearing journal carefully, to avoid damaging the crankshaft.

6. Check the bearing clearance of all the rod bearings, fitting them to the crankshaft bearing journals. Follow the procedure in the crankshaft installation above.

7. After the bearings have been fitted, apply a light coating of assembly oil to the journals and bearings.

8. Turn the crankshaft until the appropriate bearing journal is at the bottom of its stroke, then push the piston assembly all the way down until the connecting rod bearing seats on the crankshaft journal. Be careful not to allow the bearing cap screws to strike the crankshaft bearing journals and damage them.

9. After the piston and connecting rod assemblies have been installed, check the connecting rod side clearance on each crankshaft journal.

10. Prime and install the oil pump and the oil pump intake tube.

Camshaft, Lifters And Timing Assembly

1. Install the camshaft.
2. Install the lifters/followers into their bores.
3. Install the timing gears/chain assembly.

Cylinder Head(s)

1. Install the cylinder head(s) using new gaskets.
2. Assemble the rest of the valve train (pushrods and rocker arms and/or shafts).

Engine Covers and Components

Install the timing cover(s) and oil pan. Refer to your notes and drawings made prior to disassembly and install all of the components that were removed. Install the engine into the vehicle.

Engine Start-up and Break-in

STARTING THE ENGINE

Now that the engine is installed and every wire and hose is properly connected, go back and double check that all coolant and vacuum hoses are con-

nected. Check that you oil drain plug is installed and properly tightened. If not already done, install a new oil filter onto the engine. Fill the crankcase with the proper amount and grade of engine oil. Fill the cooling system with a 50/50 mixture of coolant/water.

1. Connect the vehicle battery.
2. Start the engine. Keep your eye on your oil pressure indicator; if it does not indicate oil pressure within 10 seconds of starting, turn the vehicle off.

✳✳ WARNING

Damage to the engine can result if it is allowed to run with no oil pressure. Check the engine oil level to make sure that it is full. Check for any leaks and if found, repair the leaks before continuing. If there is still no indication of oil pressure, you may need to prime the system.

3. Confirm that there are no fluid leaks (oil or other).
4. Allow the engine to reach normal operating temperature (the upper radiator hose will be hot to the touch).
5. If necessary, set the ignition timing.
6. Install any remaining components such as the air cleaner (if removed for ignition timing) or body panels which were removed.

BREAKING IT IN

Make the first miles on the new engine, easy ones. Vary the speed but do not accelerate hard. Most importantly, do not lug the engine, and avoid sustained high speeds until at least 100 miles. Check the engine oil and coolant levels frequently. Expect the engine to use a little oil until the rings seat. Change the oil and filter at 500 miles, 1500 miles, then every 3000 miles past that.

KEEP IT MAINTAINED

Now that you have just gone through all of that hard work, keep yourself from doing it all over again by thoroughly maintaining it. Not that you may not have maintained it before, heck you could have had one to two hundred thousand miles on it before doing this. However, you may have bought the vehicle used, and the previous owner did not keep up on maintenance. Which is why you just went through all of that hard work. See?

ENGINE MECHANICAL SPECIFICATIONS

Component	U.S.	Metric
Bore × Stroke		
2.5L	4.0000 in. × 3.0000 in.	101.6mm × 76.2mm
2.8L	3.5039 in. × 2.9921 in.	89.0mm × 76.0mm
3.1L	3.5030 in. × 3.3122 in.	88.9mm × 84.1mm
3.4L	3.6220 in. × 3.3122 in.	91.9mm × 84.1mm
5.0L	3.7360 in. × 3.4800 in.	94.9mm × 88.4mm
5.7L	4.0000 in. × 3.4800 in.	101.6mm × 88.4mm
Displacement		
2.5L	150.8 cu. in.	2471.1 cc
2.8L	173.1 cu. in.	2836.8 cc
3.1L	191.5 cu. in.	3138.6 cc
3.4L	204.8 cu. in.	3355.5 cc
5.0L	305.2 cu. in.	5001.2 cc
5.7L	349.8 cu. in.	5732.9 cc
Camshaft bearing ID		
2.5L	1.8697-1.8717 in.	47.4904-47.5411mm
2.8L	1.8687-1.8737 in.	47.4660-47.5910mm
3.4L	1.8710-1.8720 in.	47.5230-47.5490mm
Camshaft end-play		
2.5L	0.0015-0.0050 in.	0.0381-0.1270mm
5.0L	0.0040-0.0120 in.	0.1016-0.3048mm
5.7L	0.0040-0.0120 in.	0.1016-0.3048mm
Camshaft journal-to-bearing clearance		
2.5L	0.0007-0.0027 in.	0.0178-0.0686mm
2.8L	0.0010-0.0040 in.	0.0254-0.1016mm
3.1L	0.0010-0.0040 in.	0.0254-0.1016mm
3.4L	0.0010-0.0040 in.	0.0254-0.1016mm
Camshaft journal diameter		
2.5L	1.8690 in.	47.4726mm
2.8L	1.8677-1.8697 in.	47.4400-47.4900mm
3.1L	1.8677-1.8697 in.	47.4400-47.4900mm
3.4L	1.8710-1.8720 in.	47.5230-47.5490mm
5.0L	1.8682-1.8692 in.	47.4523-47.4777mm
5.7L	1.8682-1.8692 in.	47.4523-47.4777mm
Camshaft lobe lift		
2.5L		
Intake	0.3980 in.	10.3124mm
Exhaust	0.3980 in.	10.3124mm
2.8L		
1982-84		
Intake	0.2311 in.	5.8700mm
Exhaust	0.2626 in.	6.6700mm
1985-89		
Intake	0.2626 in.	6.6700mm
Exhaust	0.2732 in.	6.9400mm
3.1L		
Intake	0.2626 in.	6.6700mm
Exhaust	0.2732 in.	6.9400mm
3.4L		
Intake	0.2626 in.	6.6700mm
Exhaust	0.2732 in.	6.9400mm

82603C00

ENGINE MECHANICAL SPECIFICATIONS

Component	U.S.	Metric
5.0L		
1982		
Intake		
LU5	0.2600 in.	6.6040mm
LG4	0.2380 in.	6.0452mm
Exhaust		
LU5	0.2730 in.	6.9342mm
LG4	0.2600 in.	6.6040mm
1983-84		
Intake		
L69	0.2690 in.	6.8326mm
LG4	0.2380 in.	6.0452mm
Exhaust		
L69	0.2760 in.	7.0104mm
LG4	0.2600 in.	6.6040mm
1985		
Intake		
LG4	0.2690 in.	6.8326mm
LB9	0.2340 in.	5.9436mm
Exhaust		
L69	0.2760 in.	7.0104mm
LG4	0.2570 in.	6.5278mm
LB9	0.2760 in.	7.0104mm
1986		
Intake		
L69	0.2690 in.	6.8326mm
LG4	0.2340 in.	5.9436mm
LB9	0.2690 in.	6.8326mm
Exhaust		
L69	0.2760 in.	7.0104mm
LG4	0.2570 in.	6.5278mm
LB9	0.2760 in.	7.0104mm
1987		
Intake		
LG4	0.2340 in.	5.9436mm
LB9	0.2690 in.	6.8326mm
Exhaust		
LG4	0.2570 in.	6.5278mm
LB9	0.2760 in.	7.0104mm
1988-90		
Intake		
L03	0.2340 in.	5.9436mm
LB9	0.2690 in.	6.8326mm
Exhaust		
L03	0.2570 in.	6.5278mm
LB9	0.2760 in.	7.0104mm
1991-92		
Intake		
L03	0.2340 in.	5.9436mm
LB9	0.2750 in.	6.9850mm
Exhaust		
L03	0.2570 in.	6.5278mm
LB9	0.2850 in.	7.2390mm

82603C0A

ENGINE MECHANICAL SPECIFICATIONS

Component	U.S.	Metric
5.7L		
1986-90		
Intake	0.2730 in.	6.9342mm
Exhaust	0.2820 in.	7.1628mm
1991-92		
Intake	0.2750 in.	6.9850mm
Exhaust	0.2850 in.	7.2390mm
1993-94		
Intake	0.3000 in.	7.6200mm
Exhaust	0.3000 in.	7.6200mm
Connecting rod bearing bore ID		
2.5L	2.0005-2.0026 in.	50.8127-50.8660mm
2.8L		
1982-84	2.0008-2.0020 in.	50.8200-50.8500mm
1985-89	2.0007-2.0021 in.	50.8190-50.8530mm
3.1L	1.9997-2.0030 in.	50.7924-50.8762mm
3.4L	1.9998-2.0026 in.	50.7949-50.8660mm
5.0L	2.1006-2.1028 in.	53.3552-53.4111mm
5.7L		
1986-92	2.1006-2.1028 in.	53.3552-53.4111mm
1993-94	2.0906-2.1033 in.	53.1012-53.4238mm
Connecting rod lower end bearing clearance		
2.5L	0.0005-0.0026 in.	0.0127-0.0660mm
2.8L		
1982-84	0.0014-0.0036 in.	0.0360-0.0910mm
1985-89	0.0014-0.0037 in.	0.0350-0.0950mm
3.1L		
1990	0.0014-0.0036 in.	0.0350-0.0930mm
1991-92	0.0011-0.0033 in.	0.0279-0.0838mm
3.4L	0.0011-0.0032 in.	0.0279-0.0813mm
5.0L		
1982-85	0.0020-0.0030 in.	0.0508-0.0762mm
1986-89	0.0018-0.0039 in.	0.0457-0.0991mm
1990-92	0.0013-0.0035 in.	0.0330-0.0889mm
5.7L	0.0013-0.0035 in.	0.0330-0.0889mm
Connecting rod-to-crankshaft side clearance		
2.5L	0.0060-0.0220 in.	0.1524-0.5588mm
2.8L	0.0063-0.0173 in.	0.1600-0.4400mm
3.1L		
1990	0.0140-0.0270 in.	0.3556-0.6858mm
1991	0.0140-0.0290 in.	0.3556-0.7366mm
1992	0.0080-0.0170 in.	0.2932-0.4400mm
3.4L	0.0070-0.0170 in.	0.1778-0.4400mm
5.0L		
1982-89	0.0080-0.0140 in.	0.2032-0.3556mm
1990-92	0.0060-0.0140 in.	0.1524-0.3556mm
5.7L	0.0060-0.0140 in.	0.1524-0.3556mm

82603C0B

ENGINE MECHANICAL SPECIFICATIONS

Component	U.S.	Metric
Connecting rod journal diameter		
2.5L	2.0000 in.	50.8000mm
2.8L	1.9983-1.9994 in.	50.7840-50.7580mm
3.1L	1.9983-1.9994 in.	50.7840-50.7580mm
3.4L	1.9987-1.9994 in.	50.7670-50.7580mm
5.0L		
1982-89	2.0986-2.0998 in.	53.3044-53.3350mm
1990-92	2.0893-2.0998 in.	53.0682-53.3349mm
5.7L		
1986-89	2.0986-2.0998 in.	53.3044-53.3350mm
1990-94	2.0893-2.0998 in.	53.0682-53.3349mm
Connecting rod journal taper (max.)		
2.5L	0.0005 in.	0.0127mm
2.8L	0.0002 in.	0.0050mm
3.1L	0.0002 in.	0.0050mm
3.4L	0.0002 in.	0.0050mm
5.0L	0.0010 in.	0.0254mm
5.7L	0.0010 in.	0.0254mm
Crankshaft end-play		
2.8L		
1982-85	0.0035-0.0085 in.	0.0889-0.2159mm
1986-89	0.0020-0.0067 in.	0.0500-0.1700mm
3.1L	0.0024-0.0087 in.	0.0600-0.2209mm
3.4L	0.0024-0.0083 in.	0.0600-0.2108mm
5.0L		
1982-89	0.0024-0.0083 in.	0.0600-0.2108mm
1990-92	0.0020-0.0060 in.	0.0500-0.1524mm
5.7L		
1986-89	0.0010-0.0070 in.	0.0254-0.1778mm
1990-94	0.0010-0.0070 in.	0.0254-0.1778mm
Cylinder bore diameter		
2.5L	4.0000 in.	101.6mm
2.8L	3.5036-3.5067 in.	88.9920-89.0700mm
3.1L	3.5046-3.5053 in.	89.0168-89.0346mm
3.4L	3.6228-3.6235 in.	92.0190-92.0369mm
5.0L	3.7350-3.7385 in.	94.8690-94.9579mm
5.7L	3.9995-4.0026 in.	101.5873-101.6635mm
Cylinder bore max. taper		
2.5L	0.0005 in.	0.0127mm
2.8L	0.0008 in.	0.0200mm
3.1L	0.0005 in.	0.0127mm
3.4L	0.0003 in.	0.0076mm
5.0L	0.0010 in.	0.0254mm
5.7L	0.0010 in.	0.0254mm
Cylinder bore out-of-round (max.)		
2.5L		
1982	0.0014 in.	0.0356mm
1983-86	0.0010 in.	0.0254mm
2.8L	0.0008 in.	0.0200mm
3.1L	0.0005 in.	0.0127mm
3.4L	0.0003 in.	0.0076mm
5.0L	0.0020 in.	0.0508mm
5.7L	0.0020 in.	0.0508mm

82603C0C

ENGINE MECHANICAL SPECIFICATIONS

Component	U.S.	Metric
Main bearing bore diameter		
2.5L	2.3005–2.3022 in.	58.4327–58.4759mm
2.8L		
1982–84	2.4954–2.4976 in.	63.3840–63.4400mm
1985–89	2.6489–2.6514 in.	67.2820–67.3460mm
3.1L	2.6485–2.6510 in.	67.2719–67.3354mm
3.4L		
5.0L	2.6485–2.6513 in.	67.2719–67.3430mm
No. 1	2.4492–2.4513 in.	62.2097–62.2630mm
Nos. 2, 3, 4	2.4491–2.4510 in.	62.2071–62.2554mm
No. 5	2.4504–2.4518 in.	62.2402–62.2757mm
5.7L		
No. 1	2.4492–2.4513 in.	62.2097–62.2630mm
Nos. 2, 3, 4	2.4491–2.4510 in.	62.2071–62.2554mm
No. 5	2.4504–2.4518 in.	62.2402–62.2757mm
Main bearing clearance		
2.5L	0.0005–0.0022 in.	0.0127–0.0559mm
2.8L		
1982–84	0.0017–0.0030 in.	0.0440–0.0760mm
1985–86	0.0021–0.0033 in.	0.0540–0.0840mm
1987–89	0.0016–0.0032 in.	0.0410–0.0810mm
3.1L		
1990	0.0012–0.0027 in.	0.0302–0.0686mm
1991–92	0.0012–0.0030 in.	0.0302–0.0760mm
3.4L	0.0012–0.0030 in.	0.0302–0.0760mm
5.0L		
1982–88		
No. 1	0.0010–0.0015 in.	0.0254–0.0381mm
Nos. 2, 3, 4	0.0010–0.0020 in.	0.0254–0.0508mm
No. 5	0.0025–0.0030 in.	0.0635–0.0762mm
1989–92		
No. 1	0.0010–0.0015 in.	0.0254–0.0381mm
Nos. 2, 3, 4	0.0010–0.0025 in.	0.0254–0.0635mm
No. 5	0.0025–0.0035 in.	0.0635–0.0889mm
5.7L		
1986–88		
No. 1	0.0010–0.0015 in.	0.0254–0.0381mm
Nos. 2, 3, 4	0.0010–0.0020 in.	0.0254–0.0508mm
No. 5	0.0025–0.0030 in.	0.0635–0.0762mm
1989–94		
No. 1	0.0010–0.0015 in.	0.0254–0.0381mm
Nos. 2, 3, 4	0.0010–0.0025 in.	0.0254–0.0635mm
No. 5	0.0025–0.0035 in.	0.0635–0.0889mm
Main bearing journal diameter		
2.5L	2.3000 in.	59.1820mm
2.8L		
1982	2.4937–2.4946 in.	63.3400–63.3640mm
1983–84		
LE2 and LH7	2.4937–2.4946 in.	63.3400–63.3640mm
LL1 and LC1		
Nos. 1, 2, 4	2.4937–2.4946 in.	63.3400–63.3640mm
No. 3	2.4930–2.4941 in.	63.3220–63.3510mm
1985–89	2.6473–2.6482 in.	67.2410–67.2650mm
3.1L	2.6473–2.6482 in.	67.2410–67.2650mm
3.4L	2.6473–2.6483 in.	67.2410–67.2668mm

82603C0D

ENGINE MECHANICAL SPECIFICATIONS

Component	U.S.	Metric
5.0L		
No. 1	2.6473–2.6483 in.	67.2410–67.2668mm
Nos. 2, 3, 4	2.4484–2.4493 in.	62.1894–62.2122mm
No. 5	2.4481–2.4490 in.	62.1817–62.2046mm
5.7L		
No. 1	2.4479–2.4488 in.	62.1766–62.1995mm
Nos. 2, 3, 4	2.4484–2.4493 in.	62.1894–62.2122mm
No. 5	2.4481–2.4490 in.	62.1817–62.2046mm
	2.4479–2.4488 in.	62.1766–62.1995mm
Main bearing journal runout (max.)		
2.5L	0.0005 in.	0.0127mm
2.8L	0.0002 in.	0.0050mm
3.1L	0.0002 in.	0.0050mm
3.4L	0.0002 in.	0.0050mm
5.0L	0.0010 in.	0.0254mm
5.7L	0.0010 in.	0.0254mm
Main bearing journal taper (max.)		
2.5L	0.0005 in.	0.0127mm
2.8L	0.0002 in.	0.0050mm
3.1L	0.0002 in.	0.0050mm
3.4L	0.0002 in.	0.0050mm
5.0L	0.0010 in.	0.0254mm
5.7L	0.0010 in.	0.0254mm
Oil pump gear backlash		
2.5L	0.0090–0.0150 in.	0.2286–0.3810mm
2.8L	0.0037–0.0077 in.	0.0940–0.1956mm
3.1L		
3.4L	0.0004–0.0007 in.	0.0102–0.0178mm
5.0L	0.0004–0.0007 in.	0.0102–0.0178mm
5.7L		
Oil pump gear diameter		
2.5L	1.4960–1.5000 in.	37.9984–38.1000mm
2.8L	1.4980–1.5000 in.	38.0500–38.1000mm
3.4L	1.4980–1.5000 in.	38.0500–38.1000mm
5.0L	1.5290–1.5310 in.	38.8366–38.8874mm
5.7L	1.5290–1.5310 in.	38.366–38.8874mm
Oil pump gear length		
2.5L	0.9990–1.0020 in.	25.3746–25.4508mm
2.8L	1.1988–1.2000 in.	30.4800–30.4500mm
3.4L	1.1988–1.2000 in.	30.4800–30.4500mm
5.0L	1.5075–1.5095 in.	38.2905–38.3413mm
5.7L	1.5075–1.5095 in.	38.2905–38.3413mm
Oil pump gear side clearance		
2.5L	0.0040 in. max.	0.1016mm max.
2.8L	0.0031–0.0039 in.	0.0800–0.1000mm
3.4L	0.0031–0.0039 in.	0.0800–0.1000mm
5.0L	0.0015–0.0045 in.	0.0381–0.1143mm
5.7L	0.0015–0.0045 in.	0.0381–0.1143mm

82603C0E

ENGINE MECHANICAL SPECIFICATIONS

Component	U.S.	Metric
Oil pump gear end clearance		
2.5L	0.0020-0.0051 in.	0.0500-0.1300mm
2.8L	0.0020-0.0051 in.	0.0500-0.1300mm
3.4L	0.0020-0.0060 in.	0.0500-0.1524mm
5.0L	0.0015-0.0085 in.	0.0381-0.2159mm
5.7L	0.0015-0.0085 in.	0.0381-0.2159mm
Oil pump gear pocket depth		
2.5L	0.9950-0.9980 in.	25.2730-25.3492mm
2.8L	1.1953-1.1984 in.	30.3600-30.4400mm
3.4L	1.2029-1.2051 in.	30.5131-30.6100mm
5.0L	1.5010-1.5060 in.	38.1254-38.2524mm
5.7L	1.5010-1.5060 in.	38.1254-38.2524mm
Oil pump gear pocket diameter		
2.5L	1.5031-1.5059 in.	38.1800-38.2500mm
2.8L	1.5031-1.5059 in.	38.1800-38.2500mm
3.4L	1.5040-1.5059 in.	38.2016-38.2500mm
5.0L	1.5340-1.5390 in.	38.9636-39.0906mm
5.7L	1.5340-1.5390 in.	38.9636-39.0906mm
Oil pump relief valve-to-housing clearance		
2.8L	0.0015-0.0035 in.	0.0380-0.0890mm
3.4L	0.0015-0.0035 in.	0.0380-0.0890mm
5.0L	0.0025-0.0050 in.	0.0635-0.1270mm
5.7L	0.0025-0.0050 in.	0.0635-0.1270mm
Piston diameter (centerline)		
2.5L		
1982-84	3.9971-3.9975 in.	101.5260-101.5360mm
1985-86	3.9986-3.9973 in.	101.5644-101.5441mm
2.8L		
1982-84	3.4990-3.5040 in.	88.8750-89.0010mm
1985-89	3.4656-3.5030 in.	88.0270-88.9750mm
3.1L	3.5024-3.5034 in.	88.9610-88.9864mm
3.4L	3.6211-3.6217 in.	91.9770-91.9920mm
5.0L		
1982	3.7357-3.7402 in.	94.8868-95.0011mm
1983-92	3.7323-3.7358 in.	94.8004-94.8893mm
5.7L	3.9970-3.9990 in.	101.5238-101.5746mm
Piston-to-bore or liner clearance		
2.5L		
1982-84	0.0025-0.0033 in.	0.0635-0.0838mm
1985-86	0.0015-0.0022 in.	0.0356-0.0559mm
2.8L		
1982-84	0.0017-0.0027 in.	0.0430-0.0690mm
1985-89	0.0007-0.0017 in.	0.0700-0.0430mm
3.1L		
1990-91	0.0012-0.0029 in.	0.0305-0.0737mm
1992	0.0012-0.0026 in.	0.0305-0.0660mm
3.4L	0.0011-0.0024 in.	0.0279-0.0690mm
5.0L		
1982-89	0.0007-0.0017 in.	0.0178-0.0432mm
1990-92	0.0007-0.0021 in.	0.0178-0.0533mm
5.7L		
1986-89	0.0025-0.0035 in.	0.0635-0.0889mm
1990-92	0.0007-0.0021 in.	0.0178-0.0533mm
1993-94	0.0010-0.0027 in.	0.0254-0.0686mm

82603C0F

ENGINE MECHANICAL SPECIFICATIONS

Component	U.S.	Metric
Piston pin bore diameter in piston		
2.5L	0.9383-0.9425 in.	23.8328-23.9395mm
2.8L	0.9055-0.9059 in.	23.0002-23.0106mm
3.1L	0.9056-0.9062 in.	23.0022-23.0175mm
3.4L	0.9057-0.9063 in.	23.0048-23.0200mm
5.0L	0.9273-0.9308 in.	23.5534-23.6423mm
5.7L		
1986-92	0.9273-0.9308 in.	23.5534-23.6423mm
1993-94	0.9275-0.9279 in.	23.5585-23.5687mm
Piston pin diameter		
2.5L	0.9380-0.9420 in.	23.8252-23.9268mm
2.8L	0.9053-0.9056 in.	22.9937-23.0015mm
3.1L	0.9052-0.9054 in.	22.9921-22.9972mm
3.4L	0.9052-0.9054 in.	22.9921-22.9972mm
5.0L	0.9270-0.9273 in.	23.5458-23.5534mm
5.7L		
1982-92	0.9270-0.9273 in.	23.5458-23.5534mm
1993-94	0.9270-0.9271 in.	23.5458-23.5483mm
Piston pin-to-piston bore clearance		
2.5L		
1982	0.0003-0.0005 in.	0.0076-0.0127mm
1983-86	0.0002-0.0004 in.	0.0051-0.0091mm
2.8L	0.0003-0.004 in.	0.0065-0.0091mm
3.1L		
1990-91	0.0004-0.0008 in.	0.0091-0.0203mm
1992	0.0002-0.0007 in.	0.0051-0.0178mm
3.4L	0.0005-0.0009 in.	0.0127-0.0229mm
5.0L		
1982-90	0.0003-0.0004 in.	0.0065-0.0091mm
1991-92	0.0002-0.0006 in.	0.0051-0.0152mm
5.7L		
1986-90	0.0003-0.0004 in.	0.0065-0.0091mm
1991-94	0.0005-0.0008 in.	0.0127-0.0203mm
Piston pin-to-rod clearance		
2.5L		press fit
2.8L		press fit
3.1L		press fit
3.4L		press fit
5.0L	0.0008-0.0016 in.	0.0203-0.0406mm
5.7L	0.0008-0.0016 in.	0.0203-0.0406mm
Piston ring end gap		
2.5L		
1982		
Top	0.0100-0.0220 in.	0.2540-0.5589mm
Middle	0.0100-0.0270 in.	0.2540-0.6858mm
Oil	0.0150-0.0550 in.	0.3810-1.3970mm
1983-86		
Top	0.0100-0.0200 in.	0.2540-0.5100mm
Middle	0.0100-0.0200 in.	0.2540-0.5100mm
Oil	0.0200-0.0600 in.	0.5100-1.5240mm

82603C0G

ENGINE MECHANICAL SPECIFICATIONS

Component			U.S.	Metric
2.8L				
	Top		0.0098–0.0197 in.	0.2500–0.5000mm
	Middle		0.0098–0.0197 in.	0.2500–0.5000mm
	Oil		0.0200–0.0551 in.	0.5100–1.4000mm
3.1L				
	1990			
		Top	0.0098–0.0197 in.	0.2500–0.5000mm
		Middle	0.0098–0.0197 in.	0.2500–0.5000mm
		Oil	0.0100–0.0300 in.	0.5100–0.7620mm
	1991			
		Top	0.0098–0.0197 in.	0.2500–0.5000mm
		Middle	0.0200–0.0280 in.	0.5100–0.7112mm
		Oil	0.0100–0.0300 in.	0.2540–0.7620mm
	1992			
		Top	0.0070–0.0160 in.	0.1778–0.4064mm
		Middle	0.0200–0.0280 in.	0.5100–0.7112mm
		Oil	0.0100–0.0300 in.	0.2540–0.7620mm
3.4L				
	Top		0.0070–0.0160 in.	0.1800–0.4100mm
	Middle		0.0190–0.0290 in.	0.4800–0.7400mm
	Oil		0.0100–0.0300 in.	0.2540–0.7620mm
5.0L				
	1982			
		Top	0.0100–0.0200 in.	0.2540–0.5589mm
		Middle	0.0150–0.0250 in.	0.2540–0.6350mm
		Oil	0.0150–0.0550 in.	0.3810–1.3970mm
	1983–84			
		Top	0.0100–0.0200 in.	0.2540–0.5589mm
		Middle	0.0100–0.0200 in.	0.2540–0.5589mm
		Oil	0.0150–0.0550 in.	0.3810–1.3970mm
	1985–90			
		Top	0.0100–0.0200 in.	0.2540–0.5589mm
		Middle	0.0100–0.0250 in.	0.2540–0.6350mm
		Oil	0.0150–0.0550 in.	0.3810–1.3970mm
	1991			
		Top	0.0100–0.0200 in.	0.2540–0.5589mm
		Middle	0.0100–0.0250 in.	0.2540–0.6350mm
		Oil	0.0100–0.0300 in.	0.2540–0.7620mm
	1992			
		Top	0.0100–0.0200 in.	0.2540–0.5589mm
		Middle	0.0180–0.0260 in.	0.4572–0.6604mm
		Oil	0.0100–0.0300 in.	0.2540–0.7620mm
5.7L				
	1986–90			
		Top	0.0100–0.0200 in.	0.2540–0.5589mm
		Middle	0.0100–0.0200 in.	0.2540–0.6350mm
		Oil	0.0150–0.0550 in.	0.3810–1.3970mm
	1991–94			
		Top	0.0100–0.0200 in.	0.2540–0.5589mm
		Middle	0.0180–0.0260 in.	0.4572–0.6604mm
		Oil	0.0100–0.0300 in.	0.2540–0.7620mm

82603C0H

ENGINE MECHANICAL SPECIFICATIONS

Component			U.S.	Metric
Piston ring side clearance				
2.5L				
	1982			
		Top	0.0015–0.0030 in.	0.0381–0.0762mm
		Middle	0.0015–0.0030 in.	0.0381–0.0762mm
		Oil	snug	
	1983–86			
		Top	0.0020–0.0030 in.	0.0510–0.0762mm
		Middle	0.0010–0.0030 in.	0.0254–0.0762mm
		Oil	0.0150–0.0550 in.	0.3810–1.3970mm
2.8L				
	1982			
		Top	0.0012–0.0028 in.	0.0300–0.0700mm
		Middle	0.0016–0.0037 in.	0.0400–0.0950mm
		Oil	0.0078 in. max.	0.1990mm max.
	1983–84			
		Top	0.0012–0.0031 in.	0.0300–0.0800mm
		Middle	0.0012–0.0031 in.	0.0300–0.0800mm
		Oil	0.0078 in. max.	0.1990mm max.
	1985–89			
		Top	0.0012–0.0028 in.	0.0300–0.0700mm
		Middle	0.0016–0.0037 in.	0.0400–0.0950mm
		Oil	0.0078 in. max.	0.1990mm max.
3.1L				
	Top		0.0020–0.0035 in.	0.0508–0.0889mm
	Middle		0.0020–0.0035 in.	0.0508–0.0889mm
	Oil		0.0078 in. max.	0.1990mm max.
3.4L				
	Top		0.0020–0.0035 in.	0.0508–0.0889mm
	Middle		0.0020–0.0035 in.	0.0508–0.0889mm
	Oil		0.0078 in. max.	0.1990mm max.
5.0L				
	Top		0.0012–0.0032 in.	0.0300–0.0813mm
	Middle		0.0012–0.0032 in.	0.0300–0.0813mm
	Oil		0.0020–0.0070 in.	0.0508–0.1778mm
5.7L				
	Top		0.0012–0.0032 in.	0.0300–0.0813mm
	Middle		0.0012–0.0032 in.	0.0300–0.0813mm
	Oil		0.0020–0.0070 in.	0.0508–0.1778mm
Rocker arm lift ratio				
	2.5L		1.75:1	
	2.8L		1.50:1	
	3.1L		1.50:1	
	3.4L		1.50:1	
	5.0L		1.50:1	
	5.7L		1.50:1	
Valve face angle				
	2.5L		45 degrees	
	2.8L		45 degrees	
	3.1L		45 degrees	
	3.4L		45 degrees	
	5.0L		45 degrees	
	5.7L		45 degrees	

82603C0I

ENGINE MECHANICAL SPECIFICATIONS

Component	U.S.	Metric
Valve face minimum margin		
All engines	0.03125 in.	0.7938mm
Valve seat angle		
2.5L	46 degrees	
3.1L	46 degrees	
3.4L	46 degrees	
5.0L	46 degrees	
5.7L	46 degrees	
Valve seat runout (max.)		
2.8L	0.0020 in.	0.0500mm
3.1L	0.0020 in.	0.0500mm
3.4L	0.0010 in.	0.0254mm
5.0L	0.0020 in.	0.0500mm
5.7L	0.0020 in.	0.0500mm
Valve seat width		
2.5L		
Intake	0.0353-0.0747 in.	0.8966-1.8974mm
Exhaust	0.0580-0.0971 in.	1.4732-2.4663mm
2.8L		
Intake	0.0492-0.0591 in.	0.2500-1.5000mm
Exhaust	0.0630-0.0750 in.	1.6000-1.9000mm
3.1L		
Intake	0.0492-0.0591 in.	0.2500-1.5000mm
Exhaust	0.0630-0.0750 in.	1.6000-1.9000mm
3.4L		
Intake	0.0610-0.0730 in.	1.5494-1.8542mm
Exhaust	0.0670-0.0790 in.	1.7018-1.0066mm
5.0L		
Intake	0.0313-0.0625 in.	0.7938-1.5875mm
Exhaust	0.0625-0.0938 in.	1.5875-2.3813mm
5.7L		
1986-92		
Intake	0.0313-0.0625 in.	0.7938-1.5875mm
Exhaust	0.0625-0.0938 in.	1.5875-2.3813mm
1993-94		
Intake	0.0300-0.0500 in.	0.7620-1.2700mm
Exhaust	0.0600-0.0800 in.	1.5240-2.0320mm
Valve spring compression pressure		
2.5L		
1982-84	122-180 lbs. @ 1.254 in.	55-82 kg @ 31.85mm
1985-86	170-180 lbs. @ 1.260 in.	77-82 kg @ 32mm
3.1L	195 lbs. @ 1.18 in.	88 kg @ 30mm
1990	195 lbs. @ 1.181 in.	88 kg @ 30mm
1991-92	189 lbs. @ 1.200 in.	86 kg @ 30mm
3.4L	190 lbs. @ 1.200 in.	86 kg @ 30mm

82603CUU

ENGINE MECHANICAL SPECIFICATIONS

Component	U.S.	Metric
5.0L		
1982-85	194-206 lbs. @ 1.25 in.	88-93 kg @ 31.75mm
1986-92	194-206 lbs. @ 1.25 in.	88-93 kg @ 31.75mm
Intake	194-206 lbs. @ 1.25 in.	88-93 kg @ 31.75mm
Exhaust	194-206 lbs. @ 1.15 in.	88-93 kg @ 29.46mm
5.7L		
1986-92		
Intake	194-206 lbs. @ 1.25 in.	88-93 kg @ 31.75mm
Exhaust	194-206 lbs. @ 1.16 in.	88-93 kg @ 29.46mm
1993-94		
Intake	252-272 lbs. @ 1.31 in.	114-123 kg @ 33mm
Exhaust	252-272 lbs. @ 1.31 in.	114-123 kg @ 33mm
Valve spring free length (approx.)		
2.5L	2.0800 in.	52.8mm
2.8L	1.9094 in.	48.5mm
3.1L	1.9094 in.	48.5mm
3.4L	1.9094 in.	48.5mm
5.0L	2.0300 in.	51.6mm
5.7L		
1986-92	2.0300 in.	51.6mm
1993-94	2.0100 in.	51.1mm
Valve spring installed height		
2.5L		
1982	1.6600 in.	42.1640mm
1983-86	1.6900 in.	42.9260mm
2.8L	1.5748 in.	40.0000mm
3.1L		
1990	1.5748 in.	40.0000mm
1991-92	1.6100 in.	40.8940mm
3.4L	1.6100 in.	40.8940mm
5.0L		
1982-85	1.7188 in.	43.6563mm
1986-91		
Intake	1.5938 in.	40.4813mm
Exhaust	1.7000 in.	43.1800mm
1992		
5.7L		
1986-91		
Intake	1.7188 in.	43.6563mm
Exhaust	1.5938 in.	40.4813mm
1992	1.7000 in.	43.1800mm
1993-94	1.7800 in.	45.2120mm
Valve stem-to-guide clearance		
2.5L	0.0010-0.0027 in.	0.0254-0.6858mm
2.8L	0.0010-0.0027 in.	0.0260-0.0680mm
3.1L		
1990	0.0010-0.0027 in.	0.0260-0.0680mm
1991-92		
Intake	0.0014-0.0025 in.	0.0356-0.0635mm
Exhaust	0.0016-0.0029 in.	0.0406-0.0737mm
3.4L		
Intake	0.0014-0.0027 in.	0.0356-0.0680mm
Exhaust	0.0015-0.0029 in.	0.0381-0.0737mm
5.0L	0.0010-0.0027 in.	0.0260-0.0680mm
5.7L	0.0010-0.0027 in.	0.0260-0.0680mm

82603CJK

TORQUE SPECIFICATIONS

Component	U.S.	Metric
Alternator adjusting bolt	25 ft. lbs.	34 Nm
Alternator bracket-to-block or head		
2.8L	40 ft. lbs.	54 Nm
3.1L		
nut	18 ft. lbs.	25 Nm
bolt	37 ft. lbs.	50 Nm
Alternator pivot bolt	30 ft. lbs.	41 Nm
Camshaft position sensor	89 inch lbs.	10 Nm
Camshaft retainer plate		
All	9 ft. lbs.	12 Nm
Camshaft sprocket-to-camshaft		
2.8L		
1982–87	20 ft. lbs.	27 Nm
1988–89	25 ft. lbs.	35 Nm
3.1L	21 ft. lbs.	28 Nm
3.4L	18 ft. lbs.	25 Nm
5.0L		
1982–84	20 ft. lbs.	27 Nm
1985–88	23 ft. lbs.	31 Nm
1989–92	21 ft. lbs.	28 Nm
5.7L		
1986–88	23 ft. lbs.	31 Nm
1989–94	21 ft. lbs.	28 Nm
Camshaft thrust plate bolts		
2.5L		
1982–85	85 inch lbs.	9 Nm
1986	90 inch lbs.	10 Nm
Connecting rod nuts		
2.5L	32 ft. lbs.	44 Nm
2.8L		
1982–84	40 ft. lbs.	54 Nm
1985–89	45 ft. lbs.	60 Nm
3.1L	39 ft. lbs.	53 Nm
3.4L	37 ft. lbs.	50 Nm
5.0L	45 ft. lbs.	61 Nm
5.7L	45 ft. lbs.	61 Nm
Crankshaft pulley		
2.8L	30 ft. lbs.	41 Nm
3.1L	37 ft. lbs.	50 Nm
3.4L	37 ft. lbs.	50 Nm
5.0L, 5.7L	43 ft. lbs.	58 Nm
Cylinder head bolts		
2.5L		
1982–83		
Step 1	25 ft. lbs.	34 Nm
Step 2	50 ft. lbs.	68 Nm
Step 3	85 ft. lbs.	115 Nm
1984–85		
Step 1	30 ft. lbs.	40 Nm
Step 2	60 ft. lbs.	82 Nm
Step 3	92 ft. lbs.	125 Nm

86343C99

TORQUE SPECIFICATIONS

Component	U.S.	Metric
Cylinder head bolts		
1986		
Step 1	18 ft. lbs.	25 Nm
Step 2 exc. No. 9	22 ft. lbs.	30 Nm
No. 9	29 ft. lbs.	40 Nm
Step 3 exc. No. 9	+ 120 degree turn	
No. 9	+ 90 degree turn	
2.8L		
1982–84		
Step 1	25 ft. lbs.	34 Nm
Step 2	50 ft. lbs.	68 Nm
Step 3	75 ft. lbs.	102 Nm
1985–87		
Step 1	30 ft. lbs.	40 Nm
Step 2	60 ft. lbs.	82 Nm
Step 3	90 ft. lbs.	122 Nm
1988–89		
Step 1	40 ft. lbs.	55 Nm
Step 2	+ 90 turn	
3.1L		
Step 1	40 ft. lbs.	55 Nm
Step 2	+ 90 turn	
3.4L		
Step 1	40 ft. lbs.	55 Nm
Step 2	+ 90 turn	
5.0L		
1982–84		
Step 1	25 ft. lbs.	34 Nm
Step 2	50 ft. lbs.	68 Nm
Step 3	65 ft. lbs.	88 Nm
1985–88		
Step 1	25 ft. lbs.	34 Nm
Step 2	50 ft. lbs.	68 Nm
Step 3	75 ft. lbs.	102 Nm
1989–92		
Step 1	25 ft. lbs.	34 Nm
Step 2	50 ft. lbs.	68 Nm
Step 3	68 ft. lbs.	92 Nm
5.7L		
1986–88		
Step 1	25 ft. lbs.	34 Nm
Step 2	50 ft. lbs.	68 Nm
Step 3	75 ft. lbs.	102 Nm
1989–92		
Step 1	25 ft. lbs.	34 Nm
Step 2	50 ft. lbs.	68 Nm
Step 3	68 ft. lbs.	92 Nm
1993–94		
Step 1	25 ft. lbs.	34 Nm
Step 2	50 ft. lbs.	68 Nm
Step 3	65 ft. lbs.	88 Nm

85343G9A

TORQUE SPECIFICATIONS

Component	U.S.	Metric
Damper-to-crankshaft		
2.5L		
1982–83	160 ft. lbs.	212 Nm
1984–85	200 ft. lbs.	260 Nm
1986	162 ft. lbs.	220 Nm
2.8L	85 ft. lbs.	115 Nm
3.1L		
1990	76 ft. lbs.	103 Nm
1991–92	70 ft. lbs.	95 Nm
3.4L	58 ft. lbs.	79 Nm
5.0L		
1982–88	60 ft. lbs.	82 Nm
1989–92	70 ft. lbs.	95 Nm
5.7L		
1986–88	60 ft. lbs.	82 Nm
1989–92	70 ft. lbs.	95 Nm
Damper bolt		
1993–94	60 ft. lbs.	81 Nm
Damper hub bolts	75 ft. lbs.	102 Nm
Distributor clamp bolt		
2.5L		
1982–85	22 ft. lbs.	30 Nm
1986	15 ft. lbs.	20 Nm
2.8L	30 ft. lbs.	41 Nm
3.1L	25 ft. lbs.	34 Nm
5.0L		
1982–84	20 ft. lbs.	27 Nm
1985–92	35 ft. lbs.	48 Nm
5.7L		
1986–92	35 ft. lbs.	48 Nm
1993	100 inch lbs.	11 Nm
1994	9 ft. lbs.	12 Nm
Electric cooling fan-to-radiator support		
All	20 ft. lbs.	27 Nm
Engine fan clutch-to-water pump hub		
All	18 ft. lbs.	24 Nm
Engine front cover		
2.8L		
1982–84		
1.25	18 ft. lbs.	24 Nm
1.50	30 ft. lbs.	41 Nm
1985–89		
1.25 x 40	22 ft. lbs.	30 Nm
1.25 x 70	22 ft. lbs.	30 Nm
1.25 x 27	24 ft. lbs.	32 Nm
1.50 x 75	35 ft. lbs.	48 Nm
3.1L	15 ft. lbs.	21 Nm
3.4L	15 ft. lbs.	21 Nm

8534399B

TORQUE SPECIFICATIONS

Component	U.S.	Metric
Engine front cover		
5.0L		
1982–84	80 inch lbs.	9 Nm
1985	94 inch lbs.	11 Nm
1986–88	11 ft. lbs.	14 Nm
1989–92	8 ft. lbs.	11 Nm
5.7L		
1986–88	11 ft. lbs.	14 Nm
1989–92	8 ft. lbs.	11 Nm
1993–94	100 inch lbs.	11 Nm
3.4L		
Engine mounting bracket		
2.8L	92 ft. lbs.	125 Nm
5.0L, 5.7L	38 ft. lbs.	52 Nm
Engine mount nuts		
All	30 ft. lbs.	41 Nm
Engine mount through-bolts		
3.1L	50 ft. lbs.	68 Nm
3.4		
bolt	70 ft. lbs.	95 Nm
nut	59 ft. lbs.	80 Nm
5.0L, 5.7L		
1982–92	50 ft. lbs.	68 Nm
1993–94		
bolt	70 ft. lbs.	95 Nm
nut	59 ft. lbs.	80 Nm
Engine mount torque strut		
2.8L	40 ft. lbs.	54 Nm
Engine rear cover		
2.8L	9 ft. lbs.	12 Nm
3.1L	89 inch lbs.	10 Nm
3.4L	89 inch lbs.	10 Nm
Engine side cover		
2.5L	90 inch lbs.	10 Nm
Exhaust manifold-to-cylinder head		
2.5L		
1982–85	44 ft. lbs.	60 Nm
1986		
4 outer bolts	32 ft. lbs.	43 Nm
3 center bolts	37 ft. lbs.	50 Nm
2.8L		
1982–84	28 ft. lbs.	38 Nm
1985–89	31 ft. lbs.	42 Nm
3.1L	25 ft. lbs.	34 Nm
3.4L	18 ft. lbs.	25 Nm
5.0L		
1982–84	20 ft. lbs.	27 Nm
1985–88		
4 outer bolts	26 ft. lbs.	35 Nm
2 inner bolts	32 ft. lbs.	44 Nm
1988–92		
Center bolts	20 ft. lbs.	27 Nm
Outer	26 ft. lbs.	35 Nm

8534399C

TORQUE SPECIFICATIONS

Component	U.S.	Metric
Cylinder head bolts		
5.7L		
1986-88		
4 outer bolts	26 ft. lbs.	35 Nm
2 inner bolts	32 ft. lbs.	44 Nm
1988-92		
Center bolts	20 ft. lbs.	27 Nm
Outer	26 ft. lbs.	35 Nm
1993	26 ft. lbs.	35 Nm
1994	35 ft. lbs.	47 Nm
Flywheel-to-crankshaft		
2.5L		
1982-85	44 ft. lbs.	60 Nm
1986	55 ft. lbs.	75 Nm
2.8L		
1982-88		
Automatic	35 ft. lbs.	47 Nm
Manual	55 ft. lbs.	75 Nm
1989	59 ft. lbs.	80 Nm
3.1L	52 ft. lbs.	71 Nm
3.4L	61 ft. lbs.	83 Nm
5.0L		
1982-84	60 ft. lbs.	82 Nm
1985	70 ft. lbs.	95 Nm
1986-88	85 ft. lbs.	115 Nm
1989-92	74 ft. lbs.	100 Nm
5.7L		
1986-88	85 ft. lbs.	115 Nm
1989-94	74 ft. lbs.	100 Nm
Fuel pump mounting bolts		
2.5L, 2.8L	18 ft. lbs.	25 Nm
Intake manifold-to-cylinder head		
2.5L		
1982-85	29 ft. lbs.	40 Nm
1986		
Cap bolts	28 ft. lbs.	38 Nm
Stud-head bolts		
Except upper left	25 ft. lbs.	34 Nm
Upper left	37 ft. lbs.	50 Nm
2.8L 1982-87	25 ft. lbs.	34 Nm
1988		
Lower	25 ft. lbs.	34 Nm
Upper	22 ft. lbs.	30 Nm
1989		
Lower	25 ft. lbs.	34 Nm
Upper	18 ft. lbs.	24 Nm
3.1L		
Lower	19 ft. lbs.	26 Nm
Upper	15 ft. lbs.	21 Nm

85343590D

TORQUE SPECIFICATIONS

Component	U.S.	Metric
Intake manifold-to-cylinder head		
3.4L		
1993		
Lower		
bolt	22 ft. lbs.	30 Nm
nut	22 ft. lbs.	30 Nm
stud	89 inch lbs.	10 Nm
Upper	18 ft. lbs.	25 Nm
1994		
Lower	22 ft. lbs.	30 Nm
Upper	18 ft. lbs.	25 Nm
5.0L		
1982-84	30 ft. lbs.	41 Nm
1985-88	45 ft. lbs.	61 Nm
1989-91	35 ft. lbs.	47 Nm
1992		
Step 1	89 inch lbs.	10 Nm
Step 2	35 ft. lbs.	47 Nm
5.7L		
1986-88	45 ft. lbs.	61 Nm
1989-91	35 ft. lbs.	47 Nm
1992		
Step 1	89 inch lbs.	10 Nm
Step 2	35 ft. lbs.	47 Nm
1993-94		
Step 1	71 inch lbs.	8 Nm
Step 2	35 ft. lbs.	47 Nm
Main bearing cap bolts		
2.5L	70 ft. lbs.	95 Nm
2.8L		
1982-84	74 ft. lbs.	100 Nm
1985-89	83 ft. lbs.	112 Nm
3.1L	73 ft. lbs.	99 Nm
3.4L		
Step 1	37 ft. lbs.	50 Nm
Step 2	+ 77 degrees (⅛ turn)	
5.0L		
1982-84	70 ft. lbs.	95 Nm
1985	75 ft. lbs.	102 Nm
1986		
outer	75 ft. lbs.	102 Nm
inner	85 ft. lbs.	115 Nm
1987-88	85 ft. lbs.	115 Nm
1989-92	77 ft. lbs.	105 Nm
5.7L		
1986		
outer	75 ft. lbs.	102 Nm
inner	85 ft. lbs.	115 Nm
1987-88	85 ft. lbs.	115 Nm
1989-94	77 ft. lbs.	105 Nm

85343990E

TORQUE SPECIFICATIONS

Component	U.S.	Metric
Oil filter stud		
2.8L		
1982-88	34 ft. lbs.	46 Nm
1989	70 ft. lbs.	95 Nm
3.4L	50 ft. lbs.	68 Nm
3.1L, 5.0L, 5.7L		
1990-94	63 ft. lbs.	85 Nm
Oil pan bolts		
2.5L		
1982-84	75 inch lbs.	8 Nm
1985	53 inch lbs.	6 Nm
1986	90 inch lbs.	10 Nm
2.8L		
1.00	9 ft. lbs.	12 Nm
1.25	22 ft. lbs.	30 Nm
1985-86		
1.25 x 14	30 ft. lbs.	40 Nm
1.00 x 16	15 ft. lbs.	20 Nm
1987-89		
1.25 x 14	22 ft. lbs.	30 Nm
1.00 x 16	9 ft. lbs.	12 Nm
3.1L		
Rear 2 bolts	18 ft. lbs.	25 Nm
All the rest	89 inch lbs.	10 Nm
3.4L		
1993		
Rear 2 bolts	18 ft. lbs.	25 Nm
All the rest	89 inch lbs.	10 Nm
1994		
Front corners	24 ft. lbs.	33 Nm
Rear corners	18 ft. lbs.	25 Nm
Side bolts	89 inch lbs.	10 Nm
5.0L		
1982-84		
5/16-18	14 ft. lbs.	10 Nm
1/4-20	80 inch lbs.	9 Nm
1985-88		
5/16-18 stud	10 inch lbs.	1 Nm
5/16-18 nut	15 ft. lbs.	11 Nm
1/4-20 bolt	90 inch lbs.	5 Nm
1989-92		
Bolts	8 ft. lbs.	11 Nm
Nuts	17 ft. lbs.	23 Nm
5.7L		
1986-88		
5/16-18 stud	10 inch lbs.	1 Nm
5/16-18 nut	15 ft. lbs.	11 Nm
1/4-20 bolt	90 inch lbs.	5 Nm
1989-92		
Bolts	8 ft. lbs.	11 Nm
Nuts	17 ft. lbs.	23 Nm
1993-94		
Corner bolts	15 ft. lbs.	20 Nm
Side bolts	100 inch lbs.	11 Nm

85343399F

TORQUE SPECIFICATIONS

Component	U.S.	Metric
Oil pan drain plug		
2.5L	25 ft. lbs.	34 Nm
2.8L	20 ft. lbs.	27 Nm
3.1L, 3.4L	18 ft. lbs.	25 Nm
5.0L, 5.7L	16 ft. lbs.	22 Nm
Oil pickup tube-to-pump		
2.5L	37 ft. lbs.	50 Nm
Oil pump cover		
2.5L	10 ft. lbs.	14 Nm
2.8L	9 ft. lbs.	12 Nm
3.4L	89 inch lbs.	10 Nm
5.0L	80 inch lbs.	9 Nm
5.7L	80 inch lbs.	9 Nm
Oil pump-to-block		
2.5L	22 ft. lbs.	30 Nm
2.8L	35 ft. lbs.	47 Nm
3.1L	30 ft. lbs.	41 Nm
3.4L	30 ft. lbs.	41 Nm
5.0L		
1982-84	65 ft. lbs.	88 Nm
1985-88	70 ft. lbs.	95 Nm
1989-92	65 ft. lbs.	88 Nm
5.7L		
1986-88	70 ft. lbs.	95 Nm
1989-94	65 ft. lbs.	88 Nm
Rear oil seal retainer		
3.1L, 5.0L, 5.7L	11 ft. lbs.	15 Nm
Rocker arm cover		
2.5L	72 inch lbs.	8 Nm
2.8L		
1982-84	9 ft. lbs.	12 Nm
1985-89	15 ft. lbs.	20 Nm
3.1L	10 ft. lbs.	14 Nm
3.4L	89 inch lbs.	10 Nm
5.0L		
1982-84	45 inch lbs.	5 Nm
1985-86		
Nuts	65 inch lbs.	4 Nm
Studs	10 inch lbs.	1 Nm
1987-88	9 ft. lbs.	12 Nm
1989	72 inch lbs.	8 Nm
1990	89 inch lbs.	10 Nm
1991-92	95 inch lbs.	11 Nm
5.7L		
1986		
Nuts	65 inch lbs.	4 Nm
Studs	10 inch lbs.	1 Nm
1987-88	9 ft. lbs.	12 Nm
1989	72 inch lbs.	8 Nm
1990	89 inch lbs.	10 Nm
1991-92	95 inch lbs.	10.5 Nm
1993-94	100 inch lbs.	11 Nm

85343399G

TORQUE SPECIFICATIONS

Component	U.S.	Metric
Rocker arm stud/nut		
2.5L	20 ft. lbs.	27 Nm
2.8L		
1982–84	49 ft. lbs.	66 Nm
1985–89	11 inch lbs.	14 Nm
3.1L	89 inch lbs.	10 Nm
5.0L		
1982–87	11 ft. lbs.	14 Nm
5.7L		
1986–87	11 ft. lbs.	14 Nm
Spark plugs		
2.8L		
1982–88	15 ft. lbs.	20 Nm
1989	25 ft. lbs.	34 Nm
3.1L	25 ft. lbs.	34 Nm
3.4L	23 ft. lbs.	31 Nm
5.0L, 5.7L		
1982–92	22 ft. lbs.	30 Nm
1993–94	11 ft. lbs.	15 Nm
Starter mounting bolts		
All	37 ft. lbs.	50 Nm
Thermostat housing bolts		
2.5L	20 ft. lbs.	27 Nm
2.8L		
1982–84	30 ft. lbs.	41 Nm
1985–88	18 ft. lbs.	24 Nm
1989	22 ft. lbs.	30 Nm
3.1L	18 ft. lbs.	25 Nm
3.4L	15 ft. lbs.	21 Nm
5.0L		
1982	25 ft. lbs.	34 Nm
1983–87		
Carbureted engines	23 ft. lbs.	17 Nm
Fuel injected engines	30 ft. lbs.	22 Nm
1988	30 ft. lbs.	22 Nm
1989–92	21 ft. lbs.	28 Nm
5.7L		
1986–88	30 ft. lbs.	22 Nm
1989–94	25 ft. lbs.	34 Nm
Timing chain tensioner-to-block		
2.8L	19 ft. lbs.	24 Nm
3.1L	15 ft. lbs.	21 Nm
3.4L		
1993	18 ft. lbs.	25 Nm
1994	15 ft. lbs.	21 Nm
Timing gear case		
2.5L	90 inch lbs.	10 Nm
Valve lifter retainer		
5.0L, 5.7L		
1990	12 ft. lbs.	16 Nm
1991–94	15 ft. lbs.	20 Nm

8534399H

USING A VACUUM GAUGE

White needle = steady needle   *Dark needle = drifting needle*

The vacuum gauge is one of the most useful and easy-to-use diagnostic tools. It is inexpensive, easy to hook up, and provides valuable information about the condition of your engine.

Indication: Normal engine in good condition

Gauge reading: Steady, from 17–22 in./Hg.

Indication: Sticking valve or ignition miss

Gauge reading: Needle fluctuates from 15–20 in./Hg. at idle

Indication: Late ignition or valve timing, low compression, stuck throttle valve, leaking carburetor or manifold gasket.

Gauge reading: Low (15–20 in./Hg.) but steady

Indication: Improper carburetor adjustment, or minor intake leak at carburetor or manifold

NOTE: Bad fuel injector O-rings may also cause this reading.

Gauge reading: Drifting needle

Indication: Weak valve springs, worn valve stem guides, or leaky cylinder head gasket (vibrating excessively at all speeds).

NOTE: A plugged catalytic converter may also cause this reading.

Gauge reading: Needle fluctuates as engine speed increases

Indication: Burnt valve or improper valve clearance. The needle will drop when the defective valve operates.

Gauge reading: Steady needle, but drops regularly

Indication: Choked muffler or obstruction in system. Speed up the engine. Choked muffler will exhibit a slow drop of vacuum to zero.

Gauge reading: Gradual drop in reading at idle

Indication: Worn valve guides

Gauge reading: Needle vibrates excessively at idle, but steadies as engine speed increases

TCCS3C01

Troubleshooting Engine Mechanical Problems

Problem	Cause	Solution
External oil leaks	• Cylinder head cover RTV sealant broken or improperly seated	• Replace sealant; inspect cylinder head cover sealant flange and cylinder head sealant surface for distortion and cracks
	• Oil filler cap leaking or missing	• Replace cap
	• Oil filter gasket broken or improperly seated	• Replace oil filter
	• Oil pan side gasket broken, improperly seated or opening in RTV sealant	• Replace gasket or repair opening in sealant; inspect oil pan gasket flange for distortion
	• Oil pan front oil seal broken or improperly seated	• Replace seal; inspect timing case cover and oil pan seal flange for distortion
	• Oil pan rear oil seal broken or improperly seated	• Replace seal; inspect oil pan rear oil seal flange; inspect rear main bearing cap for cracks, plugged oil return channels, or distortion in seal groove
	• Timing case cover oil seal broken or improperly seated	• Replace seal
	• Excess oil pressure because of restricted PCV valve	• Replace PCV valve
	• Oil pan drain plug loose or has stripped threads	• Repair as necessary and tighten
	• Rear oil gallery plug loose	• Use appropriate sealant on gallery plug and tighten
	• Rear camshaft plug loose or improperly seated	• Seat camshaft plug or replace and seal, as necessary
Excessive oil consumption	• Oil level too high	• Drain oil to specified level
	• Oil with wrong viscosity being used	• Replace with specified oil
	• PCV valve stuck closed	• Replace PCV valve
	• Valve stem oil deflectors (or seals) are damaged, missing, or incorrect type	• Replace valve stem oil deflectors
	• Valve stems or valve guides worn	• Measure stem-to-guide clearance and repair as necessary
	• Poorly fitted or missing valve cover baffles	• Replace valve cover
	• Piston rings broken or missing	• Replace broken or missing rings
	• Scuffed piston	• Replace piston
	• Incorrect piston ring gap	• Measure ring gap, repair as necessary
	• Piston rings sticking or excessively loose in grooves	• Measure ring side clearance, repair as necessary
	• Compression rings installed upside down	• Repair as necessary
	• Cylinder walls worn, scored, or glazed	• Repair as necessary

TCCS3C02

Troubleshooting Engine Mechanical Problems

Problem	Cause	Solution
Excessive oil consumption (cont.)	• Piston ring gaps not properly staggered	• Repair as necessary
	• Excessive main or connecting rod bearing clearance	• Measure bearing clearance, repair as necessary
No oil pressure	• Low oil level	• Add oil to correct level
	• Oil pressure gauge, warning lamp or sending unit inaccurate	• Replace oil pressure gauge or warning lamp
	• Oil pump malfunction	• Replace oil pump
	• Oil pressure relief valve sticking	• Remove and inspect oil pressure relief valve assembly
	• Oil passages on pressure side of pump obstructed	• Inspect oil passages for obstruction
	• Oil pickup screen or tube obstructed	• Inspect oil pickup for obstruction
	• Loose oil inlet tube	• Tighten or seal inlet tube
Low oil pressure	• Low oil level	• Add oil to correct level
	• Inaccurate gauge, warning lamp or sending unit	• Replace oil pressure gauge or warning lamp
	• Oil excessively thin because of dilution, poor quality, or improper grade	• Drain and refill crankcase with recommended oil
	• Excessive oil temperature	• Correct cause of overheating engine
	• Oil pressure relief spring weak or sticking	• Remove and inspect oil pressure relief valve assembly
	• Oil inlet tube and screen assembly has restriction or air leak	• Remove and inspect oil inlet tube and screen assembly. (Fill inlet tube with lacquer thinner to locate leaks.)
	• Excessive oil pump clearance	• Measure clearances
	• Excessive main, rod, or camshaft bearing clearance	• Measure bearing clearances, repair as necessary
High oil pressure	• Improper oil viscosity	• Drain and refill crankcase with correct viscosity oil
	• Oil pressure gauge or sending unit inaccurate	• Replace oil pressure gauge
	• Oil pressure relief valve sticking closed	• Remove and inspect oil pressure relief valve assembly
Main bearing noise	• Insufficient oil supply	• Inspect for low oil level and low oil pressure
	• Main bearing clearance excessive	• Measure main bearing clearance, repair as necessary
	• Bearing insert missing	• Replace missing insert
	• Crankshaft end-play excessive	• Measure end-play, repair as necessary
	• Improperly tightened main bearing cap bolts	• Tighten bolts with specified torque
	• Loose flywheel or drive plate	• Tighten flywheel or drive plate attaching bolts
	• Loose or damaged vibration damper	• Repair as necessary

TCCS3C03

Troubleshooting Engine Mechanical Problems

Problem	Cause	Solution
Connecting rod bearing noise	• Insufficient oil supply	• Inspect for low oil level and low oil pressure
	• Carbon build-up on piston	• Remove carbon from piston crown
	• Bearing clearance excessive or bearing missing	• Measure clearance, repair as necessary
	• Crankshaft connecting rod journal out-of-round	• Measure journal dimensions, repair or replace as necessary
	• Misaligned connecting rod or cap	• Repair as necessary
	• Connecting rod bolts tightened improperly	• Tighten bolts with specified torque
Piston noise	• Piston-to-cylinder wall clearance excessive (scuffed piston)	• Measure clearance and examine piston
	• Cylinder walls excessively tapered or out-of-round	• Measure cylinder wall dimensions, rebore cylinder
	• Piston ring broken	• Replace all rings on piston
	• Loose or seized piston pin	• Measure piston-to-pin clearance, repair as necessary
	• Connecting rods misaligned	• Measure rod alignment, straighten or replace
	• Piston ring side clearance excessively loose or tight	• Measure ring side clearance, repair as necessary
	• Carbon build-up on piston is excessive	• Remove carbon from piston
Valve actuating component noise	• Insufficient oil supply	• Check for: (a) Low oil level (b) Low oil pressure (c) Wrong hydraulic tappets (d) Restricted oil gallery (e) Excessive tappet to bore clearance
	• Rocker arms or pivots worn	• Replace worn rocker arms or pivots
	• Foreign objects or chips in hydraulic tappets	• Clean tappets
	• Excessive tappet leak-down	• Replace valve tappet
	• Tappet face worn	• Replace tappet; inspect corresponding cam lobe for wear
	• Broken or cocked valve springs	• Properly seat cocked springs; replace broken springs
	• Stem-to-guide clearance excessive	• Measure stem-to-guide clearance, repair as required
	• Valve bent	• Replace valve
	• Loose rocker arms	• Check and repair as necessary
	• Valve seat runout excessive	• Regrind valve seat/valves
	• Missing valve lock	• Install valve lock
	• Excessive engine oil	• Correct oil level

TCCS3C04

Troubleshooting Engine Performance

Problem	Cause	Solution
Hard starting (engine cranks normally)	• Faulty engine control system component • Faulty fuel pump • Faulty fuel system component • Faulty ignition coil • Improper spark plug gap • Incorrect ignition timing • Incorrect valve timing	• Repair or replace as necessary • Replace fuel pump • Repair or replace as necessary • Test and replace as necessary • Adjust gap • Adjust timing • Check valve timing; repair as necessary
Rough idle or stalling	• Incorrect curb or fast idle speed • Incorrect ignition timing • Improper feedback system operation • Faulty EGR valve operation • Faulty PCV valve air flow • Faulty TAC vacuum motor or valve • Air leak into manifold vacuum • Faulty distributor rotor or cap • Improperly seated valves • Incorrect ignition wiring • Faulty ignition coil • Restricted air vent or idle passages • Restricted air cleaner	• Adjust curb or fast idle speed (If possible) • Adjust timing to specification • Refer to Chapter 4 • Test EGR system and replace as necessary • Test PCV valve and replace as necessary • Repair as necessary • Inspect manifold vacuum connections and repair as necessary • Replace rotor or cap (Distributor systems only) • Test cylinder compression, repair as necessary • Inspect wiring and correct as necessary • Test coil and replace as necessary • Clean passages • Clean or replace air cleaner filter element
Faulty low-speed operation	• Restricted idle air vents and passages • Restricted air cleaner • Faulty spark plugs • Dirty, corroded, or loose ignition secondary circuit wire connections • Improper feedback system operation • Faulty ignition coil high voltage wire • Faulty distributor cap	• Clean air vents and passages • Clean or replace air cleaner filter element • Clean or replace spark plugs • Clean or tighten secondary circuit wire connections • Refer to Chapter 4 • Replace ignition coil high voltage wire (Distributor systems only) • Replace cap (Distributor systems only)
Faulty acceleration	• Incorrect ignition timing • Faulty fuel system component • Faulty spark plug(s) • Improperly seated valves • Faulty ignition coil	• Adjust timing • Repair or replace as necessary • Clean or replace spark plug(s) • Test cylinder compression, repair as necessary • Test coil and replace as necessary

TCCS3C05

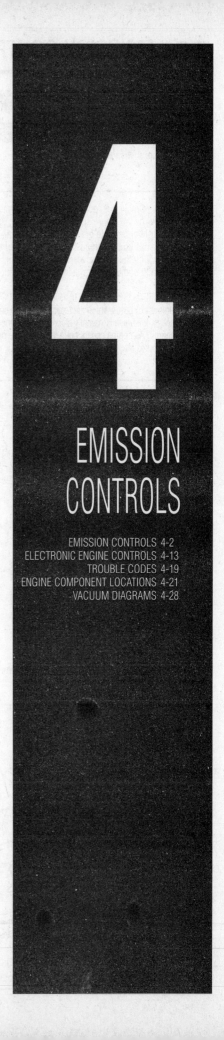

4

EMISSION CONTROLS

EMISSION CONTROLS

Crankcase Ventilation System

▶ **See Figures 1 thru 6**

OPERATION

The Positive Crankcase Ventilation (PCV) system is used to control crankcase blow-by vapors. As the engine is running, clean, filtered air is drawn through the air filter and into the crankcase. As the air passes through the crankcase, it picks up the combustion gases and carries them out of the crankcase, through the PCV valve, and into the induction system. As they enter the intake manifold, they are drawn into the combustion chamber where they are reburned.

The most critical component in the system is the PCV valve. This valve controls the amount of gases which are recycled into the combustion chamber. At low engine speeds, the valve is partially closed, limiting the flow of gases into the intake manifold. As engine speed increases, the valve opens to admit greater quantities of gases into the intake manifold. If the PCV valve becomes clogged, the system is designed to allow excessive amounts of blow-by gases to back flow through the crankcase tube into the air cleaner to be consumed by normal combustion.

SERVICE

Inspect the PCV system hose and connections at each tune-up and replace any deteriorated hoses. Check the PCV valve at every tune-up and replace it at 30,000 mile intervals.

TESTING

1. Remove the PCV valve from the intake manifold or valve cover.
2. Run the engine at idle.
3. Place your thumb over the end of the valve. Check for vacuum. If there is no vacuum at the valve, check for plugged valve or vacuum lines.
4. Shut off the engine. Shake the valve and listen for the rattle. If valve doesn't rattle, replace it.

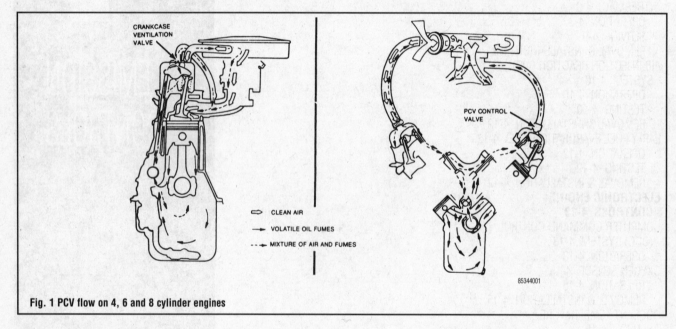

CLEAN AIR

VOLATILE OIL FUMES

MIXTURE OF AIR AND FUMES

85344001

Fig. 1 PCV flow on 4, 6 and 8 cylinder engines

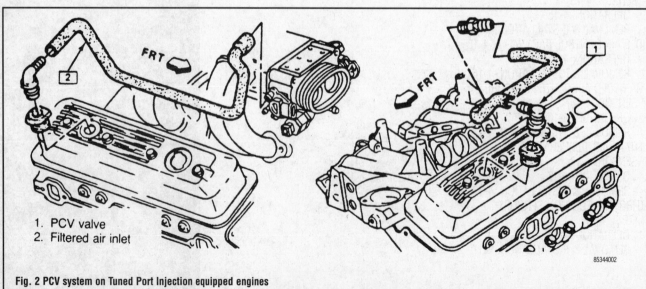

1. PCV valve
2. Filtered air inlet

85344002

Fig. 2 PCV system on Tuned Port Injection equipped engines

REMOVAL & INSTALLATION

PCV System Filter

1. To replace the PCV filter disconnect the hose, if equipped, attached to the filter at the air cleaner and remove the air cleaner cover. Slide the spring clamp off of the filter and remove it from the air cleaner.

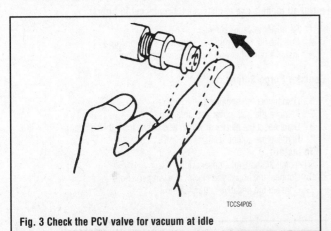

TCCS4P05

Fig. 3 Check the PCV valve for vacuum at idle

2. Inspect the rubber grommet in the valve cover and the hose for signs of deterioration, brittleness and cracking. Replace as necessary.
3. Installation is the reverse of removal.

PCV Valve

1. Disconnect the hose or pipe from the PCV valve.
2. Gently pull the PCV valve out of the grommet in the valve cover or intake manifold.
3. Installation is the reverse of removal.

Evaporative Emission Controls

▶ **See Figures 7 thru 13**

OPERATION

This system reduces the amount of gasoline vapors escaping into the atmosphere. Some models employ a purge control solenoid which is controlled by the ECM, to open and close the EEC system. Other models use a canister mounted vacuum purge valve; when the engine vacuum reaches a certain pressure, the valve opens allowing the gas vapors to be drawn off to the carburetor for burning.

Carbureted models use an exhaust tube from the float bowl to the charcoal canister; fuel injected models eliminate the fuel bowl tube (as no float bowl is

85344007

Fig. 4 PCV filter location on most carbureted and throttle body injected engines

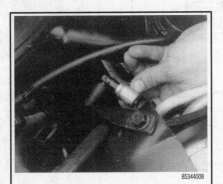

85344008

Fig. 5 Most PCV valves are located in the rocker arm covers

85344009

Fig. 6 Once the valve has been withdrawn from the rocker cover, it can be removed from the hose and replaced

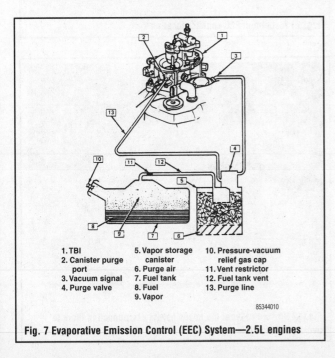

1. TBI	5. Vapor storage canister	10. Pressure-vacuum relief gas cap
2. Canister purge port	6. Purge air	11. Vent restrictor
3. Vacuum signal	7. Fuel tank	12. Fuel tank vent
4. Purge valve	8. Fuel	13. Purge line
	9. Vapor	

85344010

Fig. 7 Evaporative Emission Control (EEC) System—2.5L engines

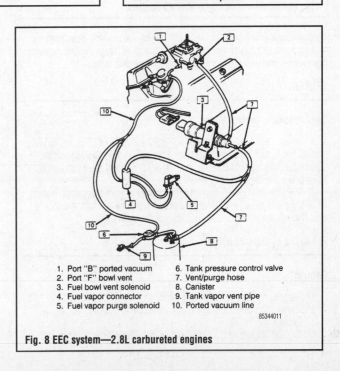

1. Port "B" ported vacuum	6. Tank pressure control valve
2. Port "F" bowl vent	7. Vent/purge hose
3. Fuel bowl vent solenoid	8. Canister
4. Fuel vapor connector	9. Tank vapor vent pipe
5. Fuel vapor purge solenoid	10. Ported vacuum line

85344011

Fig. 8 EEC system—2.8L carbureted engines

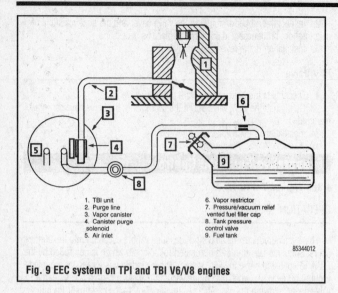

1. TBI unit
2. Purge line
3. Vapor canister
4. Canister purge solenoid
5. Air inlet
6. Vapor restrictor
7. Pressure/vacuum relief vented fuel filler cap
8. Tank pressure control valve
9. Fuel tank

85344012

Fig. 9 EEC system on TPI and TBI V6/V8 engines

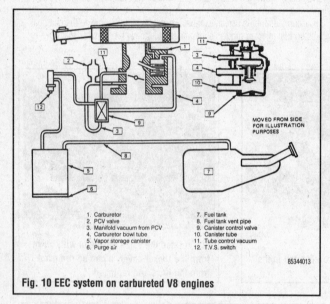

1. Carburetor
2. PCV valve
3. Manifold vacuum from PCV
4. Carburetor bowl tube
5. Vapor storage canister
6. Purge air
7. Fuel tank
8. Fuel tank vent pipe
9. Canister control valve
10. Canister tube
11. Tube control vacuum
12. T.V.S. switch

MOVED FROM SIDE
FOR ILLUSTRATION
PURPOSES

85344013

Fig. 10 EEC system on carbureted V8 engines

used on fuel injection systems). Fuel vapors from the gas tank travel from the tank to the vapor canister, where they are collected. Although the system varies from vehicle-to-vehicle, the operations are basically the same.

TESTING

Tank Pressure Control Valve

1. Using a hand-held vacuum pump, apply a vacuum of 15 in. Hg. (51 kPa) through the control vacuum signal tube to the purge valve diaphragm. If the diaphragm does not hold 5 in. Hg. at least for 10 seconds, the diaphragm is leaking. Replace the control valve.

2. With the vacuum still applied to the control vacuum tube, attach a short piece of hose to the valve's tank tube side and blow into the hose. Air should pass through the valve. If it does not, replace the control valve.

REMOVAL & INSTALLATION

Canister

1. Disconnect the negative battery cable.
2. Loosen the screw holding the canister retaining bracket.
3. Remove the canister.
4. Tag and disconnect the hoses leading from the canister.

To install:
5. Connect the hoses to the canister according to the tags.
6. Install the canister into the retaining bracket.
7. Tighten the screw holding the canister retaining bracket.
8. Reconnect the negative battery cable.

Filter

➡ **Not all models use canisters with replaceable filters.**

1. Remove the vapor canister.
2. Pull the filter out from the bottom of the canister.
3. Install a new filter and then replace the canister.

Canister Purge Solenoid

1. Disconnect the negative battery cable.
2. Remove the bolt, cover and solenoid.
3. Disconnect the electrical wiring and hoses from the solenoid.
4. Remove the solenoid.
To install:
5. Install the solenoid, cover and bolt.
6. Connect the hoses and electrical wiring solenoid.
7. Connect the negative battery cable.

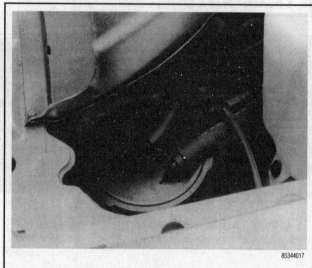

85344017

Fig. 11 A common EEC canister location

85344018

Fig. 12 Be sure to label the hoses before disconnecting them to avoid confusion later

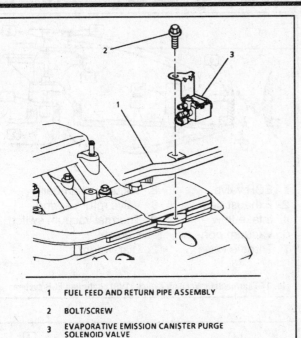

1 FUEL FEED AND RETURN PIPE ASSEMBLY

2 BOLT/SCREW

3 EVAPORATIVE EMISSION CANISTER PURGE
   SOLENOID VALVE

85344020

Fig. 13 A common canister purge solenoid location

Tank Pressure Control Valve

1. Disconnect the hoses from the control valve.
2. Remove the mounting hardware.
3. Remove the control valve from the vehicle.
4. Installation is the reverse of the removal procedure. Refer to the Vehicle Emission Control Information (VECI) label, located in the engine compartment (if present) or the diagrams found later in this section, for proper routing of the vacuum hoses.

Exhaust Gas Recirculation (EGR) System

▸ **See Figures 14 thru 27**

OPERATION

All models are equipped with this system, which consists of a metering valve, a vacuum line to the carburetor or intake manifold, and cast-in exhaust passages in the intake manifold. The EGR valve is controlled by vacuum, which opens and closes in response to the vacuum signals to admit exhaust gases into the air/fuel mixture. The exhaust gases lower peak combustion temperatures, reducing the formation of NOx. The valve is closed at idle and wide open throttle, but is open between the two extreme positions.

There are actually four types of EGR systems: Ported, Positive Back-Pressure, Negative Backpressure and Digital. The principle of all the systems are the same; the only difference is in the method used to control how the EGR valve opens.

Too much EGR flow at idle, cruise or during cold operation may result in the engine stalling after cold start, the engine stalling at idle after deceleration, vehicle surge during cruise and rough idle. If the EGR valve is always open, the vehicle may not idle. Too little or no EGR flow allows combustion temperatures to rise, which could result in spark knock (detonation), engine overheating and/or emission test failure.

A Thermal Vacuum Switch (TVS) or vacuum control solenoid may sometimes be used in combination with the EGR valve. The TVS will close off vacuum during cold operation. A vacuum control solenoid uses Pulse Width Modulation (PWM) to turn the solenoid ON and OFF numerous times a second and varies the amount of ON time (pulse width) to vary the amount of ported vacuum supplied the EGR valve.

Ported Valve

In the ported system, the amount of exhaust gas admitted into the intake manifold depends on a ported vacuum signal. A ported vacuum signal is one taken from the carburetor above the throttle plates; thus, the vacuum signal (amount of vacuum) is dependent on how far the throttle plates are opened. When the throttle is closed (idle or deceleration) there is no vacuum signal. Thus, the EGR valve is closed, and no exhaust gas enters the intake manifold. As the throttle is opened, a vacuum is produced, which opens the EGR valve, admitting exhaust gas into the intake manifold.

Positive Backpressure Valve

This valve operates the same as the ported, except, it has an internal air bleed that acts as a vacuum regulator. The bleed valve controls the amount of vacuum inside the vacuum chamber during operation. When the valve receives sufficient exhaust backpressure through the hollow shaft, it closes the bleed; at this point the EGR valve opens.

➡ **This valve will not open, with vacuum applied to it, while the engine is idling or stopped.**

Negative Backpressure Valve

This valve is similar to the positive backpressure type, except, the bleed valve spring is moved from above the diaphragm to below it. The bleed valve is normally closed.

At certain manifold pressures, the EGR valve will open. When the manifold vacuum combines with the negative exhaust backpressure, the bleed hole opens and the EGR valve closes.

➡ **This valve will open when vacuum is applied and the engine is not running.**

Digital EGR Valve

The digital EGR valve, used on 3.1L (VIN T) engines, is designed to control the flow of EGR independent of intake manifold vacuum. The valve controls EGR flow through 3 solenoid-opened orifices, which increase in size, to produce 7 possible combinations. When a solenoid is energized, the armature with attached shaft and swivel pintle, is lifted, opening the orifice.

The digital EGR valve is opened by the ECM "quad-driver" (QDR), grounding each solenoid circuit individually. The flow of EGR is regulated by the ECM which uses information from the Coolant Temperature Sensor (CTS), Throttle Position Sensor (TPS) and the Manifold Absolute Pressure (MAP) sensor to determine the appropriate rate of flow for a particular engine operating condition.

IDENTIFICATION

- Positive backpressure EGR valves will have a "P" stamped on the top side of the valve below the date built

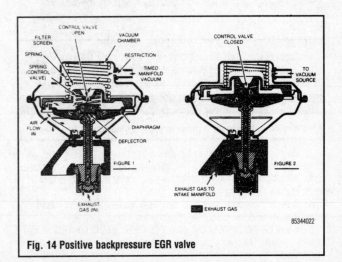

Fig. 14 Positive backpressure EGR valve

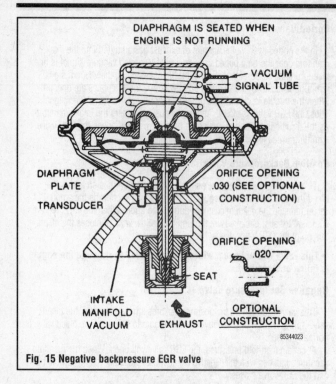

Fig. 15 Negative backpressure EGR valve

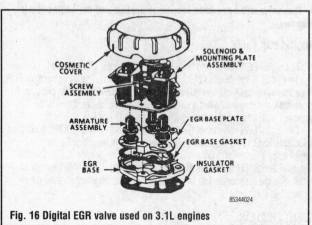

Fig. 16 Digital EGR valve used on 3.1L engines

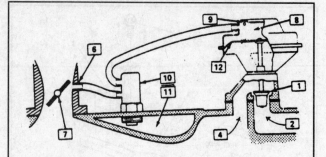

1. EGR valve
2. Exhaust gas
4. Intake flow
6. Vacuum port
7. Throttle valve
8. Vacuum chamber
9. Valve return spring
10. Thermal vacuum switch
11. Coolant
12. Diaphragm

Fig. 17 Thermostatic Vacuum Switch (TVS) controlled EGR system

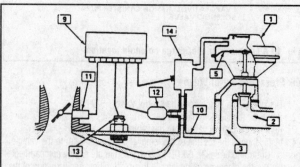

1. EGR valve
2. Exhaust gas
3. Intake air
5. Diaphragm
9. Electronic control module
10. Manifold vacuum
12. Manifold pressure sensor
13. Coolant temperature sensor
14. EGR control solenoid

Fig. 18 Solenoid controlled EGR system

- Negative backpressure EGR valves will have a "N" stamped on the top side of the valve below the date built
- Port EGR valves have no identification stamped below the date built

SERVICE

1. Check to see if the EGR valve diaphragm moves freely. Use your finger to reach up under the valve and push on the diaphragm. If it doesn't move freely, the valve should be replaced. The use of a mirror will aid the inspection process.

❊❊ CAUTION

If the engine is hot, wear a glove to protect your hand.

2. Install a vacuum gauge into the vacuum line between the EGR valve and the vacuum source. Start the engine and allow it to reach operating temperature.

3. With the car in either **P** or **N**, increase the engine speed until at least 5 in. Hg is showing on the gauge.

4. Remove the vacuum hose from the EGR valve. The diaphragm should move downward (valve closed). The engine speed should increase.

5. Install the vacuum hose and watch for the EGR valve to open (diaphragm moving upward). The engine speed should decrease to its former level, indicating exhaust recirculation.

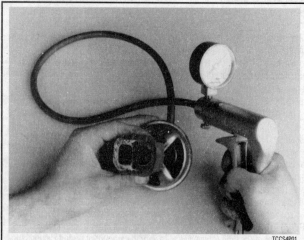

Fig. 19 Some EGR valves may be tested using a vacuum pump by watching for diaphragm movement

6. If the diaphragm doesn't move, check engine vacuum; it should be at least 5 in. Hg with the throttle open and engine running.

7. Check to see that the engine is at normal operating temperature.

8. Check for vacuum at the EGR hose. If no vacuum is present, check the hose for leaks, breaks, kinks, improper connections, etc., and replace as necessary.

9. If the diaphragm moves, but the engine speed doesn't change, check the EGR passages in the intake manifold for blockage.

REMOVAL & INSTALLATION

EGR Valve

EXCEPT 3.1L ENGINE

1. Disconnect the negative battery cable.
2. Remove the air cleaner assembly, if necessary.

➡If equipped with the 5.0L (VIN F) and 5.7L (VIN 8) engines with Tuned Port Injection (TPI), it will be necessary to remove the intake plenum to gain access to the EGR valve.

3. Tag and disconnect the necessary hoses and wiring to gain access to the EGR valve.
4. Remove the EGR valve retaining bolts.

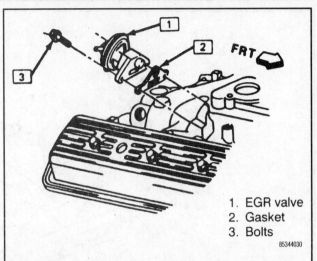

1. EGR valve
2. Gasket
3. Bolts

85344030

Fig. 22 EGR valve location on carbureted and throttle body injected V8 engines

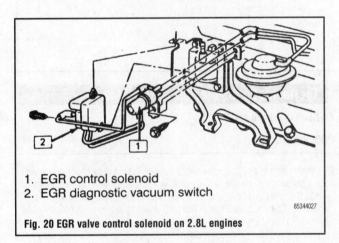

1. EGR control solenoid
2. EGR diagnostic vacuum switch

85344027

Fig. 20 EGR valve control solenoid on 2.8L engines

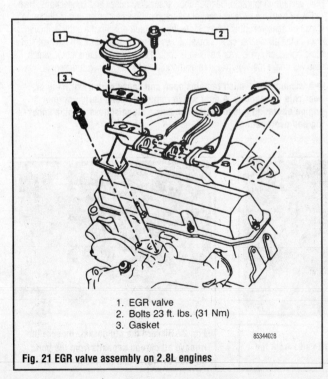

1. EGR valve
2. Bolts 23 ft. lbs. (31 Nm)
3. Gasket

85344028

Fig. 21 EGR valve assembly on 2.8L engines

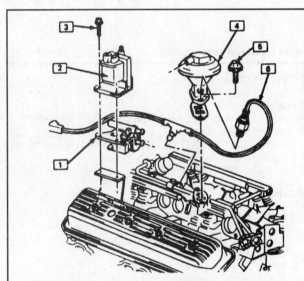

1. EGR solenoid
2. Coil
3. Bolt 16 ft. lbs. (21 Nm)
4. EGR valve
5. Bolts
6. EGR diagnostic temp. switch 105 inch lbs. (12 Nm)

85344031

Fig. 23 EGR valve and solenoid assembly on Tuned Port Injection engines

5. Remove the EGR valve. Discard the gasket.
6. Buff the exhaust deposits from the mounting surface and around the valve using a wire wheel.
7. Remove deposits from the valve outlet.
8. Clean the mounting surfaces of the intake manifold and valve assembly.

To install:
9. Install a new EGR gasket.
10. Install the EGR valve to the manifold.
11. Install the retaining bolts.
12. Connect the wiring and hoses.
13. Install the air cleaner assembly.
14. Connect the negative battery cable.

3.1L ENGINE

1. Disconnect the negative battery cable.
2. Disconnect the electrical wiring at the solenoid.

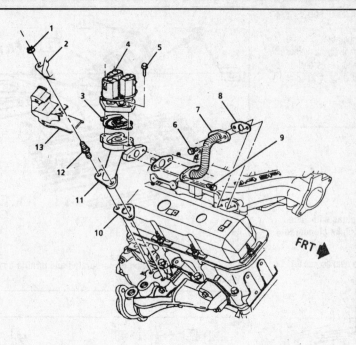

Fig. 24 Digital EGR valve assembly

1	SHIELD NUT
2	SHIELD
3	GASKET
4	DIGITAL EGR VALUE ASSEMBLY
5	BOLT/SCREW (2)
6	BOLT/SCREW (4)
7	TUBE ASSEMBLY
8	GASKET
9	BOLT/SCREW (4)
10	GASKET
11	ADAPTOR
12	STUD (2)
13	SHIELD

85344032

3. Remove the 2 base-to-flange bolts.
4. Remove the digital EGR valve.

To install:

5. Install the gasket with "UP" readable after positioning on the adapter.
6. Install the digital EGR valve.
7. Install the 2 base-to-flange bolts. Tighten the bolts to 11 ft. lbs (15 Nm) first, then torque to 22 ft. lbs. (30 Nm).
8. Connect the negative battery cable.

EGR Solenoid

1. Disconnect the negative battery cable.
2. Remove the air cleaner, as required.
3. Disconnect the electrical wiring at the solenoid.
4. Disconnect the vacuum hoses.
5. Remove the retaining bolts and the solenoid.
6. Remove the filter, as required.

To install:

7. If removed, install the filter.
8. Install the solenoid and retaining bolts.
9. Connect the vacuum hoses.
10. Connect the electrical wiring.
11. If removed, install the air cleaner.
12. Connect the negative battery cable.

Thermostatic Air Cleaner (THERMAC)

▶ **See Figures 28 and 29**

OPERATION

This system is designed to warm the air entering the carburetor when under-hood temperatures are low, and to maintain a controlled air temperature into the carburetor or throttle body at all times. By allowing preheated air to enter, the amount of time the choke is on is reduced, resulting in better fuel economy and lower emissions. Engine warm-up time is also reduced.

The THERMAC system is composed of the air cleaner body, a filter, sensor unit, vacuum diaphragm, damper door, associated hoses and connections. Heat radiating from the exhaust manifold is trapped by a heat stove and is ducted to the air cleaner to supply heated air to the carburetor or throttle body. A movable door in the air cleaner case snorkel allows air to be drawn in from the heat stove (cold operation). The door position is controlled by the vacuum motor, which receives intake manifold vacuum as modulated by the temperature sensor.

➡ **A vacuum door which remains open can cause carburetor icing or poor cold driveability. A door which remains closed during normal engine operating temperatures can cause sluggishness, engine knocking and overheating.**

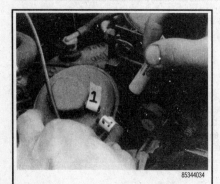

85344034

Fig. 25 Disconnect and label the EGR valve vacuum hose

85344035

Fig. 26 Removing the EGR valve from the engine

85344036

Fig. 27 Discard the old gasket. Be sure the remove all carbon deposits from the ports on the EGR valve and the mounting surface

SERVICE

1. Check the vacuum hoses for leaks, kinks, breaks, or improper connections and correct any defects.

2. With the engine off, check the position of the damper door within the snorkel. A mirror can be used to make this job easier. The damper door should be open to admit outside air.

3. Apply at least 7 in. Hg of vacuum to the damper diaphragm unit. The door should close. If it doesn't, check the diaphragm linkage for binding and correct hookup.

4. With the vacuum still applied and the door closed, clamp the tube to trap the vacuum. If the door doesn't remain closed, there is a leak in the diaphragm assembly.

REMOVAL & INSTALLATION

Vacuum Motor

1. Remove the air cleaner.
2. Disconnect the vacuum hose from the motor.
3. Drill out the spot welds with a ⅛ inch (3mm) bit, then enlarge as necessary to remove the retaining strap.
4. Remove the retaining strap.
5. Lift up the motor and cock it to one side to unhook the motor linkage at the control damper assembly.
To install:
6. In order to install the new vacuum motor, drill a ⁷⁄₆₄ inch (2.8mm) hole in the snorkel tube as the center of the vacuum motor retaining strap.

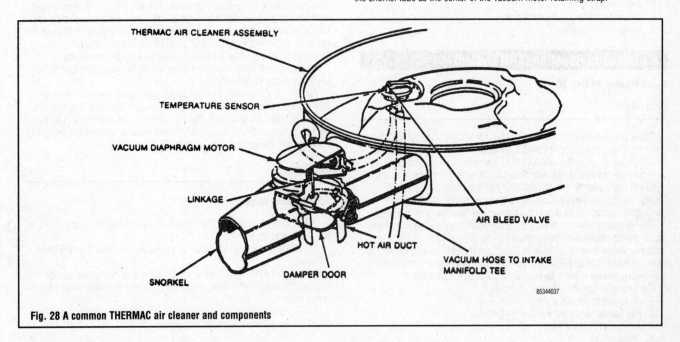

Fig. 28 A common THERMAC air cleaner and components

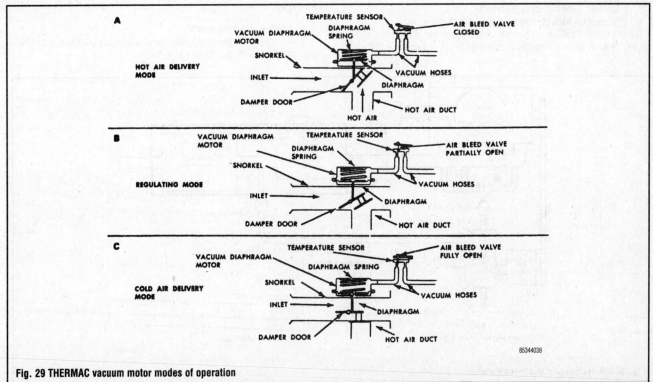

Fig. 29 THERMAC vacuum motor modes of operation

7. Insert the vacuum motor linkage into the control damper assembly.

8. Use the motor retaining strap and a sheet metal screw to secure the retaining strap and motor to the snorkel tube.

➡**Make sure the screw does not interfere with the operation of the damper assembly. Shorten the screw if necessary.**

Temperature Sensor

1. Remove the air cleaner.
2. Disconnect the hoses at the air cleaner.
3. Pry up the tabs on the sensor retaining clip and remove the clip and sensor from the air cleaner.

To install:

4. Position sensor into air cleaner.
5. Install retaining clip.
6. Connect the hoses to the air cleaner.
7. Install the air cleaner.

Air Injection Reaction (AIR) System

▶ **See Figures 30 thru 36**

OPERATION

The AIR management system is used to provide additional oxygen to continue the combustion process after the exhaust gases leave the combustion chamber. Air is injected into either the exhaust port(s), the exhaust manifold(s) or the catalytic converter by an engine driven air pump. The system is in operation at all times and will bypass air only momentarily during deceleration and at high speeds. The bypass function is performed by the air control valve, while the check valve protects the air pump by preventing any backflow of exhaust gases.

The AIR system helps reduce HC and CO content in the exhaust gases by injecting air into the exhaust ports during cold engine operation. This air injection also helps the catalytic converter to reach the proper temperature quicker during warmup. When the engine is warm (Closed Loop), the AIR system injects air into the beds of a three-way converter to lower the HC and the CO content in the exhaust.

The system utilizes the following components:

1. An engine driven AIR pump.
2. AIR Control valves (Air Control, Air Switching).
3. Air flow and control hoses.
4. Check valves.
5. A dual-bed, three-way catalytic converter.
6. A deceleration back-fire control valve— 2.8L engine only.

The belt driven, vane-type air pump is located at the front of the engine and supplies clean air to the AIR system for purposes already stated. When the engine is cold, the Electronic Control Module (ECM) energizes an AIR control solenoid. This allows air to flow to the AIR switching valve. The AIR switching valve is then energized to direct air to the exhaust ports.

When the engine is warm, the ECM de-energizes the AIR switching valve, thus directing the air between the beds of the catalytic converter. This provides additional oxygen for the oxidizing catalyst in the second bed to decrease HC and CO, while at the same time keeping oxygen levels low in the first bed, enabling the reducing catalyst to effectively decrease the levels of NOx.

If the AIR control valve detects a rapid increase in manifold vacuum (deceleration), certain operating modes (wide open throttle, etc.) or if the ECM self-diagnostic system detects any problem in the system, air is diverted to the air cleaner or directly into the atmosphere.

The primary purpose of the ECM's divert mode is to prevent backfiring. Throttle closure at the beginning of deceleration will temporarily create air/fuel mixtures which are too rich to burn completely. These mixtures become burnable when they reach the exhaust if combined with the injection air. The next firing of the engine will ignite this mixture causing an exhaust backfire. Momentary diverting of the injection air from the exhaust prevents this.

The AIR system check valves and hoses should be checked periodically for any leaks, cracks or deterioration.

On the 2.8L engine only, an anti-backfire (gulp) valve is used to allow air flow into the intake manifold. This is used to help prevent backfire during high vacuum deceleration conditions. The extra air enters the intake system to lean the rich air/fuel mixture. The valve is operated by the intake manifold vacuum to allow air from the air filter to flow into the intake manifold.

TESTING

Anti-Backfire Valve

1. Remove the air cleaner and plug the air cleaner vacuum source. Connect a tachometer to the engine.
2. With the engine idling, remove the vacuum signal hose from the intake manifold.
3. Reconnect the signal hose and listen for air flow through the ventilation tube into the anti-backfire valve. A speed drop should be noticed when the hose is reconnected.
4. If these conditions are not found, check hoses for restrictions or leaks. If hoses are OK, replace the anti-backfire valve.

Air Pump

1. Check the drive belt tension.
2. Increase the engine speed and observe an increase in air flow. If air flow does not increase, replace the air pump.

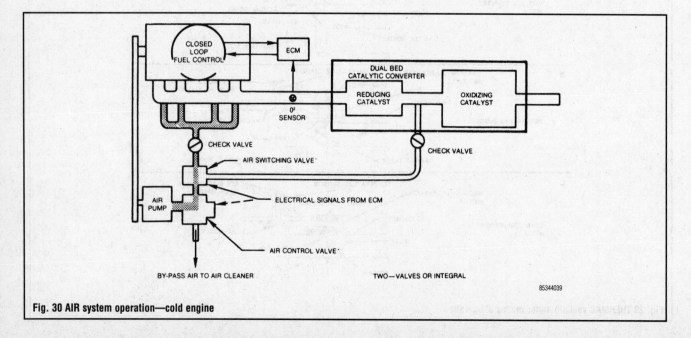

85344039

Fig. 30 AIR system operation—cold engine

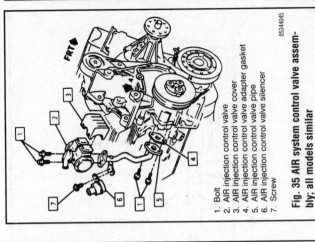

85344045

1. Bolt
2. AIR injection control valve
3. AIR injection control valve cover
4. AIR injection control valve adapter gasket
5. AIR injection control valve pipe
6. AIR injection control valve silencer
7. Screw

Fig. 35 AIR system control valve assembly; all models similar

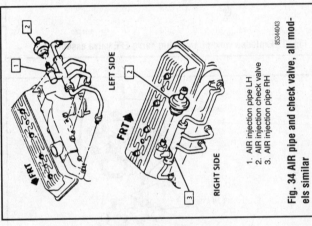

85344043

1. AIR injection pipe LH
2. AIR injection check valve
3. AIR injection pipe RH

Fig. 34 AIR pipe and check valve, all models similar

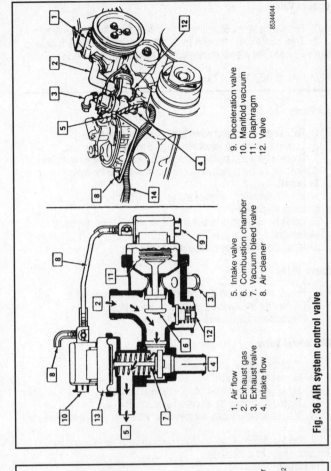

85344044

9. Deceleration valve
10. Manifold vacuum
11. Diaphragm
12. Valve

5. Intake valve
6. Combustion chamber
7. Vacuum bleed valve
8. Air cleaner

1. Air flow
2. Exhaust gas
3. Exhaust valve
4. Intake flow

Fig. 36 AIR system control valve

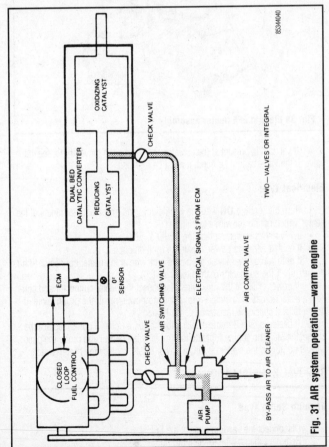

85344040

TWO—VALVES OR INTEGRAL

Fig. 31 AIR system operation—warm engine

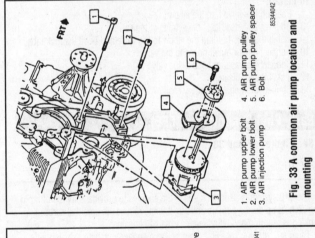

85344042

1. AIR pump upper bolt
2. AIR pump lower bolt
3. AIR injection pump
4. AIR pump pulley
5. AIR pump pulley spacer
6. Bolt

Fig. 33 A common air pump location and mounting

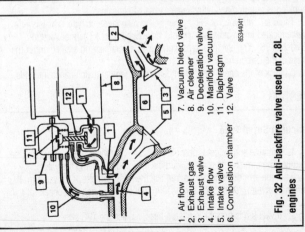

85344041

1. Air flow
2. Exhaust gas
3. Exhaust valve
4. Intake flow
5. Intake valve
6. Combustion chamber
7. Vacuum bleed valve
8. Air cleaner
9. Deceleration valve
10. Manifold vacuum
11. Diaphragm
12. Valve

Fig. 32 Anti-backfire valve used on 2.8L engines

Control Valve

1. Remove the hoses. Blow through the valve (toward the cylinder head).
2. Then, suck through the valve (or blow through the other side). If air flows in one direction, the valve is operative. If not, replace the control valve.

REMOVAL & INSTALLATION

Air Pump

1. Remove the AIR control valves and/or adapter at the pump.
2. Loosen the air pump adjustment bolt and remove the drive belt.
3. Unscrew the pump mounting bolts and then remove the pump pulley.
4. Unscrew the pump mounting bolts and then remove the pump.

To install:

5. Position the pump into place and secure it with the mounting bolts.
6. Install the pump pulley.
7. Install the air pump drive belt and adjust pump belt with the pump adjustment bolt.
8. Install the AIR control valves and/or adapter.

Check Valve

1. Release the clamp and disconnect the air hoses from the valve.
2. Unscrew the check valve from the air injection pipe.
3. Installation is in the reverse order of removal.

Air Control Valve

1. Disconnect the negative battery cable.
2. Remove the air cleaner.
3. Tag and disconnect the vacuum hose from the valve.
4. Tag and disconnect the air outlet hoses from the valve.
5. Bend back the lock tabs and then remove the bolts holding the elbow to the valve.
6. Tag and disconnect any electrical connections at the valve and then remove the valve from the elbow.

To install:

7. Position the valve into the elbow.
8. Connect any electrical connections at the valve.
9. Install the bolts holding the elbow to the valve and bend the lock tabs.
10. Connect the air outlet hoses to the valve.
11. Connect the vacuum hose to the valve.
12. Install the air cleaner.
13. Connect the negative battery cable.

Early Fuel Evaporation (EFE)

♦ **See Figures 37 and 38**

OPERATION

The EFE system is used on some of the engines to provide a source of rapid engine heat up during cold operations. It helps reduce the time that carburetor choking is required and helps reduce exhaust emissions.

There are two types of EFE systems. The vacuum servo type, consists of a valve located in the exhaust manifold, an actuator and a Thermal Vacuum Switch (TVS). The electrical type, consists of a ceramic grid located under the base of the carburetor.

A check of the operation should be made at regular maintenance intervals.

TESTING

Vacuum Servo Type

1. With the engine cold, observe the position of the actuator arm. Start the engine. The arm should move toward the diaphragm (closing the valve).
2. If the arm does not move, remove the hose and check for vacuum. If still no vacuum, remove the top hose from the TVS switch and check for vacuum.
3. If vacuum is present in the top hose, replace the TVS switch.

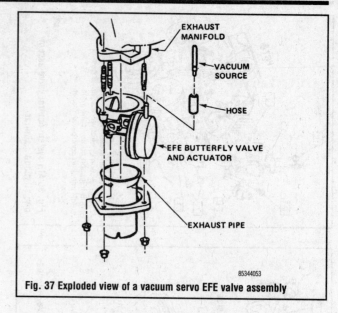

Fig. 37 Exploded view of a vacuum servo EFE valve assembly

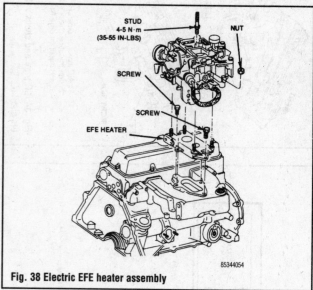

Fig. 38 Electric EFE heater assembly

4. If vacuum is present at the actuator and it does not move, try to free the valve. If the valve cannot be freed, it must be replaced.

Electrical Type

1. Turn the ignition **ON** with the engine cold and probe both terminals of the heater switch connector with a test light.
   - If 1 wire has power, replace the heater switch.
   - If neither wire has power, repair the ignition circuit.
   - If both wires have power, probe the pink wire at the heater connector (if no power, repair the connector of the heater switch).
2. If power exists at the pink wire, disconnect the heater connector and connect a tester across the harness terminal. If no power, repair the ground wire; if power exists, check the resistance of the heater.
3. If heater is over 3 ohms, replace the heater. If under 3 ohms, replace the connector, start the engine (operate to normal temperature) and probe the pink wire. If no power, the system is OK; if power exists, replace the heater switch.

REMOVAL & INSTALLATION

Vacuum Servo Type

1. Disconnect the vacuum hose at the EFE.
2. Remove exhaust pipe to manifold nuts.

3. Remove the crossover pipe. Complete removal is not always necessary.

4. Remove the EFE valve.

To install:

5. Position the EFE valve into place.
6. Install the crossover pipe.
7. Install the exhaust pipe to manifold nuts.
8. Connect the vacuum hose at the EFE.

Electrical Type

1. Remove the air cleaner and disconnect the negative battery cable.
2. Tag, then disengage all electrical, vacuum and fuel connections from the carburetor.
3. Disconnect the EFE heater electrical lead.
4. Remove the carburetor.
5. Lift off the EFE heater grid.

To install:

6. Position the EFE heater grid onto the manifold.
7. Install the carburetor.
8. Connect the EFE heater electrical lead.
9. Connect all electrical, vacuum and fuel connection to the carburetor.
10. Install the air cleaner and connect the negative battery cable.

Electric EFE Relay

1. Disconnect the negative battery cable.
2. Remove the retaining bracket.
3. Tag and disconnect all electrical connections.
4. Unscrew the retaining bolts and remove the relay.

To install:

5. Position the relay into place and secure the relay with the retaining bolt.
6. Attach all electrical connections.
7. Install the retaining bracket.
8. Connect the negative battery cable.

ELECTRONIC ENGINE CONTROLS

Computer Command Control (CCC) System

▶ **See Figures 39, 40, 41 and 42**

The Computer Command Control (CCC) System is an electronically controlled exhaust emission system that can monitor and control a large number of interrelated emission control systems. It can monitor various engine/vehicle operating conditions and then use this information to control multiple engine related systems. The CCC system is thereby making constant adjustments to maintain optimum vehicle performance under all normal driving conditions while at the same time allowing the catalytic converter to effectively control the emissions of HC, CO and NOx.

OPERATION

The Electronic Control Module (ECM) is required to maintain the exhaust emissions at acceptable levels. The module is a small, solid state computer which receives signals from many sources and sensors; it uses these data to

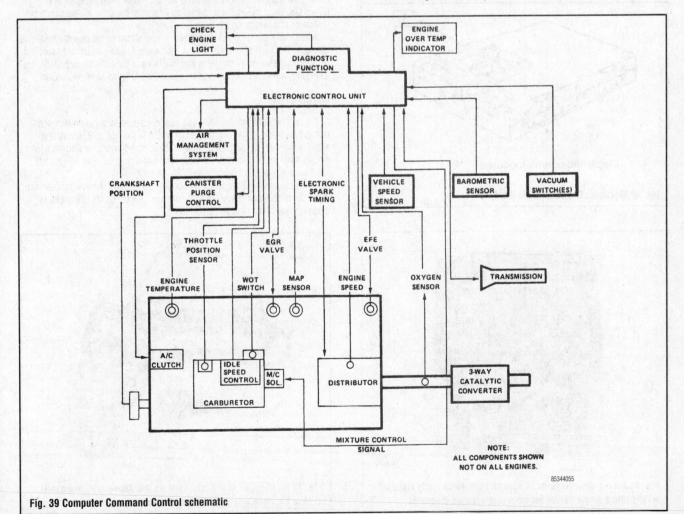

Fig. 39 Computer Command Control schematic

make judgements about operating conditions and then control output signals to the fuel and emission systems to match the current requirements.

Inputs are received from many sources to form a complete picture of engine operating conditions. Some inputs are simply Yes or No messages, such as that from the Park/Neutral switch; the vehicle is either in gear or in Park/Neutral; there are no other choices. Other data is sent in quantitative input, such as engine rpm or coolant temperature. The ECM is pre-programmed to recognize acceptable ranges or combinations of signals and control the outputs to control emissions while providing good driveability and economy. The ECM also monitors some output circuits, making sure that the components function as commanded. For proper engine operation, it is essential that all input and output components function properly and communicate properly with the ECM.

Since the control module is programmed to recognize the presence and value of electrical inputs, it will also note the lack of a signal or a radical change in values. It will, for example, react to the loss of signal from the vehicle speed sensor or note that engine coolant temperature has risen beyond acceptable (programmed) limits. Once a fault is recognized, a numeric code is assigned and held in memory. The SERVICE ENGINE SOON Malfunction Indicator Lamp (MIL), will illuminate to advise the operator that the system has detected a fault.

More than one code may be stored. Although not every engine uses every code, possible codes range from 12–999. Additionally, the same code may carry different meanings relative to each engine or engine family. For example, on the 3.3L (VIN N) engine, code 46 indicates a fault found in the power steering pressure switch circuit. The same code on the 5.7L (VIN F) engine indicates a fault in the VATS anti-theft system.

In the event of an ECM failure, the system will default to a pre-programmed set of values. These are compromise values which allow the engine to operate, although possibly at reduced efficiency. This is variously known as the default, limp-in/limp-home or back-up mode. Driveability is almost always affected when the ECM enters this mode.

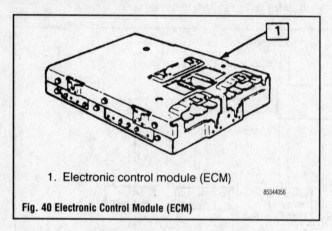

1. Electronic control module (ECM)

85344056

Fig. 40 Electronic Control Module (ECM)

Learning Ability

The ECM can compensate for minor variations within the fuel system through the block learn and fuel integrator systems. The fuel integrator monitors the oxygen sensor output voltage, adding or subtracting fuel to drive the mixture rich or lean as needed to reach the ideal air fuel ratio of 14.7:1. The integrator values may be read with a scan tool; the display will range from 0–255 and should center on 128 if the oxygen sensor is indicating a 14.7:1 mixture.

The temporary nature of the integrator's control is expanded by the block learn function. The name is derived from the fact that the entire engine operating range (load vs. rpm) is divided into sections or blocks. Within each memory block is stored the correct fuel delivery value for that combination of load and engine speed. Once the operating range enters a certain block, that stored value controls the fuel delivery unless the integrator steps in to change it. If changes are made by the integrator, the new value is memorized and stored within the block. As the block learn makes the correction, the integrator correction will be reduced until the integrator returns to 128; the block learn then controls the fuel delivery with the new value.

The next time the engine operates within the block's range, the new value will be used. The block learn data can also be read by a scan tool; the range is the same as the integrator and should also center on 128. In this way, the systems can compensate for engine wear, small air or vacuum leaks or reduced combustion.

Any time the battery is disconnected, the block learn values are lost and must be relearned by the ECM. This loss of corrected values may be noticed as a significant change in driveability. To re-teach the system, make certain the engine is fully warmed up. Drive the vehicle at part throttle using moderate acceleration and idle until normal performance is felt.

Malfunction Indicator Lamp

The primary function of the MIL is to advise the operator and the technician that a fault is detected, and, in most cases, a code is stored. Under normal conditions, the malfunction indicator lamp will illuminate when the ignition is turned **ON**. Once the engine is started and running, the ECM will perform a system check and extinguish the lamp if no fault is found.

Additionally, the lamp can be used to retrieve stored codes after the system is placed in the Diagnostic Mode. Codes are transmitted as a series of flashes with short or long pauses. When the system is placed in the Field Service Mode, the dash lamp will indicate open loop or closed loop function to the technician.

Intermittents

If a fault occurs intermittently, such as a loose connector pin breaking contact as the vehicle hits a bump, the ECM will note the fault as it occurs and energize the dash warning lamp. If the problem self-corrects, as with the terminal pin again making contact, the dash lamp will extinguish after 10 seconds but a code will remain stored in the ECM memory.

When an unexpected code appears during diagnostics, it may have been set during an intermittent failure that self-corrected; the codes are still useful in diagnosis and should not be discounted.

TCCS4P06

Fig. 41 Among other features, a scan tool combines many standard testers into a single device for quick and accurate diagnosis

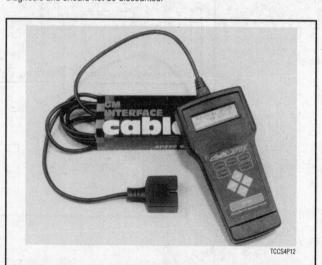

TCCS4P12

Fig. 42 Inexpensive scan tools, such as this Auto Xray®, are available to interface with your General Motors vehicle

Oxygen Sensor

▶ **See Figures 43 and 44**

OPERATION

An oxygen sensor is used on all models. The sensor protrudes into the exhaust stream and monitors the oxygen content of the exhaust gases. The difference between the oxygen content of the exhaust gases and that of the outside air generates a voltage signal to the ECM. The ECM monitors this voltage and, depending upon the value of the signal received, issues a command to adjust for a rich or a lean condition.

No attempt should ever be made to measure the voltage output of the sensor. The current drain of any conventional voltmeter would be such that it would permanently damage the sensor.

REMOVAL & INSTALLATION

The sensor may be difficult to remove when the engine temperature is below 120°F (48°C). Excessive removal force may damage the threads in the exhaust manifold or pipe; follow the removal procedure carefully.

1. Disconnect the negative battery cable.
2. Locate the oxygen sensor. It protrudes from the exhaust manifold (it looks somewhat like a spark plug).
3. Disconnect the electrical wiring from the oxygen sensor harness.
4. Spray a commercial solvent onto the sensor threads and allow it to soak in for at least five minutes.
5. Carefully remove the sensor with a special oxygen sensor socket.
To install:
6. First coat the new sensor's threads with GM anti-seize compound No. 5613695 or the equivalent. This is not a conventional anti-seize paste. The use of a regular compound may electrically insulate the sensor, rendering it inoperative. You must coat the threads with an electrically conductive anti-seize compound. Installation torque is 30 ft. lbs. (41 Nm). Do not overtighten.
7. Reconnect the electrical wiring. Be careful not to damage the electrical pigtail. Check the sensor boot for proper fit and installation.
8. Reconnect the negative battery cable.

Coolant Temperature Sensor

▶ **See Figure 45**

OPERATION

Most engine functions are affected by the coolant temperature. Determining whether the engine is hot or cold is largely dependent on the temperature of the coolant. An accurate temperature signal to the ECM is supplied by the coolant temperature sensor. The coolant temperature sensor is a thermistor mounted in the engine coolant stream. A thermistor is an electrical device that varies its resistance in relation to changes in temperature. Low coolant temperature produces a high resistance and high coolant temperature produces low resistance. The ECM supplies a signal of 5 volts to the coolant temperature sensor through a resistor in the ECM and measures the voltage. The voltage will be high when the engine is cold and low when the engine is hot.

REMOVAL & INSTALLATION

1. Disconnect the negative battery cable.
2. Drain the cooling system to an appropriate and clean container for reuse.
3. Disconnect the electrical wiring from the coolant temperature sensor.
4. Remove the coolant temperature sensor.
To install:
5. Install the coolant temperature sensor.
6. Connect the electrical wiring.
7. Fill the cooling system.
8. Connect the negative battery cable.
9. Start the engine and check for leaks.

Idle Air Control (IAC) Valve

▶ **See Figures 46, 47 and 48**

OPERATION

Engine idle speeds are controlled by the ECM through the IAC valve mounted on the throttle body. The ECM sends voltage pulses to the IAC motor windings causing the IAC motor shaft and pintle to move **IN** or **OUT** a given distance (number of steps) for each pulse (called counts). The movement of the pintle controls the airflow around the throttle plate, which in turn, controls engine idle speed. IAC valve pintle position counts can be observed using a scan tool. Zero counts correspond to a fully closed passage, while 140 counts or more corresponds to full flow.

Idle speed can be categorized in 2 ways: actual (controlled) idle speed and minimum idle speed. Controlled idle speed is obtained by the ECM positioning the IAC valve pintle. Resulting idle speed is determined by total air flow (IAC/passage + PCV + throttle valve + calibrated vacuum leaks). Controlled idle speed is specified at normal operating conditions, which consists of engine coolant at normal operating temperature, air conditioning compressor **OFF**, manual transmission in neutral or automatic transmission in **D**.

Minimum idle air speed is set at the factory with a stop screw. This setting allows a certain amount of air to bypass the throttle valves regardless of IAC

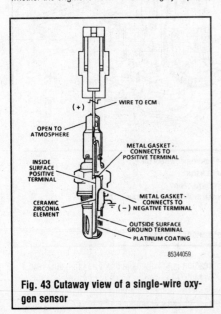

85344059

Fig. 43 Cutaway view of a single-wire oxygen sensor

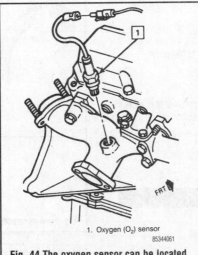

1. Oxygen (O₂) sensor

85344061

Fig. 44 The oxygen sensor can be located on either the left, right or both exhaust manifolds

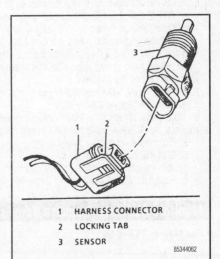

1	HARNESS CONNECTOR
2	LOCKING TAB
3	SENSOR

85344062

Fig. 45 Coolant temperature sensor. The intake air temperature sensor is similar in appearance

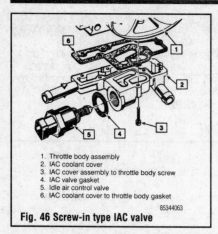

1. Throttle body assembly
2. IAC coolant cover
3. IAC cover assembly to throttle body screw
4. IAC valve gasket
5. Idle air control valve
6. IAC coolant cover to throttle body gasket

85344063

Fig. 46 Screw-in type IAC valve

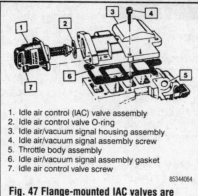

1. Idle air control (IAC) valve assembly
2. Idle air control valve O-ring
3. Idle air/vacuum signal housing assembly
4. Idle air/vacuum signal assembly screw
5. Throttle body assembly
6. Idle air/vacuum signal assembly gasket
7. Idle air control valve screw

85344064

Fig. 47 Flange-mounted IAC valves are retained by a screw

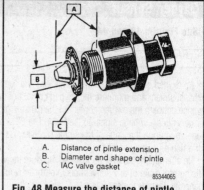

A. Distance of pintle extension
B. Diameter and shape of pintle
C. IAC valve gasket

85344065

Fig. 48 Measure the distance of pintle extension when installing a new IAC valve

valve pintle positioning. A combination of this air flow and IAC pintle positioning allows the ECM to control engine idle speed. During normal engine idle operation, the IAC valve pintle is positioned a calibrated number of steps (counts) from the seat. No adjustment is required during routine maintenance. Tampering with the minimum idle speed adjustment may result in premature failure of the IAC valve or improperly controlled engine idle operation.

REMOVAL & INSTALLATION

➥**On some models it may be necessary to remove the air inlet assembly.**

1. Disconnect the negative battery cable. Disconnect the IAC valve electrical wiring.
2. Remove the IAC valve by performing the following:
   a. On thread-mounted units, use a 1¼ inch (32mm) wrench.
   b. On flange-mounted units, remove the mounting screw assemblies.
3. Remove the IAC valve gasket or O-ring and discard.
To install:
4. Clean the mounting surfaces by performing the following:
   a. If servicing a thread-mounted valve, remove the old gasket material from the surface of the throttle body to ensure proper sealing of the new gasket.
   b. If servicing a flange-mounted valve, clean the IAC valve surfaces on the throttle body to assure proper seal of the new O-ring and contact of the IAC valve flange.
5. If installing a new IAC valve, measure the distance between the tip of the IAC valve pintle and the mounting flange. If the distance is greater than 1.102 inch (28mm), use finger pressure to slowly retract the pintle. The force required to retract the pintle of a new valve will not cause damage to the valve. If reinstalling the original IAC valve, do not attempt to adjust the pintle in this manner.
6. Install the IAC valve into the throttle body by performing the following:
   a. With thread-mounted valves, install with a new gasket. Using a 1¼ inch (32mm) wrench, tighten to 13 ft. lbs. (18 Nm).
   b. With flange-mounted valves, lubricate a new O-ring with transmission fluid and install on the IAC valve. Install the IAC valve to the throttle body. Install the mounting screws using a suitable thread locking compound. Tighten to 28 inch lbs. (3 Nm).
7. Connect the IAC valve electrical wiring.
8. Connect the negative battery cable.
9. No physical adjustment of the IAC valve assembly is required after installation. Reset the IAC valve pintle position by performing the following:
   a. Depress the accelerator pedal slightly.
   b. Start the engine and run for 5 seconds.
   c. Turn the ignition switch to the **OFF** position for 10 seconds.
   d. Restart the engine and check for proper idle operation.

Manifold Absolute Pressure Sensor

♦ **See Figures 49 and 50**

OPERATION

The MAP sensor measures the changes in intake manifold pressure, which result from engine load/speed changes and converts this information to a volt-

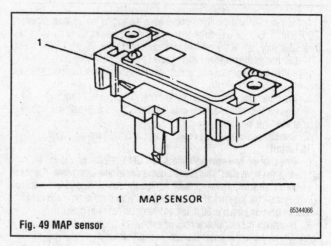

1 MAP SENSOR

85344066

Fig. 49 MAP sensor

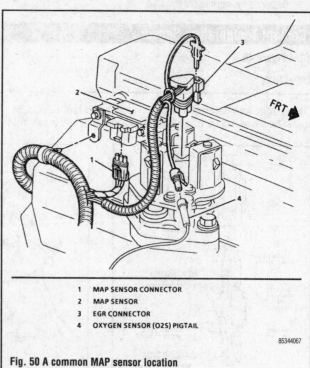

1 MAP SENSOR CONNECTOR
2 MAP SENSOR
3 EGR CONNECTOR
4 OXYGEN SENSOR (O2S) PIGTAIL

85344067

Fig. 50 A common MAP sensor location

age output. The MAP sensor reading is the opposite of a vacuum gauge reading: when manifold pressure is high, MAP sensor value is high and vacuum is low. A MAP sensor will produce a low output on engine coast-down with a closed throttle while a wide open throttle will produce a high output. The high output is produced because the pressure inside the manifold is the same as outside the manifold, so 100 percent of the outside air pressure is measured.

The MAP sensor is also used to measure barometric pressure under certain conditions, which allows the ECM to automatically adjust for different altitudes.

The MAP sensor changes the 5 volt signal supplied by the ECM, which reads the change and uses the information to control fuel delivery and ignition timing.

REMOVAL & INSTALLATION

1. Disconnect the negative battery cable.
2. Disconnect the vacuum connection.
3. Release the electrical wiring locking tab and disconnect the connector.
4. Remove the bolts or release the MAP sensor locking tabs and remove the sensor.

To install:
5. Install the bolts or snap sensor onto the bracket.
6. Connect the MAP sensor electrical wiring.
7. Connect the MAP sensor vacuum harness connector.
8. Connect the negative battery cable.

Intake Air Temperature (IAT) Sensor

◗ **See Figures 51, 52 and 53**

OPERATION

The IAT sensor is a thermistor which supplies intake air temperature information to the ECM. The sensor produces high resistance at low temperatures and

Throttle Position Sensor (TPS)

◗ **See Figure 54**

OPERATION

The TPS is mounted to the throttle body, opposite the throttle lever and is connected to the throttle shaft. Its function is to sense the current throttle valve position and relay that information to the ECM. Throttle position information allows the ECM to generate the required injector control signals. The TPS consists of a potentiometer which alters the flow of voltage according to the position of a wiper on the variable resistor windings, in proportion to the movement of the throttle shaft.

REMOVAL & INSTALLATION

1. Disconnect the negative battery cable.
2. Disconnect the TPS electrical wiring.
3. Remove the mounting screws.
4. Remove the TPS and, if equipped, sensor seal from the throttle body.

To install:
5. Place the TPS in position. Align the TPS lever with the sensor drive lever on the throttle body.
6. Install the TPS mounting screws.
7. Connect the electrical wiring.
8. Connect the negative battery cable.

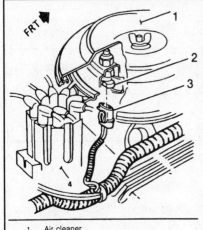

1. Air cleaner
2. Intake Air TGemperature (IAT) sensor
3. Harness connector to ECM
4. Distributor

85344068

Fig. 51 Intake air temperature sensor location on some TBI engines

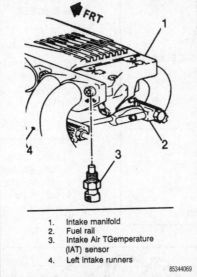

1. Intake manifold
2. Fuel rail
3. Intake Air TGemperature (IAT) sensor
4. Left intake runners

85344069

Fig. 52 Intake air temperature sensor location on Tuned Port Injection engines

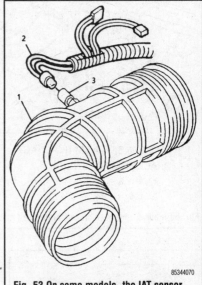

85344070

Fig. 53 On some models, the IAT sensor may be located on the air intake hose

low resistance at high temperatures. The ECM supplies a 5 volt signal to the sensor and measures the output voltage. The voltage signal will be low when the air is cold and high when the air is hot. On some models, this sensor is also known as the Manifold Air Temperature (MAT) sensor.

REMOVAL & INSTALLATION

1. Disconnect the negative battery cable.
2. Detach the sensor electrical connector locking tab.
3. Carefully remove the sensor.

To install:
4. Install the sensor.
5. Connect the electrical wiring.
6. Connect the negative battery cable.

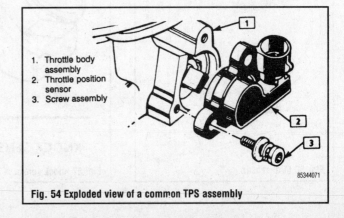

1. Throttle body assembly
2. Throttle position sensor
3. Screw assembly

85344071

Fig. 54 Exploded view of a common TPS assembly

Mass Air Flow (MAF) Sensor

▶ See Figures 55 and 56

OPERATION

The Mass Air Flow (MAF) sensor, found on some fuel injected engines, measures the amount of air passing through it. The ECM uses this information to determine the operating condition of the engine, to control fuel delivery. A large quantity of air indicates acceleration, while a small quantity indicates deceleration or idle.

The MAF sensor used on these vehicles is of the hot-wire type. Current is supplied to the sensing wire to maintain a calibrated temperature, and as air flow increases or decreases the current will vary. This varying current is directly proportional to air mass.

REMOVAL & INSTALLATION

1. Disconnect the negative battery cable.
2. Disconnect the sensor electrical connection.
3. Loosen the clamps and remove the air intake hoses from the MAF sensor.
4. Remove the sensor from the vehicle. On some models it will be necessary to remove the sensor-to-bracket attaching bolts.

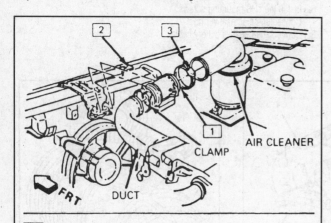

1	MAF SENSOR ASM (PONTIAC)
2	BRACKET MAF SENSOR
3	CLAMP 1.4-2.0 N·m (1-1.4 LBS. FT.)

85344073

Fig. 55 Mass Air Flow sensor mounting, all models similar

5. Installation is the reverse of removal.

Knock Sensor

▶ See Figure 57

OPERATION

The knock sensor is usually mounted to the right lower side of the engine block. When spark knock or pinging is present, the sensor produces a voltage signal which is sent to the ECM. The ECM will then retard the ignition timing based on these signals.

REMOVAL & INSTALLATION

1. Disconnect the negative battery cable.
2. Drain the engine coolant.
3. Raise and properly support the vehicle.
4. Disconnect the knock sensor wiring harness.
5. Remove the knock sensor from the engine block.

✷✷ CAUTION

The knock sensor is mounted in the engine block cooling passage. Engine coolant in the block will drain when the sensor is removed.

6. Installation is the reverse of removal. Tighten the sensor to 14 ft. lbs (19 Nm).

Vehicle Speed Sensor (VSS)

▶ See Figure 58

OPERATION

The VSS is located on the transmission and sends a pulsing voltage signal to the ECM which is converted to miles per hour. This sensor mainly controls the operation of the TCC system, shift light, cruise control and activation of the EGR system.

REMOVAL & INSTALLATION

1. Disconnect the negative battery cable.
2. Raise and safely support the vehicle.
3. Disconnect the VSS electrical wiring.
4. Remove the retaining bolt.
5. Have a clean container to catch the transmission fluid and remove the VSS.
6. Remove and discard the O-ring.

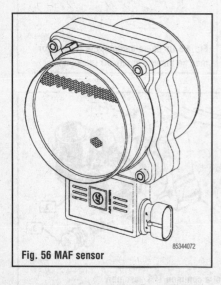

85344072

Fig. 56 MAF sensor

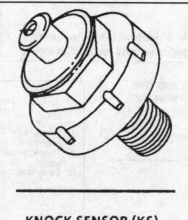

KNOCK SENSOR (KS)

85344074

Fig. 57 Knock sensor

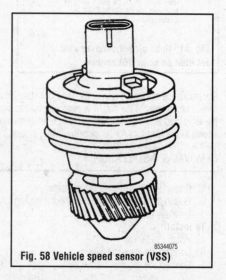

85344075

Fig. 58 Vehicle speed sensor (VSS)

To install:

7. Lubricate a new O-ring with a thin film of transmission fluid. Install the O-ring and VSS.

8. Install the retaining bolt.

9. Connect the electrical wiring.
10. Lower the vehicle.
11. Connect the negative battery cable.
12. Refill transmission to proper level.

TROUBLE CODES

Self Diagnostics

▶ See Figures 59 and 60

READING CODES

➡ The following procedure applies to models with the 12 pin diagnostic connector only.

1. Turn the ignition switch **OFF**. Locate the Assembly Line Diagnostic Link (ALDL), usually under the instrument panel. It may be within a plastic cover or housing labeled DIAGNOSTIC CONNECTOR. This link is used to communicate with the ECM.

2. Use a small jumper wire to connect Terminal B of the ALDL to Terminal A. As the ALDL connector is viewed from the front, Terminal A is on the extreme right of the upper row; Terminal B is second from the right on the upper row.

3. After the terminals are connected, turn the ignition switch to the **ON** position but do not start the engine. The dash warning lamp should begin to flash Code 12. The code will display as one flash, a pause and two flashes. Code 12 is not a fault code. It is used as a system acknowledgment or handshake code; its presence indicates that the ECM can communicate as requested. Code 12 is used to begin every diagnostic sequence.

4. After Code 12 has been transmitted 3 times, the fault codes, if any, will each be flashed in the same manner three times. The codes are stored and transmitted in numeric order from lowest to highest.

➡ The order of codes in the memory does not indicate the order of occurrence.

5. If one or more codes are stored, record them. At the end of the procedure, perform a visual and physical check of each system.

6. Switch the ignition **OFF** when finished with code retrieval.

Visual and Physical Underhood Inspection

A detailed examination of connectors, wiring and vacuum hoses can often lead to a repair without further diagnosis. This step relies on the skill of the technician performing it; a careful inspector will check the undersides of hoses as well as the integrity of hard-to-reach hoses blocked by the air cleaner or other component. Wiring should be checked carefully for any sign of strain, burning, crimping, or terminal pull-out from a connector. Checking connectors at components or in harnesses is required; usually, pushing them together will reveal a loose fit. It is important to note that the fault code indicates a fault or loss of signal within that system, not necessarily the specific component. Due to the intricacy of the systems and the special testing equipment required, it is recommended to have a qualified technician perform any further testing, if needed.

FIELD SERVICE MODE

On fuel injected models, if the ALDL terminal B is grounded to terminal A with the engine running, the system enters the Field Service Mode. In this mode, the MIL will indicate whether the system is operating in open loop or closed loop.

If working in open loop, the MIL will flash rapidly 2½ times per second. In closed loop, the flash rate slows to once per second. Additionally, if the system is running lean in closed loop, the lamp will be off most of the cycle. A rich condition in closed loop will cause the lamp to remain lit for most of the one second cycle.

When operating in the Field Service Mode, additional codes cannot be stored by the ECM. The closed loop timer is bypassed in this mode.

CLEARING CODES

Stored fault codes may be erased from memory at any time by removing power from the ECM for at least 30 seconds. It may be necessary to clear stored codes during diagnosis to check for any recurrence during a test drive, but the stored should be written down when retrieved. The codes may still be required for subsequent troubleshooting. Whenever a repair is complete, the stored codes must be erased and the vehicle test driven to confirm correct operation and repair.

➡ The ignition switch must be OFF any time power is disconnected or restored to the ECM. Severe damage may result if this precaution is not observed.

Depending on the electric distribution of the particular vehicle, power to the ECM may be disconnected by removing the ECM fuse in the fusebox or disconnecting the inline ECM power lead at the positive battery terminal. Disconnecting the negative battery cable to clear codes will achieve the desired result, but this will also clear other memory data in the vehicle such as radio presets or seat memory.

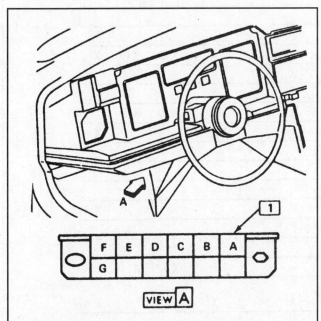

1. ALCL Connector
A. Ground
B. Diagnostic "Test Terminal"
C. A.I.R.
E. Serial data
F. T.C.C.
G. Fuel pump

85344076

Fig. 59 Diagnostic connector location shown with a 12 pin connector

DIAGNOSTIC TROUBLE CODES

Trouble Codes	4-2.5L (2)	6-2.8L (1)	6-2.8L (5)	6-3.1L (T)	8-5.0L (E)	8-5.0L (F)	8-5.0L (G)	8-5.0L (H)	8-5.7L (8)
12—Speed reference pulse	X⑤	X⑤	X⑤	X⑤	X⑤	X⑤	X⑤	X⑤	X⑤
13—Oxygen sensor	X	X	X	X	X	X	X	X	X
14—CTS (Temp HI)	X	X	X	X	X	X	X	X	X
15—CTS (Temp LO)	X	X		X	X	X	X	X	X
16—System volts HI									
21—TPS (Volts HI)	X	X	X	X	X	X	X	X	X
22—TPS (Volts LO)	X		X	X	X	X			X
23—MAT (Temp LO)			X	X	X	X			X
23—M/C solenoid (open or ground)		X					X	X	
24—VSS	X	X	X	X	X	X	X	X	X
24B—Park/neutral switch									
25—MAT (Temp HI)			X	X	X	X			X
26—Quad-driver									
27/28—Gear switch									
28/29—Gear switch									
31—Park/neutral switch									
31—Wastegate overboost									
31—Canister purge (Volts HI)									
32—EGR failure		X①	X	X	X	X	X①	X①	X
33—MAP (Volts HI/Vac LO)	X			X	X				
33—MAF (gm/sec HI)			X			X			X
34—MAP (Volts LO/Vac HI)	X	X②		X	X		X②	X②	
34—MAF (gm/sec HI)			X			X			X
35—Idle speed error									
35—IAC				X					
36—Close throttle air flow HI									
36—MAF burn-off						X			X
38—Brake switch									
39—TCC									
41—1 X reference		X					X	X	
41—Cylinder select error/ MEM-CAL			X	X		X			X
41—Cam sensor									
42—EST	X	X	X	X	X	X	X	X	X
43—ESC		X		X	X	X	X	X	X
44—Oxygen sensor (lean)	X	X	X	X	X	X	X	X	X
45—Oxygen sensor (rich)	X	X	X	X	X	X	X	X	X
46—Power steering press switch									
46—VATS				X		X			X
48—Misfire diagnosis									

82604078

Fig. 60 Diagnostic trouble codes

ENGINE COMPONENT LOCATIONS

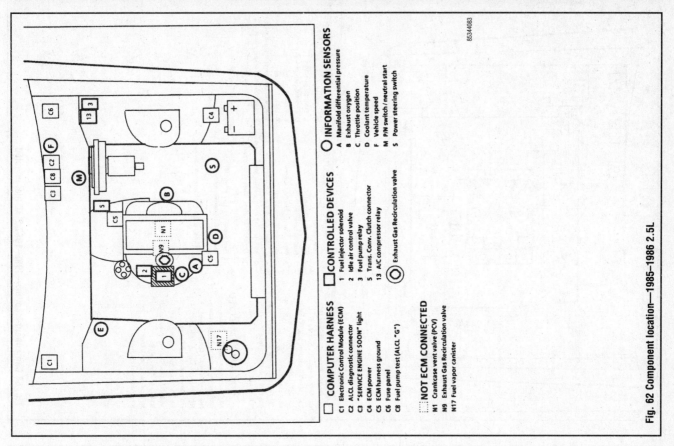

○ INFORMATION SENSORS

A Manifold differential pressure
B Exhaust oxygen
C Throttle position
D Coolant temperature
F Vehicle speed
M P/N switch/neutral start
S Power steering switch

□ CONTROLLED DEVICES

1 Fuel injector solenoid
2 Idle air control valve
3 Fuel pump relay
5 Trans. Conv. Clutch connector
13 A/C compressor relay
◎ Exhaust Gas Recirculation valve

□ COMPUTER HARNESS

C1 Electronic Control Module (ECM)
C2 ALCL diagnostic connector
C3 "SERVICE ENGINE SOON" light
C4 ECM power
C5 ECM harness ground
C6 Fuse panel
C8 Fuel pump test (ALCL "G")

□ NOT ECM CONNECTED

N1 Crankcase vent valve (PCV)
N9 Exhaust Gas Recirculation valve
N17 Fuel vapor canister

85344083

Fig. 62 Component location—1985–1986 2.5L

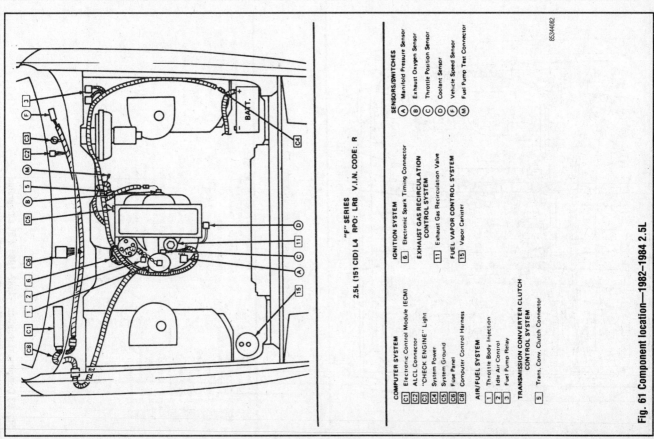

COMPUTER SYSTEM

C1 Electronic Control Module (ECM)
C2 ALCL Connector
C3 "CHECK ENGINE" Light
C4 System Power
C5 System Ground
C6 Fuse Panel
C8 Computer Control Harness

AIR/FUEL SYSTEM

1 Throttle Body Injection
2 Idle Air Control
3 Fuel Pump Relay

TRANSMISSION CONVERTER CLUTCH CONTROL SYSTEM

5 Trans. Conv. Clutch Connector

IGNITION SYSTEM

6 Electronic Spark Timing Connector

EXHAUST GAS RECIRCULATION CONTROL SYSTEM

11 Exhaust Gas Recirculation Valve

FUEL VAPOR CONTROL SYSTEM

15 Vapor Canister

SENSORS/SWITCHES

A Manifold Pressure Sensor
B Exhaust Oxygen Sensor
C Throttle Position Sensor
D Coolant Sensor
F Vehicle Speed Sensor
M Fuel Pump Test Connector

2.5L (151 CID) L4 RPO: LR8 V.I.N. CODE: R

"F" SERIES

85344082

Fig. 61 Component location—1982–1984 2.5L

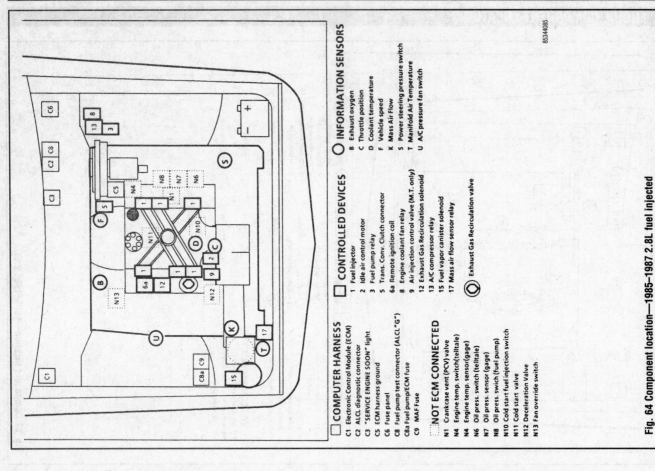

COMPUTER HARNESS
C1 Electronic Control Module (ECM)
C2 ALCL diagnostic connector
C3 "SERVICE ENGINE SOON" light
C5 ECM harness ground
C6 Fuse panel
C8 Fuel pump test connector (ALCL "G")
C8a Fuel pump/ECM fuse
C9 MAF Fuse

NOT ECM CONNECTED
N1 Crankcase vent (PCV) valve
N4 Engine temp. switch(telltale)
N6 Engine temp. sensor(gage)
N6 Oil press. switch (telltale)
N7 Oil press. sensor (gage)
N8 Oil press. swich (fuel pump)
N10 Cold start fuel injection switch
N11 Cold start valve
N12 Deceleration valve
N13 Fan override switch

CONTROLLED DEVICES
1 Fuel injector
2 Idle air control motor
3 Fuel pump relay
5 Trans. Conv. Clutch connector
6a Remote ignition coil
8 Engine coolant fan relay
9 Air injection control valve (M.T. only)
12 Exhaust Gas Recirculation solenoid
13 A/C compressor relay
15 Fuel vapor canister solenoid
17 Mass air flow sensor relay

⊙ Exhaust Gas Recirculation valve

INFORMATION SENSORS
B Exhaust oxygen
C Throttle position
D Coolant temperature
F Vehicle speed
K Mass Air Flow
S Power steering pressure switch
T Manifold Air Temperature
U A/C pressure fan switch

Fig. 64 Component location—1985–1987 2.8L fuel injected

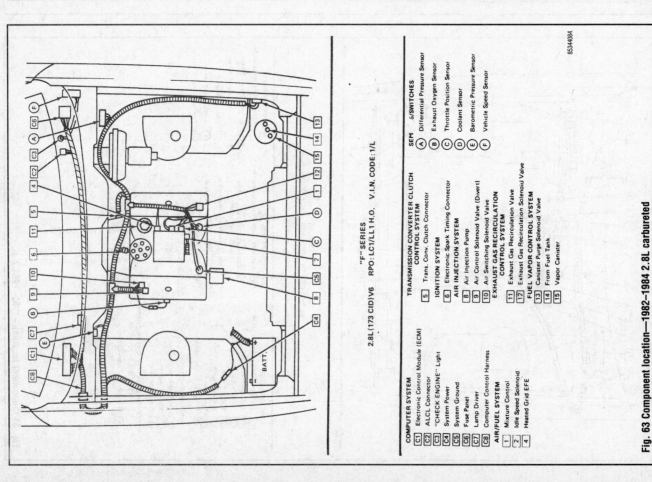

COMPUTER SYSTEM
C1 Electronic Control Module (ECM)
C2 ALCL Connector
C3 "CHECK ENGINE" Light
C4 System Power
C5 System Ground
C6 Fuse Panel
C7 Lamp Driver
C8 Computer Control Harness

AIR/FUEL SYSTEM
1 Mixture Control
2 Idle Speed Solenoid
4 Heated Grid EFE

2.8L (173 CID)V6   "F" SERIES
RPO: LC1/LL1 H.O.   V.I.N. CODE: 1/L

**TRANSMISSION CONVERTER CLUTCH
CONTROL SYSTEM**
5 Trans. Conv. Clutch Connector

IGNITION SYSTEM
6 Electronic Spark Timing Connector

AIR INJECTION SYSTEM
8 Air Injection Pump
9 Air Control Solenoid Valve (Divert)
10 Air Switching Solenoid Valve

**EXHAUST GAS RECIRCULATION
CONTROL SYSTEM**
11 Exhaust Gas Recirculation Valve
12 Exhaust Gas Recirculation Solenoid Valve

FUEL VAPOR CONTROL SYSTEM
13 Canister Purge Solenoid Valve
14 From Fuel Tank
15 Vapor Canister

SEM   s/SWITCHES
A Differential Pressure Sensor
B Exhaust Oxygen Sensor
C Throttle Position Sensor
D Coolant Sensor
E Barometric Pressure Sensor
F Vehicle Speed Sensor

Fig. 63 Component location—1982–1984 2.8L carbureted

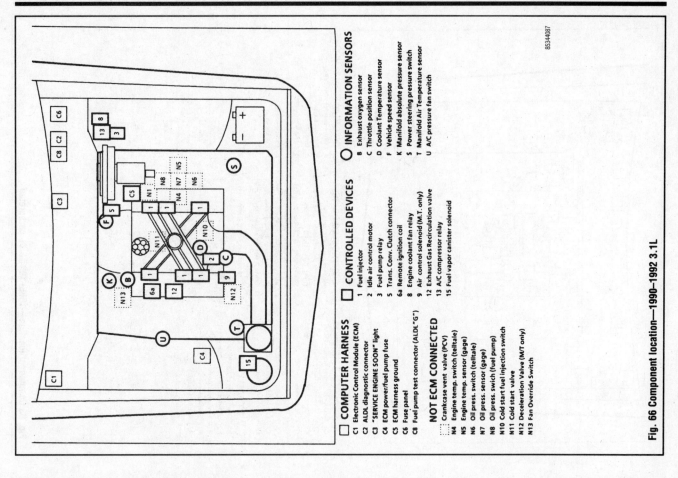

□ **COMPUTER HARNESS**

C1 Electronic Control Module (ECM)
C2 ALDL diagnostic connector
C3 "SERVICE ENGINE SOON" light
C4 ECM power/fuel pump fuse
C5 ECM harness ground
C6 Fuse panel
C8 Fuel pump test connector (ALDL "G")

NOT ECM CONNECTED

N1 Crankcase vent valve (PCV)
N4 Engine temp. switch (telltale)
N5 Engine temp. sensor (gage)
N6 Oil press. switch (telltale)
N7 Oil press. sensor (gage)
N8 Oil press. switch (fuel pump)
N10 Cold start fuel injection switch
N11 Cold start valve
N12 Deceleration Valve (M/T only)
N13 Fan Override Switch

□ **CONTROLLED DEVICES**

1 Fuel injector
2 Idle air control motor
3 Fuel pump relay
5 Trans. Conv. Clutch connector
6a Remote ignition coil
8 Engine coolant fan relay
9 Air control solenoid (M.T. only)
12 Exhaust Gas Recirculation valve
13 A/C compressor relay
15 Fuel vapor canister solenoid

○ **INFORMATION SENSORS**

B Exhaust oxygen sensor
C Throttle position sensor
D Coolant Temperature sensor
F Vehicle speed sensor
K Manifold absolute pressure sensor
S Power steering pressure switch
T Manifold Air Temperature sensor
U A/C pressure fan switch

85344087

Fig. 66 Component location—1990–1992 3.1L

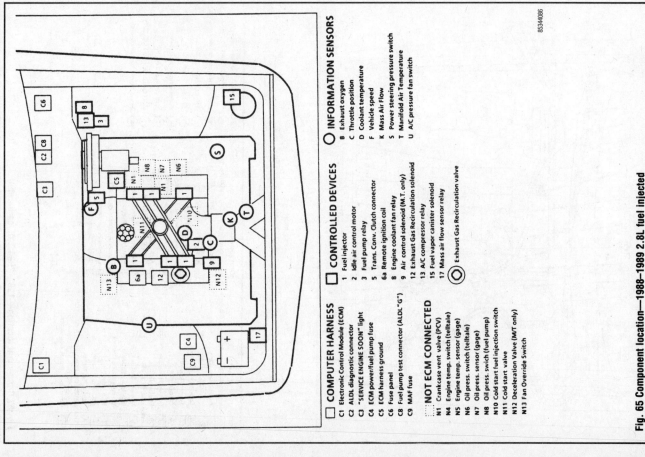

□ **COMPUTER HARNESS**

C1 Electronic Control Module (ECM)
C2 ALDL diagnostic connector
C3 "SERVICE ENGINE SOON" light
C4 ECM power/fuel pump fuse
C5 ECM harness ground
C6 Fuse panel
C8 Fuel pump test connector (ALDL "G")
C9 MAF fuse

NOT ECM CONNECTED

N1 Crankcase vent valve (PCV)
N4 Engine temp. switch (telltale)
N5 Engine temp. sensor (gage)
N6 Oil press. switch (telltale)
N7 Oil press. sensor (gage)
N8 Oil press. swich (fuel pump)
N10 Cold start fuel injection switch
N11 Cold start valve
N12 Deceleration Valve (M/T only)
N13 Fan Override Switch

□ **CONTROLLED DEVICES**

1 Fuel injector
2 Idle air control motor
3 Fuel pump relay
5 Trans. Conv. Clutch connector
6a Remote ignition coil
8 Engine coolant fan relay
9 Air control solenoid (M.T. only)
12 Exhaust Gas Recirculation solenoid
13 A/C compressor relay
15 Fuel vapor canister solenoid
17 Mass air flow sensor relay
◎ Exhaust Gas Recirculation valve

○ **INFORMATION SENSORS**

B Exhaust oxygen
C Throttle position
D Coolant temperature
F Vehicle speed
K Mass Air Flow
S Power steering pressure switch
T Manifold Air Temperature
U A/C pressure fan switch

85344086

Fig. 65 Component location—1988–1989 2.8L fuel injected

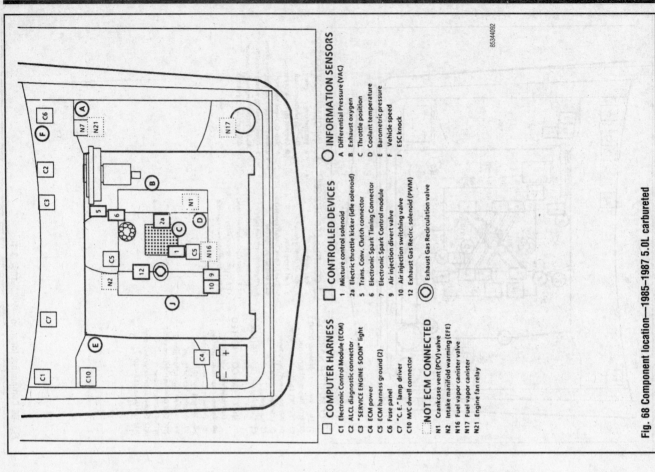

□ **COMPUTER HARNESS**

- C1 Electronic Control Module (ECM)
- C2 ALCL diagnostic connector
- C3 "SERVICE ENGINE SOON" light
- C4 ECM power
- C5 ECM harness ground (2)
- C6 Fuse panel
- C7 "C. E." lamp driver
- C10 M/C dwell connector

□ **CONTROLLED DEVICES**

- 1 Mixture control solenoid
- 2a Electric throttle kicker (idle solenoid)
- 5 Trans. Conv. Clutch connector
- 6 Electronic Spark Timing Connector
- 7 Electronic Spark Control module
- 9 Air injection switching valve
- 10 Air injection divert valve
- 12 Exhaust Gas Recirc. solenoid (PWM)

○ **Exhaust Gas Recirculation valve**

○ **INFORMATION SENSORS**

- A Differential Pressure (VAC)
- B Exhaust oxygen
- C Throttle position
- E Coolant temperature
- E Barometric pressure
- F Vehicle speed
- J ESC knock

□ **NOT ECM CONNECTED**

- N1 Crankcase vent (PCV) valve
- N2 Intake manifold warming (EFE)
- N16 Fuel vapor canister valve
- N17 Fuel vapor canister
- N21 Engine fan relay

85344092

Fig. 68 Component location—1985–1987 5.0L carbureted

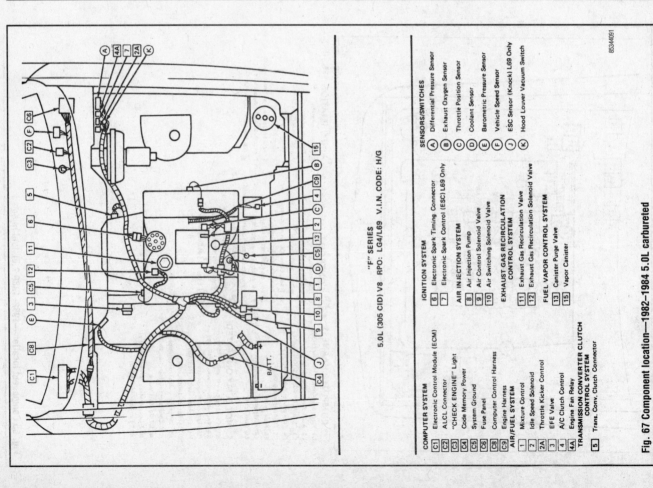

5.0L (305 CID) V8   "F" SERIES   RPO: LG4/L69   V.I.N. CODE: H/G

COMPUTER SYSTEM

- C1 Electronic Control Module (ECM)
- C2 ALCL Connector
- C3 "CHECK ENGINE" Light
- C4 Code Memory Power
- C5 System Ground
- C6 Fuse Panel
- C8 Computer Control Harness
- C9 Engine Harness

AIR/FUEL SYSTEM

- 1 Mixture Control
- 2 Idle Speed Solenoid
- 2A Throttle Kicker Control
- 3 EFE Valve
- 4 A/C Clutch Control
- 4A Engine Fan Relay

TRANSMISSION CONVERTER CLUTCH CONTROL SYSTEM

- 5 Trans. Conv. Clutch Connector

IGNITION SYSTEM

- 6 Electronic Spark Timing Connector
- 7 Electronic Spark Control (ESC) L69 Only

AIR INJECTION SYSTEM

- 8 Air Injection Pump
- 9 Air Control Solenoid Valve
- 10 Air Switching Solenoid Valve

EXHAUST GAS RECIRCULATION CONTROL SYSTEM

- 11 Exhaust Gas Recirculation Valve
- 12 Exhaust Gas Recirculation Solenoid Valve

FUEL VAPOR CONTROL SYSTEM

- 13 Canister Purge Valve
- 15 Vapor Canister

SENSORS/SWITCHES

- A Differential Pressure Sensor
- B Exhaust Oxygen Sensor
- C Throttle Position Sensor
- D Coolant Sensor
- E Barometric Pressure Sensor
- F Vehicle Speed Sensor
- J ESC Sensor (Knock) L69 Only
- K Hood Louver Vacuum Switch

85344091

Fig. 67 Component location—1982–1984 5.0L carbureted

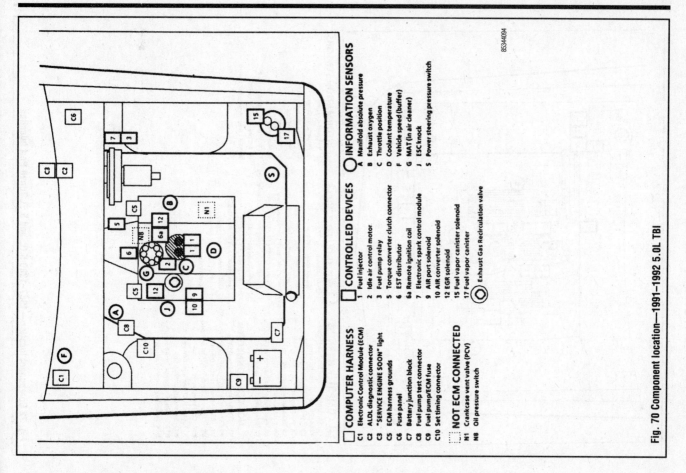

COMPUTER HARNESS
- C1 Electronic Control Module (ECM)
- C2 ALDL diagnostic connector
- C3 "SERVICE ENGINE SOON" light
- C5 ECM harness grounds
- C6 Fuse panel
- C7 Battery junction block
- C8 Fuel pump test connector
- C9 Fuel pump/ECM fuse
- C10 Set timing connector

NOT ECM CONNECTED
- N1 Crankcase vent valve (PCV)
- N8 Oil pressure switch

CONTROLLED DEVICES
- 1 Fuel injector
- 2 Idle air control motor
- 3 Fuel pump relay
- 5 Torque converter clutch connector
- 6 EST distributor
- 6a Remote ignition coil
- 7 Electronic spark control module
- 9 AIR port solenoid
- 10 AIR converter solenoid
- 12 EGR solenoid
- 15 Fuel vapor canister solenoid
- 17 Fuel vapor canister

INFORMATION SENSORS
- A Manifold absolute pressure
- B Exhaust oxygen
- C Throttle position
- D Coolant temperature
- F Vehicle speed (buffer)
- G MAT (in air cleaner)
- J ESC knock
- S Power steering pressure switch

◎ Exhaust Gas Recirculation valve

Fig. 70 Component location—1991–1992 5.0L TBI

85344094

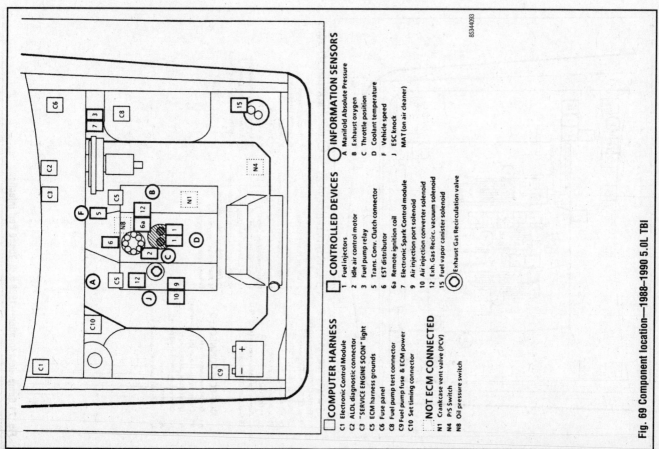

COMPUTER HARNESS
- C1 Electronic Control Module
- C2 ALDL diagnostic connector
- C3 "SERVICE ENGINE SOON" light
- C5 ECM harness grounds
- C6 Fuse panel
- C8 Fuel pump test connector
- C9 Fuel pump fuse & ECM power
- C10 Set timing connector

NOT ECM CONNECTED
- N1 Crankcase vent valve (PCV)
- N4 P/S Switch
- N8 Oil pressure switch

CONTROLLED DEVICES
- 1 Fuel injectors
- 2 Idle air control motor
- 3 Fuel pump relay
- 5 Trans. Conv. Clutch connector
- 6 EST distributor
- 6a Remote ignition coil
- 7 Electronic Spark Control module
- 9 Air injection port solenoid
- 10 Air injection converter solenoid
- 12 Exh. Gas Recirc. vacuum solenoid
- 15 Fuel vapor canister solenoid

INFORMATION SENSORS
- A Manifold Absolute Pressure
- B Exhaust oxygen
- C Throttle position
- D Coolant temperature
- F Vehicle speed
- J ESC knock
- M MAT (on air cleaner)

◎ Exhaust Gas Recirculation valve

Fig. 69 Component location—1988–1990 5.0L TBI

85344093

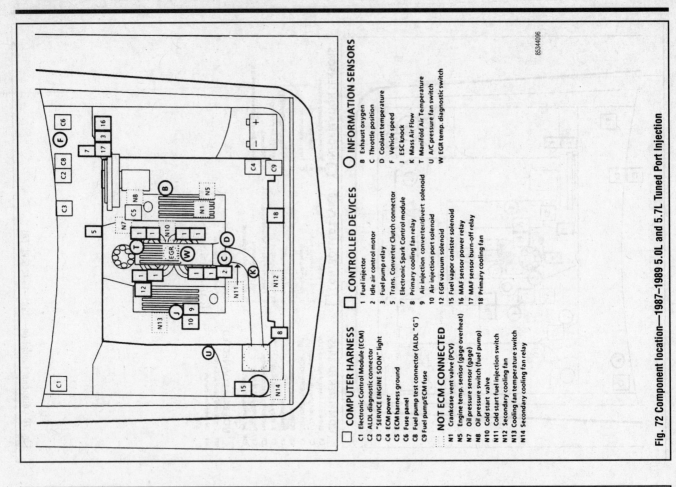

☐ COMPUTER HARNESS
- C1 Electronic Control Module (ECM)
- C2 ALDL diagnostic connector
- C3 "SERVICE ENGINE SOON" light
- C4 ECM power
- C5 ECM harness ground
- C6 Fuse panel
- C8 Fuel pump test connector (ALDL "G")
- C9 Fuel pump/ECM fuse

☐ CONTROLLED DEVICES
- 1 Fuel injector
- 2 Idle air control motor
- 3 Fuel pump relay
- 5 Trans. Converter Clutch connector
- 7 Electronic Spark Control module
- 8 Primary cooling fan relay
- 9 Air injection converter/divert solenoid
- 10 Air injection port solenoid
- 12 EGR vacuum solenoid
- 15 Fuel vapor canister solenoid
- 16 MAF sensor power relay
- 17 MAF sensor burn-off relay
- 18 Primary cooling fan

⬭ INFORMATION SENSORS
- B Exhaust oxygen
- C Throttle position
- D Coolant temperature
- F Vehicle speed
- J ESC knock
- K Mass Air Flow
- T Manifold Air Temperature
- U A/C pressure fan switch
- W EGR temp. diagnostic switch

⋯ NOT ECM CONNECTED
- N1 Crankcase vent valve (PCV)
- N5 Engine temp. sensor (gage overheat)
- N7 Oil pressure sensor (gage)
- N8 Oil pressure switch (fuel pump)
- N10 Cold start valve
- N11 Cold start fuel injection switch
- N12 Secondary cooling fan
- N13 Cooling fan temperature switch
- N14 Secondary cooling fan relay

Fig. 72 Component location—1987–1989 5.0L and 5.7L Tuned Port Injection

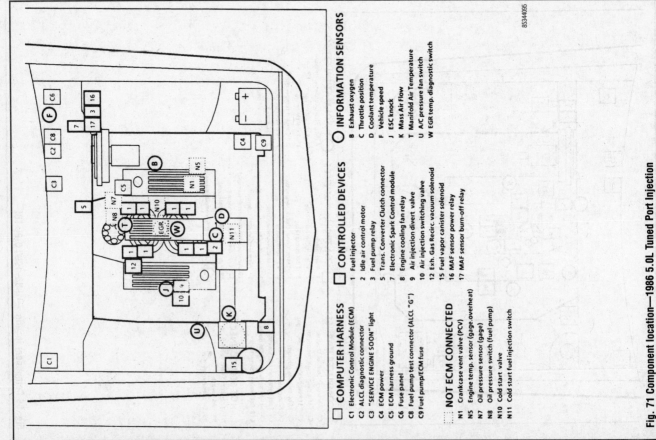

☐ COMPUTER HARNESS
- C1 Electronic Control Module (ECM)
- C2 ALCL diagnostic connector
- C3 "SERVICE ENGINE SOON" light
- C4 ECM power
- C5 ECM harness ground
- C6 Fuse panel
- C8 Fuel pump test connector (ALCL "G")
- C9 Fuel pump/ECM fuse

☐ CONTROLLED DEVICES
- 1 Fuel injector
- 2 Idle air control motor
- 3 Fuel pump relay
- 5 Trans. Converter Clutch connector
- 7 Electronic Spark Control module
- 8 Engine cooling fan relay
- 9 Air injection divert valve
- 10 Air injection switching valve
- 12 Exh. Gas Recirc. vacuum solenoid
- 15 Fuel vapor canister solenoid
- 16 MAF sensor power relay
- 17 MAF sensor burn-off relay

⬭ INFORMATION SENSORS
- B Exhaust oxygen
- C Throttle position
- D Coolant temperature
- F Vehicle speed
- J ESC knock
- K Mass Air Flow
- T Manifold Air Temperature
- U A/C pressure fan switch
- W EGR temp. diagnostic switch

⋯ NOT ECM CONNECTED
- N1 Crankcase vent valve (PCV)
- N5 Engine temp. sensor (gage-overheat)
- N7 Oil pressure sensor (gage)
- N8 Oil pressure switch (fuel pump)
- N10 Cold start valve
- N11 Cold start fuel injection switch

Fig. 71 Component location—1986 5.0L Tuned Port Injection

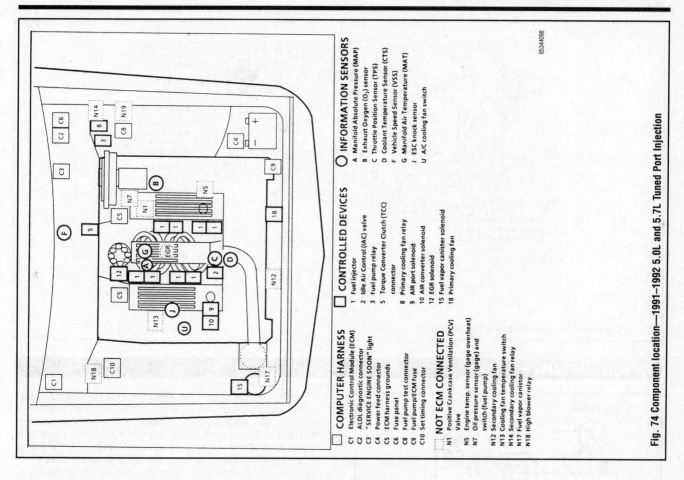

85344098

COMPUTER HARNESS

C1 Electronic Control Module (ECM)
C2 ALDL diagnostic connector
C3 "SERVICE ENGINE SOON" light
C4 Power feed connector
C5 ECM harness grounds
C6 Fuse panel
C8 Fuel pump test connector
C9 Fuel pump/ECM fuse
C10 Set timing connector

NOT ECM CONNECTED

N1 Positive Crankcase Ventilation (PCV) Valve
N5 Engine temp. sensor (gage overheat)
N7 Oil pressure sensor (gage) and switch (fuel pump)
N12 Secondary cooling fan
N13 Cooling fan temperature switch
N14 Secondary cooling fan relay
N17 Fuel vapor canister
N18 High blower relay

▣ CONTROLLED DEVICES

1   Fuel injector
2   Idle Air Control (IAC) valve
3   Fuel pump relay
5   Torque Converter Clutch (TCC) connector
8   Primary cooling fan relay
9   AIR port solenoid
10 AIR converter solenoid
12 EGR solenoid
15 Fuel vapor canister solenoid
18 Primary cooling fan

◯ INFORMATION SENSORS

A   Manifold Absolute Pressure (MAP)
B   Exhaust Oxygen (O₂) sensor
C   Throttle Position Sensor (TPS)
D   Coolant Temperature Sensor (CTS)
F   Vehicle Speed Sensor (VSS)
G   Manifold Air Temperature (MAT)
J   ESC knock sensor
U   A/C cooling fan switch

Fig. 74 Component location—1991–1992 5.0L and 5.7L Tuned Port Injection

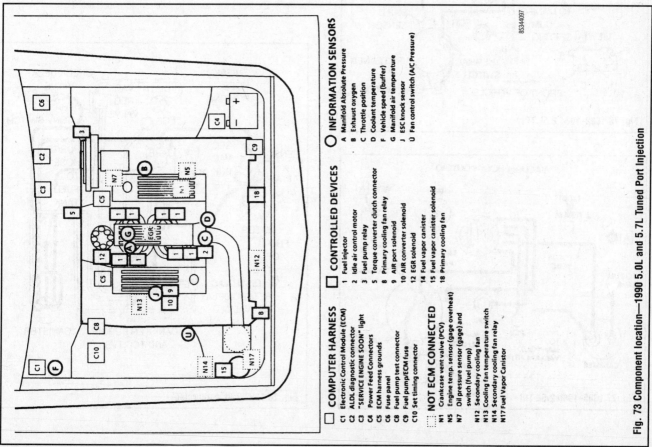

85344097

COMPUTER HARNESS

C1 Electronic Control Module (ECM)
C2 ALDL diagnostic connector
C3 "SERVICE ENGINE SOON" light
C4 Power Feed Connectors
C5 ECM harness grounds
C6 Fuse panel
C8 Fuel pump test connector
C9 Fuel pump/ECM fuse
C10 Set timing connector

NOT ECM CONNECTED

N1 Crankcase vent valve (PCV)
N5 Engine temp. sensor (gage overheat)
N7 Oil pressure sensor (gage) and switch (fuel pump)
N12 Secondary cooling fan
N13 Cooling fan temperature switch
N14 Secondary cooling fan relay
N17 Fuel Vapor Canister

▣ CONTROLLED DEVICES

1   Fuel injector
2   Idle air control motor
3   Fuel pump relay
5   Torque converter clutch connector
8   Primary cooling fan relay
9   AIR port solenoid
10 AIR converter solenoid
12 EGR solenoid
14 Fuel vapor canister
15 Fuel vapor canister solenoid
18 Primary cooling fan

◯ INFORMATION SENSORS

A   Manifold Absolute Pressure
B   Exhaust oxygen
C   Throttle position
D   Coolant temperature
F   Vehicle speed (buffer)
G   Manifold air temperature
J   ESC knock sensor
U   Fan control switch (A/C Pressure)

Fig. 73 Component location—1990 5.0L and 5.7L Tuned Port Injection

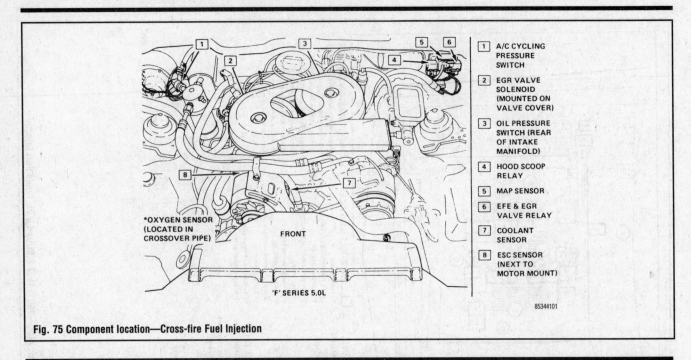

1. A/C CYCLING PRESSURE SWITCH
2. EGR VALVE SOLENOID (MOUNTED ON VALVE COVER)
3. OIL PRESSURE SWITCH (REAR OF INTAKE MANIFOLD)
4. HOOD SCOOP RELAY
5. MAP SENSOR
6. EFE & EGR VALVE RELAY
7. COOLANT SENSOR
8. ESC SENSOR (NEXT TO MOTOR MOUNT)

*OXYGEN SENSOR (LOCATED IN CROSSOVER PIPE)

FRONT

'F' SERIES 5.0L

85344101

Fig. 75 Component location—Cross-fire Fuel Injection

VACUUM DIAGRAMS

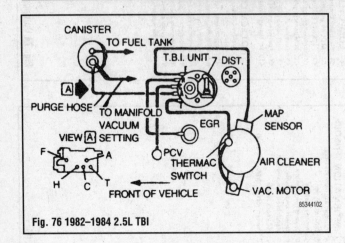

Fig. 76 1982–1984 2.5L TBI

Following are vacuum diagrams for most of the engine and emissions package combinations covered by this manual. Because vacuum circuits will vary based on various engine and vehicle options, always refer first to the vehicle emission control information label, if present. Should the label be missing, or should vehicle be equipped with a different engine from the vehicle's original equipment, refer to the diagrams below for the same or similar configuration. If you wish to obtain a replacement emissions label, most manufacturers make the labels available for purchase. The labels can usually be ordered from a local dealer.

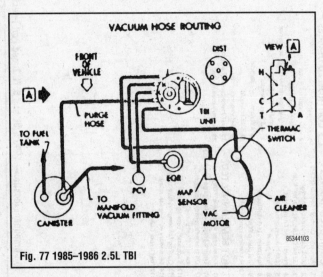

Fig. 77 1985–1986 2.5L TBI

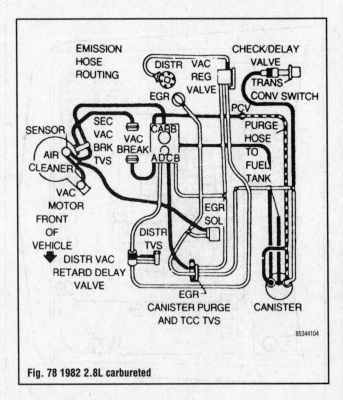

Fig. 78 1982 2.8L carbureted

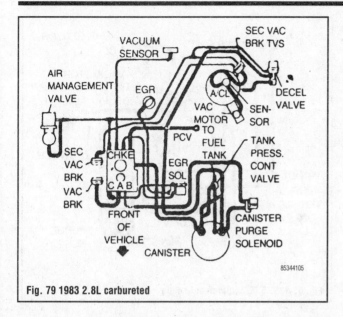

Fig. 79 1983 2.8L carbureted

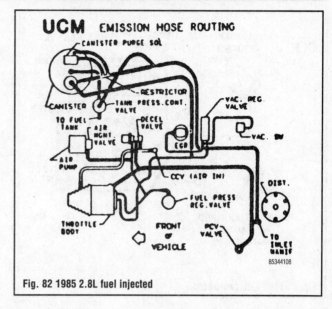

Fig. 82 1985 2.8L fuel injected

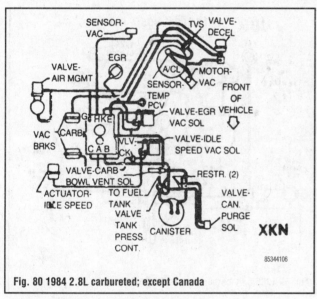

Fig. 80 1984 2.8L carbureted; except Canada

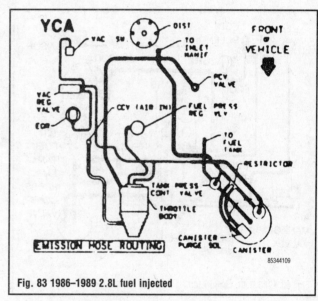

Fig. 83 1986–1989 2.8L fuel injected

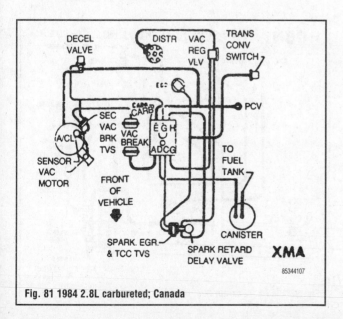

Fig. 81 1984 2.8L carbureted; Canada

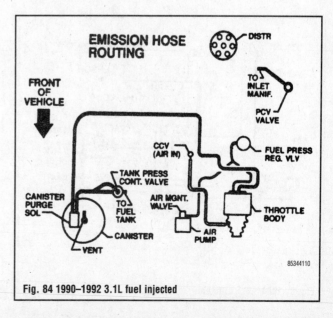

Fig. 84 1990–1992 3.1L fuel injected

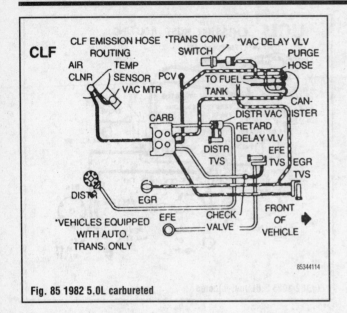

Fig. 85 1982 5.0L carbureted

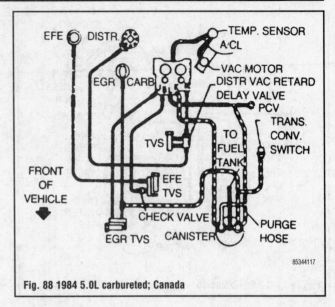

Fig. 88 1984 5.0L carbureted; Canada

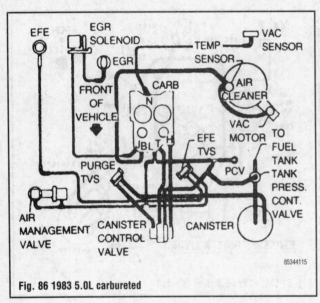

Fig. 86 1983 5.0L carbureted

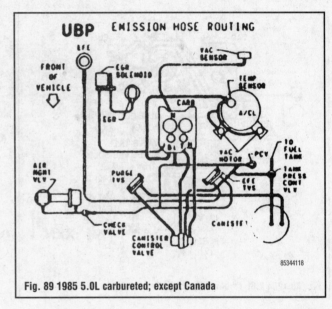

Fig. 89 1985 5.0L carbureted; except Canada

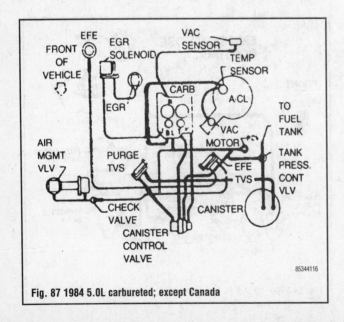

Fig. 87 1984 5.0L carbureted; except Canada

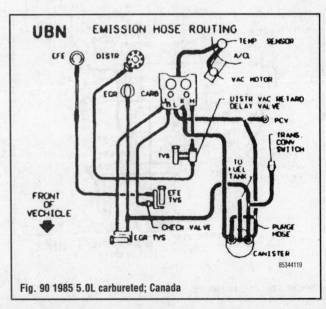

Fig. 90 1985 5.0L carbureted; Canada

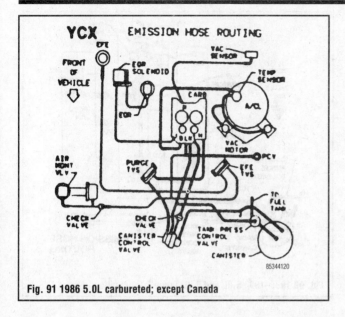

Fig. 91 1986 5.0L carbureted; except Canada

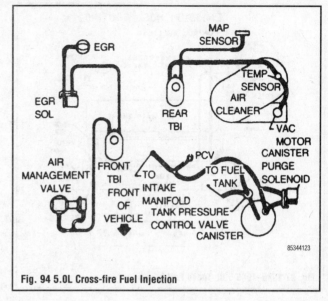

Fig. 94 5.0L Cross-fire Fuel Injection

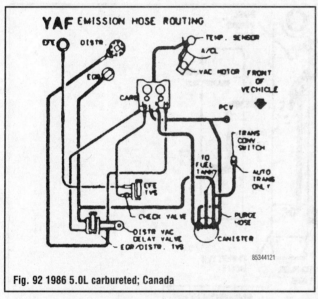

Fig. 92 1986 5.0L carbureted; Canada

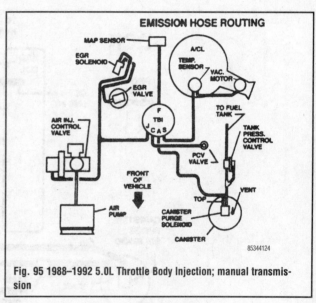

Fig. 95 1988–1992 5.0L Throttle Body Injection; manual transmission

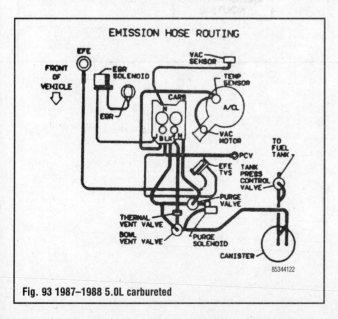

Fig. 93 1987–1988 5.0L carbureted

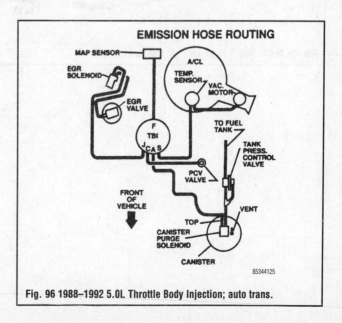

Fig. 96 1988–1992 5.0L Throttle Body Injection; auto trans.

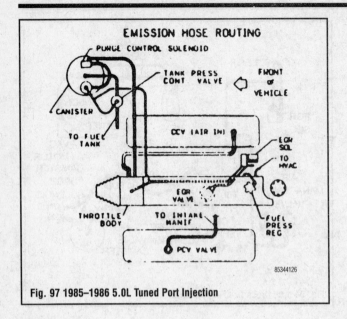

Fig. 97 1985–1986 5.0L Tuned Port Injection

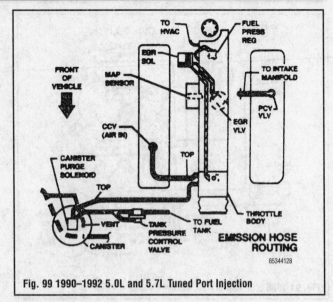

Fig. 99 1990–1992 5.0L and 5.7L Tuned Port Injection

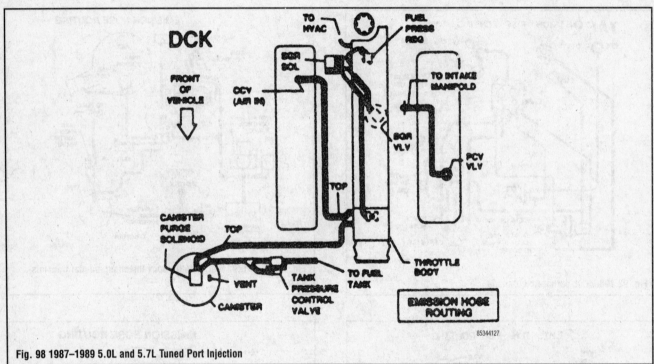

Fig. 98 1987–1989 5.0L and 5.7L Tuned Port Injection

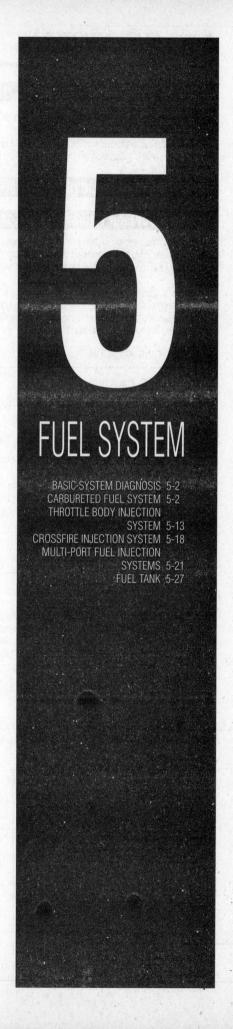

5

FUEL SYSTEM

BASIC FUEL SYSTEM DIAGNOSIS

When there is a problem starting or driving a vehicle, two of the most important checks involve the ignition and the fuel systems. The questions most mechanics attempt to answer first, "is there spark?" and "is there fuel?" will often lead to solving most basic problems. For ignition system diagnosis and testing, please refer to the information on engine electrical components and ignition systems found earlier in this manual. If the ignition system checks out (there is spark), then you must determine if the fuel system is operating properly (is there fuel?).

CARBURETED FUEL SYSTEM

Mechanical Fuel Pump

All fuel pumps used on carbureted V6 and V8 engines are of the diaphragm type and are serviced by replacement only. No adjustments or repairs are possible. The fuel pump is mounted on the left front (V6) and right front (V8) of the engine.

The fuel pumps are also equipped with vapor return lines for purposes of emission control and to reduce vapor lock. All pumps are operated by an eccentric on the camshaft. On V6 and V8 engines, a pushrod between the camshaft eccentric and the fuel pump operates the pump.

REMOVAL & INSTALLATION

▶ **See Figures 1, 2 and 3**

➡**When disconnecting the fuel pump outlet fitting, always use two wrenches to avoid twisting the line.**

1. Disconnect the fuel intake and outlet lines at the pump, then plug the pump intake line.
2. Remove the two pump mounting bolts and lockwashers; remove the pump and its gasket.
3. If the fuel pushrod is to be removed from the V8, remove the two adapter bolts and lockwashers, then remove the adapter and its gasket.
4. Install the fuel pump with a new gasket reversing the removal procedure. Coat the mating surfaces with sealer.
5. Connect the fuel lines and check for leaks.

TESTING

To determine if the pump is in good condition, tests for both volume and pressure should be performed. The tests are made with the pump installed, the engine at normal operating temperature and operating at idle speed. Never replace a fuel pump without first performing these simple tests.

Ensure the fuel filter has been changed at the specified interval. If in doubt, install a new filter first. Always check for broken or deteriorated fuel hoses. If a line has a crack or split, the pump may be operating properly, but the pump will only draw air, not fuel.

Pressure Test

1. Disconnect the fuel line at the carburetor, then connect a fuel pump pressure gauge. Ensure the carburetor float bowl has a sufficient amount of gasoline.

2. Start the engine and check the pressure with the engine at idle. If the pump has a vapor return hose, squeeze it off so that an accurate reading can be obtained. Pressure should be 5½–6½ psi.
3. If the pressure is incorrect, replace the pump. If it is within specifications, go on to the volume test.

Volume Test

1. Disconnect the pressure gauge. Run the fuel line into a graduated container.
2. Run the engine at idle until one pint of gasoline has been pumped. One pint should be delivered in 30 seconds or less. There is normally enough fuel in the carburetor float bowl to perform this test, but refill it if necessary.
3. If the delivery rate is below the minimum, check the lines for restrictions or leaks, then replace the pump.

Carburetors

The V6 engine is equipped with the Rochester E2SE carburetor, V8 engines use the E4ME and E4MC. These carburetors are of the downdraft design and are used in conjunction with the CCC system for fuel control. They have special design features for optimum air/fuel mixture control during all ranges of engine operation.

An electric solenoid in the carburetor controls the air/fuel ratio. The solenoid is connected to an Electronic Control Module (ECM) which is an on-board computer. The ECM provides a controlling signal to the solenoid. The solenoid controls the metering rod(s) and an idle air bleed valve, thereby closely controlling the air/fuel ratio throughout the operating range of the engine.

MODEL IDENTIFICATION

General Motors Rochester carburetors are identified by their model code. The first number indicates the number of barrels, while one of the last letters indicates the type of choke used. These are V for the manifold mounted choke coil, C for the choke coil mounted in the carburetor body, and E for electric choke, also mounted on the carburetor. Model codes ending in A indicate an altitude-compensating carburetor.

➡**Because of their intricate nature and computer controls, the E2SE, E4ME and E4MC carburetors should only be serviced by a qualified technician.**

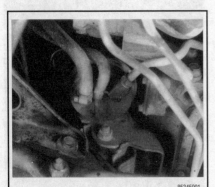
Fig. 1 Most fuel pumps are more easily accessed from underneath the car

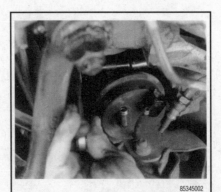
Fig. 2 Removing the fuel pump attaching bolts

Fig. 3 Be careful not to spill fuel when removing the pump from the engine

PRELIMINARY CHECKS

The following should be observed before attempting any adjustments.

1. Thoroughly warm the engine. If the engine is cold, be sure that it reaches operating temperature.

2. Check the torque of all carburetor mounting nuts and assembly screws. Also check the intake manifold-to-cylinder head bolts. If air is leaking at any of these points, any attempts at adjustment will inevitably lead to frustration.

3. Check the manifold heat control valve (if used) to be sure that it is free.

4. Check and adjust the choke as necessary.

5. Adjust the idle speed and mixture. If the mixture screws are capped, don't adjust them unless all other causes of rough idle have been eliminated. If any adjustments are performed that might possibly change the idle speed or mixture, adjust the idle and mixture again when you are finished.

➡**Before you make any carburetor adjustments make sure that the engine is in tune. Many problems which are thought to be carburetor related can be traced to an engine which is simply out-of-tune. Any trouble in these areas will have symptoms like those of carburetor problems.**

ADJUSTMENTS

Fast Idle

ROCHESTER E2SE

1. Refer to the emission label and prepare the vehicle for adjustment.
2. Place the fast idle screw on the highest step of the fast idle cam.
3. Turn the fast idle screw to obtain the fast idle speed.

ROCHESTER E4ME AND E4MC

The fast idle adjustment must be performed according to the directions of the emissions label.

Float and Fuel Level

♦ See Figures 4 and 5

ROCHESTER E2SE

1. Remove the air horn and gasket.
2. While holding the retainer in place, push the float down lightly against the needle.
3. Place a measuring gauge on the float at the farthest point from the float hinge.
4. To adjust, remove the float and bend the arm up or down. Also check the float alignment.
5. Install the air horn and gasket.

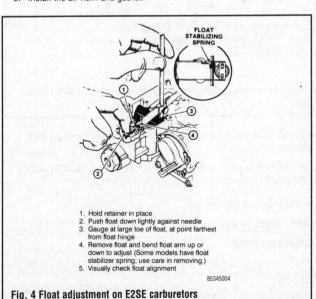

1. Hold retainer in place
2. Push float down lightly against needle
3. Gauge at large toe of float, at point farthest from float hinge
4. Remove float and bend float arm up or down to adjust (Some models have float stabilizer spring; use care in removing.)
5. Visually check float alignment

85345004

Fig. 4 Float adjustment on E2SE carburetors

ROCHESTER E4ME AND E4MC

1. Remove the air horn and gasket from the float bowl. Hold the float retainer down firmly. Push the float down (lightly) against the needle.
2. Position a T-scale over the toe of the float 1/16 in. (1.6mm) from the end of the float toe.
3. If the float level varies more than 1/16 in. (1.6mm) from the specified setting, it must be reset.

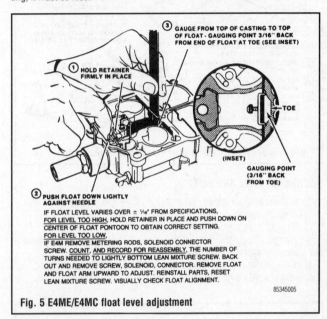

IF FLOAT LEVEL VARIES OVER ± 1/16" FROM SPECIFICATIONS, FOR LEVEL TOO HIGH, HOLD RETAINER IN PLACE AND PUSH DOWN ON CENTER OF FLOAT PONTOON TO OBTAIN CORRECT SETTING. FOR LEVEL TOO LOW, IF E4M REMOVE METERING RODS, SOLENOID CONNECTOR SCREW. COUNT, AND RECORD FOR REASSEMBLY, THE NUMBER OF TURNS NEEDED TO LIGHTLY BOTTOM LEAN MIXTURE SCREW. BACK OUT AND REMOVE SCREW, SOLENOID, CONNECTOR. REMOVE FLOAT AND FLOAT ARM UPWARD TO ADJUST. REINSTALL PARTS, RESET LEAN MIXTURE SCREW. VISUALLY CHECK FLOAT ALIGNMENT.

85345005

Fig. 5 E4ME/E4MC float level adjustment

FLOAT LEVEL TOO HIGH

1. Hold the float retainer in place.
2. Push down on the center of the float until the correct level is obtained.

FLOAT LEVEL TOO LOW

1. Lift out the metering rods and remove the solenoid connector screws.
2. Turn the lean mixture solenoid screw clockwise, counting and recording the number of turns required to seat the screw in the float bowl.
3. Turn the screw counterclockwise and remove it. Lift the solenoid and the connector from the float bowl.
4. Remove the float and bend the arm up to adjust. The float must be correctly aligned after adjustment.
5. To install the components, reverse the order of removal. Back out the solenoid mixture screw the number of turns that was recorded earlier.

Throttle Linkage

ROCHESTER E2SE

No adjustment of the throttle cable can be made.

ROCHESTER E4ME AND E4MC

Due to the design of the throttle cable, no adjustments of the throttle linkage can be made.

Choke Unloader (Primary)

♦ See Figures 6 and 7

ROCHESTER E2SE

1. Connect a rubber band to the intermediate choke lever and open the throttle to allow the choke valve to close.
2. Set up the angle gauge and set the gauge to specifications.
3. Using a vacuum source, retract the vacuum break plunger. Make sure that the air valve rod does not interfere with the retraction of the vacuum break plunger.
4. Support the vacuum break rod and make the adjustment by bending the rod.

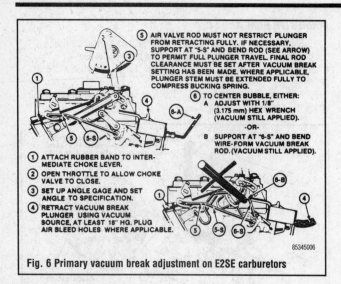

Fig. 6 Primary vacuum break adjustment on E2SE carburetors

ROCHESTER E4ME AND E4MC

1. Connect a rubber band to the green tang of the intermediate choke shaft.
2. Open the throttle to allow the choke valve to close.
3. Set up the angle gauge and set to specifications.
4. Using a vacuum source, retract the vacuum break plunger. The air valve rod must not restrict the breaker plunger from fully retracting.
5. With the vacuum applied, turn the adjusting screw until the centering bubble of the angle gauge is level.

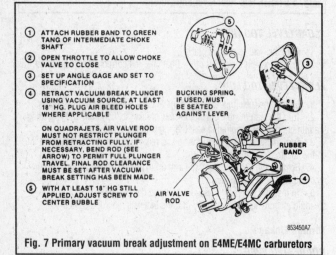

Fig. 7 Primary vacuum break adjustment on E4ME/E4MC carburetors

Choke Unloader (Secondary)

▶ See Figures 8 and 9

ROCHESTER E2SE

1. Connect a rubber band to the intermediate choke lever and open the throttle to allow the choke to close.
2. Set up the angle gauge and set the angle to specifications.
3. Using a vacuum source, retract the vacuum break plunger and retain the vacuum pressure.
4. Refer to the accompanying illustration to perform this procedure. Center the angle gauge bubble by turning an ⅛ in. (3mm) Allen wrench or bending vacuum break rod.

ROCHESTER E4ME AND E4MC

1. Connect a rubber band to the green tang of the intermediate choke shaft.
2. Open the throttle to allow the choke valve to close.
3. Set up the angle gauge and set the angle to specification.
4. Using a vacuum source, retract the vacuum break plunger.

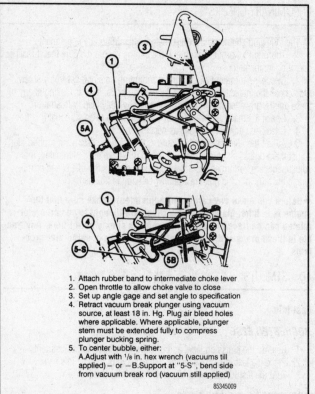

Fig. 8 Secondary vacuum break adjustment on E2SE carburetors

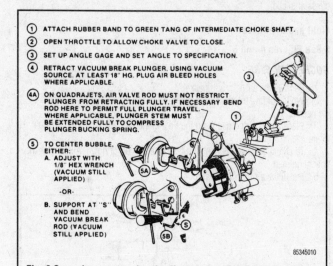

Fig. 9 Secondary vacuum break adjustment on E4ME/E4MC carburetors

➡The air valve rod must not restrict the vacuum break plunger from fully retracting.

5. With the vacuum applied, turn the adjusting screw or bend the vacuum break rod until the bubble of the angle gauge is centered.

Air Valve Spring Adjustment

▶ See Figures 10 and 11

ROCHESTER E2SE

1. If necessary, remove the intermediate choke rod to gain access to the lock screw.
2. Loosen the lock screw and turn the tension adjusting screw clockwise until the air valve opens slightly.

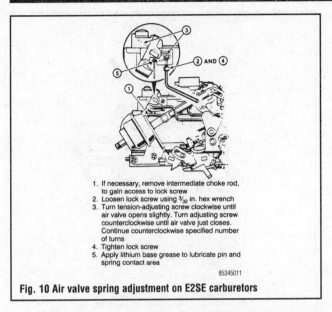

1. If necessary, remove intermediate choke rod, to gain access to lock screw
2. Loosen lock screw using ³/₃₂ in. hex wrench
3. Turn tension-adjusting screw clockwise until air valve opens slightly. Turn adjusting screw counterclockwise until air valve just closes. Continue counterclockwise specified number of turns.
4. Tighten lock screw
5. Apply lithium base grease to lubricate pin and spring contact area

Fig. 10 Air valve spring adjustment on E2SE carburetors

3. Turn the adjusting screw counterclockwise until the air valve just closes; continue turning the screw counterclockwise according to specifications.
4. Tighten the lock screw. Apply lithium grease to the spring and pin.

ROCHESTER E4ME AND E4MC

1. Loosen the lock screw and turn the tension adjusting screw counterclockwise until the air valve partly opens.
2. Turn the tension adjusting screw clockwise until the air valve just closes, then turn the screw clockwise a specified number of turns.
3. Tighten the lock screw and apply lithium grease to the spring contact area.

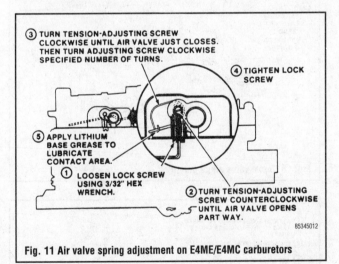

3. TURN TENSION-ADJUSTING SCREW CLOCKWISE UNTIL AIR VALVE JUST CLOSES. THEN TURN ADJUSTING SCREW CLOCKWISE SPECIFIED NUMBER OF TURNS.
4. TIGHTEN LOCK SCREW
5. APPLY LITHIUM BASE GREASE TO LUBRICATE CONTACT AREA.
1. LOOSEN LOCK SCREW USING 3/32" HEX WRENCH.
2. TURN TENSION-ADJUSTING SCREW COUNTERCLOCKWISE UNTIL AIR VALVE OPENS PART WAY.

Fig. 11 Air valve spring adjustment on E4ME/E4MC carburetors

Air Valve Rod Adjustment

▶ See Figures 12, 13 and 14

ROCHESTER E2SE

1. Set up the angle gauge on the air valve and set the angle to specification.
2. Use a vacuum source to seat the vacuum break plunger.
3. By applying light pressure to the air valve lever, rotate it in the opening direction.
4. Support the air valve rod and bend it to make the adjustment.

ROCHESTER E4ME AND E4MC

1. Using a vacuum source, seat the vacuum break plunger. The air valve must be closed.

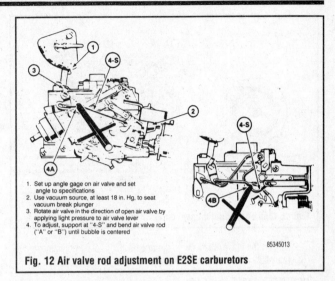

1. Set up angle gage on air valve and set angle to specifications
2. Use vacuum source, at least 18 in. Hg, to seat vacuum break plunger
3. Rotate air valve in the direction of open air valve by applying light pressure to air valve lever
4. To adjust, support at "4-S" and bend air valve rod ("A" or "B") until bubble is centered

Fig. 12 Air valve rod adjustment on E2SE carburetors

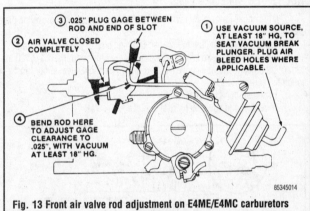

3. .025" PLUG GAGE BETWEEN ROD AND END OF SLOT
2. AIR VALVE CLOSED COMPLETELY
1. USE VACUUM SOURCE, AT LEAST 18" HG, TO SEAT VACUUM BREAK PLUNGER. PLUG AIR BLEED HOLES WHERE APPLICABLE.
4. BEND ROD HERE TO ADJUST GAGE CLEARANCE TO .025", WITH VACUUM AT LEAST 18" HG.

Fig. 13 Front air valve rod adjustment on E4ME/E4MC carburetors

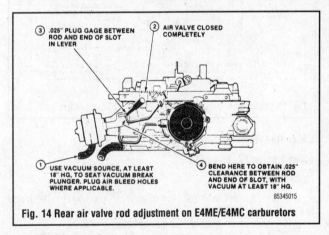

3. .025" PLUG GAGE BETWEEN ROD AND END OF SLOT IN LEVER
2. AIR VALVE CLOSED COMPLETELY
1. USE VACUUM SOURCE, AT LEAST 18" HG, TO SEAT VACUUM BREAK PLUNGER. PLUG AIR BLEED HOLES WHERE APPLICABLE.
4. BEND HERE TO OBTAIN .025" CLEARANCE BETWEEN ROD AND END OF SLOT, WITH VACUUM AT LEAST 18" HG.

Fig. 14 Rear air valve rod adjustment on E4ME/E4MC carburetors

2. Insert a 0.025 in. (0.635mm) plug gauge between the rod and the end of the slot.
3. To adjust, bend the air valve rod.

Choke Lever Adjustment

▶ See Figures 15 and 16

ROCHESTER E2SE

1. If the choke cover is riveted, drill out the rivets and remove the choke cover with the spring assembly.
2. Place the fast idle screw on the high step of the fast idle cam. Push the intermediate choke lever until the choke valve is closed.
3. Place a 0.085 in. (2.16mm) plug gauge in the choke housing hole and move the choke lever to touch the plug gauge.

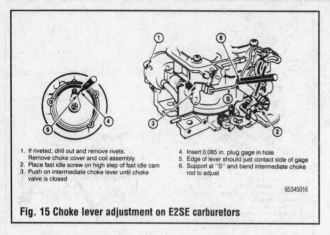

1. If riveted, drill out and remove rivets.
   Remove choke cover and coil assembly
2. Place fast idle screw on high step of fast idle cam
3. Push on intermediate choke lever until choke
   valve is closed
4. Insert 0.085 in. plug gage in hole
5. Edge of lever should just contact side of gage
6. Support at "S" and bend intermediate choke
   rod to adjust

85345016

Fig. 15 Choke lever adjustment on E2SE carburetors

4. Support the intermediate choke rod and bend it to make adjustment.
5. To install choke cover, use pop rivets.

ROCHESTER E4ME AND E4MC

1. If the choke cover plate is riveted, drill out the rivets and remove the plate assembly.
2. Place the fast idle cam follower on the high step of the fast idle cam.
3. Lift up on the choke lever to close the choke valve and insert a 0.120 in. (3mm) plug gauge into the choke housing hole. The choke lever should just touch the gauge.
4. To adjust, bend the choke rod.
5. To replace the cover plate, rivet in place.

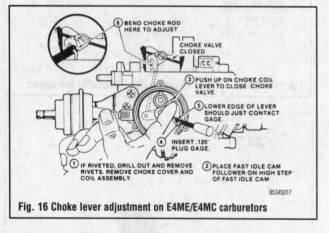

85345017

Fig. 16 Choke lever adjustment on E4ME/E4MC carburetors

Choke Rod Fast Idle Cam Adjustment

▶ **See Figures 17, 18 and 19**

ROCHESTER E2SE

1. Attach a rubber band to the intermediate choke lever and open the throttle to allow the choke plate to close.
2. Set up the angle gauge and set the angle to specifications.
3. Place the fast idle screw on the second step of the cam, against the high step.
4. Move the choke shaft lever, to open the choke valve, make contact with the black closing tang.
5. Support the fast idle cam rod and bend the rod to make the adjustment. Adjustment is completed when the bubble of the angle gauge is level.

ROCHESTER E4ME AND E4MC

1. Connect a rubber band to the green tang of the intermediate choke shaft.
2. Open the throttle to allow the choke valve to close.
3. Set up the angle gauge and set the angle to specifications.
4. Place the cam follower on the second step of the fast idle cam, against the rise of the first step. If the cam follower does not contact the cam, turn the fast idle screw additional turns.

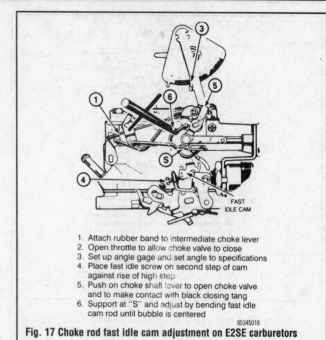

1. Attach rubber band to intermediate choke lever
2. Open throttle to allow choke valve to close
3. Set up angle gage and set angle to specifications
4. Place fast idle screw on second step of cam against rise of high step
5. Push on choke shaft lever to open choke valve and to make contact with black closing tang
6. Support at "S" and adjust by bending fast idle cam rod until bubble is centered

85345018

Fig. 17 Choke rod fast idle cam adjustment on E2SE carburetors

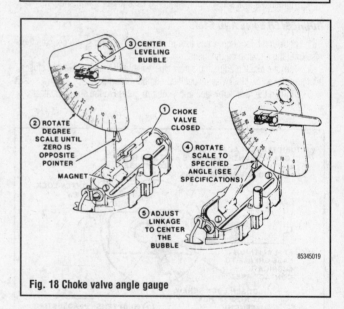

3. CENTER LEVELING BUBBLE

2. ROTATE DEGREE SCALE UNTIL ZERO IS OPPOSITE POINTER

MAGNET

1. CHOKE VALVE CLOSED

4. ROTATE SCALE TO SPECIFIED ANGLE (SEE SPECIFICATIONS)

5. ADJUST LINKAGE TO CENTER THE BUBBLE

85345019

Fig. 18 Choke valve angle gauge

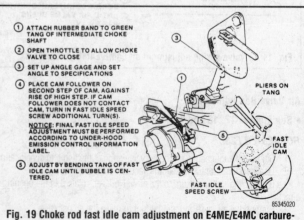

1. ATTACH RUBBER BAND TO GREEN TANG OF INTERMEDIATE CHOKE SHAFT
2. OPEN THROTTLE TO ALLOW CHOKE VALVE TO CLOSE
3. SET UP ANGLE GAGE AND SET ANGLE TO SPECIFICATIONS
4. PLACE CAM FOLLOWER ON SECOND STEP OF CAM, AGAINST RISE OF HIGH STEP. IF CAM FOLLOWER DOES NOT CONTACT CAM, TURN IN FAST IDLE SPEED SCREW ADDITIONAL TURN(S).
   NOTICE: FINAL FAST IDLE SPEED ADJUSTMENT MUST BE PERFORMED ACCORDING TO UNDER-HOOD EMISSION CONTROL INFORMATION LABEL.
5. ADJUST BY BENDING TANG OF FAST IDLE CAM UNTIL BUBBLE IS CENTERED

PLIERS ON TANG

FAST IDLE CAM

FAST IDLE SPEED SCREW

85345020

Fig. 19 Choke rod fast idle cam adjustment on E4ME/E4MC carburetors

5. To adjust, bend the tang of the fast idle cam until the gauge bubble is centered.

→**The final fast idle speed adjustment must be performed according to the emission control label.**

Unloader Adjustment

♦ **See Figures 20 and 21**

ROCHESTER E2SE

1. Connect a rubber band to the intermediate choke lever and open throttle to allow the choke to close.
2. Set up the angle gauge and set the angle to specifications.
3. Hold the throttle lever in wide-open position and push on the choke lever to open the choke, making contact with the black closing tang.
4. To adjust, bend the tang until the bubble of the angle gauge is centered.

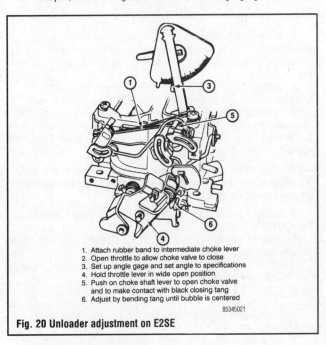

1. Attach rubber band to intermediate choke lever
2. Open throttle to allow choke valve to close
3. Set up angle gage and set angle to specifications
4. Hold throttle lever in wide open position
5. Push on choke shaft lever to open choke valve and to make contact with black closing tang
6. Adjust by bending tang until bubble is centered

85345021

Fig. 20 Unloader adjustment on E2SE

ROCHESTER E4ME AND E4MC

1. Connect a rubber band to the green tang of the intermediate shaft.
2. Open the throttle to allow the choke valve to close.
3. Set up the angle gauge and set the angle to specification.
4. Hold the secondary lockout lever away from the pin.
5. Hold the throttle lever in the wide-open position.
6. To adjust, bend the tang of the fast idle lever until the bubble of the angle gauge is centered.

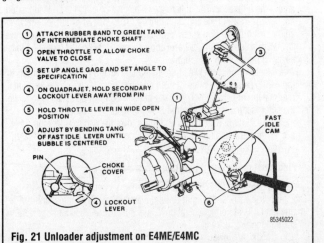

1. ATTACH RUBBER BAND TO GREEN TANG OF INTERMEDIATE CHOKE SHAFT
2. OPEN THROTTLE TO ALLOW CHOKE VALVE TO CLOSE
3. SET UP ANGLE GAGE AND SET ANGLE TO SPECIFICATION
4. ON QUADRAJET, HOLD SECONDARY LOCKOUT LEVER AWAY FROM PIN
5. HOLD THROTTLE LEVER IN WIDE OPEN POSITION
6. ADJUST BY BENDING TANG OF FAST IDLE LEVER UNTIL BUBBLE IS CENTERED

PIN
CHOKE COVER
FAST IDLE CAM
LOCKOUT LEVER

85345022

Fig. 21 Unloader adjustment on E4ME/E4MC

Secondary Lockout Adjustment

♦ **See Figures 22 and 23**

ROCHESTER E2SE

1. Push down on the intermediate choke lever to hold the choke valve wide-open.
2. Open the throttle lever until the end of the secondary actuating lever is opposite the toe of the lockout lever.
3. Insert a 0.025 in. (0.635mm) plug gauge.
4. To adjust, bend the lockout lever tang into contact with the fast idle cam.

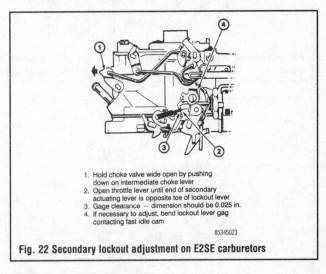

1. Hold choke valve wide open by pushing down on intermediate choke lever
2. Open throttle lever until end of secondary actuating lever is opposite toe of lockout lever
3. Gage clearance — dimension should be 0.025 in.
4. If necessary to adjust, bend lockout lever gag contacting fast idle cam

85345023

Fig. 22 Secondary lockout adjustment on E2SE carburetors

ROCHESTER E4ME AND E4MC

1. With the choke and the throttle valves closed, insert a 0.015 in. (0.38mm) plug gauge between the lockout lever and the pin. To establish clearance, bend the pin.
2. Push down on the fast idle cam and hold the choke valve wide open.
3. Insert a 0.015 in. (0.38mm) plug gauge sideways between the lockout lever and the pin. To adjust, file the end of the pin.

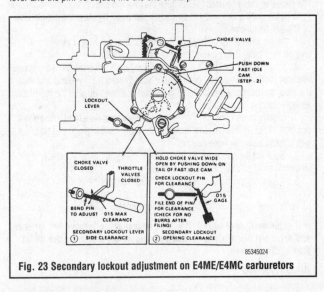

CHOKE VALVE
PUSH DOWN FAST IDLE CAM (STEP 2)
LOCKOUT LEVER

CHOKE VALVE CLOSED
THROTTLE VALVES CLOSED
BEND PIN TO ADJUST
.015 MAX CLEARANCE
SECONDARY LOCKOUT LEVER
① SIDE CLEARANCE

HOLD CHOKE VALVE WIDE OPEN BY PUSHING DOWN ON TAIL OF FAST IDLE CAM
CHECK LOCKOUT PIN FOR CLEARANCE
FILE END OF PIN FOR CLEARANCE (CHECK FOR NO BURRS AFTER FILING)
.015 GAGE
SECONDARY LOCKOUT ② OPENING CLEARANCE

85345024

Fig. 23 Secondary lockout adjustment on E4ME/E4MC carburetors

Mixture Control (M/C) Solenoid

♦ **See Figures 24, 25, 26 and 27**

TRAVEL TEST

These procedures are performed on four barrel models only. Before checking the mixture control solenoid travel, it may be necessary to modify the float gauge J–9789–130 or equivalent (used to externally check the float level). This should be done by filing or grinding sufficient material off the gauge to

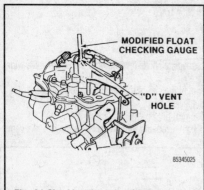

Fig. 24 Checking the solenoid plunger travel

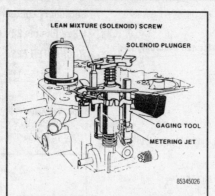

Fig. 25 Installing the mixture control solenoid gauging tool

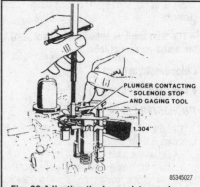

Fig. 26 Adjusting the lean mixture solenoid screw

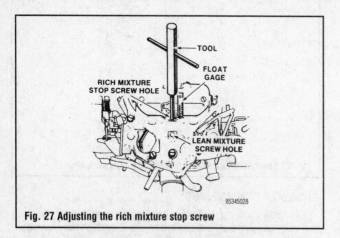

Fig. 27 Adjusting the rich mixture stop screw

allow for insertion down the vertical D-shaped hole in the air horn casting (located next to the idle air bleed valve cover).

Check that the gauge freely enters the D-shaped vent hole and does not bind. The gauge will also be used to determine the total mixture control solenoid travel.

With the engine OFF and the air cleaner removed, measure the control solenoid travel as follows:

1. Insert a modified float gauge J–9789–130 or equivalent down the D-shaped vent hole. Press down on the gauge and release it.

2. Observe that the gauge moves freely and does not bind. With the gauge released (solenoid in the up position), be sure to read it at eye level and record the mark on the gauge (in inches/millimeters) that lines up with the top of the air horn casting (upper edge).

3. Lightly press down on the gauge until bottomed (solenoid in the down position). Record (in inches/millimeters) the mark on the gauge that lines up with the top of the air horn casting.

4. Subtract the gauge up dimension from gauge dimension. Record the difference (in inches/millimeters). This difference is total solenoid travel.

5. If total solenoid travel is not within $\frac{3}{32}$–$\frac{5}{32}$ in. (2.4–3.9mm), perform the mixture control solenoid adjustments. If the difference is within specifications, proceed to the idle air bleed valve adjustment.

➡ **If adjustment is required, it will be necessary to remove the air horn and drive out the mixture control solenoid screw plug from the under side of the air horn.**

ADJUSTMENTS

Before making adjustment to mixture control solenoid, verify that the plunger travel is not correct.

1. Remove air horn, mixture control solenoid plunger, air horn gasket and plastic filler block, using normal service procedures.

2. Check carburetor for cause of incorrect mixture:
   a. M/C solenoid bore or plunger worn or sticking
   b. Metering rods for incorrect part number, sticking or rods or springs not installed properly
   c. Foreign material in jets

3. Remove throttle side metering rod. Install mixture control solenoid gauging tool, J–33815–1, BT–8253–A, or equivalent, over the throttle side metering jet rod guide and temporarily reinstall the solenoid plunger into the solenoid body.

4. Holding the solenoid plunger in the **DOWN** position, use tool J–28696–10, BT–7928, or equivalent, to turn lean mixture solenoid screw counterclockwise until the plunger breaks contact with the gauging tool. Turn slowly clockwise until the plunger makes contact with the gauging tool. The adjustment is correct when the solenoid plunger is contacting both the solenoid stop and the gauging tool.

➡ **If the total difference in adjustment required less than $\frac{3}{4}$ turn of the lean mixture solenoid screw, the original setting was within the manufacturer's specifications.**

5. Remove solenoid plunger and gauging tool and reinstall metering rod and plastic filler block.

6. Invert air horn and remove rich mixture stop screw from bottom side of air horn, using tool J–28696–4, BT–7967–A, or equivalent.

7. Remove lean mixture screw plug and the rich mixture stop screw plug from air horn, using a punch.

8. Reinstall rich mixture stop screw in air horn and bottom lightly, then back screw out $\frac{1}{4}$ turn.

9. Reinstall air horn gasket, mixture control solenoid plunger and air horn to carburetor.

10. Adjust the M/C solenoid plunger travel as follows:
    a. Insert float gauge down D-shaped vent hole. Press down on gauge and release, observing that the gauge moves freely and does not bind. With gauge released, (plunger UP position), read at eye level and record the reading of the gauge mark (in inches/millimeters) that lines up with the top of air horn casting, (upper edge).
    b. Lightly press down on gauge until bottomed, (plunger DOWN position). Read and record (in inches/millimeters) the reading of the gauge mark that lines up with top of air horn casting.
    c. Subtract gauge **UP** position from the gauge **DOWN** position and record the difference. This difference is the total plunger travel. Insert external float gauge in vent hole and, with tool J–28696–10, BT–7928, or equivalent, adjust rich mixture stop screw to obtain $\frac{5}{32}$ in. (3.9mm) total plunger travel.

11. With solenoid plunger travel correctly set, install plugs (supplied in service kits) in the air horn, as follows:
    a. Install plug, hollow end down, into the access hole for the lean mixture (solenoid) screw. Use suitably sized punch to drive plug into the air horn until the top of plug is even with the lower. Plug must be installed to retain the screw setting and to prevent fuel vapor loss.
    b. Install plug, with hollow end down, over the rich mixture stop screw access hole and drive plug into place so that the top of the plug is $\frac{3}{16}$ in. (4.7mm) below the surface of the air horn casting.

➡ **Plug must be installed to retain screw setting.**

12. To check the M/C solenoid dwell, first disconnect vacuum line to the canister purge valve and plug it. Ground diagnostic TEST terminal and run engine until it is at normal operation temperature (upper radiator hose hot) and in closed loop.

13. Check M/C dwell at 3000 rpm. If within 10–50 degrees, calibration is

complete. If higher than 50 degrees, check the carburetor for a cause of rich condition. If below 10 degrees, look for a cause of lean engine condition such as vacuum leaks. If none are found, check for the cause of a lean carburetor.

Idle Air Valve

▶ **See Figures 28 and 29**

A cover is in place over the idle air bleed valve. Also, the access holes to the idle mixture needles are sealed with hardened plugs. This is done to seal the factory settings, during original equipment production. These items are NOT to be removed unless required for cleaning, part replacement, improper dwell readings or if the System Performance Check indicates the carburetor is the cause of the trouble.

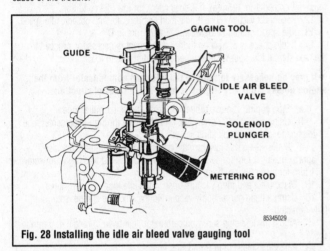

Fig. 28 Installing the idle air bleed valve gauging tool

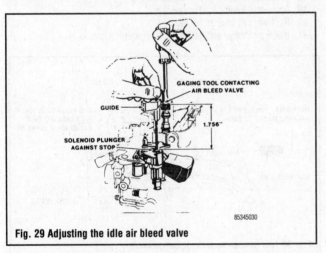

Fig. 29 Adjusting the idle air bleed valve

ROCHESTER E4ME AND E4MC

1. With engine **OFF**, cover the internal bowl vents and inlet to bleed valve and the carburetor air intakes with masking tape. This is done to prevent metal chips from entering.
2. Carefully drill rivet head of idle air bleed cover, with 0.110 in. (2.8mm) drill bit.
3. Remove rivet head and all pieces of rivet.
4. Lift cover off air bleed valve and blow out any metal shavings, or use a magnet to remove excess metal.

❋❋ CAUTION

Always wear eye protection when using compressed air.

5. Remove masking tape.
6. Start engine and allow it to reach normal operating temperature.
7. Disconnect the vacuum hose from the canister purge valve and plug it.
8. While idling in **D** for automatic transmission or **N** for manual transmission, slowly turn the valve counterclockwise or clockwise, until the dwell reading varies within the 25–35 degree range, attempting to be as close to 30 degrees as possible.

➡**Perform this step carefully. The air bleed valve is very sensitive and should be turned in ⅛ turn increments only.**

9. If the dwell reading does not vary and is not within the 25–35 degree range, it will be necessary to remove the plugs and to adjust the idle mixture needles.

Idle Mixture

▶ **See Figures 30, 31 and 32**

E2SE CARBURETORS

1. Remove the carburetor from the engine.
2. Remove the plugs covering the idle mixture needles.
3. Turn the mixture needle in until slightly seated, then back it out 4 turns.
4. If the plug in the air horn covering the idle air bleed has been removed, replace the air horn. If the plug is still in place, do not remove it.
5. Remove the vent stack screen assembly to gain access to the lean mixture screw.
6. Using tool J-28696-10 or equivalent, turn the lean mixture screw in until lightly seated, then back out 2½ turns.
7. Install the carburetor on the engine.
8. Disconnect the bowl vent line at the carburetor.
9. Disconnect the EGR hose and canister purge hose at the carburetor. Cap the ports on the carburetor.
10. Find the hose from port D of the carburetor to the temperature sensor and secondary vacuum break thermal vacuum switch. Disconnect and plug the vacuum hose going to the air cleaner.
11. Connect the positive lead of a dwell meter to the mixture control solenoid test lead (green connector). Connect the other lead to ground. Set the meter to the 6 cylinder position.
12. Run the engine on the high step of the fast idle cam until the cooling fan starts to cycle.

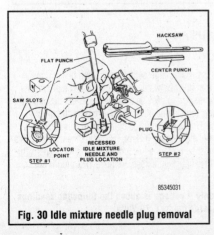

Fig. 30 Idle mixture needle plug removal

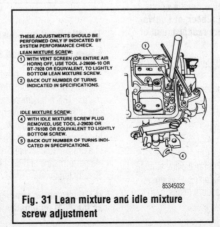

Fig. 31 Lean mixture and idle mixture screw adjustment

Fig. 32 Mixture needle and spring

13. Run the engine at 3,000 rpm and adjust the lean mixture screw slowly. Allow the reading to stabilize, obtain an average dwell of 35 degrees. It is normal for the dwell to vary in a narrow range.

14. Return to idle.

15. Adjust the idle mixture screw to obtain an average dwell of 25 degrees. Allow time for the reading to stabilize.

16. Run the engine at 3,000 rpm and note the dwell reading. It should be varying with an average reading of 35 degrees. If it does not, repeat the earlier steps.

E4ME CARBURETORS (ELECTRIC CHOKE)

1. Using tool J–29030, BT–7610–B, or equivalent, turn both idle mixture needles clockwise until they are lightly seated, then turn each mixture needle counterclockwise 3 turns.

2. Reinstall carburetor on engine using a new flange mounting gasket, but do not install air cleaner and gasket at this time.

3. Disconnect the vacuum hose to canister purge valve and plug it. Readjust the idle air bleed valve to finalize correct dwell reading.

4. Connect the positive lead of a dwell meter to the mixture control solenoid test lead (green connector). Connect the other lead to ground. Set the meter to the 6 cylinder position.

5. Start engine and run until fully warm, then repeat the idle air bleed valve adjustment.

6. If unable to set dwell to 25–35 degrees and the dwell is below 25 degrees, turn both mixture needles counterclockwise an additional turn. If dwell is above 35 degrees, turn both mixture needles clockwise an additional turn. Readjust idle air bleed valve to obtain dwell limits. Repeat as needed.

7. After adjustments are complete, seal the idle mixture needle openings in the throttle body, using silicone sealant, RTV rubber, or equivalent. The sealer is required to discourage unnecessary adjustment of the setting and to prevent fuel vapor loss in that area. Reconnect canister vacuum hose.

8. On vehicles without an Idle Load Compensator (ILC), adjust curb idle speed if necessary.

9. Check, and if necessary, adjust fast idle speed as described on Vehicle Emission Control Information (VECI) label.

E4MC CARBURETOR (HOT AIR CHOKE)

1. Using tool J–29030–B, BT–7610–B, or equivalent, turn each idle mixture needle clockwise until lightly seated, then turn each mixture needle counterclockwise 3 turns.

2. Reinstall carburetor on engine, using a new flange mounting gasket, but do not install air cleaner or gasket at this time.

3. Disconnect vacuum hose to canister purge valve and plug it.

4. Connect the positive lead of a dwell meter to the mixture control solenoid test lead (green connector). Connect the other lead to ground. Set the meter to the 6 cylinder position.

5. Start engine and allow it to reach normal operating temperature.

6. While idling in **D** (**N** for manual transmission), adjust both mixture needles equally, in ⅛ turn increments, until dwell reading varies within the 25–35 degree range, attempting to be as close to 30 degrees as possible.

7. If reading is too low, turn mixture needles counterclockwise. If reading is too high, turn mixture needles clockwise. Allow time for dwell reading to stabilize after each adjustment.

➡ After adjustments are complete, seal the idle mixture needle openings in the throttle body, using silicone sealant, RTV rubber, or equivalent. The sealer is required to discourage unnecessary readjustment of the setting and prevent fuel vapor loss in that area.

8. On vehicles without a carburetor-mounted Idle Load Compensator (ILC), adjust curb idle speed if necessary.

9. Check, and if necessary, adjust fast idle speed, as described on the Vehicle Emission Control Information (VECI) label.

Idle Load Compensator

▶ See Figure 33

The idle load compensator is adjusted at the factory. Do not make any adjustments unless diagnosis leads to it, or curb idle speed is not to specification.

1. Take certain ignition timing, mixture adjustment, vacuum hoses, fuel pressure and CCC system meets specifications.

2. Remove air cleaner and plug hose to thermal vacuum valve.

3. Connect a tachometer.

4. Disconnect and plug hose to EGR valve.

5. Disconnect and plug hose to canister purge port.

6. Disconnect and plug hose to idle load compensator.

7. Back out idle stop screw on carburetor 3 turns.

8. Turn air conditioning OFF.

9. Block drive wheels, set parking brake, place transmission in **P**, start and warm engine to normal operating temperature. Make certain choke is **OPEN**.

10. With engine **RUNNING** place transmission in **D** and idle load compensator fully extended (no vacuum applied). Using tool J–29607, or equivalent, adjust plunger to obtain 650–750 rpm. Locknut on plunger must be held with a wrench to prevent damage to guide tabs.

11. Measure distance from the locknut to tip of the plunger. This distance must not exceed 1 in. (25mm). If it does check for low idle condition.

12. Reconnect vacuum hose to idle load compensator and observe idle speed.

13. Idle speed should be between 425–475 rpm in **D**.

14. If idle speed is correct no further adjustment is necessary, proceed to the next step. If idle speed is still incorrect continue as follows:

➡ It may be necessary to remove the idle load compensator from the engine unless a hex key wrench is modified to clear obstructions.

a. Stop engine, remove rubber cap from the center outlet tube.

b. Using a 0.90 in. (23mm) hex wrench, insert through open center tube to engage idle speed adjusting screw.

c. If idle speed was low, turn the adjusting screw counterclockwise approximately 1 turn for every 85 rpm low. If idle speed was high turn screw 1 turn for every 85 rpm high.

15. Disconnect and plug vacuum hose to the idle load compensator.

16. Using a hand pump, apply vacuum to the idle load compensator until fully retracted.

17. Adjust the idle stop screw on carburetor float bowl to obtain 450 rpm in **D**.

18. Place transmission in **P** and stop engine.

19. Reconnect the idle load compensator.

20. Reconnect all vacuum hoses.

21. Install air cleaner and gasket. Remove wheel blocks.

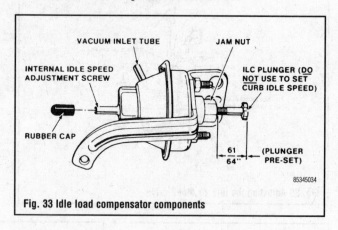

Fig. 33 Idle load compensator components

Throttle Position Sensor (TPS)

▶ See Figures 34 and 35

Before the throttle position sensor voltage output setting can be accurately checked or adjusted the idle rpm must be within specifications. The plug covering the TPS adjustment screw is used to provide a tamper-resistant design and retain the factory setting during vehicle operation. Do not remove the plug unless diagnosis indicates the TPS is not adjusted correctly, or it is necessary to replace the air horn assembly, float bowl, TPS, or TPS adjustment screw. This is a critical adjustment that must be performed accurately to ensure proper vehicle performance and control of exhaust emissions. Remove TPS plug if not already removed.

➡ Adjustment is required only if voltage is above the following readings, as the ECM automatically zeros below 0.70 Volts.

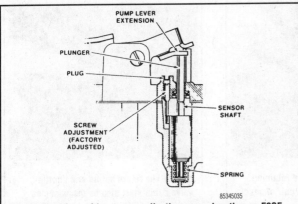

Fig. 34 Throttle position sensor adjusting screw location on E2SE carburetors

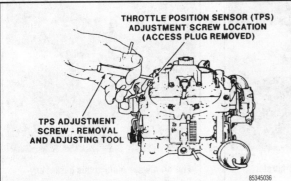

Fig. 35 Throttle position sensor adjusting screw location on E4ME/E4MC carburetors

1. Using a 5/64 in. (2mm) drill bit, carefully drill a hole in the steel or aluminum plug. Be sure to drill only far enough to start a self tapping screw, the approximate drilling depth is 1/16–1/8 in. (1.6–3mm).

➡**Use care in drilling so as not to damage the TPS adjustment screw head.**

2. Start a long self tapping screw (No. 8 x 1/2 in.) into the drilled pilot hole in the plug. Turn the screw in only enough to ensure a good thread engagement in the drilled hole.

3. Place a suitable tool between the screw head and the air horn casting. Then pry against the screw head to remove the plug. A small slide hammer may also be used in this procedure. Be sure to discard the plug when it has been removed.

4. Connect a suitable digital voltmeter (J–29125 or equivalent) from the TPS connector center terminal (B) to the bottom terminal (C).

➡**Jumper wires for access can be made using terminals 12014836 and 12014837 or equivalent. Make jumper wires up with 16 gauge (1.0mm), 18 gauge (0.8mm) or 20 gauge (0.5mm) wire approximately 6 in. (152mm) long.**

5. With the ignition **ON** and the engine stopped, install the TPS adjustment screw and turn the screw with a suitable tool to obtain the specified voltage at the specified throttle position with the A/C controls in the **OFF** position.
    a. 2.8L — 0.30 volts at curb idle position
    b. 5.0L — 0.40 volts at curb idle position

6. After the adjustment has been made, install a new plug kit (supplied in the service kits), into the air horn. Drive the plug into place until it is flush with the raised pump lever boss on the casting. Clear trouble code memory after adjustment.

➡**The plug must be installed to retain the TPS adjustment screw setting. If a plug kit is not available, remove the TPS adjusting screw and apply thread sealer adhesive X–10 or equivalent to the screw threads. Now repeat the TPS adjustment procedure to obtain the correct TPS voltage.**

REMOVAL & INSTALLATION

▶ **See Figures 36 thru 46**

Always replace all internal gaskets that are removed. Flooding, stumble on acceleration and other performance complaints are in many instances, caused by presence of dirt, water, or other foreign matter in carburetor. To aid in diagnosis, carburetor should be carefully removed from engine without draining fuel from bowl. Contents of fuel bowl may then be examined for contamination as carburetor is disassembled. Check the fuel filter.

Rochester E2SE

1. Remove air cleaner and gasket.
2. Disconnect fuel pipe and vacuum lines.
3. Disconnect electrical connectors.
4. Disconnect accelerator linkage.
5. If equipped with automatic transmission, disconnect downshift cable.
6. If equipped with cruise control, disconnect linkage.
7. Remove carburetor attaching bolts.
8. Remove carburetor and EFE heater/insulator (if used).
9. Inspect EFE heater/insulator for damage. Be certain throttle body and EFE heater/insulator surfaces are clean.

To install:

10. Install EFE heater/insulator.
11. Install carburetor and tighten nuts alternately to the correct torque.
12. Connect downshift cable, as required.
13. Attach the cruise control cable, as required.
14. Connect accelerator linkage.
15. Connect electrical connections.
16. Connect fuel pipe sand vacuum hoses.
17. Check base (slow) and fast idle.
18. Install the air cleaner.

Fig. 36 Remove the air cleaner for access to the carburetor

Fig. 37 Use a back-up wrench when disconnecting fuel lines

Fig. 38 If the retaining clip on the connector is broken off like this one, it should be replaced

Fig. 39 The vacuum modulator line behind the carburetor must also be disconnected, if equipped

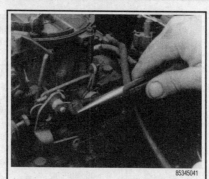

Fig. 40 The accelerator cable retaining clip can be removed using a pair of needle nose pliers

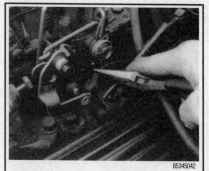

Fig. 41 The return spring and throttle valve cable must also be disconnected from the linkage

Fig. 42 Removing the rear carburetor attaching bolts (note: a long extension is helpful here)

Fig. 43 Removing the front carburetor attaching bolts

Fig. 44 Always replace this gasket any-time the carburetor is removed

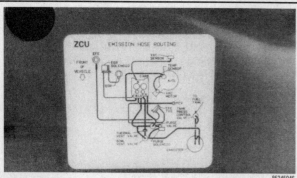

Fig. 45 The emission hose routing sticker under the hood is helpful when installing the carburetor

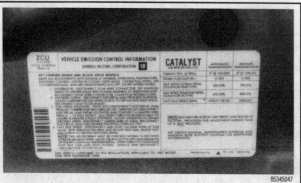

Fig. 46 The adjustment specifications on the emission control infor-mation label must always be followed

Rochester E4ME and E4MC

1. Disconnect the battery and remove the air cleaner.
2. Disconnect the accelerator linkage.
3. Disconnect the transmission detent cable.
4. If equipped, remove the cruise control cable.
5. Tag and detach all of the necessary vacuum lines and electrical connections.
6. Disconnect the fuel line at the carburetor inlet.
7. Remove the attaching bolts and remove the carburetor.

To install:

8. Position the carburetor onto the manifold and install the attaching bolts.
9. Connect the fuel line at the carburetor inlet.
10. Attach all of the vacuum lines and electrical connections, as tagged during removal.
11. If equipped, install the cruise control.
12. Connect the transmission detent cable.
13. Connect the accelerator linkage.
14. Install the air cleaner and connect the battery.

OVERHAUL

Carburetor overhaul kits are recommended for each overhaul. These kits contain all gaskets and new parts to replace those which deteriorate most rapidly. Failure to replace all parts supplied with the kit (especially gaskets) can result in poor performance later.

Some carburetor manufacturers supply overhaul kits for three basic types: minor repair; major repair; and gasket kits. Certain parts may be expected in most kits based on the desired degree of overhaul.

Minor Repair Kits:

- All gaskets
- Float needle valve
- All diaphragms
- Spring for the pump diaphragm

Major Repair Kits:
- All jets and gaskets
- All diaphragms
- Float needle valve
- Pump ball valve
- Float
- Complete intermediate rod
- Intermediate pump lever
- Some cover hold-down screws and washers

Gasket kits:
- All gaskets

Efficient carburetion depends greatly on careful cleaning and inspection during overhaul, since dirt, gum, water, or varnish in or on the carburetor parts are often responsible for poor performance.

Overhaul your carburetor in a clean, dust-free area. Carefully disassemble the carburetor, referring often to the exploded views and directions packaged with the rebuilding kit. Keep all similar and look-alike parts separated during disassembly and cleaning to avoid accidental interchange during assembly. Make a note of all jet sizes.

When the carburetor is disassembled, wash all parts (except diaphragms, electric components, pump plunger, and any other plastic, leather, fiber, or rubber parts) in clean carburetor solvent. Do not leave parts in the solvent any longer than is necessary to sufficiently loosen the deposits. Excessive cleaning may remove the special finish from the float bowl and choke valve bodies, leaving these parts unfit for service. Rinse all parts in clean solvent and blow them dry with compressed air or allow them to air dry. Wipe clean all cork, plastic, leather, and fiber parts with a clean, lint-free cloth.

Blow out all passages and jets with compressed air and be sure that there are no restrictions or blockages. Never use wire or similar tools to clean jets, fuel passages, or air bleeds. Clean all jets and valves separately to avoid accidental interchange.

Check all parts for wear or damage. If wear or damage is found, replace the defective parts. Especially check the following:
1. Check the float needle and seat for wear.
2. Check the float hinge pin for wear and the float(s) for dents or distortion. Replace the float if fuel has leaked into it.
3. Check the throttle and choke shaft bores for wear or an out-of-round condition. Damage or wear to the throttle arm, shaft, or shaft bore will often require replacement of the throttle body. These parts require a close tolerance of fit; wear may allow air leakage, which could affect starting and idling.

➡ **Throttle shafts and bushings are not included in overhaul kits. They can be purchased separately or repaired by a qualified carburetor overhaul shop.**

4. Inspect the idle mixture adjusting needles for burrs or grooves. Any such condition requires replacement of the needle, since you will not be able to obtain a satisfactory idle.
5. Test the accelerator pump check valves. They should pass air one way but not the other. Test for proper seating by blowing and sucking on the valve. Replace the valve check ball and spring as necessary. If the valve is satisfactory, wash the valve parts again to remove breath moisture.
6. Check the bowl cover for warped surfaces with a straightedge.
7. Closely inspect the accelerator pump plunger for wear and damage, replacing as necessary.

8. After the carburetor is assembled, check the choke valve for freedom of operation.
9. Check, repair or replace parts, if the following problems are encountered:

Flooding
- Inspect the float valve and seat for dirt, deep wear grooves, scores and improper sealing
- Inspect the float valve pull clip for proper installation; be careful not to bend the pull clip
- Inspect the float, the float arms and the hinge pin for distortion, binds, and burrs. Check the density of the material in the float; if heavier than normal, replace the float
- Clean or replace the fuel inlet filter and check the valve assembly

Hesitation
- Inspect the pump plunger for cracks, scores or cup excessive wear. A used pump cup will shrink when dry. If dried out, soak in fuel for 8 hours before testing
- Inspect the pump duration and return springs for weakness or distortion
- Check the pump passages and the jet(s) for dirt, improper seating of the discharge checkball or the temperature bypass disc and/or scores in the pump-well. Check the condition of the pump discharge check ball spring, replace as necessary
- Check the pump linkage for excessive wear; repair or replace as necessary

Hard Starting-Poor Cold Operation
- Check the choke valve and linkage for excessive wear, binds or distortion
- Test the vacuum break diaphragm(s) for leaks
- Clean or replace the fuel filter
- Inspect the float valve for sticking, dirt, etc.
- Also check the items under "Flooding"

Poor Performance-Poor Gas Mileage
- Clean all fuel and vacuum passages in the castings
- Check the choke valve for freedom of movement
- Check the Mixture Control (M/C) solenoid for sticking, binding or leaking
- Check the air valve and secondary metering rod for binding conditions. If the air valve or metering rod is damaged or the metering rod adjustment is changed from the factory setting, the air horn assembly must be replaced. Also check the air valve lever spring for proper installation

Rough Idle
- Inspect the gasket and gasket mating surfaces on the casting for nicks, burrs or damage to the sealing beads
- Check the operation and sealing of the mixture control solenoid
- Clean all of the idle field passages
- If removed, inspect the idle mixture needle for ridges, burrs or being bent
- Check the throttle lever and valves for binds, nicks. or other damage
- Check all of the diaphragms for possible ruptures or leaks

After cleaning and checking all components, reassemble the carburetor, using new parts and referring to the exploded view. When reassembling, make sure that all screws and jets are tight in their seats, but do not overtighten as the tips will be distorted. Tighten all screws gradually, in rotation. Do not tighten needle valves into their seats; uneven jetting will result. Always use new gaskets. Be sure to follow all assembly and adjustment procedures.

➡ **Before performing any service on the carburetor, it is essential that it be placed on a suitable holding fixture, such as tool J–9789–118, BY–30–15 or equivalent. Without the use of the holding fixture, it is possible to damage throttle valves or other parts of the carburetor.**

THROTTLE BODY INJECTION SYSTEM

System Description

The throttle body injection (TBI) system used on 2.5L (VIN 2) and 5.0L (VIN E) engines is centrally located on the intake manifold. Its function is to supply the correct air/fuel mixture to the engine, as directed by the Engine Control Module (ECM).

The TBI unit consists of two relatively simple casting assemblies: a throttle body and a fuel metering assembly. Components include, a pressure regulator, idle air control valve, fuel injector(s), throttle position sensor, fuel inlet and a fuel return fitting.

The Throttle Body Injection identification number is stamped on the lower mounting flange located near the TPS. The number is in alphabetical code and should be noted before servicing the unit.

An oxygen sensor in the exhaust system functions to provide feedback information to the ECM as to oxygen content in the exhaust. The ECM then uses this information to modify fuel delivery to achieve as near as possible an ideal air/fuel ratio of 14.7:1. This ratio permits the catalytic converter to become more effective in reducing emissions while providing acceptable driveability.

Should you encounter any type of engine performance problem, have a complete CCC system test performed by a qualified, professional technician. If the fault lies in the injection system, you can use the following procedures to remove the TBI unit and replace the defective component(s).

Relieving Fuel System Pressure

1. Disconnect the negative battery cable to prevent fuel discharge if the key is accidentally turned to the RUN position.

2. Loosen the fuel filler cap to relieve fuel tank pressure and do not tighten until service has been completed.

3. Fuel system pressure is automatically relieved when the engine is turned OFF. No further action is necessary.

➡ **When disconnecting fuel lines, there may still be a small amount of fuel released. Cover the fuel line connection with a shop cloth to collect the fuel, then place the cloth in an approved container.**

Electric Fuel Pump

REMOVAL & INSTALLATION

▶ **See Figures 47 and 48**

The fuel pump is part of the fuel sender assembly located inside the fuel tank.

1. Release the fuel system pressure and disconnect the negative battery cable.

2. Drain the fuel tank, then raise and safely support the vehicle.

3. Remove the fuel tank from the vehicle.

4. Clean the area surrounding the sender assembly to prevent contamination of the fuel system.

5. Remove the fuel sender from the tank as follows:

   a. Use tool J–24187 or equivalent to remove the sending unit retaining cam. Remove the fuel sender and O-rings from the tank. Discard the O-rings.

6. If necessary, separate the fuel pump from the sending unit assembly.

To install:

7. If removed, install the fuel pump to the sending unit. If the strainer was removed, it must be replaced with a new one.

8. Inspect and clean the O-ring mating surfaces.

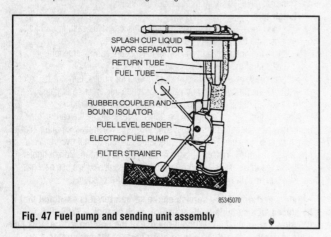

Fig. 47 Fuel pump and sending unit assembly

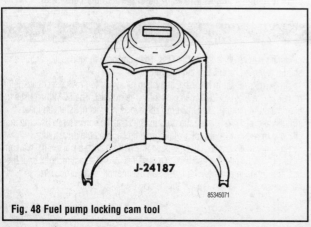

Fig. 48 Fuel pump locking cam tool

9. Install a new O-ring in the groove around the tank opening. If applicable, install a new O-ring on the fuel sender feed tube.

10. Install the fuel sender assembly as follows:

    a. The fuel pump strainer must be in a horizontal position, and when installed, must not block the travel of the float arm. Gently fold the strainer over itself and slowly position the sending assembly in the tank so the strainer is not damaged or trapped by the sump walls.

11. Install the retaining cam using tool J–24187 or equivalent.

12. Install the fuel tank assembly.

13. Lower the vehicle.

14. Fill the fuel tank, tighten the fuel filler cap and connect the negative battery cable.

TESTING

▶ **See Figure 49**

1. Turn the engine OFF and relieve the fuel pressure.

2. Remove the air cleaner and plug the THERMAC vacuum port on TBI.

3. Install a fuel pressure gauge between the throttle body unit and the fuel line. Use a back-up wrench to hold fuel nut on the TBI when removing the fuel line.

4. Start the car and observe the fuel pressure reading. It should be 9–13 psi (62–90 kPa).

5. Relieve the fuel pressure.

6. Remove the fuel pressure gauge.

7. Reinstall the fuel line.

8. Start the car and check for fuel leaks.

9. Remove plug covering THERMAC vacuum port on the TBI and install the air cleaner.

Fig. 49 Fuel pressure can be checked using an inexpensive pressure/vacuum gauge

Throttle Body

REMOVAL & INSTALLATION

▶ **See Figures 50 and 51**

1. Relieve the fuel system pressure.

2. Disconnect the THERMAC hose from the engine fitting and remove the air cleaner.

3. Detach the electrical connectors at the idle air control, throttle position sensor, and the injector.

4. Disconnect the throttle linkage, return spring, and cruise control (if equipped).

5. Disconnect the throttle body vacuum hoses, fuel supply and fuel return lines.

6. Disconnect the 3 bolts securing the throttle body and remove the throttle body.

7. To install, reverse the removal procedures. Replace the manifold gasket and O-rings.

8. Perform the minimum idle speed adjustment, if necessary.

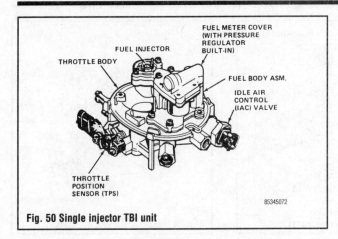

FUEL METER COVER
(WITH PRESSURE
REGULATOR
BUILT-IN)

FUEL INJECTOR

THROTTLE BODY

FUEL BODY ASM.

IDLE AIR
CONTROL
(IAC) VALVE

THROTTLE
POSITION
SENSOR (TPS)

85345072

Fig. 50 Single injector TBI unit

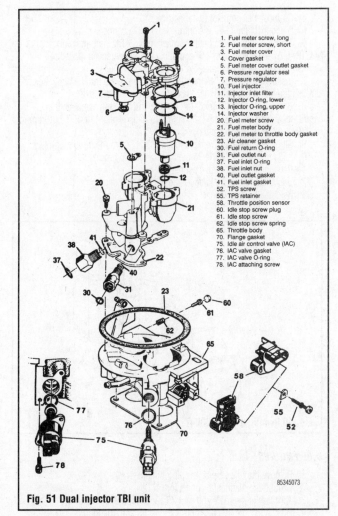

1. Fuel meter screw, long
2. Fuel meter screw, short
3. Fuel meter cover
4. Cover gasket
5. Fuel meter cover outlet gasket
6. Pressure regulator seal
7. Pressure regulator
10. Fuel injector
11. Injector inlet filter
12. Injector O-ring, lower
13. Injector O-ring, upper
14. Injector washer
20. Fuel meter screw
21. Fuel meter body
22. Fuel meter to throttle body gasket
23. Air cleaner gasket
30. Fuel return O-ring
31. Fuel outlet nut
37. Fuel inlet O-ring
38. Fuel inlet nut
40. Fuel outlet gasket
41. Fuel inlet gasket
52. TPS screw
55. TPS retainer
58. Throttle position sensor
60. Idle stop screw plug
61. Idle stop screw
62. Idle stop screw spring
65. Throttle body
70. Flange gasket
75. Idle air control valve (IAC)
76. IAC valve gasket
77. IAC valve O-ring
78. IAC attaching screw

85345073

Fig. 51 Dual injector TBI unit

INJECTOR REPLACEMENT

▶ **See Figures 52, 53 and 54**

➡ **Use care in removing injectors to prevent damage to the electrical connector pins on top of the injector, the fuel injector fuel filter and nozzle. The fuel injector is serviced as a complete assembly only and should never be immersed in any type of cleaner.**

Single Injector Units

1. Relieve the fuel system pressure.
2. Remove the air cleaner.

3. Detach the injector connector by squeezing the two tabs together and pulling straight up.
4. Remove the screws securing the fuel meter cover. Note the location of any short screws for correct placement during reassembly.

✳✳ CAUTION

DO NOT remove the four screws securing the pressure regulator to the fuel meter cover. The fuel pressure regulator includes a large spring under heavy tension which could cause personal injury if released.

5. With the old fuel meter gasket in place to prevent damage to the casting, use a prytool and fulcrum to pry the injector carefully until it is free from the fuel meter body.
6. Remove the injector.
7. Remove the large O-ring and steel back-up washer at the top of the injector cavity in the fuel meter body.
8. Remove the small O-ring located at the bottom of the injector cavity.

To Install:

9. Lubricate the new, small O-ring with automatic transmission fluid; then, push the new O-ring on the nozzle end of the injector up against the injector fuel filter.
10. Install the steel backup washer in the recess of the fuel meter body. Lubricate the new large O-ring with automatic transmission fluid, then install the O-ring directly above the backup washer, pressing the O-ring down into the cavity recess. The O-ring is properly installed when it is flush with the casting surface.

✳✳ WARNING

Do not attempt to reverse this procedure and install the backup washer and O-ring after the injector is located in the cavity. To do so will prevent proper seating of the O-ring in the cavity recess which could result in a fuel leak and possible fire.

11. Install the injector by using a pushing/twisting motion to center the nozzle O-ring in the bottom of the injector cavity and aligning the raised lug on the injector base with the notch cast into the fuel meter body. Push down on the injector making sure it is fully seated in the cavity. Injector installation is correct when the lug is seated in the notch and the electrical terminals are parallel to the throttle shaft.
12. Using new gaskets on the fuel meter cover and a new dust seal, install the cover to the fuel meter body. The two short screws are located adjacent to the injector.
13. Connect the injector electrical connector by pushing straight down until seated firmly in place.
14. Connect the negative battery cable.
15. With the engine OFF and the ignition ON, check for fuel leaks.
16. Install the air cleaner.

Dual Injector Units

1. Relieve the fuel system pressure.
2. Remove the air cleaner.
3. Disconnect the injector connector by squeezing the two tabs together and pulling straight up.
4. Remove the screws securing the fuel meter cover.

✳✳ CAUTION

DO NOT remove the four screws securing the pressure regulator to the fuel meter cover. The fuel pressure regulator includes a large spring under heavy tension which could cause personal injury if released.

5. With the old fuel meter gasket in place to prevent damage to the casting, use a suitable prytool and fulcrum to pry the injector carefully until it is free from the fuel meter body.
6. Remove the injector.
7. Remove the small O-ring from the nozzle end of the injector and discard it.

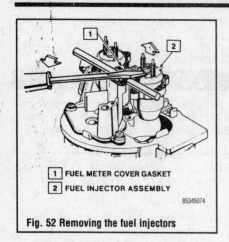

| 1 | FUEL METER COVER GASKET |
| 2 | FUEL INJECTOR ASSEMBLY |

85345074

Fig. 52 Removing the fuel injectors

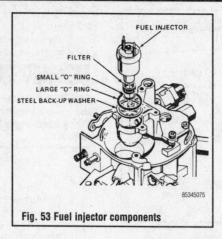

85345075

Fig. 53 Fuel injector components

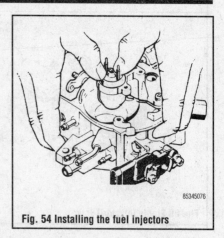

85345076

Fig. 54 Installing the fuel injectors

8. Remove the old fuel meter cover gasket and discard it.

9. Remove the upper O-ring and steel backup washer from the top of the injector cavity. Discard the O-ring.

To install:

10. Install the steel backup washer in the counterbore of the fuel meter body.

11. Lubricate the new large O-ring with clean engine oil and install it directly over the backup washer. Be sure the O-ring is seated properly and is flush with the top of the fuel meter body surface.

12. Lubricate the new small O-ring with clean engine oil and install it on the nozzle end of the injector. Push the O-ring on far enough to contact the filter.

✳✳ WARNING

Do not attempt to reverse this procedure and install the backup washer and O-ring after the injector is located in the cavity. To do so will prevent proper seating of the O-ring in the cavity recess which could result in a fuel leak and possible fire.

13. Install the injector by aligning the raised lug on the injector base with the notch cast into the fuel meter body. Push down on the injector making sure it is fully seated in the cavity. Injector installation is correct when the lug is seated in the notch and the electrical terminals are parallel to the throttle shaft.

14. Using new gaskets on the fuel meter cover and a new dust seal, install the cover to the fuel meter body. Use an appropriate thread locking compound on the cover attaching screws.

15. Connect the injector electrical connector by pushing straight down until seated firmly in place.

16. Connect the negative battery cable.

17. With the engine OFF and the ignition ON, check for fuel leaks.

18. Install the air cleaner.

ADJUSTMENTS

▶ **See Figures 55 and 56**

Minimum Idle Speed

➡Minimum idle speed should only be adjusted when installing a replacement throttle body. The idle stop screw is used to regulate the minimum idle speed of the engine. The throttle body is adjusted at the factory, then covered with a cap or plug to discourage unnecessary readjustment.

2.5L ENGINES

1. Remove the air cleaner and plug the THERMAC vacuum port.

2. Disconnect the TV cable from the throttle control bracket to allow access to the idle adjustment screw.

3. Remove the throttle stop screw plug or cap.

4. Connect a tachometer to the engine.

5. Disconnect the Idle Air Control (IAC) valve connector.

6. Start the engine with the transmission in PARK (auto transmission) or NEUTRAL (manual transmission) and allow the engine speed to stabilize. All accessories (A/C, rear defogger, etc.) should be OFF.

7. Install tool J–33047 in the idle air passage of the throttle body. Be certain that the tool seats fully in the passage and no air leaks exist.

8. Using a number 20 Torx® bit, turn the throttle stop screw until the engine speed is 475–525 rpm in PARK (auto transmission) or 450–500 rpm in NEUTRAL (manual transmission).

9. Stop the engine and remove tool J–33047 from the throttle body.

10. Reconnect the TV cable to the throttle control bracket.

11. Reconnect the IAC valve connector.

12. Use silicone sealant to cover the throttle stop screw.

13. Reinstall the air cleaner.

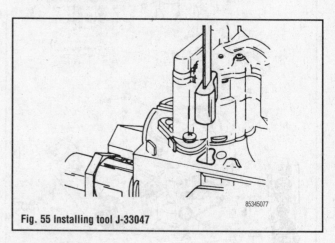

85345077

Fig. 55 Installing tool J-33047

5.0L ENGINES

1. Remove the idle stop screw plug or cap.

2. Ground the diagnostic connector (ALDL).

3. Turn the ignition **ON** and wait 45 seconds, DO NOT start the engine.

4. Disconnect the idle air control connector with the ignition **ON**.

5. Remove the ground from the diagnostic connector and disconnect the distributor set-timing connector.

6. Connect a tachometer to the engine.

7. Place the transmission in PARK (auto transmission) or NEUTRAL (manual transmission). Start and run the engine until it reaches normal operating temperature.

➡It is important that the distributor set-timing connector be disconnected to fix the spark advance at base timing. This eliminates the possibility of changes in engine speed due to variations in timing.

8. The idle speed should be 450–500 rpm, adjust as necessary.

Correct minimum idle speed adjustment is critical to vehicle performance and component durability. Incorrect minimum idle speed adjustment (too high) will cause the IAC valve pintle to constantly bottom in it's seat and result in early valve failure. If minimum idle speed is adjusted too low, the vehicle may not start in cold weather or may stall during warm-up.

9. Turn the ignition **OFF** and reconnect the IAC motor connector.
10. Reconnect the distributor set-timing connector.
11. Use silicone sealant to cover the throttle stop screw.

Throttle Position Sensor (TPS)

➡1982–1983 2.5L TBI engines are equipped with an adjustable throttle position sensor. This procedure should only be performed after replacing the TPS or diagnosis leads to incorrect TPS adjustment.

1. Remove the throttle position sensor connector and install three jumper wires between the connector and the sensor. Connect a digital voltmeter to terminals **B** and **C**.
2. Turn the ignition **ON**. It should display between 0.45–0.60 volts.
3. Adjust the TPS, if necessary, by loosening the attaching screws and rotating the TPS.
4. Tighten the screws, remove the jumper wires with the ignition **OFF** and reconnect the harness connector.
5. Start the engine and check for proper idle operation.

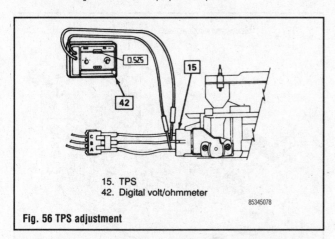

15. TPS
42. Digital volt/ohmmeter

85345078

Fig. 56 TPS adjustment

Fuel Pressure Regulator

REMOVAL & INSTALLATION

▶ **See Figures 57 and 58**

The fuel meter cover contains the pressure regulator and is only serviced as a complete preset assembly. The fuel pressure regulator is preset and plugged at the factory.

1. Relieve the fuel system pressure.
2. Remove the air cleaner.
3. Disconnect the electrical connector to the fuel injector(s).
4. Remove the fuel meter cover attaching screws and lockwashers.
5. Remove the fuel meter cover.

DO NOT remove the four screws securing the pressure regulator to the meter cover. The pressure regulator contains a large spring under

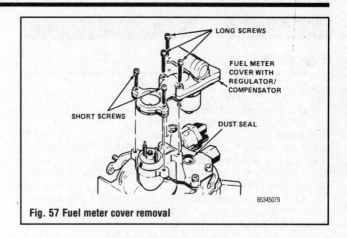

85345079

Fig. 57 Fuel meter cover removal

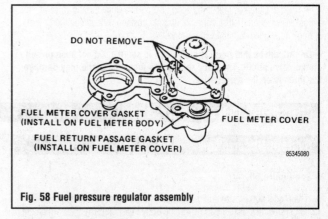

85345080

Fig. 58 Fuel pressure regulator assembly

heavy compression which could cause personal injury if released. Disassembly may also cause a fuel leak and result in a fire.

6. Discard the old gaskets and dust seal.

To install:

7. Install a new dust seal, fuel outlet passage gasket and fuel meter cover gasket.
8. Install the fuel meter cover.
9. Coat the attaching screws with a thread locking compound and tighten the screws to 27 inch lbs. (3 Nm). Install the short screws next to the injectors.
10. Reconnect the electrical connectors to the fuel injectors.
11. With the engine OFF and the ignition ON, check for fuel leaks.
12. Install the air cleaner.

Throttle Position Sensor (TPS)

REMOVAL & INSTALLATION

1. Remove the air cleaner.
2. Disconnect the electrical connector.
3. Remove the TPS attaching screws and lockwashers.
4. Remove the TPS.

To install:

5. Install the throttle position sensor. On 2.5L engines, make sure the TPS pickup lever is located above the tang on the throttle actuator lever. On 5.0L engines, line up the TPS lever with the TPS drive lever on the throttle body.
6. Install the TPS attaching screws.
7. Adjust the TPS voltage, if applicable.
8. Reconnect the electrical connector.
9. Install the air cleaner.

Idle Air Control (IAC) Valve

REMOVAL & INSTALLATION

▶ **See Figure 59**

1. Unplug the electrical connector from idle air control valve.
2. Remove the idle air control valve.

To install:

3. Before installing the idle air control valve, measure the distance that the valve is extended. Measurement should be made from the motor housing to the end of the cone. It should not exceed 28.5mm (1⅛ in.), or damage to the valve may occur when installed.

4. Identify the replacement IAC valve as being either Type 1 (with collar at electric terminal end) or Type 2 (without collar). If measuring distance is greater than specified above, proceed as follows:

- Type 1: Use finger pressure to slowly retract the pintle.
- Type 2: Compress retaining spring from valve while turning valve in with a clockwise motion. Return spring to original position with straight portion of spring end aligned with flat surface of valve.

➡ **On IAC valves that have already been in service, do not push or pull on the valve pintle. The force required to move the pintle may damage the threads on the worm drive.**

5. Use a new gasket or O-ring and install the IAC valve into the throttle body.

6. Allow the ECM to reset the idle air control valve using the procedure described earlier in this section.

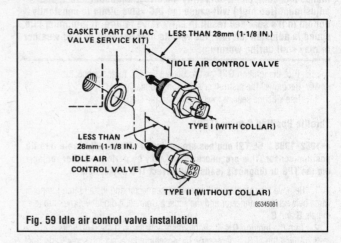

Fig. 59 Idle air control valve installation

CROSSFIRE INJECTION SYSTEM

System Description

▶ **See Figure 60**

The Model 400 Electronic Fuel Injection (EFI) system is a computer controlled system that uses a pair of Throttle Body Injection (TBI) units, which are mounted on a single manifold cover on the 5.0L (VIN 7) engine. Since each TBI feeds the cylinders on the opposite side of the engine, the system has acquired the name of Crossfire Injection.

Fuel is supplied, by an electric fuel pump located in the fuel tank, to the front TBI fuel accumulator. From the accumulator, it is carried to the rear TBI fuel pressure regulator by a connecting tube. Unused fuel is sent to the fuel tank through a separate return line.

Fuel is supplied to the engine through electronically pulsed injector valves located in the throttle body.

Relieving Fuel System Pressure

1. Remove the fuse marked "Fuel Pump" from the fuse block in the passenger compartment.

2. Crank the engine. The engine will start and run until the fuel supply remaining in the lines is exhausted. When the engines stops, engage the starter again for three seconds to assure dissipation of any remaining pressure.

3. With the ignition **OFF**, disconnect the negative battery cable to prevent fuel discharge if the key is accidentally turned to the **ON** position. Replace the fuse with the ignition **OFF**.

➡ **When disconnecting fuel lines, there may still be a small amount of fuel released. Cover the fuel line connection with a shop cloth to collect the fuel, then place the cloth in an approved container.**

Electric Fuel Pump

REMOVAL & INSTALLATION

The removal and installation procedures for the Crossfire injection system fuel pump is identical to the Throttle Body Injection (TBI) system. Please refer to the TBI fuel pump procedures earlier in this manual.

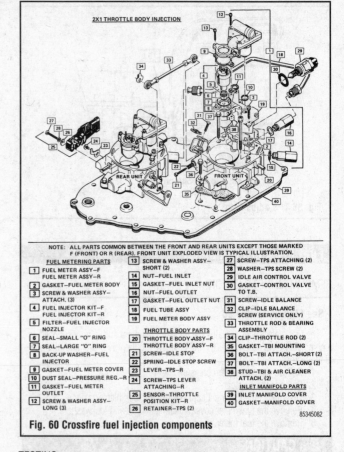

Fig. 60 Crossfire fuel injection components

TESTING

The testing procedures for the Crossfire injection system fuel pump is identical to the Throttle Body Injection (TBI) system. Please refer to the TBI fuel pump procedures earlier in this manual.

Throttle Body

REMOVAL & INSTALLATION

Front Unit

1. Relieve the fuel system pressure.
2. Remove the air cleaner assembly, noting the connection points of the vacuum lines.
3. Detach the electrical connectors at the injector and the idle air control motor.
4. Disconnect the vacuum lines from the TBI unit, noting the connection points. During installation, refer to the underhood emission control information decal for vacuum line routing information.
5. Disconnect the transmission detent cable from the TBI unit.
6. Disconnect the fuel inlet (feed) and fuel balance line connections at the front TBI unit.
7. Remove and discard the throttle control rod retaining clip from the front TBI throttle lever stud. A new clip must be used during reassembly.
8. Unbolt and remove the TBI unit.

To install:

9. Replacement of the manifold cover or either throttle body requires throttle valve synchronizing and checking of the throttle rod alignment (see "Preliminary Adjustments"). Before installing the replacement throttle body unit(s) on the engine, perform the following steps:

   a. If the tamper resistant plugs covering the throttle stop screws are in place, remove the plugs.

   b. If the front TBI unit throttle synchronizing screw has a welded retaining collar, grind off the weld.

   c. Block possible movement of the throttle lever, relieving the force of the heavy spring against the throttle synchronizing screw. This prevents the levers from coming into contact.

➡**If the lever is not blocked before the throttle synchronizing screw is removed, the screw may be damaged, and reinstallation will be accomplished only with great difficulty.**

   d. Remove the synchronizing screw and collar. Discard the collar and reinstall the screw. The blocking from the throttle lever (installed in the previous step) can now be removed.

✳ CAUTION

The collar must be removed to prevent possible interference with the air cleaner. Failure to do so could result in personal injury.

10. Use new gaskets and tighten the TBI bolts to 120–168 inch lbs. (13–19 Nm) during installation.
11. Perform the preliminary adjustments. These procedures must be followed before further assembly.
12. Reconnect the fuel lines to the TBI units. Use a backup wrench to prevent the nuts from turning in the TBI unit.
13. Reconnect the throttle cable and detent cable.
14. Reconnect all related vacuum lines.
15. Reconnect the electrical connectors.
16. With the engine OFF, depress the accelerator pedal to the floor and release. Check for free return of the pedal.
17. Check the throttle position sensor voltage and adjust if necessary.
18. Perform the Minimum Idle and Throttle Valve Synchronization adjustment procedures.

Rear Unit

1. Relieve the fuel system pressure.
2. Remove the air cleaner assembly, noting the connection points of the vacuum lines.
3. Disconnect the electrical connectors at the injector, idle air control motor, and throttle position sensor.
4. Disconnect the vacuum lines from the TBI unit, noting the connection points. During installation, refer to the underhood emission control information decal for vacuum line routing information.

5. Disconnect the throttle and cruise control (if so equipped) cables at the TBI unit.
6. Disconnect the fuel return and balance line connections from the rear TBI unit.
7. Remove and discard the throttle control rod retaining clip from the front TBI unit throttle lever stud. A new clip must be used during reassembly.

➡**One throttle rod end bearing is permanently attached to the throttle lever stud of the rear TBI unit, and must not be removed from it. If the throttle rod and bearing assembly needs replacement, The entire rear throttle body must be replaced.**

8. Unbolt and remove the TBI unit.

To install:

9. Replacement of the manifold cover or either throttle body requires throttle valve synchronizing and checking of the throttle rod alignment (see "Preliminary Adjustments"). Before installing the replacement throttle body unit(s) on the engine, perform the following steps:

   a. If the tamper resistant plugs covering the throttle stop screws are in place, remove the plugs.

   b. If the front TBI unit throttle synchronizing screw has a welded retaining collar, grind off the weld.

   c. Block possible movement of the throttle lever, relieving the force of the heavy spring against the throttle synchronizing screw. This prevents the levers from coming into contact.

➡**If the lever is not blocked before the throttle synchronizing screw is removed, the screw may be damaged, and reinstallation will be accomplished only with great difficulty.**

   d. Remove the synchronizing screw and collar. Discard the collar and reinstall the screw. The blocking from the throttle lever (installed in the previous step) can now be removed.

✳ CAUTION

The collar must be removed to prevent possible interference with the air cleaner. Failure to do so could result in personal injury.

10. Use new gaskets and tighten the TBI bolts to 120–168 inch lbs. (13–19 Nm) during installation.
11. Perform the preliminary adjustments. These procedures must be followed before further assembly.
12. Reconnect the fuel lines to the TBI units. Use a backup wrench to prevent the nuts from turning in the TBI unit.
13. Reconnect the throttle cable and the cruise control cable.
14. Reconnect all related vacuum lines.
15. Reconnect the electrical connectors.
16. With the engine OFF, depress the accelerator pedal to the floor and release. Check for free return of the pedal.
17. Check the throttle position sensor voltage and adjust if necessary.
18. Perform the Minimum Idle and Throttle Valve Synchronization adjustment procedures.

INJECTOR REPLACEMENT

The removal and installation procedures for the Crossfire injection system's fuel injector is identical to the Throttle Body Injection (TBI) system. Please refer to the TBI fuel injector procedures earlier in this manual.

ADJUSTMENTS

▶ **See Figures 61, 62, 63, 64 and 65**

Preliminary Adjustments

➡**The preliminary adjustments are performed if tampering with the idle speed or synchronization is evident and when either of the throttle bodies or the manifold cover have been replaced. They must be performed BEFORE the Minimum Idle and Throttle Valve Synchronizing procedure.**

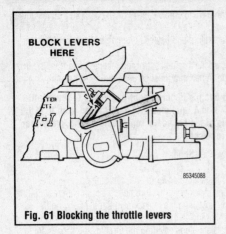

Fig. 61 Blocking the throttle levers

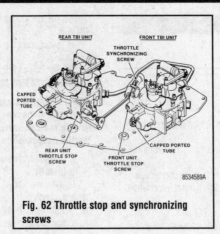

Fig. 62 Throttle stop and synchronizing screws

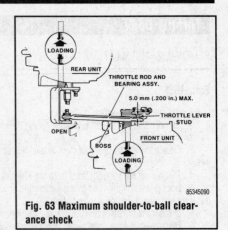

Fig. 63 Maximum shoulder-to-ball clearance check

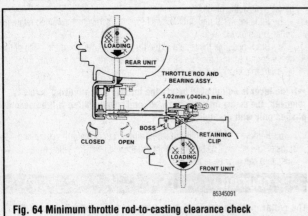

Fig. 64 Minimum throttle rod-to-casting clearance check

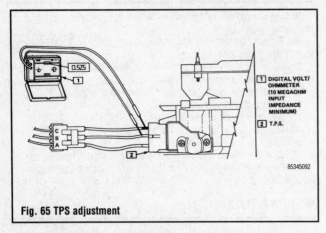

Fig. 65 TPS adjustment

THROTTLE VALVE SYNCHRONIZING

1. Turn BOTH front and rear unit throttle stop screws counterclockwise enough to break contact with the related throttle lever tangs.

2. Adjust the throttle synchronizing screw to allow BOTH throttle valves to close. The throttle rod end bearing will move freely on the front unit throttle lever stud when both valves are closed.

3. Turn the front unit throttle stop screw clockwise slowly until it makes contact with the throttle lever tang. Turn the screw clockwise an additional ¼ turn.

4. Turn the rear unit throttle stop screw clockwise slowly until it makes contact with the throttle lever tang. Turn the screw an additional ½ turn.

THROTTLE ROD ALIGNMENT CHECK

➡The throttle rod alignment check procedure is followed only if a replacement manifold cover or TBI unit has been installed. If not, proceed to "Minimum Idle and Throttle Valve Synchronizing".

1. Actuate the rear unit throttle lever to bring both units to the wide open throttle position, loading the throttle valves. Move the throttle rod toward the front unit casting boss.

2. Check the clearance between the shoulder of the stud and the side of the ball surface. Maximum clearance must not exceed 0.200 in. (5mm). If the clearance is greater, the assembly (manifold cover, TBI unit or throttle body) must be replaced and the preliminary adjustments repeated.

3. Use needle-nose pliers to install a NEW throttle rod and bearing assembly retaining clip.

4. Move both front and rear throttle levers through the total throttle travel, loading both valves.

5. Check the clearance between the throttle rod and the front unit throttle body casting boss. If minimum clearance is less than 0.040 in. (1.02mm), the assembly must be replaced. If minimum clearance is at least 0.040 in. (1.02mm), proceed with assembly.

Minimum Idle and Throttle Valve Synchronizing

➡The throttle position of each throttle body must be balanced so that the throttle plates are synchronized and open simultaneously. These adjustment procedures must be followed AFTER performing the "Preliminary Adjustments".

1. Remove the air cleaner and plug the vacuum port on the rear TBI unit for the thermostatic air cleaner.

2. Remove the tamper resistant plugs covering both unit throttle stop screws, if necessary.

3. Block the drive wheels and apply the parking brake.

4. Connect a tachometer to measure rpm.

5. Start the engine and allow the engine rpm to stabilize at normal operating temperature.

6. Have a helper apply the brakes and place the transmission in DRIVE.

7. Plug the idle air passages of each throttle body with plugs (J–33047 or equivalent). Make sure the plugs are seated fully in the passage so that no air leaks exist. The engine rpm should decrease below curb idle speed. If the engine rpm does not decrease, check for a vacuum leak.

8. Remove the cap from the ported tube on the rear TBI unit and connect a vacuum gauge or water manometer.

9. Adjust the rear unit throttle stop screw to obtain approximately ½ in. Hg as read on the vacuum gauge, or 6 in. H$_2$O as read on the manometer. If not able to adjust to this level, check that the front unit throttle stop is not limiting throttle travel.

10. Remove the vacuum gauge or manometer from the rear unit and install the cap on the ported vacuum tube.

11. Remove the cap from the ported vacuum tube on the front TBI unit and install the gauge or manometer as before. If the reading is not the same as the rear unit, proceed as follows:

   a. Locate the throttle synchronizing screw and collar on the front TBI unit. The screw may be welded to discourage tampering with this adjustment. Break the weld, if necessary, and install a new screw with a thread sealing compound applied.

   b. Adjust the screw to obtain approximately ½ in. Hg as read on the vacuum gauge, or 6 in. H$_2$O on the manometer.

12. Remove the gauge or manometer from the ported tube and reinstall the cap.

13. Adjust the rear throttle stop screw to obtain 475 rpm, with the transmission in **D** and the parking brake applied. On manual transmission models, leave the gear selector in **N**.

14. Turn the ignition OFF and place automatic transmission in **N**.

15. Remove idle air passage plugs.

16. Start the engine. It may run at a high rpm but the engine speed should decrease when the idle air control valves close the air passages. Stop the engine when the rpm decreases.

17. The throttle position sensor (TPS) voltage should be checked and adjusted, if necessary.

18. Connect the vacuum line to the TBI unit and install the air cleaner.

19. Reset the idle speed control motors by driving the vehicle to 45 mph.

Throttle Position Sensor (TPS)

➡An accurate digital voltmeter is needed to perform this adjustment.

1. Remove the air cleaner.
2. Disconnect the TPS electrical connector.
3. Install three jumper wires between the TPS and the TPS wiring terminal connections.
4. Turn the ignition ON, engine stopped, measure the voltage between terminals B and C.
5. The display should read between 0.45–0.60 volts.
6. Loosen the screws and rotate the TPS to obtain the correct voltage, if necessary.
7. Tighten the TPS screws and turn the ignition OFF. Remove the jumpers.
8. Reconnect the wiring to the TPS.
9. Install the air cleaner.

Fuel Pressure Regulator

REMOVAL & INSTALLATION

The removal and installation procedures for the Crossfire injection system's fuel pressure regulator is identical to the Throttle Body Injection (TBI) system. Please refer to the TBI fuel pressure regulator procedures earlier in this manual.

Throttle Position Sensor (TPS)

REMOVAL & INSTALLATION

1. Remove the air cleaner.
2. Disconnect the electrical connector.
3. Remove the TPS attaching screws and lockwashers.
4. Remove the TPS.

To install:

5. Install the throttle position sensor. Make sure the TPS pickup lever is located above the tang on the throttle actuator lever.
6. Install the TPS attaching screws.
7. Adjust the TPS voltage.
8. Reconnect the electrical connector.
9. Install the air cleaner.

MULTI-PORT FUEL INJECTION SYSTEMS

System Descriptions

The Multi-Port Fuel Injection (MPFI or MFI) systems were first introduced on the 1985 models. They may be called different names (Port Fuel Injection-PFI, Tuned Port Injection-TPI, Sequential Fuel Injection-SFI), however, all of the systems are similar in operation.

The systems are controlled by an Electronic Control Module (ECM) which monitors the engine operations and generates output signals to provide the correct air/fuel mixture, ignition timing and idle speed. Input information to the ECM is provided by the oxygen sensor, temperature sensors, detonation sensor, mass air flow sensor and throttle position sensor. A system may use all or some of these sensors, depending on the year and engine application. The ECM also

Idle Air Control Valve

REMOVAL & INSTALLATION

◆ **See Figures 66 and 67**

1. Remove the air cleaner.
2. Detach the electrical connection from the idle air control assembly.
3. Using a 1¼ in. wrench, remove the IAC valve from the throttle body. On IAC valves secured with screws, remove the attaching screws.

➡**Before installing a NEW IAC valve, measure the distance that the conical valve is extended. Measurement should be made from the motor housing to the end of the cone. Distance should be no greater than 1¼ in. (32mm). If the cone is extended too far, damage may result when the motor is installed. If necessary, push on the end of cone until it is retracted the correct distance.**

4. Installation is the reverse of removal. Torque threaded valves to 13 ft. lbs. (17 Nm).

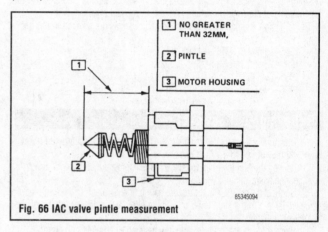

Fig. 66 IAC valve pintle measurement

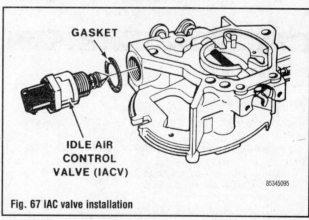

Fig. 67 IAC valve installation

receives information concerning engine rpm, road speed, transmission gear position, power steering and air conditioning status.

All of the systems use multiple injectors, aimed at the intake valve at each intake port, rather than the centrally located injector(s) found on the earlier Throttle Body Injection (TBI) and Crossfire Injection systems. The injectors are mounted on a fuel rail and are activated by a signal from the electronic control module. The injector is a solenoid-operated valve which remains open depending on the width of the electronic pulses (length of the signal) from the ECM; the longer the open time, the more fuel is injected. In this manner, the air/fuel mixture can be precisely controlled for maximum performance with minimum emissions.

There are two different types of fuel management systems used on the multi-port fuel injection engines. The mass air flow system and the speed density system.

The mass air flow systems measure the mass of air that is drawn into the engine cylinders, rather than just the volume. The sensor contains a hot-wire sensing unit, which is made up of an electronic balanced bridge network. Whenever current is supplied to the sensor, the bridge is energized and the sensing hot-wire is heated. As the air enters the mass air flow sensor, it passes over and cools the hot wire. When the hot wire is cooled, it's resistance changes and additional current is needed to keep the bridge network balanced. This increase in current is sent to the computer as a voltage signal and is used to calculate the mass of the incoming air. The ECM uses this information to determine the duration of fuel injection pulse, ignition timing and EGR operation.

The speed density systems calculate the volume of air moving through the intake. The ECM establishes the speed factor through a signal from the ignition module. The Manifold or Intake Air Temperature (MAT/IAT) and the Engine Coolant Temperature (ECT) sensors work together to assure that proper temperature information gets to the ECM while the Manifold Absolute Pressure (MAP) sensor monitors the changes in manifold pressure which results from changes in engine loading. These three sensors contribute to the density factor. Together, these inputs (engine speed, coolant temperature sensor, etc . . .) are the major determinants of the air/fuel mixture delivered by the fuel injection system.

The following engines and fuel management systems are covered in this section:

- 1985–1989 2.8L MPFI—Mass Air Flow
- 1990–1992 3.1L MPFI—Speed Density
- 1985–1989 5.0L and 5.7L TPI—Mass Air Flow
- 1990–1992 5.0L and 5.7L TPI—Speed Density

Relieving Fuel System Pressure

1. Disconnect the negative battery cable to prevent fuel discharge if the key is accidentally turned to the RUN position.
2. Loosen the fuel filler cap to relieve the tank pressure and do not tighten until service has been completed.
3. Connect J–34730–1 fuel pressure gauge or equivalent, to the fuel pressure test valve. Wrap a shop towel around the fitting while connecting the gauge to prevent spillage.
4. Place the end of the bleed hose into a suitable container and open the valve to relieve the fuel system pressure.

Electric Fuel Pump

REMOVAL & INSTALLATION

♦ See Figures 68 and 69

The fuel pump is part of the fuel sender assembly located inside the fuel tank.

1. Release the fuel system pressure and disconnect the negative battery cable.
2. Drain the fuel tank, then raise and safely support the vehicle.
3. Remove the fuel tank from the vehicle.

4. Clean the area surrounding the sender assembly to prevent contamination of the fuel system.
5. Using tool J–24187 or equivalent, remove the sending unit retaining cam. Remove the fuel sender and O-rings from the tank. Discard the O-rings.
6. If necessary, separate the fuel pump from the sending unit assembly.

To install:
7. If removed, install the fuel pump to the sending unit. If the strainer was removed, it must be replaced with a new one.
8. Inspect and clean the O-ring mating surfaces.
9. Install a new O-ring in the groove around the tank opening. If applicable, install a new O-ring on the fuel sender feed tube.
10. Install the fuel sender assembly as follows:
    a. The fuel pump strainer must be in a horizontal position, and when installed, must not block the travel of the float arm. Gently fold the strainer over itself and slowly position the sending assembly in the tank so the strainer is not damaged or trapped by the sump walls.
11. Install the retaining cam using tool J–24187 or equivalent.
12. Install the fuel tank assembly.
13. Lower the vehicle.
14. Fill the fuel tank, tighten the fuel filler cap and connect the negative battery cable.
15. Turn the ignition switch to the ON position for 2 seconds, OFF for 10 seconds, then back to the ON position. Check for fuel leaks.

TESTING

♦ See Figure 70

1. Relieve the fuel system pressure and check that there is an adequate quantity of fuel in the tank.
2. Connect a fuel pressure gauge to the pressure connector fitting located on the end of the fuel rail.
3. Make sure the ignition switch has been in the OFF position for at least 10 seconds and that all accessories are OFF.
4. Turn the ignition switch ON and the pump will run for about 2 seconds. Note the system pressure with the pump running, it should be between 40–47 psi.

➡ **The ignition switch may have to be cycled to the ON position more than once to obtain maximum pressure. It is also normal for the pressure to drop slightly when the pump first stops, but it should then hold steady.**

5. If the pressure is not as specified, verify that fuel pump operation is heard in the tank.
6. If fuel pump operation is not heard, inspect the fuel pump relay and wiring.
7. If fuel pump operation is heard, inspect the filter and lines for restriction.
8. Start the engine and make sure the pressure decreases about 3–10 psi at idle.
9. If fuel pressure does not decrease, inspect the fuel pressure regulator and hose.
10. Disconnect the fuel pressure gauge.

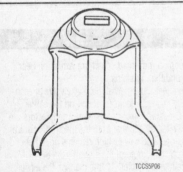

TCCS5P06

Fig. 68 A special tool is usually available to remove or install the fuel pump locking cam

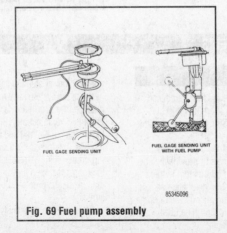

FUEL GAGE SENDING UNIT

FUEL GAGE SENDING UNIT WITH FUEL PUMP

85345096

Fig. 69 Fuel pump assembly

TCCS4P04

Fig. 70 Fuel pressure can be checked using an inexpensive pressure/vacuum gauge

Throttle Body

REMOVAL & INSTALLATION

▶ **See Figures 71, 72 and 73**

1. Disconnect the negative (–) battery cable and partially drain the radiator.
2. Remove the air inlet duct and unplug the IAC and TPS electrical connectors.
3. Label and disconnect the vacuum and coolant lines.
4. Disconnect the accelerator, throttle valve (transmission control) and cruise control cables, as applicable.
5. Remove the throttle body attaching bolts, then separate the throttle body from the plenum.
6. Discard the gasket.

To install:

7. Install the throttle body to the plenum using a new gasket. Tighten the bolts to specification.
8. Engage the accelerator, throttle valve and cruise control cables, as necessary. Make sure that the linkages do not hold the throttle open.
9. Connect the vacuum and coolant lines.
10. Install the air inlet duct and plug the IAC and TPS electrical connectors into their sockets.
11. Connect the negative (–) battery cable and refill the radiator.
12. With the engine OFF, check to see that the accelerator pedal is free. Depress the pedal to the floor and release.

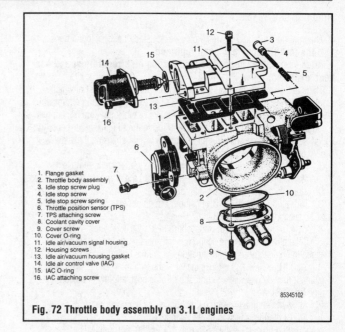

1. Flange gasket
2. Throttle body assembly
3. Idle stop screw plug
4. Idle stop screw
5. Idle stop screw spring
6. Throttle position sensor (TPS)
7. TPS attaching screw
8. Coolant cavity cover
9. Cover screw
10. Cover O-ring
11. Idle air/vacuum signal housing
12. Housing screws
13. Idle air/vacuum housing gasket
14. Idle air control valve (IAC)
15. IAC O-ring
16. IAC attaching screw

85345102

Fig. 72 Throttle body assembly on 3.1L engines

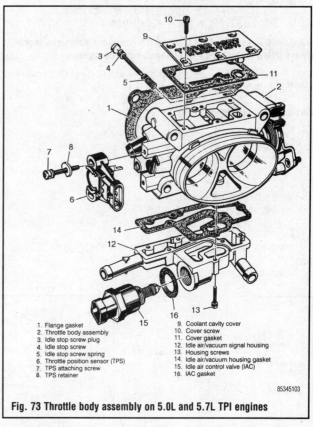

1. Flange gasket
2. Throttle body assembly
3. Idle stop screw plug
4. Idle stop screw
5. Idle stop screw spring
6. Throttle position sensor (TPS)
7. TPS attaching screw
8. TPS retainer
9. Coolant cavity cover
10. Cover screw
11. Cover gasket
12. Idle air/vacuum signal housing
13. Housing screws
14. Idle air/vacuum housing gasket
15. Idle air control valve (IAC)
16. IAC gasket

85345103

Fig. 73 Throttle body assembly on 5.0L and 5.7L TPI engines

ADJUSTMENTS

IAC Valve Position

The ECM will need to relearn the Idle Air Control (IAC) valve position anytime battery power has been interrupted to it. A scan tool must be used on 3.1L engines to update the ECM with the correct IAC valve position and provide a stable idle speed. The IAC valve position on others can be reset by starting and running the engine for 5 seconds, then turning the ignition OFF for 10 seconds. Start the engine again and check for proper operation.

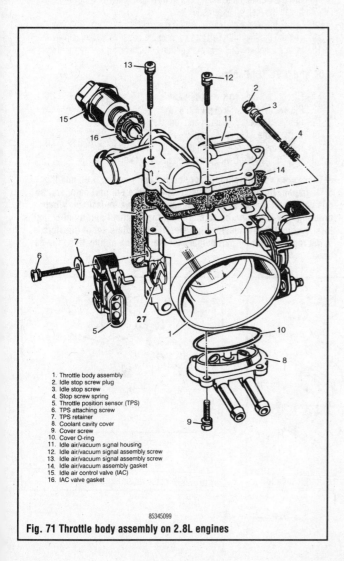

1. Throttle body assembly
2. Idle stop screw plug
3. Idle stop screw
4. Stop screw spring
5. Throttle position sensor (TPS)
6. TPS attaching screw
7. TPS retainer
8. Coolant cavity cover
9. Cover screw
10. Cover O-ring
11. Idle air/vacuum signal housing
12. Idle air/vacuum signal assembly screw
13. Idle air/vacuum signal assembly screw
14. Idle air/vacuum assembly gasket
15. Idle air control valve (IAC)
16. IAC valve gasket

85345099

Fig. 71 Throttle body assembly on 2.8L engines

Minimum Idle Speed

The minimum idle speed should only be adjusted under two conditions:

If the throttle body has been replaced.

After every other possible cause for the incorrect idle speed has been explored.

There are many possible causes for incorrect idle speed, most of which require a high level of diagnostic skill as well as expensive testing equipment. Check the vehicle for vacuum leaks, incorrect valve or ignition timing, deposit accumulation in the throttle bore or valve, sticking throttle linkage or bent throttle valves. If the vehicle will still not idle properly after checking these areas, it should be diagnosed by a professional.

1. Pierce the idle stop screw with an awl. Apply leverage to remove it.
2. Make sure the IAC valve is connected. Short the A and B terminals of the ALDL connector together with a length of wire.
3. Turn the ignition to the ON position, but do not start the engine. Wait at least 30 seconds before proceeding.
4. With the ignition ON, disconnect the IAC valve connector.
5. Separate the set-timing connector. This eliminates the possibility of changes in engine speed due to variations of engine timing.
6. Start the engine and remove the wire shorting the A and B terminals together. It may be necessary to hold the throttle open slightly to prevent the engine from stalling.
7. Allow the engine to reach normal operating temperature.
8. Adjust the idle speed to the following:
   a. 2.8L Engines — 450–550 rpm A/T or 550–650 rpm M/T
   b. 3.1L Engines — Refer to the underhood emissions sticker
   c. 5.0L and 5.7L TPI engines — 400–450 rpm.

➡**If these figures differ from those on the underhood emissions sticker, always follow the specifications on the emissions sticker.**

9. Turn the ignition OFF and connect the IAC valve harness. On models up to 1989, adjust the Throttle Position Sensor.

Throttle Position Sensor (TPS)

1. Install three jumper wires between the TPS and the harness connector.
2. Use a digital voltmeter connected to terminals A and B of the TPS.
3. Turn the ignition switch ON, but do not start the engine.
4. Loosen the TPS attaching screws and adjust the sensor to the following:
   a. 2.8L Engines — 0.50–0.60 volts
   b. 5.0L and 5.7L TPI Engines — 0.47–0.61 volts
5. Tighten the attaching screws, then check that the reading has not been disturbed.
6. With the ignition OFF, remove the jumper wires. Reconnect the TPS harness.
7. Start the engine and check for proper operation.

Fuel Injectors

REMOVAL & INSTALLATION

◗ **See Figures 74, 75 and 76**

➡**Use care in removing injectors to prevent damage to the electrical connector pins and the nozzle. The fuel injector is serviced as a complete assembly only. Since it is an electrical component, DO NOT immerse it in a cleaner.**

2.8L and 3.1L Engines

1. Disconnect the negative battery cable.
2. Relieve the fuel system pressure.
3. Remove the intake plenum and the fuel rail assembly.
4. Rotate the injector retaining clip to the unlocked position and remove the injector. Discard the O-rings and the injector retaining clip.

➡**Different injectors are calibrated for different flow rates. When ordering new injectors, be sure to order the identical part number that is inscribed on the old injector.**

To install:

5. Lubricate the new O-ring seals with engine oil and install them on the injector. Assemble a new retaining clip on the injector.
6. Install the injector into the fuel rail socket with the electrical connections facing outward. Rotate the retaining clip to the lock position.
7. Install the fuel rail assembly.
8. Install the intake plenum with new gaskets.
9. Tighten the fuel filler cap and connect the negative battery cable.
10. With the engine OFF and the ignition ON, check for fuel leaks.

5.0L and 5.7L TPI Engines

1. Disconnect the negative battery cable.
2. Relieve the fuel system pressure.
3. Remove the intake plenum and runners.
4. Remove the fuel rail assembly.
5. Rotate the injector retaining clip to the unlocked position and remove the injector. Discard the O-rings and the injector retaining clip.

➡**There are two different injector part numbers for the 5.0L and the 5.7L engine. Do not intermix injectors with different part numbers, as this will result in engine roughness and excessive emissions. When ordering new injectors, be sure to order the identical part number that is inscribed on the old injector. However, if a complete set of injectors is being replaced, either part number for that engine application may be used.**

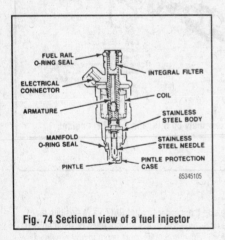

Fig. 74 Sectional view of a fuel injector

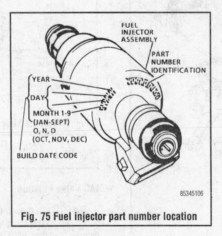

Fig. 75 Fuel injector part number location

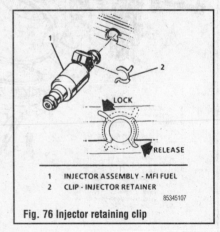

Fig. 76 Injector retaining clip

To install:

6. Lubricate the new O-ring seals with engine oil and install them on the injector. Assemble a new retaining clip on the injector.

7. Install the injector into the fuel rail socket with the electrical connections facing outward. Rotate the retaining clip to the lock position.

8. Install the fuel rail assembly.

9. Install the intake plenum and runners with new gaskets.

10. Tighten the fuel filler cap and connect the negative battery cable.

11. With the engine OFF and the ignition ON, check for fuel leaks.

Fuel Rail Assembly

REMOVAL & INSTALLATION

▶ **See Figures 77, 78 and 79**

➡**When servicing the fuel system, be sure to relieve the pressure of the system and drain the fuel into an approved container. Cap all open fuel lines and plug any other open passages. DO NOT allow dirt or other contaminants to enter the system.**

2.8L and 3.1L Engines

1. Disconnect the negative battery cable.
2. Relieve the fuel system pressure.
3. Remove the intake plenum.
4. Clean the fuel rail assembly to prevent dirt from entering the system.
5. Remove the cold start tube at the fuel rail fitting. Use a backup wrench on the fuel rail fitting to prevent it from turning.
6. Disconnect the fuel feed and return lines at the rail.
7. Disconnect the vacuum hose at the pressure regulator.
8. Unplug the electrical connectors.
9. Loosen and remove the fuel rail attaching bolts.
10. Remove the fuel rail assembly from the intake manifold.
11. Discard all of the O-ring seals that are exposed during this procedure.

To install:

12. Lubricate with clean engine oil, then install the injector nozzle O-rings.

13. Install the fuel rail assembly. Tilt the assembly to install the injectors.

14. Tighten the fuel rail attaching bolts to specification.

15. Engage the injector electrical connectors. Rotate each injector as required to avoid stretching the harness.

16. Connect the vacuum hose to the pressure regulator.

17. Connect the fuel feed and return lines. New O-rings must be used.

18. Install a new O-ring seal on the cold start tube. Thread the tube nut to the fitting on the fuel rail. Use a backup wrench on the fuel rail fitting to prevent it from turning.

19. Temporarily connect the negative battery terminal.

   a. With the engine OFF and the ignition ON, check for fuel leaks. Repair as necessary.

   b. Disconnect the negative battery cable.

20. Install the intake plenum using new gaskets.

21. Connect the negative battery cable.

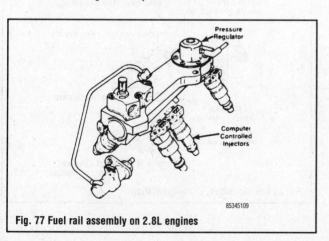

Fig. 77 Fuel rail assembly on 2.8L engines

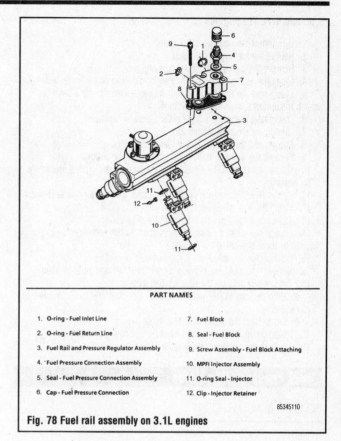

PART NAMES	
1. O-ring - Fuel Inlet Line	7. Fuel Block
2. O-ring - Fuel Return Line	8. Seal - Fuel Block
3. Fuel Rail and Pressure Regulator Assembly	9. Screw Assembly - Fuel Block Attaching
4. Fuel Pressure Connection Assembly	10. MPFI Injector Assembly
5. Seal - Fuel Pressure Connection Assembly	11. O-ring Seal - Injector
6. Cap - Fuel Pressure Connection	12. Clip - Injector Retainer

Fig. 78 Fuel rail assembly on 3.1L engines

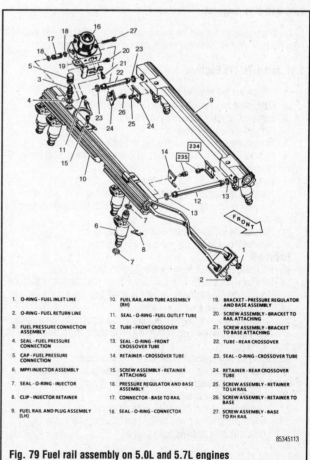

1. O-RING - FUEL INLET LINE	10. FUEL RAIL AND TUBE ASSEMBLY (RH)	19. BRACKET - PRESSURE REGULATOR AND BASE ASSEMBLY
2. O-RING - FUEL RETURN LINE	11. SEAL - O-RING - FUEL OUTLET TUBE	20. SCREW ASSEMBLY - BRACKET TO RAIL ATTACHING
3. FUEL PRESSURE CONNECTION ASSEMBLY	12. TUBE - FRONT CROSSOVER	21. SCREW ASSEMBLY - BRACKET TO BASE ATTACHING
4. SEAL - FUEL PRESSURE CONNECTION	13. SEAL - O-RING - FRONT CROSSOVER TUBE	22. TUBE - REAR CROSSOVER
5. CAP - FUEL PRESSURE CONNECTION	14. RETAINER - CROSSOVER TUBE	23. SEAL - O-RING - CROSSOVER TUBE
6. MPFI INJECTOR ASSEMBLY	15. SCREW ASSEMBLY - RETAINER ATTACHING	24. RETAINER - REAR CROSSOVER TUBE
7. SEAL - O-RING - INJECTOR	16. PRESSURE REGULATOR AND BASE ASSEMBLY	25. SCREW ASSEMBLY - RETAINER TO LH RAIL
8. CLIP - INJECTOR RETAINER	17. CONNECTOR - BASE TO RAIL	26. SCREW ASSEMBLY - RETAINER TO BASE
9. FUEL RAIL AND PLUG ASSEMBLY (LH)	18. SEAL - O-RING - CONNECTOR	27. SCREW ASSEMBLY - BASE TO RH RAIL

Fig. 79 Fuel rail assembly on 5.0L and 5.7L engines

5.0L and 5.7L TPI Engines

1. Disconnect the negative battery cable.
2. Relieve the fuel system pressure.
3. Remove the intake plenum and runners.
4. Clean the fuel rail assembly to prevent dirt from entering the system.
5. Disconnect the fuel feed and return lines at the rail. Use a back-up wrench to support the fuel rail tube fittings.
6. Disconnect the vacuum hose at the pressure regulator.
7. Unplug the electrical connectors.
8. Loosen and remove the fuel rail attaching bolts.
9. Remove the fuel rail assembly from the intake manifold.
10. Discard all of the O-ring seals that are exposed during this procedure.

To install:
11. Lubricate with clean engine oil, then install the injector nozzle O-rings.
12. Install the fuel rail assembly in the intake manifold.
13. Tighten the fuel rail attaching bolts to specification.
14. Engage the injector electrical connectors. Rotate each injector as required to avoid stretching the harness.
15. Connect the vacuum hose to the pressure regulator.
16. Connect the fuel feed and return lines. New O-rings must be used.
17. Temporarily connect the negative battery terminal.
   a. With the engine OFF and the ignition ON, check for fuel leaks. Repair as necessary.
   b. Disconnect the negative battery cable.
18. Install the intake plenum and runners. Use new gaskets.
19. Connect the negative battery cable.

Fuel Pressure Regulator

REMOVAL & INSTALLATION

2.8L and 3.1L Engines

The pressure regulator and the fuel rail are serviced as a complete assembly only. DO NOT attempt to remove the regulator cover from the fuel rail.

5.0L and 5.7L TPI Engines

1. Disconnect the negative battery cable.
2. Relieve the fuel system pressure.
3. Remove the intake plenum and runners.
4. Remove the fuel rail assembly.
5. Remove the rear crossover retainer and base attaching screw.
6. Remove the rear crossover tube and O-ring from the regulator base. Discard the O-ring.
7. Remove the pressure regulator bracket.
8. Remove the pressure regulator base-to-rail screw.
9. Separate the regulator base from the fuel rail, then disconnect from the fuel outlet tube.
10. Remove the fuel outlet tube O-ring and discard.
11. Remove the regulator base-to-fuel rail connector.

To install:
12. Lubricate and install new regulator base-to-fuel rail O-rings.
13. Lubricate a new outlet tube O-ring and install it on the end of the tube.
14. Connect the regulator base to the fuel outlet tube, then to the fuel rail.
15. Finger-tighten the base-to-rail screw.
16. Install the pressure regulator bracket. Finger-tighten the screws only.
17. Lubricate a new rear crossover tube O-ring and install it on the end of the tube.
18. Install the rear crossover tube to the regulator base.
19. Install the crossover tube retainer and finger-tighten the screw.
20. Tighten all attaching screws to 44 inch lbs. (5 Nm).
21. Install the fuel rail assembly.
22. Temporarily connect the negative battery cable.
   a. With the engine OFF and the ignition ON, check for fuel leaks.
   b. Disconnect the negative battery cable.

23. Install the intake plenum and runners.
24. Connect the negative battery cable.

Idle Air Control Valve

REMOVAL & INSTALLATION

▶ **See Figures 80 and 81**

1. Unplug the electrical connector from idle air control valve.
2. Remove the idle air control valve.

To install:
3. Before installing the idle air control valve, measure the distance that the valve is extended. Measurement should be made from the motor housing to the end of the cone. It should not exceed 28.5mm (1⅛ in.), or damage to the valve may occur when installed.
4. On 1985–1992 models, identify the replacement IAC valve as being either Type 1 (with collar at electric terminal end) or Type 2 (without collar). If measuring distance is greater than specified above, proceed as follows:
   • Type 1: Use finger pressure to slowly retract the pintle.
   • Type 2: Compress retaining spring from valve while turning valve in with a clockwise motion. Return spring to original position with straight portion of spring end aligned with flat surface of valve.

➡**On IAC valves that have already been in service, do not push or pull on the valve pintle. The force required to move the pintle may damage the threads on the worm drive.**

5. Use a new gasket or O-ring and install the IAC valve into the throttle body.
6. Allow the ECM to reset the idle air control valve using the procedure described earlier in this section.

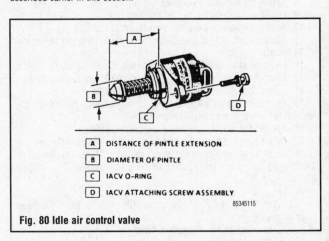

A	DISTANCE OF PINTLE EXTENSION
B	DIAMETER OF PINTLE
C	IACV O-RING
D	IACV ATTACHING SCREW ASSEMBLY

85345115

Fig. 80 Idle air control valve

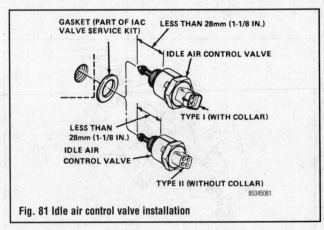

GASKET (PART OF IAC VALVE SERVICE KIT)

LESS THAN 28mm (1-1/8 IN.)

IDLE AIR CONTROL VALVE

TYPE I (WITH COLLAR)

LESS THAN 28mm (1-1/8 IN.)

IDLE AIR CONTROL VALVE

TYPE II (WITHOUT COLLAR)

85345081

Fig. 81 Idle air control valve installation

Throttle Position Sensor (TPS)

REMOVAL & INSTALLATION

1. Disconnect the negative battery cable.
2. Detach the electrical connector from the sensor.
3. Remove the attaching screws, lockwashers and retainers. Some models use a seal between the throttle body and the sensor, do not lose this!
4. Remove the throttle position sensor.

To install:
5. Install the throttle position sensor seal, if applicable.
6. With the throttle valve in the normal closed idle position, install the sensor on the throttle body assembly. Make sure the sensor pickup lever is properly located on the throttle actuator lever.
7. Install the retainers, screws and lockwashers using a thread locking compound. On models up to 1989, DO NOT tighten the screws until the sensor is adjusted. Follow the procedures outlined earlier in this section.

Cold Start Valve

REMOVAL & INSTALLATION

▶ **See Figure 82**

1. Disconnect the negative battery cable.
2. Relieve the fuel system pressure.
3. Remove the intake manifold plenum.
4. Unplug the electrical connection.
5. Clean the fuel rail around the cold start valve tube fitting.

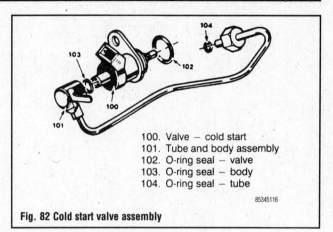

100. Valve — cold start
101. Tube and body assembly
102. O-ring seal — valve
103. O-ring seal — body
104. O-ring seal — tube

85345116

Fig. 82 Cold start valve assembly

6. Remove the tube fitting from the fuel rail. Use a backup wrench to prevent it from turning.
7. Remove the cold start valve retaining bolt and remove the valve from the intake manifold.

To install:
8. Use new O-rings and install the valve and bolt.
9. Connect the wiring harness.
10. Connect the cold start tube at the fuel rail. Use a wrench to prevent it from turning.
11. Install the intake manifold plenum.
12. Connect the negative battery cable. With the engine OFF and the ignition ON, check for fuel leaks.

FUEL TANK

Tank Assembly

REMOVAL & INSTALLATION

▶ **See Figures 83 and 84**

1. Disconnect the negative battery cable.
2. Relieve the fuel system pressure.
3. Drain the fuel from the tank into an approved container. Use a hand-operated pump to drain the fuel through the filler neck.
4. Safely raise and support the vehicle.
5. Remove the fuel filler neck shield.
6. Remove the rear axle assembly.
7. Remove the rear portion of the exhaust system.
8. Remove the exhaust heat shield.
9. Clean all the fuel pipes and hoses in the surrounding areas to prevent contamination of the fuel system.
10. Disconnect the rear fuel feed, fuel return, vapor, and vent hoses at the fuel sender assembly.
11. Separate the electrical connection.
12. With the aid of an assistant, support the fuel tank.
13. Remove the fuel tank strap front attaching bolts. Do not bend the straps as this will damage them.
14. Remove the tank straps and the fuel tank.

To install:
15. Hook the rear end of the fuel tank straps into the underbody bracket.
16. With the aid of an assistant, position and support the fuel tank with the straps. Loosely install the front fuel tank attaching bolts.
17. Engage the electrical connection.
18. Connect the fuel hoses and lines separated during removal.

19. Install the muffler heat shield and the exhaust system.
20. Install the rear axle and the fuel filler neck shield.
21. Lower the vehicle.
22. Add fuel and install the filler cap.
23. Connect the negative battery cable.
24. With the engine OFF, turn the ignition switch to the ON position for 2 seconds, then turn it to the OFF position for 10 seconds. Again turn it to the ON position and check for fuel leaks.

SENDING UNIT REPLACEMENT

1. Remove the fuel tank.
2. Clean the area surrounding the sender assembly to prevent contamination of the fuel system.
3. Using tool J–24187 or equivalent, remove the sending unit retaining cam. Remove the fuel sender and O-rings from the tank. Discard the O-rings.
4. If necessary, separate the fuel pump from the sending unit assembly.

To install:
5. If removed, install the fuel pump to the sending unit. If the strainer was removed, it must be replaced with a new one.
6. Inspect and clean the O-ring mating surfaces.
7. Install a new O-ring in the groove around the tank opening. If applicable, install a new O-ring on the fuel sender feed tube.
8. Install the fuel sender assembly as follows:
   a. The fuel pump strainer must be in a horizontal position, and when installed, must not block the travel of the float arm. Gently fold the strainer over itself and slowly position the sending assembly in the tank so the strainer is not damaged or trapped by the sump walls.
9. Install the retaining cam using tool J–24187 or equivalent.
10. Install the fuel tank assembly.

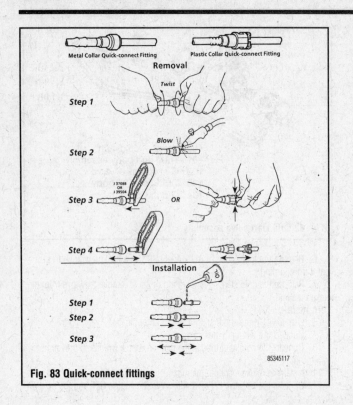

Fig. 83 Quick-connect fittings

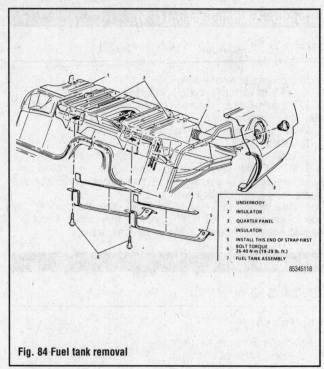

1 UNDERBODY
2 INSULATOR
3 QUARTER PANEL
4 INSULATOR
5 INSTALL THIS END OF STRAP FIRST
6 BOLT TORQUE 26-40 N·m (19-29 lb. ft.)
7 FUEL TANK ASSEMBLY

Fig. 84 Fuel tank removal

E2SE CARBURETOR SPECIFICATIONS

Year	Carburetor Identification	Float Level (in.)	Pump Rod (in.)	Air Valve Spring (Turns)	Choke Coil Level (in.)	Fast Idle Cam (deg.)	Air Valve Rod (deg.)	Primary Vacuum Break (deg.)	Choke Setting (notches)	Secondary Vacuum Break (deg.)	Choke Unloader (deg.)
1982	17082390	13/32	Fixed	1	0.085	17°	1°	26°	Fixed	34°	35°
	17082391	13/32	Fixed	1	0.085	25°	1°	29°	Fixed	35°	35°
	17082490	13/32	Fixed	1	0.085	17°	1°	26°	Fixed	34°	35°
	17082491	13/32	Fixed	1	0.085	25°	1°	29°	Fixed	35°	35°
1983	17083356	13/32	Fixed	1	0.085	22°	1°	25°	Fixed	35°	30°
	17083357	13/32	Fixed	1	0.085	22°	1°	25°	Fixed	35°	30°
	17083358	13/32	Fixed	1	0.085	22°	1°	25°	Fixed	35°	30°
	17083359	13/32	Fixed	1	0.085	22°	1°	25°	Fixed	35°	30°
	17083368	1/8	Fixed	1	0.085	22°	1°	25°	Fixed	35°	30°
	17083370	1/8	Fixed	1	0.085	22°	1°	25°	Fixed	35°	30°
	17083450	1/8	Fixed	1	0.085	28°	1°	27°	Fixed	35°	45°
	17083451	1/8	Fixed	1	0.085	28°	1°	27°	Fixed	35°	45°
	17083452	1/8	Fixed	1	0.085	28°	1°	27°	Fixed	35°	45°
	17083453	1/8	Fixed	1	0.085	28°	1°	27°	Fixed	35°	45°
	17083454	1/8	Fixed	1	0.085	28°	1°	27°	Fixed	35°	45°
	17083455	1/8	Fixed	1	0.085	28°	1°	27°	Fixed	35°	45°
	17083456	1/8	Fixed	1	0.085	28°	1°	27°	Fixed	35°	45°
	17083630	1/4	Fixed	1	0.085	28°	1°	27°	Fixed	35°	45°
	17083631	1/4	Fixed	1	0.085	28°	1°	27°	Fixed	35°	45°
	17083632	1/4	Fixed	1	0.085	28°	1°	27°	Fixed	35°	45°
	17083633	1/4	Fixed	1	0.085	28°	1°	27°	Fixed	35°	45°
	17083634	1/4	Fixed	1	0.085	28°	1°	27°	Fixed	35°	45°
	17083635	1/4	Fixed	1	0.085	28°	1°	27°	Fixed	35°	45°
	17083636	1/4	Fixed	1	0.085	28°	1°	27°	Fixed	35°	45°
	17083650	1/8	Fixed	1/2	0.085	28°	1°	27°	Fixed	35°	45°
1984	17072683	9/32	Fixed	1/2	0.085	28°	1°	25°	Fixed	35°	45°
	17074812	9/32	Fixed	1/2	0.085	28°	1°	25°	Fixed	35°	45°
	17084356	9/32	Fixed	3/4	0.085	22°	1°	25°	Fixed	30°	30°
	17084357	9/32	Fixed	3/4	0.085	22°	1°	25°	Fixed	30°	30°
	17084358	9/32	Fixed	3/4	0.085	22°	1°	25°	Fixed	30°	30°
	17084359	9/32	Fixed	3/4	0.085	22°	1°	25°	Fixed	30°	30°
	17084368	1/8	Fixed	3/4	0.085	22°	1°	25°	Fixed	30°	30°
	17084370	1/8	Fixed	3/4	0.085	22°	1°	25°	Fixed	30°	30°
	17084430	11/32	Fixed	1	0.085	15°	1°	26°	Fixed	38°	42°
	17084431	11/32	Fixed	1	0.085	15°	1°	26°	Fixed	38°	42°
	17084434	11/32	Fixed	1	0.085	15°	1°	26°	Fixed	38°	42°
	17084435	11/32	Fixed	1	0.085	15°	1°	26°	Fixed	38°	42°
	17084452	5/32	Fixed	1/2	0.085	28°	1°	25°	Fixed	35°	45°
	17084453	5/32	Fixed	1/2	0.085	28°	1°	25°	Fixed	35°	45°
	17084455	5/32	Fixed	1/2	0.085	28°	1°	25°	Fixed	35°	45°

E4ME and E4MC CARBURETOR SPECIFICATIONS

Year	Carburetor Identification	Float Level (in.)	Air Valve Spring (turn)	Pump Rod (in.)	Primary Vacuum Break (deg.)	Secondary Vacuum Break (deg.)	Air Valve Rod (in.)	Choke Rod (deg.)	Choke Unloader (deg.)	Fast Idle Speed (rpm)
1982	17082202	11/32	7/8	Fixed	27°	—	.025	20°	38°	①
	17082204	11/32	7/8	Fixed	27°	—	.025	20°	38°	①
	17082203	11/32	7/8	Fixed	27°	—	.025	38°	38°	①
	17082207	11/32	7/8	Fixed	27°	—	.025	38°	38°	①
1983	17083204	11/32	7/8	Fixed	—	27°	.025	20°	38°	②
	17083206	11/32	7/8	Fixed	—	27°	.025	20°	38°	②
	17083207	11/32	7/8	Fixed	—	27°	.025	38°	38°	②
	17083218	11/32	7/8	Fixed	—	27°	.025	20°	38°	②
	17083236	11/32	7/8	Fixed	—	27°	.025	20°	38°	②
	17083506	7/16	7/8	Fixed	27°	36°	.025	20°	36°	②
	17083508	7/16	7/8	Fixed	27°	36°	.025	20°	36°	②
	17083524	7/16	7/8	Fixed	25°	36°	.025	20°	36°	②
	17083526	7/16	7/8	Fixed	25°	36°	.025	20°	36°	②
1984	17084201	11/32	7/8	Fixed	27°	—	.025	20°	38°	②
	17084205	11/32	7/8	Fixed	27°	—	.025	38°	38°	②
	17084208	11/32	7/8	Fixed	27°	—	.025	20°	38°	②
	17084209	11/32	7/8	Fixed	27°	—	.025	38°	38°	②
	17084210	11/32	7/8	Fixed	27°	—	.025	20°	38°	②
	17084507	7/16	1	Fixed	27°	36°	.025	20°	36°	②
	17084509	7/16	1	Fixed	27°	36°	.025	20°	36°	②
	17084525	7/16	1	Fixed	25°	36°	.025	20°	36°	②
	17084527	7/16	1	Fixed	25°	36°	.025	20°	36°	②
1985	17084201	11/32	7/8	Fixed	27°	—	.025	20°	38°	②
	17084205	11/32	7/8	Fixed	27°	—	.025	38°	38°	②
	17084208	11/32	7/8	Fixed	27°	—	.025	20°	38°	②
	17084209	11/32	7/8	Fixed	27°	—	.025	38°	38°	②
	17084210	11/32	7/8	Fixed	27°	—	.025	20°	38°	②
	17084507	7/16	1	Fixed	27°	36°	.025	20°	36°	②
	17084509	7/16	1	Fixed	27°	36°	.025	20°	36°	②
	17084525	7/16	1	Fixed	25°	36°	.025	20°	36°	②
	17084527	7/16	1	Fixed	25°	36°	.025	20°	36°	②
1986	17084201	11/32	7/8	Fixed	27°	—	.025	20°	38°	②
	17084205	11/32	7/8	Fixed	27°	—	.025	38°	38°	②
	17084208	11/32	7/8	Fixed	27°	—	.025	20°	38°	②
	17084209	11/32	7/8	Fixed	27°	—	.025	38°	38°	②
	17084210	11/32	7/8	Fixed	27°	—	.025	20°	38°	②
	17084507	7/16	1	Fixed	27°	36°	.025	20°	36°	②
	17084509	7/16	1	Fixed	27°	36°	.025	20°	36°	②
	17084525	7/16	1	Fixed	25°	36°	.025	20°	36°	②
	17084527	7/16	1	Fixed	25°	36°	.025	20°	36°	②

85345301

E4ME and E4MC CARBURETOR SPECIFICATIONS

Year	Carburetor Identification	Float Level (in.)	Air Valve Spring (turn)	Pump Rod (in.)	Primary Vacuum Break (deg.)	Secondary Vacuum Break (deg.)	Air Valve Rod (in.)	Choke Rod (deg.)	Choke Unloader (deg.)	Fast Idle Speed (rpm)
1987	17084201	$^{11}/_{32}$	$^{7}/_{8}$	Fixed	27°	—	.025	20°	38°	②
	17084205	$^{11}/_{32}$	$^{7}/_{8}$	Fixed	27°	—	.025	38°	38°	②
	17084208	$^{11}/_{32}$	$^{7}/_{8}$	Fixed	27°	—	.025	20°	38°	②
	17084209	$^{11}/_{32}$	$^{7}/_{8}$	Fixed	27°	—	.025	38°	38°	②
	17084210	$^{11}/_{32}$	$^{7}/_{8}$	Fixed	27°	—	.025	20°	38°	②
	17084507	$^{7}/_{16}$	1	Fixed	27°	36°	.025	20°	36°	②
	17084509	$^{7}/_{16}$	1	Fixed	27°	36°	.025	20°	36°	②
	17084525	$^{7}/_{16}$	1	Fixed	25°	36°	.025	20°	36°	②
	17084527	$^{7}/_{16}$	1	Fixed	25°	36°	.025	20°	36°	②

① 3 turns after contacting lever for preliminary setting
② Refer to Emission Label

8534531A

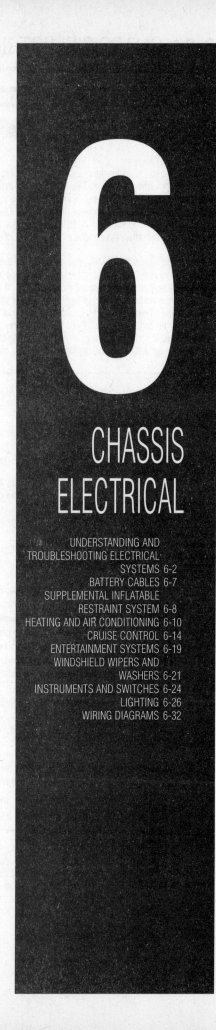

6

CHASSIS ELECTRICAL

UNDERSTANDING AND TROUBLESHOOTING ELECTRICAL SYSTEMS

Basic Electrical Theory

▶ See Figure 1

For any 12 volt, negative ground, electrical system to operate, the electricity must travel in a complete circuit. This simply means that current (power) from the positive (+) terminal of the battery must eventually return to the negative (-) terminal of the battery. Along the way, this current will travel through wires, fuses, switches and components. If, for any reason, the flow of current through the circuit is interrupted, the component fed by that circuit will cease to function properly.

Perhaps the easiest way to visualize a circuit is to think of connecting a light bulb (with two wires attached to it) to the battery—one wire attached to the negative (-) terminal of the battery and the other wire to the positive (+) terminal. With the two wires touching the battery terminals, the circuit would be complete and the light bulb would illuminate. Electricity would follow a path from the battery to the bulb and back to the battery. It's easy to see that with longer wires on our light bulb, it could be mounted anywhere. Further, one wire could be fitted with a switch so that the light could be turned on and off.

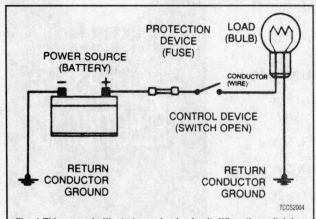

Fig. 1 This example illustrates a simple circuit. When the switch is closed, power from the positive (+) battery terminal flows through the fuse and the switch, and then to the light bulb. The light illuminates and the circuit is completed through the ground wire back to the negative (-) battery terminal. In reality, the two ground points shown in the illustration are attached to the metal frame of the vehicle, which completes the circuit back to the battery

The normal automotive circuit differs from this simple example in two ways. First, instead of having a return wire from the bulb to the battery, the current travels through the frame of the vehicle. Since the negative (-) battery cable is attached to the frame (made of electrically conductive metal), the frame of the vehicle can serve as a ground wire to complete the circuit. Secondly, most automotive circuits contain multiple components which receive power from a single circuit. This lessens the amount of wire needed to power components on the vehicle.

HOW DOES ELECTRICITY WORK: THE WATER ANALOGY

Electricity is the flow of electrons—the subatomic particles that constitute the outer shell of an atom. Electrons spin in an orbit around the center core of an atom. The center core is comprised of protons (positive charge) and neutrons (neutral charge). Electrons have a negative charge and balance out the positive charge of the protons. When an outside force causes the number of electrons to unbalance the charge of the protons, the electrons will split off the atom and look for another atom to balance out. If this imbalance is kept up, electrons will continue to move and an electrical flow will exist.

Many people have been taught electrical theory using an analogy with water. In a comparison with water flowing through a pipe, the electrons would be the water and the wire is the pipe.

The flow of electricity can be measured much like the flow of water through a pipe. The unit of measurement used is amperes, frequently abbreviated as amps (a). You can compare amperage to the volume of water flowing through a pipe. When connected to a circuit, an ammeter will measure the actual amount of current flowing through the circuit. When relatively few electrons flow through a circuit, the amperage is low. When many electrons flow, the amperage is high.

Water pressure is measured in units such as pounds per square inch (psi); The electrical pressure is measured in units called volts (v). When a voltmeter is connected to a circuit, it is measuring the electrical pressure.

The actual flow of electricity depends not only on voltage and amperage, but also on the resistance of the circuit. The higher the resistance, the higher the force necessary to push the current through the circuit. The standard unit for measuring resistance is an ohm. Resistance in a circuit varies depending on the amount and type of components used in the circuit. The main factors which determine resistance are:

• Material—some materials have more resistance than others. Those with high resistance are said to be insulators. Rubber materials (or rubber-like plastics) are some of the most common insulators used in vehicles as they have a very high resistance to electricity. Very low resistance materials are said to be conductors. Copper wire is among the best conductors. Silver is actually a superior conductor to copper and is used in some relay contacts, but its high cost prohibits its use as common wiring. Most automotive wiring is made of copper.

• Size—the larger the wire size being used, the less resistance the wire will have. This is why components which use large amounts of electricity usually have large wires supplying current to them.

• Length—for a given thickness of wire, the longer the wire, the greater the resistance. The shorter the wire, the less the resistance. When determining the proper wire for a circuit, both size and length must be considered to design a circuit that can handle the current needs of the component.

• Temperature—with many materials, the higher the temperature, the greater the resistance (positive temperature coefficient). Some materials exhibit the opposite trait of lower resistance with higher temperatures (negative temperature coefficient). These principles are used in many of the sensors on the engine.

OHM'S LAW

There is a direct relationship between current, voltage and resistance. The relationship between current, voltage and resistance can be summed up by a statement known as Ohm's law.

Voltage (E) is equal to amperage (I) times resistance (R): $E = I \times R$

Other forms of the formula are $R = E/I$ and $I = E/R$

In each of these formulas, E is the voltage in volts, I is the current in amps and R is the resistance in ohms. The basic point to remember is that as the resistance of a circuit goes up, the amount of current that flows in the circuit will go down, if voltage remains the same.

The amount of work that the electricity can perform is expressed as power. The unit of power is the watt (w). The relationship between power, voltage and current is expressed as:

Power (w) is equal to amperage (I) times voltage (E): $W = I \times E$

This is only true for direct current (DC) circuits; The alternating current formula is a tad different, but since the electrical circuits in most vehicles are DC type, we need not get into AC circuit theory.

Electrical Components

POWER SOURCE

Power is supplied to the vehicle by two devices: The battery and the alternator. The battery supplies electrical power during starting or during periods when the current demand of the vehicle's electrical system exceeds the output capacity of the alternator. The alternator supplies electrical current when the engine is running. Just not does the alternator supply the current needs of the vehicle, but it recharges the battery.

The Battery

In most modern vehicles, the battery is a lead/acid electrochemical device consisting of six 2 volt subsections (cells) connected in series, so that the unit is capable of producing approximately 12 volts of electrical pressure. Each subsection consists of a series of positive and negative plates held a short distance apart in a solution of sulfuric acid and water.

The two types of plates are of dissimilar metals. This sets up a chemical reaction, and it is this reaction which produces current flow from the battery when its positive and negative terminals are connected to an electrical load. The power removed from the battery is replaced by the alternator, restoring the battery to its original chemical state.

The Alternator

On some vehicles there isn't an alternator, but a generator. The difference is that an alternator supplies alternating current which is then changed to direct current for use on the vehicle, while a generator produces direct current. Alternators tend to be more efficient and that is why they are used.

Alternators and generators are devices that consist of coils of wires wound together making big electromagnets. One group of coils spins within another set and the interaction of the magnetic fields causes a current to flow. This current is then drawn off the coils and fed into the vehicles electrical system.

GROUND

Two types of grounds are used in automotive electric circuits. Direct ground components are grounded to the frame through their mounting points. All other components use some sort of ground wire which is attached to the frame or chassis of the vehicle. The electrical current runs through the chassis of the vehicle and returns to the battery through the ground (-) cable; if you look, you'll see that the battery ground cable connects between the battery and the frame or chassis of the vehicle.

➡It should be noted that a good percentage of electrical problems can be traced to bad grounds.

PROTECTIVE DEVICES

◗ **See Figure 2**

It is possible for large surges of current to pass through the electrical system of your vehicle. If this surge of current were to reach the load in the circuit, the surge could burn it out or severely damage it. It can also overload the wiring, causing the harness to get hot and melt the insulation. To prevent this, fuses, circuit breakers and/or fusible links are connected into the supply wires of the electrical system. These items are nothing more than a built-in weak spot in the system. When an abnormal amount of current flows through the system, these protective devices work as follows to protect the circuit:

- Fuse—when an excessive electrical current passes through a fuse, the fuse "blows" (the conductor melts) and opens the circuit, preventing the passage of current.
- Circuit Breaker—a circuit breaker is basically a self-repairing fuse. It will open the circuit in the same fashion as a fuse, but when the surge subsides, the circuit breaker can be reset and does not need replacement.
- Fusible Link—a fusible link (fuse link or main link) is a short length of special, high temperature insulated wire that acts as a fuse. When an excessive electrical current passes through a fusible link, the thin gauge wire inside the link melts, creating an intentional open to protect the circuit. To repair the circuit, the link must be replaced. Some newer type fusible links are housed in plug-in modules, which are simply replaced like a fuse, while older type fusible links must be cut and spliced if they melt. Since this link is very early in the electrical path, it's the first place to look if nothing on the vehicle works, yet the battery seems to be charged and is properly connected.

⁑⁑ CAUTION

Always replace fuses, circuit breakers and fusible links with identically rated components. Under no circumstances should a component of higher or lower amperage rating be substituted.

SWITCHES & RELAYS

◗ **See Figures 3 and 4**

Switches are used in electrical circuits to control the passage of current. The most common use is to open and close circuits between the battery and the various electric devices in the system. Switches are rated according to the amount of amperage they can handle. If a sufficient amperage rated switch is not used in a circuit, the switch could overload and cause damage.

Some electrical components which require a large amount of current to operate use a special switch called a relay. Since these circuits carry a large amount of current, the thickness of the wire in the circuit is also greater. If this large wire were connected from the load to the control switch, the switch would have to carry the high amperage load and the fairing or dash would be twice as large to accommodate the increased size of the wiring harness. To prevent these problems, a relay is used.

Relays are composed of a coil and a set of contacts. When the coil has a current passed though it, a magnetic field is formed and this field causes the contacts to move together, completing the circuit. Most relays are normally open, preventing current from passing through the circuit, but they can take any electrical form depending on the job they are intended to do. Relays can be considered "remote control switches." They allow a smaller current to operate devices that require higher amperages. When a small current operates the coil, a larger current is allowed to pass by the contacts. Some common circuits which may use relays are the horn, headlights, starter, electric fuel pump and other high draw circuits.

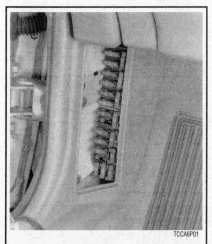

Fig. 2 Most vehicles use one or more fuse panels. This one is located on the driver's side kick panel

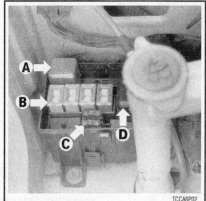

A. Relay
B. Fusible Link
C. Fuse
D. Flasher

Fig. 3 The underhood fuse and relay panel usually contains fuses, relays, flashers and fusible links

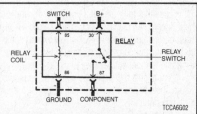

Fig. 4 Relays are composed of a coil and a switch. These two components are linked together so that when one operates, the other operates at the same time. The large wires in the circuit are connected from the battery to one side of the relay switch (B+) and from the opposite side of the relay switch to the load (component). Smaller wires are connected from the relay coil to the control switch for the circuit and from the opposite side of the relay coil to ground

LOAD

Every electrical circuit must include a "load" (something to use the electricity coming from the source). Without this load, the battery would attempt to deliver its entire power supply from one pole to another. This is called a "short circuit." All this electricity would take a short cut to ground and cause a great amount of damage to other components in the circuit by developing a tremendous amount of heat. This condition could develop sufficient heat to melt the insulation on all the surrounding wires and reduce a multiple wire cable to a lump of plastic and copper.

WIRING & HARNESSES

The average vehicle contains meters and meters of wiring, with hundreds of individual connections. To protect the many wires from damage and to keep them from becoming a confusing tangle, they are organized into bundles, enclosed in plastic or taped together and called wiring harnesses. Different harnesses serve different parts of the vehicle. Individual wires are color coded to help trace them through a harness where sections are hidden from view.

Automotive wiring or circuit conductors can be either single strand wire, multi-strand wire or printed circuitry. Single strand wire has a solid metal core and is usually used inside such components as alternators, motors, relays and other devices. Multi-strand wire has a core made of many small strands of wire twisted together into a single conductor. Most of the wiring in an automotive electrical system is made up of multi-strand wire, either as a single conductor or grouped together in a harness. All wiring is color coded on the insulator, either as a solid color or as a colored wire with an identification stripe. A printed circuit is a thin film of copper or other conductor that is printed on an insulator backing. Occasionally, a printed circuit is sandwiched between two sheets of plastic for more protection and flexibility. A complete printed circuit, consisting of conductors, insulating material and connectors for lamps or other components is called a printed circuit board. Printed circuitry is used in place of individual wires or harnesses in places where space is limited, such as behind instrument panels.

Since automotive electrical systems are very sensitive to changes in resistance, the selection of properly sized wires is critical when systems are repaired. A loose or corroded connection or a replacement wire that is too small for the circuit will add extra resistance and an additional voltage drop to the circuit.

The wire gauge number is an expression of the cross-section area of the conductor. Vehicles from countries that use the metric system will typically describe the wire size as its cross-sectional area in square millimeters. In this method, the larger the wire, the greater the number. Another common system for expressing wire size is the American Wire Gauge (AWG) system. As gauge number increases, area decreases and the wire becomes smaller. An 18 gauge wire is smaller than a 4 gauge wire. A wire with a higher gauge number will carry less current than a wire with a lower gauge number. Gauge wire size refers to the size of the strands of the conductor, not the size of the complete wire with insulator. It is possible, therefore, to have two wires of the same gauge with different diameters because one may have thicker insulation than the other.

It is essential to understand how a circuit works before trying to figure out why it doesn't. An electrical schematic shows the electrical current paths when a circuit is operating properly. Schematics break the entire electrical system down into individual circuits. In a schematic, usually no attempt is made to represent wiring and components as they physically appear on the vehicle; switches and other components are shown as simply as possible. Face views of harness connectors show the cavity or terminal locations in all multi-pin connectors to help locate test points.

CONNECTORS

▶ **See Figures 5 and 6**

Three types of connectors are commonly used in automotive applications—weatherproof, molded and hard shell.

• Weatherproof—these connectors are most commonly used where the connector is exposed to the elements. Terminals are protected against moisture and dirt by sealing rings which provide a weathertight seal. All repairs require the use of a special terminal and the tool required to service it. Unlike standard blade type terminals, these weatherproof terminals cannot be straightened once they are bent. Make certain that the connectors are properly seated and all of the sealing rings are in place when connecting leads.

Fig. 5 Hard shell (left) and weatherproof (right) connectors have replaceable terminals

Fig. 6 Weatherproof connectors are most commonly used in the engine compartment or where the connector is exposed to the elements

• Molded—these connectors require complete replacement of the connector if found to be defective. This means splicing a new connector assembly into the harness. All splices should be soldered to insure proper contact. Use care when probing the connections or replacing terminals in them, as it is possible to create a short circuit between opposite terminals. If this happens to the wrong terminal pair, it is possible to damage certain components. Always use jumper wires between connectors for circuit checking and NEVER probe through weatherproof seals.

• Hard Shell—unlike molded connectors, the terminal contacts in hard-shell connectors can be replaced. Replacement usually involves the use of a special terminal removal tool that depresses the locking tangs (barbs) on the connector terminal and allows the connector to be removed from the rear of the shell. The connector shell should be replaced if it shows any evidence of burning, melting, cracks, or breaks. Replace individual terminals that are burnt, corroded, distorted or loose.

Test Equipment

Pinpointing the exact cause of trouble in an electrical circuit is most times accomplished by the use of special test equipment. The following describes different types of commonly used test equipment and briefly explains how to use them in diagnosis. In addition to the information covered below, the tool manufacturer's instructions booklet (provided with the tester) should be read and clearly understood before attempting any test procedures.

JUMPER WIRES

Jumper wires are simple, yet extremely valuable, pieces of test equipment. They are basically test wires which are used to bypass sections of a circuit. Although jumper wires can be purchased, they are usually fabricated from lengths of standard automotive wire and whatever type of connector (alligator clip, spade connector or pin connector) that is required for the particular application being tested. In cramped, hard-to-reach areas, it is advisable to have insulated boots over the jumper wire terminals in order to prevent accidental grounding. It is also advisable to include a standard automotive fuse in any jumper wire. This is commonly referred to as a "fused jumper". By inserting an in-line fuse holder between a set of test leads, a fused jumper wire can be used for bypassing open circuits. Use a 5 amp fuse to provide protection against voltage spikes.

Jumper wires are used primarily to locate open electrical circuits, on either the ground (-) side of the circuit or on the power (+) side. If an electrical component fails to operate, connect the jumper wire between the component and a good ground. If the component operates only with the jumper installed, the ground circuit is open. If the ground circuit is good, but the component does not operate, the circuit between the power feed and component may be open. By moving the jumper wire successively back from the component toward the power source, you can isolate the area of the circuit where the open is located. When the component stops functioning, or the power is cut off, the open is in the segment of wire between the jumper and the point previously tested.

You can sometimes connect the jumper wire directly from the battery to the "hot" terminal of the component, but first make sure the component uses 12 volts in operation. Some electrical components, such as fuel injectors or sensors, are designed to operate on about 4 to 5 volts, and running 12 volts directly to these components will cause damage.

TEST LIGHTS

▶ **See Figure 7**

The test light is used to check circuits and components while electrical current is flowing through them. It is used for voltage and ground tests. To use a 12 volt test light, connect the ground clip to a good ground and probe wherever necessary with the pick. The test light will illuminate when voltage is detected. This does not necessarily mean that 12 volts (or any particular amount of voltage) is present; it only means that some voltage is present. It is advisable before using the test light to touch its ground clip and probe across the battery posts or terminals to make sure the light is operating properly.

Like the jumper wire, the 12 volt test light is used to isolate opens in circuits. But, whereas the jumper wire is used to bypass the open to operate the load, the 12 volt test light is used to locate the presence of voltage in a circuit. If the test light illuminates, there is power up to that point in the circuit; if the test light does not illuminate, there is an open circuit (no power). Move the test light in successive steps back toward the power source until the light in the handle illuminates. The open is between the probe and a point which was previously probed.

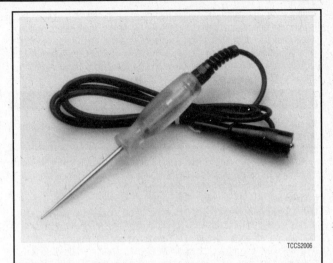

TCCS2006

Fig. 7 A 12 volt test light is used to detect the presence of voltage in a circuit

The self-powered test light is similar in design to the 12 volt test light, but contains a 1.5 volt penlight battery in the handle. It is most often used in place of a multimeter to check for open or short circuits when power is isolated from the circuit (continuity test).

The battery in a self-powered test light does not provide much current. A weak battery may not provide enough power to illuminate the test light even when a complete circuit is made (especially if there is high resistance in the circuit). Always make sure that the test battery is strong. To check the battery, briefly touch the ground clip to the probe; if the light glows brightly, the battery is strong enough for testing.

➡**A self-powered test light should not be used on any computer controlled system or component. The small amount of electricity transmitted by the test light is enough to damage many electronic automotive components.**

MULTIMETERS

Multimeters are an extremely useful tool for troubleshooting electrical problems. They can be purchased in either analog or digital form and have a price range to suit any budget. A multimeter is a voltmeter, ammeter and ohmmeter (along with other features) combined into one instrument. It is often used when testing solid state circuits because of its high input impedance (usually 10 megaohms or more). A brief description of the multimeter main test functions follows:

• Voltmeter—the voltmeter is used to measure voltage at any point in a circuit, or to measure the voltage drop across any part of a circuit. Voltmeters usually have various scales and a selector switch to allow the reading of different voltage ranges. The voltmeter has a positive and a negative lead. To avoid damage to the meter, always connect the negative lead to the negative (-) side of the circuit (to ground or nearest the ground side of the circuit) and connect the positive lead to the positive (+) side of the circuit (to the power source or the nearest power source). Note that the negative voltmeter lead will always be black and that the positive voltmeter will always be some color other than black (usually red).

• Ohmmeter—the ohmmeter is designed to read resistance (measured in ohms) in a circuit or component. Most ohmmeters will have a selector switch which permits the measurement of different ranges of resistance (usually the selector switch allows the multiplication of the meter reading by 10, 100, 1,000 and 10,000). Some ohmmeters are "auto-ranging" which means the meter itself will determine which scale to use. Since the meters are powered by an internal battery, the ohmmeter can be used like a self-powered test light. When the ohmmeter is connected, current from the ohmmeter flows through the circuit or component being tested. Since the ohmmeter's internal resistance and voltage are known values, the amount of current flow through the meter depends on the resistance of the circuit or component being tested. The ohmmeter can also be used to perform a continuity test for suspected open circuits. In using the meter for making continuity checks, do not be concerned with the actual resistance readings. Zero resistance, or any ohm reading, indicates continuity in the circuit. Infinite resistance indicates an opening in the circuit. A high resistance reading where there should be none indicates a problem in the circuit. Checks for short circuits are made in the same manner as checks for open circuits, except that the circuit must be isolated from both power and normal ground. Infinite resistance indicates no continuity, while zero resistance indicates a dead short.

❄❄ WARNING

Never use an ohmmeter to check the resistance of a component or wire while there is voltage applied to the circuit.

• Ammeter—an ammeter measures the amount of current flowing through a circuit in units called amperes or amps. At normal operating voltage, most circuits have a characteristic amount of amperes, called "current draw" which can be measured using an ammeter. By referring to a specified current draw rating, then measuring the amperes and comparing the two values, one can determine what is happening within the circuit to aid in diagnosis. An open circuit, for example, will not allow any current to flow, so the ammeter reading will be zero. A damaged component or circuit will have an increased current draw, so the reading will be high. The ammeter is always connected in series with the circuit being tested. All of the current that normally flows through the circuit must also flow through the ammeter; if there is any other path for the current to follow, the ammeter reading will not be accurate. The ammeter itself has very little resistance to current flow and, therefore, will not affect the circuit, but it will measure current draw only when the circuit is closed and electricity is flowing. Excessive current draw can blow fuses and drain the battery, while a reduced current draw can cause motors to run slowly, lights to dim and other components to not operate properly.

Troubleshooting Electrical Systems

When diagnosing a specific problem, organized troubleshooting is a must. The complexity of a modern automotive vehicle demands that you approach any problem in a logical, organized manner. There are certain troubleshooting techniques, however, which are standard:

• Establish when the problem occurs. Does the problem appear only under certain conditions? Were there any noises, odors or other unusual symptoms? Isolate the problem area. To do this, make some simple tests and observations, then eliminate the systems that are working properly. Check for obvious problems, such as broken wires and loose or dirty connections. Always check the obvious before assuming something complicated is the cause.

• Test for problems systematically to determine the cause once the problem area is isolated. Are all the components functioning properly? Is there power going to electrical switches and motors. Performing careful, systematic checks will often turn up most causes on the first inspection, without wasting time checking components that have little or no relationship to the problem.

• Test all repairs after the work is done to make sure that the problem is fixed. Some causes can be traced to more than one component, so a careful verification of repair work is important in order to pick up additional malfunctions that may cause a problem to reappear or a different problem to arise. A blown fuse, for example, is a simple problem that may require more than another fuse to repair. If you don't look for a problem that caused a fuse to blow, a shorted wire (for example) may go undetected.

Experience has shown that most problems tend to be the result of a fairly simple and obvious cause, such as loose or corroded connectors, bad grounds or damaged wire insulation which causes a short. This makes careful visual inspection of components during testing essential to quick and accurate troubleshooting.

Testing

OPEN CIRCUITS

▶ See Figure 8

This test already assumes the existence of an open in the circuit and it is used to help locate the open portion.
1. Isolate the circuit from power and ground.
2. Connect the self-powered test light or ohmmeter ground clip to the ground side of the circuit and probe sections of the circuit sequentially.

3. If the light is out or there is infinite resistance, the open is between the probe and the circuit ground.
4. If the light is on or the meter shows continuity, the open is between the probe and the end of the circuit toward the power source.

SHORT CIRCUITS

➡**Never use a self-powered test light to perform checks for opens or shorts when power is applied to the circuit under test. The test light can be damaged by outside power.**

1. Isolate the circuit from power and ground.
2. Connect the self-powered test light or ohmmeter ground clip to a good ground and probe any easy-to-reach point in the circuit.
3. If the light comes on or there is continuity, there is a short somewhere in the circuit.
4. To isolate the short, probe a test point at either end of the isolated circuit (the light should be on or the meter should indicate continuity).
5. Leave the test light probe engaged and sequentially open connectors or switches, remove parts, etc. until the light goes out or continuity is broken.
6. When the light goes out, the short is between the last two circuit components which were opened.

VOLTAGE

This test determines voltage available from the battery and should be the first step in any electrical troubleshooting procedure after visual inspection. Many electrical problems, especially on computer controlled systems, can be caused by a low state of charge in the battery. Excessive corrosion at the battery cable terminals can cause poor contact that will prevent proper charging and full battery current flow.
1. Set the voltmeter selector switch to the 20V position.
2. Connect the multimeter negative lead to the battery's negative (-) post or terminal and the positive lead to the battery's positive (+) post or terminal.
3. Turn the ignition switch **ON** to provide a load.
4. A well charged battery should register over 12 volts. If the meter reads below 11.5 volts, the battery power may be insufficient to operate the electrical system properly.

VOLTAGE DROP

▶ See Figure 9

When current flows through a load, the voltage beyond the load drops. This voltage drop is due to the resistance created by the load and also by small resistances created by corrosion at the connectors and damaged insulation on the wires. The maximum allowable voltage drop under load is critical, especially if there is more than one load in the circuit, since all voltage drops are cumulative.
1. Set the voltmeter selector switch to the 20 volt position.
2. Connect the multimeter negative lead to a good ground.
3. Operate the circuit and check the voltage prior to the first component (load).
4. There should be little or no voltage drop in the circuit prior to the first component. If a voltage drop exists, the wire or connectors in the circuit are suspect.
5. While operating the first component in the circuit, probe the ground side of the component with the positive meter lead and observe the voltage readings. A small voltage drop should be noticed. This voltage drop is caused by the resistance of the component.
6. Repeat the test for each component (load) down the circuit.
7. If a large voltage drop is noticed, the preceding component, wire or connector is suspect.

RESISTANCE

▶ See Figures 10 and 11

❄❄ WARNING

Never use an ohmmeter with power applied to the circuit. The ohmmeter is designed to operate on its own power supply. The normal 12 volt electrical system voltage could damage the meter!

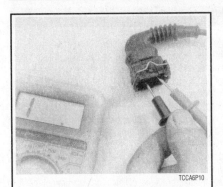

Fig. 8 The infinite reading on this multimeter indicates that the circuit is open

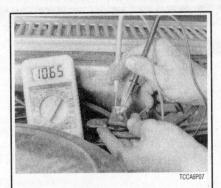

Fig. 9 This voltage drop test revealed high resistance (low voltage) in the circuit

Fig. 10 Checking the resistance of a coolant temperature sensor with an ohmmeter. Reading is 1.04 kilohms

1. Isolate the circuit from the vehicle's power source.
2. Ensure that the ignition key is **OFF** when disconnecting any components or the battery.
3. Where necessary, also isolate at least one side of the circuit to be checked, in order to avoid reading parallel resistances. Parallel circuit resistances will always give a lower reading than the actual resistance of either of the branches.
4. Connect the meter leads to both sides of the circuit (wire or component) and read the actual measured ohms on the meter scale. Make sure the selector switch is set to the proper ohm scale for the circuit being tested, to avoid misreading the ohmmeter test value.

Wire and Connector Repair

Almost anyone can replace damaged wires, as long as the proper tools and parts are available. Wire and terminals are available to fit almost any need. Even the specialized weatherproof, molded and hard shell connectors are now available from aftermarket suppliers.

Be sure the ends of all the wires are fitted with the proper terminal hardware and connectors. Wrapping a wire around a stud is never a permanent solution and will only cause trouble later. Replace wires one at a time to avoid confusion. Always route wires exactly the same as the factory.

➡**If connector repair is necessary, only attempt it if you have the proper tools. Weatherproof and hard shell connectors require special tools to release the pins inside the connector. Attempting to repair these connectors with conventional hand tools will damage them.**

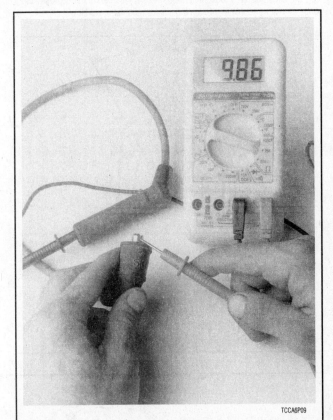

Fig. 11 Spark plug wires can be checked for excessive resistance using an ohmmeter

BATTERY CABLES

Disconnecting the Cables

When working on any electrical component on the vehicle, it is always a good idea to disconnect the negative (-) battery cable. This will prevent potential damage to many sensitive electrical components such as the Engine Control Module (ECM), radio, alternator, etc.

➡**Any time you disengage the battery cables, it is recommended that you disconnect the negative (-) battery cable first. This will prevent your accidentally grounding the positive (+) terminal to the body of the vehicle when disconnecting it, thereby preventing damage to the above mentioned components.**

Before you disconnect the cable(s), first turn the ignition to the **OFF** position. This will prevent a draw on the battery which could cause arcing (electricity trying to ground itself to the body of a vehicle, just like a spark plug jumping the gap) and, of course, damaging some components such as the alternator diodes.

When the battery cable(s) are reconnected (negative cable last), be sure to check that your lights, windshield wipers and other electrically operated safety components are all working correctly. If your vehicle contains an Electronically Tuned Radio (ETR), don't forget to also reset your radio stations. Ditto for the clock.

SUPPLEMENTAL INFLATABLE RESTRAINT SYSTEM

General Information

▶ **See Figure 12**

All 1990–1992 models are equipped with an airbag system. The Supplemental Inflatable Restraint (SIR) system helps supplement the protection offered by the seat belts by deploying an air bag from the center of the steering wheel. The air bag deploys when the vehicle is involved in a frontal crash of sufficient force up to 30 degrees off the centerline of the vehicle. To further absorb the crash energy, there is a knee bolster located beneath the instrument panel and the steering column is collapsible.

SYSTEM OPERATION

The main portions of the SIR system are the deployment loops and the Diagnostic Energy Reserve Module (DERM). The main function of the deployment loops is to supply current through the inflator module(s), which will cause

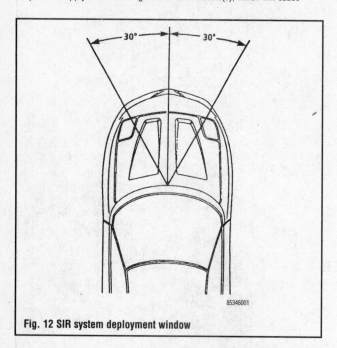

Fig. 12 SIR system deployment window

deployment of the air bag(s) in the event of a frontal crash of sufficient force. The arming sensor, SIR coil assembly (driver side only), passenger inflator module jumper (passenger side only), inflator module(s), passenger compartment discriminating sensor and forward discriminating sensor make up the deployment loops.

The DERM has two functions. One to supply the deployment loops with a 36 volt reserve to ensure sufficient energy is available to deploy the airbag(s) if the battery voltage feed to the arming sensor is lost during a frontal crash. Another function is SIR electrical system diagnostics.

The arming sensor switches power to the inflator module(s) on the high side (power side) of the deployment loops. Either of the discriminating sensors can supply ground to the inflator module(s) on the low side (ground side) of the loop. The inflator module(s) are only supplied sufficient current to deploy when the arming sensor and at least one of the two discriminating sensors are closed simultaneously.

SYSTEM COMPONENTS

▶ **See Figures 13 and 14**

Diagnostic Energy Reserve Module

The DERM is designed to perform the following functions in the SIR system:
- Energy Reserve — Maintains 36 volt energy reserve(s) to provide deployment energy when the vehicle voltage is low or lost in a frontal impact
- Malfunction Detection — Performs diagnostic monitoring of the SIR system electrical components
- Malfunction Recording — Provides diagnostic trouble code information
- Frontal Crash Recording — Records the SIR system status during a frontal crash

Warning Lamp

The "INFL REST" or "AIR BAG" warning lamp is used to do the following:
- Verify lamp and DERM operation by flashing seven to nine times when the ignition key is first turned ON
- Warn the driver of SIR electrical system faults which could potentially affect the operation of the SIR system
- Provide diagnostic information by flashing the fault codes when the diagnostic mode is enabled

Arming Sensor

The arming sensor is a protective switch located in the power feed side of the deployment loop. It is calibrated to close at low level velocity changes (lower

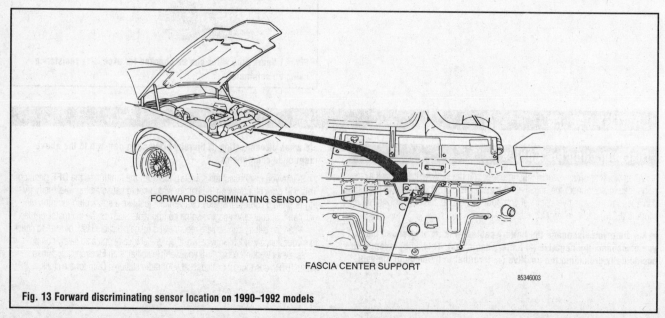

FORWARD DISCRIMINATING SENSOR

FASCIA CENTER SUPPORT

85346003

Fig. 13 Forward discriminating sensor location on 1990–1992 models

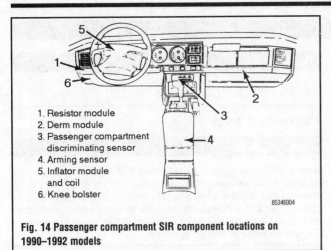

1. Resistor module
2. Derm module
3. Passenger compartment
   discriminating sensor
4. Arming sensor
5. Inflator module
   and coil
6. Knee bolster

85346004

Fig. 14 Passenger compartment SIR component locations on 1990–1992 models

than the discriminating sensors). This assures that the inflator module is connected directly to the 36 volt output of the DERM or battery voltage feed when either of the discriminating sensors close.

Discriminating Sensors

The discriminating sensors are wired in parallel on the ground side of the deployment loop. These sensors are calibrated to close with velocity changes which are severe enough to warrant deployment.

SIR Coil Assembly

The SIR coil assembly consists of two current carrying coils. They are attached to the steering column and allow rotation of the steering wheel while maintaining continuous contact of the deployment loop to the inflator module.

Inflator Modules

Each inflator module consists of an inflatable bag and an inflator (a canister of gas generating material with an initiating device). When the vehicle is in a frontal crash of sufficient force, current flows through the deployment loops. Current flowing through the initiator ignites the material in the inflator module. The gas produced from this reaction rapidly inflates the air bag.

SERVICE PRECAUTIONS

▶ **See Figures 15 and 16**

The DERM can maintain sufficient voltage to cause a deployment for up to 10 minutes after the ignition switch is turned OFF or the battery is disconnected. **Always disable the system when performing service procedures ON OR NEAR the system and it's components.**

�֎ CAUTION

The disarming and arming procedures must be followed in the order listed to temporarily disable the SIR system. Failure to do so could result in possible air bag deployment, personal injury or otherwise unneeded SIR system repairs.

DISARMING THE SYSTEM

1. Turn the steering wheel so that the vehicle's wheels are pointing straight ahead.
2. Turn the ignition switch to the LOCK position.
3. Remove the SIR or AIR BAG fuse from the fuse panel.
4. Remove the left side trim panel, then remove the Connector Position Assurance (CPA) device and disconnect the yellow two-way SIR harness connector at the base of the steering column.
5. On vehicles with passenger side air bags, remove the glove box door then disconnect the yellow two-way connector located near the yellow 24-way DERM harness connector.

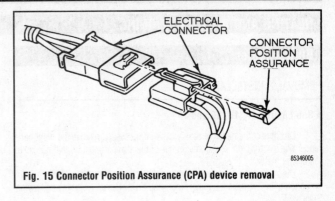

ELECTRICAL
CONNECTOR

CONNECTOR
POSITION
ASSURANCE

85346005

Fig. 15 Connector Position Assurance (CPA) device removal

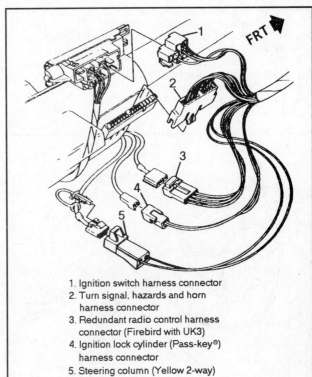

FRT

1. Ignition switch harness connector
2. Turn signal, hazards and horn
   harness connector
3. Redundant radio control harness
   connector (Firebird with UK3)
4. Ignition lock cylinder (Pass-key®)
   harness connector
5. Steering column (Yellow 2-way)
   harness connector

85346006

Fig. 16 Drivers side yellow two way SIR connector location. The connector on the passenger side air bag is located behind the glove compartment

➡With the fuse removed and the ignition switch ON, the air bag warning lamp will be on. This is normal and does not indicate a SIR system malfunction.

ARMING THE SYSTEM

1. Turn the ignition key to the LOCK position and remove the key.
2. On vehicles with a passenger side air bag, reconnect the yellow two-way connector assembly located near the yellow 24-way DERM harness connector. Install the glove box door assembly.
3. Connect the yellow two-way connector assembly at the base of the steering column.

➡**Always be sure to reinstall the Connector Position Assurance (CPA) device.**

4. Install the left side trim panel and reinstall the fuse in the fuse block.
5. Turn the ignition key to the RUN position and verify that the warning lamp flashes seven to nine times and then turns OFF. If it does not operate as described, have the system repaired by a qualified technician.

HEATING AND AIR CONDITIONING

Blower Motor

REMOVAL & INSTALLATION

▶ **See Figures 17, 18, 19 and 20**

1. Disconnect the negative battery cable. If necessary, remove the diagonal fender brace at the right rear corner of the engine compartment to gain access to the blower motor.
2. Disconnect the electrical wiring from the blower motor. If equipped with air conditioning, remove the blower relay and bracket as an assembly and swing them aside.
3. Remove the blower motor cooling tube.
4. Remove the blower motor retaining screws.
5. Remove the blower motor and fan as an assembly from the case.

To install:
6. Position the blower motor into place and install the retaining screws.
7. Install the blower motor cooling tube.
8. Connect all the electrical connections.
9. Connect the negative battery cable.

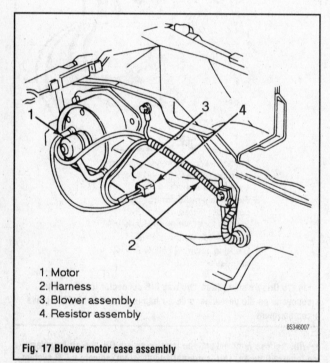

1. Motor
2. Harness
3. Blower assembly
4. Resistor assembly

85346007

Fig. 17 Blower motor case assembly

Heater Core

REMOVAL & INSTALLATION

▶ **See Figures 21 thru 26**

❊ CAUTION

When draining the coolant, keep in mind that cats and dogs are attracted by the ethylene glycol antifreeze, and are quite likely to drink any that is left in an uncovered container or in puddles on the ground. This will prove fatal in sufficient quantity. Always drain the coolant into a sealable container. Coolant should be reused unless it is contaminated or several years old.

1. Drain the cooling system.
2. Remove both heater hoses.
3. Remove the lower right hush panel.
4. Remove the lower right instrument panel and the ESC module if necessary.
5. Remove the lower right instrument panel-to-cowl screw.
6. Remove the heater case screws.

➡**The upper left screw may be reached with a long socket extension. Carefully lift the lower right corner of the instrument panel to align the extension.**

7. Remove the case cover.
8. Remove the support plate and baffle screws.
9. Remove the heater core and baffle plate from the housing.

To install:
10. Position the heater core and baffle plate into the housing.
11. Install the support plate and baffle screws.
12. Install the case cover.
13. Install the heater case screws.
14. Install the lower right instrument panel-to-cowl screw.
15. Install the lower right instrument panel and the ESC module if necessary.
16. Install the lower right hush panel.
17. Install both heater hoses.
18. Fill the cooling system and check for leaks.

Hot Water Valve

REMOVAL & INSTALLATION

▶ **See Figures 27 and 28**

➡**Not all model years and engine applications use hot water valves.**

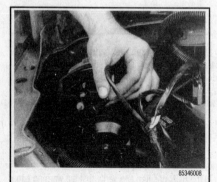

85346008

Fig. 18 Disconnect the blower motor electrical connector by pulling it straight out

85346009

Fig. 19 Removing the blower motor attaching bolts

85346010

Fig. 20 Be sure to remove the blower motor cooling tube before removing the motor from the case

1. Drain the coolant.
2. Disconnect the vacuum hose at the hot water valve by sliding the tab of the connector past the L-shaped bend in the actuator vacuum tube. Then, slide the hose connector off the tube while continuing to hold the tab back against the connector end.
3. Disconnect the heater hoses from the valve.

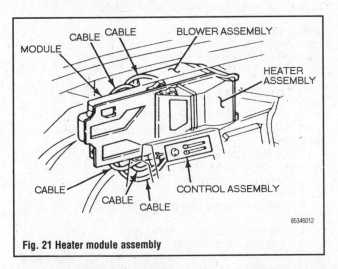

Fig. 21 Heater module assembly

To install:

4. Install the valve with the vacuum actuator facing up. The heater hoses will hold the valve in position.
5. Install the vacuum hose to the actuator.
6. Refill the cooling system. Run the engine long enough to purge any trapped air, then add more coolant if necessary.
7. Check for leaks.

Air Conditioning Components

REMOVAL & INSTALLATION

Repair or service of air conditioning components is not covered by this manual, because of the risk of personal injury or death, and because of the legal ramifications of servicing these components without the proper EPA certification and experience. Cost, personal injury or death, environmental damage, and legal considerations (such as the fact that it is a federal crime to vent refrigerant into the atmosphere), dictate that the A/C components on your vehicle should be serviced only by a Motor Vehicle Air Conditioning (MVAC) trained, and EPA certified automotive technician.

➡️**If your vehicle's A/C system uses R-12 refrigerant and is in need of recharging, the A/C system can be converted over to R-134a refrigerant (less environmentally harmful and expensive). Refer to Section 1 for additional information on R-12 to R-134a conversions, and for additional considerations dealing with your vehicle's A/C system.**

Fig. 22 Removing the heater core inlet hoses

Fig. 23 Removing the sound insulator attaching screws

Fig. 24 Once the sound insulator has been removed, the heater module can be accessed

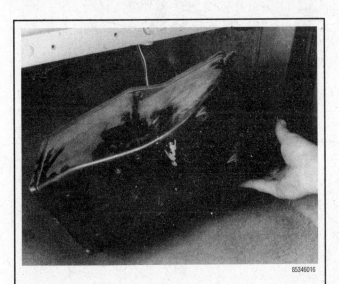

Fig. 25 Removing the heater module cover

Fig. 26 Be careful not to allow any coolant to drain on the carpet when removing the heater core

Control Cables

REMOVAL & INSTALLATION

♦ **See Figures 29, 30, 31, 32 and 33**

➥Some of the following cables will not be used on all models and model years.

Left and Right Air Vent Cables

1. Remove the left and right sound insulators.
2. Remove the screws attaching the cables to the steering column cover.
3. Disengage the cable clamps at the vent ducts.
4. Disengage the Z-shaped cable ends from the vent valve levers.
5. Remove the air vent cables noting their positions for installation.

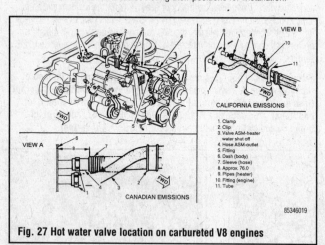

1. Clamp
2. Clip
3. Valve ASM-heater water shut off
4. Hose ASM-outlet
5. Fitting
6. Dash (body)
7. Sleeve (hose)
8. Approx. 76.0
9. Pipes (heater)
10. Fitting (engine)
11. Tube

Fig. 27 Hot water valve location on carbureted V8 engines

To install:

6. Place the cables in position under the instrument panel.
7. Engage the Z-shaped cable ends to the vent valve levers.
8. Snap the cable clamps into the slot of the bracket formed on the vent ducts.
9. Attach the air vent cables at the steering column cover.
10. Install the sound insulators and test cable operation.

Vent Control Cable

1. Remove the right side sound insulator.
2. Remove the push nut retainer holding the cable self-adjusting clip to the vent valve lever pin.
3. Disengage the cable clamp from the slot in the bracket on the heater module.
4. Remove the radio and heater control panel trim plate.
5. Remove the heater control head attaching screws and remove the control head.
6. Pull the vent control cable clip from the control assembly, then tilt the assembly to slip the vent control cable end loop off the pin of the mode lever.
7. Remove the vent control cable.

To install:

8. Install the vent control cable to the control assembly and install the control head.
9. Install the radio and heater control trim plate.
10. Fit the cable self-adjusting clip onto the vent valve lever pin.
11. Snap the cable clamp into the slot in the bracket on the heater module.
12. Install the push nut retainer to the vent valve lever pin.
13. Install the right side sound insulator.
14. Check operation and adjust the cable if necessary.

Defrost Control Cable

1. Remove the left side sound insulator.
2. Remove the push nut retainer holding the cable self-adjusting clip to the defroster valve lever pin at the heater module.

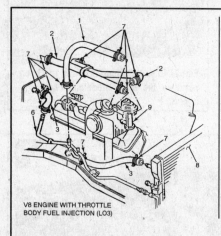

V8 ENGINE WITH THROTTLE BODY FUEL INJECTION (LO3)

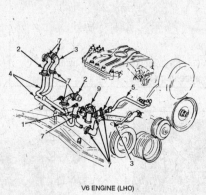

V6 ENGINE (LHO)

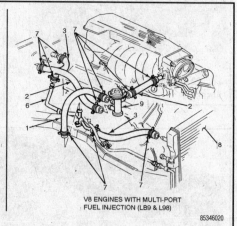

V8 ENGINES WITH MULTI-PORT FUEL INJECTION (LB9 & L98)

Fig. 28 Hot water valve location on fuel injected engines

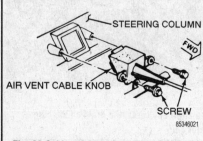

Fig. 29 Cable attachment at the steering column cover

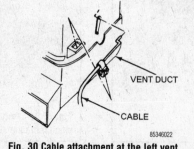

Fig. 30 Cable attachment at the left vent duct

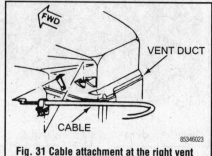

Fig. 31 Cable attachment at the right vent duct

3. Disengage the cable clamp from the slot in the bracket on the heater module.

4. Remove the radio and heater control trim plate.

5. Remove the control head assembly.

6. Disconnect the defroster control cable by pulling the cable clip from the control assembly. Then tilt the control assembly to slip the control cable end loop off the pin of the mode lever.

7. Remove the cable.

To install:

8. Install the defroster control cable to the control assembly and install the control head.

9. Install the radio and heater control trim plate.

10. Fit the cable self-adjusting clip onto the defroster valve lever pin.

11. Snap the cable clamp into the slot in the bracket on the heater module.

12. Install the push nut retainer to the defroster valve lever pin.

13. Install the left side sound insulator.

14. Check operation and adjust the cable if necessary.

Temperature Control Cable

1. Remove the right side sound insulator.

2. Remove the cable cover attaching screws and remove the cover.

3. Remove the push nut retainer holding the cable self-adjusting clip to the temperature valve lever pin.

4. Disengage the cable clamp from the slot in the bracket on the heater module.

5. Remove the radio and heater control panel trim plate.

6. Remove the heater control head attaching screws and remove the control head.

7. Remove the temperature control cable push nut retainer.

8. Pull the temperature control cable clip from the control assembly, then tilt the assembly to slip the vent control cable end loop off the pin of the mode lever.

9. Remove the temperature control cable.

To install:

10. Install the temperature control cable to the control assembly. Install the cable push nut retainer and install the control head.

11. Install the radio and heater control trim plate.

12. Fit the cable self-adjusting clip onto the temperature valve lever pin.

13. Snap the cable clamp into the slot in the bracket on the heater module.

14. Install the push nut retainer to the temperature valve lever pin.

15. Install the cable cover.

16. Install the right side sound insulator.

17. Check operation and adjust the cable if necessary.

ADJUSTMENTS

The control cables are connected at the heater module to the air valve that each cable operates. The cable ends are attached to the air valve crank arm by a self-adjusting clip that grips the cable core firmly. Adjustment can be accomplished by moving the mode lever (to adjust the vent or defrost control cables) or the temperature lever (to adjust the temperature control cable) briskly back and forth to both extremes of lever travel in the control assembly. When the cable is properly adjusted, the air valve may be heard hitting it's stop at both extremes of travel.

Control Head

REMOVAL & INSTALLATION

▶ **See Figures 34 and 35**

1. Disconnect the negative battery cable.

2. Remove the air conditioning/radio console trim plate.

3. Remove the control head retaining screws.

4. Pull the assembly forward, disconnect the electrical and vacuum connections. Remove the temperature control cable.

5. Remove the control assembly from the vehicle.

To install:

6. Position the control head into the vehicle.

7. Install the temperature control cable.

8. Connect the electrical and vacuum connections and push the assembly rearward.

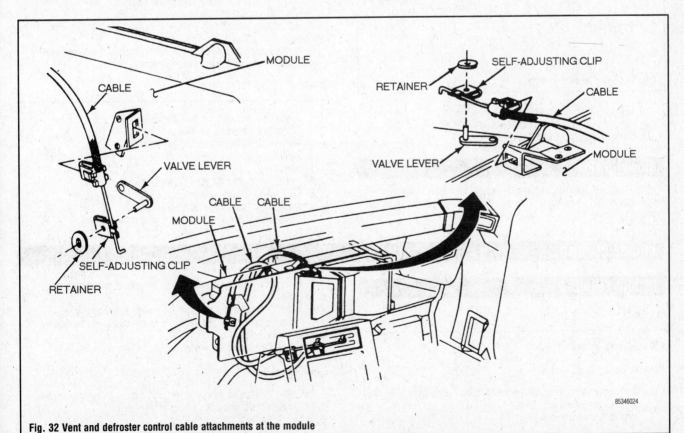

Fig. 32 Vent and defroster control cable attachments at the module

85346024

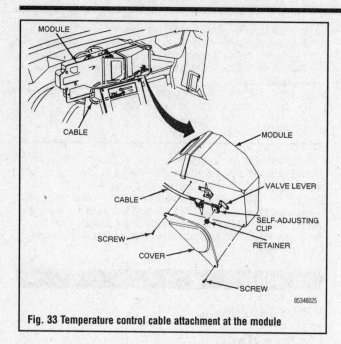

Fig. 33 Temperature control cable attachment at the module

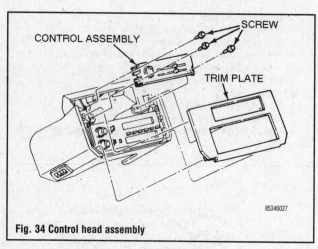

Fig. 34 Control head assembly

9. Install the control head retaining screws.
10. Install the air conditioning/radio console trim plate.
11. Connect the negative battery cable.

Blower Switch

With the control head removed from the vehicle, the blower switch may be removed by pulling the blower switch knob off and removing the retaining clip or retaining screws.

CRUISE CONTROL

Control Switches

REMOVAL & INSTALLATION

▶ **See Figures 36 and 37**

Release Switch

1. At the brake switch, remove either the 2 electrical connectors or the electrical connector and the vacuum hose.
2. Remove the switch from the retainer.

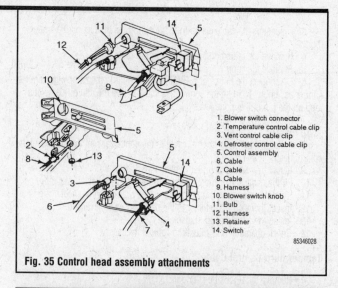

1. Blower switch connector
2. Temperature control cable clip
3. Vent control cable clip
4. Defroster control cable clip
5. Control assembly
6. Cable
7. Cable
8. Cable
9. Harness
10. Blower switch knob
11. Bulb
12. Harness
13. Retainer
14. Switch

Fig. 35 Control head assembly attachments

Vacuum Motors

OPERATION

Used on certain heating and air conditioning systems, the vacuum actuators operate the air doors determining the different modes. The actuator consists of a spring loaded diaphragm connected to a lever. When vacuum is applied to the diaphragm, the lever moves the control door to its appropriate position. When the lever on the control panel is moved to another position, vacuum is cut off and the spring returns the actuator lever to its normal position.

TESTING

1. Disconnect the vacuum line from the actuator.
2. Attach a hand held vacuum pump to the actuator.
3. Apply vacuum to the actuator.
4. The actuator lever should move to its engaged position and remain there while vacuum is applied.
5. When vacuum is released it should move back to its normal position.
6. The lever should operate smoothly and not bind.

REMOVAL & INSTALLATION

1. Remove the vacuum lines from the actuator.
2. Disconnect the linkage from the actuator.
3. Remove the hardware attaching the actuator.
4. Remove the actuator.
To install:
5. Install the actuator and attaching hardware.
6. Connect the linkage to the actuator.
7. Connect the vacuum lines to the actuator.
8. Test system to confirm proper functioning of the actuator.

3. Remove the tubular retainer from the brake pedal mounting bracket.
To install:
4. Install the tubular retainer to the brake pedal mounting bracket.
5. Press the brake pedal and install the release switch into the retainer until fully seated in the clips.
6. Connect the wiring and/or vacuum lines. Adjust the switch.

Engagement Switch

The engagement switch cannot be serviced. The complete multi-function lever (turn signal lever) must be replaced as an assembly.

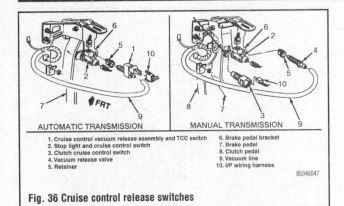

1. Cruise control vacuum release assembly and TCC switch
2. Stop light and cruise control switch
3. Clutch cruise control switch
4. Vacuum release valve
5. Retainer
6. Brake pedal bracket
7. Brake pedal
8. Clutch pedal
9. Vacuum line
10. I/P wiring harness

85346047

Fig. 36 Cruise control release switches

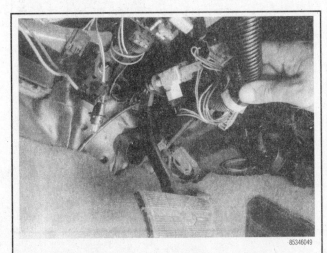

85346049

Fig. 37 Cruise control release switch location; all models similar

ADJUSTMENT

1. Depress the brake pedal and check that the release switch is fully seated in the clips.
2. Slowly pull the brake pedal back to the at-rest position; the switch and valve assembly will move within the clips to the adjusted position.
3. Measure pedal travel and check switch engagement. The electric brake release switch contacts must open at less than 1 inch (25.4 mm) of pedal travel. The vacuum release should engage between ⅝ and 1 inch (16–25mm) of pedal travel.

Servo

REMOVAL & INSTALLATION

▶ **See Figures 38 thru 46**

1. Disconnect the electrical connector and vacuum hoses at the servo.
2. Disconnect the actuating chain, cable or rod from the servo.
3. Remove the screws holding the vacuum servo and solenoid unit to the bracket, then remove the unit.
   To install:
4. Connect the large diameter brake release vacuum line to the servo unit. Connect the vacuum hose from the vacuum control valve to the servo unit.
5. Connect the actuating chain, rod or cable to the servo.
6. Install the servo unit to the bracket; tighten the screws to 12 inch lbs. (1.4 Nm).
7. Install the electrical connector to the servo.
8. Adjust the cable, rod or chain.

ADJUSTMENTS

➡ **Do not stretch cables or chains to make pins fit or holes align. This will prevent the engine from returning to idle.**

Cable Type

1. Check that the cable is properly installed and that the throttle is closed to the idle position.
2. Pull the servo end of the cable toward the linkage bracket of the servo. Place the servo connector in one of the 6 holes in the bracket which allows the least amount of slack and does not move the throttle linkage.
3. Install the retainer clip. Check that the throttle linkage is still in the idle position.

Rod With Screw Adjuster

1. Inspect the rod assembly for proper attachment to the servo and throttle stud. Make certain the throttle is at idle.
2. Adjust the slotted bracket or the rod to obtain a clearance of 0.02–0.04 in. (0.5–1.0mm) between the throttle stud and the end of the bracket slot.
3. Install the retainer clip; make certain the throttle is still at idle.

Rod With Adjustment Holes

1. Inspect the rod to be sure it is securely connected to the servo and throttle linkage; make certain the throttle is at idle.
2. Install the retainer pin in the hole which provides the least slack between the servo bracket and the retainer.
3. Check the throttle; it must still be in the idle position.

Chain and Cable

CHAIN AT THROTTLE

1. Check for proper installation of cable assembly. Inspect the throttle; it must be in the idle position.
2. Install the chain in the swivel so that the slack does not exceed ½ the diameter of the ball stud.
3. Install the retainer on the swivel and make sure the throttle has not moved from idle.

CHAIN AT SERVO

1. Check for proper installation of cable assembly. Inspect the throttle; it must be in the idle position.
2. Install the cable on the third link of the chain; adjust the jam nuts of the servo until there is no noticeable slack in the chain.
3. Tighten the jam nuts and check that the throttle has not moved out of the idle position.

Module

REMOVAL & INSTALLATION

▶ **See Figure 47**

1984–1992 Models

➡ **The module is mounted next to the heater and A/C duct on most models, but is integral with the ECM on certain late-model engines.**

1. Disconnect the negative battery cable.
2. Remove the right side sound insulator.
3. Remove the module attaching screws and remove the module.
4. Disconnect the electrical connector.
   To install:
5. Connect the electrical connector.
6. Install the cruise control module and the attaching screws.
7. Install the right side sound insulator.
8. Connect the negative battery cable.

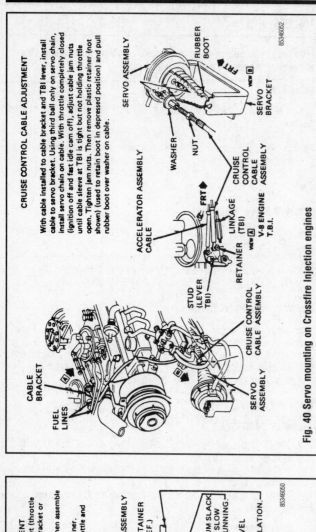

CRUISE CONTROL CABLE ADJUSTMENT

With cable installed to cable bracket and TBI lever, install cable to servo bracket. Using third ball only on servo chain, install servo chain on cable. With throttle completely closed (ignition off and fast idle cam off), adjust cable jam nuts until cable sleeve at TBI is tight but not holding throttle open. Tighten jam nuts. Then remove plastic retainer (not shown) (used to retain boot in depressed position) and pull rubber boot over washer on cable.

Fig. 40 Servo mounting on Crossfire Injection engines

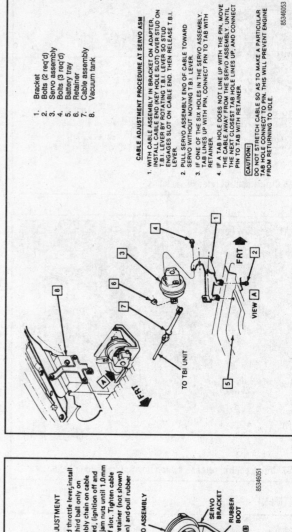

CABLE ADJUSTMENT PROCEDURE AT SERVO ASM

1. WITH CABLE ASSEMBLY IN BRACKET ON ADAPTER, INSTALL CABLE END (KEY HOLE SLOT) OVER STUD ON T.B.I. LEVER BY ROTATING T.B.I. LEVER SO STUD ENGAGES SLOT ON CABLE END. THEN RELEASE T.B.I. LEVER.
2. PULL SERVO ASSEMBLY END OF CABLE TOWARD SERVO WITHOUT MOVING T.B.I. LEVER.
3. IF ONE OF THE SIX HOLES IN THE SERVO ASSEMBLY TAB LINES UP WITH PIN, CONNECT PIN TO TAB WITH RETAINER.
4. IF A TAB HOLE DOES NOT LINE UP WITH THE PIN, MOVE THE CABLE AWAY FROM THE SERVO ASSEMBLY, UNTIL THE NEXT CLOSEST TAB HOLE LINES UP, AND CONNECT PIN TO TAB WITH RETAINER.

CAUTION:
DO NOT STRETCH CABLE SO AS TO MAKE A PARTICULAR TAB HOLE CONNECT TO PIN. THIS WILL PREVENT ENGINE FROM RETURNING TO IDLE.

1. Bracket
2. Bolts (2 req'd)
3. Servo assembly
4. Bolts (3 req'd)
5. Battery tray
6. Retainer
7. Cable assembly
8. Vacuum tank

Fig. 41 Servo mounting on 1985–1986 2.5L engines

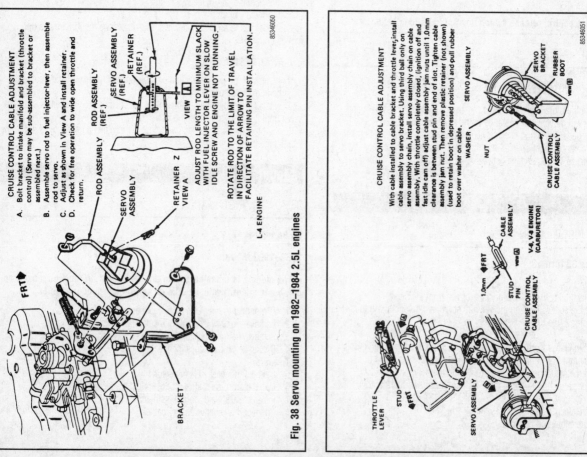

CRUISE CONTROL CABLE ADJUSTMENT

A. Bolt bracket to intake manifold and bracket (throttle control) (Servo may be sub-assembled to bracket or assembled next.)
B. Assemble servo rod to fuel injector-lever, then assemble rod to servo.
C. Adjust as shown in View A and install retainer.
D. Check for free operation to wide open throttle and return.

ADJUST ROD LENGTH TO MINIMUM SLACK WITH FUEL INJECTOR LEVER ON SLOW IDLE SCREW AND ENGINE NOT RUNNING.

ROTATE ROD TO THE LIMIT OF TRAVEL IN DIRECTION OF ARROW TO FACILITATE RETAINING PIN INSTALLATION.

L-4 ENGINE

Fig. 38 Servo mounting on 1982–1984 2.5L engines

CRUISE CONTROL CABLE ADJUSTMENT

With cable installed to cable bracket and throttle lever, install cable assembly to servo bracket. Using third ball only on servo assembly chain, install servo assembly chain on cable assembly. With throttle completely closed, (ignition off and fast idle cam off) adjust cable assembly jam nuts until 1.0mm clearance is between stud pin and end of slot. Tighten cable assembly jam nut. Then remove plastic retainer (not shown) (used to retain boot in depressed position) and assembly boot over washer on cable.

Fig. 39 Servo mounting on 1982–1984 carbureted V6 and V8 engines

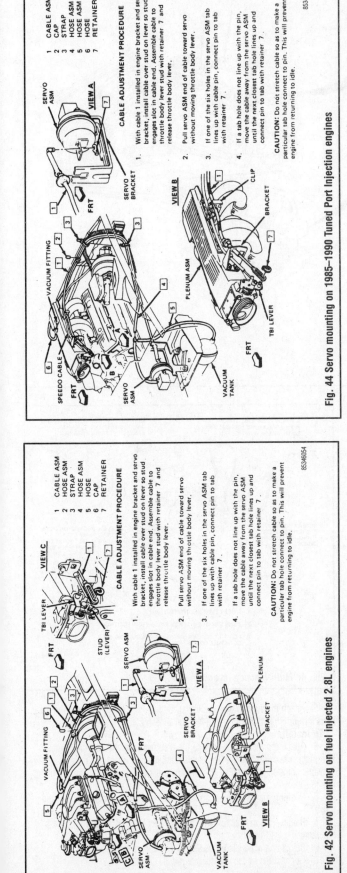

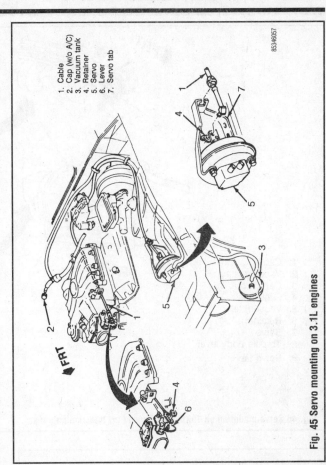

Fig. 45 Servo mounting on 3.1L engines

1. Cable
2. Cap (w/o A/C)
3. Vacuum tank
4. Retainer
5. Servo
6. Lever
7. Servo tab

Fig. 44 Servo mounting on 1985–1990 Tuned Port Injection engines

1. CABLE ASM
2. CAP
3. STRAP
4. HOSE ASM
5. HOSE ASM
6. HOSE
7. RETAINER

CABLE ADJUSTMENT PROCEDURE

With cable 1 installed in engine bracket and servo bracket, install cable over stud on lever so stud engages slot in cable end. Assemble cable to throttle body lever stud with retainer 7 and release throttle body lever.

1. Pull servo ASM end of cable toward servo without moving throttle body lever.
2. If one of the six holes in the servo ASM tab lines up with cable pin, connect pin to tab with retainer 7.
3. If a tab hole does not line up with the pin, move the cable away from the servo ASM until the next closest tab hole lines up and connect pin to tab with retainer 7.

CAUTION: Do not stretch cable so as to make a particular tab hole connect to pin. This will prevent engine from returning to idle.

Fig. 42 Servo mounting on fuel injected 2.8L engines

1. CABLE ASM
2. HOSE ASM
3. STRAP
4. HOSE ASM
5. HOSE
6. CAP
7. RETAINER

CABLE ADJUSTMENT PROCEDURE

With cable 1 installed in engine bracket and servo bracket, install cable over stud on lever so stud engages slot in cable end. Assemble cable to throttle body lever stud with retainer 7 and release throttle body lever.

1. Pull servo ASM end of cable toward servo without moving throttle body lever.
2. If one of the six holes in the servo ASM tab lines up with cable pin, connect pin to tab with retainer 7.
3. If a tab hole does not line up with the pin, move the cable away from the servo ASM until the next closest tab hole lines up and connect pin to tab with retainer 7.

CAUTION: Do not stretch cable so as to make a particular tab hole connect to pin. This will prevent engine from returning to idle.

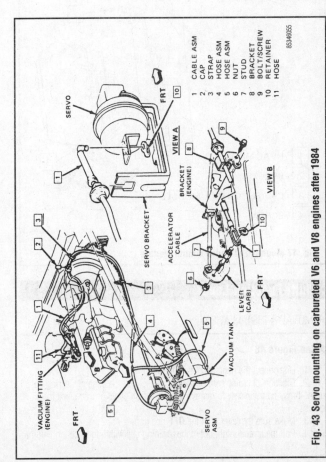

Fig. 43 Servo mounting on carbureted V6 and V8 engines after 1984

1. CABLE ASM
2. CAP
3. STRAP
4. HOSE ASM
5. HOSE ASM
6. NUT
7. STUD
8. BRACKET
9. BOLT/SCREW
10. RETAINER
11. HOSE

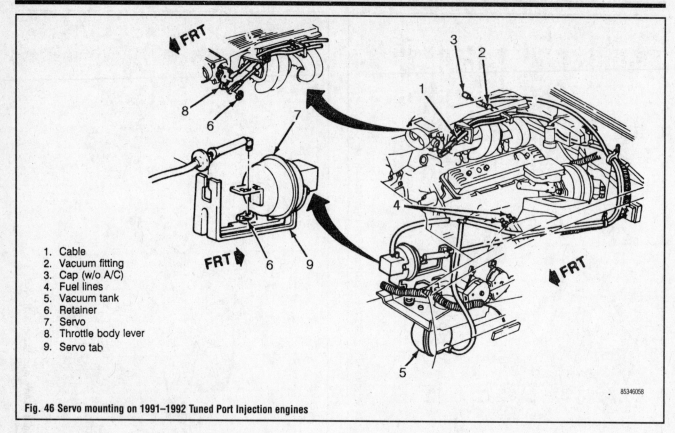

1. Cable
2. Vacuum fitting
3. Cap (w/o A/C)
4. Fuel lines
5. Vacuum tank
6. Retainer
7. Servo
8. Throttle body lever
9. Servo tab

85346058

Fig. 46 Servo mounting on 1991–1992 Tuned Port Injection engines

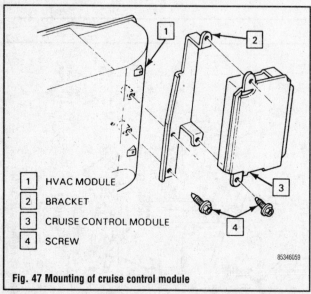

1 HVAC MODULE
2 BRACKET
3 CRUISE CONTROL MODULE
4 SCREW

85346059

Fig. 47 Mounting of cruise control module

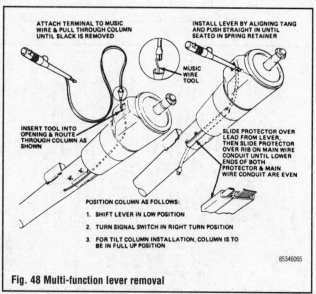

85346065

Fig. 48 Multi-function lever removal

Multi-Function Lever

REMOVAL & INSTALLATION

▶ **See Figure 48**

1. Disconnect the negative battery terminal.
2. Disconnect cruise control switch connector at the base of steering column. It may be necessary to remove an under dash panel or trim piece for access.
3. Make sure the lever is in the **OFF** position.
4. Pull the lever straight out of the retaining clip within the steering column.

5. Attach mechanic's wire or similar to the connector; gently pull the harness through the column, leaving the pull wire in place.

To install:

6. Attach the mechanic's wire to the connector. Gently pull the harness into place, checking that the harness is completely clear of any moving or movable components such as tilt column, telescoping column, brake pedal linkage, etc.
7. Position the lever and push it squarely into the retainer until it snaps in place.
8. Remove the mechanics' wire and connect the cruise control harness connector.
9. Reinstall any panels or insulation which were removed for access.
10. Connect the negative battery terminal.

ENTERTAINMENT SYSTEMS

Radio

REMOVAL & INSTALLATION

▶ **See Figures 49, 50, 51, 52 and 53**

1. Disconnect the negative battery cable.
2. Remove the heater/radio trim panel.
3. Remove the radio to console attaching screws.
4. Remove the radio and disconnect the electrical connector.

To install:

5. Connect the electrical connector.
6. Install the radio to console attaching screws.
7. Install the heater/radio trim panel.
8. Connect the negative battery cable.

➥**Always connect the speakers before applying power to the radio as radio damage may result.**

Speakers

REMOVAL & INSTALLATION

▶ **See Figure 54**

Front

1. Remove the instrument panel pad.
2. Remove the speaker attaching screws.
3. Remove the speaker and disconnect the electrical connector.
4. Installation is the reverse of removal.

Rear

1. Remove the coat hook screw and the coat hook.
2. Remove the speaker cover trim panel by pushing it straight up towards the roof.

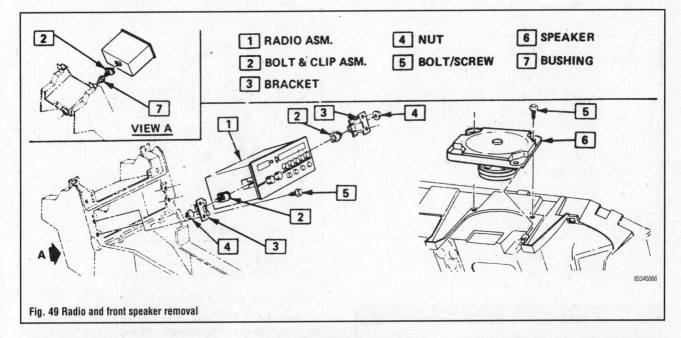

1	RADIO ASM.	**4**	NUT	**6**	SPEAKER
2	BOLT & CLIP ASM.	**5**	BOLT/SCREW	**7**	BUSHING
3	BRACKET				

Fig. 49 Radio and front speaker removal

Fig. 50 Removing the radio trim plate

Fig. 51 Remove the radio attaching screws

Fig. 52 Pull the radio out far enough to reach the connectors behind it

Fig. 53 Disconnecting the radio connectors

Fig. 54 Rear speaker removal

1. SPEAKER RETAINER ASSEMBLY SCREWS
2. SPEAKER TO SPEAKER RETAINER SCREWS
3. ELECTRICAL CONNECTOR

1.	Body and cable assy.
2.	Fixed antenna
3.	Nut
4.	Bezel
5.	Screw
6.	Bracket
7.	Antenna assembly
8.	Bracket (installed)
9.	Insulator (installed)
10.	Screw

Fig. 55 Antenna mounting

3. Remove the speaker attaching screws and remove the speaker.
4. Disconnect the electrical connector.
5. Installation is the reverse of removal.

Antenna

REMOVAL & INSTALLATION

▶ See Figure 55

➡Placement of tape on the right inner door edge will help prevent scratches during the antenna removal and installation procedure.

1. Disconnect the negative battery terminal.
2. Remove the right side lower instrument panel sound insulator and disconnect the antenna connection from the radio.
3. Raise and safely support the vehicle.
4. Disconnect the instrument panel harness from the radio.
5. Disconnect the power antenna lead, if equipped.
6. Disconnect the power antenna wire from the relay, if equipped.
7. Remove the right fender wheelhouse.
8. Loosen the fender-to-body attaching bolts and block the fender out.
9. Remove the antenna bezel and nut.

10. Remove the antenna assembly mounting screws.
11. Remove the grommet from the bulkhead and pull the harness from the vehicle interior.
12. Remove the antenna assembly from the vehicle.

➡In some cases, if the vehicle is equipped with a power antenna, it may be repaired. Seek a professional radio shop for proper repair of the antenna assembly.

To install:
13. Install the antenna assembly into the vehicle.
14. Install the grommet and the harness into the vehicle interior.
15. Install the antenna assembly mounting screws.
16. Install the antenna bezel and nut.
17. Remove the fender block, tighten the fender-to-body attaching bolts. Ensure any shims for the fender are reinstalled.
18. Install the right fender wheelhouse.
19. Lower the vehicle.
20. Connect the power antenna wire to the relay, if equipped.
21. Connect the power antenna lead, if equipped.
22. Connect the instrument panel harness to the radio.
23. Connect the antenna connection to the radio. Install the right side lower instrument panel sound insulator
24. Connect the negative battery cable.

WINDSHIELD WIPERS AND WASHERS

Blade and Arm

REMOVAL & INSTALLATION

♦ **See Figures 56 thru 61**

Blade

If the wiper assembly has a press type release tab at the center, simply depress the tab and remove the blade. If the blade has no release tab, use a screwdriver to depress the spring at the center. This will release the assembly. To install the assembly, position the blade over the pin at the tip of the arm and press until the spring retainer engages the groove in the pin.

To remove the element, either depress the release button or squeeze the spring type retainer clip at the outer end together, then slide the blade element out. Just slide the new element in until it latches.

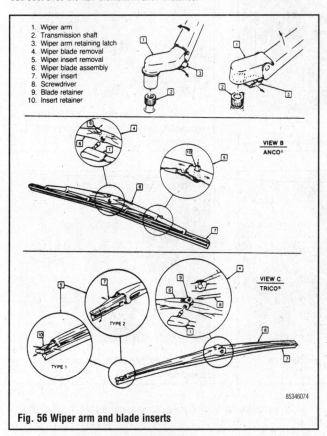

1. Wiper arm
2. Transmission shaft
3. Wiper arm retaining latch
4. Wiper blade removal
5. Wiper insert removal
6. Wiper blade assembly
7. Wiper insert
8. Screwdriver
9. Blade retainer
10. Insert retainer

VIEW B
ANCO®

VIEW C
TRICO®

TYPE 2

TYPE 1

85346074

Fig. 56 Wiper arm and blade inserts

Arm

Removal of the wiper arms requires the use of a special tool, GM J-8966 or its equivalent. Versions of this tool are generally available in auto parts stores.

1. Insert the tool under the wiper arm and lever the arm off the shaft.

➡**Raising the hood on most later models will facilitate easier wiper arm removal.**

2. Disconnect the washer hose from the arm (if so equipped). Remove the arm.
3. Installation is in the reverse order of removal. Be sure that the motor is in the park position before installing the arms.

Windshield Wiper Motor

REMOVAL & INSTALLATION

♦ **See Figures 62, 63, 64, 65 and 66**

1. Disconnect the negative battery cable at the battery.
2. Remove the screen or grille that covers the cowl area.
3. Working under the hood, disconnect the motor wiring. Then, reach through the cowl opening and loosen, but do not remove, the nuts which attach the transmission drive link to the motor crank arm. Then, disconnect the drive link from the crank arm.

85346075

Fig. 57 Most wiper blade and insert assemblies are retained with a lock tab

85346076

Fig. 58 Removing the wiper blade and insert assembly

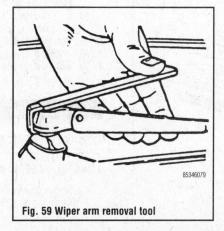

85346079

Fig. 59 Wiper arm removal tool

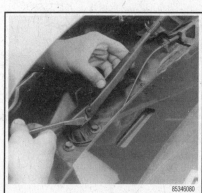

85346080

Fig. 60 Use a small prybar or screwdriver to lift the arm locktab

4. Remove the three motor attaching screws, and remove the motor, guiding the crank arm through the hole.

To install:

5. Position the motor, guiding the crank arm through the hole, and install the 3 motor attaching screws.

6. Connect the drive link to the crank arm and connect the motor wiring.

➥**The motor must be in the park position before assembling the crank arm to the transmission drive link(s).**

7. Install the screen or grille that covers the cowl area.

8. Connect the negative battery cable at the battery.

Rear Window Wiper Motor

REMOVAL & INSTALLATION

▶ **See Figure 67**

1. Remove the wiper arm blade using tool J-8966 or equivalent.

2. Remove the nut and spacer on the wiper motor shaft.

3. Raise the lid and remove the lift window trim panel.

4. Disconnect the electrical connectors to the wiper motor.

5. Remove the rivets holding the motor support to the lift window panel and remove the assembly from the car.

Fig. 61 Be sure to line up the splines on the driveshaft with the grooves in the arm when installing

Fig. 62 Removing the cowl screen

Fig. 63 When disconnecting the electrical connector, be careful not to damage the retaining tang

Fig. 64 Disconnecting the drive link from the crank arm

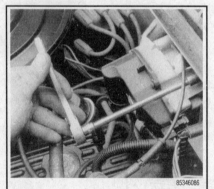

Fig. 65 Removing the motor attaching bolts

Fig. 66 Removing the wiper motor from the cowl

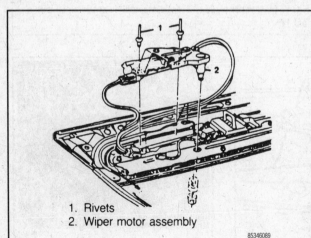

1. Rivets
2. Wiper motor assembly

Fig. 67 Rear wiper motor assembly

6. To remove the motor, remove the screws retaining wiper motor to motor support.

To install:

7. Position the motor onto the motor support and install the screws.

8. Install the motor support with the motor onto the lift window panel and secure it with rivets or nuts/bolts.

9. Connect the electrical connectors to the wiper motor.

10. Install the lift window trim panel and lower the lid.

11. Install the nut and spacer on the wiper motor shaft.

12. Install the wiper arm blade.

Wiper Linkage

REMOVAL & INSTALLATION

▶ **See Figures 68, 69 and 70**

1. Remove the wiper arms and blades. Remove the cowl screen or grille.

2. Disconnect the wiring from the wiper motor. Loosen, but do not remove

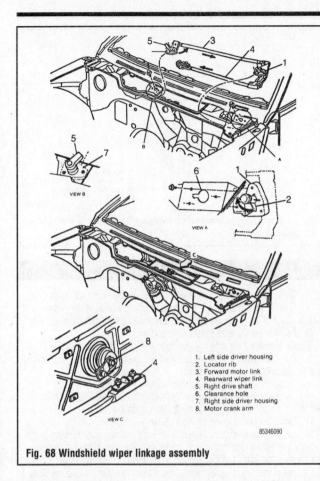

Fig. 68 Windshield wiper linkage assembly

1. Left side driver housing
2. Locator rib
3. Forward motor link
4. Rearward wiper link
5. Right drive shaft
6. Clearance hole
7. Right side driver housing
8. Motor crank arm

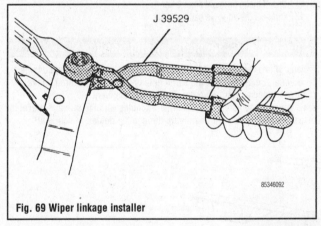

Fig. 69 Wiper linkage installer

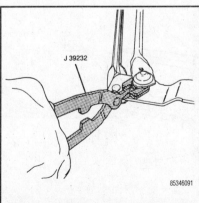

Fig. 70 Using the wiper linkage separator

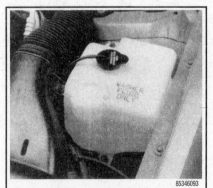

Fig. 71 A common washer reservoir location

Fig. 72 Removing the washer reservoir attaching screws

the nuts which attach the transmission drive link to the motor crank arm. Then, disconnect the drive link from the arm.

3. Remove the transmission-to-body attaching screws from both the right and left sides of the car.

4. Guide the transmissions and linkage out through the cowl opening.

To install:

5. Guide the transmissions and linkage in through the cowl opening.

6. Install the transmission attaching screws to both the right and left sides of the car.

7. Connect the drive link to the arm. Tighten the nuts which attach the transmission drive link to the motor crank arm. Connect the wiring to the wiper motor.

8. Install the cowl screen or grille.

9. Install the wiper arms and blades.

Washer Fluid Reservoir

REMOVAL & INSTALLATION

▶ See Figures 71, 72 and 73

1. Drain the reservoir.
2. Disconnect the washer pump electrical connector, if equipped.
3. Disconnect the hoses.
4. Remove the attaching bolts and remove the reservoir.
5. Installation is the reverse of removal.

Washer Pump

REMOVAL & INSTALLATION

▶ See Figure 74

Pump On Wiper Motor

1. Using a screwdriver, lift the washer pump retainer clip on the wiper motor cover.

2. Pull the washer pump from the cover.

To install:

3. Position the washer pump to the cover. Be sure to push the washer pump all the way into the female socket.

4. Install the washer pump retainer clip on the wiper motor cover.

Pump In Washer Tank

1. Drain the washer tank and disconnect the wire connectors.
2. Disconnect and remove the reservoir
3. Remove the washer pump from the reservoir.
4. Installation is the reverse of the removal procedure. Ensure pump is pushed fully into the reservoir.

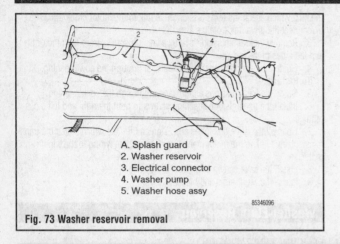

A. Splash guard
2. Washer reservoir
3. Electrical connector
4. Washer pump
5. Washer hose assy

85346096

Fig. 73 Washer reservoir removal

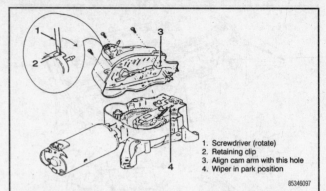

1. Screwdriver (rotate)
2. Retaining clip
3. Align cam arm with this hole
4. Wiper in park position

85346097

Fig. 74 Washer pump removal on models with the pump mounted on the wiper motor

INSTRUMENTS AND SWITCHES

Instrument Cluster

REMOVAL & INSTALLATION

▶ See Figures 75 and 76

Sport Coupe Model

1. Disconnect the negative battery cable.
2. Remove the instrument cluster bezel.
3. Remove the cluster attachment screws.
4. Pull the cluster out. Disconnect the speedometer cable and electrical connections.
5. Remove the cluster lens.
6. Install the cluster lens.
7. Connect the speedometer and electrical connections.
8. Push the cluster in.
9. Install the cluster attachment screws.
10. Install the instrument cluster bezel.
11. Connect the negative battery cable.

Berlinetta Model

1. Disconnect the negative battery cable.
2. Remove the instrument cluster bezel.

3. Remove the 8 steering column trim cover screws and trim cover.
4. Remove the right and left hand pod attaching screws at the bottom front of each pod. Pull the pods rearward and disconnect the electrical connection.
5. Remove the 5 cluster lens screws and lens.
6. Remove the 2 steering column bolts and lower the column.
7. Pull the instrument cluster rearward and disconnect the electrical connection. Remove the instrument cluster.
8. To install, position the instrument cluster into place.
9. Connect the electrical connection and push the cluster forward.
10. Lift the column and install the 2 steering column bolts.
11. Install the lens and install the 5 cluster lens screws.
12. Connect the electrical connection to each pod and push forward. Install the right and left hand pod attaching screws at the bottom front of each pod. Pull the pods rearward and disconnect the electrical connection.
13. Install the trim cover and install the 8 steering column trim cover screws.
14. Install the instrument cluster bezel.
15. Connect the negative battery cable.

Speedometer, Tachometer and Gauges

➡Federal law requires that the odometer in any replacement speedometer/odometer must register the same mileage as that registered on the removed speedometer/odometer. Service replacement speedometer/odometers and odometer modules with the mileage preset to actual vehicle mileage are available through the dealer. In nearly all

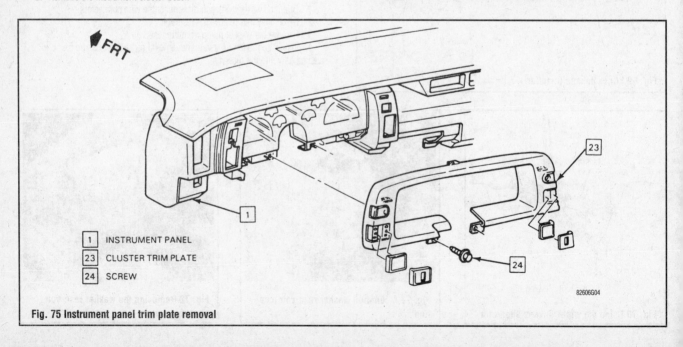

1	INSTRUMENT PANEL
23	CLUSTER TRIM PLATE
24	SCREW

82606G04

Fig. 75 Instrument panel trim plate removal

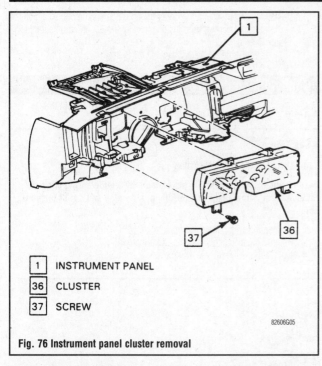

Fig. 76 Instrument panel cluster removal

1	INSTRUMENT PANEL
36	CLUSTER
37	SCREW

82606G05

cases, the mileage continues to accumulate in the odometer memory even if the odometer does not display mileage. This mileage can usually be verified by the dealer. Contact the dealer for instructions to receive a replacement speedometer/odometer with preset mileage. If the actual vehicle mileage cannot be verified, the dealer will supply a speedometer/odometer with a display set to zero miles. In addition, an odometer mileage sticker is supplied with the replacement odometer. The sticker must display the estimated vehicle mileage and is to be affixed to the driver's door.

REMOVAL & INSTALLATION

1. The gauges can be removed from the cluster assembly by:
   a. Removing the cluster lens.
   b. Removing the printed circuit board from the back of the cluster.
   c. Removing the gauge attaching screws.
2. Installation is the reverse of removal.

Speedometer Cable

REMOVAL & INSTALLATION

1. Disconnect the negative battery cable at the battery.
2. On models without cruise control, disconnect the speedometer cable strap at the power brake booster. On models with cruise control, disconnect the speedometer cable at the cruise control transducer.
3. Remove the instrument cluster trim plate.
4. Remove the instrument cluster attaching screws and pull the cluster out far enough to gain access to the rear of the speedometer head.
5. Reach beneath the cable connection at the speedometer head, push in on the cable retaining spring, and disconnect the cable from the speedometer.
6. Slide the old cable out of the speedometer cable casing. If the cable is broken, remove the cable from both ends of the casing. Using a short piece of the old cable to fit the speedometer connection, turn the speedometer to increase the speed indicated on the dial and check for any binding during rotation. If binding is noted, the speedometer must be removed for repair or replacement. Check the entire cable casing for extreme bends, chafing, breaks, etc., and replace if necessary.
   To install:
7. Wipe the cable clean using a lint free cloth.
8. If the old casing is to be reused, flush the casing with petroleum spirits and blow dry with compressed air.

9. Lubricate the speedometer cable with an appropriate lubricant, being sure to cover the lower thirds of the cable.
10. Insert the cable into the casing, then connect the cable and casing assembly to the speedometer.
11. Install the instrument cluster, then install the cluster attaching screws.
12. Install the instrument cluster trim plate.
13. On models without cruise control, connect the speedometer cable strap at the power brake booster. On models with cruise control, connect the speedometer cable at the cruise control transducer.
14. Connect the negative battery cable at the battery.

Wiper Switch

REMOVAL & INSTALLATION

➡ **The wiper switch is part of the multi-function lever, located on the steering wheel column.**

1. Disconnect the electrical connector of the multi-function lever, located under the instrument panel.
2. Remove the protective cover from the wire.
3. Grasp the lever firmly, twist and pull (the tang on the lever must align with the socket) the lever straight out.
4. Pull the wire through the steering column.
   To install:
5. Slide a music wire tool through the steering column and connect the lever wire to the tool wire; pull the wire through the steering column.
6. Push the control lever into the spring loaded socket (be sure to align the tang).
7. Install the protective cover to the wire.
8. Connect the electrical connector of the multi-function lever.

Headlight Switch

REMOVAL & INSTALLATION

♦ **See Figure 77**

1. Disconnect the negative battery cable at the battery.
2. Remove the four screws from inside the defroster duct (instrument panel pad securing screws).

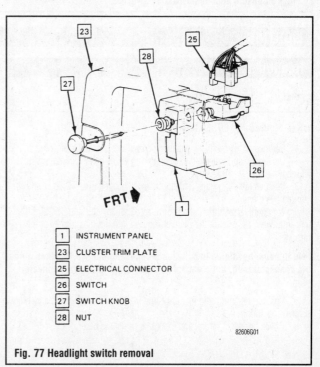

1	INSTRUMENT PANEL
23	CLUSTER TRIM PLATE
25	ELECTRICAL CONNECTOR
26	SWITCH
27	SWITCH KNOB
28	NUT

82606G01

Fig. 77 Headlight switch removal

3. Remove the screws which are under the lip of the instrument panel pad.

4. Remove the instrument panel pad.

5. On models equipped with air conditioning, remove the instrument panel cluster bezel and the cluster.

6. Remove the radio speaker bracket.

7. Pull the headlamp switch knob to the **ON** position, depress the locking button for the knob and shaft (located on the switch), and remove the knob and shaft.

8. Remove the switch bezel (retainer).

9. Disconnect the wiring from the switch and remove the switch.

10. To install, position the switch into place and connect the wiring to the switch.

11. Install the switch bezel (retainer).

12. Push the headlamp switch knob into the switch. (It may be necessary to depress the knob release button.

13. Install the radio speaker bracket.

14. On models equipped with air conditioning, install the instrument panel cluster bezel and the cluster.

15. Install the instrument panel pad.

16. Install the screws which are under the lip of the instrument panel pad.

17. Install the four screws from inside the defroster duct (instrument panel pad securing screws).

18. Connect the negative battery cable at the battery.

Console Mounted Switches

REMOVAL & INSTALLATION

▶ **See Figure 78**

1. Disconnect the negative battery cable.

➡ **The switches are secured in the console by simple spring clips. To remove them, simply pull or carefully pry them up and out of the console.**

2. Unsnap the switch from the console.
3. Remove the electrical connector from the switch.
4. Installation is the reverse of removal.

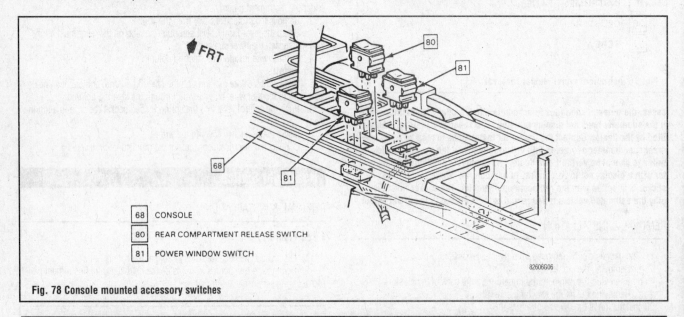

68	CONSOLE
80	REAR COMPARTMENT RELEASE SWITCH
81	POWER WINDOW SWITCH

82606G06

Fig. 78 Console mounted accessory switches

LIGHTING

Headlights

REMOVAL & INSTALLATION

▶ **See Figures 79, 80, 81 and 82**

1. Remove headlamp bezel retaining screws and remove bezel.

2. Disengage spring from the retaining ring with a cotter pin removal tool and remove two attaching screws.

3. Remove retaining ring, disconnect sealed beam unit at wiring connector and remove the unit.

4. To install, attach the connector to replacement unit and position the unit in place making sure the number molded into the lens face is at the top.

➡ **In the dual headlamp installation the inboard unit (No. 1) takes a double connector plug, the outboard unit (No. 2) takes a triple connector plug.**

5. Position retaining ring into place and install the retaining ring attaching screws and spring.

6. Check operation of unit and install the headlamp bezel.

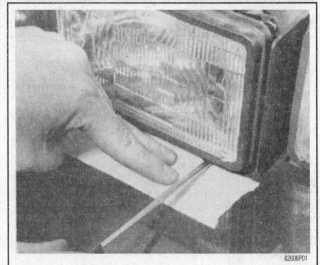

82606P01

Fig. 79 Headlight removal—the lower bezel mounting screws only need to be loosened, not removed

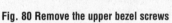

Fig. 80 Remove the upper bezel screws

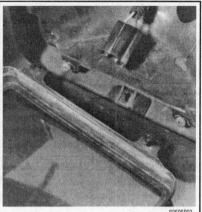

Fig. 81 Headlight and bezel removed and notice the lower bezel screw slots for ease of removal

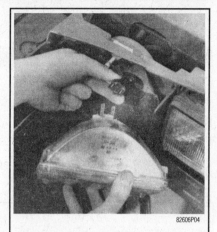

Fig. 82 Plug headlight in and ensure the headlight is right side up

AIMING THE HEADLIGHTS

▶ **See Figures 83, 84, 85 and 86**

The headlights must be properly aimed to provide the best, safest road illumination. The lights should be checked for proper aim and adjusted as necessary. Certain state and local authorities have requirements for headlight aiming; these should be checked before adjustment is made.

✳ CAUTION

About once a year, when the headlights are replaced or any time front end work is performed on your vehicle, the headlight should be accurately aimed by a reputable repair shop using the proper equipment. Headlights not properly aimed can make it virtually impossible to see and may blind other drivers on the road, possibly causing an accident. Note that the following procedure is a temporary fix, until you can take your vehicle to a repair shop for a proper adjustment.

Headlight adjustment may be temporarily made using a wall, as described below, or on the rear of another vehicle. When adjusted, the lights should not glare in oncoming car or truck windshields, nor should they illuminate the passenger compartment of vehicles driving in front of you. These adjustments are rough and should always be fine-tuned by a repair shop which is equipped with headlight aiming tools. Improper adjustments may be both dangerous and illegal.

For most of the vehicles covered by this manual, horizontal and vertical aiming of each sealed beam unit is provided by two adjusting screws which move the retaining ring and adjusting plate against the tension of a coil spring. There is no adjustment for focus; this is done during headlight manufacturing.

➡**Because the composite headlight assembly is bolted into position, no adjustment should be necessary or possible. Some applications, however, may be bolted to an adjuster plate or may be retained by adjusting screws. If so, follow this procedure when adjusting the lights, BUT always have the adjustment checked by a reputable shop.**

Before removing the headlight bulb or disturbing the headlamp in any way, note the current settings in order to ease headlight adjustment upon reassembly. If the high or low beam setting of the old lamp still works, this can be done using the wall of a garage or a building:

1. Park the vehicle on a level surface, with the fuel tank about ½ full and with the vehicle empty of all extra cargo (unless normally carried). The vehicle should be facing a wall which is no less than 6 feet (1.8m) high and 12 feet (3.7m) wide. The front of the vehicle should be about 25 feet from the wall.

2. If aiming is to be performed outdoors, it is advisable to wait until dusk in order to properly see the headlight beams on the wall. If done in a garage, darken the area around the wall as much as possible by closing shades or hanging cloth over the windows.

3. Turn the headlights **ON** and mark the wall at the center of each light's low

beam, then switch on the bright lights and mark the center of each light's high beam. A short length of masking tape which is visible from the front of the vehicle may be used. Although marking all four positions is advisable, marking one position from each light should be sufficient.

4. If neither beam on one side is working, and if another like-sized vehicle is available, park the second one in the exact spot where the vehicle was and mark the beams using the same-side light. Then switch the vehicles so the one to be aimed is back in the original spot. It must be parked no closer to or farther away from the wall than the second vehicle.

5. Perform any necessary repairs, but make sure the vehicle is not moved, or is returned to the exact spot from which the lights were marked. Turn the headlights **ON** and adjust the beams to match the marks on the wall.

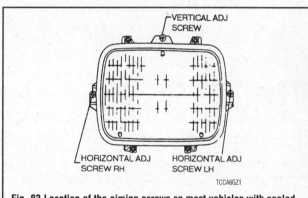

Fig. 83 Location of the aiming screws on most vehicles with sealed beam headlights

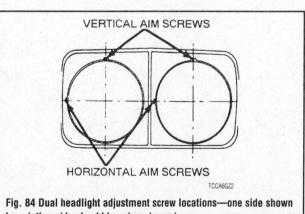

Fig. 84 Dual headlight adjustment screw locations—one side shown here (other side should be mirror image)

6. Have the headlight adjustment checked as soon as possible by a reputable repair shop.

Signal and Marker Lights

REMOVAL & INSTALLATION

Front Parking and Turn Signal

▶ See Figure 87

1. Reach around to the back side of the light assembly and unlock the bulb holder/wiring harness by grasping the bulb holder/wiring harness and turning it counterclockwise approximately ¼ turn.
2. Remove the bulb holder/wiring harness assembly.
3. To install, insert the bulb holder/wiring harness assembly into the light assembly and locking the holder by turning it ¼ turn clockwise.

Front Marker Lights

▶ See Figures 88, 89 and 90

1. Remove the six screws from the filler panel under the front fascia.
2. Remove the filler panel.
3. Remove the socket from the lamp assembly.
4. Remove the bulb from the socket.
5. Installation is the reverse of removal.

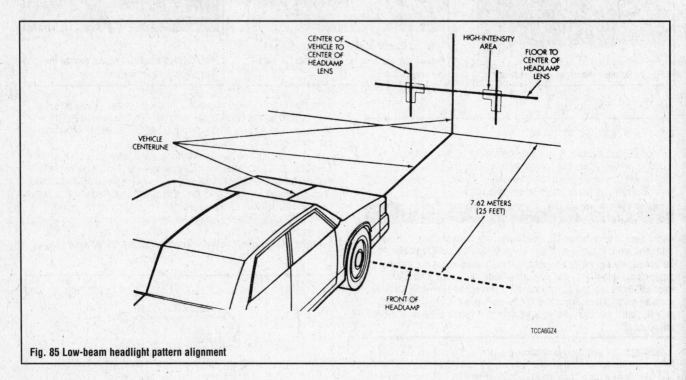

Fig. 85 Low-beam headlight pattern alignment

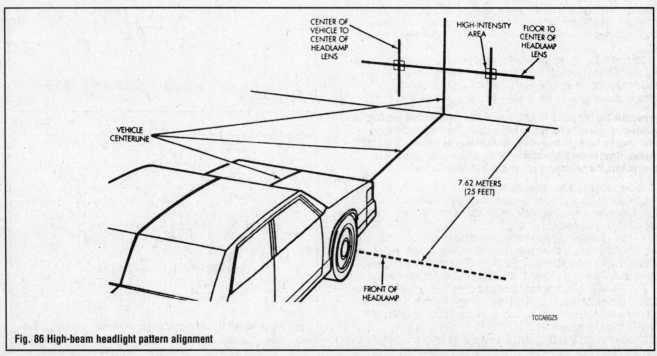

Fig. 86 High-beam headlight pattern alignment

Rear Marker Lights

▶ **See Figure 91**

1. Open the hatch.
2. Remove the fasteners from the rear trim panel.
3. Remove the trim panel.
4. Remove the socket from the lens assembly.
5. Remove the bulb from the socket.
6. Installation is the reverse of removal.

Rear Turn Signal, Brake and Parking Lights

▶ **See Figures 92, 93 and 94**

1. Remove the rear compartment trim assembly.
2. Remove the plastic wing nuts from the tail lamp assembly.

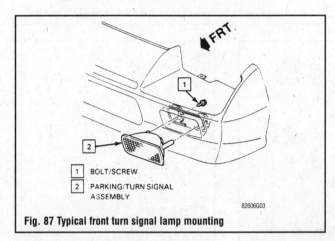

Fig. 87 Typical front turn signal lamp mounting

3. Remove the tail lamp assembly.
4. Remove the socket(s) from the assembly.
5. Remove the bulb(s) from the socket(s).
6. Installation is the reverse of removal.

High Mount Brake Light

▶ **See Figures 95, 96 and 97**

1986 MODELS

1. Remove the screw securing the cover.
2. Remove the cover.
3. Remove the bulb.
4. Installation is the reverse of removal.

1987–1990 MODELS

1. Remove the screws securing the lens assembly.
2. Remove the bulb from the lamp assembly.
3. Installation is the reverse of removal.

1991–1992 MODELS

1. Remove the two screws from the lamp assembly.
2. Remove the lamp assembly from the bracket.
3. Remove the bulb from the socket.
4. Installation is the reverse of removal.

Dome Light

▶ **See Figure 97**

1. Remove the courtesy lamp fuse.
2. Remove the lens by gently squeezing the edge and pulling down.
3. Remove the bulb.
4. Installation is the reverse of removal.

Fig. 88 Remove the six filler panel bolts

Fig. 89 Removing the filler panel from the vehicle

Fig. 90 Once the filler panel has been removed, the front side marker light can be replaced

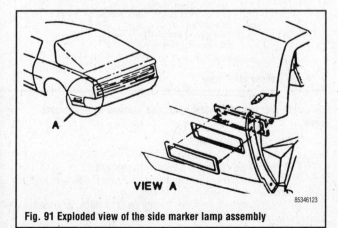

Fig. 91 Exploded view of the side marker lamp assembly

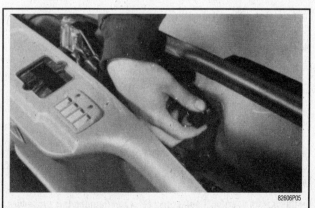

Fig. 92 Remove the tail light bezel attaching screws

Fig. 93 There are attaching screws hidden in the rear corner

Fig. 94 Push the thumb-lock and turn the lamp assembly to remove

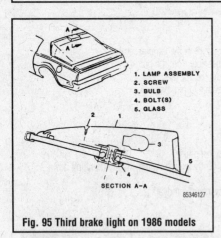

1. LAMP ASSEMBLY
2. SCREW
3. BULB
4. BOLT(S)
5. GLASS

SECTION A-A

Fig. 95 Third brake light on 1986 models

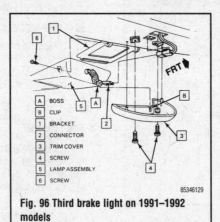

A	BOSS
B	CLIP
1	BRACKET
2	CONNECTOR
3	TRIM COVER
4	SCREW
5	LAMP ASSEMBLY
6	SCREW

Fig. 96 Third brake light on 1991–1992 models

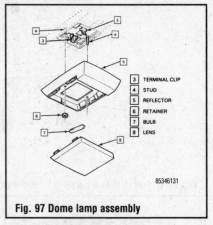

3. TERMINAL CLIP
4. STUD
5. REFLECTOR
6. RETAINER
7. BULB
8. LENS

Fig. 97 Dome lamp assembly

Passenger Area Lamps

The passenger area courtesy lamps can be replaced by first removing the appropriate trim panel, then removing the bulb from the socket. Most panels are fastened by screws or snap-fasteners. Be careful not to force the trim panel off, as you may damage it. Do not pry with tools which may damage the panel, use tools designed for panel removal only.

License Plate Lights

▶ See Figure 98

1. Remove the screws securing the lamp assembly to the bumper.
2. Remove the bulb from the socket.
3. Installation is the reverse of removal.

Fog Lights

REMOVAL & INSTALLATION

▶ See Figure 99

1. Remove the two screws attaching the lamp assembly to the front impact bar.
2. Remove the lamp assembly from the impact bar.
3. Disconnect the electrical connector.
4. Remove the two lens attaching screws.
5. Remove the bulb.
6. Installation is the reverse of removal.

AIMING

▶ See Figure 100

➡Check with your local authorities before performing this procedure. Most areas have standards for proper adjustment. We recommend,

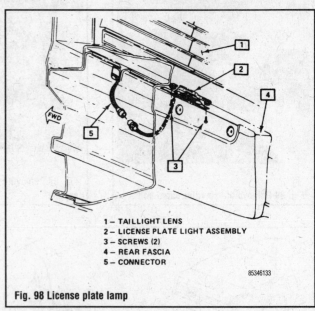

1 – TAILLIGHT LENS
2 – LICENSE PLATE LIGHT ASSEMBLY
3 – SCREWS (2)
4 – REAR FASCIA
5 – CONNECTOR

Fig. 98 License plate lamp

for safety, that the adjustment always be checked by a reputable shop.

1. Prepare the vehicle as follows:
    a. Make sure all components are in place.
    b. Make sure the vehicle has a ½ tank of fuel or less.
    c. Move the vehicle to a level area and park 25 feet (7.6 m) away from a target screen.
2. With the fog lamps on, measure from the center of the fog lamp assembly to the ground line.

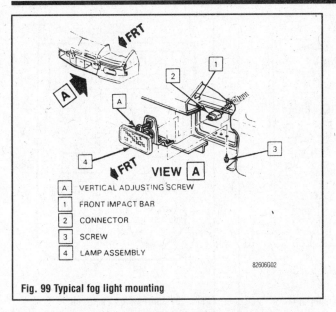

Fig. 99 Typical fog light mounting

A	VERTICAL ADJUSTING SCREW
1	FRONT IMPACT BAR
2	CONNECTOR
3	SCREW
4	LAMP ASSEMBLY

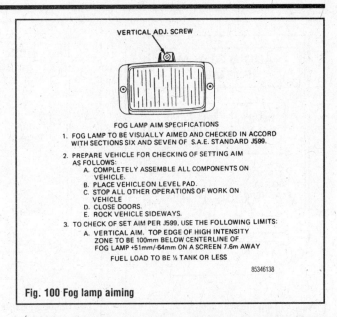

Fig. 100 Fog lamp aiming

FOG LAMP AIM SPECIFICATIONS

1. FOG LAMP TO BE VISUALLY AIMED AND CHECKED IN ACCORD WITH SECTIONS SIX AND SEVEN OF S.A.E. STANDARD J599.
2. PREPARE VEHICLE FOR CHECKING OF SETTING AIM AS FOLLOWS:
   A. COMPLETELY ASSEMBLE ALL COMPONENTS ON VEHICLE.
   B. PLACE VEHICLE ON LEVEL PAD.
   C. STOP ALL OTHER OPERATIONS OF WORK ON VEHICLE
   D. CLOSE DOORS.
   E. ROCK VEHICLE SIDEWAYS.
3. TO CHECK OF SET AIM PER J599, USE THE FOLLOWING LIMITS:
   A. VERTICAL AIM. TOP EDGE OF HIGH INTENSITY ZONE TO BE 100mm BELOW CENTERLINE OF FOG LAMP +51mm/-64mm ON A SCREEN 7.6m AWAY
   FUEL LOAD TO BE ½ TANK OR LESS

3. Top edge of the high intensity zone should be 4 inches (102 mm) below the centerline of the fog lamp assembly.

4. Adjust if necessary.

Fuse Block

▶ See Figures 101 thru 107

The fuse block on some models is located under the instrument panel next to the steering wheel and is a swing down unit. Other models have the fuse block located on the left side of the dash.

Each fuse block uses miniature fuses which are designed for increased circuit protection and greater reliability. The compact fuse is a blade terminal design which allows easy pull-out/push-in removal and replacement.

Although the fuses are interchangeable, the amperage values are not. The values are usually molded in bold, color coded, easy to read numbers on the fuse body. Use only fuses of equal replacement valve.

A blown fuse can easily be checked by visual inspection or by continuity checking.

Fusible Links

In addition to circuit breakers and fuses, the wiring harness incorporates fusible links to protect the wiring. Links are used rather than a fuse, in wiring circuits that are not normally fused, such as the ignition circuit. The fusible

Fig. 101 The fuse block is located behind this access panel

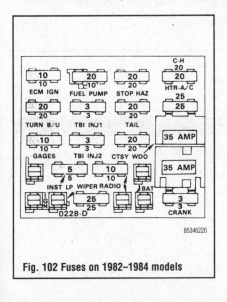

Fig. 102 Fuses on 1982–1984 models

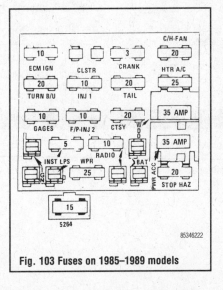

Fig. 103 Fuses on 1985–1989 models

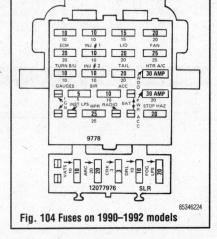

Fig. 104 Fuses on 1990–1992 models

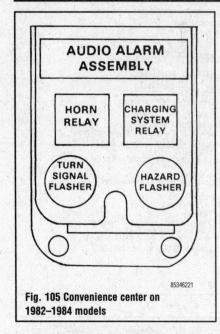

Fig. 105 Convenience center on 1982–1984 models

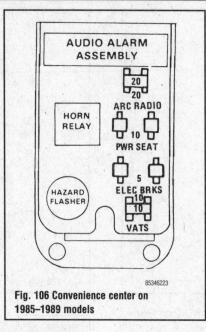

Fig. 106 Convenience center on 1985–1989 models

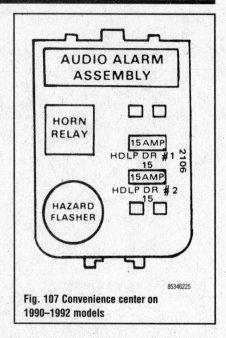

Fig. 107 Convenience center on 1990–1992 models

links are color coded red in the charging and load circuits to match the color coding of the circuits they protect. Each link is four gauges smaller than the cable it protects, and is marked on the insulation with the gauge size because the insulation makes it appear heavier than it really is. The engine compartment wiring harness has several fusible links. The same size wire with a special Hypalon insulation must be used when replacing a fusible link.

➡ **For more details, see the information on fusible links at the beginning of this section.**

The links are located in the following areas:
1. A molded splice at the starter solenoid **Bat** terminal, a 14 gauge red wire.
2. A 16 gauge red fusible link at the junction block to protect the unfused wiring of 12 gauge or larger wire. This link stops at the bulkhead connector.
3. The alternator warning light and field circuitry is protected by a 20 gauge red wire fusible link used in the battery feed-to-voltage regulator number 3 terminal. The link is installed as a molded splice in the circuit at the junction block.
4. The ammeter circuit is protected by two 20 gauge fusible links installed as molded splices in the circuit at the junction block and battery to starter circuit.

REPLACEMENT

1. Determine the circuit that is damaged.
2. Disconnect the negative battery terminal.
3. Cut the damaged fuse link from the harness and discard it.
4. Identify and procure the proper fuse link and butt connectors.
5. Strip the wire about ½ in. (13mm) on each end.
6. Connect the fusible link and crimp the butt connectors making sure that the wires are secure.

7. Solder each connection with resin core solder, and wrap the connections with plastic electrical tape.
8. Reinstall the wire in the harness.
9. Connect the negative battery terminal and test the system for proper operation.

Circuit Breakers

Various circuit breakers are located under the instrument panel. In order to gain access to these components, it may be necessary to first remove the under dash padding. Most of the circuit breakers are located in the convenience center or the fuse panel.

Buzzers, Relays, and Flashers

The electrical protection devices are located in the convenience center, which is a swing down unit located under the instrument panel. All units are serviced by plug-in replacements.

TURN SIGNAL FLASHER

The turn signal flasher is located inside the convenience center. In order to gain access to the turn signal flasher, it may be necessary to first remove the under dash padding.

HAZARD FLASHER

The hazard flasher is located inside the convenience center. In order to gain access to the turn signal flasher, it may be necessary to first remove the under dash padding.

WIRING DIAGRAMS

The following wiring diagrams are provided to help troubleshoot electrical problems and as a an additional source to help understand the complex wiring utilized by these vehicles. No attempt has been made to illustrate most components as they physically appear, instead, representations are used to simplify the diagram. When working on a system, locate the component and use the wire color codes to help trace the circuit.

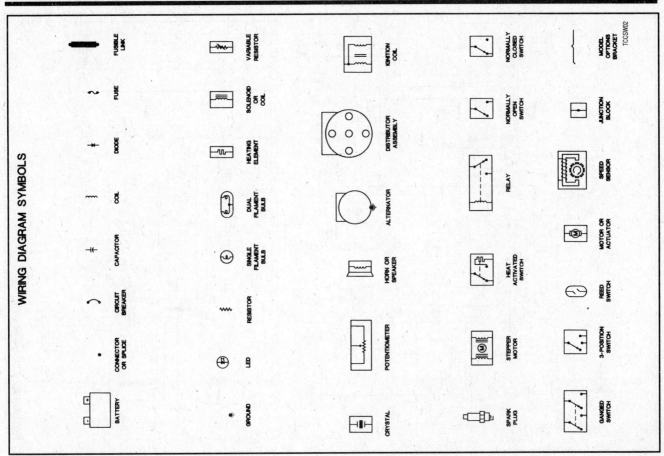

WIRING DIAGRAM SYMBOLS

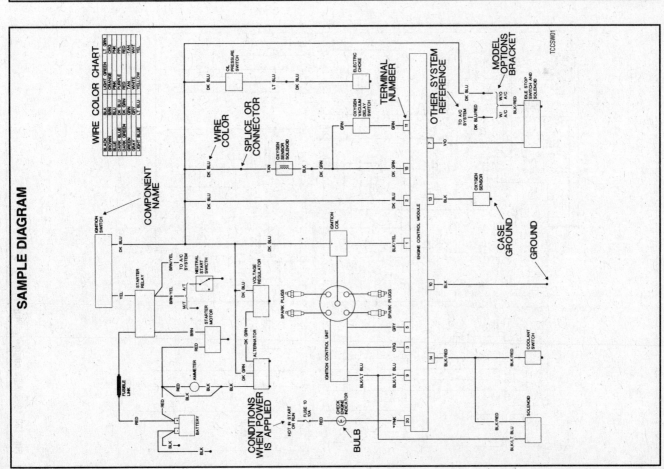

SAMPLE DIAGRAM

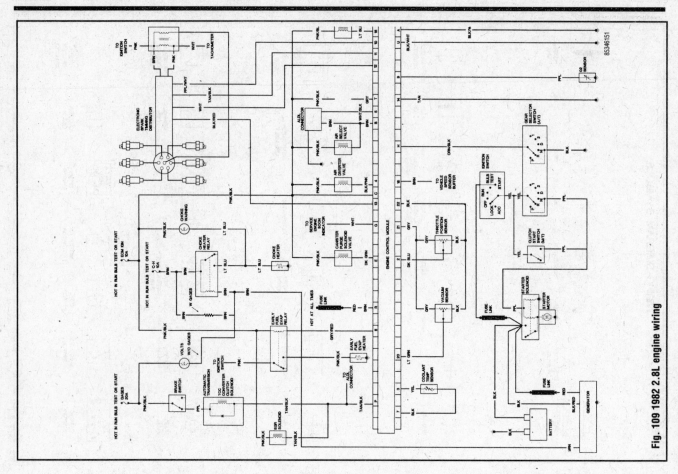

Fig. 109 1982 2.8L engine wiring

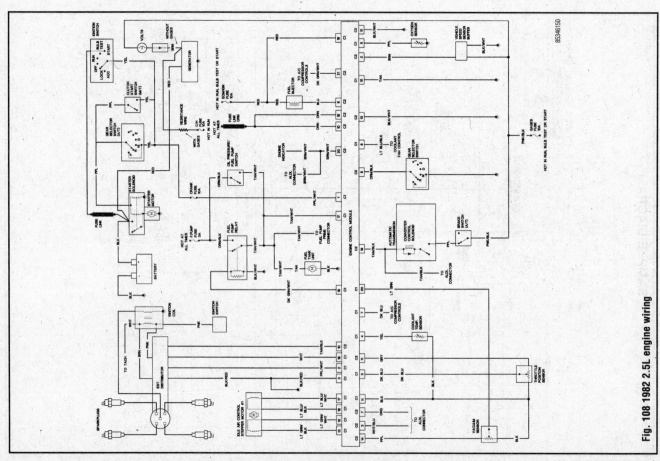

Fig. 108 1982 2.5L engine wiring

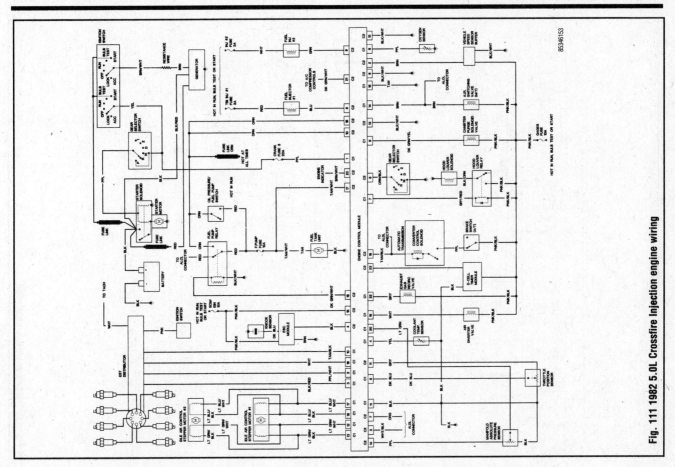

Fig. 111 1982 5.0L Crossfire Injection engine wiring

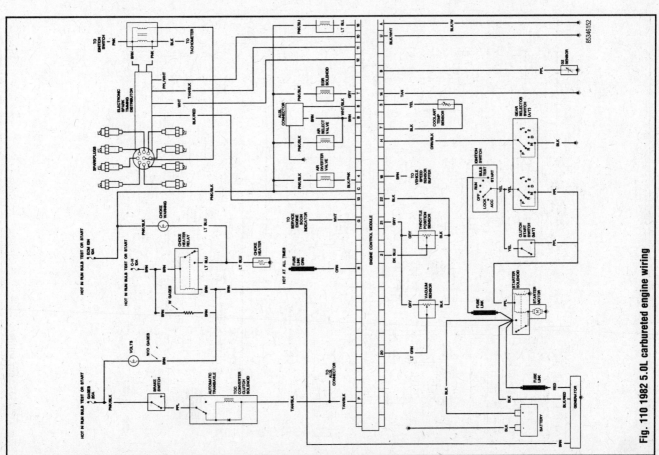

Fig. 110 1982 5.0L carbureted engine wiring

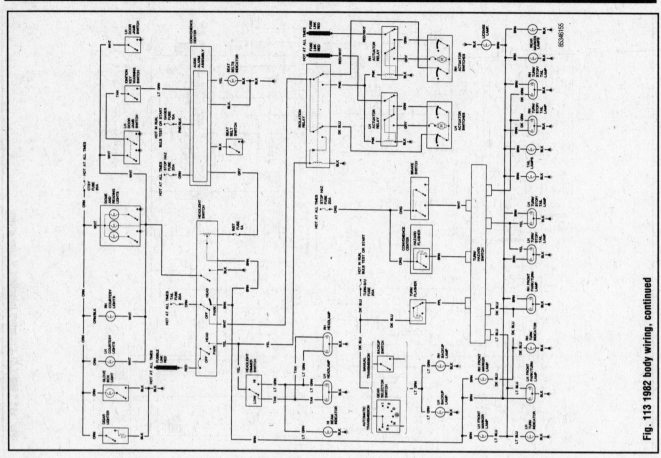

Fig. 113 1982 body wiring, continued

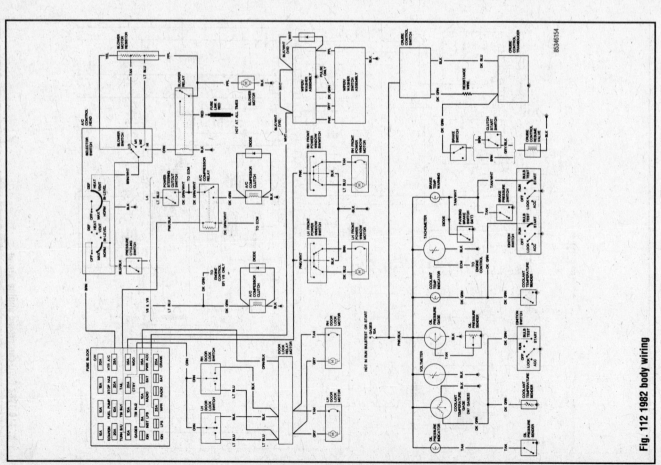

Fig. 112 1982 body wiring

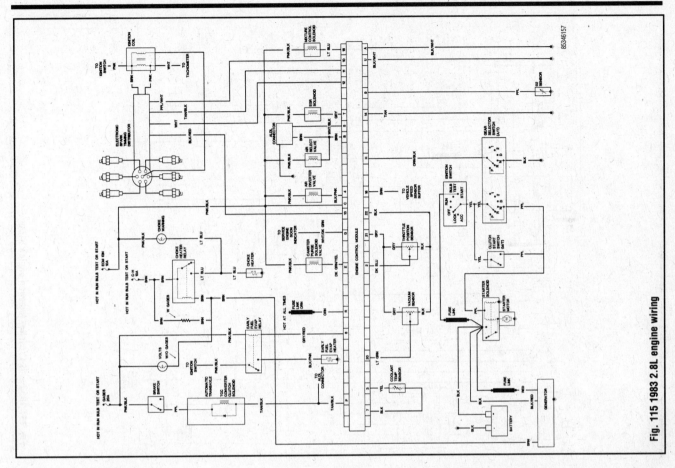

Fig. 115 1983 2.8L engine wiring

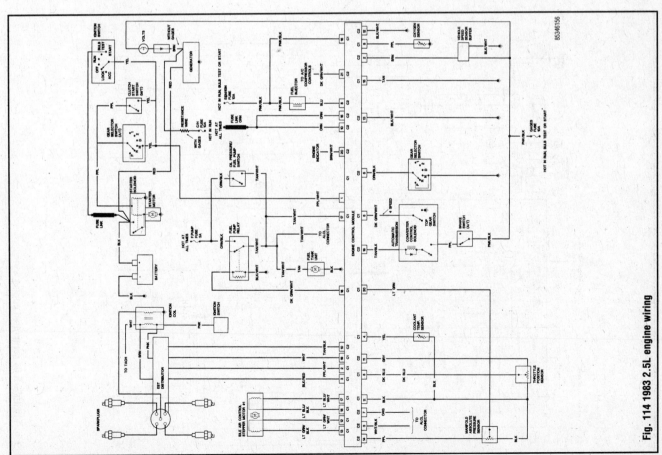

Fig. 114 1983 2.5L engine wiring

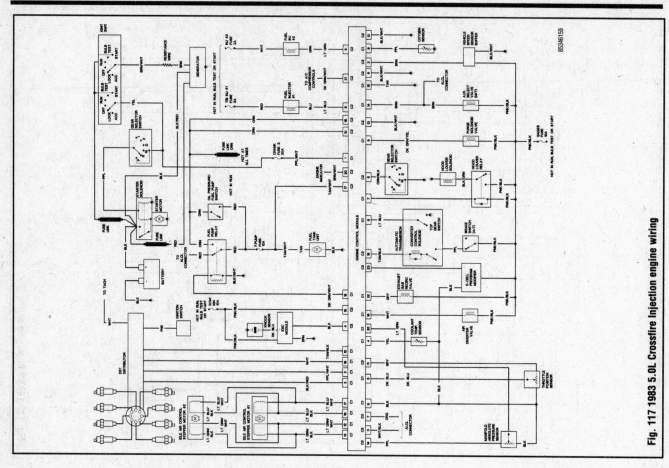

Fig. 117 1983 5.0L Crossfire Injection engine wiring

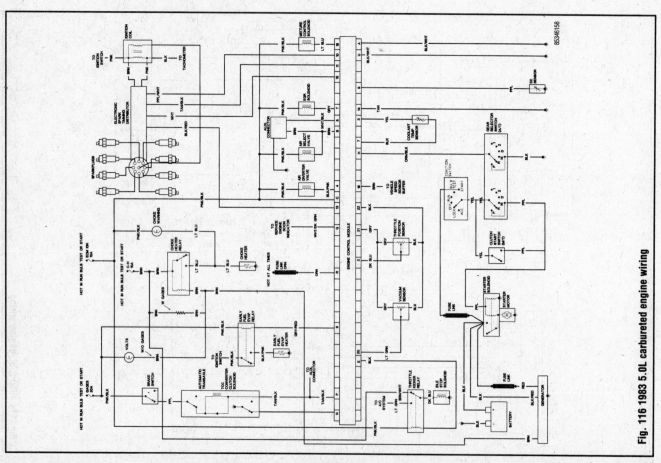

Fig. 116 1983 5.0L carbureted engine wiring

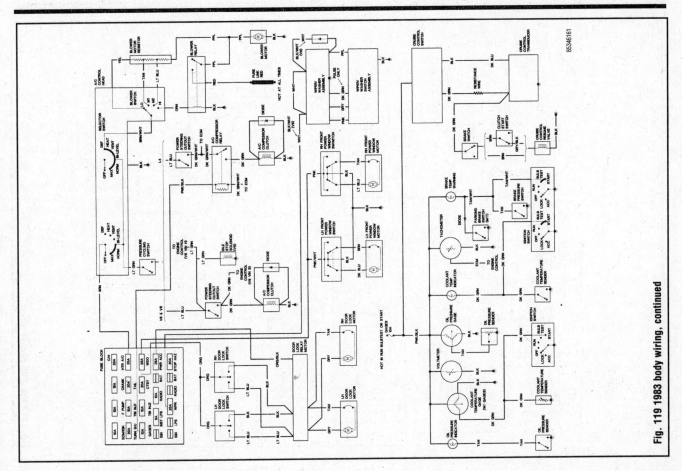

Fig. 119 1983 body wiring, continued

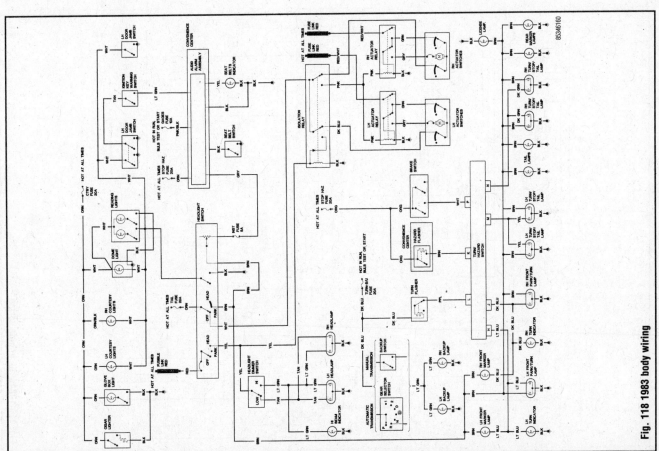

Fig. 118 1983 body wiring

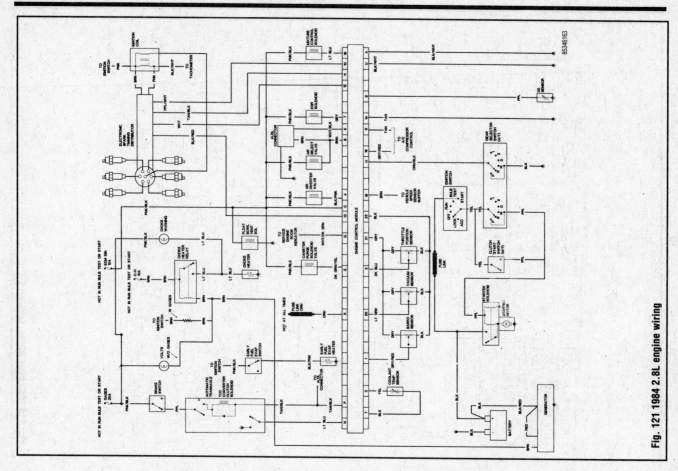

Fig. 121 1984 2.8L engine wiring

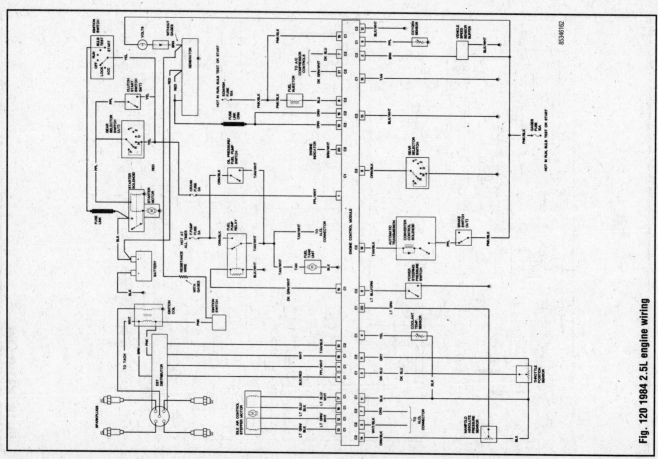

Fig. 120 1984 2.5L engine wiring

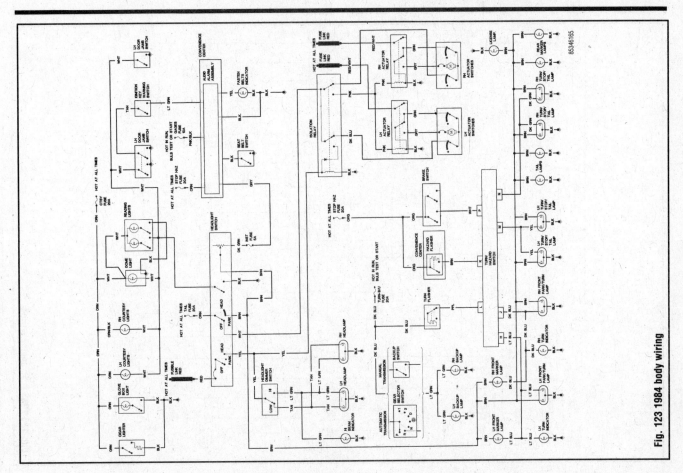

Fig. 123 1984 body wiring

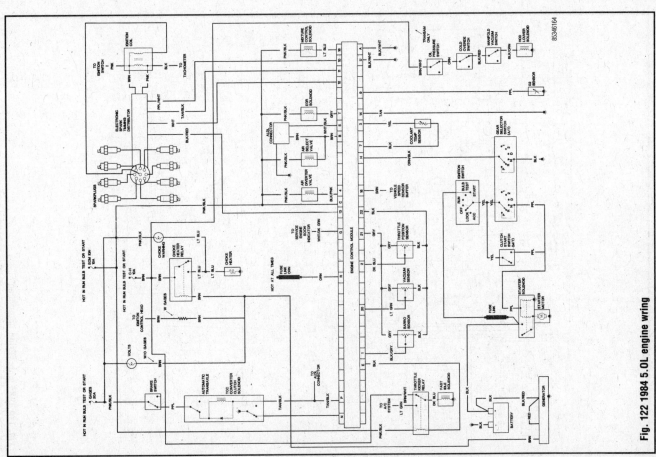

Fig. 122 1984 5.0L engine wiring

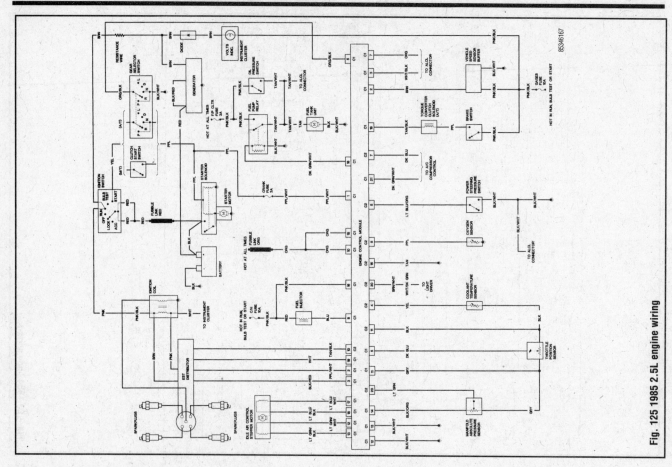

Fig. 125 1985 2.5L engine wiring

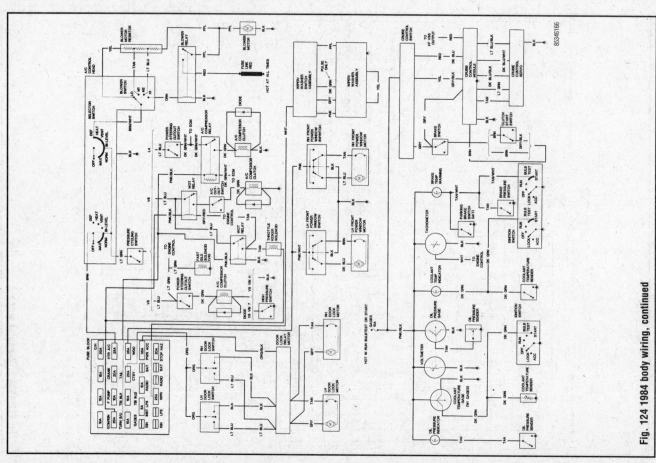

Fig. 124 1984 body wiring, continued

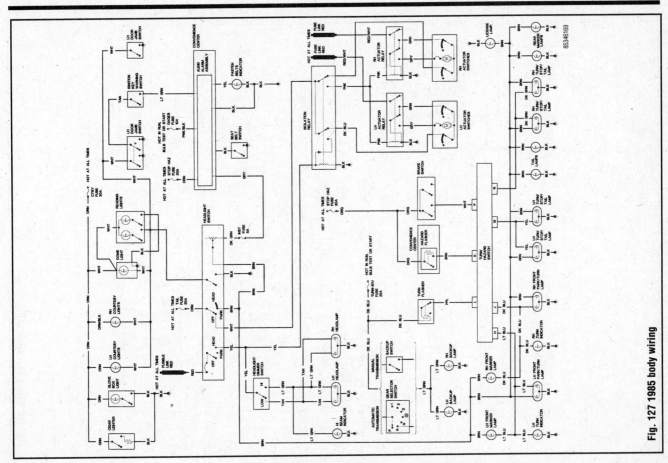

Fig. 127 1985 body wiring

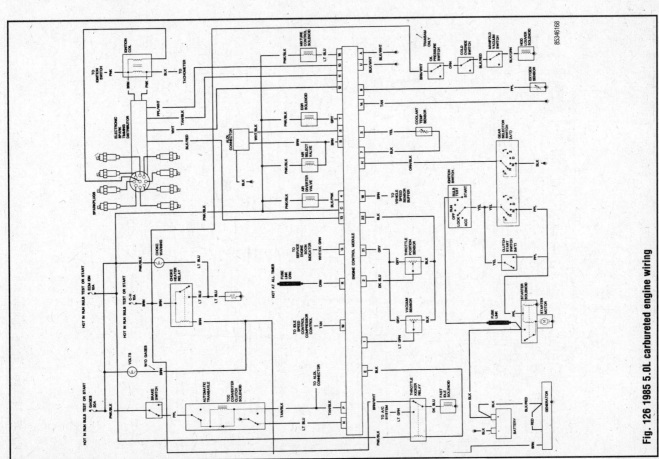

Fig. 126 1985 5.0L carbureted engine wiring

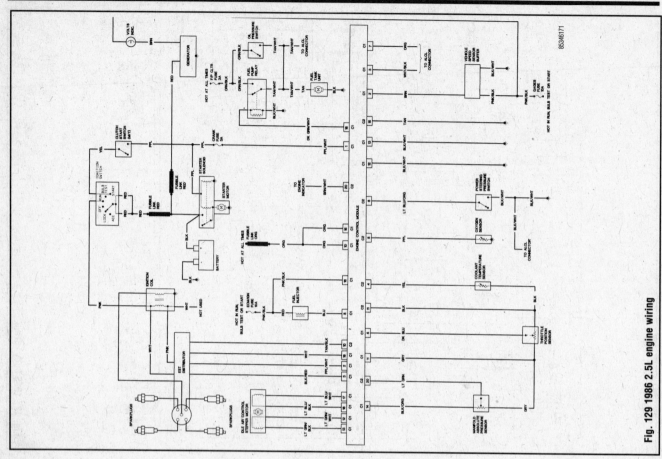

Fig. 129 1986 2.5L engine wiring

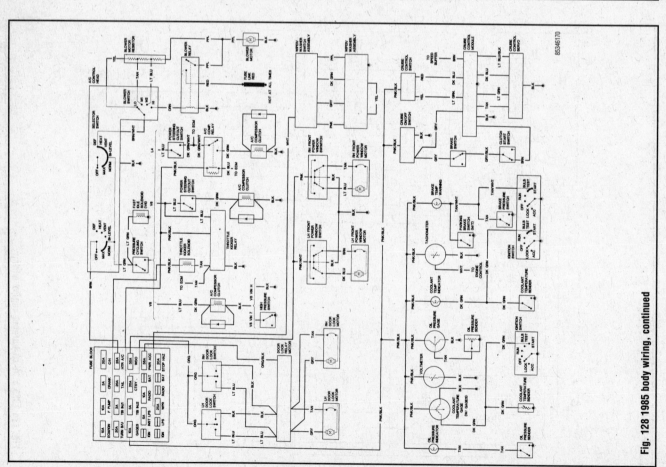

Fig. 128 1985 body wiring, continued

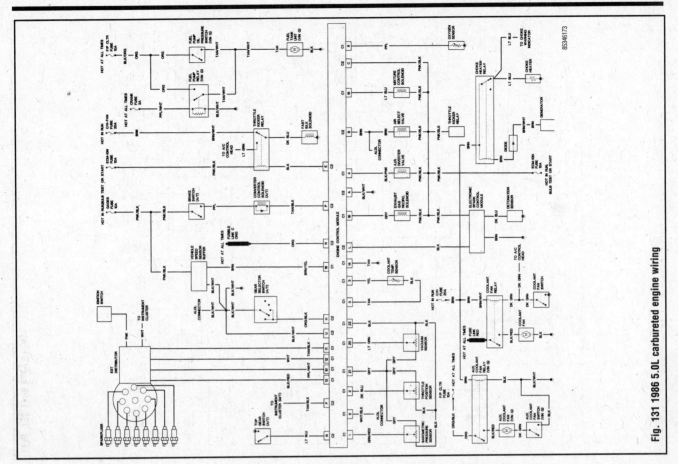

Fig. 131 1986 5.0L carbureted engine wiring

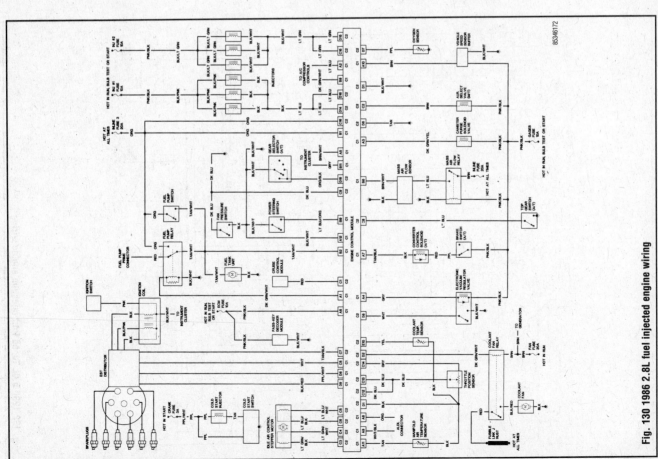

Fig. 130 1986 2.8L fuel injected engine wiring

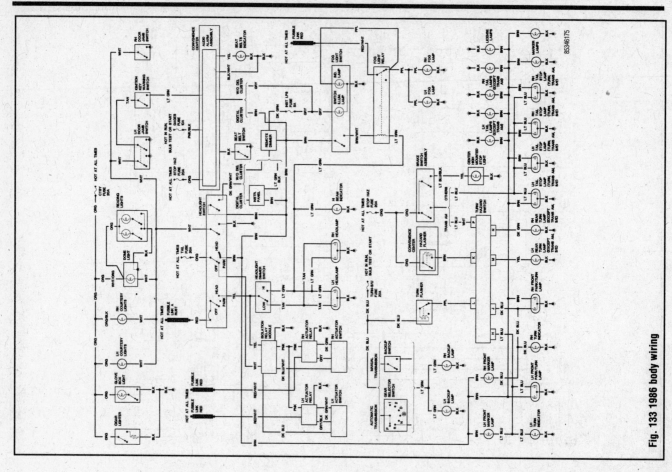

Fig. 133 1986 body wiring

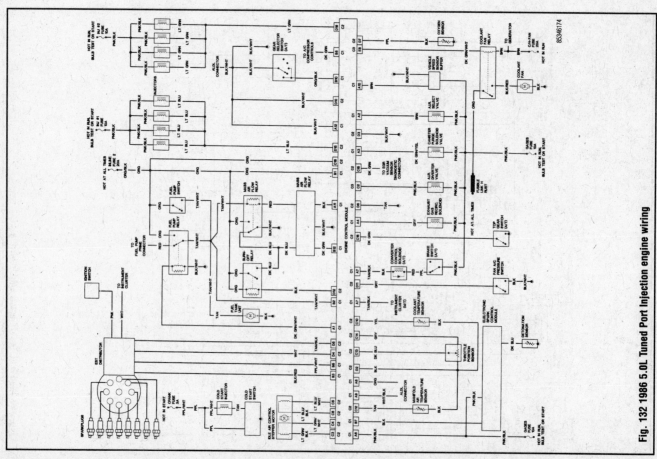

Fig. 132 1986 5.0L Tuned Port Injection engine wiring

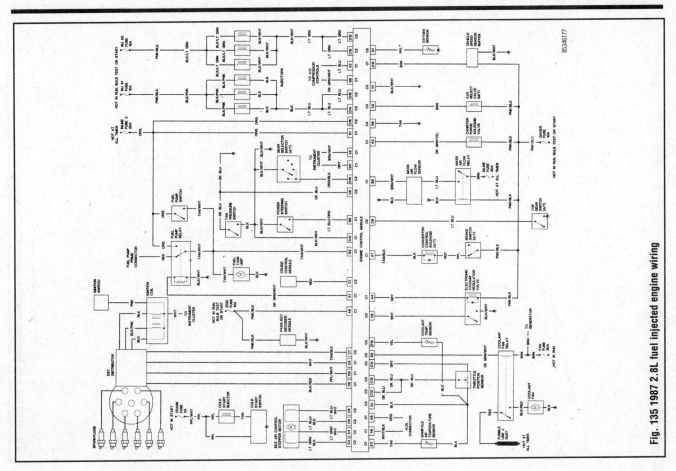

Fig. 135 1987 2.8L fuel injected engine wiring

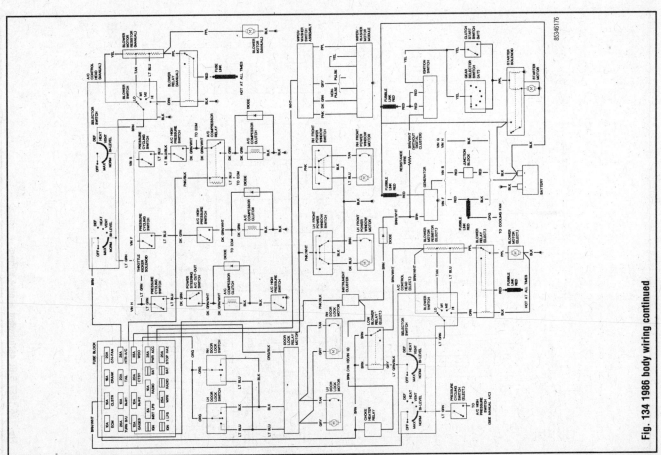

Fig. 134 1986 body wiring continued

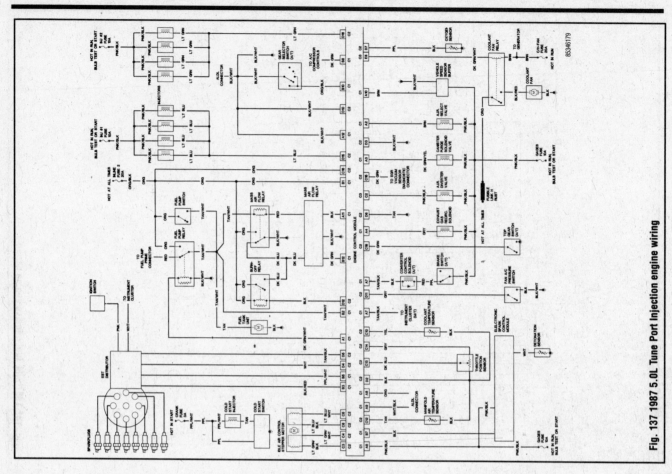

Fig. 137 1987 5.0L Tune Port Injection engine wiring

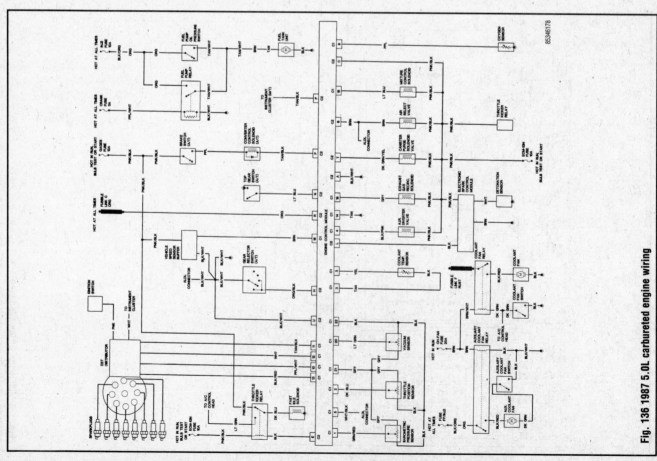

Fig. 136 1987 5.0L carbureted engine wiring

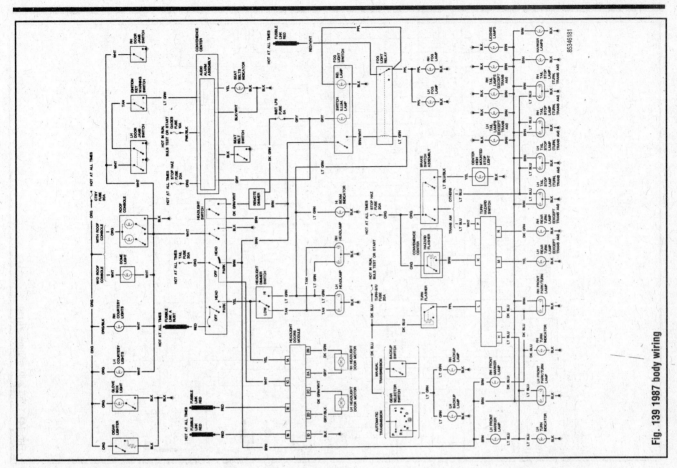

Fig. 139 1987 body wiring

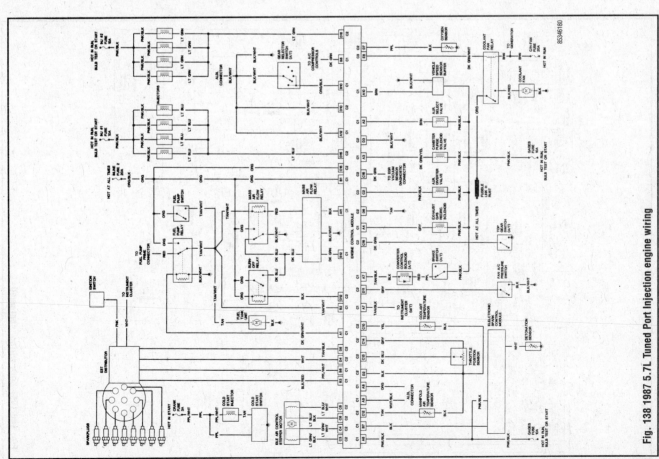

Fig. 138 1987 5.7L Tuned Port Injection engine wiring

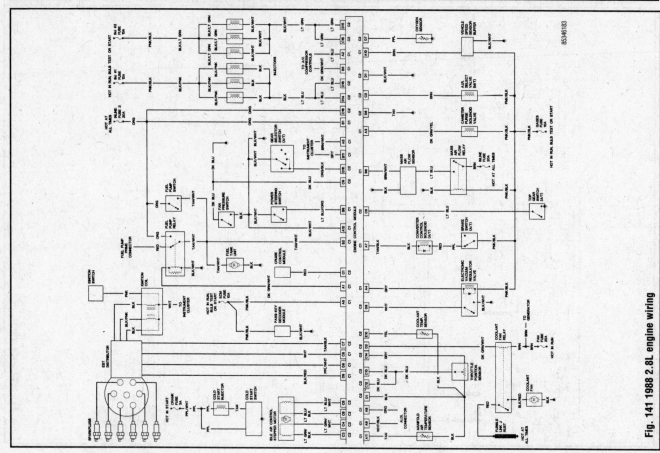

Fig. 141 1988 2.8L engine wiring

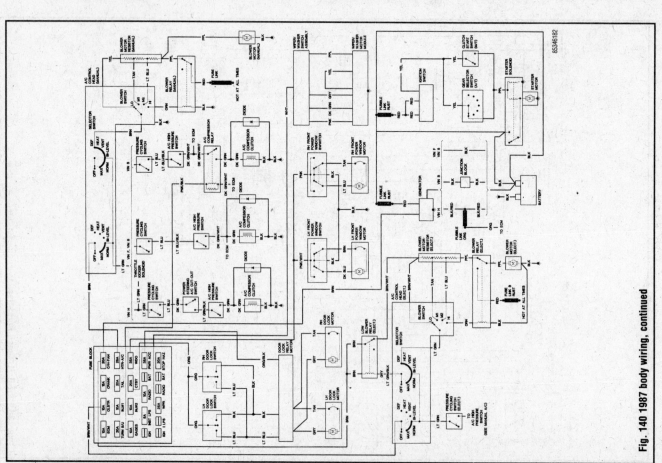

Fig. 140 1987 body wiring, continued

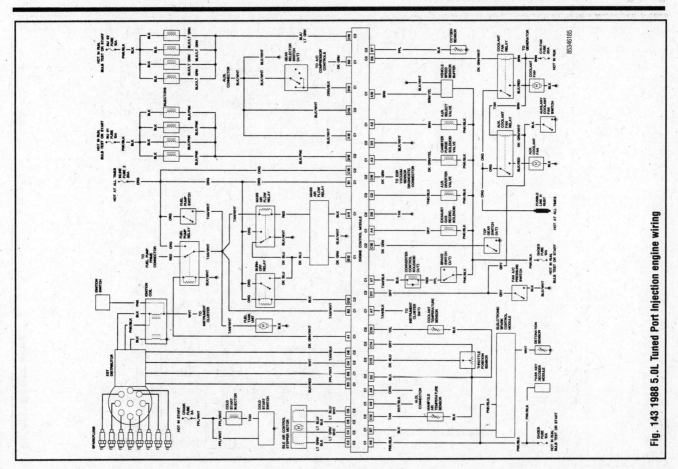

Fig. 143 1988 5.0L Tuned Port Injection engine wiring

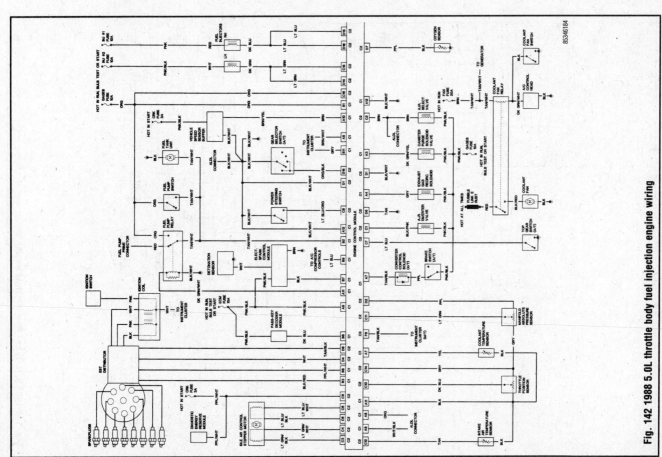

Fig. 142 1988 5.0L throttle body fuel injection engine wiring

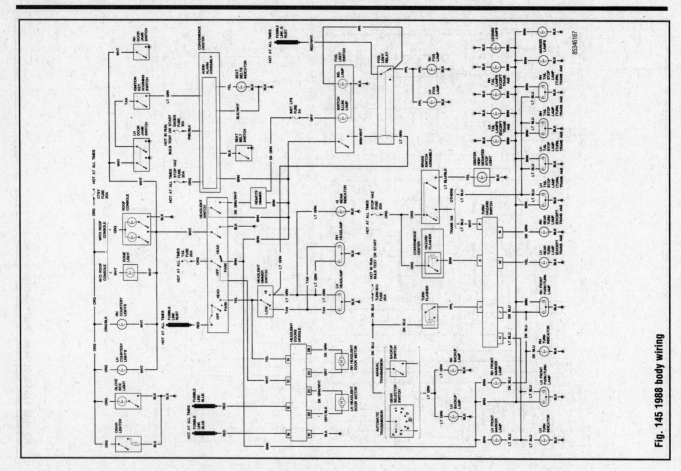

Fig. 145 1988 body wiring

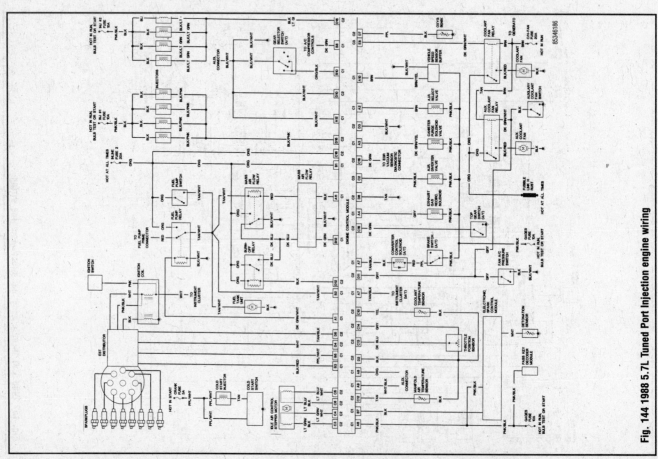

Fig. 144 1988 5.7L Tuned Port Injection engine wiring

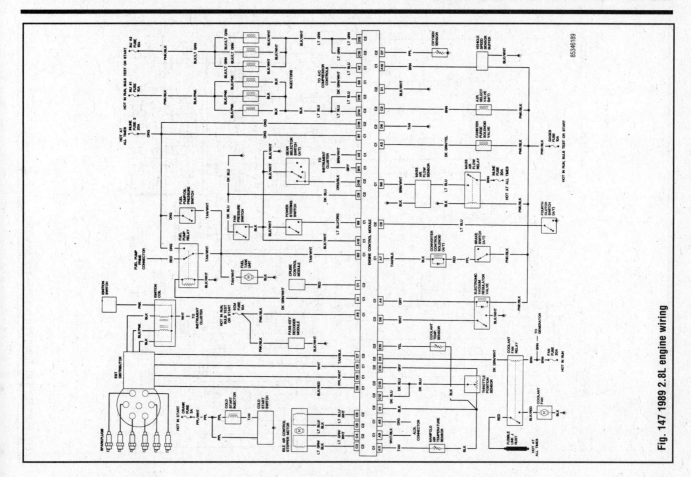

Fig. 147 1989 2.8L engine wiring

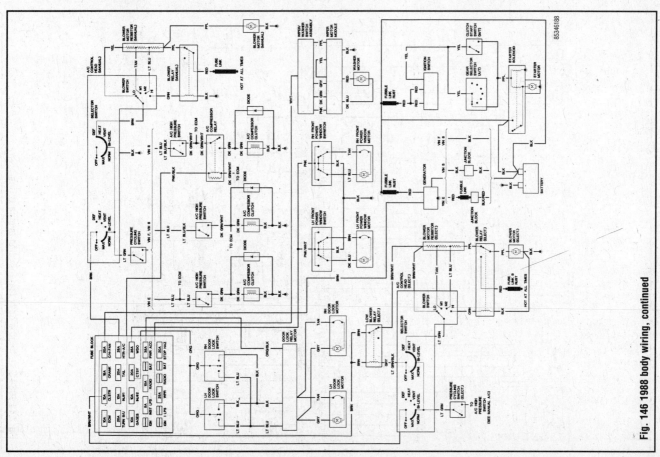

Fig. 146 1988 body wiring, continued

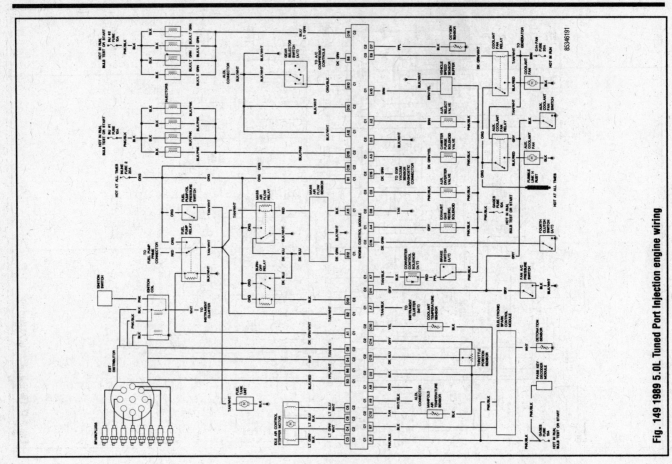

Fig. 149 1989 5.0L Tuned Port Injection engine wiring

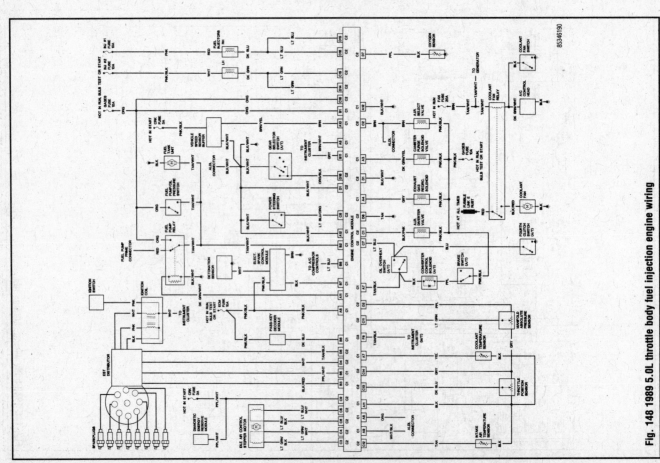

Fig. 148 1989 5.0L throttle body fuel injection engine wiring

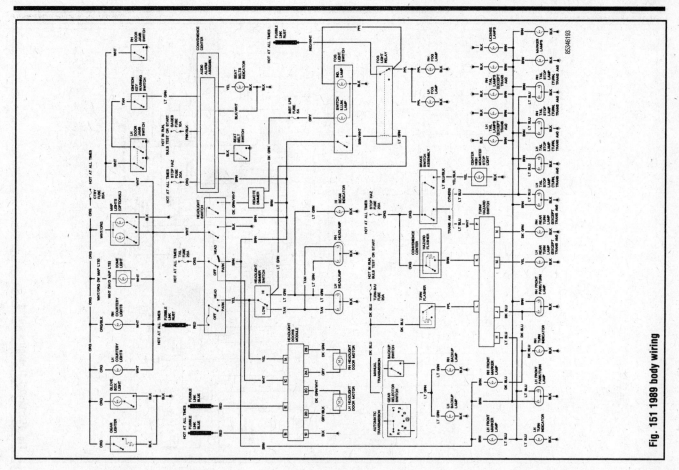

Fig. 151 1989 body wiring

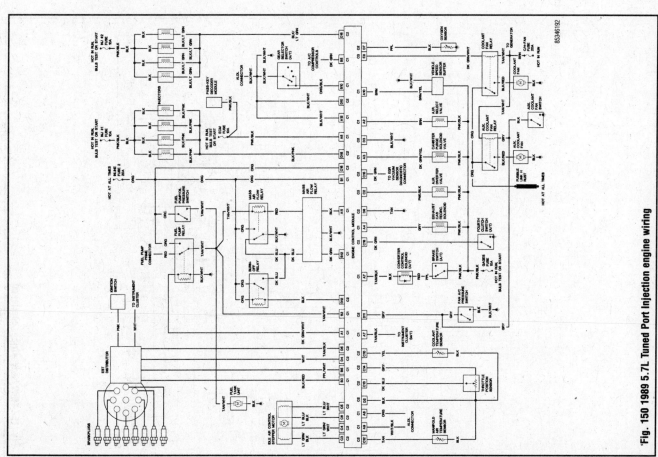

Fig. 150 1989 5.7L Tuned Port Injection engine wiring

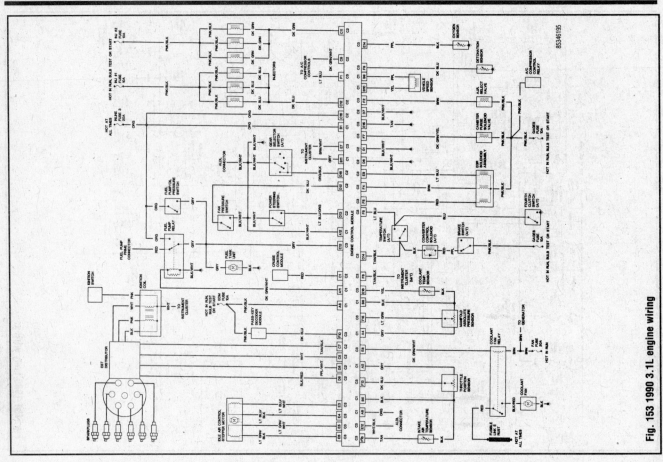

Fig. 153 1990 3.1L engine wiring

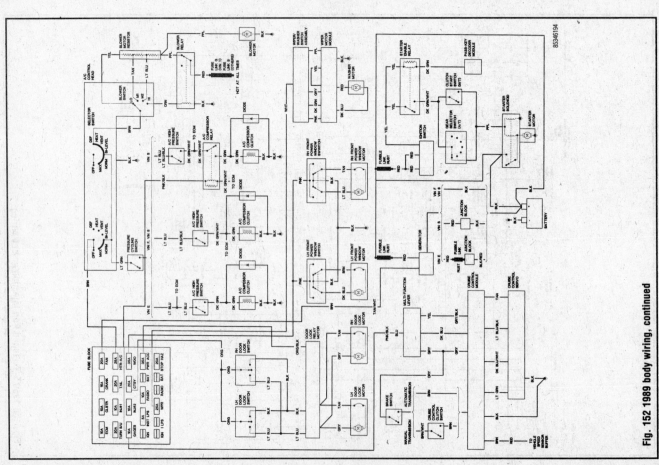

Fig. 152 1989 body wiring, continued

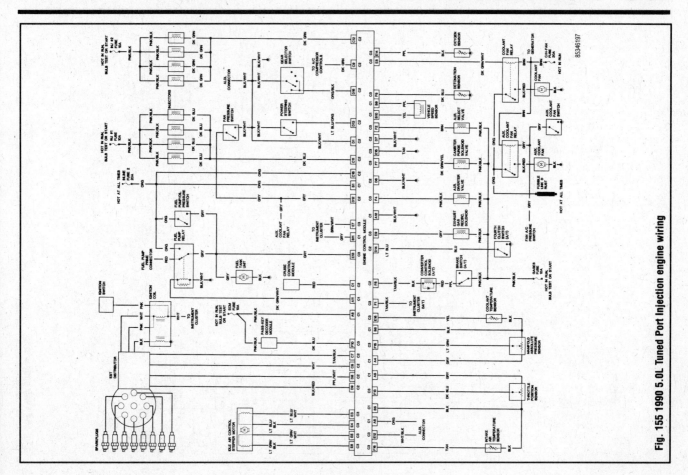

Fig. 155 1990 5.0L Tuned Port Injection engine wiring

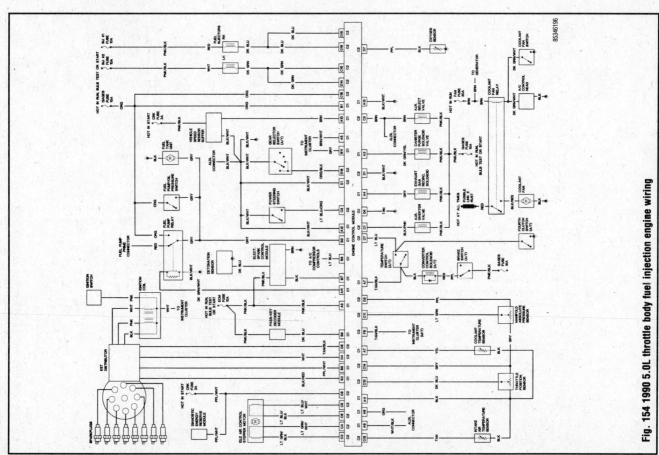

Fig. 154 1990 5.0L throttle body fuel injection engine wiring

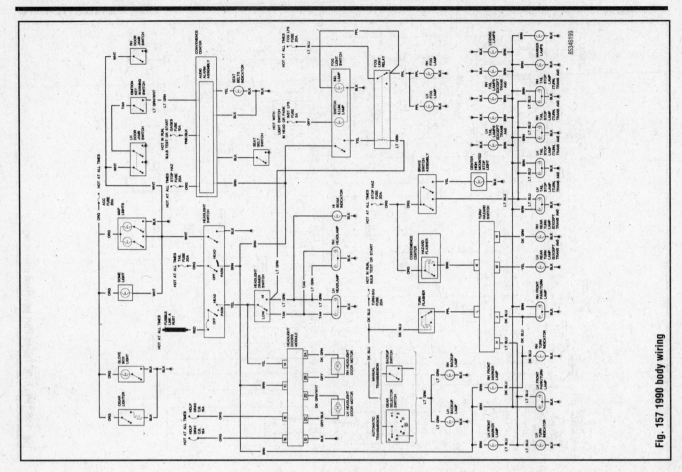

Fig. 157 1990 body wiring

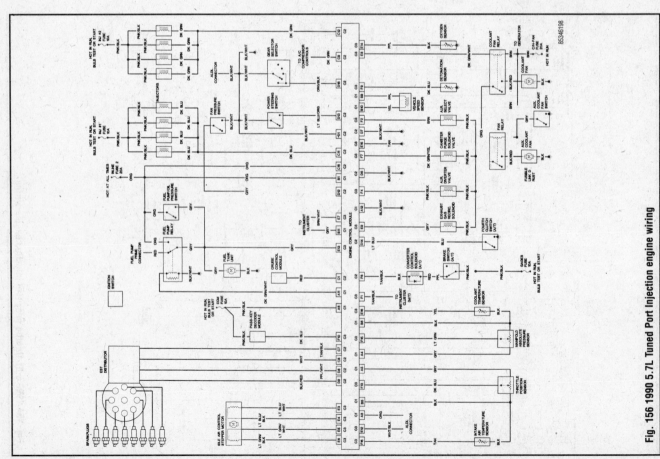

Fig. 156 1990 5.7L Tuned Port Injection engine wiring

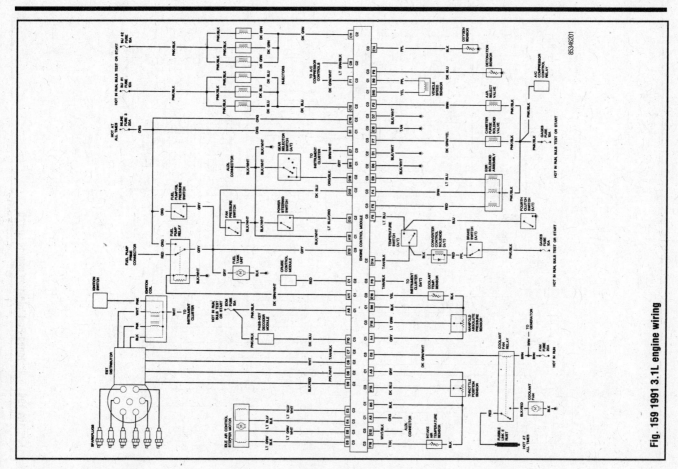

Fig. 159 1991 3.1L engine wiring

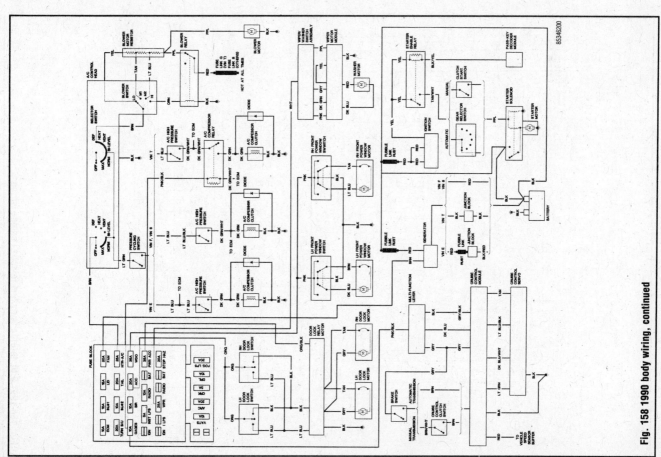

Fig. 158 1990 body wiring, continued

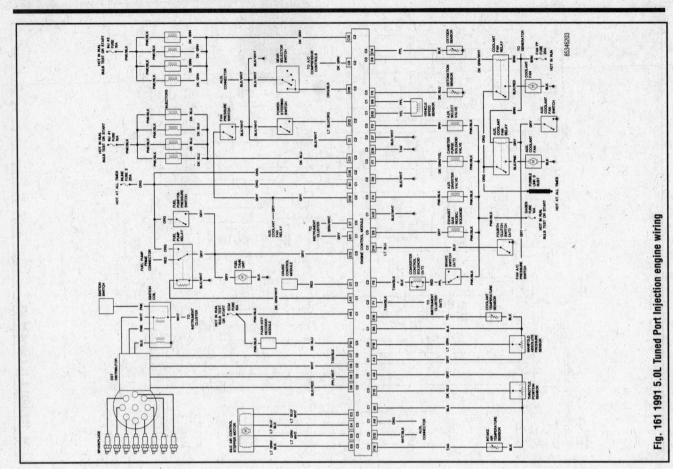

Fig. 161 1991 5.0L Tuned Port Injection engine wiring

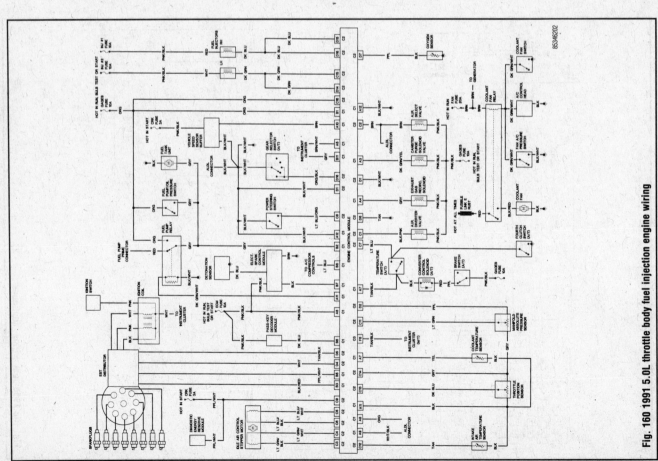

Fig. 160 1991 5.0L throttle body fuel injection engine wiring

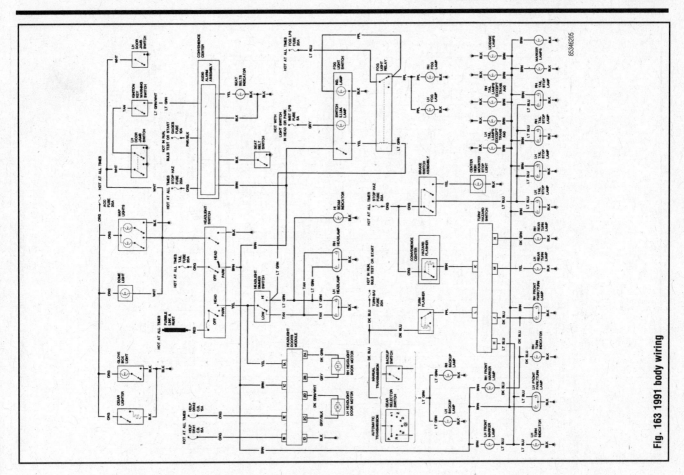

Fig. 163 1991 body wiring

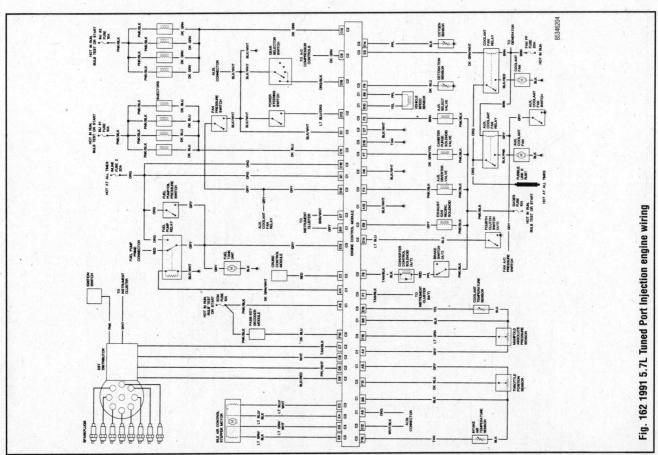

Fig. 162 1991 5.7L Tuned Port Injection engine wiring

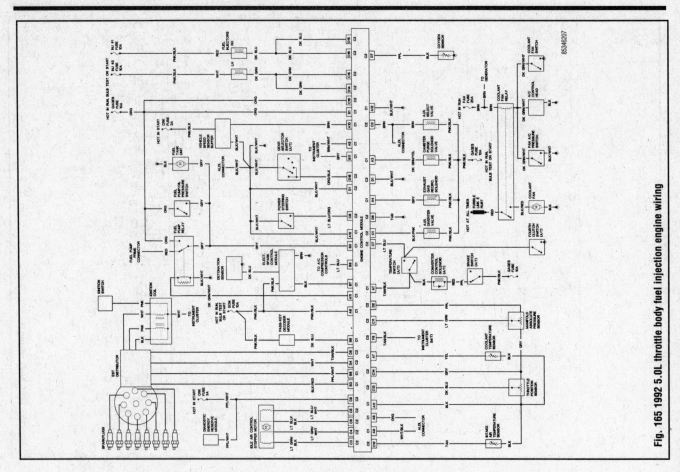

Fig. 165 1992 5.0L throttle body fuel injection engine wiring

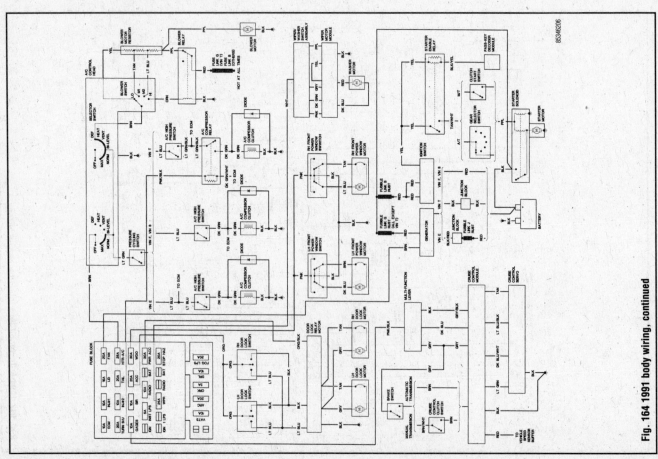

Fig. 164 1991 body wiring, continued

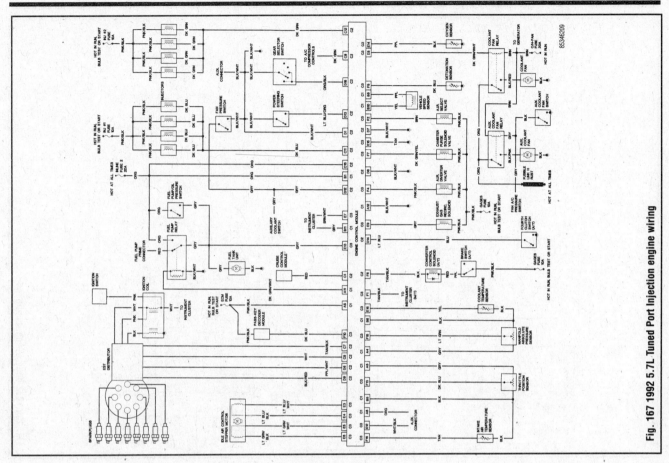

Fig. 167 1992 5.7L Tuned Port Injection engine wiring

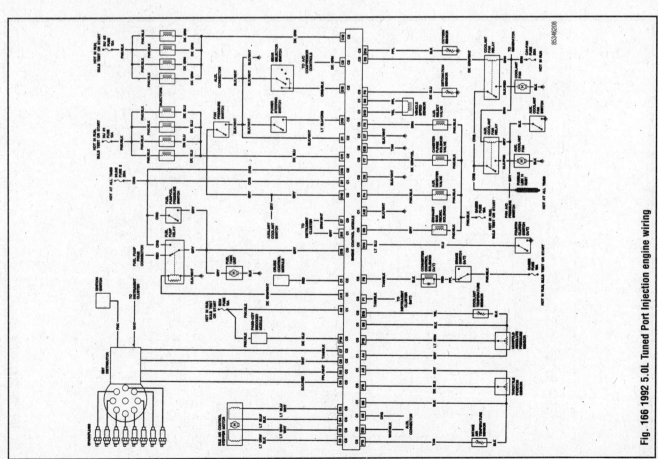

Fig. 166 1992 5.0L Tuned Port Injection engine wiring

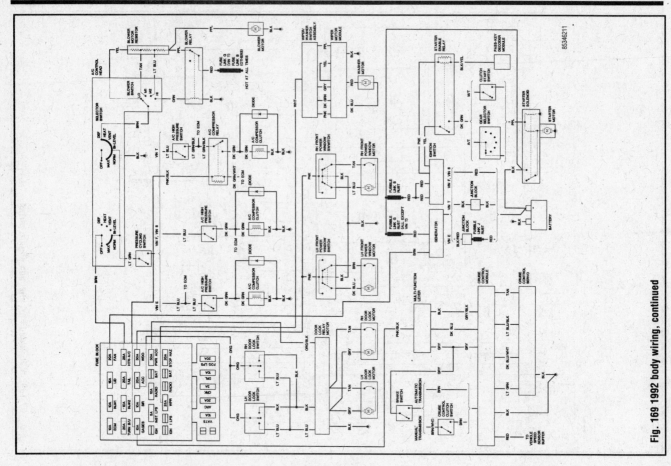

Fig. 169 1992 body wiring, continued

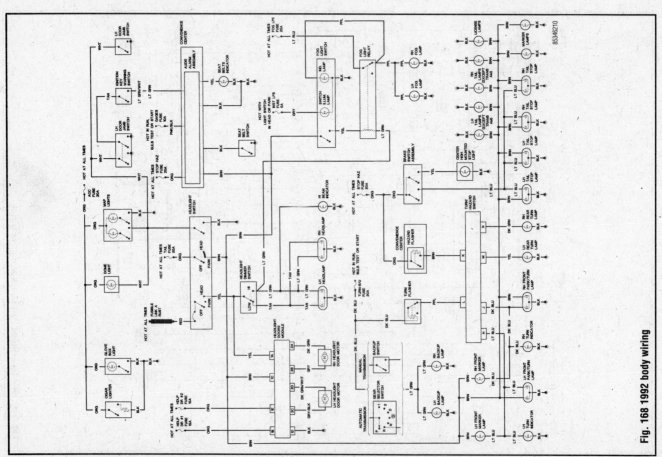

Fig. 168 1992 body wiring

7

DRIVE TRAIN

MANUAL TRANSMISSION

Understanding the Manual Transmission

Because of the way an internal combustion engine breathes, it can produce torque (or twisting force) only within a narrow speed range. Most overhead valve pushrod engines must turn at about 2500 rpm to produce their peak torque. Often by 4500 rpm, they are producing so little torque that continued increases in engine speed produce no power increases. The torque peak on overhead camshaft engines is, generally, much higher, but much narrower. The manual transmission and clutch are employed to vary the relationship between engine RPM and the speed of the wheels so that adequate power can be produced under all circumstances. The clutch allows engine torque to be applied to the transmission input shaft gradually, due to mechanical slippage. The vehicle can, consequently, be started smoothly from a full stop. The transmission changes the ratio between the rotating speeds of the engine and the wheels by the use of gears. 4-speed or 5-speed transmissions are most common. The lower gears allow full engine power to be applied to the rear wheels during acceleration at low speeds. The clutch driveplate is a thin disc, the center of which is splined to the transmission input shaft. Both sides of the disc are covered with a layer of material which is similar to brake lining and which is capable of allowing slippage without roughness or excessive noise. The clutch cover is bolted to the engine flywheel and incorporates a diaphragm spring which provides the pressure to engage the clutch. The cover also houses the pressure plate. When the clutch pedal is released, the driven disc is sandwiched between the pressure plate and the smooth surface of the flywheel, thus forcing the disc to turn at the same speed as the engine crankshaft. The transmission contains a mainshaft which passes all the way through the transmission, from the clutch to the driveshaft. This shaft is separated at one point, so that front and rear portions can turn at different speeds. Power is transmitted by a countershaft in the lower gears and reverse. The gears of the countershaft mesh with gears on the mainshaft, allowing power to be carried from one to the other. Countershaft gears are often integral with that shaft, while several of the mainshaft gears can either rotate independently of the shaft or be locked to it. Shifting from one gear to the next causes one of the gears to be freed from rotating with the shaft and locks another to it. Gears are locked and unlocked by internal dog clutches which slide between the center of the gear and the shaft. The forward gears usually employ synchronizers; friction members which smoothly bring gear and shaft to the same speed before the toothed dog clutches are engaged.

Adjustments

LINKAGE

4-Speed Transmission

▶ See Figure 1

➡ **All terms used in the following procedure match those which are used in the accompanying illustration. No linkage adjustment is possible on the 5-speed transmissions.**

1. Disconnect the negative battery cable at the battery.
2. Place the shift control lever (F) in Neutral.
3. Raise the vehicle and support it safely with jackstands.
4. Remove the swivel retainers (P) from the levers (E, H, and J).
5. Remove the swivels (S) from the shifter assembly (G), and loosen the swivel locknuts (R and T).
6. Make sure that levers L, M, and N are in their Neutral positions (center detents).
7. Align the holes of levers E, H, and J with the notch in the shifter assembly (G). Insert an alignment gauge (J–33195) to hold the levers in this position.
8. Insert swivel S into lever E and install washer Q. Secure with retainer P.
9. Apply rearward pressure (Z) to lever N. Tighten locknuts R and T (at the same time) against swivel S to 25 ft. lbs. (34 Nm).
10. Repeat steps 8 and 9 for rod D and levers J and M.
11. Repeat steps 8 and 9 for rod K and levers H and L.
12. Remove the alignment gauge, lower the vehicle, and check the operation of the shifting mechanism.
13. Reconnect the negative battery cable.

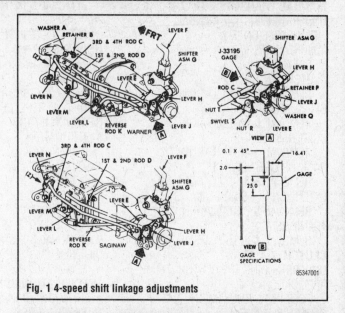

Fig. 1 4-speed shift linkage adjustments

Clutch Switch

REMOVAL & INSTALLATION

▶ See Figure 2

1. Disconnect the negative battery cable.
2. Remove the sound insulator on 1988–89 vehicles or the console trim plate on 1990–92 vehicles.
3. Unplug the clutch switch connector.
4. Remove the switch attaching bolt and remove the clutch switch.
5. Installation is the reverse of the removal procedure. The switch will automatically adjust when depressed for the first time.

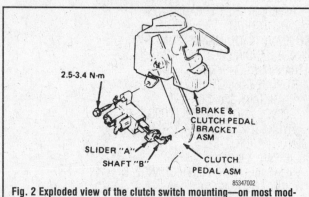

Fig. 2 Exploded view of the clutch switch mounting—on most models, the clutch switch adjusts automatically

Speed Sensor

REMOVAL & INSTALLATION

5-Speed Transmission

1. Disconnect the negative battery cable.
2. Disconnect the electrical connector.
3. Remove the attaching bolt and remove the sensor.
4. Installation is the reverse of the removal procedure. The bolt torque is 89 inch lbs. (10 Nm).

Shift Handle

REMOVAL & INSTALLATION

▶ **See Figure 3**

1. Disconnect the negative battery cable.
2. Raise and safely support the vehicle.
3. Disconnect the shift rods from the control lever.
4. Lower the vehicle. Remove the shifter knob.
5. Remove the parking lever grip.
6. Remove the console cover.
7. Remove the shifter boot.
8. Remove the shifter mounting bolts and remove the shifter assembly.
9. Installation is the reverse of the removal procedure. Adjust the linkage as detailed earlier.

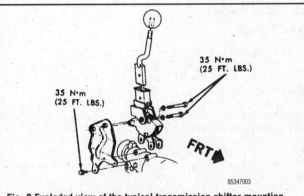

Fig. 3 Exploded view of the typical transmission shifter mounting

Back-up Light Switch

REMOVAL & INSTALLATION

1. Disconnect the negative battery terminal from the battery.
2. At the left-rear of the transmission, the back-up light switch is threaded into the transmission case. The speed sensor is held in with a separate bracket. Disconnect the electrical connector from the back-up light switch.
3. Remove the back-up light switch from the transmission.
4. To install, reverse the removal procedures. Coat the threads with Teflon® tape. Please refer to the torque chart for specifications. Place the gear shift lever in the reverse position and check that the back-up lights work.

Extension Housing Seal

REMOVAL & INSTALLATION

▶ **See Figure 4**

This seal controls transmission oil leakage around the driveshaft. Continued failure of this seal usually indicates a worn output shaft bushing. If so, there will be signs of the same wear on the driveshaft where it contacts the seal and bushing. The seal is available and is fairly simple to install, with the proper tool.

1. Raise and safely support the rear of the vehicle to minimize transmission oil loss when the driveshaft is removed.
2. Unbolt the driveshaft from the differential and center support bearing, if equipped. Wrap tape around the bearing cups to keep them in place on the universal joint and slide the shaft out of the transmission.
3. Use an small pry tool to carefully pry out the old seal. Be careful not to insert the tool too far into the housing or the bushing will be damaged.
4. Use an oil seal installation tool to evenly drive the new seal into the housing. Make sure the tool only contacts the outer metal portion of the seal.
5. Install the driveshaft. Torque the universal bearing cup retainer bolts to 15 ft. lbs. (20 Nm).

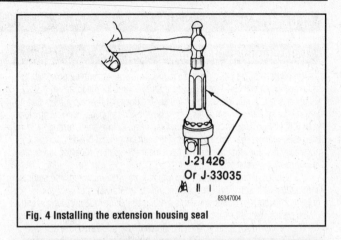

Fig. 4 Installing the extension housing seal

Transmission

REMOVAL & INSTALLATION

➡ **On 5-speed transmissions remove the shift lever boot and the shift lever prior to transmission removal.**

1. Disconnect the negative battery cable at the battery.
2. Raise the vehicle and support it safely with jackstands.
3. Drain the lubricant from the transmission.
4. Remove the torque arm from the vehicle as outlined under Rear Suspension in Section 8 of this manual.
5. Mark the driveshaft and the rear axle pinion flange to indicate their relationship. Unbolt the rear universal joint straps. Lower the rear of the driveshaft, being careful to keep the universal joint caps in place. Withdraw the driveshaft from the transmission and remove it from the vehicle.
6. Disconnect the speedometer cable and the electrical connectors from the transmission.
7. Remove the exhaust pipe brace.
8. Remove the transmission shifter support attaching bolts from the transmission.
9. On 4-speed transmissions only, disconnect the shift linkage at the shifter.
10. Raise the transmission slightly with a jack, then remove the crossmember attaching bolts.
11. Remove the transmission mount attaching bolts, then remove the mount and crossmember from the vehicle.
12. Remove the transmission attaching bolts, then with the aid of an assistant, move the transmission rearward and downward out of the vehicle.

To install:

13. Apply a light coating of high temperature grease to the main drive gear bearing retainer and to the splined portion of the main drive gear. This will assure free movement of the clutch and transmission components during assembly.
14. Install the transmission and secure with transmission mounting bolts Torque transmission-to-clutch housing bolts to 55 ft. lbs. (74 Nm).
15. Install the mount and crossmember into the vehicle, then install the transmission mount attaching bolts. Torque both the mount-to-crossmember bolts and the mount-to-transmission bolts to 35 ft. lbs. (47 Nm).
16. Install the crossmember attaching bolts. Torque the crossmember-to-body bolts to 35 ft. lbs.
17. On 4-speed transmissions only, connect the shift linkage at the shifter and adjust the shift linkage.
18. Install the transmission shifter support attaching bolts to the transmission. Torque shifter bracket-to-extension housing to 25 ft. lbs. (35 Nm).
19. Install the exhaust pipe brace.
20. Connect the speedometer cable and the electrical connectors to the transmission.
21. Install the driveshaft into the transmission. Then, align the marks on the driveshaft and the rear axle pinion flange. Bolt the rear universal joint straps.
22. Install the torque arm into the vehicle.
23. Fill the transmission with lubricant. Then install the filler plug and torque to 15 ft. lbs. (20 Nm).
24. Lower the vehicle.
25. Connect the negative battery cable at the battery.

CLUTCH

Understanding the Clutch

The purpose of the clutch is to disconnect and connect engine power at the transmission. A vehicle at rest requires a lot of engine torque to get all that weight moving. An internal combustion engine does not develop a high starting torque (unlike steam engines) so it must be allowed to operate without any load until it builds up enough torque to move the vehicle. To a point, torque increases with engine rpm. The clutch allows the engine to build up torque by physically disconnecting the engine from the transmission, relieving the engine of any load or resistance.

The transfer of engine power to the transmission (the load) must be smooth and gradual; if it weren't, drive line components would wear out or break quickly. This gradual power transfer is made possible by gradually releasing the clutch pedal. The clutch disc and pressure plate are the connecting link between the engine and transmission. When the clutch pedal is released, the disc and plate contact each other (the clutch is engaged) physically joining the engine and transmission. When the pedal is pushed in, the disc and plate separate (the clutch is disengaged) disconnecting the engine from the transmission.

Most clutch assemblies consists of the flywheel, the clutch disc, the clutch pressure plate, the throw out bearing and fork, the actuating linkage and the pedal. The flywheel and clutch pressure plate (driving members) are connected to the engine crankshaft and rotate with it. The clutch disc is located between the flywheel and pressure plate, and is splined to the transmission shaft. A driving member is one that is attached to the engine and transfers engine power to a driven member (clutch disc) on the transmission shaft. A driving member (pressure plate) rotates (drives) a driven member (clutch disc) on contact and, in so doing, turns the transmission shaft.

There is a circular diaphragm spring within the pressure plate cover (transmission side). In a relaxed state (when the clutch pedal is fully released) this spring is convex; that is, it is dished outward toward the transmission. Pushing in the clutch pedal actuates the attached linkage. Connected to the other end of this is the throw out fork, which hold the throw out bearing. When the clutch pedal is depressed, the clutch linkage pushes the fork and bearing forward to contact the diaphragm spring of the pressure plate. The outer edges of the spring are secured to the pressure plate and are pivoted on rings so that when the center of the spring is compressed by the throw out bearing, the outer edges bow outward and, by so doing, pull the pressure plate in the same direction — away from the clutch disc. This action separates the disc from the plate, disengaging the clutch and allowing the transmission to be shifted into another gear. A coil type clutch return spring attached to the clutch pedal arm permits full release of the pedal. Releasing the pedal pulls the throw out bearing away from the diaphragm spring resulting in a reversal of spring position. As bearing pressure is gradually released from the spring center, the outer edges of the spring bow outward, pushing the pressure plate into closer contact with the clutch disc. As the disc and plate move closer together, friction between the two increases and slippage is reduced until, when full spring pressure is applied (by fully releasing the pedal) the speed of the disc and plate are the same. This stops all slipping, creating a direct connection between the plate and disc which results in the transfer of power from the engine to the transmission. The clutch disc is now rotating with the pressure plate at engine speed and, because it is splined to the transmission shaft, the shaft now turns at the same engine speed.

The clutch is operating properly if:

1. It will stall the engine when released with the vehicle held stationary.
2. The shift lever can be moved freely between 1st and reverse gears when the vehicle is stationary and the clutch disengaged.

Application

All 1982–83 vehicles use a mechanical (non-hydraulic) clutch; 1984–92 models use a hydraulic clutch. With the hydraulic clutch, no adjustment of the clutch pedal or the linkage is required. On the mechanical type, the only required adjustment is to maintain the proper clutch pedal freeplay. The freeplay adjustment is very important, for it determines the engaging and disengaging characteristics of the clutch assembly.

The clutch assembly consists of: a flywheel, a pressure plate, a throwout bearing and fork, a clutch pedal, and an actuating lever (non-hydraulic) or a master cylinder/slave cylinder (hydraulic).

The hydraulic system utilizes a remote reservoir which is mounted to the power brake booster, a master cylinder mounted to the cowl panel and a slave cylinder that is mounted to the bell housing. The system is operated directly by the clutch pedal. When adding fluid to the reservoir, always use a type which meets DOT 3 specifications.

✳✳ CAUTION

The clutch driven disc contains asbestos, which has been determined to be a cancer causing agent. Never clean clutch surfaces with compressed air! Avoid inhaling any dust from any clutch surface! When cleaning clutch surfaces, use a commercially available brake cleaning fluid.

FREE-PLAY ADJUSTMENT

Mechanical Linkage

▶ See Figure 5

1. Disconnect the return spring at the clutch fork.
2. Hold the pedal against the rubber bumper on the dash brace.
3. Push the clutch fork so that the throwout bearing lightly contacts the pressure plate fingers.
4. Loosen the locknut and adjust the length of the rod so that the swivel or rod can slip freely into the gauge hole in the lever. Increase the length of the rod until all free-play is removed.
5. Remove the rod or swivel from the gauge hole and insert it in the other (original) hole on the lever. Install the retainer and tighten the locknut.
6. Install the return spring and check freeplay measurement at the pedal pad.

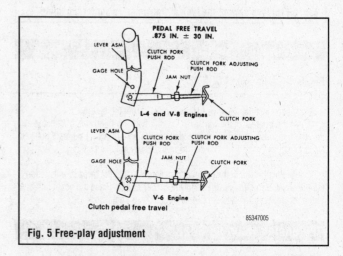

Fig. 5 Free-play adjustment

Clutch Pedal

REMOVAL & INSTALLATION

▶ See Figures 6 and 7

1. Disconnect the negative battery cable.
2. Disconnect the clutch return spring.
3. Remove the hush panel under the dash.
4. If equipped, remove the cruise control switch at the pedal.
5. Disconnect and remove the neutral start switch at the pedal.
6. Remove the turn signal and hazard warning flasher mounting bracket.
7. Disconnect the clutch pedal rod from the pedal.
8. Remove the clutch pedal pivot bolt far enough to permit removal of pedal assembly.
9. Clean all parts and relubricate. Install in reverse of removal.

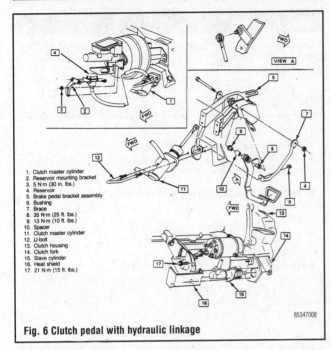

1. Clutch master cylinder
2. Reservoir mounting bracket
3. 5 N·m (30 in. lbs.)
4. Reservoir
5. Brake pedal bracket assembly
6. Bushing
7. Brace
8. 35 N·m (25 ft. lbs.)
9. 13 N·m (10 ft. lbs.)
10. Spacer
11. Clutch master cylinder
12. U-bolt
13. Clutch housing
14. Clutch fork
15. Slave cylinder
16. Heat shield
17. 21 N·m (15 ft. lbs.)

Fig. 6 Clutch pedal with hydraulic linkage

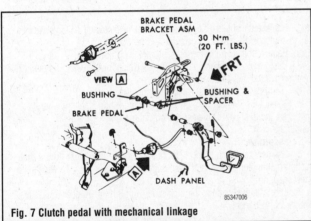

Fig. 7 Clutch pedal with mechanical linkage

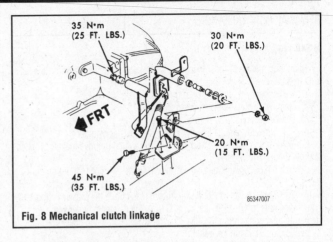

Fig. 8 Mechanical clutch linkage

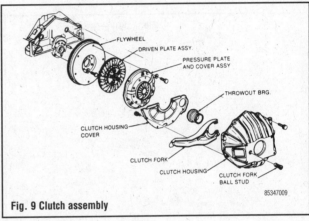

Fig. 9 Clutch assembly

Clutch Linkage

REMOVAL & INSTALLATION

⧫ **See Figure 8**

1. Disconnect the negative battery cable.
2. Disconnect the return spring and rods from the pedal and fork assembly.
3. Loosen the outboard ball stud nut and slide stud out of the bracket slot.
4. Move the cross shaft outboard, as required to clear inboard ball stud, then lift out from the vehicle.
5. Inspect the nylon bushing and anti-rattle O-ring for wear and replace as required.
6. Installation is the reverse of the removal procedure. Adjust linkage as previously outlined.

Driven Disc and Pressure Plate

REMOVAL & INSTALLATION

⧫ **See Figure 9**

1. Support engine and remove the transmission (as outlined in this section).
2. Disconnect the clutch fork push rod and spring.

3. Remove the flywheel housing.
4. Slide the clutch fork from the ball stud and remove the fork from the dust boot. The ball stud is threaded into the clutch housing and may be replaced, if necessary.
5. Install an alignment tool to support the clutch assembly during removal. Mark the flywheel and clutch cover for reinstallation, if they do not already have **X** marks.
6. Loosen the clutch-to-flywheel attaching bolts evenly, one turn at a time, until spring pressure is released. Remove the bolts and clutch assembly.

To install:

7. Clean the pressure plate and flywheel face.
8. Support the clutch disc and pressure plate with an alignment tool. The driven disc is installed with the damper springs on the transmission side.
9. Turn the clutch assembly until the mark on the cover lines up with the mark on the flywheel, then install the bolts. Tighten down evenly and gradually to avoid distortion.
10. Remove the alignment tool.
11. Lubricate the ball socket and fork fingers at the release bearing end with high melting point grease. Lubricate the recess on the inside of the throwout bearing and throwout fork groove with a light coat of graphite grease.
12. Install the clutch fork and dust boot into the housing. Install the throwout bearing to the throwout fork. Install the flywheel housing. Install the transmission.
13. Connect the fork push rod and spring. Lubricate the spring and pushrod ends.
14. Adjust the shift linkage and clutch pedal free-play.

Master Cylinder

➡**Before removing the hydraulic components for repair, remove the clutch housing dust cover to verify the malfunction. Measure the movement of the slave cylinder push rod by pushing the clutch pedal to the floor; the minimum movement should be 14mm. Do not replace the cylinder if its movement exceeds the minimum.**

REMOVAL & INSTALLATION

♦ **See Figure 10**

The clutch master cylinder is located in the engine compartment, on the left side of the firewall, above the steering column.

1. Disconnect negative battery terminal from the battery.
2. Remove hush panel from under the dash.
3. Disconnect push rod from clutch pedal.
4. Disconnect hydraulic line from the clutch master cylinder.
5. Remove the master cylinder-to-cowl brace nuts. Remove master cylinder and overhaul (if necessary).
6. Using a putty knife, clean the master cylinder and cowl mounting surfaces.
7. To install, reverse the removal procedures. Torque the master cylinder-to-cowl brace nuts to 10–15 ft. lbs. (14–20 Nm). Fill master cylinder with new hydraulic fluid conforming to DOT 3 specifications. Bleed and check the hydraulic clutch system for leaks.

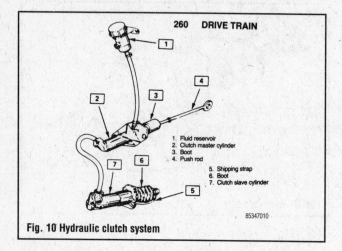

260   DRIVE TRAIN

1. Fluid reservoir
2. Clutch master cylinder
3. Boot
4. Push rod

5. Shipping strap
6. Boot
7. Clutch slave cylinder

85347010

Fig. 10 Hydraulic clutch system

OVERHAUL

1. Remove the filler cap and drain fluid from the master cylinder.
2. Remove the reservoir and seal from the master cylinder. Pull back the dust cover and remove the snapring.
3. Remove the push rod assembly. Using a block of wood, tap the master cylinder on it to eject the plunger assembly from the cylinder bore.
4. Remove the seal (carefully) from the front of the plunger assembly, ensuring no damage occurs to the plunger surfaces.
5. From the rear of the plunger assembly, remove the spring, the support, the seal and the shim.
6. Using clean brake fluid, clean all of the parts.
7. Inspect the cylinder bore and the plunger for ridges, pitting and/or scratches, the dust cover for wear and cracking; replace the parts if any of the conditions exist.

To assemble:

8. Use new seals, lubricate all of the parts in clean brake fluid, fit the plunger seal to the plunger and reverse the disassembly procedures.
9. Insert the plunger assembly, valve end leading into the cylinder bore (easing the entrance of the plunger seal).
10. Position the push rod assembly into the cylinder bore, then install a new snapring to retain the push rod. Install dust cover onto the master cylinder. Lubricate the inside of the dust cover with Girling® Rubber Grease or equivalent.

➡ **Be careful not to use any lubricant that will deteriorate rubber dust covers or seals.**

On vehicles equipped with a hydraulic clutch release mechanism, the slave cylinder is located on the left side of the bellhousing and controls the clutch release fork operation.

REMOVAL & INSTALLATION

1. Disconnect the negative battery cable.
2. Raise and safely support the front of the vehicle on jackstands.
3. Disconnect the hydraulic line from clutch master cylinder. Remove the line-to-chassis screw and the clip from the chassis.

➡ **Be sure to plug the line opening to keep dirt and moisture out of the system.**

4. Remove the slave cylinder-to-bellhousing nuts.
5. Remove the push rod and the slave cylinder from the vehicle, then overhaul it (if necessary).
6. To install, reverse the removal procedures. Lubricate leading end of the slave cylinder with Girling® Rubber Lube or equivalent. Torque the slave cylinder-to-bellhousing nuts to 10–15 ft. lbs. (14–20 Nm). Fill the master cylinder with new brake fluid conforming to DOT 3 specifications. Bleed the hydraulic system.

OVERHAUL

1. Remove the shield, the pushrod and the dust cover from the slave cylinder, then inspect the cover for damage or deterioration.
2. Remove the snapring form the end of the cylinder bore.
3. Using a block of wood, tap the slave cylinder on it to eject the plunger, then remove the seal and the spring.
4. Using clean brake fluid, clean all of the parts.
5. Inspect the cylinder bore and the plunger for ridges, pitting and/or scratches, the dust cover for wear and cracking; replace the parts if any of the conditions exist.

To assemble:

6. Use new seals and lubricate all of the parts in clean brake fluid. Install the spring, the plunger seal and the plunger into the cylinder bore, then install a new snapring.
7. Lubricate the inside of the dust cover with Girling® Rubber Grease or equivalent, then install it into the slave cylinder.

➡ **Be careful not to use any lubricant that will deteriorate rubber dust covers or seals.**

BLEEDING THE HYDRAULIC CLUTCH

Bleeding air from the hydraulic clutch system is necessary whenever any part of the system has been disconnected or the fluid level (in the reservoir) has been allowed to fall so low that air has been drawn into the master cylinder.

1. Fill master cylinder reservoir with new brake fluid conforming to DOT 3 specifications.
2. Raise and safely support the front of the vehicle on jackstands.
3. Fully depress clutch pedal and open the bleeder screw.
4. Close the bleeder screw and release clutch pedal.
5. Repeat the procedure until all of the air is evacuated from the system. Check and refill master cylinder reservoir as required to prevent air from being drawn through the master cylinder.

➡ **Never release a depressed clutch pedal with the bleeder screw open or air will be drawn into the system.**

AUTOMATIC TRANSMISSION

Understanding Automatic Transmissions

The automatic transmission allows engine torque and power to be transmitted to the rear wheels within a narrow range of engine operating speeds. It will allow the engine to turn fast enough to produce plenty of power and torque at very low speeds, while keeping it at a sensible rpm at high vehicle speeds (and it does this job without driver assistance). The transmission uses a light fluid as the medium for the transmission of power. This fluid also works in the operation of various hydraulic control circuits and as a lubricant. Because the transmission fluid performs all of these functions, trouble within the unit can easily travel from one part to another. For this reason, and because of the complexity and unusual operating principles of the transmission, a very sound understanding of the basic principles of operation will simplify troubleshooting.

TORQUE CONVERTER

♦ **See Figure 11**

The torque converter replaces the conventional clutch. It has three functions:
1. It allows the engine to idle with the vehicle at a standstill, even with the transmission in gear.
2. It allows the transmission to shift from range-to-range smoothly, without requiring that the driver close the throttle during the shift.
3. It multiplies engine torque to an increasing extent as vehicle speed drops and throttle opening is increased. This has the effect of making the transmission more responsive and reduces the amount of shifting required.

The torque converter is a metal case which is shaped like a sphere that has been flattened on opposite sides. It is bolted to the rear end of the engine's crankshaft. Generally, the entire metal case rotates at engine speed and serves as the engine's flywheel. The case contains three sets of blades. One set is attached directly to the case. This set forms the torus or pump. Another set is directly connected to the output shaft, and forms the turbine. The third set is mounted on a hub which, in turn, is mounted on a stationary shaft through a

one-way clutch. This third set is known as the stator. A pump, which is driven by the converter hub at engine speed, keeps the torque converter full of transmission fluid at all times. Fluid flows continuously through the unit to provide cooling. Under low speed acceleration, the torque converter functions as follows:

The torus is turning faster than the turbine. It picks up fluid at the center of the converter and, through centrifugal force, slings it outward. Since the outer edge of the converter moves faster than the portions at the center, the fluid picks up speed. The fluid then enters the outer edge of the turbine blades. It then travels back toward the center of the converter case along the turbine blades. In impinging upon the turbine blades, the fluid loses the energy picked up in the torus. If the fluid was now returned directly into the torus, both halves of the converter would have to turn at approximately the same speed at all times, and torque input and output would both be the same. In flowing through the torus and turbine, the fluid picks up two types of flow, or flow in two separate directions. It flows through the turbine blades, and it spins with the engine. The stator, whose blades are stationary when the vehicle is being accelerated at low speeds, converts one type of flow into another. Instead of allowing the fluid to flow straight back into the torus, the stator's curved blades turn the fluid almost 90° toward the direction of rotation of the engine. Thus the fluid does not flow as fast toward the torus, but is already spinning when the torus picks it up. This has the effect of allowing the torus to turn much faster than the turbine. This difference in speed may be compared to the difference in speed between the smaller and larger gears in any gear train. The result is that engine power output is higher, and engine torque is multiplied. As the speed of the turbine increases, the fluid spins faster and faster in the direction of engine rotation. As a result, the ability of the stator to redirect the fluid flow is reduced. Under cruising conditions, the stator is eventually forced to rotate on its one-way clutch in the direction of engine rotation. Under these conditions, the torque converter begins to behave almost like a solid shaft, with the torus and turbine speeds being almost equal.

PLANETARY GEARBOX

♦ **See Figures 12, 13 and 14**

The ability of the torque converter to multiply engine torque is limited. Also, the unit tends to be more efficient when the turbine is rotating at relatively high speeds. Therefore, a planetary gearbox is used to carry the power output of the turbine to the driveshaft.

Planetary gears function very similarly to conventional transmission gears. However, their construction is different in that three elements make up one gear system, and, in that all three elements are different from one another. The three elements are: an outer gear that is shaped like a hoop, with teeth cut into the inner surface; a sun gear, mounted on a shaft and located at the very center of the outer gear; and a set of three planet gears, held by pins in a ring-like planet carrier, meshing with both the sun gear and the outer gear. Either the outer gear or the sun gear may be held stationary, providing more than one possible torque multiplication factor for each set of gears. Also, if all three gears are forced to rotate at the same speed, the gearset forms, in effect, a solid shaft.

Most automatics use the planetary gears to provide various reductions ratios. Bands and clutches are used to hold various portions of the gearsets to the

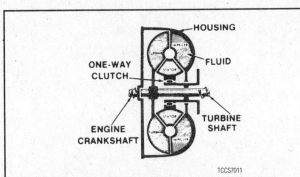

Fig. 11 The torque converter housing is rotated by the engine's crankshaft, and turns the impeller—The impeller then spins the turbine, which gives motion to the turbine shaft, driving the gears

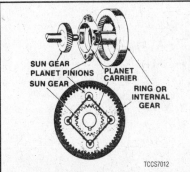

Fig. 12 Planetary gears work in a similar fashion to manual transmission gears, but are composed of three parts

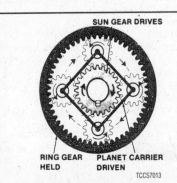

Fig. 13 Planetary gears in the maximum reduction (low) range. The ring gear is held and a lower gear ratio is obtained

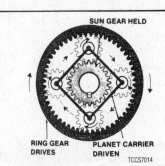

Fig. 14 Planetary gears in the minimum reduction (drive) range. The ring gear is allowed to revolve, providing a higher gear ratio

transmission case or to the shaft on which they are mounted. Shifting is accomplished, then, by changing the portion of each planetary gearset which is held to the transmission case or to the shaft.

SERVOS AND ACCUMULATORS

◆ See Figure 15

The servos are hydraulic pistons and cylinders. They resemble the hydraulic actuators used on many other machines, such as bulldozers. Hydraulic fluid enters the cylinder, under pressure, and forces the piston to move to engage the band or clutches.

The accumulators are used to cushion the engagement of the servos. The transmission fluid must pass through the accumulator on the way to the servo. The accumulator housing contains a thin piston which is sprung away from the discharge passage of the accumulator. When fluid passes through the accumulator on the way to the servo, it must move the piston against spring pressure, and this action smooths out the action of the servo.

TCCS7015

Fig. 15 Servos, operated by pressure, are used to apply or release the bands, to either hold the ring gear or allow it to rotate

HYDRAULIC CONTROL SYSTEM

The hydraulic pressure used to operate the servos comes from the main transmission oil pump. This fluid is channeled to the various servos through the shift valves. There is generally a manual shift valve which is operated by the transmission selector lever and an automatic shift valve for each automatic upshift the transmission provides.

➡**Many new transmissions are electronically controlled. On these models, electrical solenoids are used to better control the hydraulic fluid. Usually, the solenoids are regulated by an electronic control module.**

There are two pressures which affect the operation of these valves. One is the governor pressure which is effected by vehicle speed. The other is the modulator pressure which is effected by intake manifold vacuum or throttle position. Governor pressure rises with an increase in vehicle speed, and modulator pressure rises as the throttle is opened wider. By responding to these two pressures, the shift valves cause the upshift points to be delayed with increased throttle opening to make the best use of the engine's power output. Most transmissions also make use of an auxiliary circuit for downshifting. This circuit may be actuated by the throttle linkage the vacuum line which actuates the modulator, by a cable or by a solenoid. It applies pressure to a special downshift surface on the shift valve or valves. The transmission modulator also governs the line pressure, used to actuate the servos. In this way, the clutches and bands will be actuated with a force matching the torque output of the engine.

Identification

Two types of transmissions are used on the vehicles; Turbo Hydra-Matic 200C 3-speed and Turbo Hydra-Matic 700-R4 4-speed. Beginning in 1991, the 700-R4 was redesignated the 4L60.

Fluid Pan

REMOVAL, FLUID/FILTER CHANGE, & INSTALLATION

Refer to Section 1 for fluid pan procedures.

Adjustments

BANDS

There are no band adjustments possible or required.

SHIFT CONTROL CABLE

◆ See Figures 16 and 17

1. Place the control lever in **N**.
2. Raise the car and support it with jackstands.
3. Loosen the cable attachment at the shift lever.
4. Rotate the shift lever clockwise to the park detent and then back to neutral.
5. Tighten cable attachment to 11 ft. lbs. (15 Nm).

➡**The lever must be held out of P when tightening the nut.**

SHIFT LINKAGE

1. Place the manual shaft of the transmission in **N**. Place the console shift lever in **N**.
2. Install the cable in the slot of the shift lever. Adjust the cable so that the pin has free movement.
3. Install and tighten the nut to the pin.

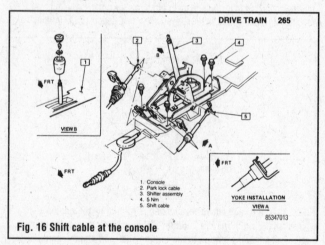

DRIVE TRAIN 265

1. Console
2. Park lock cable
3. Shifter assembly
4. 5 Nm
5. Shift cable

YOKE INSTALLATION
VIEW A

VIEW B

85347013

Fig. 16 Shift cable at the console

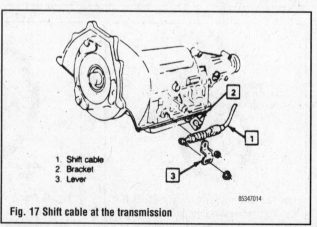

1. Shift cable
2. Bracket
3. Lever

85347014

Fig. 17 Shift cable at the transmission

THROTTLE VALVE CABLE

▶ **See Figures 18 and 19**

1. After installation of the cable to the transmission, engine bracket, and the cable actuating lever, check to assure that the cable slider is in the zero or fully re-adjusted position.

2. If cable slider is not in zero or fully re-adjusted, depress and hold the metal re-adjust tab. Move the slider back through the fitting in the direction away from the cable actuating lever until the slider stops against the fitting. Release the metal re-adjust tab.

3. Rotate the cable actuating lever to its full travel position.

4. The slider must move (ratchet) forward when the lever is rotated to the full travel position.

5. Release the lever.

Neutral Start/Back-Up Light Switch

REPLACEMENT & ADJUSTMENT

▶ **See Figure 20**

1. Remove the console trim from the console.

2. Disconnect the electrical connector from the switch.

3. Remove the 2 attaching screws from the switch and remove the switch.

4. To install a new switch:

   a. Place the switch onto the transmission control shifter and loosely install the attaching screws. Position the transmission control shifter assembly in the **N** notch in the detent plate.

   b. Assemble the switch to the transmission control shifter assembly by inserting the carrier tang into the hole in the shifter lever.

   c. Install the attaching screws and tighten.

   d. Move the transmission control shifter assembly out of **N** position. This will shear the switch internal plastic pin.

5. To install the original switch:

   a. Place the switch onto the transmission control shifter and loosely install the attaching screws. Position the transmission control shifter assembly in the **N** notch in the detent plate.

   b. Rotate the switch on the shifter assembly to align the service adjustment hole with the carrier tang hole. Insert a ³⁄₃₂ in. (2.38mm) diameter gauge pin to a depth of ⁷⁄₁₆ in. (15mm) and tighten attaching screws.

   c. Remove the gauge pin.

6. Connect the electrical connector to the switch.

7. Install the console trim to the console.

Park Lock Cable

REMOVAL & INSTALLATION

1982–83 Models

▶ **See Figure 21**

1. Remove the console and steering column covers. Remove cable retaining screw from the steering column slider and disconnect the cable.

2. At the shifter bracket, pull out the lock button on the cable housing and remove the yoke.

3. Disconnect the cable from the shifter.

To install:

4. Place the shifter lever in **P**. Rotate the steering column shift bowl to the **P** position and lock the column.

5. Connect the cable to the shifter.

6. Install the yoke and push in the lock button on the cable bracket.

7. Connect the cable and install cable retaining screw to the steering column slider.

8. Install the console and steering column covers.

1984–89 Models

▶ **See Figure 22**

1. Place the shifter lever in the **P** position. Remove the negative battery cable.

2. Turn the key to **RUN**. Release the cable from the inhibitor switch by inserting a screwdriver into the switch slot.

3. Push the cable lock button to the **UP** position and remove the cable from the park lever lock pin.

4. Depress the 2 cable connector latches at the shifter base and remove the cable. Remove the cable clips.

To install:

5. Place the shifter lever into the **P** position and the ignition key to the **RUN** position.

6. After installing the cable ends, push the cable connector nose toward the connector as far as possible and push down the lock button.

7. Complete the installation by reversing the removal procedure.

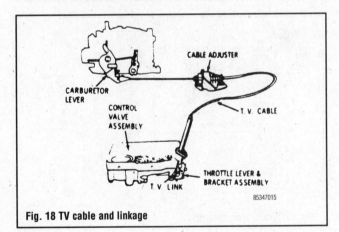

Fig. 18 TV cable and linkage

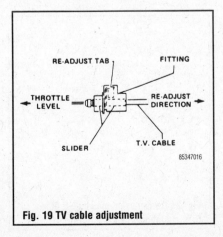

Fig. 19 TV cable adjustment

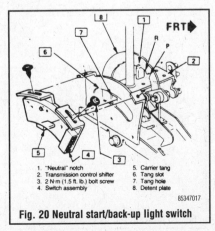

1. "Neutral" notch
2. Transmission control shifter
3. 2 N·m (1.5 ft. lb.) bolt screw
4. Switch assembly
5. Carrier tang
6. Tang slot
7. Tang hole
8. Detent plate

Fig. 20 Neutral start/back-up light switch

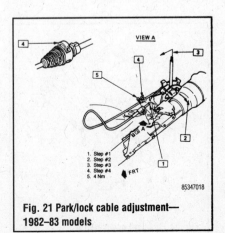

1. Step #1
2. Step #2
3. Step #3
4. Step #4
5. 4 N·m

Fig. 21 Park/lock cable adjustment— 1982–83 models

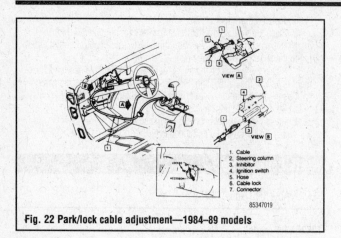

1. Cable
2. Steering column
3. Inhibitor
4. Ignition switch
5. Hose
6. Cable lock
7. Connector

85347019

Fig. 22 Park/lock cable adjustment—1984–89 models

1990–92 Models

1. Place the shifter lever in the **P** position. Remove the negative battery cable.
2. Turn the key to **RUN**.
3. Remove the left side instrument panel sound insulator and kick panels.
4. Remove the floor console.
5. Remove the cable nut and clip. Remove the cable from the bracket, move the button to the **UP** position and unsnap the cable end from the lever lock pin.
6. Lower the steering column. Remove the cable clips.

To install:

7. Place the shifter lever into the **P** position and the ignition key to the **RUN** position.
8. After installing the cable ends, push the cable connector nose toward the connector as far as possible and push down the lock button.
9. Complete the installation by reversing the removal procedure.

Extension Housing Seal (in Vehicle)

REMOVAL & INSTALLATION

This seal controls transmission oil leakage around the driveshaft. Continued failure of this seal usually indicates a worn output shaft bushing. If so, there will be signs of the same wear on the driveshaft where it contacts the seal and bushing. The seal is available and is fairly simple to install, with the proper tool.

1. Raise and safely support rear of the vehicle to minimize transmission oil loss when the driveshaft is removed.
2. Unbolt the driveshaft from the differential and center support bearing, if equipped. Wrap tape around the bearing cups to keep them in place on the universal joint and slide the shaft out of the transmission.
3. Use a small pry tool to carefully pry out the old seal. Be careful not to insert the tool too far into the housing or the bushing will be damaged.
4. Use an oil seal installation tool to evenly drive the new seal into the housing. Make sure the tool only contacts the outer metal portion of the seal.

5. Install the driveshaft. Torque the universal bearing cup retainer bolts to 15 ft. lbs. (20 Nm). Recheck fluid level.

Transmission

REMOVAL & INSTALLATION

▶ **See Figures 23 thru 28**

1. Disconnect the negative battery cable at the battery.
2. Remove the air cleaner assembly.
3. Disconnect the throttle valve (TV) control cable at the carburetor.
4. Remove the transmission oil dipstick. Unbolt and remove the dipstick tube.
5. Raise the vehicle and support it safely with jackstands.

➡ **In order to provide adequate clearance for transmission removal, it may be necessary to raise both the front and the rear of the vehicle.**

6. Mark the relationship between the driveshaft and the rear pinion flange so that the driveshaft may be reinstalled in its original position.
7. Unbolt the universal joint straps from the pinion flange (use care to keep the universal joint caps in place), lower and remove the driveshaft from the vehicle. Place a transmission tailshaft plug or rag in place of the driveshaft to keep the transmission fluid from draining out.
8. Disconnect the catalytic converter support bracket at the transmission.
9. Disconnect the speedometer cable, electrical connectors and the shift control cable from the transmission.

✳ CAUTION

During the next step, rear spring force will cause the torque arm to move toward the floor pan. When disconnecting the arm from the transmission, carefully place a piece of wood between the floor pan and the torque arm. This will prevent possible personal injury and/or floor pan damage.

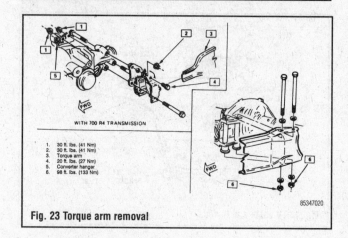

WITH 700 R4 TRANSMISSION

1. 30 ft. lbs. (41 Nm)
2. 30 ft. lbs. (41 Nm)
3. Torque arm
4. 20 ft. lbs. (27 Nm)
5. Converter hanger
6. 98 ft. lbs. (133 Nm)

85347020

Fig. 23 Torque arm removal

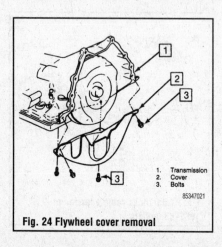

1. Transmission
2. Cover
3. Bolts

85347021

Fig. 24 Flywheel cover removal

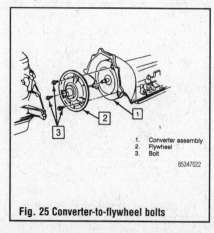

1. Converter assembly
2. Flywheel
3. Bolt

85347022

Fig. 25 Converter-to-flywheel bolts

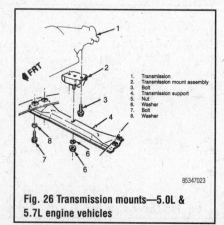

1. Transmission
2. Transmission mount assembly
3. Bolt
4. Transmission support
5. Nut
6. Washer
7. Bolt
8. Washer

85347023

Fig. 26 Transmission mounts—5.0L & 5.7L engine vehicles

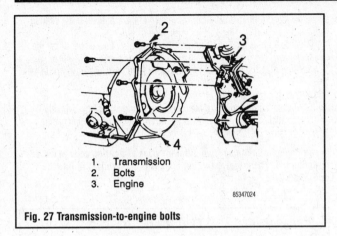

1. Transmission
2. Bolts
3. Engine

85347024

Fig. 27 Transmission-to-engine bolts

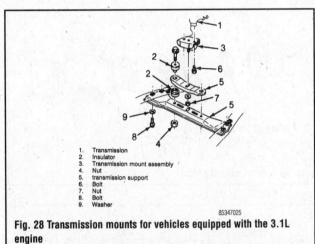

1. Transmission
2. Insulator
3. Transmission mount assembly
4. Nut
5. transmission support
6. Bolt
7. Nut
8. Bolt
9. Washer

85347025

Fig. 28 Transmission mounts for vehicles equipped with the 3.1L engine

10. Remove the torque arm-to-transmission bolts.
11. Remove the flywheel cover, then mark the relationship between the torque converter and the flywheel so that these parts may be reassembled in the same relationship.

12. Remove the torque converter-to-flywheel attaching bolts.
13. Support the transmission with a jack, then remove the transmission mount bolt.
14. Unbolt and remove the transmission crossmember.
15. Lower the transmission slightly. Disconnect the throttle valve cable and oil cooler lines from the transmission.
16. Support the engine using GM special tool BT–6424 or its equivalent. Remove the transmission-to-engine mounting bolts.

✳✳ CAUTION

The transmission must be secured to the transmission jack.

17. Remove the transmission from the vehicle. Be careful not to damage the oil cooler lines, throttle valve cable, or the shift control cable. Also, keep the rear of the transmission lower than the front to avoid the possibility of the torque converter disengaging from the transmission.

To install:
18. Position the transmission and converter into place.
19. Install the transmission-to-engine mounting bolts.
20. Connect the throttle valve cable and oil cooler lines to the transmission.
21. Install the transmission crossmember and secure with bolts.
22. Install the transmission mount bolt.
23. Matchmark the torque converter-to-flywheel. Install the torque converter-to-flywheel attaching bolts.

➡Before installing the converter-to-flywheel bolts, be sure that the weld nuts on the converter are flush with the flywheel, and that the converter rotates freely by hand in this position.

24. Install the flywheel cover.
25. Install the torque arm-to-transmission bolts.
26. Connect the speedometer cable, electrical connectors and the shift control cable from the transmission.
27. Connect the catalytic converter support bracket at the transmission.
28. Align the matchmark made earlier, then install the driveshaft to the axle pinion. Bolt the universal joint straps to the pinion flange.
29. Lower the vehicle.
30. Install the dipstick tube using a new dipstick tube O-ring and secure with the bolt. Install the transmission oil dipstick.
31. Connect the throttle valve (TV) control cable at the carburetor.
32. Install the air cleaner assembly.
33. Connect the negative battery cable at the battery.

DRIVELINE

Driveshaft and U-Joints

The U-joint is secured to the yoke in one of two ways. Dana and Cleveland shafts use a conventional snapring to hold each bearing cup in the yoke. The snapring fits into a groove located in each yoke end just on top of each bearing cup. The Saginaw design shaft secures its U-joints in another way. Nylon material is injected through a small hole in the yoke and flows along a circular groove between the U-joint and the yoke, creating a synthetic snapring. Disassembly of the Saginaw U-joint requires the joint to be pressed from the yoke. This results in damage to the bearing cups and destruction of the nylon rings.

Replacement kits include new bearing cups and conventional snaprings to replace the original nylon rings. These replacement rings must go inboard of the yoke in contrast to outboard mounting of the Dana and Cleveland designs. Previous service to the Saginaw U-joints can be recognized by the presence of snaprings inboard of the yoke.

Bad U-joints, requiring replacement, will produce a clunking sound when the car is put into gear. This is due to worn needle bearings or a scored trunnion end possibly caused by improper lubrication during assembly. Camaro U-joints require no periodic maintenance and therefore have no lubrication fittings.

Driveshaft

REMOVAL & INSTALLATION

◆ **See Figure 29**

1. Raise the vehicle and safely support it on jackstands. Paint a reference line from the rear end of the driveshaft to the companion flange so that they can be reassembled in the same position.
2. Disconnect the rear universal joint by removing the U-bolts, retaining straps, or the flange bolts.
3. To prevent loss of the needle bearings, tape the bearing caps to the trunnion.
4. Remove the driveshaft from the transmission by sliding it rearward.

➡Do not be alarmed by oil leakage at the transmission output shaft. This oil is there to lubricate the splines of the front yoke.

To install:
5. Check the yoke seal in the transmission case extension and replace it if necessary. See the transmission section for replacement procedures.

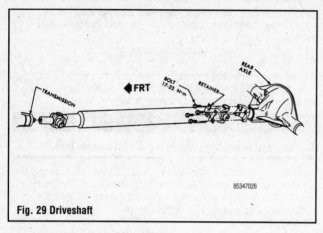

Fig. 29 Driveshaft

6. Position the driveshaft and insert the front yoke into the transmission so the splines mesh with the transmission shaft splines.

7. Using reference marks made during removal, align the driveshaft with the companion flange and secure it with U-bolts or, retaining straps.

U-JOINT REPLACEMENT

♦ **See Figures 30, 31, 32, 33 and 34**

1. Support the driveshaft horizontally in line with the base plate of a press.

2. Place the U-joint so the lower ear of the shaft yoke is supported on a 1⅛ in. (29mm) socket.

3. Remove the lower bearing cap out of the yoke ear by placing tool J–9522–3 or equivalent, on the open horizontal bearing caps and pressing the lower bearing cap out of the yoke ear.

➡ **This will shear the nylon injector ring, if the original U-joint is being removed. There are no bearing retaining grooves in the production bearing caps, therefore they cannot be reused. If a replacement U-joint is being removed, be sure to remove the retaining clips from the U-joint.**

4. If the bearing cap is not completely removed, lift tool J–9522–3 and insert tool J–9522–5 or equivalent between the bearing cap and seal, then continue pressing the U-joint out of the yoke.

5. Repeat the procedure for the opposite side.

6. Remove the spider from the yoke.

To install:

7. Install 1 bearing cap part way into 1 side of the yoke. Turn this yoke ear to the bottom.

8. Using tool J–9522–3 or equivalent, seat the trunnion into the bearing cap.

9. Install the opposite bearing cap partially onto the trunnion.

10. Ensure both trunnions are straight and true in the bearing caps.

11. Press the spider against the opposite bearing cap, while working the

spider back and forth to ensure free movement of the trunnions in the bearing caps.

12. If trunnion is binding, the needle bearings have tipped over under the end of the cap.

13. Stop pressing when 1 bearing cap clears the retainer groove inside the yoke.

14. Install a retaining ring.

15. Repeat the procedure for the remaining bearing caps and U-joints.

16. Installation of the driveshaft is the reverse of the removal procedure. Tighten the strap bolts to 16 ft. lbs. (22 Nm).

➡ **The Saginaw shaft uses two different sizes of bearing cups at the differential end. The larger cups (the ones with the groove) fit into the driveshaft yoke.**

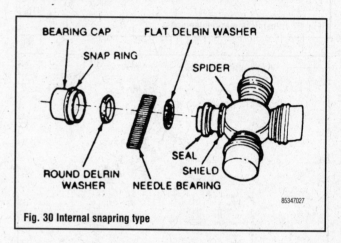

Fig. 30 Internal snapring type

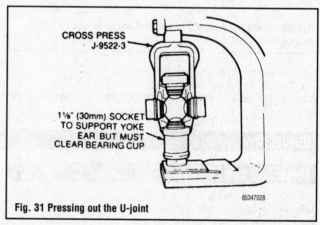

Fig. 31 Pressing out the U-joint

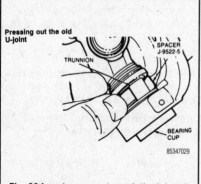

Fig. 32 Insert a spacer to push the joint all the way out

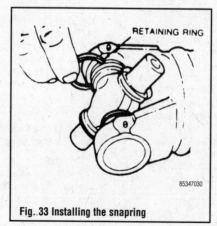

Fig. 33 Installing the snapring

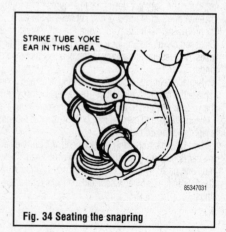

Fig. 34 Seating the snapring

REAR AXLE

Identification

▶ **See Figure 35**

The rear axle code and the manufacturers code, plus the date built, is stamped on the forward side of the right axle tube. Any reports made on the rear axle assemblies must include the full code letters and the date built numbers. The Limited-slip differentials are identified by a tag attached to the lower right section of the axle.

Determining Axle Ratio

An axle ratio is obtained by dividing the number of teeth on the drive pinion gear into the number of teeth on the ring gear. For instance, on a 4.11 ratio, the driveshaft will turn 4.11 times for every turn of the rear wheel.

The most accurate way to determine the axle ratio is to drain the differential, remove the cover, and count the number of teeth on the ring and pinion.

An easier method is to jack and support the car so that both rear wheels are off the ground. Make a chalk mark on the rear wheel and the driveshaft. Block the front wheels and put the transmission in Neutral. Turn the rear wheel one complete revolution and count the number of turns made by the driveshaft. The number of driveshaft rotations is the axle ratio. More accuracy can be obtained by going more than one tire revolution and dividing the result by the number of tire rotations.

The axle ratio is also identified by the axle serial number prefix on the axle; the axle ratios are listed in dealer's parts books according to prefix number. Some axles have a tag on the cover.

Axle Shaft, Bearing and Seal

Axle shafts are the last link in the chain of components working to transmit engine power to the rear wheels. The splined end of each shaft meshes with the internal splines of each differential side gear. As the side gears turn, so do the axle shafts, and, since they are also connected, so do the wheels.

Each shaft passes through the side gear and is locked into place by either a C-lock or flange plate bolted to the end of the axle housing with pressed on bearings. As the name implies, the C-lock is a flat, C-shaped piece of metal that fits into a groove at the end of the shaft. A round pinion shaft is wedged in between the end of the shafts. This pinion shaft prevents the shafts from sliding inward and makes the C-locks functional by pushing them tightly against each side gear. Removing this pinion shaft allows the shafts to slide inward making the C-locks accessible for removal. Once the C-locks are removed, the axle shafts can be pulled from the car.

The wheel end of each shaft is flanged and pressed into it are five wheel lug bolts serving to hold on the wheel. Each axle shaft is supported by an axle bearing (wheel bearing) and oil seal located within the axle shaft housing just to the outside of the brake backing plate.

REMOVAL & INSTALLATION

Except Borg-Warner Rear Assembly

▶ **See Figures 36 thru 45**

1. Raise and support the vehicle safely. Remove the rear wheels and drums or rotors.
2. Remove the carrier cover and drain the gear oil into a suitable container.
3. Remove the rear axle pinion shaft lock screw. Remove the rear axle pinion shaft.
4. Push the flanged end of the axle shaft into the axle housing and remove the C-clip from the opposite end of the shaft.
5. Remove the axle shaft from the axle housing.
6. Using a suitable tool, remove the oil seal from the axle housing. Be careful not to damage the housing.

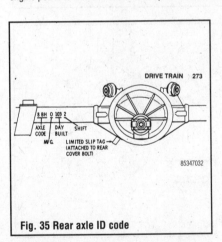

Fig. 35 Rear axle ID code

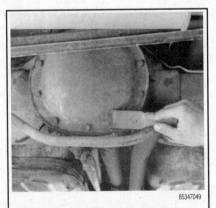
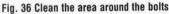

Fig. 36 Clean the area around the bolts

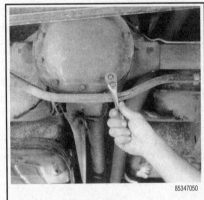

Fig. 37 Bolt removal

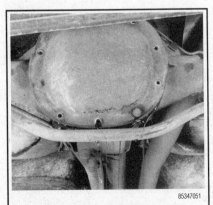

Fig. 38 The fluid will begin to seep out

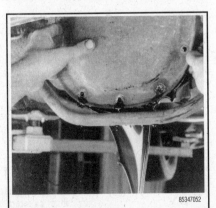

Fig. 39 Pry the cover away

Fig. 40 Cover removal

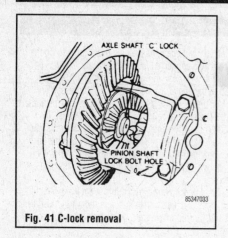

Fig. 41 C-lock removal

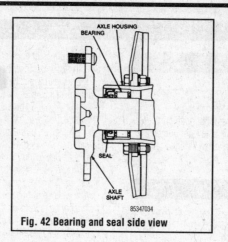

Fig. 42 Bearing and seal side view

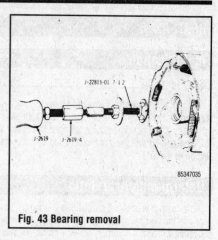

Fig. 43 Bearing removal

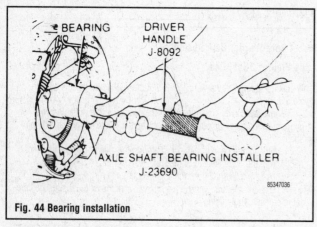

Fig. 44 Bearing installation

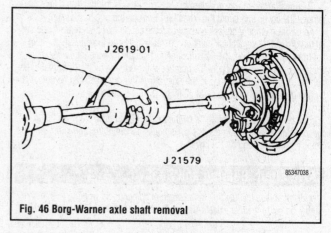

Fig. 46 Borg-Warner axle shaft removal

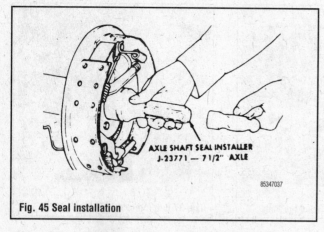

Fig. 45 Seal installation

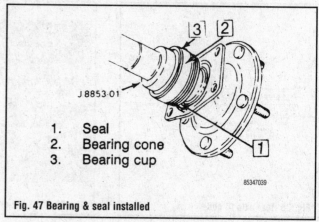

1. Seal
2. Bearing cone
3. Bearing cup

Fig. 47 Bearing & seal installed

7. Install tool J–22813–01 or equivalent, into the bore of the axle housing and position it behind the bearing, ensure the tangs of the tool engage the outer race. Remove the bearing using a slide hammer.

8. Installation is the reverse of the removal procedure. Lubricate the new bearing and sealing lips with gear lube before installing. Tighten the pinion gear shaft lock screw to 27 ft. lbs. (36 Nm). Tighten the carrier cover bolts to 22 ft. lbs. (30 Nm).

Borg-Warner Rear Assembly

♦ See Figures 46 and 47

➡The Borg-Warner axle assembly can be quickly identified by checking the axle code. The Borg-Warner axle numbers are 4EW, 4EU and 4ET on 1988 vehicles, BET, BEU and BEW on 1989 vehicles and 9EQ and 9ER on 1990 vehicles.

1. Raise the vehicle and support is safely.

2. Remove the rear wheels and drums or rotors. Remove the brake components as required.

3. Remove the 4 nuts attaching the brake anchor plate and outer bearing retainer to the axle housing.

4. Remove the axle shaft and wheel bearing assembly using axle shaft removal tool J–21595 and slide hammer J–2619 or equivalent.

5. To remove the inner bearing retainer and the bearing from the axle shaft, split the retainer with a chisel, then remove it from the shaft. Using tool J–22912–01, press the bearing off the shaft.

6. Installation is the reverse of the removal procedure. Make sure the axle seal is installed with the spring side facing the center of the axle. Tighten the backing plate bolts to 36 ft. lbs. (49 Nm).

➡There are right (black banded) and left (gold banded) axle seals and they cannot be interchanged.

Pinion Seal

REMOVAL & INSTALLATION

Except Borg-Warner Rear Axle

♦ **See Figures 48, 49 and 50**

1. Raise and safely support the vehicle.
2. Remove both rear wheel and tire assemblies.
3. Matchmark the driveshaft and pinion yoke so they may be reassembled in the same position. Remove the driveshaft.
4. Using a suitable punch, mark the position of the pinion yoke, pinion shaft and nut so proper reinstallation preload can be maintained.
5. Using a suitable tool, hold the pinion flange in place, then remove the pinion flange nut and washer.
6. Place a container under the differential to catch any fluid that may drain from the rear axle. Using a suitable tool, remove the pinion yoke.
7. Use a suitable tool to remove the pinion seal.

To install:

8. Inspect the sealing surfaces of the pinion yoke for nicks or damage and replace, as necessary. Examine the carrier bore and remove any burrs that may cause leaks around the outside of the seal.
9. Install the seal using a suitable installer.
10. Apply a seal lubricant to the outer diameter of the pinion flange and the sealing lip of the new seal.
11. Install the pinion yoke on the drive pinion by taping with a soft-face hammer until a few pinion threads project through the pinion yoke.
12. Install the washer and pinion flange nut. While holding the pinion yoke, tighten the nut to the same position as marked earlier, then tighten an additional ¹⁄₁₆ in. (1.6mm) turn beyond the marks.
13. Install the driveshaft.
14. Install the rear wheels and tires. Check and add the correct lubricant, as necessary.

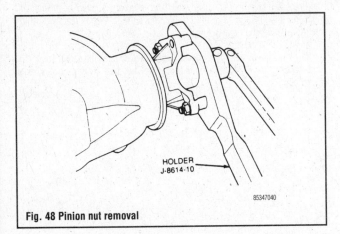

Fig. 48 Pinion nut removal

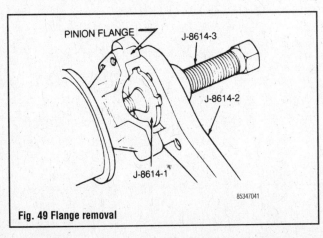

Fig. 49 Flange removal

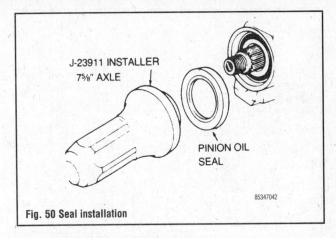

Fig. 50 Seal installation

Borg-Warner Rear Axle

1. Raise and safely support the vehicle.
2. Remove both rear wheel and tire assemblies.
3. Matchmark the driveshaft and pinion yoke so they may be reassembled in the same position. Remove the driveshaft.
4. Using a beam-type inch pound torque wrench on the pinion yoke nut, measure and record the amount of pinion bearing, axle bearings and seal preload. Turn the torque wrench smoothly for several rotations and record the amount of preload as the assembly is turning, not the initial force required to start the assembly moving.

➡ **Preload is measured as the amount of torque required to turn the assembly.**

5. Using a suitable tool to hold the pinion yoke in place, remove the pinion yoke nut and washer.
6. Place a suitable container under the differential to catch any fluid that may drain from the rear axle. Using a suitable tool, remove the pinion flange.
7. Use a suitable tool to remove the pinion seal.

To install:

8. Inspect the seal surface of the pinion flange for tool marks, nicks or damage and replace, as necessary. Examine the carrier bore and remove any burrs that might cause leaks around the outside of the seal.
9. Install the seal 0.010 in. (0.25mm) below the flange surface using a suitable seal installer.
10. Apply suitable seal lubricant to the outer diameter of the pinion flange and the sealing lip of the new seal.
11. Install the pinion flange on the drive pinion by taping with a soft hammer until a few pinion threads project through the pinion flange.
12. Install the washer and pinion flange nut. While holding the pinion flange, tighten the nut a little at a time and turn the drive pinion several revolutions after each tightening, to set the bearing rollers. Check the preload each time with a suitable inch pound torque wrench until the preload is 5 inch lbs. (0.6 Nm) more then the reading obtained during disassembly.
13. Install the driveshaft.
14. Install the rear wheels and tires. Check and add the correct lubricant, as necessary.

Axle Housing

REMOVAL & INSTALLATION

♦ **See Figure 51**

1. Raise the vehicle and support it safely. Be sure that the rear axle assembly is supported safely.
2. Disconnect shock absorbers from axle. Remove the wheel assemblies.
3. Mark driveshaft and pinion flange, then disconnect driveshaft and support out of the way.
4. Remove brake line junction block bolt at axle housing. If necessary, disconnect the brake lines at the junction block.
5. Disconnect the upper control arms from the axle housing.

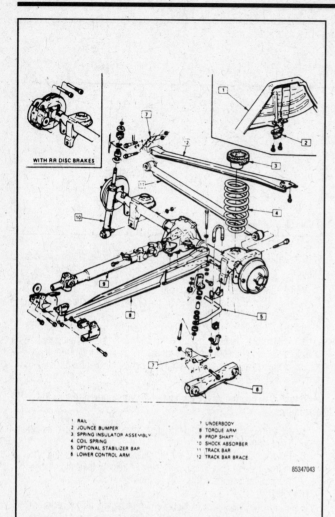

WITH RR DISC BRAKES

1	RAIL	7	UNDERBODY
2	JOUNCE BUMPER	8	TORQUE ARM
3	SPRING INSULATOR ASSEMBLY	9	PROP SHAFT
4	COIL SPRING	10	SHOCK ABSORBER
5	OPTIONAL STABILIZER BAR	11	TRACK BAR
6	LOWER CONTROL ARM	12	TRACK BAR BRACE

85347043

Fig. 51 Exploded view of the rear axle and rear suspension component mounting

6. Lower the rear axle assembly. Remove the springs.

7. Continue lowering the rear axle assembly and remove it from the vehicle.

To install:

8. Position the rear axle assembly into place and install the springs.

9. Connect the upper control arms to the axle housing.

10. Install the brake line junction block bolt at the axle housing. Connect any brake lines that were disconnected.

11. Install and secure the driveshaft aligning the match marks made earlier.

12. Connect the shock absorbers to the axle and install the wheel assemblies.

13. Lower the vehicle and replace any lost rear axle fluid.

Differential Assembly

REMOVAL & INSTALLATION

1. Raise and safely support the vehicle.

2. Place a suitable container under the differential. Remove the carrier cover and drain the gear oil.

3. Remove the drive axles.

4. Mark the differential bearing caps **L** and **R** to make sure they will be reassembled in their original location.

5. Using a suitable tool, remove the differential carrier. Be careful not to damage the gasket sealing surface when removing the unit. Place the right and left bearing outer races of the side bearing assemblies and shims in sets with the marked differential bearings caps so they can be reinstalled in their original positions.

To install:

6. Inspect the differential carrier housing for foreign material. Check the ring and pinion for chipped teeth, excessive wear and scoring. Check the carrier bearings visually and by feel. Clean the differential housing and replace components, as necessary.

7. Install the differential carrier. Check the carrier bearing preload along with the ring and pinion backlash, then adjust, as necessary. Tighten the differential bearing cap bolts to 55 ft. lbs. (75 Nm) except on Borg-Warner rear axles which are tightened to 40 ft. lbs. (54 Nm).

8. Install the axles.

9. Install the carrier cover using a new gasket. Tighten the carrier cover bolts to 20 ft. lbs. (27 Nm). Add the proper type and quantity of gear oil to axle assembly.

AUTOMATIC TRANSMISSION TORQUE SPECIFICATIONS

Component	U.S.	Metric
200C		
Control valve-to-case	9-12 ft. lbs.	13-17 Nm
Converter housing lower cover	84 inch lbs.	10 Nm
Converter-to-flex plate	35 ft. lbs.	47 Nm
Cooler line connectors	26-30 ft. lbs.	35-40 Nm
Final drive-to-transmission	30 ft. lbs.	41 Nm
Governor pressure switch	5-10 ft. lbs.	7-14 Nm
Oil pan-to-case	10-13 ft. lbs.	14-18 Nm
Oil screen-to-case	9-12 ft. lbs.	13-17 Nm
Park bracket-to-case	15-20 ft. lbs.	20-27 Nm
Pump cover-to-body	15-20 ft. lbs.	20-27 Nm
Pump-to-case	15-20 ft. lbs.	20-27 Nm
Solenoid-to-pump	24-48 inch lbs.	3-5 Nm
Speedometer gear retainer	6-10 ft. lbs.	8-14 Nm
Throttle lever link	9-12 ft. lbs.	13-17 Nm
Transmission-to-engine	35 ft. lbs.	47 Nm
700-R4 (4L60)		
Control valve-to-case	9-12 ft. lbs.	13-17 Nm
Converter housing lower cover	84 inch lbs.	10 Nm
Converter-to-flex plate	35 ft. lbs.	47 Nm
Cooler line connectors	26-30 ft. lbs.	35-40 Nm
Final drive-to-transmission	30 ft. lbs.	41 Nm
Governor pressure switch	5-10 ft. lbs.	7-14 Nm
Oil pan-to-case	10-13 ft. lbs.	14-18 Nm
Oil screen-to-case	9-12 ft. lbs.	13-17 Nm
Park bracket-to-case	15-20 ft. lbs.	20-27 Nm
Pump cover-to-body	15-20 ft. lbs.	20-27 Nm
Pump-to-case	15-20 ft. lbs.	20-27 Nm
Solenoid-to-pump	24-48 inch lbs.	3-5 Nm
Speedometer gear retainer	6-10 ft. lbs.	8-14 Nm
Throttle lever link	9-12 ft. lbs.	13-17 Nm
Transmission-to-engine	35 ft. lbs.	47 Nm

8347C99

MANUAL TRANSMISSION TORQUE SPECIFICATIONS

Component	U.S.	Metric
76mm 4-speed		
Cover-to-case	15 ft. lbs.	20 Nm
Crossmember-to-frame	35 ft. lbs.	50 Nm
Drive gear retainer	15 ft. lbs.	20 Nm
Extension housing bolts	45 ft. lbs.	60 Nm
Filler plug	15 ft. lbs.	20 Nm
Mount-to-crossmember	35 ft. lbs.	50 Nm
Mount-to-transmission	35 ft. lbs.	50 Nm
Shift lever-to-shifter shaft	25 ft. lbs.	30 Nm
Transmission-to-clutch housing	55 ft. lbs.	75 Nm
77mm 4-speed		
Cover-to-case	10-13 ft. lbs.	50 Nm
Crossmember-to-frame	35 ft. lbs.	40 Nm
Damper	30 ft. lbs.	20 Nm
Drive gear retainer	15 ft. lbs.	30 Nm
Extension housing bolts	25 ft. lbs.	27 Nm
Filler plug	20 ft. lbs.	20 Nm
Front bearing retainer	5 ft. lbs.	50 Nm
Mount-to-crossmember	35 ft. lbs.	40 Nm
Mount-to-transmission	30 ft. lbs.	27 Nm
Reverse pivot bolt	20 ft. lbs.	30 Nm
Shift lever-to-shifter shaft	25 ft. lbs.	30 Nm
Transmission-to-engine	30 ft. lbs.	40 Nm
77mm 5-speed		
Back-up switch	28 ft. lbs.	38 Nm
Cover-to-case	10 ft. lbs.	13 Nm
Crossmember-to-frame	35 ft. lbs.	50 Nm
Damper	30 ft. lbs.	40 Nm
Drive gear retainer	15 ft. lbs.	20 Nm
Extension housing bolts	20 ft. lbs.	30 Nm
Filler plug	15 ft. lbs.	20 Nm
Front bearing retainer	15 ft. lbs.	20 Nm
Mount-to-crossmember	30 ft. lbs.	50 Nm
Mount-to-transmission	30 ft. lbs.	40 Nm
Reverse lockout	13 ft. lbs.	18 Nm
Reverse pivot bolt	20 ft. lbs.	27 Nm
Shift lever-to-shifter shaft	20 ft. lbs.	30 Nm
Speed sensor	89 inch lbs.	10 Nm
Transmission-to-engine	30 ft. lbs.	40 Nm
83mm 4-speed		
Cover-to-case	15 ft. lbs.	20 Nm
Crossmember-to-frame	35 ft. lbs.	50 Nm
Drive gear retainer	18 ft. lbs.	25 Nm
Extension housing bolts	40 ft. lbs.	55 Nm
Extension housing-to-rear retainer	25 ft. lbs.	35 Nm
Filler plug	15 ft. lbs.	20 Nm
Mount-to-crossmember	35 ft. lbs.	50 Nm
Mount-to-transmission	35 ft. lbs.	50 Nm
Rear bearing retainer	25 ft. lbs.	35 Nm
Shift lever-to-shifter shaft	25 ft. lbs.	25 Nm
Side cover	18 ft. lbs.	25 Nm
Transmission-to-clutch housing	55 ft. lbs.	75 Nm

8347998B

CLUTCH TORQUE SPECIFICATIONS

Component	U.S.	Metric
Clutch housing-to-engine	55 ft. lbs.	75 Nm
Clutch reservoir bracket	30 inch lbs.	5 Nm
Heat shield	15 ft. lbs.	21 Nm
Master cylinder-to-firewall	10 ft. lbs.	13 Nm
Neutral start switch	26 inch lbs.	3 Nm
Pedal-to-bracket	25 ft. lbs.	35 Nm
Pressure plate-to-flywheel		
4-cyl.	68 ft. lbs.	92 Nm
V6	50 ft. lbs.	70 Nm
V8	60 ft. lbs.	81 Nm
Slave cylinder-to-clutch housing	15 ft. lbs.	21 Nm
Starter-to-clutch housing	30 ft. lbs.	41 Nm

8534799A

MANUAL TRANSMISSION TORQUE SPECIFICATIONS

Component	U.S.	Metric
85mm 6-speed		
Back-up switch	15 ft. lbs.	20 Nm
Cover-to-case	15 ft. lbs.	20 Nm
Crossmember-to-frame	35 ft. lbs.	50 Nm
Drive gear retainer	18 ft. lbs.	25 Nm
Extension housing-to-case	40 ft. lbs.	55 Nm
Extension housing-to-rear retainer	25 ft. lbs.	35 Nm
Filler plug	15 ft. lbs.	20 Nm
Mount-to-crossmember	35 ft. lbs.	50 Nm
Mount-to-transmission	35 ft. lbs.	50 Nm
Rear bearing retainer	25 ft. lbs.	35 Nm
Reverse lockout	13 ft. lbs.	18 Nm
Shift lever-to-shifter shaft	18 ft. lbs.	25 Nm
Side cover	18 ft. lbs.	25 Nm
Speed sensor	89 inch lbs.	10 Nm
Transmission-to-clutch housing	26 ft. lbs.	75 Nm
Borg-Warner T5 5-speed		
Back-up switch	15 ft. lbs.	20 Nm
Cover-to-case	115 inch lbs.	13 Nm
Crossmember-to-frame	35 ft. lbs.	50 Nm
Drive gear retainer	18 ft. lbs.	25 Nm
Extension housing-to-case	22 ft. lbs.	30 Nm
Filler plug	20 ft. lbs.	27 Nm
Front bearing retainer	15 ft. lbs.	20 Nm
Mount-to-crossmember	35 ft. lbs.	50 Nm
Mount-to-transmission	40 ft. lbs.	54 Nm
Rear bearing retainer	25 ft. lbs.	35 Nm
Reverse lockout	13 ft. lbs.	18 Nm
Shift lever-to-shifter shaft	18 ft. lbs.	25 Nm
Side cover	18 ft. lbs.	25 Nm
Speed sensor	89 inch lbs.	10 Nm
Transmission-to-clutch housing	26 ft. lbs.	75 Nm
Borg-Warner T56 6-speed		
Adapter plate-to-transmission	26 ft. lbs.	35 Nm
Back-up switch	20 ft. lbs.	27 Nm
Cover-to-case	15 ft. lbs.	20 Nm
Crossmember-to-frame	35 ft. lbs.	50 Nm
Drive gear retainer	18 ft. lbs.	25 Nm
Extension housing-to-case	26 ft. lbs.	35 Nm
Extension housing-to-rear retainer	25 ft. lbs.	35 Nm
Filler plug	20 ft. lbs.	27 Nm
Mount-to-crossmember	35 ft. lbs.	50 Nm
Mount-to-transmission	35 ft. lbs.	50 Nm
Rear bearing retainer	25 ft. lbs.	35 Nm
Reverse lockout	13 ft. lbs.	18 Nm
Shift lever	15 ft. lbs.	20 Nm
Side cover	18 ft. lbs.	25 Nm
Speed sensor	89 inch lbs.	10 Nm

85347C

REAR DRIVE AXLE TORQUE SPECIFICATIONS

Component	U.S.	Metric
7.625 inch axle		
Brake backing plate bolts	35 ft. lbs.	48 Nm
Differential bearing cap bolts	60 ft. lbs.	81 Nm
Differential cover bolts	30 ft. lbs.	41 Nm
Differential ring gear bolts ①	90 ft. lbs.	120 Nm
Filler plug	20 ft. lbs.	27 Nm
Pinion lockbolt	20 ft. lbs.	27 Nm
7.5 inch axle		
Brake backing plate bolts	35 ft. lbs.	48 Nm
Differential bearing cap bolts	60 ft. lbs.	81 Nm
Differential cover bolts	30 ft. lbs.	41 Nm
Differential ring gear bolts ①		
1982–83	80 ft. lbs.	108 Nm
1984–85	90 ft. lbs.	120 Nm
Filler plug	20 ft. lbs.	27 Nm
Pinion lockbolt	20 ft. lbs.	27 Nm
7.75 inch axle		
Axle shaft retainer nuts	31 ft. lbs.	40 Nm
Back-up switch	35 ft. lbs.	48 Nm
Brake backing plate bolts	10 ft. lbs.	14 Nm
Breather	40 ft. lbs.	52 Nm
Differential bearing cap bolts	29 ft. lbs.	38 Nm
Differential case half bolts	20 ft. lbs.	26 Nm
Differential cover bolts	101 ft. lbs.	131 Nm
Differential ring gear bolts ①	20 ft. lbs.	27 Nm
Filler plug		

① Use thread locking compound

85347990D

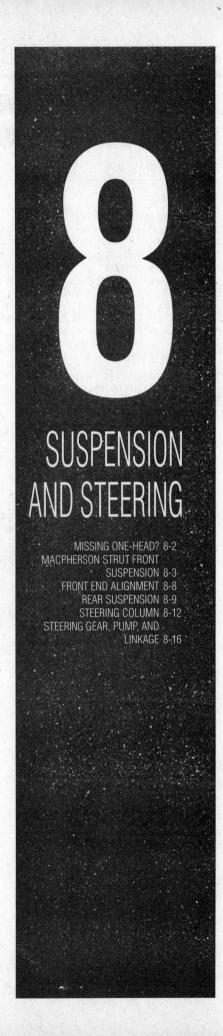

8

SUSPENSION AND STEERING

WHEELS

Wheel Assembly

REMOVAL & INSTALLATION

◆ See Figure 1

1. Park the vehicle on a level surface.
2. Remove the jack, tire iron and, if necessary, the spare tire from their storage compartments.
3. Check the owner's manual or refer to Section 1 of this manual for the jacking points on your vehicle. Then, place the jack in the proper position.
4. If equipped with lug nut trim caps, remove them by either unscrewing or pulling them off the lug nuts, as appropriate. Consult the owner's manual, if necessary.
5. If equipped with a wheel cover or hub cap, insert the tapered end of the tire iron in the groove and pry off the cover.
6. Apply the parking brake and block the diagonally opposite wheel with a wheel chock or two.

➡**Wheel chocks may be purchased at your local auto parts store, or a block of wood cut into wedges may be used. If possible, keep one or two of the chocks in your tire storage compartment, in case any of the tires has to be removed on the side of the road.**

7. If equipped with an automatic transmission, place the selector lever in **P** or Park; with a manual transmission, place the shifter in Reverse.
8. With the tires still on the ground, use the tire iron/wrench to break the lug nuts loose.

➡**If a nut is stuck, never use heat to loosen it or damage to the wheel and bearings may occur. If the nuts are seized, one or two heavy hammer blows directly on the end of the bolt usually loosens the rust. Be careful, as continued pounding will likely damage the brake drum or rotor.**

9. Using the jack, raise the vehicle until the tire is clear of the ground. Support the vehicle safely using jackstands.
10. Remove the lug nuts, then remove the tire and wheel assembly.

To install:

11. Make sure the wheel and hub mating surfaces, as well as the wheel lug studs, are clean and free of all foreign material. Always remove rust from the wheel mounting surface and the brake rotor or drum. Failure to do so may cause the lug nuts to loosen in service.
12. Install the tire and wheel assembly and hand-tighten the lug nuts.
13. Using the tire wrench, tighten all the lug nuts, in a crisscross pattern, until they are snug.
14. Raise the vehicle and withdraw the jackstand, then lower the vehicle.
15. Using a torque wrench, tighten the lug nuts in a crisscross pattern to 100 ft. lbs. (140 Nm) for 1982–85 vehicles with aluminum wheels, 80 ft. lbs. (110 Nm) for 1982–85 vehicles with steel wheels, 80 ft. lbs. (110 Nm) for 1986–91 vehicles or 100 ft. lbs. (140 Nm) for 1992 vehicles. Check your owner's manual or refer to Section 1 of this manual for the proper tightening sequence.

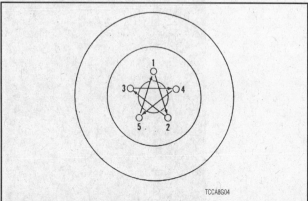

Fig. 1 Typical wheel lug tightening sequence

TCCA8G04

Do not overtighten the lug nuts, as this may cause the wheel studs to stretch or the brake disc (rotor) to warp.

16. If so equipped, install the wheel cover or hub cap. Make sure the valve stem protrudes through the proper opening before tapping the wheel cover into position.
17. If equipped, install the lug nut trim caps by pushing them or screwing them on, as applicable.
18. Remove the jack from under the vehicle, and place the jack and tire iron/wrench in their storage compartments. Remove the wheel chock(s).
19. If you have removed a flat or damaged tire, place it in the storage compartment of the vehicle and take it to your local repair station to have it fixed or replaced as soon as possible.

INSPECTION

Inspect the tires for lacerations, puncture marks, nails and other sharp objects. Repair or replace as necessary. Also check the tires for treadwear and air pressure as outlined in Check the wheel assemblies for dents, cracks, rust and metal fatigue. Repair or replace as necessary.

Wheel Lug Studs

REMOVAL & INSTALLATION

With Disc Brakes

◆ See Figures 2, 3 and 4

1. Raise and support the appropriate end of the vehicle safely using jackstands, then remove the wheel.
2. Remove the brake pads and caliper. Support the caliper aside using wire or a coat hanger. For details, please refer to Section 9 of this manual.
3. Remove the outer wheel bearing and lift off the rotor. For details on wheel bearing removal, installation and adjustment, please refer to Section 1 of this manual.
4. Properly support the rotor using press bars, then drive the stud out using an arbor press.

➡**If a press is not available, CAREFULLY drive the old stud out using a blunt drift. MAKE SURE the rotor is properly and evenly supported or it may be damaged.**

To install:

5. Clean the stud hole with a wire brush and start the new stud with a hammer and drift pin. Do not use any lubricant or thread sealer.
6. Finish installing the stud with the press.

➡**If a press is not available, start the lug stud through the bore in the hub, then position about 4 flat washers over the stud and thread the lug nut. Hold the hub/rotor while tightening the lug nut, and the stud should be drawn into position. MAKE SURE THE STUD IS FULLY SEATED, then remove the lug nut and washers.**

7. Install the rotor and adjust the wheel bearings.
8. Install the brake caliper and pads.
9. Install the wheel, then remove the jackstands and carefully lower the vehicle.
10. Tighten the lug nuts to the proper torque.

With Drum Brakes

◆ See Figures 5, 6 and 7

1. Raise the vehicle and safely support it with jackstands, then remove the wheel.
2. Remove the brake drum.
3. If necessary to provide clearance, remove the brake shoes, as outlined in Section 9 of this manual.

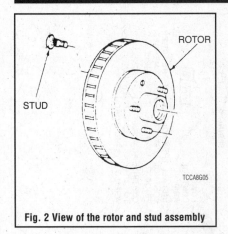

Fig. 2 View of the rotor and stud assembly

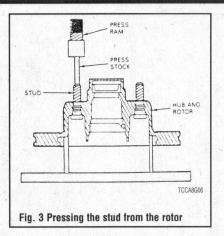

Fig. 3 Pressing the stud from the rotor

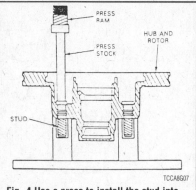

Fig. 4 Use a press to install the stud into the rotor

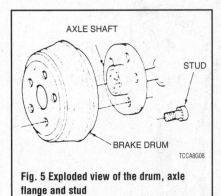

Fig. 5 Exploded view of the drum, axle flange and stud

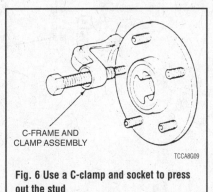

Fig. 6 Use a C-clamp and socket to press out the stud

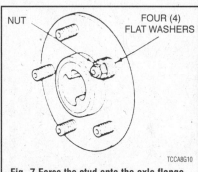

Fig. 7 Force the stud onto the axle flange using washers and a lug nut

4. Using a large C-clamp and socket, press the stud from the axle flange.
5. Coat the serrated part of the stud with liquid soap and place it into the hole.

To install:

6. Position about 4 flat washers over the stud and thread the lug nut. Hold the flange while tightening the lug nut, and the stud should be drawn into position. MAKE SURE THE STUD IS FULLY SEATED, then remove the lug nut and washers.

7. If applicable, install the brake shoes.
8. Install the brake drum.
9. Install the wheel, then remove the jackstands and carefully lower the vehicle.
10. Tighten the lug nuts to the proper torque.

MACPHERSON STRUT FRONT SUSPENSION

▶ See Figure 8

1982–92 Camaros are equipped with a front suspension consisting of a pivoting lower control arm on which are mounted a coil spring and a MacPherson strut. The strut and spring are separate. The spring upper end bears on a fixed crossmember; the strut upper end is located in a strut tower on the fender.

Coil Springs

REMOVAL & INSTALLATION

▶ See Figure 9

1. Raise the front of the vehicle and support it on jackstands.
2. Remove the road wheel(s).
3. Disconnect the stabilizer link from the lower control arm.
4. If the steering gear hinders removal procedures, detach the unit and move it out of the way.
5. Disconnect the tie rod from the steering knuckle using a ball joint remover.
6. Using an internal fit coil spring compressor, compress the coil spring so that it is loose in its seat.

✳ CAUTION

Be sure to follow manufacturer's instructions when using spring compressor. Coil springs in a compressed state contain enormous energy which, if released accidentally, could cause serious injury.

7. To remove the coil spring, disconnect the lower control arm from the crossmember at the pivot bolts. If additional clearance is necessary, disconnect the lower control arm from the steering knuckle at the ball joint.

To install:

8. Compress the coil spring until spring height is the same as when removed, then position the spring on the control arm. Make sure the lower end of the coil spring is properly positioned in the lower control arm and that the upper end fits correctly in its pad.
9. Connect the lower control arm from the steering knuckle at the ball joint. Connect the lower control arm from the crossmember at the pivot bolts and install the coil spring.
10. Connect the tie rod to the steering knuckle.
11. Attach the steering gear unit.
12. Connect the stabilizer link to the lower control arm.
13. Install the wheel(s).
14. Lower the vehicle.

Struts

REMOVAL & INSTALLATION

▶ See Figures 10, 11, 12 and 13

1. Place the ignition key in the unlocked position so that the front wheels can be moved.
2. From inside the engine compartment, remove the upper strut to upper mount nut.

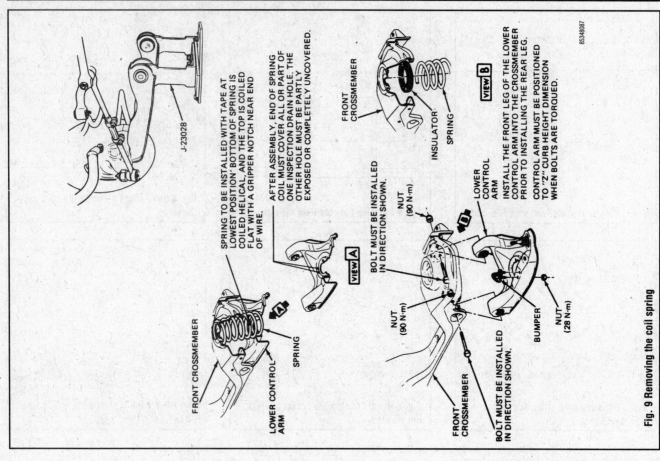

SPRING TO BE INSTALLED WITH TAPE AT LOWEST POSITION, BOTTOM OF SPRING IS COILED HELICAL, AND THE TOP IS COILED FLAT WITH A GRIPPER NOTCH NEAR END OF WIRE.

AFTER ASSEMBLY, END OF SPRING COIL MUST COVER ALL OR PART OF ONE INSPECTION DRAIN HOLE, THE OTHER HOLE MUST BE PARTLY EXPOSED OR COMPLETELY UNCOVERED.

FRONT CROSSMEMBER

SPRING

LOWER CONTROL ARM

VIEW A

BOLT MUST BE INSTALLED IN DIRECTION SHOWN.

NUT (90 N·m)

NUT (90 N·m)

FRONT CROSSMEMBER

BOLT MUST BE INSTALLED IN DIRECTION SHOWN.

BUMPER

NUT (28 N·m)

INSTALL THE FRONT LEG OF THE LOWER CONTROL ARM INTO THE CROSSMEMBER PRIOR TO INSTALLING THE REAR LEG.

CONTROL ARM MUST BE POSITIONED TO "Z" CURB HEIGHT DIMENSION WHEN BOLTS ARE TORQUED.

LOWER CONTROL ARM

VIEW B

FRONT CROSSMEMBER

INSULATOR

SPRING

J-23028

Fig. 9 Removing the coil spring

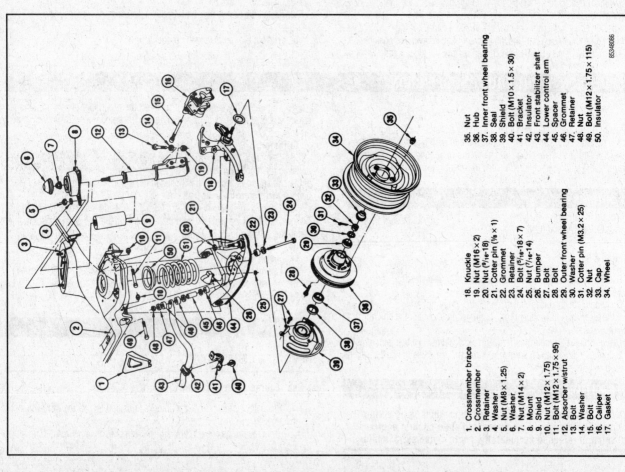

1. Crossmember brace
2. Crossmember
3. Retainer
4. Washer
5. Nut (M8 × 1.25)
6. Washer
7. Nut (M14 × 2)
8. Mount
9. Shield
10. Nut (M12 × 1.75)
11. Bolt (M12 × 1.75 × 95)
12. Absorber w/strut
13. Bolt
14. Washer
15. Bolt
16. Caliper
17. Gasket
18. Knuckle
19. Nut (M16 × 2)
20. Nut (9/16-18)
21. Cotter pin (5/16 × 1)
22. Grommet
23. Retainer
24. Bolt (5/16-18 × 7)
25. Nut (7/16-14)
26. Bumper
27. Bolt
28. Bolt
29. Outer front wheel bearing
30. Washer
31. Cotter pin (M3.2 × 25)
32. Nut
33. Cap
34. Wheel
35. Nut
36. Hub
37. Inner front wheel bearing
38. Seal
39. Shield
40. Bolt (M10 × 1.5 × 30)
41. Bracket
42. Insulator
43. Front stabilizer shaft
44. Lower control arm
45. Spacer
46. Grommet
47. Retainer
48. Nut
49. Bolt (M12 × 1.75 × 115)
50. Insulator

Fig. 8 MacPherson strut front suspension

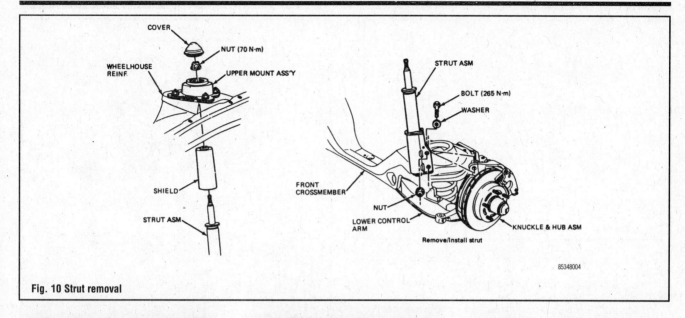

Fig. 10 Strut removal

Fig. 11 Matchmarking the strut brace position

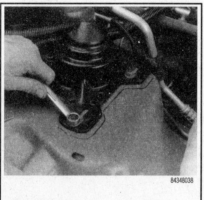

Fig. 12 Removing the strut brace nuts

Fig. 13 Lifting out the strut

⁙ CAUTION

Do not attempt to move the vehicle with the upper strut fastener disconnected.

   3. Raise the front of the vehicle and position safety stands under the vehicle.

   4. Remove the wheel and tire assembly.

   5. Remove the brake caliper without disconnecting the fluid hose, and hang out of the way on a wire. Do not allow the caliper to hang by its fluid hose.

   6. Remove the two lower bolts attaching the strut to the steering knuckle.

   7. Lift the strut up from the steering knuckle to compress the rod, then pull down and remove the strut.

To install:

   8. Half extend the rod through the upper mount, then hand-start the upper fastener, engaging as many threads as possible.

   9. Extend the strut and position it onto the steering knuckle.

  10. Install the lower mount bolts hand-tight.

  11. Tighten the upper fastener fully.

  12. Fully tighten the lower bolts only when the front suspension is on the ground. Torque the steering knuckle-to-strut nuts to 125 ft. lbs. (170 Nm) followed by a 120 degree turn. Do not exceed a final torque of 148 Ft. lbs. (200 Nm).

  13. Install the brake caliper

  14. Install the wheel and tire assembly.

  15. Lower the front of the vehicle.

  16. From inside the engine compartment, tighten the upper strut to upper mount nut to 44 ft. lbs. (60 Nm).

  17. Have the front end aligned.

OVERHAUL

   The OEM domestic struts are serviced by replacement of the entire unit. There is no strut cartridge to replace.

Lower Ball Joint

INSPECTION

➡**Before performing this inspection, make sure the wheel bearings are adjusted correctly and that the control arm bushings are in good condition.**

   1. Jack the car up under the front lower control arm at the spring seat.

   2. Raise the car until there is 1–2 in. (25–51mm) of clearance under the wheel.

   3. Insert a bar under the wheel and pry upward. If the wheel raises more than 1/8 in. (3mm), the ball joints are worn. Determine if the lower ball joint is worn by visual inspection while prying on the wheel.

REMOVAL & INSTALLATION

◗ **See Figure 14**

➡**To prevent component damage, an on-car ball joint press, such as Kent-Moore tool J–9519–23 should be used.**

   1. Raise and safely support the vehicle, then remove the wheel.

   2. Support the lower control arm spring seat with a jack.

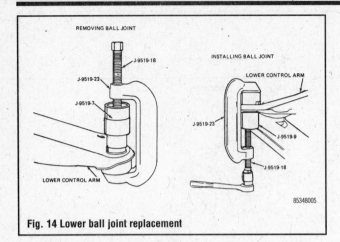

Fig. 14 Lower ball joint replacement

3. Loosen the lower ball stud nut. Break the ball stud loose. Remove the ball stud nut.

4. Remove the ball stud from the steering knuckle. Support the steering knuckle aside using a hanger or wire.

5. Using a ball joint press, remove the ball joint from the lower control arm.

To install:

6. Install the new ball joint, using the press.

7. Install the ball stud in the steering knuckle boss.

8. Install the nut on the ball stud, tightening to 77 ft. lbs. (105 Nm) on all models. Continue to tighten the nut until the cotter pin holes align and install the pin. Do not back off the nut to align the holes.

9. Install the lube fitting and grease the new joint.

Stabilizer Shaft

REMOVAL & INSTALLATION

▶ **See Figure 15**

1. Raise the car and safely support on jackstands.
2. Remove the link bolt, nut, grommet, spacer and retainers.
3. Remove the insulators and brackets.
4. Remove the stabilizer shaft.

To install:

5. Position the stabilizer shaft into place and install the insulators and brackets.

6. Hold the stabilizer shaft approximately 55mm from the bottom of the side rail and torque the bracket bolts to 37 ft. lbs. (50 Nm).

7. Install the bolt, nut, grommets, spacer and retainers.

8. Lower the car.

Lower Control Arm

REMOVAL & INSTALLATION

1. Raise the car and safely support on jackstands.
2. Remove the wheel and tire.
3. Remove the stabilizer link and bushings at the lower control arm.
4. Remove the pivot bolt nuts. DO NOT remove the pivot bolts at this time.
5. Install tool J–23028 or equivalent adapter to the jack and place into position with tool J–23028 or equivalent adapter supporting bushings.
6. Install the jackstand under the outside frame rail on the opposite side of the vehicle.
7. Raise tool J–23028 or equivalent adapter enough to remove both pivot bolts.
8. Lower tool J–23028 or equivalent adapter.

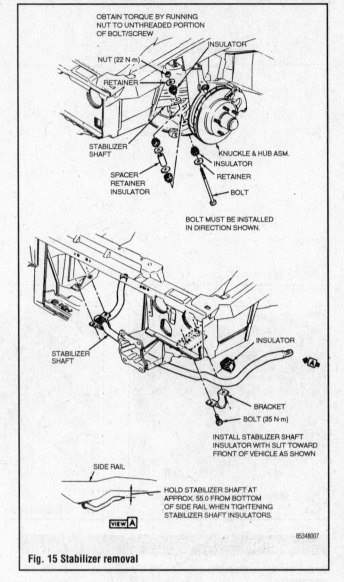

Fig. 15 Stabilizer removal

9. Remove the spring and insulator tape insulator to the spring.
10. Remove the ball joint from the knuckle.
11. To install, reverse the removal procedure.

Steering Knuckle and Spindle

REMOVAL & INSTALLATION

▶ **See Figure 16**

1. Siphon some brake fluid from the master cylinder. Raise and support the vehicle.

2. Remove the wheel and tire. Remove the brake hose from the strut.

3. Remove the caliper and support on a wire. Refer to Section 9 for procedures, then remove the hub-and-disc.

4. Remove the splash shield. Disconnect the tie rod from the steering knuckle.

5. Support the lower control arm and disconnect the ball joint from the steering knuckle using tool J–24292A.

6. Remove the 2 bolts securing the strut to the steering knuckle and remove the steering knuckle.

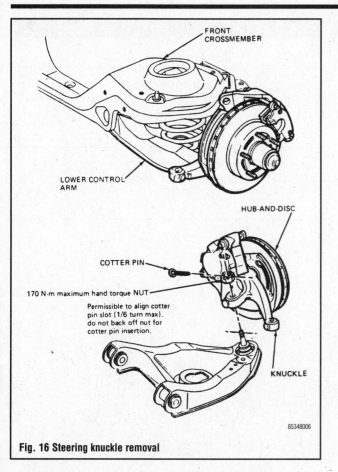

Fig. 16 Steering knuckle removal

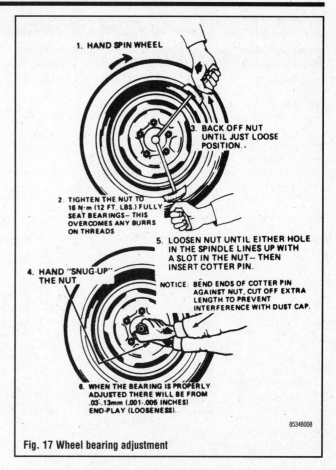

Fig. 17 Wheel bearing adjustment

To install:

7. Place the steering knuckle into position and install the 2 bolts securing the strut to the steering knuckle.

8. Support the lower control arm and connect the ball joint to the steering knuckle.

9. Connect the tie rod to the steering knuckle. Install the splash shield.

10. Install the caliper.

11. Install the brake hose from the strut. Install the wheel and tire.

12. Lower the vehicle and refill the master cylinder with brake fluid.

Front Wheel Bearings

ADJUSTMENT

▶ **See Figure 17**

1. Raise the car and support it at the lower arm.

2. Remove the hub dust cover and spindle cotter pin. Loosen the nut.

3. While spinning the wheel, snug the nut down to seat the bearings. Do not exert over 12 ft. lbs. (16 Nm) of force on the nut.

4. Back the nut off ¼ turn or until it is just loose. Line up the cotter pin hole in the spindle with the hole in the nut.

5. Insert a new cotter pin. Endplay should be between 0.001–0.005 in. (0.03–0.13mm). If play exceeds this tolerance, the wheel bearings should be replaced.

REMOVAL & INSTALLATION

1. Raise the car and support it at the lower arm. Remove the wheel. Remove the brake caliper and support it on a wire.

2. Remove the dust cap, cotter pin, castle nut, thrust washer and outside wheel bearing. Pull the disc/hub assembly from the steering knuckle.

3. Pry out the inner seal and remove the inner bearing. If necessary to remove the inner bearing races, use a hammer and a brass drift to drive the bearing races from the hub.

4. Clean all parts in kerosene or equivalent, DO NOT use gasoline. After cleaning, check parts for excessive wear and replace damaged parts.

5. Smear grease inside of hub. Install the bearing races into hub, using a hammer and a brass drift. Drive the races in until they seat against the shoulder of the hub.

6. Pack the bearings with grease and install the inner bearing in the hub. Install a new grease seal, be careful not to damage the seal.

7. Install the disc/hub assembly onto the steering knuckle. Install the outer bearing, thrust washer and castle nut. Tighten the nut until the wheel does not turn freely.

8. Back off the nut until the wheel turns freely and install the cotter pin. Install the dust cap, caliper and wheel. Lower the car.

PACKING

Clean the wheel bearings thoroughly with solvent and check their condition before installation.

✺✺ CAUTION

Do not blow the bearing dry with compressed air as this could allow the bearing to turn without lubrication.

Apply a sizable amount of lubricant to the palm of one hand. Using your other hand, work the bearing into the lubricant so that the grease is pushed through the rollers and out the other side. Keep rotating the bearing while continuing to push the lubricant through it.

FRONT END ALIGNMENT

Description

▶ **See Figure 18**

CAMBER

Camber is the inward or outward tilting of the front wheels from the vertical. When the wheels tilt outward at the top, the camber is said to be positive (+). When the wheels tilt inward at the top, the camber is said to be negative (−). The amount of tilt is measured in degrees from the vertical and this measurement is called the camber angle.

CASTER

Caster is the tilting of the front steering axis either forward or backward from the vertical. A backward tilt is said to be positive (+) and a forward tilt is said to be negative (−).

TOE

Toe is the turning in of the front wheels. The actual amount of toe-in or toe-out is normally only a fraction of a degree. The purpose of toe is to ensure parallel rolling of the front wheels. Excessive toe-in or toe-out will cause tire wear.

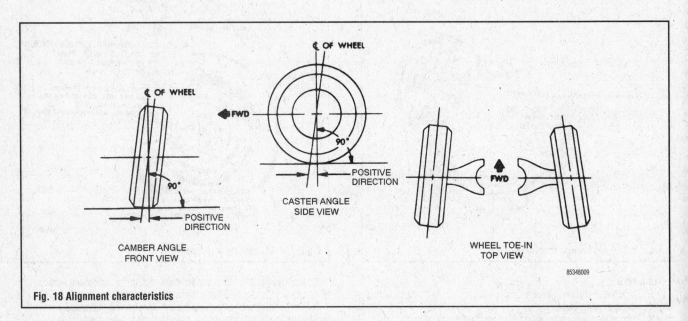

Fig. 18 Alignment characteristics

An alignment verification label on the upper mount-to-wheelhouse tower verifies the accuracy of camber and caster adjustment. If a steering problem exists, it is important to check other possible causes before adjusting camber or caster.

② Using reliable alignment equipment, follow the manufacturer's instructions to obtain camber and caster readings. Adjust the camber by rotating the turnbuckle on J-29724 to allow the mount assembly to move inboard or outboard.

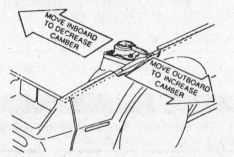

④ When the correct camber and caster readings are obtained, tighten the (3) nuts attaching the mount assembly to 28 N·m. Remove J-29724. Install the fender bolt and dust cap.

① Remove dust cap and fender bolt. Attach J-29724, using original fender bolt. Tighten the turnbuckle. Loosen (3) nuts attaching mount assembly.

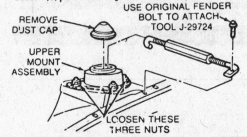

③ After obtaining the correct camber reading, caster can be adjusted by lightly tapping the mount assembly forward or rearward.

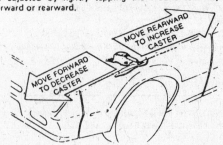

Fig. 19 Caster & camber adjustments

Adjustment

CASTER/CAMBER

▶ **See Figure 19**

Caster and camber can be adjusted by moving the position of the upper strut mount assembly. Moving the mount forward/rearward adjusts caster. Movement inboard/outboard adjusts camber.

TOE

▶ **See Figure 20**

1. Loosen the clamp bolts at each end of the steering tie rod adjustable sleeves.
2. With the steering wheel set straight ahead, turn the adjusting sleeves to obtain the proper adjustment.
3. When the adjustment has been completed, check to see that the number of threads showing on each end of the sleeve are equal. Also check that tie rod end housings are at the right angles to the steering arm.

REAR SUSPENSION

▶ **See Figure 21**

Coil Springs

REMOVAL & INSTALLATION

1. Raise the car by the frame so that the rear axle can be independently raised and lowered.
2. Support the rear axle with a floor jack.
3. If equipped with brake hose attaching brackets, disconnect the brackets allowing the hoses to hang free. Do not disconnect the hoses. Perform this step only if the hoses would otherwise be stretched and damaged when the axle is lowered.
4. Disconnect the track bar from the axle.
5. Remove the lower shock absorber bolts and lower the axle. Make sure the axle is supported securely on the floor jack and that there is no chance of the axle slipping after the shock absorbers are disconnected.

➡ **On vehicles equipped with a 4-cylinder engine, remove the driveshaft.**

6. Lower the axle and remove the coil spring. Do not lower the axle past the limits of the brake lines or the lines will be damaged.

To install:
7. Position spring with the axle lowered.
8. On vehicles equipped with 4-cylinder engines, install the driveshaft.
9. Raise the axle and install the lower shock absorber bolts.
10. Connect the track bar to the axle.
11. Connect the brake hose attaching brackets, if removed.
12. Remove the support from the rear axle.
13. Lower the vehicle.

Shock Absorbers

REMOVAL & INSTALLATION

▶ **See Figures 22 and 23**

1. Jack up the car to a convenient working height. Support the axle assembly with jackstands.
2. Disconnect the upper shock attaching nuts.
3. Remove the lower shock to axle mounting bolt.
4. Remove the shock absorber.

To install:
5. Position the shock into place.
6. Install the lower shock to axle mounting bolt. Torque to 70 ft. lbs. (95 Nm).

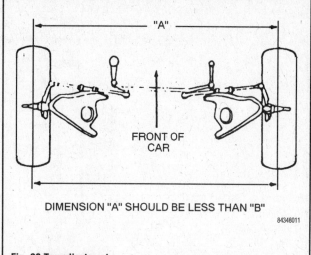

DIMENSION "A" SHOULD BE LESS THAN "B"

84348011

Fig. 20 Toe adjustment

7. Connect the upper shock attaching nuts. Torque the upper nuts to 13 ft. lbs. (17 Nm).
8. Lower the car.

TESTING

Visually inspect the shock absorber. If there is evidence of leakage and the shock absorber is covered with oil, the shock is defective and should be replaced.

If there is no sign of excessive leakage (a small amount of weeping is normal) bounce the car at one corner by pressing down on the fender or bumper and releasing. When you have the car bouncing as much as you can, release it. The car should stop bouncing after the first rebound. If the bouncing continues past the center point of the bounce more than once, the shock absorbers are worn and should be replaced.

Track Bar

REMOVAL & INSTALLATION

▶ **See Figure 24**

1. Raise the rear of the vehicle, place jackstands under the rear axle, then lower the jack so that the stands are supporting all of the weight.
2. Remove the track bar mounting fasteners. Remove the track bar.

To install:
3. Clean all of the track bar fasteners.
4. Position the track bar in the body bracket, then loosely install the bolt and the nut.
5. Position the track bar to the axle assembly, then install the bolt and the nut. Torque the bolt to 59 ft. lbs. (80 Nm).
6. Torque the body bracket nut to 78 ft. lbs. (105 Nm).

Track Bar Brace

REMOVAL & INSTALLATION

1. Raise the rear of the vehicle, place jackstands under the rear axle, then lower the jack so that the stands are supporting all of the weight.
2. Remove the heat shield screws from the track bar brace.
3. Remove the three track bar brace-to-body brace screws.
4. Remove the track bar-to-body bracket fasteners and remove the track bar brace.

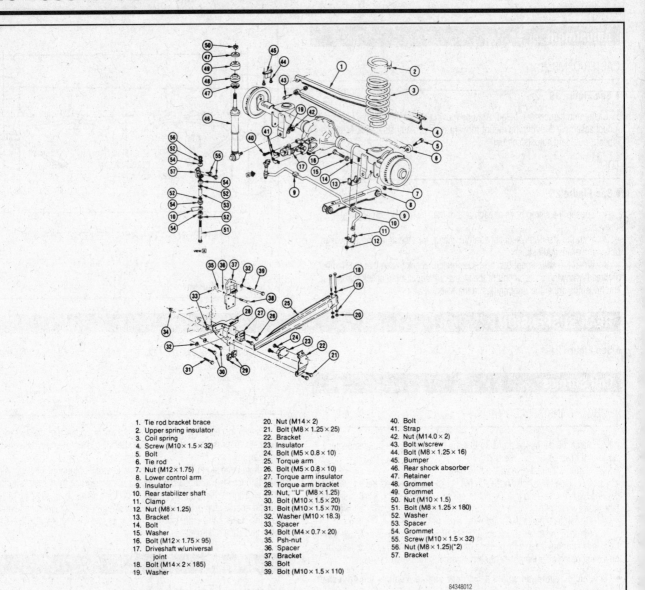

1. Tie rod bracket brace	20. Nut (M14 × 2)	40. Bolt
2. Upper spring insulator	21. Bolt (M8 × 1.25 × 25)	41. Strap
3. Coil spring	22. Bracket	42. Nut (M14.0 × 2)
4. Screw (M10 × 1.5 × 32)	23. Insulator	43. Bolt w/screw
5. Bolt	24. Bolt (M5 × 0.8 × 10)	44. Bolt (M8 × 1.25 × 16)
6. Tie rod	25. Torque arm	45. Bumper
7. Nut (M12 × 1.75)	26. Bolt (M5 × 0.8 × 10)	46. Rear shock absorber
8. Lower control arm	27. Torque arm insulator	47. Retainer
9. Insulator	28. Torque arm bracket	48. Grommet
10. Rear stabilizer shaft	29. Nut, "U" (M8 × 1.25)	49. Grommet
11. Clamp	30. Bolt (M10 × 1.5 × 20)	50. Nut (M10 × 1.5)
12. Nut (M8 × 1.25)	31. Bolt (M10 × 1.5 × 70)	51. Bolt (M8 × 1.25 × 180)
13. Bracket	32. Washer (M10 × 18.3)	52. Washer
14. Bolt	33. Spacer	53. Spacer
15. Washer	34. Bolt (M4 × 0.7 × 20)	54. Grommet
16. Bolt (M12 × 1.75 × 95)	35. Psh-nut	55. Screw (M10 × 1.5 × 32)
17. Driveshaft w/universal	36. Spacer	56. Nut (M8 × 1.25)(*2)
joint	37. Bracket	57. Bracket
18. Bolt (M14 × 2 × 185)	38. Bolt	
19. Washer	39. Bolt (M10 × 1.5 × 110)	

84348012

Fig. 21 Rear suspension (exploded view)

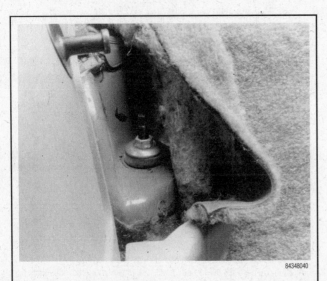

Fig. 22 Rear shock upper mount

Fig. 23 Rear shock lower mount

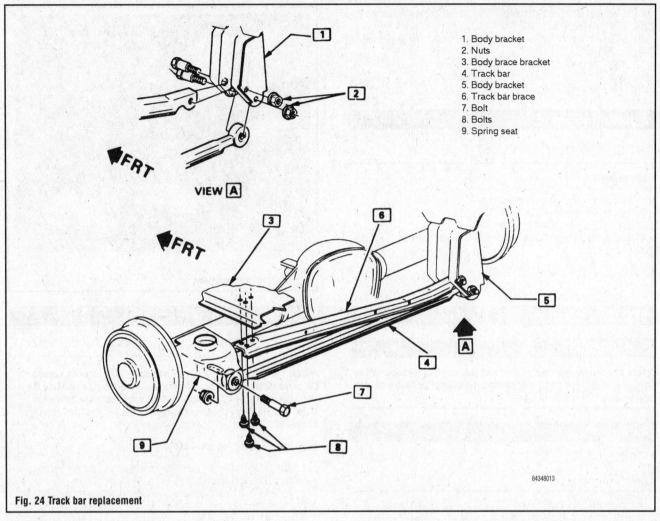

1. Body bracket
2. Nuts
3. Body brace bracket
4. Track bar
5. Body bracket
6. Track bar brace
7. Bolt
8. Bolts
9. Spring seat

VIEW A

FRT

Fig. 24 Track bar replacement

To install:
5. Place the track bar brace into position.
6. Install the track bar-to-body bracket fasteners.
7. Install the three track bar brace-to-body brace screws.
8. Install the heat shield screws to the track bar brace.
9. Lower the vehicle.

Control Arm

REMOVAL & INSTALLATION

➡ Remove/reinstall only one lower control arm at a time. If both arms are removed at the same time, the axle could roll or slip sideways, making reinstallation of the arms very difficult.

1. Raise the rear of the vehicle, place jackstands under the rear axle, then lower the jack so that the stands are supporting all of the weight.
2. Remove the control arm attaching fasteners, then remove the control arm.
3. Installation is a simple matter of bolting the arm into place. Torque the 3 bolts at the body brace bracket to 35 ft. lbs. (47 Nm) and the nut at the body bracket to 61 ft. lbs. (83 Nm).

Torque Arm

REMOVAL & INSTALLATION

➡ The coil springs must be removed BEFORE the torque arm. If the torque arm is removed first, vehicle damage will result. In order to proceed, the vehicle must be supported in a manner which will allow the rear axle height to be adjusted independently of the body height.

1. Remove the track bar mounting bolt at the axle assembly, then loosen the track bar bolt at the body brace.
2. Disconnect the rear brake hose clip at the axle assembly, which will allow additional drop of the axle.
3. Remove the lower attaching nuts from both rear shock absorbers.
4. Disconnect the shock absorbers from their lower attaching points.
5. On models with four cylinder engines, remove the driveshaft.
6. Carefully lower the rear axle assembly and remove the rear coil springs.

✳✳ CAUTION

DO NOT overstretch the brake hose when lowering the axle-damage to the hose will result.

7. Remove the torque arm rear attaching bolts.
8. Remove the front torque arm outer bracket.
9. Remove the torque arm from the vehicle.
To install:
10. Place the torque arm in position and loosely install the rear torque arm bolts.
11. Install the front torque arm bracket and torque the nuts to 31 ft. lbs. (42 Nm).
12. Torque the rear torque arm nuts to 100 ft. lbs. (135 Nm).
13. Place the rear springs and insulators in position, then raise the rear axle assembly until all of the weight is supported by the spring.
14. Attach the shock absorbers to the rear axle and torque the fasteners to 70 ft. lbs. (95 Nm).

15. Clean and reinstall the track bar mounting bolt at the axle. Torque the bolt to 59 ft. lbs. (80 Nm).

16. Clean and reinstall the track bar-to-body brace nut. Torque the nut to 78 ft. lbs. (105 Nm).

17. Install the brake line clip to the underbody.

18. On four cylinder models, reinstall the driveshaft.

19. Lower the vehicle.

Stabilizer (Sway) Bar

REMOVAL & INSTALLATION

▶ See Figure 25

1. Raise and support the rear end on jackstands.
2. Disconnect the end link bolts.
3. Remove the U-bolts and insulators.
4. Installation is the reverse of removal. Please refer to the torque specifications chart.

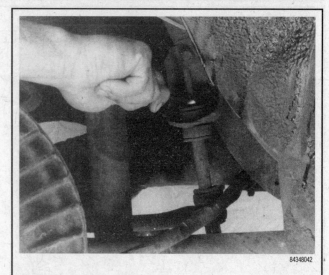

Fig. 25 Stabilizer end links

STEERING COLUMN

✳✳ WARNING

Before attempting any repairs involving the steering wheel or disassembly of it, ensure that the Supplemental Inflatable Restraint (Air Bag) system is properly disarmed.

Air Bag

▶ See Figure 26

DISARMING

1. Turn the steering wheel to align the wheels in the straight-ahead position.
2. Turn the ignition switch to the **LOCK** position.
3. Remove the SIR air bag fuse from the fuse block.
4. Remove the left side trim panel and disconnect the yellow 2-way SIR harness wire connector at the base of the steering column.
   To enable system:
5. Turn the ignition switch to the **LOCK** position.
6. Reconnect the yellow 2-way connector at the base of the steering column.
7. Reinstall the SIR fuse and the left side trim panel.
8. Turn the ignition switch to the **RUN** position.
9. Verify the SIR indicator light flashes 7–9 times, if not as specified, inspect system for malfunction or contact the manufacturer.

➡For more details on the SIR system—including disarming instructions for passenger bags—please refer to Section 6 of this manual.

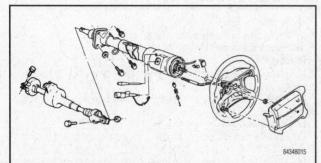

Fig. 26 Air bag-equipped steering column

SUPPLEMENTAL INFLATABLE RESTRAINT (SIR) COIL ASSEMBLY

➡After performing repairs on the internals of the steering column the coil assembly must be centered in order to avoid damaging the coil or accidental deployment of the air bag. There are 2 different styles of coils, one rotates clockwise and the other rotates counterclockwise.

Adjustment (Centering the Coil)

1. With the system properly disarmed, hold the coil assembly with the clear bottom up to see the coil ribbon.
2. While holding the coil assembly, depress the lock spring and rotate the hub in the direction of the arrow until it stops. The coil should now be wound up snug against the center hub.
3. Rotate the coil assembly in the opposite direction approximately 2½ turns and release the lock spring between the locking tabs in front of the arrow.
4. Install the coil assembly onto the steering shaft.

Steering Wheel

REMOVAL & INSTALLATION

➡If the vehicle is equipped with a SIR (Air Bag) system, ensure that the proper disarming procedure is followed.

1982–89 VEHICLES

▶ See Figure 27

1. Disconnect the negative battery cable.
2. Remove the horn pad.
3. Disconnect the horn contact lead.
4. Remove the retainer and steering wheel nut.
5. Using a suitable steering wheel puller, remove the steering wheel.
6. Installation is the reverse of the removal procedure. Tighten the steering wheel nut to 31 ft. lbs. (42 Nm).

1990–92 VEHICLES

✳✳ CAUTION

The vehicle is equipped with a Supplemental Inflatable Restraint (SIR) system, follow the recommended disarming procedures before

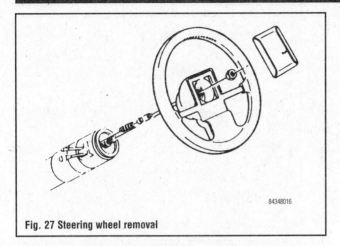

84348016

Fig. 27 Steering wheel removal

performing any work on or around the system. Failure to do so may result in possible deployment of the air bag and/or personal injury.

1. Disconnect the negative battery cable.
2. Disable the Supplemental Inflatable Restraint (SIR) system as follows:
   a. Turn the steering wheel so the vehicle's wheels are pointing straight-ahead.
   b. Remove the left sound insulator by removing the nut from the stud and gently prying the insulator from the knee bolster.
   c. Disconnect the Connector Position Assurance (CPA) clip and yellow 2-way SIR harness connector at the base of the steering column.
   d. Remove the SIR fuse from the fuse block.
3. Loosen the screws and locknuts from the back of the steering wheel using a suitable Torx® driver or equivalent, until the inflator module can be released from the steering wheel. Remove the inflator module from the steering wheel.

✶✶ CAUTION

When carrying a live inflator module, ensure the bag and trim cover are pointed away from the body. In case of an accidental deployment, the bag will then deploy with minimal chance of injury. When placing a live inflator module on a bench or other surface, always place the bag and trim cover up, away from the surface. This is necessary so a free space is provided to allow the air bag to expand in the unlikely event of accidental deployment. Otherwise, personal injury may result. Also, never carry the inflator module by the wires or connector on the underside of the module.

4. Disconnect the coil assembly connector and CPA clip from the inflator module terminal.
5. Remove the steering wheel locking nut.
6. Using a suitable puller, remove the steering wheel and disconnect the horn contact. When attaching the steering wheel puller, use care to prevent threading the side screws into the coil assembly and damaging the coil assembly.

To install:

7. Route the coil assembly connector through the steering wheel.
8. Connect the horn contact and install the steering wheel. When installing the steering wheel, align the block tooth on the steering wheel with the block tooth on the steering shaft within 1 female serration.
9. Install the steering wheel locking nut. Tighten the nut to 31 ft. lbs. (42 Nm).
10. Connect the coil assembly connector and CPA clip to the inflator module terminal.
11. Install the inflator module. Ensure the wiring is not exposed or trapped between the inflator module and the steering wheel. Tighten the inflator module screws to 25 inch lbs. (2.8 Nm).
12. Connect the negative battery cable.
13. Enable the SIR system as follows:
   a. Connect the yellow 2-way SIR harness connector to base of the steering column and CPA.
   b. Install the left sound insulator.
   c. Install the SIR fuse in the fuse block.
   d. Turn the ignition switch to the **RUN** position and verify that the inflatable restraint indicator flashes 7–9 times and then turns **OFF**. If the indicator does not respond as stated, a problem within the SIR system is indicated.

Turn Signal Switch

REMOVAL & INSTALLATION

Standard Columns Without Air Bag

1. Remove the steering wheel as previously outlined. Remove the trim cover.
2. Pry the cover off, and lift the cover off the shaft.
3. Position the U-shaped lockplate compressing tool on the end of the steering shaft and compress the lock plate by turning the shaft nut clockwise. Pry the wire snapring out of the shaft groove.
4. Remove the tool and lift the lockplate off the shaft.
5. Remove the canceling cam assembly and upper bearing preload spring from the shaft.
6. Remove the turn signal lever. Push the flasher knob in and unscrew it. On models equipped with a button and a knob, remove the button retaining screw, then remove the button, spring, and knob.
7. Pull the switch connector out the mast jacket and tape the upper part to facilitate switch removal. Attach a long piece of wire to the turn signal switch connector. When installing the turn signal switch, feed this wire through the column first, and then use this wire to pull the switch connector into position. On tilt wheels, place the turn signal and shifter housing in low position and remove the harness cover.
8. Remove the three switch mounting screws. Remove the switch by pulling it straight up while guiding the wiring harness cover through the column.

To install:

9. Install the replacement switch by working the connector and cover down through the housing and under the bracket. On tilt models, the connector is worked down through the housing, under the bracket, and then the cover is installed on the harness.
10. Install the switch mounting screws and the connector on the mast jacket bracket. Install the column-to-dash trim plate.
11. Install the flasher knob and the turn signal lever.
12. With the turn signal lever in neutral and the flasher knob out, slide the upper bearing preload spring, and canceling cam assembly onto the shaft.
13. Position the lock plate on the shaft and press it down until a new snapring can be inserted in the shaft groove. Always use a new snapring when assembling.
14. Install the cover and the steering wheel.

Tilt Columns Without Air Bag

◆ See Figure 28

✶✶ CAUTION

All elements of energy-absorbing (telescopic) steering columns are very sensitive to damage. Do not strike any part of the column (nuts, bolts, etc.) as this could ruin the entire assembly.

1. Disconnect the battery cable.
2. Remove the steering wheel as outlined earlier.
3. Remove the cover from the steering column shaft.
4. Press down on the lockplate and pry the snapring from the shaft.
5. Remove the lockplate and the canceling cam.
6. Remove the upper bearing preload spring.
7. Remove the turn signal lever and the hazard flasher knob.
8. Lift up on the tilt lever and position the housing in its central position.
9. Remove the switch attaching screws.
10. Remove the lower trim cap from the instrument panel and disconnect the turn signal connector from the wiring harness.
11. Remove the four bolts which secure the bracket assembly to the jacket.
12. Loosen the screw that holds the shift indicator needle and disconnect the clip from the link.
13. Remove the two nuts from the column support bracket while holding the column in position. Remove the bracket assembly and wire protector from the wiring, then loosely install the support column bracket.
14. Tape the turn signal wires at the connector to keep them fit and parallel.
15. Carefully remove the turn signal switch and wiring from the column.

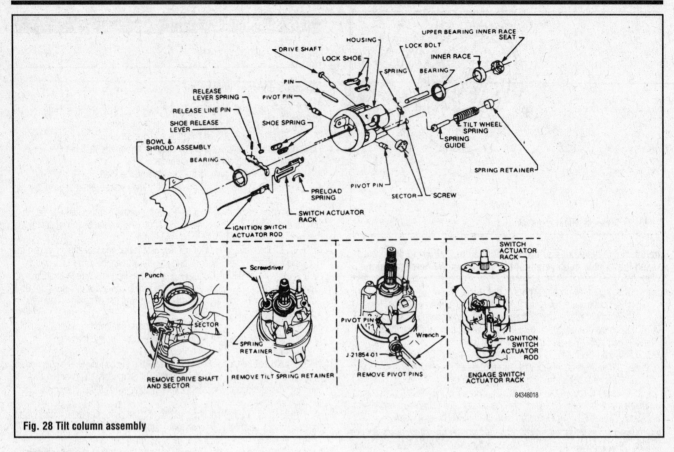

Fig. 28 Tilt column assembly

To install:

16. Carefully install the turn signal switch and wiring into the column.

17. Remove the tape from the turn signal wires.

18. Install the wire protector and, while holding the column in position, install the two nuts to the column support bracket.

19. Connect the clip to the link and tighten the screw that holds the shift indicator needle.

20. Install the four bolts which secure the bracket assembly to the jacket.

21. Connect the turn signal connector to the wiring harness and install the lower trim cap to the instrument panel.

22. Install the switch attaching screws.

23. Install the turn signal lever and the hazard flasher knob.

24. Install the upper bearing preload spring.

25. Install the lockplate and the canceling cam.

26. Press down on the lockplate and install the snapring to the shaft using a new snapring.

27. Install the cover to the steering column shaft.

28. Install the steering wheel.

29. Connect the battery cable.

Steering Column With Air Bag

♦ **See Figure 29**

1. Properly disable the SIR air bag system.

2. Disconnect the negative battery cable.

3. Remove the inflator module.

4. Remove the steering wheel.

5. Ensure the steering wheel is locked in the straight-ahead position and remove the coil assembly retaining ring.

6. Pull the coil assembly out and allow it to hang.

7. Using a suitable tool, depress the lock plate to gain access to the snapring. Remove the snapring and remove the lockplate.

8. Remove the turn signal canceling cam, upper bearing spring and signal switch arm.

9. Remove the hazard warning knob, turn signal lever and steering column wiring protector.

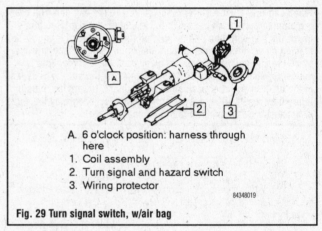

A. 6 o'clock position: harness through here
1. Coil assembly
2. Turn signal and hazard switch
3. Wiring protector

Fig. 29 Turn signal switch, w/air bag

10. Disconnect the turn signal switch connector from the harness connector.

11. Remove the switch retaining screws and remove the turn signal switch.

12. Installation is the reverse of the removal procedure. Make certain to follow the SIR coil adjustment procedure previously described.

Ignition Switch

REPLACEMENT

♦ **See Figure 30**

The switch is located inside the channel section of the brake pedal support and is completely inaccessible without first lowering the steering column. The switch is actuated by a rod and rack assembly. A gear on the end of the lock cylinder engages the toothed upper end of the rod.

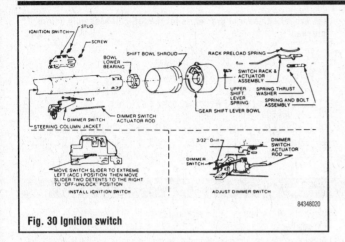

Fig. 30 Ignition switch

1. Lower the steering column; be sure to properly support it.
2. Put the switch in the **Off-Unlocked** position. The **Off-Unlocked** position is two detents from the top.
3. Remove the two switch screws and remove the switch assembly.

To install:

4. Before installing, place the new switch in the **Off-Unlocked** position. Make sure the lock cylinder and actuating rod are in the **Off-Unlocked** (second detent from the top) position.
5. Install the activating rod into the switch and assemble the switch on the column. Tighten the mounting screws. Use only the specified screws since overlength screws could impair the collapsibility of the column.
6. Reinstall the steering column.

Ignition Lock Cylinder

REMOVAL AND INSTALLATION

▶ See Figures 31 and 32

1. Properly disable the SIR air bag system, if equipped.
2. Place the lock in the **Run** position.
3. Remove the lock plate, turn signal switch and buzzer switch.
4. Remove the screw and lock cylinder.

✳✳ CAUTION

If the screw is dropped on removal, it could fall into the column, requiring complete disassembly to retrieve the screw.

To install:

5. Rotate the cylinder clockwise to align cylinder key with the keyway in the housing.
6. Push the lock all the way in.
7. Install the screw. Tighten the screw to 14 inch lbs. (1.5 Nm) for adjustable columns and 25 inch lbs. (2.8 Nm) for standard columns. Re-center the SIR coil assembly as previously directed.

Steering Column

REMOVAL & INSTALLATION

➡The front of the dash mounting plates must be loosened whenever the steering column is to be lowered from the instrument panel.

1. Disconnect the negative battery cable.
2. On 1990–92 vehicles, disable the Supplemental Inflatable Restraint (SIR) system as follows:

    a. Turn the steering wheel so the vehicle's wheels are pointing straight-ahead.

➡The wheels of the vehicle must be in the straight-ahead position and the steering column in the locked position before proceeding with

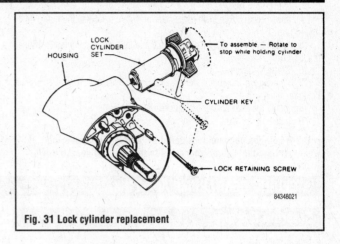

Fig. 31 Lock cylinder replacement

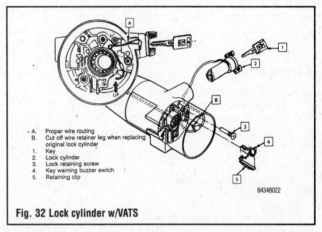

A. Proper wire routing
B. Cut off wire retainer leg when replacing original lock cylinder
1. Key
2. Lock cylinder
3. Lock retaining screw
4. Key warning buzzer switch
5. Retaining clip

Fig. 32 Lock cylinder w/VATS

steering column removal. Failure to follow this procedure will cause the SIR coil to become uncentered, resulting in damage to the coil assembly.

    b. Remove the SIR fuse from the fuse block.

    c. Remove the left sound insulator by removing the nut from the stud and gently prying the insulator from the knee bolster.

    d. Disconnect the Connector Position Assurance (CPA) and yellow 2-way SIR harness connector at the base of the steering column.

3. Remove the nut and bolt from the upper intermediate shaft coupling. Separate the coupling from the lower end of the steering column.
4. Remove the steering wheel, if the column is to be replaced or repaired on the bench.
5. Remove the knee bolster and bracket, if equipped.
6. Remove the bolts attaching the toe plate to the cowl.
7. Disconnect the electrical connectors.
8. Remove the capsule nuts attaching the steering column support bracket to the instrument panel.
9. Disconnect the park lock cable from the ignition switch inhibitor, if equipped with automatic transmission.
10. Remove the steering column from the vehicle.

To install:

➡If a replacement steering column is being installed, do not remove the anti-rotation pin until after the steering column has been connected to the steering gear. Removing the anti-rotation pin before the steering column is connected to the steering gear may damage the SIR coil assembly.

11. Position the steering column in the vehicle.
12. Connect the park lock cable to the ignition switch inhibitor on vehicles with automatic transmission.
13. Install the capsule nuts attaching the steering column support bracket to the instrument panel and tighten to 20 ft. lbs. (27 Nm).
14. Install the nut and bolt to the upper intermediate shaft coupling attach-

ing the upper intermediate shaft to the steering column. Tighten the nut to 44 ft. lbs. (60 Nm).

15. Install the bolts attaching the toe plate to the cowl and tighten to 58 inch lbs. (6.5 Nm).

16. Connect the electrical connectors.

17. Remove the anti-rotation pin if a service replacement steering column is being installed.

18. Install the knee bolster and bracket, if equipped.

19. Install the sound insulator panel.

➡ **If SIR coil has become uncentered by turning of the steering wheel without the column connected to the steering gear, follow** the proper adjustment procedure for the SIR coil assembly before proceeding.

20. Install the steering wheel.

21. Connect the negative battery cable.

22. Enable the SIR system as follows:

 a. Connect the yellow 2-way SIR harness connector to the base of the steering column and CPA clip and install the SIR fuse.

 b. Install the left sound insulator.

 c. Turn the ignition switch to the **RUN** position and verify that the inflatable restraint indicator flashes 7–9 times and then turns **OFF**. If the indicator does not respond as stated, a problem within the SIR system is indicated.

STEERING GEAR, PUMP AND LINKAGE

Steering Linkage

▸ **See Figure 33**

REMOVAL & INSTALLATION

Pitman Arm

▸ **See Figure 34**

1. Raise the vehicle and support safely on jackstands.
2. Remove the nut from the Pitman arm ball stud.
3. Remove the relay rod from the Pitman arm by using a tool such as J–24319–01 or equivalent. Pull down on the relay rod to remove it from the stud.
4. Remove the Pitman arm nut from the Pitman shaft and mark the relation of the arm position to the shaft.
5. Remove the Pitman arm with tool J–5504 or tool J–6632 or equivalent. DO NOT HAMMER ON THE PULLER.

To install:

6. Position the Pitman arm on the Pitman shaft, lining up the marks made upon removal.
7. Position the relay rod on the Pitman arm. Use J–29193 or J–29194 or equivalent to seat the tapers. A torque of 15 ft. lbs. (20 Nm) is required. With the tapers seated, remove the tool, then install a prevailing torque nut, and tighten to 35 ft. lbs. (48 Nm).
8. Set the relay rod height. Torque the idler arm-to-frame mounting bolts to 61 ft. lbs. (83 Nm).
9. Lower the vehicle.

Idler Arm

1. Raise the vehicle and support safely on jackstands.
2. Remove the idler arm to frame nuts, washers, and bolts.
3. Remove the nut from the idler arm to relay rod ball stud.
4. Remove the relay rod from the idler arm by using J-24319–01 or equivalent.
5. Remove the idler arm.

To install:

6. Position the idler arm on the frame and LOOSELY install the mounting bolts, washers and nuts.
7. Install the relay rod to the idler arm, making certain seal is on the stud. Use J–29193 or J–29194 or equivalent to seat the tapers. A torque of 15 ft. lbs. (20 Nm) is required. With the tapers seated, remove the tool, then install a prevailing torque nut, and tighten to 35 ft. lbs. (48 Nm).
8. Set the relay rod height. Torque the idler arm-to-frame mounting bolts to 61 ft. lbs. (83 Nm).
9. Lower the vehicle.

Relay Rod

▸ **See Figures 35, 36 and 37**

During production, the installed position of the relay rod is carefully controlled to assure that the rod is at the proper height. Both the left end and the right end of the relay rod must be held at the same height. The side-to-side height is controlled by adjusting the position of the idler arm

Whenever disconnecting the relay rod assembly, it is important to first scribe the position of the idler arm-to-frame, and to reinstall the idler arm in the same position. Be sure to prevent the idler support from turning in the bushing, since that motion could result in improper relay rod height.

Whenever replacing the relay rod, or the idler arm, or the Pitman arm, it is mandatory to establish the correct height.

1. Raise the vehicle and support safely on jackstands.
2. Remove the inner ends of the tie rods from the relay rod.
3. Remove the nut from the relay rod ball stud attachment at Pitman arm.
4. Detach the relay rod from the Pitman arm by using tool such as J–24319–01 or equivalent. Shift the steering linkage as required to free the Pitman arm from the relay rod.
5. Remove the nut from the idler arm and remove the relay rod from the idler arm.

To install:

6. Install the relay rod to idler arm, making certain idler stud seal is in place. Use J–29193 or J–29194 or equivalent to seat the tapers. A torque of 15 ft. lbs. (20 Nm) is required. With the tapers seated, remove the tool, then install a prevailing torque nut, and tighten to 35 ft. lbs. (48 Nm).
7. Raise the end of the rod and install on the Pitman arm. Use J–29193 or J–29194 or equivalent to seat the tapers. A torque of 15 ft. lbs. (20 Nm) is required. With the tapers seated, remove the tool, then install a prevailing torque nut, and tighten to 35 ft. lbs. (48 Nm).
8. Install the tie rod ends to the relay rod. Lubricate the tie rod ends.
9. Install the damper, if equipped.
10. Set the relay rod height. Torque the idler arm-to-frame mounting bolts to 61 ft. lbs. (83 Nm).
11. Lower the vehicle.
12. Check and, if necessary, adjust front end alignment.

Tie Rod Ends

▸ **See Figure 38**

1. Raise the vehicle and support safely on jackstands.
2. Remove the cotter pins from the ball studs and remove the castellated nuts.
3. Remove the outer ball stud by using the ball stud puller. If necessary, pull downward on the tie rod to disconnect it from the steering arm.
4. Remove the inner ball stud from the relay rod using a similar procedure.
5. Remove the tie rod end or ends to be replaced by loosening the clamp bolt and unscrewing them.

To install:

6. Lubricate tie rod threads with chassis grease and install new tie rod(s). Make sure both ends are an equal distance from the tie rod and tighten clamp bolts.
7. Make sure ball studs, tapered surfaces, and all threaded surfaces are clean and smooth, and free of grease. Install seals on ball studs. Install ball stud in steering arm and relay rod.
8. Rotate both inner and outer tie rod housings rearward to the limit of ball joint travel before tightening clamps. Make sure clamp slots and sleeve slots are aligned before tightening clamps. Make sure tightened bolts will be in horizontal position to 45 degrees upward (in the forward direction) when the tie rod is in its normal position. Make sure the tie rod end stays in position relative to the rod during the tightening operation. Tighten the clamps, and then return the assembly to the center of its travel.

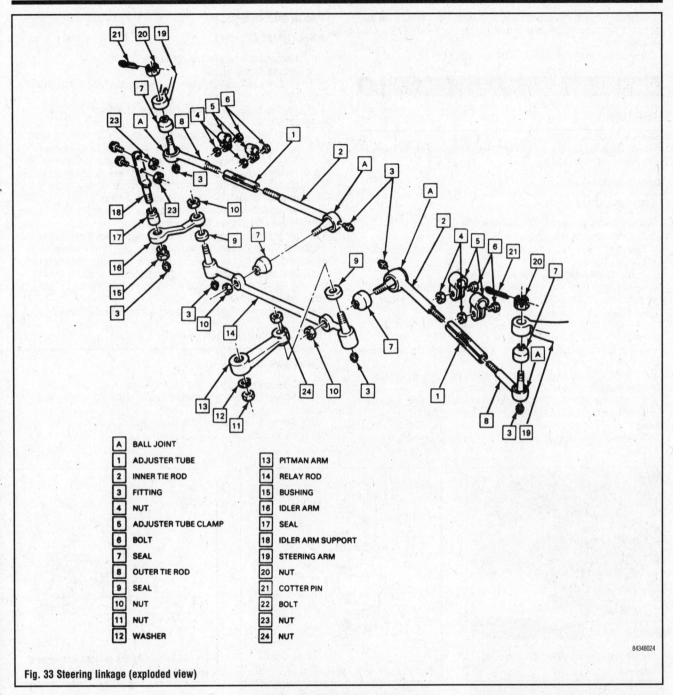

A	BALL JOINT		
1	ADJUSTER TUBE	13	PITMAN ARM
2	INNER TIE ROD	14	RELAY ROD
3	FITTING	15	BUSHING
4	NUT	16	IDLER ARM
5	ADJUSTER TUBE CLAMP	17	SEAL
6	BOLT	18	IDLER ARM SUPPORT
7	SEAL	19	STEERING ARM
8	OUTER TIE ROD	20	NUT
9	SEAL	21	COTTER PIN
10	NUT	22	BOLT
11	NUT	23	NUT
12	WASHER	24	NUT

Fig. 33 Steering linkage (exploded view)

Fig. 34 Removing the Pitman arm with the tool shown

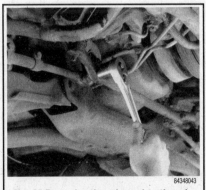

Fig. 35 Removing the relay rod-to-tie rod nut

Fig. 36 Separating the tie rod from the relay rod using a gear puller

9. Install ball stud nuts and torque to 35 ft. lbs. (47 Nm) Then tighten (do not loosen) further as required to align cotter pin holes in studs and nuts. Install new cotter pins.

10. Lubricate new tie rod ends and lower the vehicle.

Power Steering Gear

ADJUSTMENTS

➡**Adjust the worm bearing preload first, then proceed with the Pitman shaft over-center adjustment.**

Worm Bearing Preload

▶ **See Figures 39, 40, 41 and 42**

1. Disconnect the negative battery cable.
2. Remove the steering gear.
3. Rotate the stub shaft and drain the power steering fluid into a suitable container.
4. Remove the adjuster plug nut.
5. Turn the adjuster plug in (clockwise) using a suitable spanner wrench until the adjuster plug and thrust bearing are firmly bottomed in the housing. Tighten the adjuster plug to 20 ft. lbs. (27 Nm).
6. Place an index mark on the housing even with 1 of the holes in the adjuster plug.
7. Measure back counterclockwise ½ in. (13mm) and place a second mark on the housing.
8. Turn the adjuster plug counterclockwise until the hole in the adjuster plug is aligned with the second mark on the housing.
9. Install the adjuster plug nut and using a suitable punch in a notch, tighten securely. Hold the adjuster plug to maintain alignment of the marks.
10. Install the steering gear and connect the negative battery cable.

Pitman Shaft Over-Center

▶ **See Figures 43 and 44**

1. Disconnect the negative battery cable.
2. Remove the steering gear.
3. Rotate the stub shaft and drain the power steering fluid into a suitable container.
4. Turn the Pitman shaft adjuster screw counterclockwise until fully extended, then turn back 1 full turn.
5. Rotate the stub shaft from stop-to-stop and count the number of turns.
6. Starting at either stop, turn the stub shaft back half the total number of turns. This is the "Center" position of the gear. When the gear is centered, the flat on the stub shaft should face upward and be parallel with the side cover, and the master spline on the Pitman shaft should be in line with the adjuster screw.
7. Rotate the stub shaft 45 degrees each side of the center using a suitable torque wrench with the handle in the vertical position. Record the worm bearing preload measured on or near the center gear position.
8. Adjust the over-center drag torque by loosening the adjuster locknut and turning the Pitman shaft adjuster screw clockwise until the correct drag torque is obtained: Add 6–10 inch lbs. (0.7–1.1 Nm) of torque to the previously measured worm bearing preload torque. Tighten the adjuster locknut to 20 ft. lbs. (27 Nm). Prevent the adjuster screw from turning while tightening the adjuster screw locknut.
9. Install the steering gear and connect the negative battery cable.

REMOVAL & INSTALLATION

▶ **See Figure 45**

1. Disconnect the negative battery cable. Remove the coupling shield.
2. Remove the retaining bolts at the steering coupling to steering shaft flange.
3. Remove the Pitman arm nut and washer. Mark the relation of the arm position to the shaft.

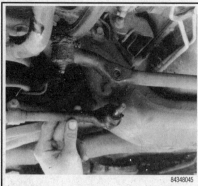
Fig. 37 Disconnecting the tie rod from the relay rod

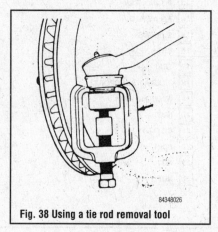
Fig. 38 Using a tie rod removal tool

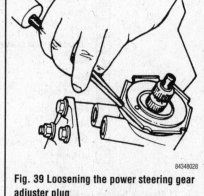
Fig. 39 Loosening the power steering gear adjuster plug

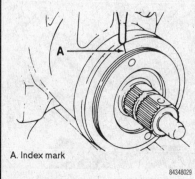
A. Index mark
Fig. 40 Marking the housing even with the adjuster plug hole

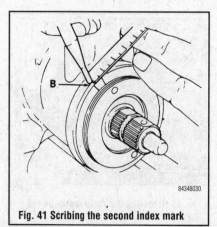
Fig. 41 Scribing the second index mark

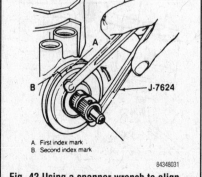
A. First index mark
B. Second index mark
Fig. 42 Using a spanner wrench to align the adjuster plug with the second mark

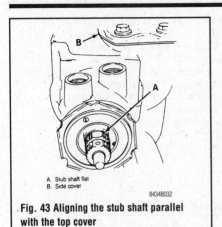

Fig. 43 Aligning the stub shaft parallel with the top cover

A. Stub shaft flat
B. Side cover

84348032

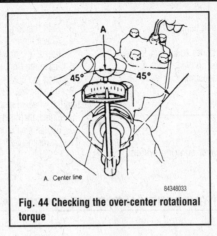

Fig. 44 Checking the over-center rotational torque

A. Center line

84348033

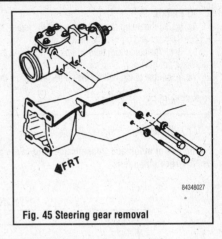

Fig. 45 Steering gear removal

84348027

4. Remove Pitman arm using special tool J–6632 or its equal.
5. Remove the steering box to frame bolts. Remove the steering box.

➥**On vehicles with power steering, remove the fluid hoses and cap them to prevent foreign material from entering the system.**

To install:

6. Position the steering box and secure with the steering box-to-frame bolts.
7. Install the Pitman arm to the matchmarks made earlier.
8. Install the Pitman arm nut and washer.
9. Install the retaining bolts at the steering coupling to steering shaft flange.
10. Install the coupling shield.
11. Connect the negative battery cable.

Power Steering Pump

REMOVAL & INSTALLATION

▶ **See Figures 46, 47 and 48**

1. Remove the hoses at the pump and tape the openings shut to prevent contamination. Position the disconnected lines in a raised position to prevent leakage.

2. Remove the pump belt. Remove the pump pulley, as required
3. Loosen the retaining bolts and any braces, and remove the pump.

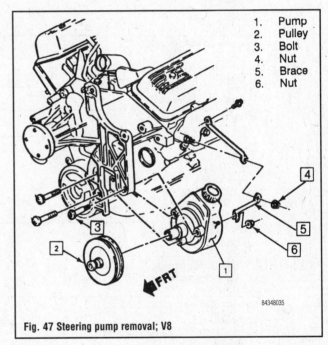

1. Pump
2. Pulley
3. Bolt
4. Nut
5. Brace
6. Nut

Fig. 47 Steering pump removal; V8

84348035

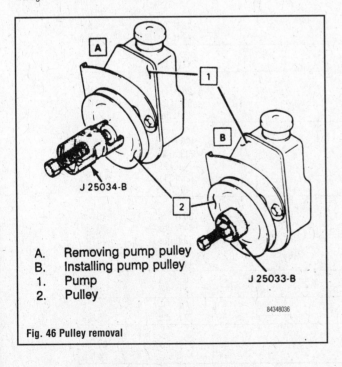

A. Removing pump pulley
B. Installing pump pulley
1. Pump
2. Pulley

J 25034-B
J 25033-B

Fig. 46 Pulley removal

84348036

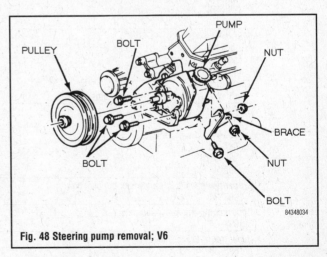

PULLEY
PUMP
BOLT
NUT
BRACE
NUT
BOLT
BOLT

Fig. 48 Steering pump removal; V6

84348034

To install:

4. Install the pump on the engine with the retaining bolt handtight.

5. Connect and tighten the hose fittings.

6. Refill the pump with fluid and bleed by turning the pulley counterclockwise (viewed from the front). Stop the bleeding when air bubbles no longer appear.

7. Install the pump belt on the pulley and adjust the tension.

SYSTEM BLEEDING

1. Fill the reservoir with power steering fluid.

➡**The use of automatic transmission fluid in the power steering system is NOT recommended.**

2. Allow the reservoir and fluid to sit undisturbed for a few minutes.

3. Start the engine, allow it to run for a moment, then turn it off.

4. Check the reservoir fluid level and add fluid if necessary.

5. Repeat the above steps until the fluid level stabilizes.

6. Raise the front of the vehicle so that the wheels are off of the ground.

7. Start the engine and increase the engine speed to about 1500 rpm.

8. Turn the front wheels right to left (and back) several times, lightly contacting the wheel stops at the ends of travel.

9. Check the reservoir fluid level. Add fluid as required.

10. Repeat step 8 until the fluid level in the reservoir stabilizes.

11. Lower the vehicle and repeat steps 8 and 9.

FRONT SUSPENSION TORQUE SPECIFICATIONS

Component	U.S.	Metric
Ball joints		
Lower		
1982–88	90 ft. lbs.	120 Nm
1989–91	83 ft. lbs.	113 Nm
1992–94	80 ft. lbs.	108 Nm
Upper		
1993–94	39 ft. lbs.	53 Nm
Lower control arm pivot nuts		
1982–84	65 ft. lbs.	90 Nm
1985–86	60 ft. lbs.	83 Nm
1987–91	67 ft. lbs.	90 Nm
1992	61 ft. lbs.	83 Nm
1993–94	96 ft. lbs.	130 Nm
Rebound bumper		
1982–94	20 ft. lbs.	27 Nm
Shock absorber		
Lower end		
1993–94	48 ft. lbs.	65 Nm
Upper end		
1993–94		
Bolt	37 ft. lbs.	50 Nm
Nut	32 ft. lbs.	43 Nm
Stabilizer bar link-to-control arm		
1982–91	15 ft. lbs.	20 Nm
1992		
w/o handling package	15 ft. lbs.	20 Nm
w/handling package	18 ft. lbs.	24 Nm
1993–94	17 ft. lbs.	23 Nm
Stabilizer bar mounting bracket-to-arm		
1993–94	41 ft. lbs.	55 Nm
Stabilizer bar mounting bracket-to-frame		
1982–84	26 ft. lbs.	35 Nm
1985–92	39 ft. lbs.	53 Nm
1993–94	41 ft. lbs.	55 Nm
Strut-to-knuckle bolts		
1982–86	195 ft. lbs.	265 Nm
1987–90	203 ft. lbs.	275 Nm
1991–92		
Step 1	125 ft. lbs.	170 Nm
Step 2 + 120 deg. turn or minimum	148 ft. lbs.	200 Nm
Strut-to-upper mount nut		
1982–84	50 ft. lbs.	70 Nm
1985–86	44 ft. lbs.	60 Nm
1987–88	52 ft. lbs.	70 Nm
1989–91	46 ft. lbs.	63 Nm
1992	44 ft. lbs.	60 Nm
Suspension frame-to-crossmember nut plug bolt		
1993–94	74 ft. lbs.	100 Nm
Upper control arm-to-support nuts		
1993–94	72 ft. lbs.	98 Nm
Upper mount-to-wheelhouse tower		
1982–88	20 ft. lbs.	27 Nm
1989–92	18 ft. lbs.	24 Nm

85348T99

REAR SUSPENSION TORQUE SPECIFICATIONS

Component	U.S.	Metric
Control arm-to-axle		
1982-87	68 ft. lbs.	93 Nm
1988	80 ft. lbs.	108 Nm
1989-92	85 ft. lbs.	115 Nm
1993-94	80 ft. lbs.	108 Nm
Control arm-to-frame		
1982-87	68 ft. lbs.	93 Nm
1988	80 ft. lbs.	108 Nm
1989-92	85 ft. lbs.	115 Nm
1993-94	80 ft. lbs.	108 Nm
Rebound bumper		
1982-94	20 ft. lbs.	27 Nm
Shock absorber		
Lower end		
1982-91	70 ft. lbs.	95 Nm
1992-94	66 ft. lbs.	90 Nm
Upper end		
1982-94	13 ft. lbs.	17 Nm
Stabilizer bar U-bolts		
1982-94	20 ft. lbs.	27 Nm
Stabilizer link-to-bar		
1982-87	12 ft. lbs.	17 Nm
1988-91	16 ft. lbs.	22 Nm
1992-94	18 ft. lbs.	24 Nm
Stabilizer link-to-frame		
1982-92	35 ft. lbs.	47 Nm
Tie rod bracket-to-left brace		
1982-92	35 ft. lbs.	47 Nm
Tie rods-to-brackets		
1993-94	75 ft. lbs.	102 Nm
Torque arm-to-axle		
1982-88	100 ft. lbs.	135 Nm
1989-94	98 ft. lbs.	133 Nm
Torque arm-to-transmission		
1982	20 ft. lbs.	27 Nm
1983-85		
200C	20 ft. lbs.	27 Nm
All others	31 ft. lbs.	42 Nm
1986-92	31 ft. lbs.	42 Nm
1993-94	37 ft. lbs.	50 Nm
Track bar-to-axle		
1982-87	93 ft. lbs.	125 Nm
1988-89	59 ft. lbs.	80 Nm
1990-91	61 ft. lbs.	83 Nm
1992	35 ft. lbs.	47 Nm

85348T9A

REAR SUSPENSION TORQUE SPECIFICATIONS

Component	U.S.	Metric
Track bar-to-frame brace		
1982-87	58 ft. lbs.	78 Nm
1988	78 ft. lbs.	105 Nm
1989-91	80 ft. lbs.	108 Nm
1992	76 ft. lbs.	103 Nm
Track bar brace-to-frame		
1982-87	58 ft. lbs.	78 Nm
1988	78 ft. lbs.	105 Nm
1989	61 ft. lbs.	83 Nm
1990-91	80 ft. lbs.	108 Nm
1992	76 ft. lbs.	103 Nm

85348T9B

WHEELS/HUBS/BEARINGS TORQUE SPECIFICATIONS

Component	U.S.	Metric
Front wheel bearings		
1982-92		
Seating torque	12 ft. lbs.	16 Nm
Back off	Until loose	
Adjusting torque	Hand tight	
Wheel hub-to-knuckle bolts		
1993-94	63 ft. lbs.	86 Nm
Wheel lug nuts		
1982-85	100 ft. lbs.	140 Nm
1988		
Aluminum wheels	80 ft. lbs.	110 Nm
Steel wheels	80 ft. lbs.	110 Nm
1986-91	80 ft. lbs.	110 Nm
1992-94	100 ft. lbs.	140 Nm

85348T9C

STEERING COMPONENTS TORQUE SPECIFICATIONS

Component	U.S.	Metric
Power steering gear		
Adjuster plug locknut		
1982-92	80 ft. lbs.	110 Nm
1993-94	55 ft. lbs.	75 Nm
Ball return guide clamp screw		
1982-92	48 inch lbs.	5 Nm
Coupling flange bolt		
1982-92	30 ft. lbs.	40 Nm
Coupling flange nuts		
1982-92	20 ft. lbs.	27 Nm
Gear-to-frame		
1982-84	80 ft. lbs.	110 Nm
1985-88	70 ft. lbs.	95 Nm
1989-91	66 ft. lbs.	90 Nm
1992	73 ft. lbs.	99 Nm
1993-94	63 ft. lbs.	85 Nm
Inner tie rod		
1993-94	74 ft. lbs.	100 Nm
Mesh load adjuster screw locknut		
1982-91	20 ft. lbs.	27 Nm
1992	36 ft. lbs.	49 Nm
Pitman shaft nut		
1982-92	185 ft. lbs.	240 Nm
Pressure hose-to-gear		
1982-92	20 ft. lbs.	27 Nm
Rack piston plug		
1982-91	75 ft. lbs.	100 Nm
1992	111 ft. lbs.	150 Nm
Return hose-to-gear		
1982-92	20 ft. lbs.	27 Nm
Side cover bolts		
1982-92	45 ft. lbs.	60 Nm
Power steering pump		
Brace-to-engine bolt		
1982-92	18 ft. lbs.	25 Nm
Brace-to-engine bolt		
1982-92	24 ft. lbs.	33 Nm
Brace-to-pump nut		
1982-92		
V6	18 ft. lbs.	25 Nm
V8	37 ft. lbs.	50 Nm
Flow control fitting		
1982-92	35 ft. lbs.	48 Nm
Fluid fitting		
1993-94	55 ft. lbs.	75 Nm
Pressure hose		
1982-92	20 ft. lbs.	27 Nm
Pump bracket bolts		
1982-92	24 ft. lbs.	33 Nm
Pump bracket-to-stud bolts		
1982-92	37 ft. lbs.	50 Nm
Pump bracket-to-stud nuts		
1982-92	24 ft. lbs.	33 Nm
Pump mounting bolts		
1993-94	43 ft. lbs.	58 Nm
Reservoir bolt		
1982-92	35 ft. lbs.	48 Nm

85348T9D

STEERING COMPONENTS TORQUE SPECIFICATIONS

Component	U.S.	Metric
Steering column		
Bracket-to-column bolt		
1982–88	30 ft. lbs.	40 Nm
Breakaway bracket-to-column nuts		
1982–88	25 ft. lbs.	34 Nm
Ignition switch screws		
1982–94	35 inch lbs.	4 Nm
Inflator module-to-steering wheel	25 inch lbs.	3 Nm
Intermediate shaft-to-flex coupling bolt		
1982–92	30 ft. lbs.	40 Nm
1993–94	35 ft. lbs.	47 Nm
Intermediate shaft-to-flex coupling nuts		
1982–89	20 ft. lbs.	27 Nm
1990–92	44 ft. lbs.	60 Nm
Intermediate shaft-to-column shaft		
1982–88	55 ft. lbs.	70 Nm
1989–92	44 ft. lbs.	60 Nm
1993–94	35 ft. lbs.	47 Nm
Lock cylinder housing		
1989	80 inch lbs.	9 Nm
Steering column shroud screws		
1982–88	100 inch lbs.	11 Nm
Steering column toe plate		
1982–88	45 inch lbs.	5 Nm
Steering wheel nut		
1982–94	30 ft. lbs.	40 Nm
Steering wheel pad screws	28 inch lbs.	4 Nm
Turn signal switch screws		
1982–89	35 inch lbs.	4 Nm
1990–92	27 inch lbs.	3 Nm
Steering linkage		
Idler arm-to-frame		
1982	50 ft. lbs.	70 Nm
1983–84	60 ft. lbs.	80 Nm
1985–91	50 ft. lbs.	70 Nm
1992	63 ft. lbs.	86 Nm
Idler arm-to-intermediate (relay) rod nut		
1982–84	40 ft. lbs.	54 Nm
1985–92	35 ft. lbs.	48 Nm
Intermediate (relay) rod-to-Pitman arm		
1982	40 ft. lbs.	54 Nm
1983–84	45 ft. lbs.	60 Nm
1985–92	35 ft. lbs.	48 Nm
Pitman arm-to-steering gear nut		
1982–92	180 ft. lbs.	250 Nm
Tie rod adjusting sleeve nuts		
1982–92	14 ft. lbs.	19 Nm
Tie rod-to-intermediate (relay) rod nut		
1982–84	40 ft. lbs.	54 Nm
1985–88	35 ft. lbs.	48 Nm
1989–92	40 ft. lbs.	54 Nm
Tie rod-to-knuckle ball stud*		
1982	40 ft. lbs.	54 Nm
1983–84	30 ft. lbs.	40 Nm
1985–94	35 ft. lbs.	48 Nm
Toerod outer end jamnut		
1993–94	50 ft. lbs.	68 Nm

*Do not back off; advance to nearest hole for cotter pin

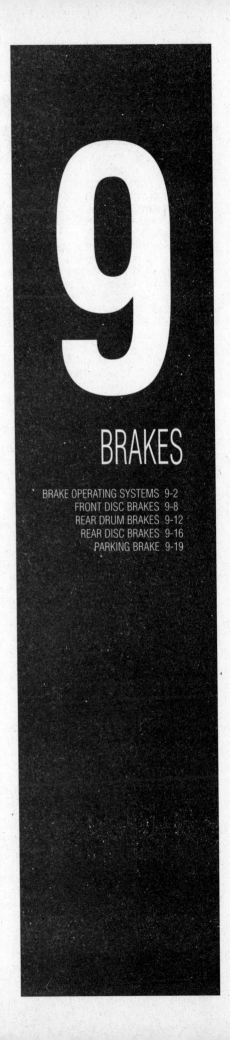

9

BRAKES

BRAKE OPERATING SYSTEM

Basic Operating Principles

Hydraulic systems are used to actuate the brakes of all modern automobiles. The system transports the power required to force the frictional surfaces of the braking system together from the pedal to the individual brake units at each wheel. A hydraulic system is used for two reasons.

First, fluid under pressure can be carried to all parts of an automobile by small pipes and flexible hoses without taking up a significant amount of room or posing routing problems.

Second, a great mechanical advantage can be given to the brake pedal end of the system, and the foot pressure required to actuate the brakes can be reduced by making the surface area of the master cylinder pistons smaller than that of any of the pistons in the wheel cylinders or calipers.

The master cylinder consists of a fluid reservoir along with a double cylinder and piston assembly. Double type master cylinders are designed to separate the front and rear braking systems hydraulically in case of a leak. The master cylinder coverts mechanical motion from the pedal into hydraulic pressure within the lines. This pressure is translated back into mechanical motion at the wheels by either the wheel cylinder (drum brakes) or the caliper (disc brakes).

Steel lines carry the brake fluid to a point on the vehicle's frame near each of the vehicle's wheels. The fluid is then carried to the calipers and wheel cylinders by flexible tubes in order to allow for suspension and steering movements.

In drum brake systems, each wheel cylinder contains two pistons, one at either end, which push outward in opposite directions and force the brake shoe into contact with the drum.

In disc brake systems, the cylinders are part of the calipers. At least one cylinder in each caliper is used to force the brake pads against the disc.

All pistons employ some type of seal, usually made of rubber, to minimize fluid leakage. A rubber dust boot seals the outer end of the cylinder against dust and dirt. The boot fits around the outer end of the piston on disc brake calipers, and around the brake actuating rod on wheel cylinders.

The hydraulic system operates as follows: When at rest, the entire system, from the piston(s) in the master cylinder to those in the wheel cylinders or calipers, is full of brake fluid. Upon application of the brake pedal, fluid trapped in front of the master cylinder piston(s) is forced through the lines to the wheel cylinders. Here, it forces the pistons outward, in the case of drum brakes, and inward toward the disc, in the case of disc brakes. The motion of the pistons is opposed by return springs mounted outside the cylinders in drum brakes, and by spring seals, in disc brakes.

Upon release of the brake pedal, a spring located inside the master cylinder immediately returns the master cylinder pistons to the normal position. The pistons contain check valves and the master cylinder has compensating ports drilled in it. These are uncovered as the pistons reach their normal position. The piston check valves allow fluid to flow toward the wheel cylinders or calipers as the pistons withdraw. Then, as the return springs force the brake pads or shoes into the released position, the excess fluid reservoir through the compensating ports. It is during the time the pedal is in the released position that any fluid that has leaked out of the system will be replaced through the compensating ports.

Dual circuit master cylinders employ two pistons, located one behind the other, in the same cylinder. The primary piston is actuated directly by mechanical linkage from the brake pedal through the power booster. The secondary piston is actuated by fluid trapped between the two pistons. If a leak develops in front of the secondary piston, it moves forward until it bottoms against the front of the master cylinder, and the fluid trapped between the pistons will operate the rear brakes. If the rear brakes develop a leak, the primary piston will move forward until direct contact with the secondary piston takes place, and it will force the secondary piston to actuate the front brakes. In either case, the brake pedal moves farther when the brakes are applied, and less braking power is available.

All dual circuit systems use a switch to warn the driver when only half of the brake system is operational. This switch is usually located in a valve body which is mounted on the firewall or the frame below the master cylinder. A hydraulic piston receives pressure from both circuits, each circuit's pressure being applied to one end of the piston. When the pressures are in balance, the piston remains stationary. When one circuit has a leak, however, the greater pressure in that circuit during application of the brakes will push the piston to one side, closing the switch and activating the brake warning light.

In disc brake systems, this valve body also contains a metering valve and, in some cases, a proportioning valve. The metering valve keeps pressure from traveling to the disc brakes on the front wheels until the brake shoes on the rear wheels have contacted the drums, ensuring that the front brakes will never be used alone. The proportioning valve controls the pressure to the rear brakes to lessen the chance of rear wheel lock-up during very hard braking.

Warning lights may be tested by depressing the brake pedal and holding it while opening one of the wheel cylinder bleeder screws. If this does not cause the light to go on, substitute a new lamp, make continuity checks, and, finally, replace the switch as necessary.

The hydraulic system may be checked for leaks by applying pressure to the pedal gradually and steadily. If the pedal sinks very slowly to the floor, the system has a leak. This is not to be confused with a springy or spongy feel due to the compression of air within the lines. If the system leaks, there will be a gradual change in the position of the pedal with a constant pressure.

Check for leaks along all lines and at wheel cylinders. If no external leaks are apparent, the problem is inside the master cylinder.

DISC BRAKES

Instead of the traditional expanding brakes that press outward against a circular drum, disc brake systems utilize a disc (rotor) with brake pads positioned on either side of it. An easily-seen analogy is the hand brake arrangement on a bicycle. The pads squeeze onto the rim of the bike wheel, slowing its motion. Automobile disc brakes use the identical principle but apply the braking effort to a separate disc instead of the wheel.

The disc (rotor) is a casting, usually equipped with cooling fins between the two braking surfaces. This enables air to circulate between the braking surfaces making them less sensitive to heat buildup and more resistant to fade. Dirt and water do not drastically affect braking action since contaminants are thrown off by the centrifugal action of the rotor or scraped off the by the pads. Also, the equal clamping action of the two brake pads tends to ensure uniform, straight line stops. Disc brakes are inherently self-adjusting. There are three general types of disc brake:

1. A fixed caliper.
2. A floating caliper.
3. A sliding caliper.

The fixed caliper design uses two pistons mounted on either side of the rotor (in each side of the caliper). The caliper is mounted rigidly and does not move.

The sliding and floating designs are quite similar. In fact, these two types are often lumped together. In both designs, the pad on the inside of the rotor is moved into contact with the rotor by hydraulic force. The caliper, which is not held in a fixed position, moves slightly, bringing the outside pad into contact with the rotor. There are various methods of attaching floating calipers. Some pivot at the bottom or top, and some slide on mounting bolts. In any event, the end result is the same.

DRUM BRAKES

Drum brakes employ two brake shoes mounted on a stationary backing plate. These shoes are positioned inside a circular drum which rotates with the wheel assembly. The shoes are held in place by springs. This allows them to slide toward the drums (when they are applied) while keeping the linings and drums in alignment. The shoes are actuated by a wheel cylinder which is mounted at the top of the backing plate. When the brakes are applied, hydraulic pressure forces the wheel cylinder's actuating links outward. Since these links bear directly against the top of the brake shoes, the tops of the shoes are then forced against the inner side of the drum. This action forces the bottoms of the two shoes to contact the brake drum by rotating the entire assembly slightly (known as servo action). When pressure within the wheel cylinder is relaxed, return springs pull the shoes back away from the drum.

Most modern drum brakes are designed to self-adjust themselves during application when the vehicle is moving in reverse. This motion causes both shoes to rotate very slightly with the drum, rocking an adjusting lever, thereby causing rotation of the adjusting screw. Some drum brake systems are designed to self-adjust during application whenever the brakes are applied. This on-board adjustment system reduces the need for maintenance adjustments and keeps both the brake function and pedal feel satisfactory.

POWER BOOSTERS

Virtually all modern vehicles use a vacuum assisted power brake system to multiply the braking force and reduce pedal effort. Since vacuum is always available when the engine is operating, the system is simple and efficient. A vacuum diaphragm is located on the front of the master cylinder and assists the driver in applying the brakes, reducing both the effort and travel he must put into moving the brake pedal.

The vacuum diaphragm housing is normally connected to the intake manifold by a vacuum hose. A check valve is placed at the point where the hose enters the diaphragm housing, so that during periods of low manifold vacuum brakes assist will not be lost.

Depressing the brake pedal closes off the vacuum source and allows atmospheric pressure to enter on one side of the diaphragm. This causes the master cylinder pistons to move and apply the brakes. When the brake pedal is released, vacuum is applied to both sides of the diaphragm and springs return the diaphragm and master cylinder pistons to the released position.

If the vacuum supply fails, the brake pedal rod will contact the end of the master cylinder actuator rod and the system will apply the brakes without any power assistance. The driver will notice that much higher pedal effort is needed to stop the car and that the pedal feels harder than usual.

Vacuum Leak Test

1. Operate the engine at idle without touching the brake pedal for at least one minute.
2. Turn off the engine and wait one minute.
3. Test for the presence of assist vacuum by depressing the brake pedal and releasing it several times. If vacuum is present in the system, light application will produce less and less pedal travel. If there is no vacuum, air is leaking into the system.

System Operation Test

1. With the engine **OFF**, pump the brake pedal until the supply vacuum is entirely gone.
2. Put light, steady pressure on the brake pedal.
3. Start the engine and let it idle. If the system is operating correctly, the brake pedal should fall toward the floor if the constant pressure is maintained.

Power brake systems may be tested for hydraulic leaks just as ordinary systems are tested.

Adjustment

DISC BRAKES

Disc brakes are self-adjusting. No adjustment is possible or necessary. Check fluid level of reservoir, for as brake pads wear, the piston moves out and the piston void must be replaced with brake fluid.

DRUM BRAKES

▶ **See Figures 1 and 2**

The drum brakes are designed to self-adjust when applied with the car moving in reverse. However, they can also be adjusted manually. This manual adjustment should also be performed whenever the linings are replaced.

1. Use a punch to knock out the lanced area in the brake backing plate. If this is done with the drum installed on the car, the drum must then be removed to clean out all metal pieces. After adjustments are complete, obtain a hole cover to prevent entry of dirt and water into the brakes.

➡ **On many vehicles the metal plate may have already been removed and replaced with a rubber plug**

2. Use an adjusting tool especially made for the purpose to turn the brake adjusting screw star wheel. Use a small screwdriver to push the adjusting lever away from star wheel when adjusting brakes. Expand the shoes until the drum can just be turned by hand. The drag should be equal at all the wheel.

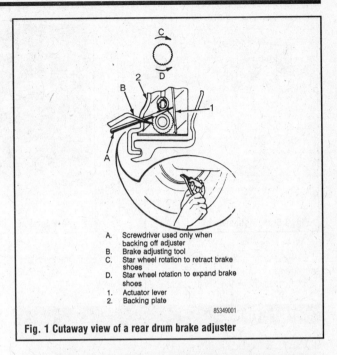

A. Screwdriver used only when backing off adjuster
B. Brake adjusting tool
C. Star wheel rotation to retract brake shoes
D. Star wheel rotation to expand brake shoes
1. Actuator lever
2. Backing plate

85349001

Fig. 1 Cutaway view of a rear drum brake adjuster

85349047

Fig. 2 Adjusting the rear drum brakes

3. Back off the adjusting screw 12 notches. If the shoes still are dragging lightly, back off the adjusting screw one or two additional notches. If the brakes still drag, the parking brake adjustment is incorrect or the parking brake is applied. Fix and start over.
4. Install the hole cover into the drum.
5. Check the parking brake adjustment.

Brake Light Switch

REMOVAL & INSTALLATION

▶ **See Figure 3**

1. Disconnect the wiring harness from the brake light switch.
2. Remove the switch.
To install:
3. Depress the braked pedal, insert the switch into the tubular clip until the switch body seats on the clip. Clicks should be heard as the threaded portion of the switch is pushed through the clip toward the brake pedal.
4. Pull the brake pedal fully rearward (towards the driver) against the pedal stop, until the click sounds can no longer be heard. The switch will be moved in the tubular clip providing adjustment.

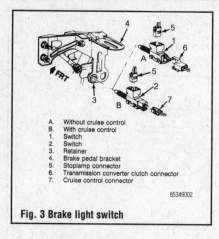

A. Without cruise control
B. With cruise control
1. Switch
2. Switch
3. Retainer
4. Brake pedal bracket
5. Stoplamp connector
6. Transmission converter clutch connector
7. Cruise control connector

85349002

Fig. 3 Brake light switch

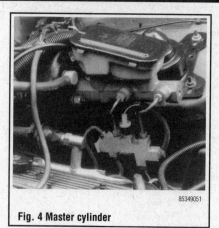

85349051

Fig. 4 Master cylinder

85349052

Fig. 5 Brake pipe removal

5. Release the brake pedal, and then repeat Step 4, to assure that no click sound remains.

6. Connect the wiring harness to the brake light switch.

Master Cylinder

REMOVAL & INSTALLATION

▶ **See Figures 4, 5 and 6**

1. Disconnect hydraulic lines at master cylinder.

2. Remove the retaining nuts and lockwashers that hold cylinder to firewall or the brake booster. Disconnect pushrod at brake pedal (non-power brakes only).

3. Remove the master cylinder, gasket and rubber boot.

4. On non-power brakes, position master cylinder on firewall, making sure pushrod goes through the rubber boot into the piston. Reconnect pushrod clevis to brake pedal. With power brakes, install the cylinder on the booster.

5. Install nuts and lockwashers. Torque nuts to 22–30 ft. lbs. (30–45 Nm).

6. Install hydraulic lines then check brake pedal free play.

7. Bleed the brakes.

OVERHAUL

▶ **See Figures 7 thru 16**

This is a tedious, time-consuming job. You can save yourself a lot of trouble by buying a rebuilt master cylinder from your dealer or parts supply house. The small difference in price between a rebuilding kit and a rebuilt part usually makes it more economical, in terms of time and work, to buy the rebuilt part.

1. Remove the reservoir cover and diaphragm. Discard any brake fluid in the reservoir.

2. Inspect the reservoir cover and diaphragm for cuts, cracks, or deformation. Replace any defective parts.

3. Depress the primary piston and remove the lock ring.

4. Direct compressed air into the outlet at the blind end of the bore and plug the other outlet to remove primary and secondary piston.

5. Remove the spring retainer and seals from the secondary piston.

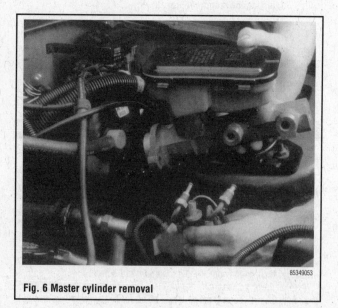

85349053

Fig. 6 Master cylinder removal

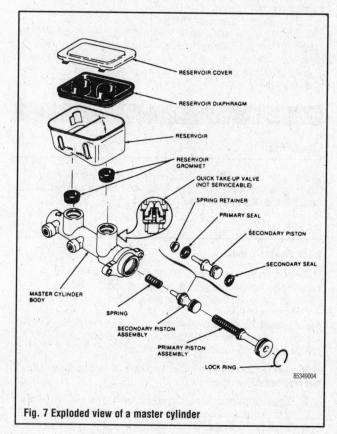

RESERVOIR COVER
RESERVOIR DIAPHRAGM
RESERVOIR
RESERVOIR GROMMET
QUICK TAKE-UP VALVE (NOT SERVICEABLE)
SPRING RETAINER
PRIMARY SEAL
SECONDARY PISTON
SECONDARY SEAL
MASTER CYLINDER BODY
SPRING
SECONDARY PISTON ASSEMBLY
PRIMARY PISTON ASSEMBLY
LOCK RING

85349004

Fig. 7 Exploded view of a master cylinder

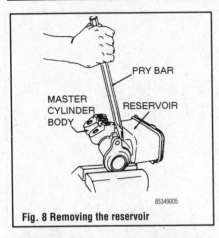

Fig. 8 Removing the reservoir

Fig. 9 Prying out the snapring

Fig. 10 Removing the snapring

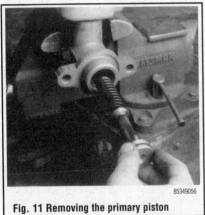

Fig. 11 Removing the primary piston

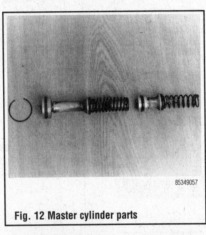

Fig. 12 Master cylinder parts

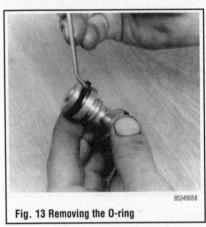

Fig. 13 Removing the O-ring

Fig. 14 Installing the secondary piston

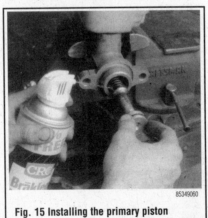

Fig. 15 Installing the primary piston

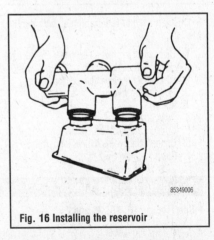

Fig. 16 Installing the reservoir

6. Clamp the master cylinder in a vise. Do not clamp it on the master cylinder body. Use a pry bar to remove the reservoir.

7. Do not attempt to remove the quick take-up valve from the body. This valve is not serviced separately.

8. Remove the reservoir grommets.

9. Inspect the master cylinder bore for corrosion. If corroded, replace the master cylinder. Do not use any abrasive on the bore.

10. Reassemble, using new seals and grommets. Lubricate all parts with brake fluid.

11. Install the reservoir grommets.

12. Install the reservoir.

13. Install the spring retainer and seals from the secondary piston.

14. Install primary and secondary piston.

15. Depress the primary piston and install the lock ring.

16. Fill with brake fluid. Install the reservoir cover and diaphragm.

17. Bleed brake system.

Power Brake Booster

REMOVAL & INSTALLATION

⬥ **See Figure 17**

1. Disconnect vacuum hose from vacuum check valve.

2. Unbolt the master cylinder and carefully move it aside without disconnecting the hydraulic lines.

3. Disconnect pushrod at brake pedal assembly.

➥**Some brake boosters may also be held on with a sealant. This can be easily removed with tar remover.**

4. Remove nuts and lockwashers that secure booster to firewall and remove booster from engine compartment.

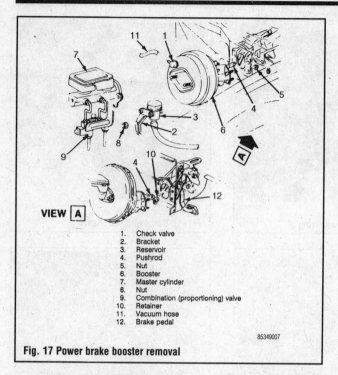

1. Check valve
2. Bracket
3. Reservoir
4. Pushrod
5. Nut
6. Booster
7. Master cylinder
8. Nut
9. Combination (proportioning) valve
10. Retainer
11. Vacuum hose
12. Brake pedal

Fig. 17 Power brake booster removal

5. Install by reversing removal procedure. Make sure to check operation of stop lights. Allow engine vacuum to build before applying brakes.

Combination Valve

REMOVAL & INSTALLATION

➡This valve is not repairable and only serviced as a complete assembly.

1. Disconnect the hydraulic lines from the valve. Plug the lines to prevent fluid loss and dirt contamination.
2. Disconnect the electrical connection.
3. Remove the valve.
To install:
4. Position the valve.
5. Connect the electrical connection.
6. Connect the hydraulic lines to the valve.
7. Bleed the brake system.

Brake Hoses and Lines

▶ **See Figures 18, 19, 20 and 21**

Metal lines and rubber brake hoses should be checked frequently for leaks and external damage. Metal lines are particularly prone to crushing and kinking under the vehicle. Any such deformation can restrict the proper flow of fluid and therefore impair braking at the wheels. Rubber hoses should be checked for cracking or scraping; such damage can create a weak spot in the hose and it could fail under pressure.

Any time the lines are removed or disconnected, extreme cleanliness must be observed. Clean all joints and connections before disassembly (use a stiff bristle brush and clean brake fluid); be sure to plug the lines and ports as soon as they are opened. New lines and hoses should be flushed clean with brake fluid before installation to remove any contamination.

REMOVAL & INSTALLATION

▶ **See Figures 22, 23, 24 and 25**

1. Disconnect the negative battery cable.
2. Raise and safely support the vehicle on jackstands.

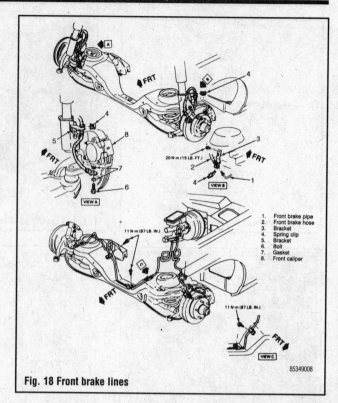

1. Front brake pipe
2. Front brake hose
3. Bracket
4. Spring clip
5. Bracket
6. Bolt
7. Gasket
8. Front caliper

Fig. 18 Front brake lines

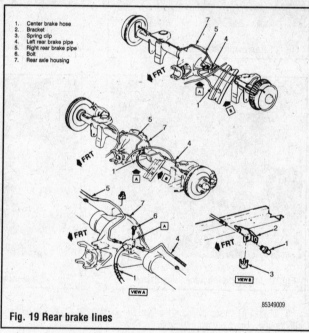

1. Center brake hose
2. Bracket
3. Spring clip
4. Left rear brake pipe
5. Right rear brake pipe
6. Bolt
7. Rear axle housing

Fig. 19 Rear brake lines

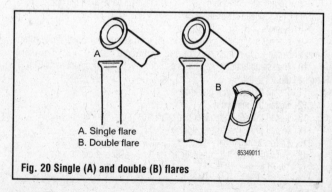

A. Single flare
B. Double flare

Fig. 20 Single (A) and double (B) flares

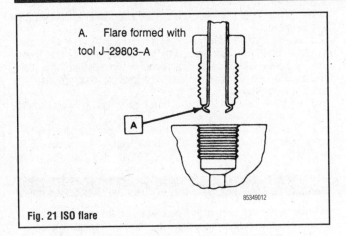

A. Flare formed with tool J–29803–A

Fig. 21 ISO flare

3. Remove any wheel and tire assemblies necessary for access to the particular line you are removing.

4. Thoroughly clean the surrounding area at the joints to be disconnected.

5. Place a suitable catch pan under the joint to be disconnected.

6. Using two wrenches (one to hold the joint and one to turn the fitting), disconnect the hose or line to be replaced.

7. Disconnect the other end of the line or hose, moving the drain pan if necessary. Always use a back-up wrench to avoid damaging the fitting.

8. Disconnect any retaining clips or brackets holding the line and remove the line from the vehicle.

➡If the brake system is to remain open for more time than it takes to swap lines, tape or plug each remaining clip and port to keep contaminants out and fluid in.

To install:

9. Install the new line or hose, starting with the end farthest from the master cylinder. Connect the other end, then confirm that both fittings are correctly threaded and turn smoothly using finger pressure. Make sure the new line will not rub against any other part. Brake lines must be at least 1/2 in. (13mm) from the steering column and other moving parts. Any protective shielding or insulators must be reinstalled in the original location.

❈❈ WARNING

Make sure the hose is NOT kinked or touching any part of the frame or suspension after installation. These conditions may cause the hose to fail prematurely.

10. Using two wrenches as before, tighten each fitting.

11. Install any retaining clips or brackets on the lines.

12. If removed, install the wheel and tire assemblies, then carefully lower the vehicle to the ground.

13. Refill the brake master cylinder reservoir with clean, fresh brake fluid, meeting DOT 3 specifications. Properly bleed the brake system.

14. Connect the negative battery cable.

Bleeding

◗ **See Figures 26 and 27**

The purpose of bleeding the brakes is to expel air trapped in the hydraulic system. The system must be bled whenever the pedal feels spongy, indicating that compressible air has entered the system. It must also be bled whenever the system has been opened, repaired or the fluid appears dirty. You will need a helper for this job.

❈❈ CAUTION

Never reuse brake fluid which has been bled from the brake system.

1. The sequence for bleeding is right rear, left rear, right front and left front. If the car has power brakes, remove the vacuum by applying the brakes several times. Do not run the engine while bleeding the brakes.

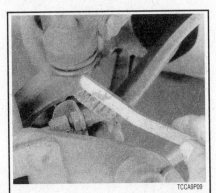

Fig. 22 Use a brush to clean the fittings of any debris

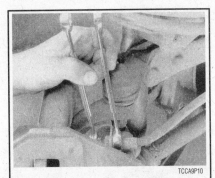

Fig. 23 Use two wrenches to loosen the fitting. If available, use flare nut type wrenches

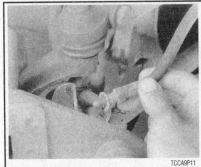

Fig. 24 Any gaskets/crush washers should be replaced with new ones during installation

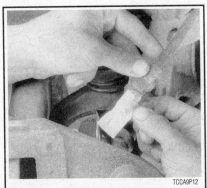

Fig. 25 Tape or plug the line to prevent contamination

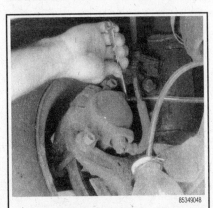

Fig. 26 Caliper bleeding

Fig. 27 Master cylinder bleeding

2. Clean all the bleeder screws. You may want to give each one a shot of penetrating solvent to loosen it; seizure is a common problem with bleeder screws, which then break off, sometimes requiring replacement of the part to which they are attached.

3. Fill the master cylinder with good quality brake fluid.

➡Brake fluid absorbs moisture from the air. Don't leave the master cylinder or the fluid container uncovered any longer than necessary. Be careful handling the fluid; it eats paint. Check the level of the fluid often when bleeding and refill the reservoirs as necessary. Don't let them run dry or you will have to repeat the process.

4. Attach a length of clear vinyl tubing to the bleeder screw on the wheel cylinder. Submerge the other end of the tube into a clear, clean jar half filled with brake fluid.

5. Have your assistant slowly depress the brake pedal. As this is done, open the bleeder screw ¾ of a turn and allow the fluid to run through the tube. Then close the bleeder screw before the pedal reaches the end of its travel. Have your assistant slowly release the pedal. Repeat this process until no air bubbles appear in the expelled fluid.

6. Repeat the procedure on the other three brakes, checking the level of fluid in the master cylinder reservoir often.

7. Upon completion, check the brake pedal for sponginess and the brake warning light for unbalanced pressure. If necessary, repeat the entire bleeding procedure.

FRONT DISC BRAKES

⁂ CAUTION

Some brake pads contain asbestos, which has been determined to be a cancer causing agent. Never clean the brake surfaces with compressed air! Avoid inhaling any dust from any brake surface! When cleaning brake surfaces, use a commercially available brake cleaning fluid.

Brake Pads

INSPECTION

The pad thickness should be inspected every time that the tires are removed for rotation. The outer pad can be checked by looking in each end, which is the point at which the highest rate of wear occurs. The inner pad can be checked by looking down through the inspection hole in the top of the caliper. If the thickness of the pad is worn to within 0.030 in. (0.8mm) of the rivet at either end of the pad, all the pads should be replaced.

➡Always replace all pads on both front wheels at the same time. Failure to do so will result in uneven braking action and premature wear.

REMOVAL & INSTALLATION

See Figures 28 thru 34

1. Siphon ⅔ of the brake fluid from the master cylinder reservoir. Loosen the wheel lug nuts and raise the car. Remove the wheel.

2. Position a C-clamp across the caliper and press on the pads. Tighten it until the caliper piston bottoms in its bore.

➡If you haven't removed some brake fluid from the master cylinder, it may overflow when the piston is retracted.

3. Remove the C-clamp.

➡There are 2 different calipers being used, a single piston or dual piston design. The single piston design uses either an Allen head bolt, regular bolt or Torx® head bolt to secure the caliper to the mounting bracket. Do not use a socket in place of the Torx® socket, otherwise

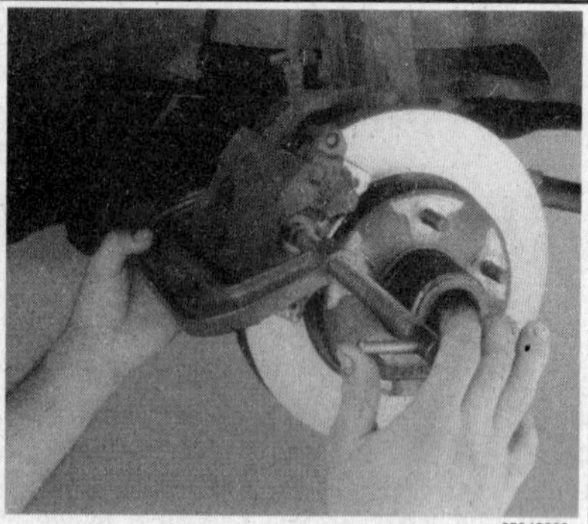

85349068

Fig. 28 Compress the piston with a C-clamp

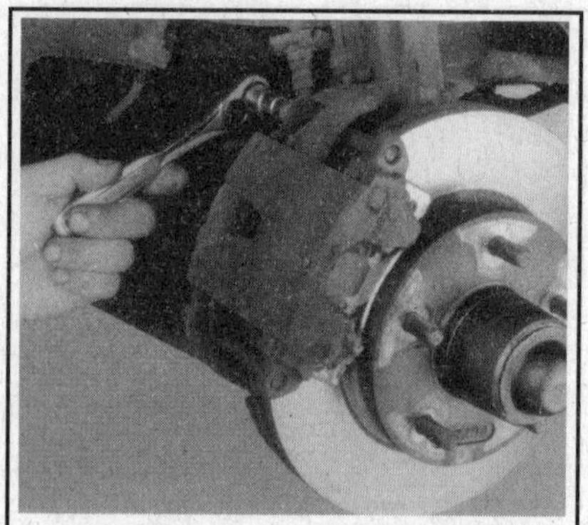

85349069

Fig. 29 Remove the caliper bolts

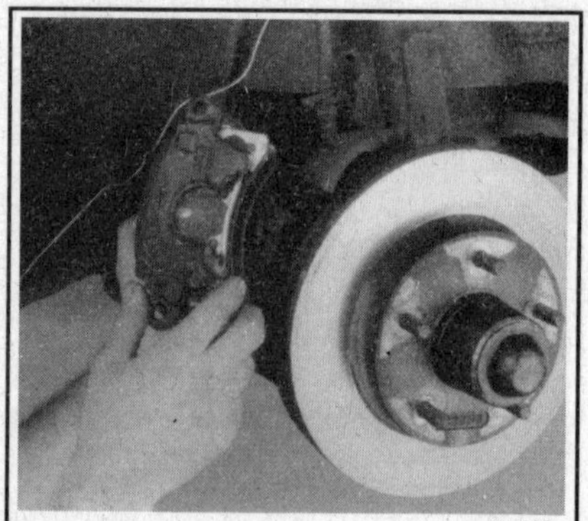

85349070

Fig. 30 Lift off the caliper

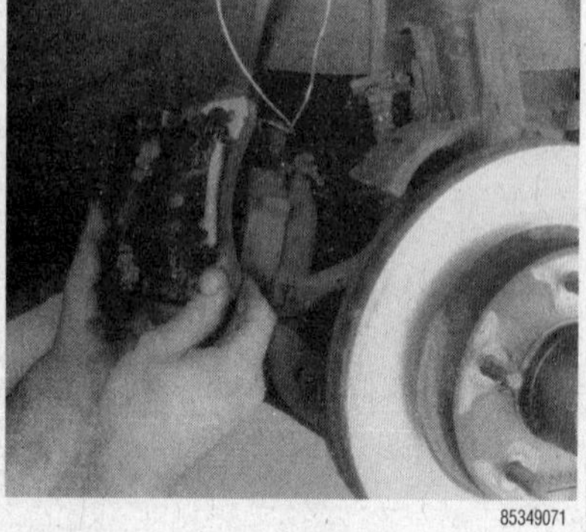

85349071

Fig. 31 Remove the inner pad

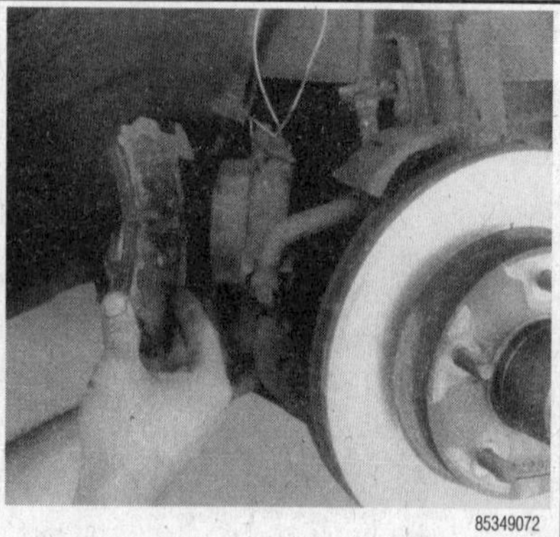

85349072

Fig. 32 Remove the outer pad

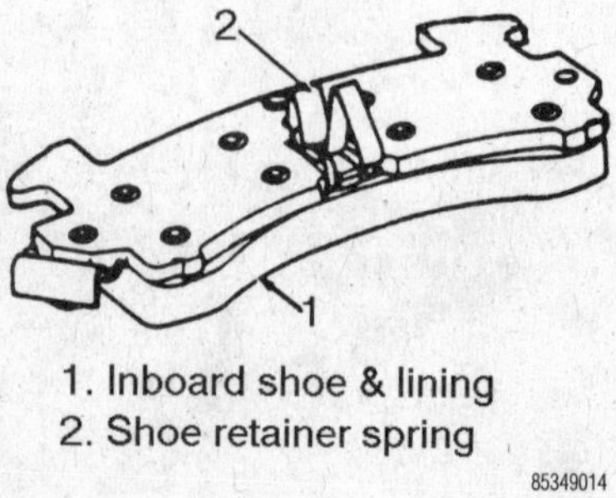
2
1
1. Inboard shoe & lining
2. Shoe retainer spring

85349014

Fig. 33 Install the inner pad retaining clip

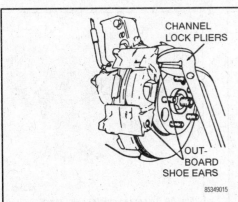

Fig. 34 Bend the outboard pad ears after installation

Fig. 35 Removing the hose retaining clip

damage to the bolt may occur. The dual piston caliper uses a slide pin and circlip to secure it to the bracket.

4. Remove the mounting bolts, if equipped with single piston caliper or the circlip and pin, if equipped with dual piston caliper. Inspect the bolts for corrosion and replace as necessary.

5. Remove the caliper from the steering knuckle and suspend it from the body of the car with a length of wire. Do not allow the caliper to hang by its hose.

6. Remove the pad retaining springs and remove the pads from the caliper.

7. Remove the plastic sleeves and the rubber bushings from the mounting bolt holes.

8. Obtain a pad replacement kit. Lubricate and install the new sleeves and bushings with a light coat of silicone grease.

9. Install the retainer spring on the inboard pad, if equipped with single piston caliper.

➡ A new spring should be included in the pad replacement kit.

10. Install the new inboard pad into the caliper with the wear sensor at the leading end of the shoe during forward wheel rotation.

11. Install the outboard pad into the caliper.

12. Use a large pair of slip joint pliers to bend the outer pad ears down over the caliper, if equipped with the single piston caliper.

13. Install the caliper onto the steering knuckle. Tighten the mounting bolts to 21–35 ft. lbs. (28–47 Nm), if equipped. Install the wheel and lower the car. Fill the master cylinder to its proper level with a good quality brake fluid.

14. Pump the brake pedal slowly and firmly 3 times with the engine running before attempting to move the vehicle; bleed the brakes as required.

Brake Caliper

REMOVAL & INSTALLATION

◆ **See Figures 35 and 36**

✶✶ CAUTION

Brake pads contain asbestos, which has been determined to be a cancer causing agent. Never clean the brake surfaces with compressed air! Avoid inhaling any dust from any brake surface! When cleaning brake surfaces, use a commercially available brake cleaning fluid.

1. Remove ⅔ of the brake fluid from the master cylinder. Raise the vehicle and remove the wheel.

2. Place a C-clamp across the caliper, positioned on the brake pads. Tighten it until the piston is forced into its bore.

3. Remove the C-clamp. Remove the bolt holding the brake hose to the caliper.

4. Remove the Allen head caliper mounting bolts. Inspect them for corrosion and replace them if necessary. Remove the caliper.

Fig. 36 Removing the hose from the retainer

To install:

5. Position the caliper with the brake pad installed and install Allen head caliper mounting bolts. Mounting bolt torque is 21–35 ft. lbs. (28–47 Nm.) for the caliper.

6. Install the bolt holding the brake hose to the caliper and tighten to 18–30 ft. lbs. (24–40 Nm.).

7. Fill the master cylinder with brake fluid.

8. Install the wheels and lower the vehicle.

✶✶ CAUTION

Before moving the vehicle, pump the brakes several times to seat the brake pad against the rotor.

OVERHAUL

◆ **See Figures 37 thru 44**

➡ Some vehicles may be equipped dual piston calipers. The procedure to overhaul the caliper is essentially the same with the exception of multiple pistons, O-rings and dust boots.

1. Remove the caliper from the vehicle and place on a clean workbench.

✶✶ CAUTION

NEVER place your fingers in front of the pistons in an attempt to catch or protect the pistons when applying compressed air. This could result in personal injury!

➡ Depending upon the vehicle, there are two different ways to remove the piston from the caliper. Refer to the brake pad replacement procedure to make sure you have the correct procedure for your vehicle.

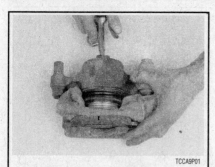

Fig. 37 For some types of calipers, use compressed air to drive the piston out of the caliper, but make sure to keep your fingers clear

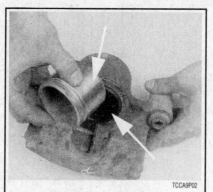

Fig. 38 Withdraw the piston from the caliper bore

Fig. 39 On some vehicles, you must remove the anti-rattle clip

Fig. 40 Use a prytool to carefully pry around the edge of the boot . . .

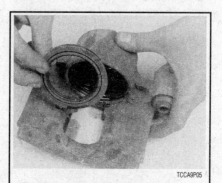

Fig. 41 . . . then remove the boot from the caliper housing, taking care not to score or damage the bore

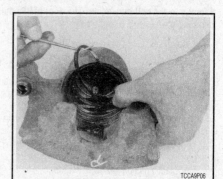

Fig. 42 Use extreme caution when removing the piston seal; DO NOT scratch the caliper bore

Fig. 43 Use the proper size driving tool and a mallet to properly seal the boots in the caliper housing

Fig. 44 There are tools, such as this Mighty-Vac, available to assist in proper brake system bleeding

2. The first method is as follows:

   a. Stuff a shop towel or a block of wood into the caliper to catch the piston.

   b. Remove the caliper piston using compressed air applied into the caliper inlet hole. Inspect the piston for scoring, nicks, corrosion and/or worn or damaged chrome plating. The piston must be replaced if any of these conditions are found.

3. For the second method, you must rotate the piston to retract it from the caliper.

4. If equipped, remove the anti-rattle clip.

5. Use a prytool to remove the caliper boot, being careful not to scratch the housing bore.

6. Remove the piston seals from the groove in the caliper bore.

7. Carefully loosen the brake bleeder valve cap and valve from the caliper housing.

8. Inspect the caliper bores, pistons and mounting threads for scoring or excessive wear.

9. Use crocus cloth to polish out light corrosion from the piston and bore.

10. Clean all parts with denatured alcohol and dry with compressed air.

To assemble:

11. Lubricate and install the bleeder valve and cap.

12. Install the new seals into the caliper bore grooves, making sure they are not twisted.

13. Lubricate the piston bore.

14. Install the pistons and boots into the bores of the calipers and push to the bottom of the bores.

15. Use a suitable driving tool to seat the boots in the housing.

16. Install the caliper in the vehicle.

17. Install the wheel and tire assembly, then carefully lower the vehicle.

18. Properly bleed the brake system.

Brake Disc (Rotor)

REMOVAL & INSTALLATION

▶ **See Figures 45, 46, 47, 48 and 49**

> ☀☀ **CAUTION**
>
> **Brake pads contain asbestos, which has been determined to be a cancer causing agent. Never clean the brake surfaces with compressed air! Avoid inhaling any dust from any brake surface! When cleaning brake surfaces, use a commercially available brake cleaning fluid.**

1. Remove the caliper by following instructions of caliper removal procedure.
2. Remove dust cap, cotter pin, castle nut, thrust washer and outside wheel bearing. Pull the disc/hub assembly from the steering knuckle.

To install:

3. Position the disc/hub assembly to the spindle/steering knuckle. Install the outside wheel bearing, thrust washer and castle nut. Tighten the castle nut until the bearing is snug. Back off the nut ¼ turn. Refer to Section 8 for details on wheel bearing removal, installation, and adjustment. Install a new cotter pin and dust cap.

4. Install the brake caliper.

INSPECTION

▶ **See Figure 50**

1. Check the rotor surface for wear, scoring, grooves or rust pitting. Rotor damage can be corrected by refacing, consult your local garage or machine shop. If the damage exceeds the minimum thickness, which is stamped on the rotor, replace the rotor.
2. Check the rotor parallelism at four or more points around the circumference, it must not vary more than 0.0005 in. (0.013mm). Make all measurements at the same distance in from the edge of the rotor. Refinish the rotor if it fails to meet specification.
3. Measure the disc runout with a dial indicator. If runout exceeds 0.004 in. (0.10mm), and the wheel bearings are okay (runout is measured with the disc on the car), the rotor must be refaced or replaced.

Fig. 45 Breaking loose the dust cap

Fig. 46 Removing the dust cap

Fig. 47 Removing the cotter pin

Fig. 48 Removing the spindle nut

Fig. 49 Removing the washer

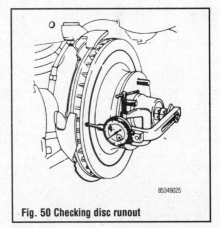

Fig. 50 Checking disc runout

REAR DRUM BRAKES

▶ **See Figure 51**

Brake Drums

REMOVAL & INSTALLATION

❋❋ CAUTION

Brake shoes may contain asbestos, which has been determined to be a cancer causing agent. Never clean the brake surfaces with compressed air! Avoid inhaling any dust from any brake surface! When cleaning brake surfaces, use a commercially available brake cleaning fluid.

1. Raise and support the car.
2. Remove the wheel or wheels.
3. Pull the brake drum off. It may be necessary to gently tap the rear edges of the drum to start it off the studs.
4. If extreme resistance to removal is encountered, it will be necessary to retract the adjusting screw. Knock out the access hole in the backing plate and turn the adjuster to retract the linings away from the drum.
5. Install a replacement hole cover before reinstalling drum.
6. Install the drums in the same position on the hub as removed.

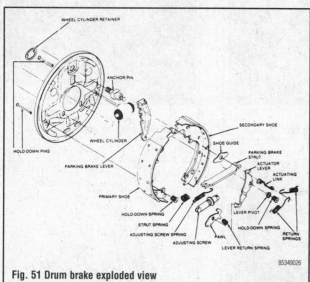

Fig. 51 Drum brake exploded view

DRUM INSPECTION

1. Check the drums for any cracks, scores, grooves, or an out-of-round condition. Replace if cracked. Slight scores can be removed with fine emery cloth while extensive scoring requires turning the drum on a lathe.
2. Never have a drum turned more than 0.060 in. (1.524mm).

Brake Shoes

ADJUSTMENT

Rotate the star wheel adjuster until a slight drag is felt between the shoes and drum, then back off 12 clicks on the adjusting wheel. Put the car in reverse and, while backing up, apply the brakes several times. This will allow the self-adjusters to complete the adjustment.

REMOVAL & INSTALLATION

▶ **See Figures 52 thru 64**

❋❋ CAUTION

Brake shoes may contain asbestos, which has been determined to be a cancer causing agent. Never clean the brake surfaces with compressed air! Avoid inhaling any dust from any brake surface! When cleaning brake surfaces, use a commercially available brake cleaning fluid.

1. Raise and safely support the vehicle.
2. Remove the wheel and tire assemblies.
3. Remove the brake drum.
4. Remove the return springs.
5. Remove the hold-down springs and pins. Remove the lever pivot.
6. Remove the actuator link while lifting up on the actuator lever.
7. Remove the actuator lever and lever return spring.
8. Remove the shoe guide, parking brake strut and strut spring.
9. Remove the brake shoes and disconnect the parking brake lever from the shoe.
10. Remove the adjusting screw assembly and spring. Remove the retaining ring, pin from the secondary shoe.

To install:

➡ **Any part or spring which may appear worn should be replace. The short shoe (primary) should be installed to the front of the vehicle and the long shoe (secondary) should be installed to the rear. After complete installation of the brake shoes a clicking sound should be heard when turning the adjusting screw or self-adjuster. Do not switch parts from the left or right brake assembly, the adjusters are designated Left and Right.**

Fig. 52 Drum brake assembly

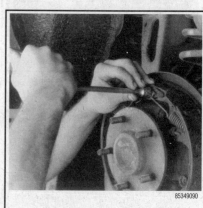

Fig. 53 Using a safe brake cleaning agent

Fig. 54 Unclipping the return springs

Fig. 55 Unclipping the parking brake cable rod

Fig. 56 Removing the rear return spring

Fig. 57 Removing the parking brake rod

Fig. 58 Removing the shoe guide plate

Fig. 59 Turning the hold-down spring lock plate

Fig. 60 Removing the hold-down springs

Fig. 61 Pulling off the shoes

Fig. 62 Separating the shoes and lower spring

Fig. 63 Disconnecting the parking brake cable from the shoe lever

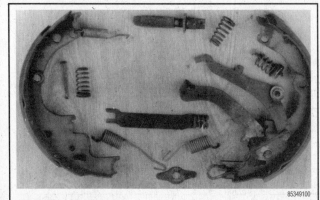

Fig. 64 Drum brake parts

11. Clean dirt from all parts and wire brush raised pads on backing plate. Lubricate backing plate pads and adjusting screw with brake grease.

12. Install the parking brake lever on the secondary shoe with the pin and new retaining ring.

13. Install the adjusting screw and spring. Lubricate the adjusting screw with brake (white) grease.

14. Clean and lubricate the contact points of the backing plate. Install the brake shoe assemblies after installing the parking brake cable on the shoe.

15. Install the parking brake strut and strut spring by spreading the shoes apart.

16. Install the shoe guide, actuator lever and lever return spring.

17. Install the hold-down pins, lever pivot and springs. Install the actuator link on the anchor pin.

18. Install the actuator link into the actuator lever while holding up on the lever.

19. Install the shoe return springs. Install the brake drum. Install the wheel and tire assemblies.

20. Adjust the brake and lower the vehicle. Check emergency brake for proper adjustment.

Wheel Cylinders

REMOVAL & INSTALLATION

▶ See Figures 65, 66 and 67

✳✳ CAUTION

Brake shoes may contain asbestos, which has been determined to be a cancer causing agent. Never clean the brake surfaces with compressed air! Avoid inhaling any dust from any brake surface! When cleaning brake surfaces, use a commercially available brake cleaning fluid.

1. Raise and support the car. Remove the wheel. Remove the brake shoes by following the Brake Shoe Replacement procedure.
2. Remove dirt from around the wheel cylinder inlet and pilot. Disconnect the inlet tube.
3. Using 2 awls, ⅛ in. (3mm) in diameter, or J29839, remove the wheel cylinder retainer. Insert the awls into the access slots between the wheel cylinder pilot and retainer. Simultaneously, bend both tabs away from each other. Remove the wheel cylinder.
   To install:
4. Place wheel cylinder into position and place a block of wood between it and the axle flange. Install a new retainer over the end of the wheel cylinder. Using a 1⅛ in. 12–point socket with an extension, drive the new retainer into position.
5. Connect the inlet tube and torque 120–280 inch lbs. (13.6–20 Nm). Complete installation by reversing the removal procedure. Bleed the brakes.

OVERHAUL

▶ See Figures 68 thru 77

Wheel cylinder overhaul kits may be available, but often at little or no savings over a reconditioned wheel cylinder. It often makes sense with these components to substitute a new or reconditioned part instead of attempting an overhaul.

If no replacement is available, or you would prefer to overhaul your wheel cylinders, the following procedure may be used. When rebuilding and installing wheel cylinders, avoid getting any contaminants into the system. Always use clean, new, high quality brake fluid. If dirty or improper fluid has been used, it will be necessary to drain the entire system, flush the system with proper brake fluid, replace all rubber components, then refill and bleed the system.

1. Remove the wheel cylinder from the vehicle and place on a clean workbench.
2. First remove and discard the old rubber boots, then withdraw the pistons. Piston cylinders are equipped with seals and a spring assembly, all located behind the pistons in the cylinder bore.
3. Remove the remaining inner components, seals and spring assembly. Compressed air may be useful in removing these components. If no compressed air is available, be VERY careful not to score the wheel cylinder bore when removing parts from it. Discard all components for which replacements were supplied in the rebuild kit.
4. Wash the cylinder and metal parts in denatured alcohol or clean brake fluid.

✳✳ WARNING

Never use a mineral-based solvent such as gasoline, kerosene or paint thinner for cleaning purposes. These solvents will swell rubber components and quickly deteriorate them.

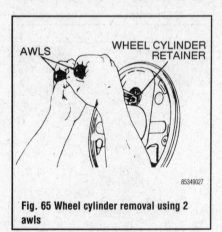

Fig. 65 Wheel cylinder removal using 2 awls

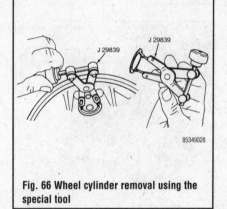

Fig. 66 Wheel cylinder removal using the special tool

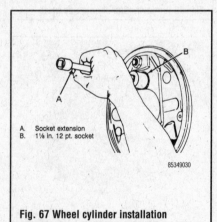

Fig. 67 Wheel cylinder installation

Fig. 68 Remove the outer boots from the wheel cylinder

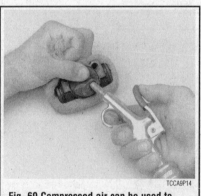

Fig. 69 Compressed air can be used to remove the pistons and seals

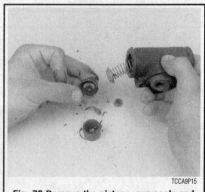

Fig. 70 Remove the pistons, cup seals and spring from the cylinder

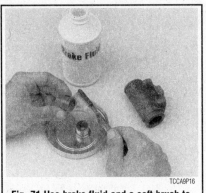

Fig. 71 Use brake fluid and a soft brush to clean the pistons . . .

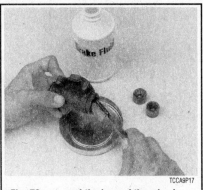

Fig. 72 . . . and the bore of the wheel cylinder

Fig. 73 Once cleaned and inspected, the wheel cylinder is ready for assembly

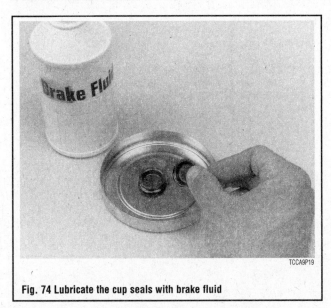

Fig. 74 Lubricate the cup seals with brake fluid

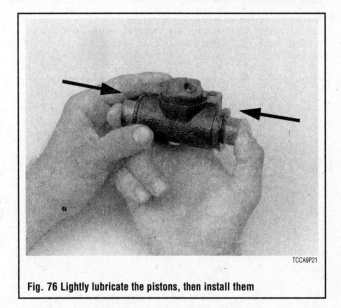

Fig. 76 Lightly lubricate the pistons, then install them

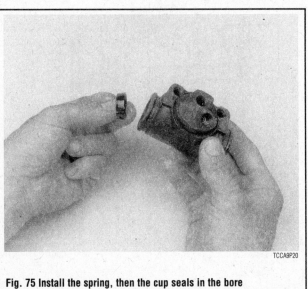
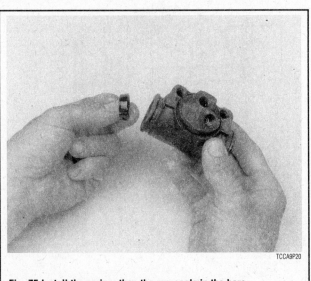

Fig. 75 Install the spring, then the cup seals in the bore

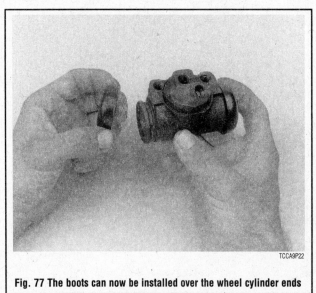

Fig. 77 The boots can now be installed over the wheel cylinder ends

5. Allow the parts to air dry or use compressed air. Do not use rags for cleaning, since lint will remain in the cylinder bore.
6. Inspect the piston and replace it if it shows scratches.
7. Lubricate the cylinder bore and seals using clean brake fluid.
8. Position the spring assembly.

9. Install the inner seals, then the pistons.
10. Insert the new boots into the counterbores by hand. Do not lubricate the boots.
11. Install the wheel cylinder.

REAR DISC BRAKES

Brake Pads

INSPECTION

Refer to the Front Disc Brake Inspection procedure.

REMOVAL & INSTALLATION

1982–88 Models

▶ See Figures 78 and 79

✳✳ CAUTION

Brake pads contain asbestos, which has been determined to be a cancer causing agent. Never clean the brake surfaces with compressed air! Avoid inhaling any dust from any brake surface! When cleaning brake surfaces, use a commercially available brake cleaning fluid.

1. To remove the brake caliper, refer to the Rear Caliper Removal procedure.
2. Remove the brake pads from the calipers. Remove the sleeves from the mounting bolts and the bushings from the caliper.

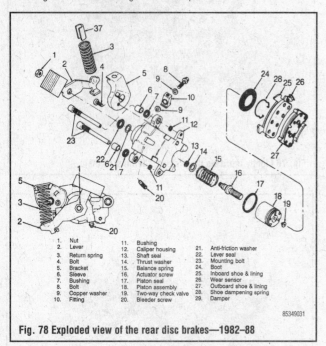

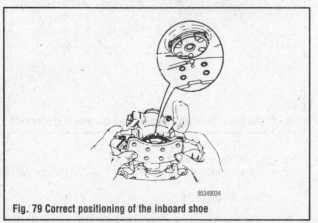

Fig. 79 Correct positioning of the inboard shoe

3. Using a small screwdriver, remove the 2-way check valve from the end of the piston. Clean and check the valve for leakage.

➡ **If leakage is noted, the caliper must be overhauled.**

To install:

4. Position the brake pads into the caliper. Lubricate and install new bushings, sleeves and check valve.
5. When installing the inner brake pad, make sure that the D-shaped tab of the pad engages with the D-shaped notch of the piston, as illustrated.
6. Upon installation of the inner pad, make sure that the wear sensor of the pad is at the leading edge of the shoe during forward wheel rotation. Slide the metal edge of the pad under the ends of the dampening spring and snap the pad into position against the piston.
7. Install the outer pad and caliper. After installing the caliper, apply the brakes, then bend the ears of the outer pad against the caliper and ensure that there is no excessive clearance.

1989–92 Models

▶ See Figure 80

1. Remove ⅔ of the brake fluid from the master cylinder reservoir.
2. Raise and safely support the vehicle.
3. Remove the wheel and tire assembly. Install 2 wheel nuts to retain the rotor.
4. Position a C-clamp and tighten until the piston bottoms in the base of the caliper housing. Make sure 1 end of the C-clamp rests on the inlet fitting bolt and the other against the outboard disc brake pad.

➡ **It is not necessary to remove the parking brake caliper lever return spring to replace the disc brake pads.**

5. Remove the upper caliper guide pin bolt and discard.
6. Rotate the caliper housing. Be careful not to strain the hose or cable conduit.
7. Remove the disc brake pads.

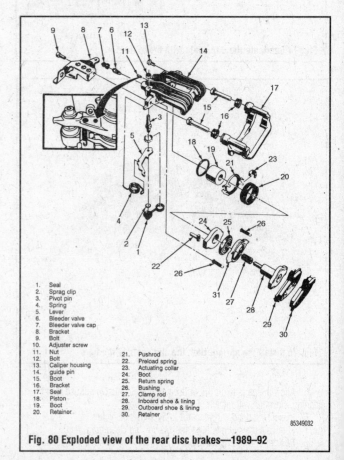

Fig. 80 Exploded view of the rear disc brakes—1989–92

To install:

8. Clean all residue from the pad guide surfaces on the mounting bracket and caliper housing. Inspect the guide pins for free movement in the mounting bracket. Replace the guide pins or boots, if they are corroded or damaged.

9. Install the disc brake pads. The outboard pad with insulator is installed toward the caliper housing. The inboard pad with the wear sensor is installed nearest the caliper piston. The wear sensor must be in the trailing position with forward wheel rotation.

10. Rotate the caliper housing into it's operating position. The springs on the outboard brake pad must not stick through the inspection hole in the caliper housing. If the springs are sticking through the inspection hole in the caliper housing, lift the caliper housing and make the necessary corrections to the outboard brake pad positions.

11. Install a new upper caliper guide pin bolt and tighten to 26 ft. lbs. (35 Nm). Tighten the lower caliper guide pin bolt to 16 ft. lbs. (22 Nm).

12. With the engine running, pump the brake pedal slowly and firmly to seat the brake pads.

13. Check the caliper parking brake levers to make sure they are against the stops on the caliper housing. If the levers are not on their stops, check the parking brake adjustment.

14. Remove the 2 wheel nuts from the rotor and install the wheel and tire assembly.

15. Lower the vehicle, check the master cylinder fluid level and road test the vehicle.

Brake Caliper

REMOVAL & INSTALLATION

✳ CAUTION

Brake pads contain asbestos, which has been determined to be a cancer causing agent. Never clean the brake surfaces with compressed air! Avoid inhaling any dust from any brake surface! When cleaning brake surfaces, use a commercially available brake cleaning fluid.

1982–88 Models

1. Remove ⅔ of the brake fluid from the master cylinder. Raise the car. Remove the wheel. Reinstall a wheel nut, with the flat side toward the rotor, to hold the rotor in place.

2. Loosen the parking brake cable at the equalizer. At the caliper, remove the parking brake cable, damper and spring from the lever.

3. Hold the parking brake lever and remove the lock nut. Remove the lever, seal and anti-friction washer.

4. Position a C-clamp over the caliper and force the piston into its bore. Remove the C-clamp. Reinstall the lever, seal and nut to the caliper.

5. Loosen the brake tube nut and disconnect the brake tube from the caliper. Plug the tube to prevent the loss of brake fluid.

➡ **At the right rear wheel, it may be necessary to remove the rear bolt from the lower control arm to allow the lower caliper mounting bolt to be removed.**

6. Remove the mounting bolts using a ⅜ in. Allen head socket. Remove the caliper and inspect the mounting bolts for corrosion. If necessary, replace the mounting bolts.

To install:

7. Place the caliper onto the rotor and install the mounting bolts. Torque the mounting bolts to 30–45 ft. lbs. (40.7–61 Nm).

8. Install a new anti-friction washer and lubricate the lever with silicone brake lube. Install the lever on the actuator with the lever pointing down. Rotate the lever toward the front of the car and hold while installing the nut. Torque the nut to 30–40 ft. lbs. (40.7–54.2 Nm), then rotate the lever back against the stop on the caliper.

9. Install damper and spring. Connect the parking brake cable. Tighten the cable at the equalizer until the lever starts to move off the stop on the caliper, then loosen the adjustment until the lever moves back against the stop.

10. Remove the nut holding the rotor in place and install the wheel. Lower the car and fill the master cylinder with brake fluid.

1989–92 Models

1. Raise and safely support the vehicle.

2. Loosen the parking brake cable at the equalizer.

3. Remove the wheel and tire assembly. Install 2 wheel nuts to retain the rotor.

4. Remove the bolt, inlet fitting and washers from the caliper housing. Plug the holes in the caliper housing and inlet fitting.

5. Remove the caliper lever return spring only if it is defective. Discard the spring if the coils are opened.

6. Disconnect the parking brake cable from the caliper lever and caliper bracket.

7. Remove the 2 caliper guide pin holes.

8. Remove the caliper housing from the rotor and mounting bracket.

To install:

9. Inspect the guide pins and boots and replace if corroded, worn or damaged. Check the inlet fitting bolt for blockage.

10. Install the caliper housing over the rotor and into the mounting bracket. Install the 2 caliper guide pin bolts. Tighten the upper caliper guide pin bolt to 26 ft. lbs. (35 Nm) and the lower guide pin bolt to 16 ft. lbs. (22 Nm).

11. Connect the parking brake cable to the caliper bracket and caliper lever. Install the caliper lever return spring, if removed.

12. Install the inlet fitting, bolt and 2 new washers to the caliper housing. Tighten the bolt to 22 ft. lbs. (30 Nm).

13. Bleed the brake system.

14. Adjust the parking brake free travel if the caliper was overhauled.

15. Lower the vehicle and cycle the parking brake.

16. Raise and safely support the vehicle.

17. Inspect the caliper parking brake levers and ensure they are against the stops on the caliper housing. If the levers are not on their stop, refer to the parking brake adjustment.

18. Remove the 2 nuts securing the rotor and then install the wheel and tire assembly. Lower the vehicle.

19. With the engine running, pump the brake pedal slowly and firmly 3 times to seat the disc brake pads. Check the hydraulic system for leaks.

OVERHAUL

1982–88 Models

▶ **See Figures 81, 82, 83, 84 and 85**

1. Remove the shoe dampening spring from the end of the piston.

2. Place the caliper in a vise. Move the parking brake lever back and forth to work the piston out of the caliper.

➡ **If the piston will not come out, remove the lever and use a wrench to rotate the adjusting screw. Rotate the screw in the direction of brake application. Remove the balance spring.**

3. Remove the nut, lever, lever seal, and anti-friction washer.

4. Press on the threaded end of the actuator screw to remove it from the housing.

5. Remove the shaft seal and washer.

6. Remove the dust boot. Be careful not to scratch the housing bore.

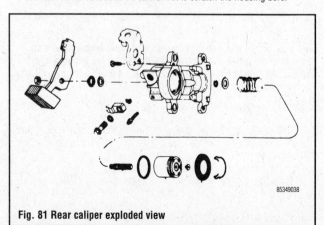

85349038

Fig. 81 Rear caliper exploded view

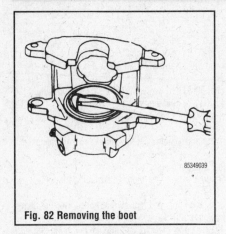

Fig. 82 Removing the boot

Fig. 83 Installing the piston

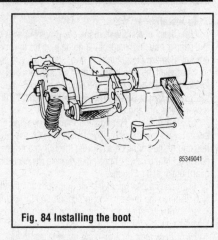

Fig. 84 Installing the boot

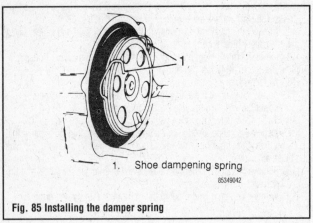

1. Shoe dampening spring

Fig. 85 Installing the damper spring

7. Remove the locator retainer if so equipped. Remove the piston locator if so equipped.

8. Remove the piston seal using a wooden or plastic tool.

9. Remove the bleeder screw, bolt, fitting, and copper washer. Remove the bracket only if it is damaged.

10. Inspect caliper bore for scoring, nicks, corrosion, and wear. Use crocus cloth for light corrosion. Replace caliper if bore will not clean up.

To install:

11. Replace the bleeder screw, bolt, fitting, and copper washer.

12. Install the piston. Lubricate seals and piston with brake fluid prior to reinstallation.

13. Install the locator retainer if so equipped. Install the piston locator if so equipped.

14. Install the dust boot.

15. Install the shaft seal and washer.

16. Install actuator screw to the housing.

17. Install the nut, lever, lever seal, and anti-friction washer. It may be necessary to rotate the parking brake lever away from the stop to install the nut. Torque the nut 30–40 ft. lbs. (41–54 Nm) and rotate the lever back to the stop.

18. Install the shoe dampening spring to the end of the piston.

➡It may be necessary to move the parking brake lever off the stop, extending the piston slightly, making the dampening spring groove accessible. If the piston is extended, push it back into the caliper before installing the caliper on the car.

1989–92 Models

1. Remove the caliper assembly. Remove the 2 collar return springs from the actuating collar. Remove the actuator collar assembly with parts attached out of the housing.

2. Remove the clamp rod and compliance bushing.

3. Remove the boot retainers, 2 boots and pushrod from the compliance bushing. Discard the retainers and boots.

4. Remove the preload spring from the retainer.

5. Using compressed air directed into the brake hose port, carefully extract piston.

✳✳ CAUTION

Do not place fingers between piston and brake shoe flange, or personal injury may occur when piston breaks free from bore. Cover caliper assembly with a rag to prevent brake fluid from spraying when piston is extracted.

6. Inspect and clean piston and bore assembly for cracks or scoring.

7. Remove the piston seal.

8. Remove the bleeder valve.

9. Remove the caliper lever pivot pin seal, sprag clip, spring and lever. Discard the clip.

10. Inspect the caliper lever for worn spots, replace as necessary.

11. Remove the 2 guide pins from the mounting bracket.

12. Clean all parts not included in the rebuild kit in denatured alcohol. Use only dry filtered compressed air to dry parts. Replace the caliper housing if badly scored or corroded.

To install:

13. Lubricate the new piston seal with clean brake fluid. Place the seal into the caliper groove, making sure the seal is not twisted.

14. Install the piston. Lubricate seals and piston with brake fluid prior to reinstallation.

15. Assemble the pushrod, 2 new boots and new retainers to the actuating collar.

16. Lightly coat the actuating collar with the lubricant provided in the rebuild kit. Do not use any other type of lubricant.

17. Install the clamp retainers firmly against the actuating collar. Bend the tabs on the retainer to hold the assembly together.

18. Install the preload spring into the boot retainers.

19. Install the clamp rod to the actuating collar and boot. Lubricate the clamp rod with the lubricant supplied in the kit.

20. Slide the clamp rod through the holes in the boot and actuating collar. The boot must be against the reaction plate on the clamp rod.

21. Lubricate and install the new compliance bushing with the lubricant supplied in the kit.

22. Install the clamp rod with assembled parts into the connecting hole in the caliper piston.

23. Install a new bleeder valve.

24. Install the pivot pin and new nut into the housing, if removed.

25. Install the caliper pivot pin seal, parking brake lever, new sprag clip and spring, in that order. The teeth of the sprag clip must face away from the lever.

26. Install the 2 collar return springs to the retainer. The retainer must enter the return springs at the end of the second coil.

27. Install the adjuster screw into the caliper housing until the actuating collar is parallel to the piston bore face of the caliper housing.

28. Lubricate and then install the guide pins and boots. Install the pads and caliper assembly.

29. Bleed the brake system.

Brake Disc (Rotor)

REMOVAL & INSTALLATION

✳✳ CAUTION

Brake pads contain asbestos, which has been determined to be a cancer causing agent. Never clean the brake surfaces with compressed air! Avoid inhaling any dust from any brake surface! When cleaning brake surfaces, use a commercially available brake cleaning fluid.

1. Raise and support the car. Remove the wheel.
2. Remove the caliper by referring to the Rear Caliper Removal procedure. Pull the brake disc from the axle.
3. To install, place the rotor onto the spindle and install caliper.
4. Install the wheel and lower the car.

PARKING BRAKE

Cables

REMOVAL & INSTALLATION

Front Cable

▶ **See Figure 86**

1. Raise the car and support it with jackstands.
2. Remove the adjusting nut at the equalizer.
3. Remove the spring retainer clip from the bracket.
4. Lower the car. Remove the upper console cover and lower console rear screws.
5. Lift the rear of the lower console for access to the cable retainer at the hand lever.
6. Remove the cable retainer pin, cable retainer, then the cable.

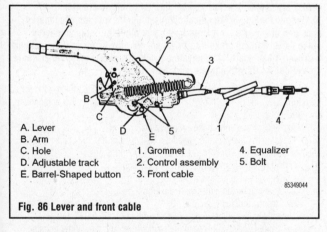

A. Lever
B. Arm
C. Hole
D. Adjustable track
E. Barrel-Shaped button

1. Grommet
2. Control assembly
3. Front cable

4. Equalizer
5. Bolt

85349044

Fig. 86 Lever and front cable

To install:
7. Position the cable retainer pin, cable retainer, then the cable.
8. Install the upper console cover and lower console rear screws. Raise the car and support it with jackstands.
9. Install the spring retainer clip from the bracket.
10. Install the adjusting nut at the equalizer.
11. Adjust the parking brake. Lower the car.

INSPECTION

1. Raise and support the car. Remove the wheel. Replace wheel nuts to hold rotor in place.
2. Check the rotor surface for wear, scoring, grooves or rust pitting. Rotor damage can be corrected by refacing, consult your local garage or machine shop. If the damage exceeds the minimum thickness, which is stamped on the rotor, replace the rotor.
3. Using a dial indicator, check the rotor parallelism at several points around the circumference. The difference must not vary more than 0.0005 in. (0.013mm). Make all measurements at the same distance in from the edge of the rotor.
4. Using the same dial indicator, measure the rotor runout. The runout should not exceed 0.004 in. (0.10mm).
5. If any of these conditions are not met, reface or replace the rotor.

Rear Cable

DRUM BRAKES

▶ **See Figure 87**

✳✳ CAUTION

Brake shoes may contain asbestos, which has been determined to be a cancer causing agent. Never clean the brake surfaces with compressed air! Avoid inhaling any dust from any brake surface! When cleaning brake surfaces, use a commercially available brake cleaning fluid.

1. Raise the car and support it with jackstands.
2. Loosen the adjusting nut at the equalizer.
3. Disengage the rear cable at the connector.
4. Remove the wheel assembly and brake drum.
5. Bend the retainer fingers.
6. Disengage the cable at the brake shoe operating lever.
To install:
7. Engage the cable at the brake shoe operating lever.
8. Bend the retainer fingers.
9. Install the wheel assembly and brake drum.
10. Engage the rear cable at the connector.

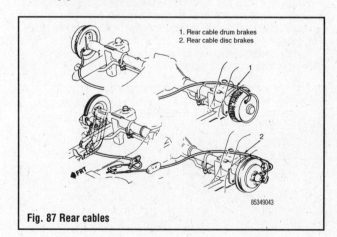

1. Rear cable drum brakes
2. Rear cable disc brakes

85349043

Fig. 87 Rear cables

11. Adjust the parking brake by the adjusting nut at the equalizer.
12. Lower the car.

DISC BRAKES

1. Raise the car and support it with jackstands.
2. Loosen the adjusting nut at the equalizer.
3. Disengage the cable at the connector.
4. Push forward on the caliper parking brake apply lever. This allows the cable to be removed from the tang. Then, release the lever.
5. Pull on the caliper parking brake apply lever to engage the cable to the tang.
6. Engage the cable at the connector.
7. Adjust the parking brake cable by the adjusting nut at the equalizer.
8. Apply the parking brake 3 times with heavy pressure and repeat adjustment.
9. Lower the car.

ADJUSTMENT

The parking brake cable is adjustable only on 1982–89 vehicles. All 1990–92 vehicles feature a self-adjusting parking brake.

Rear Drum Brakes

1. Depress the parking brake lever exactly two ratchet clicks.
2. Raise the rear of the vehicle and support safely with jackstands.
3. Tighten the brake cable adjusting nut until the left rear wheel can be turned rearward with both hands, but locks when forward rotation is attempted.
4. Release the parking brake lever; both rear wheels must turn freely in either direction without brake drag.
5. Lower the vehicle.

Rear Disc Brakes

▶ See Figures 88 and 89

1. Apply the brake pedal 3 times with a pedal force of approximately 175 lbs. (778 N). Apply and release the parking brake 3 times.
2. Raise and safely support the vehicle.
3. Check the parking brake lever for full release:
  a. Turn the ignition **ON**.
  b. The brake warning light should be **OFF**. If the brake warning light is still **ON** and the parking brake lever is completely released, pull downward on the front parking brake cable to remove slack from the lever assembly.
  c. Turn the ignition switch **OFF**.
4. Remove the rear wheels and tires. Reinstall 2 wheel nuts on each side to retain the brake rotors.
5. Pull the parking lever 4 clicks. The parking brake levers on both calipers should be against the lever stops on the caliper housings. If the levers are not against the stops, check for binding in the rear cables and/or loosen the cables at the equalizer nut until both left and right levers are against their stops.
6. Adjust the equalizer adjusting nut until the parking brake levers on both calipers just begin to move off their stops.

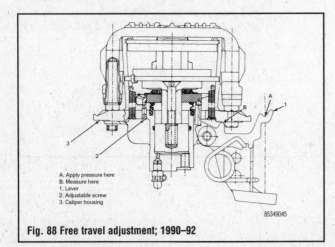

A. Apply pressure here
B. Measure here
1. Lever
2. Adjustable screw
3. Caliper housing

85349045

Fig. 88 Free travel adjustment; 1990–92

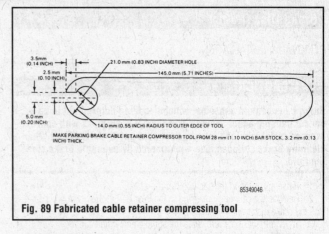

3.5mm (0.14 INCH)
2.5 mm (0.10 INCH)
5.0 mm (0.20 INCH)
21.0 mm (0.83 INCH) DIAMETER HOLE
145.0 mm (5.71 INCHES)
14.0 mm (0.55 INCH) RADIUS TO OUTER EDGE OF TOOL
MAKE PARKING BRAKE CABLE RETAINER COMPRESSOR TOOL FROM 28 mm (1.10 INCH) BAR STOCK, 3.2 mm (0.13 INCH) THICK.

85349046

Fig. 89 Fabricated cable retainer compressing tool

7. Back off the adjuster nut until the levers move back, barely touching their stops.
8. Operate the parking brake lever several times to check adjustment. After cable adjustment, the parking brake lever should travel no more than 14 ratchet clicks. The rear wheels should not turn forward when the parking brake lever is applied 8–16 ratchet clicks.
9. Release the parking brake lever. Both rear wheels must turn freely in both directions. The parking brake levers on both calipers should be resting on their stops.
10. Remove the wheel nuts retaining the rotors. Install the wheel and tire assemblies.
11. Lower the vehicle.

Parking Brake Free-Travel

ADJUSTMENT

1989–92 Models

REAR DISC BRAKES

➡Disc brake pads must be new or parallel to within 0.006 in. (0.15mm). Parking brake adjustment is not valid with heavily tapered pads and may cause caliper/parking brake binding. Replace tapered brake pads. Parking brake free-travel should only be made if the caliper has been taken apart. This adjustment will not correct a condition where the caliper levers will not return to their stops.

1. Have an assistant apply a light brake pedal load, enough to stop the rotor from turning by hand. This takes up all clearances and ensures that components are correctly aligned.
2. Apply light pressure to the caliper lever.
3. Measure the free-travel between the caliper lever and the caliper housing. The free-travel must be 0.0024–0.028 in. (0.6–0.7mm).
4. If the free-travel is incorrect, do the following:
  a. Remove the adjuster screw.
  b. Clean the thread adhesive residue from the threads.
  c. Coat the threads with adhesive.
  d. Screw in the adjuster screw far enough to obtain 0.024–0.028 in. (0.6–0.7mm) free-travel between the caliper lever and the caliper housing.
5. Have an assistant release the brake pedal, then apply the brake pedal firmly 3 times. Recheck the free-travel and adjust as necessary.

Brake Lever

REMOVAL & INSTALLATION

1982–89 Models

1. Raise and safely support the vehicle.
2. Remove the adjusting nut at the equalizer and remove the front cable from the equalizer and bracket.

3. Lower the vehicle.

4. Remove the upper console and lower console rear screws. Lift the rear of the lower console to gain access to the parking brake control.

5. Remove the pin and retainer from the control assembly and front cable.

6. Remove the cable and casing from the control assembly and bracket then remove the cable and grommet from the vehicle. Remove the parking brake lever mounting bolts and remove the assembly.

7. Installation is the reverse of the removal procedure. Adjust the parking brake.

1990–92 Models

1. Remove the carpet finish molding.
2. Remove the console assembly.

3. With the parking brake lever in the down position, rotate the arm toward the front of the vehicle until a 3mm metal pen can be inserted into the hole. Insert the metal pin into the hole, locking out the self adjuster.

4. Raise and safely support the vehicle.

5. Disconnect the rear cables from the equalizer.

6. Lower the vehicle.

7. Remove the barrel-shaped button from the adjuster track.

8. Remove the parking brake lever mounting bolts.

9. Remove the front cable and casing from the control assembly using a fabricated parking brake cable retainer compressor tool.

10. Installation is the reverse of the removal procedure. Cycle the lever to set the parking lever and cables in there proper location.

BRAKE SPECIFICATIONS

Year	Master Cylinder Bore	Disc Minimum Thickness		Disc Maximum Runout		Drum Maximum Oversize	Caliper Bore		Wheel Cylinder Bore
		Front	Rear	Front	Rear		Front	Rear	
1982	①	0.980	0.980	0.005	0.005	9.560	2.500	1.890	0.748
1983	①	0.980	0.980	0.005	0.005	9.560	2.500	1.890	0.748
1984	①	0.980	0.980	0.005	0.005	9.560	2.500	1.890	0.748
1985	①	0.980	0.980	0.005	0.005	9.560	2.500	1.870	0.748
1986	①	0.980	0.986	0.005	0.005	9.560	2.500	1.870	0.748
1987	①	0.980	0.986	0.005	0.005	9.560	2.500	1.870	0.748
1988	①	0.980	0.986	0.005	0.005	9.560	②	1.595	0.748
1989	①	0.980	0.744	0.005	0.005	9.560	②	1.595	0.748
1990	①	0.980	0.744	0.005	0.005	9.560	②	1.595	0.748
1991	①	0.980	0.744	0.005	0.005	9.560	②	1.595	0.748
1992	①	0.980	0.744	0.005	0.005	9.560	②	1.595	0.748

① With rear drums: 0.945 in.
　With rear discs: 1.000 in.
② Standard: 2.520 in.
　Heavy Duty: 1.500 in. each

85349C99A

Troubleshooting the Brake System

Problem	Cause	Solution
Low brake pedal (excessive pedal travel required for braking action.)	· Excessive clearance between rear linings and drums caused by inoperative automatic adjusters	· Make 10 to 15 alternate forward and reverse brake stops to adjust brakes. If brake pedal does not come up, repair or replace adjuster parts as necessary.
	· Worn rear brakelining	· Inspect and replace lining if worn beyond minimum thickness specification
	· Bent, distorted brakeshoes, front or rear	· Replace brakeshoes in axle sets
	· Air in hydraulic system	· Remove air from system. Refer to Brake Bleeding.
Low brake pedal (pedal may go to floor with steady pressure applied.)	· Fluid leak in hydraulic system	· Fill master cylinder to fill line; have helper apply brakes and check calipers, wheel cylinders, differential valve tubes, hoses and fittings for leaks. Repair or replace as necessary.
	· Air in hydraulic system	· Remove air from system. Refer to Brake Bleeding.
	· Incorrect or non-recommended brake fluid (fluid evaporates at below normal temp).	· Flush hydraulic system with clean brake fluid. Refill with correct-type fluid.
	· Master cylinder piston seals worn, or master cylinder bore is scored, worn or corroded	· Repair or replace master cylinder
Low brake pedal (pedal goes to floor on first application—o.k. on subsequent applications.)	· Disc brake pads sticking on abutment surfaces of anchor plate. Caused by a build-up of dirt, rust, or corrosion on abutment surfaces	· Clean abutment surfaces
Fading brake pedal (pedal height decreases with steady pressure applied.)	· Fluid leak in hydraulic system	· Fill master cylinder reservoirs to fill mark, have helper apply brakes, check calipers, wheel cylinders, differential valve, tubes, hoses, and fittings for fluid leaks. Repair or replace parts as necessary.
	· Master cylinder piston seals worn, or master cylinder bore is scored, worn or corroded	· Repair or replace master cylinder
Decreasing brake pedal travel (pedal travel required for braking action decreases and may be accompanied by a hard pedal.)	· Caliper or wheel cylinder pistons sticking or seized	· Repair or replace the calipers, or wheel cylinders
	· Master cylinder compensator ports blocked (preventing fluid return to reservoirs) or pistons sticking or seized in master cylinder bore	· Repair or replace the master cylinder
	· Power brake unit binding internally	· Test unit according to the following procedure: (a) Shift transmission into neutral and start engine (b) Increase engine speed to 1500 rpm, close throttle and fully depress brake pedal (c) Slow release brake pedal and stop engine (d) Have helper remove vacuum check valve and hose from power unit. Observe for backward movement of brake pedal. (e) If the pedal moves backward, the power unit has an internal bind—replace power unit

TCCA9C01

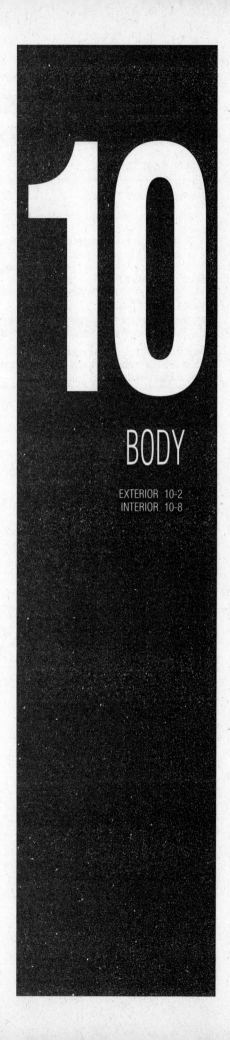

10

BODY

EXTERIOR

Doors

REMOVAL & INSTALLATION

♦ **See Figures 1 and 2**

1. On doors that are equipped with power operated components, do the following:
   a. Remove the door trim panel and inner panel water deflector.
   b. Disconnect the wire harness from all components in the door.
   c. Remove the rubber conduit from the door, then remove the wire harness from the door through the conduit access hole.
2. Tape the area (on the door pillar and body pillar) above the lower hinge with cloth backed body tape.

✷✷ CAUTION

Before performing the following step, cover the spring with a shop cloth or rag to prevent the spring from flying and possibly causing personal injury or damage.

3. Insert a long, flat-blade screwdriver under the pivot point of the hold-open link and over the top of the spring. The screwdriver should be positioned so as not to apply pressure to the hold-open link. Cover the spring with a shop cloth or rag and lift the screwdriver to disengage the spring. The spring can also be removed by using tool J–36604 (or equivalent) door hinge spring compressor tool.

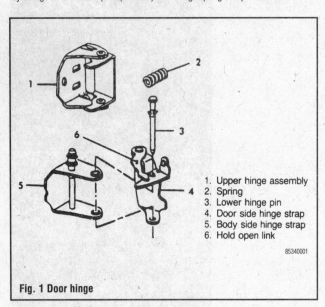

1. Upper hinge assembly
2. Spring
3. Lower hinge pin
4. Door side hinge strap
5. Body side hinge strap
6. Hold open link

85340001

Fig. 1 Door hinge

➡ The tool is stamped right side and left side. The tool stamped left side is used to service the right-hand hinge spring and vise-a-versa for the tool stamped right side.

4. With the aid of a helper to support the door, remove the lower hinge pin using a soft-headed hammer and locking type pliers. The helper can aid the hinge pin removal by raising and lowering the rear of the door.
5. Insert a bolt into the hole of the lower hinge to maintain the door attachment during upper hinge removal.
6. Using a 13mm socket, remove the upper hinge bolts from the pillar. Remove the bolt from the lower hinge and remove the door from the body.

To install:
7. Replace the hinge pin clip.
8. With the aid of a helper, position the door and insert the bolt in the hole of the lower hinge.
9. Bolt the upper hinge to the body. The lower hinge pin is installed with the pointed end down.
10. Remove the screw from the lower hinge and install the lower hinge pin. The use of tool J–36604 or equivalent is recommended for installing the hinge spring.

➡ If the spring is installed before installing the lower hinge pin, damage to the hinge bushings may result.

11. If the spring was removed using a screwdriver, install the spring as follows:
    a. Place the spring in tool J–36604 or equivalent.
    b. Place the tool and spring in a bench vise.
    c. Compress the tool in the vise and install the bolt until the spring is fully compressed.
    d. Remove the tool (with the compressed spring) from the vise and install in the proper position in the door lower hinge. A slot in one jaw fits over the hold-open link. The hole on the other jaw fits over the bubble.
    e. Remove the bolt from the tool to install the spring.
    f. Remove the tool from the door hinge (tool will fall out in three pieces). Cycle the door to check the spring operation.
12. Remove the tape from the door and the body pillars.
13. On doors with power operated components:
    a. Install the wire harness to the door through the conduit access hole, then install the rubber conduit to the door.
    b. Connect wire harness to all components in the door.
    c. Install the inner panel water deflector and door trim panel.

Hood

REMOVAL & INSTALLATION

♦ **See Figures 3 and 4**

1. Open the hood and mark the position of the hood hinge assembly-to-hood by a scribe, chalk or paint.
2. Remove the hood attaching bolts that are towards the front of the hood.

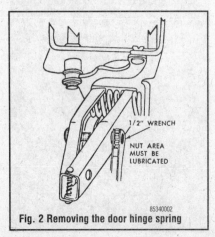

1/2" WRENCH

NUT AREA MUST BE LUBRICATED

85340002

Fig. 2 Removing the door hinge spring

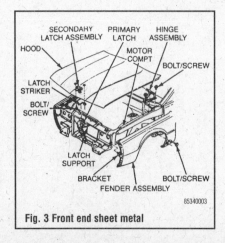

SECONDARY LATCH ASSEMBLY
PRIMARY LATCH
HINGE ASSEMBLY
HOOD
MOTOR COMPT
BOLT/SCREW
LATCH STRIKER
BOLT/SCREW
LATCH SUPPORT
BRACKET
FENDER ASSEMBLY
BOLT/SCREW

85340003

Fig. 3 Front end sheet metal

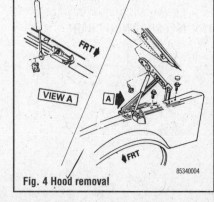

FRT
VIEW A
A
FRT

85340004

Fig. 4 Hood removal

3. Slowly loosen the remaining hood attaching bolts.

4. With the aid of a helper, remove the bolts and remove the hood. Place the hood on a protected surface.

5. Position the hood over the hood hinge assembly with the aid of a helper and install the hood attaching bolts finger tight.

6. Align the hood to the matchmarks made earlier and tighten the hood attaching bolts.

7. Close the hood and check align.

ALIGNMENT

▶ **See Figure 5**

Slotted holes are provided at all hood hinge attaching points for proper adjustment — both vertically and fore-and-aft. Vertical adjustments at the front may be made by adjusting the rubber bumpers up and down.

To adjust the hood fore-and-aft move the hood forward or rearward until the hood clearances are equal and as specified in the illustration. If the hood is not

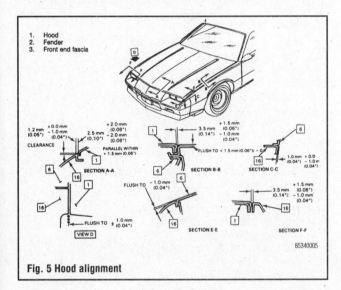

1. Hood
2. Fender
3. Front end fascia

Fig. 5 Hood alignment

properly coming into adjustment then the body panels may also need to be adjusted. To achieve the best results set the hood to any existing marks and make adjustments one at a time.

Rear Compartment Lift Window

REMOVAL & INSTALLATION

▶ **See Figures 6 and 7**

1. Prop the lid open and place a protective covering along the edges of the rear compartment opening to prevent any damage to the painted surfaces.

2. Use a 13mm socket to remove the nuts holding the glass to the hinge.

✳✳ CAUTION

Do not attempt to remove or loosen the gas support assembly attachments with the lid in any position other than fully open as personal injury may result.

3. While a helper supports the glass, disengage the gas supports from the lift window assembly and disconnect the harness connector for the electric grid defogger, if equipped.

4. With the aid of a helper, remove the lift window assembly from the body and place it on a protected surface.

5. Position the lift window assembly to the body with the aid of a helper. Install the attaching bolts and torque to 11 ft. lbs. (16 Nm).

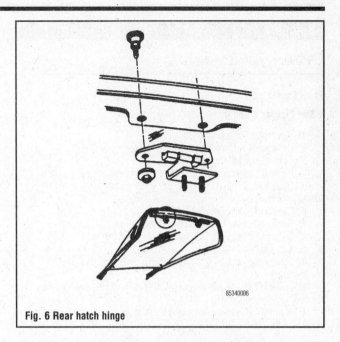

Fig. 6 Rear hatch hinge

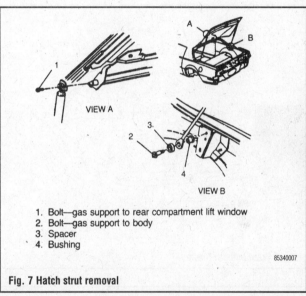

1. Bolt—gas support to rear compartment lift window
2. Bolt—gas support to body
3. Spacer
4. Bushing

Fig. 7 Hatch strut removal

✳✳ CAUTION

Do not over tighten the glass-to-hinge bolts as it could cause the glass to break resulting in personal injury! Always wear safety glasses during this operation.

6. Connect the harness connector for the electric grid defogger, if equipped, and connect the gas supports to the lift window assembly.

7. Lower the lid and check alignment.

ADJUSTMENT

The rear compartment lift window assembly height, fore and aft and side adjustments are controlled at the hinge-to-body location. This area of the body has oversize hinge attaching holes in addition to the hinge-to-body spacers. Adjustments at the hinge location must be made with the gas supports disengaged. Additional height adjustment can also be made at the lower panel by adjusting the rubber bumpers. Bolts holding hinge-to-body should be tightened to 15–20 ft. lbs. (20–28 Nm).

Bumpers

REMOVAL & INSTALLATION

Front Fascia

▶ **See Figures 8 and 9**

1. Disconnect the negative battery cable.
2. Remove the air cleaner assembly, as required.
3. Remove bumper filler panel.
4. Remove the fascia center bracket at the front end panel reinforcement.
5. Disconnect all electrical equipment, such as headlamps, turn signals, horns, fog lamps, etc.
6. Raise and safely support the vehicle.
7. Remove the front bumper fascia extension.
8. Remove the bolts from the bumper impact bar and radiator lower air baffle, if equipped.
9. Remove the push-on retainers attaching the bumper fascia to the bumper impact bar.
10. Lower the vehicle and remove the bolts attaching the outer brackets to the front end inner structure.
11. With the aid of an assistant, remove the fascia carefully as not to scratch or damage the assembly.

To install:

12. With the aid of an assistant, install the fascia carefully as not to scratch or damage the assembly.
13. Raise and safely support the vehicle.
14. Install the bolts attaching the outer brackets to the front end inner structure. Torque the bolts to 84 inch lbs. (9.5 Nm).
15. Install the push-on retainers attaching the bumper fascia to the bumper impact bar.
16. Install the bolts at the bumper impact bar and radiator lower air baffle, if equipped.
17. Install the front bumper fascia extension.
18. Connect all electrical equipment, such as headlamps, turn signals, horns, fog lamps, etc.
19. Install the fascia center bracket at the front end panel reinforcement.
20. Install bumper filler panel.
21. Install the air cleaner assembly, as required.
22. Connect the negative battery cable.

Rear

▶ **See Figure 10**

1. Disconnect the negative battery cable.
2. Open the rear compartment hatch.
3. Remove the rear left, right and center trim panel.
4. Remove the spare tire assembly.
5. Remove the left and right side tail lamps.
6. Remove the license plate bolts and bracket.
7. Remove the right and left side fascia nuts.
8. Remove the push-on retainers and lower screws.
9. With the aid of an assistant, remove the rear fascia.

To install:

10. With the aid of an assistant, install the rear fascia.
11. Install the push-on retainers and lower screws.
12. Install the right and left side fascia nuts.
13. Install the license plate bolts and bracket.
14. Install the left and right side tail lamps.
15. Install the spare tire assembly.
16. Install the rear left, right and center trim panel.
17. Close the rear compartment hatch.
18. Connect the negative battery cable.

Outside Mirrors

REMOVAL & INSTALLATION

Standard Mirrors

▶ **See Figure 11**

1. Remove the door trim panel and detach inner panel water deflector enough to gain access to the mirror retainer nuts.
2. Remove the attaching nuts from the mirror base studs and remove the mirror assembly from the door.
3. Position the mirror onto the door making sure the mirror gasket is properly aligned on the door outer panel.
4. Install the attaching nuts to the mirror base studs and tighten.
5. Install the inner panel water deflector and door trim panel.

Remote Control Mirrors

1. Remove the mirror remote control bezel and door trim panel. Detach the inner panel water deflector enough to expose the mirror and cable assembly from the door.
2. Remove the mirror base-to-door outer panel stud nuts, remove the cable from the clip and remove the mirror and cable assembly from the door.
3. Position the mirror onto the door making sure the mirror gasket is properly aligned on the door outer panel.
4. Install the cable onto the clip and install the mirror base-to-door outer panel stud nuts. Torque to 72 inch lbs. (8 Nm).
5. Install the inner panel water deflector and door trim panel.
6. Install the mirror remote control bezel.

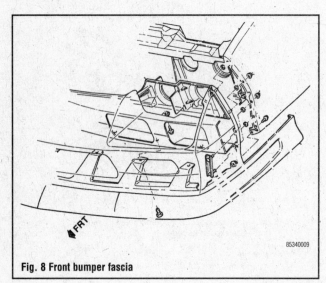

85340009

Fig. 8 Front bumper fascia

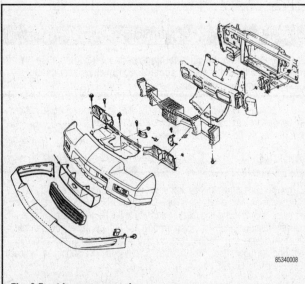

85340008

Fig. 9 Front bumper removal

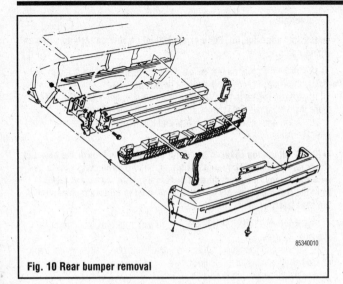

Fig. 10 Rear bumper removal

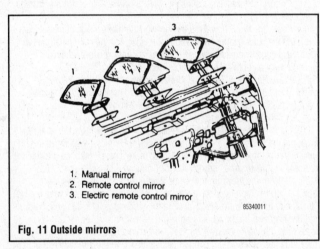

1. Manual mirror
2. Remote control mirror
3. Electirc remote control mirror

Fig. 11 Outside mirrors

Power Operated Mirrors

1. Disconnect the negative battery terminal and, from the door trim panel side, remove the remote control mirror bezel, release and remove the door panel.
2. Disconnect wire harness connection from the remote mirror electrical switch.
3. Peel back water deflector enough to detach the harness from the retaining tabs in the door.
4. Remove the mirror base-to-door stud nuts and lift mirror housing and harness assembly from the door.

To install:

5. Feed the mirror harness through the door along with the mirror assembly. Install the mirror base-to-door stud nuts and tighten.
6. Connect the mirror wire harness and install the water deflector.
7. Connect the wire harness connection to the remote mirror electrical switch.
8. Install the door panel and install the remote control mirror bezel.
9. Connect the negative battery terminal.

Fenders

REMOVAL & INSTALLATION

♦ **See Figure 12**

1. Disconnect the negative battery cable.
2. Remove the hood.
3. Raise and safely support the vehicle.

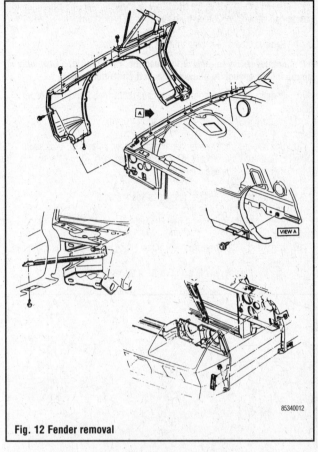

Fig. 12 Fender removal

4. Remove the lower fender bolts and inner wheel house panel.
5. Remove the rocker panel molding.
6. Remove the lower front end panel deflector-to-fender bolts.
7. Remove the bolt from the support brace.
8. Remove the front end bumper fascia-to-fender nuts and screws.
9. Remove the hood hinge-to-fender bolts.
10. Disconnect all electrical connections from horn, turn signal lamps, etc.
11. Remove the fender by sliding rearward and outward, at rear, with the aid of an assistant. Place an old blanket over the fender as to avoid scratches or dents.

To install:

12. Install the fender with the aid of an assistant. Place an old blanket over the fender as to avoid scratches or dents.
13. Connect all electrical connections to the horn, turn signal lamps, etc.
14. Install the hood hinge-to-fender bolts.
15. Install the front end bumper fascia-to-fender nuts and screws.
16. Install the bolt at the support brace.
17. Install the lower front end panel deflector-to-fender bolts.
18. Install the rocker panel molding.
19. Install the lower fender bolts and inner wheel house panel.
20. Install the hood.
21. Disconnect the negative battery cable. Align the fender and hood as necessary, placing existing shims in original positions.

Convertible Top

TOP REPLACEMENT

♦ **See Figures 13 thru 21**

1. Disconnect the negative battery cable.
2. Remove the side rails and retainers.
3. Remove the main pillar seals and retainers.
4. Remove the No. 1 bow garnish molding and retainer.

5. Remove the top from the No. 1 bow by applying heat with a heat gun to the approximately 1 in. (25mm) from the adhesive backed bow.

6. Remove the cable screws.

7. Remove the headliner from the No. 2 and 3 bows.

➡ **It is not necessary to remove the headliner from the No. 1 bow with the top folded enough to allow access to the retainer screws.**

8. Remove the screws from the underside of the Nos. 2 and 3 top cover retainers.

9. Remove the No. 2 and 3 bow top cover from the pockets in the top cover.

10. Separate the outer quarter flaps from the main pillar post, once again using the heat gun as necessary to loosen the adhesive.

11. Remove the side retention cables.

12. Remove screws.

13. Remove the elastic stays, folding the top rearward.

14. Remove the No. 5 bow seal.

15. Remove the black covered rivets from the No. 5 bow using an ⅛ in. (3mm) drill bit.

16. Remove the top cover from No. 5 bow, using heat as required to loosen the adhesive.

17. Remove the convertible top cover from the vehicle.

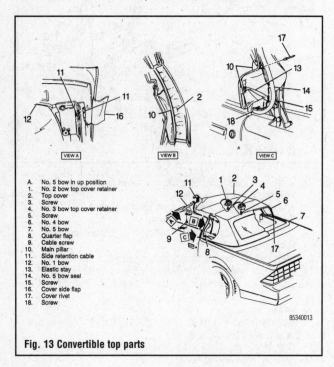

A. No. 5 bow in up position
1. No. 2 bow top cover retainer
2. Top cover
3. Screw
4. No. 3 bow top cover retainer
5. Screw
6. No. 4 bow
7. No. 5 bow
8. Quarter flap
9. Cable screw
10. Main pillar
11. Side retention cable
12. No. 1 bow
13. Elastic stay
14. No. 5 bow seal
15. Screw
16. Cover side flap
17. Cover rivet
18. Screw

85340013

Fig. 13 Convertible top parts

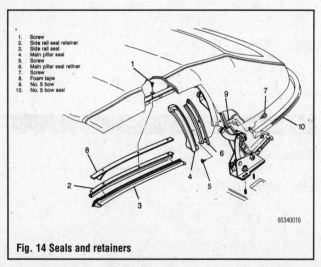

1. Screw
2. Side rail seal retainer
3. Side rail seal
4. Main pillar seal
5. Screw
6. Main pillar seal retiner
7. Screw
8. Foam tape
9. No. 5 bow
10. No. 5 bow seal

85340016

Fig. 14 Seals and retainers

To install:

➡ **Use 3M® adhesive No. 8046 or equivalent on cover attaching surfaces where noted.**

18. Install the cover on the vehicle. Slide the retention cables through the listing pockets and check cable ends for proper locations.

19. Square the top to the frame; check for evenness of quarter flap positions to the main pillar rail. Fold the top cover to the windshield header.

20. Apply adhesive to the No. 5 bow and top, raise the No. 5 bow to the full vertical position.

➡ **Glue ½ of the top cover to the No. 5 bow first, then lower the bow and check for evenness. The length of the material overhanging should be uniform. Repeat the procedure, if necessary. Trim the excess fabric from the No. 5 bow evenly at the seal channel to allow attachment of the seal later.**

21. Install new ⅛ in. (3mm) by ³⁄₁₆ in. (5mm) black aluminum rivets as shown in illustration.

22. Lower and latch the tonneau cover and No. 5 bow. Raise the No. 1 bow off the header and install the cable screws.

23. Install the No. 5 bow seal.

24. Connect the elastic stays inside of No. 5 bow seal-to-link arms. Install the screws.

25. Lower the No. 5 bow. Fold the inner quarter flaps inside of main pillar rails. Fold the outer quarter flaps around the outside of the main pillar rails to the forward edge using adhesive on the flaps and rails. Ensure seams are aligned evenly on both rails. Trim excess material.

26. Raise No. 5 bow. Raise the tonneau panel and lower No. 5 bow. Slide the No. 2 and 3 bow top cover retainers into listing pockets and align screw holes. Install the screws to the underside of No. 2 and 3 bows.

27. Install the headliner to No. 2 and 3 bows.

28. Latch the top to the windshield header and pull the top cover straight forward at the seams over the No. 1 bow to desired fullness. While maintaining tension on the top cover over the No. 1 bow, make a pencil mark on the outer surface along the forward edge of the No. 1 bow.

29. Unlatch the top from the windshield header and lower the top halfway. Pull the top cover ¼ in. (6mm) past the reference mark over the No. 1 bow and attach it to the No. 1 bow, first attaching cover side flaps. Fold the side flaps around the bow using adhesive on both the cover and bow surfaces. Fold the top cover over the No. 1 bow along the edge and over the cover side flap, once again using adhesive. Lower the top and check for proper tension, if more is needed, repeat the procedure. Trim off excess material.

30. Install all moldings, pillar seals, side seals and retainers. Replace dried out, deteriorated or cracked seals to prevent air and water leaks.

31. Adjust the top upstops and downstops, as required.

Adjustment

UPSTOP

The upstops may be adjusted to obtain proper alignment between the top latch guide pins and the windshield header receivers.

1. Lower the top. Loosen the upstop jam nut and turn screw clockwise.

2. Raise and latch the top.

3. Raise No. 5 bow to the full vertical position.

4. Turn the upstops counterclockwise until they contact the linkage.

5. Unlatch and lower the top. Tighten the upstop jam nut while holding upstop from turning.

6. Raise the top and inspect the alignment of the top latch guide pins to the header receivers.

DOWNSTOP

The downstops can be adjusted for proper clearance between the main rail and No. 4 bow when the top is lowered completely. The downstops have right angle bends and face outward.

1. Raise and latch the top.

2. Loosen the downstops nuts and adjust as required.

3. Tighten the downstop nuts while holding downstops in position.

4. Lower the top and inspect the clearance between the main rail and the No. 4 bow. Also inspect the clearance of the tonneau panel.

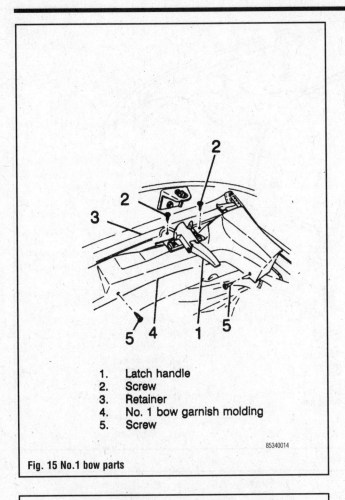

1. Latch handle
2. Screw
3. Retainer
4. No. 1 bow garnish molding
5. Screw

85340014

Fig. 15 No.1 bow parts

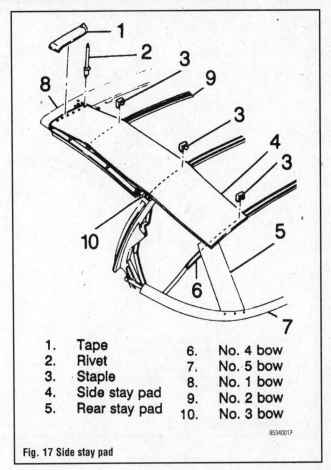

1. Tape
2. Rivet
3. Staple
4. Side stay pad
5. Rear stay pad

6. No. 4 bow
7. No. 5 bow
8. No. 1 bow
9. No. 2 bow
10. No. 3 bow

85340017

Fig. 17 Side stay pad

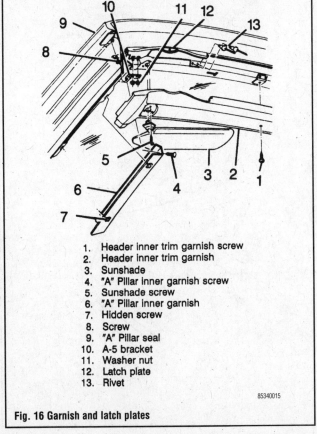

1. Header inner trim garnish screw
2. Header inner trim garnish
3. Sunshade
4. "A" Pillar inner garnish screw
5. Sunshade screw
6. "A" Pillar inner garnish
7. Hidden screw
8. Screw
9. "A" Pillar seal
10. A-5 bracket
11. Washer nut
12. Latch plate
13. Rivet

85340015

Fig. 16 Garnish and latch plates

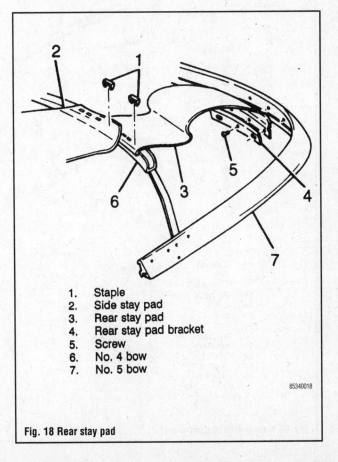

1. Staple
2. Side stay pad
3. Rear stay pad
4. Rear stay pad bracket
5. Screw
6. No. 4 bow
7. No. 5 bow

85340018

Fig. 18 Rear stay pad

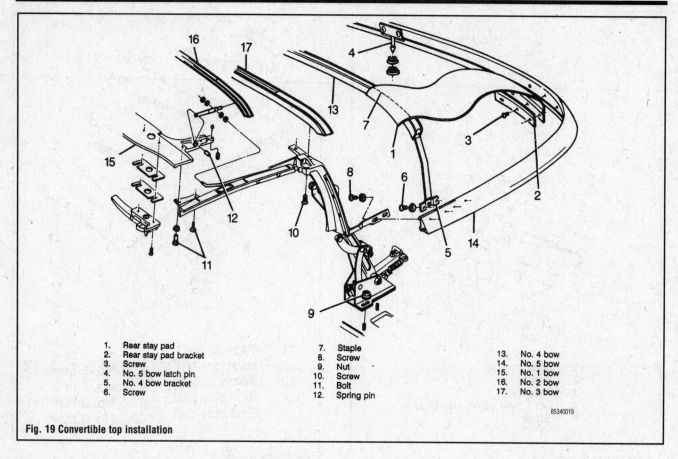

1. Rear stay pad
2. Rear stay pad bracket
3. Screw
4. No. 5 bow latch pin
5. No. 4 bow bracket
6. Screw
7. Staple
8. Screw
9. Nut
10. Screw
11. Bolt
12. Spring pin
13. No. 4 bow
14. No. 5 bow
15. No. 1 bow
16. No. 2 bow
17. No. 3 bow

85340019

Fig. 19 Convertible top installation

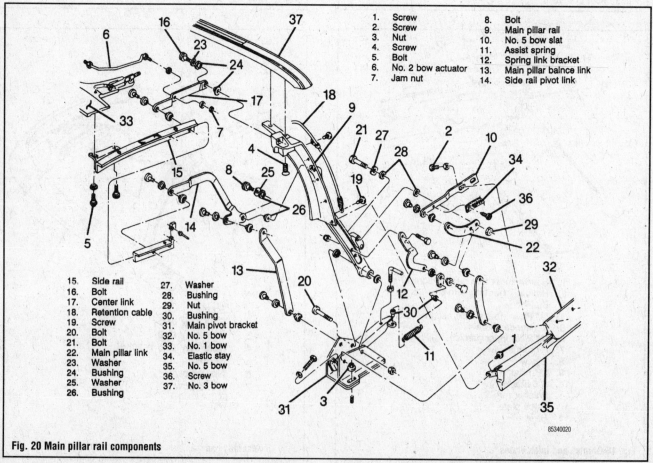

1. Screw
2. Screw
3. Nut
4. Screw
5. Bolt
6. No. 2 bow actuator
7. Jam nut
8. Bolt
9. Main pillar rail
10. No. 5 bow slat
11. Assist spring
12. Spring link bracket
13. Main pillar balnce link
14. Side rail pivot link

15. Side rail
16. Bolt
17. Center link
18. Retention cable
19. Screw
20. Bolt
21. Bolt
22. Main pillar link
23. Washer
24. Bushing
25. Washer
26. Bushing
27. Washer
28. Bushing
29. Nut
30. Bushing
31. Main pivot bracket
32. No. 5 bow
33. No. 1 bow
34. Elastic stay
35. No. 5 bow
36. Screw
37. No. 3 bow

85340020

Fig. 20 Main pillar rail components

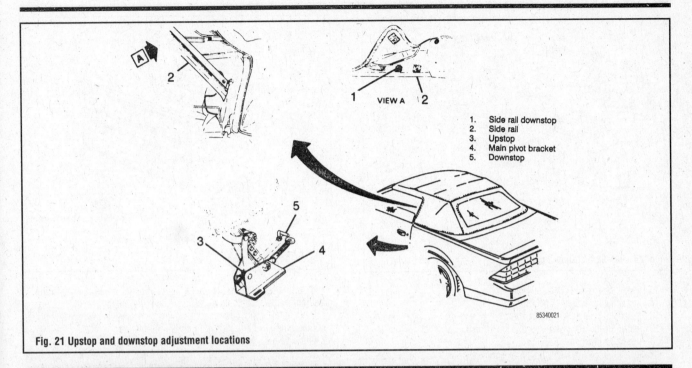

1. Side rail downstop
2. Side rail
3. Upstop
4. Main pivot bracket
5. Downstop

Fig. 21 Upstop and downstop adjustment locations

INTERIOR

Instrument Panel and Pad

REMOVAL & INSTALLATION

▶ **See Figures 22, 23 and 24**

❄❄ **CAUTION**

The 1991–92 vehicles are equipped with an Air Bag system. Proper disarming of the system is necessary before proceeding with any disassembly or repairs to the steering column, dash or electrical system or possible deployment of the air bag might occur. Refer to Section 8 for disarming procedure.

1. Properly disable the SIR air bag system, if equipped. Disconnect the negative battery cable.
2. Remove the center console.
3. Remove the screws attaching the instrument panel pad to the instrument panel.
4. Remove the daytime running light sensor electrical connector, if equipped.
5. Remove the instrument panel pad.
6. Remove the instrument panel sound insulators.
7. Remove the knee bolster and bracket.
8. Remove the instrument panel cluster.
9. Remove the steering column retaining nuts and lower the column.
10. Remove the upper and lower instrument panel to cowl screws.
11. Disconnect and remove the electrical harness at the cowl connector and under dash panel.
12. Remove the instrument panel assembly.
    To install:
13. Install the instrument panel assembly.
14. Install the electrical harness at the cowl connector and under dash panel.
15. Install the upper and lower instrument panel to cowl screws.

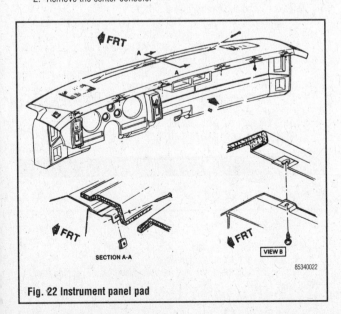

Fig. 22 Instrument panel pad

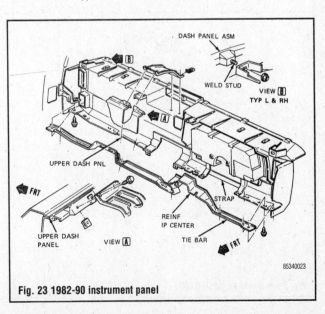

Fig. 23 1982-90 instrument panel

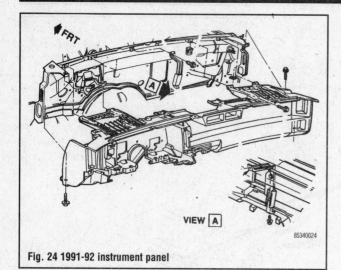

Fig. 24 1991-92 instrument panel

16. Install the steering column retaining nuts.
17. Install the instrument panel cluster.
18. Install the knee bolster and bracket.
19. Install the instrument panel sound insulators.
20. Install the instrument panel pad.
21. Install the daytime running light sensor electrical connector, if equipped.
22. Install the screws attaching the instrument panel pad to the instrument panel.
23. Install the center console.
24. Properly arm the SIR air bag system, if equipped. Disconnect the negative battery cable.

Door Panels

REMOVAL & INSTALLATION

▶ **See Figures 25 and 26**

The one-piece trim hangs over the door inner panel across the top and is secured by clips down the sides and across the bottom. It is retained by screws located in the areas of the armrest and pull handle assembly.
1. Remove all the door inside handles.
2. Remove the door inside locking rod knob.
3. Remove the screws inserted through the door armrest and pull the handle assembly into the door inner panel or armrest hanger support bracket.

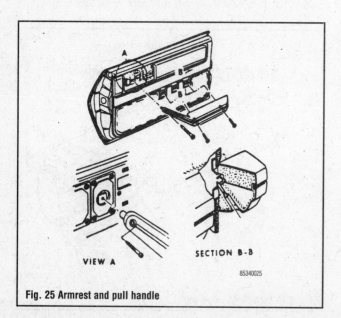

Fig. 25 Armrest and pull handle

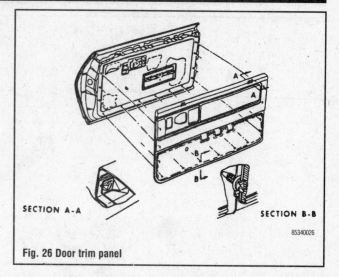

Fig. 26 Door trim panel

4. On models with remote control mirror assemblies, remove the control plate from the bezel on the trim pad and remove the control from the plate.
5. On models with power door lock controls located in the door trim panel, disconnect the wire harnesses at the switch assemblies.
6. Remove the remote control handle bezel screws.
7. Remove the screws used to hold the armrest to the inner panel.
8. Remove the screws and plastic retainers from the perimeter of the door trim panel using tool BT–7323A or equivalent and a screwdriver. To remove the trim panel, push the trim upward and outboard to disengage from the door inner panel at the beltline.
9. On models with a water deflector held in place by fasteners, use tool BT–7323A or equivalent to remove the fasteners and water deflector.
To install:
10. To install the water deflector, locate the fasteners in the holes in the door inner panel and press in place. Replace all tape which may have been applied to assist in holding the water deflector in place.
11. Before installing the door trim panel, make certain that all the trim retainers are installed securely to the panel and are not damaged. Where required, replace damaged retainers. Start the retainer flange into ¼ in. (6mm) cutout attachment hole in the trim panel, rotate the retainer until the flange is engaged fully.
12. Connect all electrical components where present.
13. To install the door trim panel, locate the top of the assembly over the upper flange of the door inner panel, inserting the door handle through the handle slot in the panel and press down on the trim panel to engage the upper retaining clips.
14. Position the trim panel to the door inner panel so the trim retainers are aligned with the attaching holes in the panel and tap the retainers into the holes with the palm of hand or a clean rubber mallet.
15. Install the screws used to hold the armrest to the inner panel.
16. Install the remote control handle bezel screws.
17. On models with power door lock controls located in the door trim panel, connect the wire harnesses at the switch assemblies.
18. On models with remote control mirror assemblies, install the control to the plate. Install the control plate to the bezel on the trim pad.
19. Install the handle assembly and install the screws inserted through the door armrest.
20. Install the door inside locking rod knob.
21. Install all the door inside handles.

Headliner

REMOVAL & INSTALLATION

▶ **See Figure 27**

1. Disconnect the negative battery cable.
2. Remove the dome lamp and sunshade.
3. Remove the coat hooks and seat belt escutcheon, by unsnapping from the headliner.

4. Remove the rear window opening molding.

5. Remove the rear quarter interior trim panels, body lock pillar panels and windshield side upper moldings.

6. Remove the headliner retaining clips and remove the headliner.

7. Installation is the reverse of the removal procedure.

Door Locks

REMOVAL & INSTALLATION

▶ **See Figures 28 and 29**

1. Raise the door window. Remove the door trim panel and detach the inner panel water deflector enough to expose the access hole.

2. Disengage the lock cylinder to the lock rod at the cylinder.

❋❋ CAUTION

If removing the lock cylinder retainer by hand, wear gloves to prevent personal injury.

3. With a screwdriver or similar tool, slide the lock cylinder retainer forward until it disengages. The retainer can also be removed by hand by grasping anti-theft shield at the top of the retainer and rotating until disengaged. Remove the lock cylinder from the door.

4. Lubricate the cylinder with the proper lubricant.

5. Position the cylinder into place and rotate it until the cylinder engages. Install the cylinder retainer.

6. Engage the lock cylinder to lock rod at the cylinder.

7. Install the inner panel water deflector and door trim panel.

Power Door Lock Actuator

REMOVAL & INSTALLATION

▶ **See Figures 30 and 31**

1. Disconnect the negative battery cable. Remove the door panel.

2. Raise the window fully. Disconnect the electrical connector from the actuator.

3. Drive the rivet center pins out using a ⅛ in. (3mm) punch and hammer, then using a ¼ in. (6mm) drill bit, remove the rivet head.

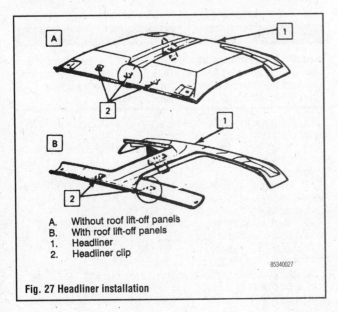

A. Without roof lift-off panels
B. With roof lift-off panels
1. Headliner
2. Headliner clip

85340027

Fig. 27 Headliner installation

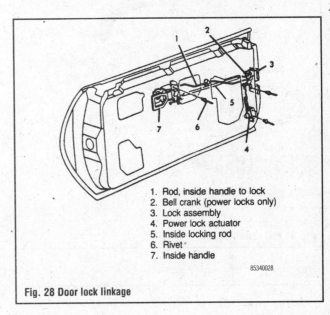

1. Rod, inside handle to lock
2. Bell crank (power locks only)
3. Lock assembly
4. Power lock actuator
5. Inside locking rod
6. Rivet
7. Inside handle

85340028

Fig. 28 Door lock linkage

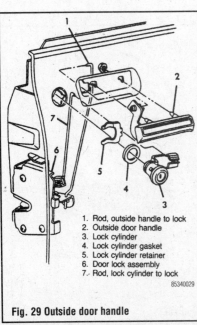

1. Rod, outside handle to lock
2. Outside door handle
3. Lock cylinder
4. Lock cylinder gasket
5. Lock cylinder retainer
6. Door lock assembly
7. Rod, lock cylinder to lock

85340029

Fig. 29 Outside door handle

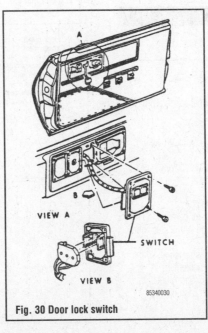

VIEW A

VIEW B

SWITCH

85340030

Fig. 30 Door lock switch

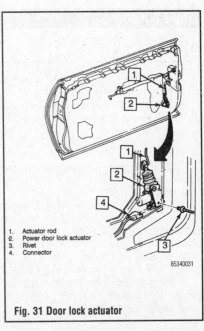

1. Actuator rod
2. Power door lock actuator
3. Rivet
4. Connector

85340031

Fig. 31 Door lock actuator

4. Remove the actuator rod and remove the door lock actuator.

5. Installation is the reverse of the removal procedure.

Rear Liftgate Pull-Down Unit

REMOVAL & INSTALLATION

♦ **See Figure 32**

1. Open the rear hatch. Disconnect the negative battery cable.

2. Remove the rear trim panel. Disconnect the electrical connector and remove the attaching screws.

3. Disconnect the unit lock cable connection from the lock cylinder.

4. Remove the unit.

5. Installation is the reverse of the removal procedure. Torque the screws to 18 ft. lbs. (24 Nm).

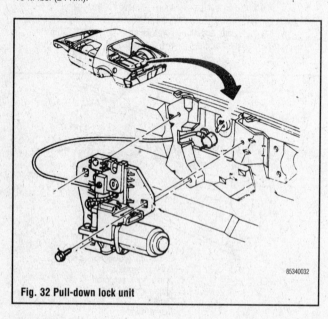

85340032

Fig. 32 Pull-down lock unit

ADJUSTMENT

Adjust the unit as necessary for proper lock striker engagement.

Door Window

REMOVAL & INSTALLATION

1. Remove the door trim panel and the inner panel water deflector.

2. Raise the window to the half-up position.

3. Punch out the center pins of the glass to sash channel attaching rivets.

4. Remove the rear guide channel through the rear access hole.

5. Remove the up stop.

6. Using a ¼ in. (6mm) drill bit, drill out the attaching rivets on sash channel.

7. Raise the glass to remove from the sash channel and remove the glass from the door.

To install:

8. Remove the drilled out rivets and shavings from the door.

9. Check the rivet bushings and retainers on the glass for damage. If necessary, remove the bushings using a flat-bladed tool covered with a cloth body tape. Install by snapping rivet retainer into the bushing.

10. Lower the glass into the door and position on the sash channel so the holes in the sash line up with the holes in the bushings and retainers.

11. Using rivet tool J–29022 or equivalent, install ¼ in. (6mm) peel type rivet (part No. 20184399 or equivalent) to retain the glass to sash channel.

12. Install the rear guide channel.

13. Install the front up stop to support on the inner panel.

14. Before installing the trim parts, check the window operation for performance and fit to roof rail weatherstrip.

15. Install the inner panel water deflector and the door trim panel.

Window Regulator and Regulator Motor

REMOVAL & INSTALLATION

♦ **See Figure 33**

1. Remove the door trim panel and inner panel water deflector.

2. Raise the window to half-up position and hold in place by inserting a rubber wedge door stops at the front and rear of the window between window and inner panel.

3. Remove the rear guide channel and inner panel cam channel.

4. Punch out the center pins of the regulator rivets; then drill out the rivets using a ¼ in. (6mm) drill bit.

5. Move the regulator rearward and disconnect wire harness from the motor (if equipped). Disengage the roller on the regulator lift arm from glass sash channel.

6. Remove the regulator through the rear access hole.

✳✳ CAUTION

If electric motor removal from the regulator is required, the sector gear must be locked in position. The regulator lift arm is under tension from the counterbalance spring and could cause personal injury if the sector gear is not locked in position.

7. Drill a hole through the regulator sector gear and backplate and install a bolt and nut to lock the sector gear in position.

8. Using a ³⁄₁₆ in. (5mm) drill bit, drill out the motor attaching rivets and remove the motor from the regulator.

To install:

9. To install the motor to the regulator, use a rivet tool J–29022 or equivalent, and install ³⁄₁₆ in. (5mm) rivets or ³⁄₁₆ in. (5mm) nuts and bolts. Remove bolt and nut used to secure the sector gear in position.

10. Place the regulator through the rear access hole into the door inner panel. If electric regulator is being installed, connect the wire connector to motor prior to installing the regulator to the inner panel.

11. Locate the lift arm roller into the glass sash channel.

12. Using rivet tool J–29022 or equivalent, rivet the regulator to the inner panel of the door using ¼ in. (6mm) ½ in. (13mm) aluminum peel type rivets (part No. 9436175 or equivalent). If rivet tool is not available, use the following nut and bolt method:

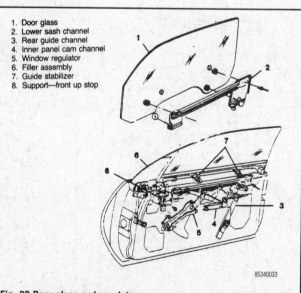

1. Door glass
2. Lower sash channel
3. Rear guide channel
4. Inner panel cam channel
5. Window regulator
6. Filler assembly
7. Guide stabilizer
8. Support—front up stop

85340033

Fig. 33 Door glass and regulator

a. Install U-clips on the regulator at the attaching locations. Be sure to install the clips with clinch nuts on the outboard side of the regulator.

b. Locate the regulator in the door inner panel. If the electric regulator is being installed, connect the wire connector to the regulator motor.

c. Locate the lift arm roller in the glass sash channel.

d. Align the regulator with clinch nuts to holes in the inner panel.

e. Attach the regulator (and motor) to the door inner panel with ¼–20 x ½ in. screws (part No. 9419723 or equivalent) into ¼ in. (6mm) nuts with integral washers. Tighten the screw to 90–125 inch lbs. (10–14 Nm) torque.

13. Install the inner panel cam channel and rear guide channel.

14. Remove the rubber wedge door stops at the front and rear of the window between window and inner panel.

15. Install the inner panel water deflector and the door trim panel.

Windshield and Fixed Glass

REMOVAL & INSTALLATION

If your windshield, or other fixed window, is cracked or chipped, you may decide to replace it with a new one yourself. However, there are two main reasons why replacement windshields and other window glass should be installed only by a professional automotive glass technician: safety and cost.

The most important reason a professional should install automotive glass is for safety. The glass in the vehicle, especially the windshield, is designed with safety in mind in case of a collision. The windshield is specially manufactured from two panes of specially-tempered glass with a thin layer of transparent plastic between them. This construction allows the glass to "give" in the event that a part of your body hits the windshield during the collision, and prevents the glass from shattering, which could cause lacerations, blinding and other harm to passengers of the vehicle. The other fixed windows are designed to be tempered so that if they break during a collision, they shatter in such a way that there are no large pointed glass pieces. The professional automotive glass technician knows how to install the glass in a vehicle so that it will function optimally during a collision. Without the proper experience, knowledge and tools, installing a piece of automotive glass yourself could lead to additional harm if an accident should ever occur.

Cost is also a factor when deciding to install automotive glass yourself. Performing this could cost you much more than a professional may charge for the same job. Since the windshield is designed to break under stress, an often life saving characteristic, windshields tend to break VERY easily when an inexperienced person attempts to install one. Do-it-yourselfers buying two, three or even four windshields from a salvage yard because they have broken them during installation are common stories. Also, since the automotive glass is designed to prevent the outside elements from entering your vehicle, improper installation can lead to water and air leaks. Annoying whining noises at highway speeds from air leaks or inside body panel rusting from water leaks can add to your stress level and subtract from your wallet. After buying two or three windshields, installing them and ending up with a leak that produces a noise while driving and water damage during rainstorms, the cost of having a professional do it correctly the first time may be much more alluring. We here at Chilton, therefore, advise that you have a professional automotive glass technician service any broken glass on your vehicle.

WINDSHIELD CHIP REPAIR

▶ See Figures 34 and 35

➡Check with your state and local authorities on the laws for state safety inspection. Some states or municipalities may not allow chip repair as a viable option for correcting stone damage to your windshield.

Although severely cracked or damaged windshields must be replaced, there is something that you can do to prolong or even prevent the need for replacement of a chipped windshield. There are many companies which offer windshield chip repair products, such as Loctite's® Bullseye™ windshield repair kit. These kits usually consist of a syringe, pedestal and a sealing adhesive. The syringe is mounted on the pedestal and is used to create a vacuum which pulls the plastic layer against the glass. This helps make the chip transparent. The adhesive is then injected which seals the chip and helps to prevent further stress cracks from developing.

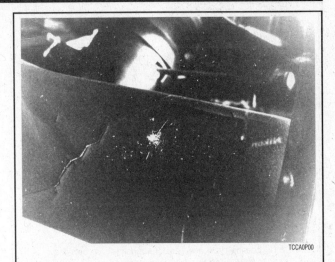

TCCA0P00

Fig. 34 Small chips on your windshield can be fixed with an aftermarket repair kit, such as the one from Loctite®

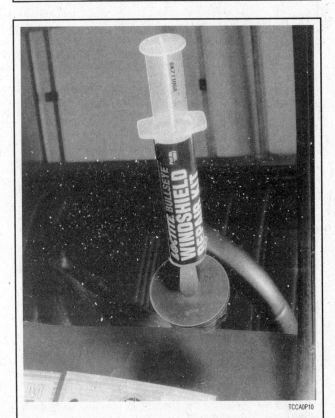

TCCA0P10

Fig. 35 Most kits use a self-stick applicator and syringe to inject the adhesive into the chip or crack

➡Always follow the specific manufacturer's instructions.

Inside Rear View Mirror

INSTALLATION

▶ See Figure 36

The rear view mirror is attached to a support which is secured to the windshield glass. This support is installed by the glass supplier using a plastic-polyvinyl.butyl adhesive.

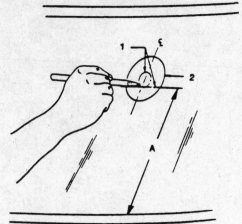

1. Locating circle and base of support line on outside glass surface
2. Circle on outside glass surface indicates area to be cleaned

85340040

Fig. 36 Locating the bonded area on the windshield

Service replacement windshield glass has the mirror support bonded to the glass assembly. To install a detached mirror support or install a new part, the following items are needed:

• Part No. 1052369, Loctite® Minute-Bond Adhesive 312 two component pack or equivalent
• Original mirror support (prepared per Steps 4 and 5 of the installation procedure) or replacement rear view mirror support
• Wax marking pencil or crayon
• Rubbing alcohol
• Clean paper towels
• Fine grit emery cloth or sandpaper (No. 320 or No. 360)
• Clean toothpick
• Six-lobed socket bit.

1. Determine the rear view mirror support position on the windshield. Support is to be located at the center of the glass 27⅛ in. (69cm) from the base of the glass to the base of the support.

2. Mark the location on the outside of the glass with wax pencil or crayon. Make a larger diameter circle around the mirror support circle on the outside of the glass surface.

3. On the inside of the glass surface, clean the large circle with a paper towel and domestic scouring cleanser, glass cleaning solution or polishing compound. Rub until the area is completely clean and dry. When dry, clean the area with an alcohol saturated paper towel to remove any traces of scouring powder or cleaning solution from this area.

4. With a piece of fine grit (No. 320 or No. 360) emery cloth or sandpaper, sand the bonding surface of the new rear view mirror support or factory installed support. If original rear view mirror support is to be reused, all traces of the factory installed adhesive must be removed prior to reinstallation.

5. Wipe the sanded mirror support with a clean paper towel saturated with alcohol and allow it to dry.

6. Follow the directions on the manufacturer's kit to prepare the rear view mirror support prior to installation on the glass.

7. Properly position the support to its premarked location, with rounded end pointed upward, press the support against the glass for 30–60 seconds, exerting steady pressure against the glass. After five minutes, any excess adhesive may be removed with an alcohol moistened paper towel or glass cleaning solution.

8. Install the mirror.

Seats

REMOVAL & INSTALLATION

1. Operate the seat to the full-forward position. If a six-way power seat is operable, operate the seat to the full-forward and up positions. Where necessary

to gain access to the adjuster-to-floor pan attaching nuts, remove the adjuster rear foot covers and/or carpet retainers.

2. Remove the track covers where necessary; then remove the adjuster-to-floor pan rear attaching nuts. Operate the seat to the full-rearward position. Remove the adjuster front foot covers; then remove the adjuster-to-floor pan front attaching nuts.

3. Remove the seat assembly from the car.

4. Check that both seat adjusters are parallel and in phase with each other.

5. Install the adjuster-to-floor pan attaching nuts by moving the seat forward and rearward and torque nuts to 15–21 ft. lbs. (20–28 Nm).

6. Check the operation of the seat assembly to full limits of travel.

Seat Belt System

REMOVAL & INSTALLATION

▶ **See Figures 37, 38, 39, 40 and 41**

1. Remove the cover from the anchor plate.
2. Remove the attaching bolt, anchor plate and washer from the door pillar.
3. Remove the bolt cover from the rear of the retractor assembly.
4. Remove the bolt retaining the retractor to the floor panel and remove the retractor.

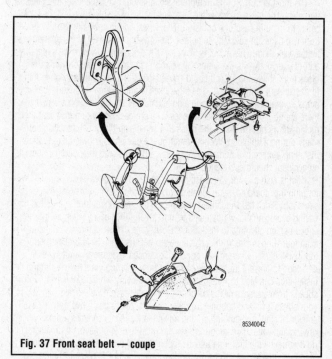

85340042

Fig. 37 Front seat belt — coupe

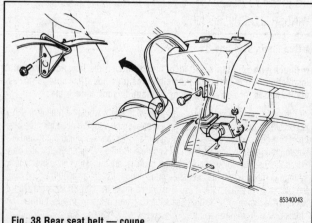

85340043

Fig. 38 Rear seat belt — coupe

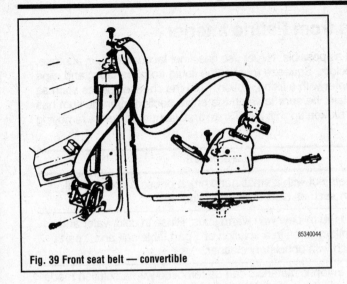

Fig. 39 Front seat belt — convertible

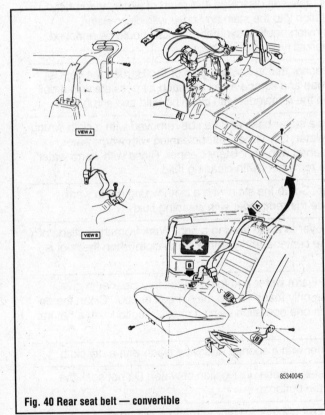

Fig. 40 Rear seat belt — convertible

5. Remove the buckle assembly from the floor panel.
6. Remove the cap which conceals the buckle assembly bolt and remove the bolt.
7. Remove the seat belt warning wire from the drivers side buckle and remove the buckle assembly from the vehicle.
8. Installation is the reverse of removal. Tighten all bolts to 31 ft. lbs. (43 Nm).

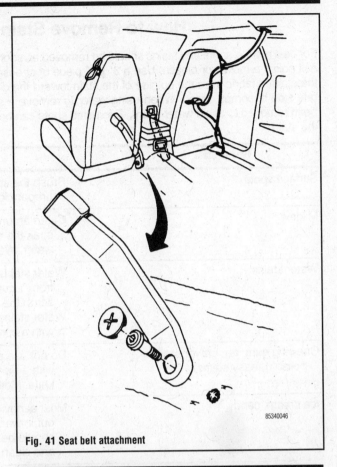

Fig. 41 Seat belt attachment

Power Seat Motor

REMOVAL & INSTALLATION

1. Remove the front seat assembly and place upside down on a clean protected surface.
2. Disconnect the motor feed wires from the motors.
3. Remove the nut securing the front of the motor support bracket to the inboard adjuster and withdraw the assembly from the adjuster and the gearnut drives.
4. Disconnect the drive cables from the motors and complete removal of the support bracket with the motor attached.
5. Grind off the peened over end(s) of the grommet assembly securing the motor to the support and separate the motor(s) as required from the support.
   To install:
6. Drill out the top end of the grommet assembly using a ³⁄₁₆ in. (5mm) drill.
7. Install the grommet assembly to the motor support bracket and secure the motor to the grommet using ³⁄₁₆ in. (5mm) rivet.
8. Install the support bracket with the motor attached and connect the drive cables to the motors.
9. Install the support bracket nuts securing the front of the motor support bracket to the inboard adjuster.
10. Connect the motor feed wires to the motors.
11. Install the front seat assembly.

How to Remove Stains from Fabric Interior

For best results, spots and stains should be removed as soon as possible. Never use gasoline, lacquer thinner, acetone, nail polish remover or bleach. Use a 3' x 3" piece of cheesecloth. Squeeze most of the liquid from the fabric and wipe the stained fabric from the outside of the stain toward the center with a lifting motion. Turn the cheesecloth as soon as one side becomes soiled. When using water to remove a stain, be sure to wash the entire section after the spot has been removed to avoid water stains. Encrusted spots can be broken up with a dull knife and vacuumed before removing the stain.

Type of Stain	How to Remove It
Surface spots	Brush the spots out with a small hand brush or use a commercial preparation such as K2R to lift the stain.
Mildew	Clean around the mildew with warm suds. Rinse in cold water and soak the mildew area in a solution of 1 part table salt and 2 parts water. Wash with upholstery cleaner.
Water stains	Water stains in fabric materials can be removed with a solution made from 1 cup of table salt dissolved in 1 quart of water. Vigorously scrub the solution into the stain and rinse with clear water. Water stains in nylon or other synthetic fabrics should be removed with a commercial type spot remover.
Chewing gum, tar, crayons, shoe polish (greasy stains)	Do not use a cleaner that will soften gum or tar. Harden the deposit with an ice cube and scrape away as much as possible with a dull knife. Moisten the remainder with cleaning fluid and scrub clean.
Ice cream, candy	Most candy has a sugar base and can be removed with a cloth wrung out in warm water. Oily candy, after cleaning with warm water, should be cleaned with upholstery cleaner. Rinse with warm water and clean the remainder with cleaning fluid.
Wine, alcohol, egg, milk, soft drink (non-greasy stains)	Do not use soap. Scrub the stain with a cloth wrung out in warm water. Remove the remainder with cleaning fluid.
Grease, oil, lipstick, butter and related stains	Use a spot remover to avoid leaving a ring. Work from the outisde of the stain to the center and dry with a clean cloth when the spot is gone.
Headliners (cloth)	Mix a solution of warm water and foam upholstery cleaner to give thick suds. Use only foam—liquid may streak or spot. Clean the entire headliner in one operation using a circular motion with a natural sponge.
Headliner (vinyl)	Use a vinyl cleaner with a sponge and wipe clean with a dry cloth.
Seats and door panels	Mix 1 pint upholstery cleaner in 1 gallon of water. Do not soak the fabric around the buttons.
Leather or vinyl fabric	Use a multi-purpose cleaner full strength and a stiff brush. Let stand 2 minutes and scrub thoroughly. Wipe with a clean, soft rag.
Nylon or synthetic fabrics	For normal stains, use the same procedures you would for washing cloth upholstery. If the fabric is extremely dirty, use a multi-purpose cleaner full strength with a stiff scrub brush. Scrub thoroughly in all directions and wipe with a cotton towel or soft rag.

85340049

GLOSSARY

AIR/FUEL RATIO: The ratio of air-to-gasoline by weight in the fuel mixture drawn into the engine.

AIR INJECTION: One method of reducing harmful exhaust emissions by injecting air into each of the exhaust ports of an engine. The fresh air entering the hot exhaust manifold causes any remaining fuel to be burned before it can exit the tailpipe.

ALTERNATOR: A device used for converting mechanical energy into electrical energy.

AMMETER: An instrument, calibrated in amperes, used to measure the flow of an electrical current in a circuit. Ammeters are always connected in series with the circuit being tested.

AMPERE: The rate of flow of electrical current present when one volt of electrical pressure is applied against one ohm of electrical resistance.

ANALOG COMPUTER: Any microprocessor that uses similar (analogous) electrical signals to make its calculations.

ARMATURE: A laminated, soft iron core wrapped by a wire that converts electrical energy to mechanical energy as in a motor or relay. When rotated in a magnetic field, it changes mechanical energy into electrical energy as in a generator.

ATMOSPHERIC PRESSURE: The pressure on the Earth's surface caused by the weight of the air in the atmosphere. At sea level, this pressure is 14.7 psi at 32°F (101 kPa at 0°C).

ATOMIZATION: The breaking down of a liquid into a fine mist that can be suspended in air.

AXIAL PLAY: Movement parallel to a shaft or bearing bore.

BACKFIRE: The sudden combustion of gases in the intake or exhaust system that results in a loud explosion.

BACKLASH: The clearance or play between two parts, such as meshed gears.

BACKPRESSURE: Restrictions in the exhaust system that slow the exit of exhaust gases from the combustion chamber.

BAKELITE: A heat resistant, plastic insulator material commonly used in printed circuit boards and transistorized components.

BALL BEARING: A bearing made up of hardened inner and outer races between which hardened steel balls roll.

BALLAST RESISTOR: A resistor in the primary ignition circuit that lowers voltage after the engine is started to reduce wear on ignition components.

BEARING: A friction reducing, supportive device usually located between a stationary part and a moving part.

BIMETAL TEMPERATURE SENSOR: Any sensor or switch made of two dissimilar types of metal that bend when heated or cooled due to the different expansion rates of the alloys. These types of sensors usually function as an on/off switch.

BLOWBY: Combustion gases, composed of water vapor and unburned fuel, that leak past the piston rings into the crankcase during normal engine operation. These gases are removed by the PCV system to prevent the buildup of harmful acids in the crankcase.

BRAKE PAD: A brake shoe and lining assembly used with disc brakes.

BRAKE SHOE: The backing for the brake lining. The term is, however, usually applied to the assembly of the brake backing and lining.

BUSHING: A liner, usually removable, for a bearing; an anti-friction liner used in place of a bearing.

CALIPER: A hydraulically activated device in a disc brake system, which is mounted straddling the brake rotor (disc). The caliper contains at least one piston and two brake pads. Hydraulic pressure on the piston(s) forces the pads against the rotor.

CAMSHAFT: A shaft in the engine on which are the lobes (cams) which operate the valves. The camshaft is driven by the crankshaft, via a belt, chain or gears, at one half the crankshaft speed.

CAPACITOR: A device which stores an electrical charge.

CARBON MONOXIDE (CO): A colorless, odorless gas given off as a normal byproduct of combustion. It is poisonous and extremely dangerous in confined areas, building up slowly to toxic levels without warning if adequate ventilation is not available.

CARBURETOR: A device, usually mounted on the intake manifold of an engine, which mixes the air and fuel in the proper proportion to allow even combustion.

CATALYTIC CONVERTER: A device installed in the exhaust system, like a muffler, that converts harmful byproducts of combustion into carbon dioxide and water vapor by means of a heat-producing chemical reaction.

CENTRIFUGAL ADVANCE: A mechanical method of advancing the spark timing by using flyweights in the distributor that react to centrifugal force generated by the distributor shaft rotation.

CHECK VALVE: Any one-way valve installed to permit the flow of air, fuel or vacuum in one direction only.

CHOKE: A device, usually a moveable valve, placed in the intake path of a carburetor to restrict the flow of air.

CIRCUIT: Any unbroken path through which an electrical current can flow. Also used to describe fuel flow in some instances.

CIRCUIT BREAKER: A switch which protects an electrical circuit from overload by opening the circuit when the current flow exceeds a predetermined level. Some circuit breakers must be reset manually, while most reset automatically.

COIL (IGNITION): A transformer in the ignition circuit which steps up the voltage provided to the spark plugs.

COMBINATION MANIFOLD: An assembly which includes both the intake and exhaust manifolds in one casting.

COMBINATION VALVE: A device used in some fuel systems that routes fuel vapors to a charcoal storage canister instead of venting them into the atmosphere. The valve relieves fuel tank pressure and allows fresh air into the tank as the fuel level drops to prevent a vapor lock situation.

COMPRESSION RATIO: The comparison of the total volume of the cylinder and combustion chamber with the piston at BDC and the piston at TDC.

CONDENSER: 1. An electrical device which acts to store an electrical charge, preventing voltage surges. 2. A radiator-like device in the air conditioning system in which refrigerant gas condenses into a liquid, giving off heat.

CONDUCTOR: Any material through which an electrical current can be transmitted easily.

CONTINUITY: Continuous or complete circuit. Can be checked with an ohmmeter.

COUNTERSHAFT: An intermediate shaft which is rotated by a mainshaft and transmits, in turn, that rotation to a working part.

CRANKCASE: The lower part of an engine in which the crankshaft and related parts operate.

CRANKSHAFT: The main driving shaft of an engine which receives reciprocating motion from the pistons and converts it to rotary motion.

CYLINDER: In an engine, the round hole in the engine block in which the piston(s) ride.

CYLINDER BLOCK: The main structural member of an engine in which is found the cylinders, crankshaft and other principal parts.

CYLINDER HEAD: The detachable portion of the engine, usually fastened to the top of the cylinder block and containing all or most of the combustion chambers. On overhead valve engines, it contains the valves and their operating parts. On overhead cam engines, it contains the camshaft as well.

DEAD CENTER: The extreme top or bottom of the piston stroke.

DETONATION: An unwanted explosion of the air/fuel mixture in the combustion chamber caused by excess heat and compression, advanced timing, or an overly lean mixture. Also referred to as "ping".

DIAPHRAGM: A thin, flexible wall separating two cavities, such as in a vacuum advance unit.

DIESELING: A condition in which hot spots in the combustion chamber cause the engine to run on after the key is turned off.

DIFFERENTIAL: A geared assembly which allows the transmission of motion between drive axles, giving one axle the ability to turn faster than the other.

DIODE: An electrical device that will allow current to flow in one direction only.

DISC BRAKE: A hydraulic braking assembly consisting of a brake disc, or rotor, mounted on an axle, and a caliper assembly containing, usually two brake pads which are activated by hydraulic pressure. The pads are forced against the sides of the disc, creating friction which slows the vehicle.

DISTRIBUTOR: A mechanically driven device on an engine which is responsible for electrically firing the spark plug at a predetermined point of the piston stroke.

DOWEL PIN: A pin, inserted in mating holes in two different parts allowing those parts to maintain a fixed relationship.

DRUM BRAKE: A braking system which consists of two brake shoes and one or two wheel cylinders, mounted on a fixed backing plate, and a brake drum, mounted on an axle, which revolves around the assembly.

DWELL: The rate, measured in degrees of shaft rotation, at which an electrical circuit cycles on and off.

ELECTRONIC CONTROL UNIT (ECU): Ignition module, module, amplifier or igniter. See Module for definition.

ELECTRONIC IGNITION: A system in which the timing and firing of the spark plugs is controlled by an electronic control unit, usually called a module. These systems have no points or condenser.

END-PLAY: The measured amount of axial movement in a shaft.

ENGINE: A device that converts heat into mechanical energy.

EXHAUST MANIFOLD: A set of cast passages or pipes which conduct exhaust gases from the engine.

FEELER GAUGE: A blade, usually metal, or precisely predetermined thickness, used to measure the clearance between two parts.

FIRING ORDER: The order in which combustion occurs in the cylinders of an engine. Also the order in which spark is distributed to the plugs by the distributor.

FLOODING: The presence of too much fuel in the intake manifold and combustion chamber which prevents the air/fuel mixture from firing, thereby causing a no-start situation.

FLYWHEEL: A disc shaped part bolted to the rear end of the crankshaft. Around the outer perimeter is affixed the ring gear. The starter drive engages the ring gear, turning the flywheel, which rotates the crankshaft, imparting the initial starting motion to the engine.

FOOT POUND (ft. lbs. or sometimes, ft.lb.): The amount of energy or work needed to raise an item weighing one pound, a distance of one foot.

FUSE: A protective device in a circuit which prevents circuit overload by breaking the circuit when a specific amperage is present. The device is constructed around a strip or wire of a lower amperage rating than the circuit it is designed to protect. When an amperage higher than that stamped on the fuse is present in the circuit, the strip or wire melts, opening the circuit.

GEAR RATIO: The ratio between the number of teeth on meshing gears.

GENERATOR: A device which converts mechanical energy into electrical energy.

HEAT RANGE: The measure of a spark plug's ability to dissipate heat from its firing end. The higher the heat range, the hotter the plug fires.

HUB: The center part of a wheel or gear.

HYDROCARBON (HC): Any chemical compound made up of hydrogen and carbon. A major pollutant formed by the engine as a byproduct of combustion.

HYDROMETER: An instrument used to measure the specific gravity of a solution.

INCH POUND (inch lbs.; sometimes in.lb. or in. lbs.): One twelfth of a foot pound.

INDUCTION: A means of transferring electrical energy in the form of a magnetic field. Principle used in the ignition coil to increase voltage.

INJECTOR: A device which receives metered fuel under relatively low pressure and is activated to inject the fuel into the engine under relatively high pressure at a predetermined time.

INPUT SHAFT: The shaft to which torque is applied, usually carrying the driving gear or gears.

INTAKE MANIFOLD: A casting of passages or pipes used to conduct air or a fuel/air mixture to the cylinders.

JOURNAL: The bearing surface within which a shaft operates.

KEY: A small block usually fitted in a notch between a shaft and a hub to prevent slippage of the two parts.

MANIFOLD: A casting of passages or set of pipes which connect the cylinders to an inlet or outlet source.

MANIFOLD VACUUM: Low pressure in an engine intake manifold formed just below the throttle plates. Manifold vacuum is highest at idle and drops under acceleration.

MASTER CYLINDER: The primary fluid pressurizing device in a hydraulic system. In automotive use, it is found in brake and hydraulic clutch systems and is pedal activated, either directly or, in a power brake system, through the power booster.

MODULE: Electronic control unit, amplifier or igniter of solid state or integrated design which controls the current flow in the ignition primary circuit based on input from the pick-up coil. When the module opens the primary circuit, high secondary voltage is induced in the coil.

NEEDLE BEARING: A bearing which consists of a number (usually a large number) of long, thin rollers.

OHM: (Ω) The unit used to measure the resistance of conductor-to-electrical flow. One ohm is the amount of resistance that limits current flow to one ampere in a circuit with one volt of pressure.

OHMMETER: An instrument used for measuring the resistance, in ohms, in an electrical circuit.

OUTPUT SHAFT: The shaft which transmits torque from a device, such as a transmission.

OVERDRIVE: A gear assembly which produces more shaft revolutions than that transmitted to it.

OVERHEAD CAMSHAFT (OHC): An engine configuration in which the camshaft is mounted on top of the cylinder head and operates the valve either directly or by means of rocker arms.

OVERHEAD VALVE (OHV): An engine configuration in which all of the valves are located in the cylinder head and the camshaft is located in the cylinder block. The camshaft operates the valves via lifters and pushrods.

OXIDES OF NITROGEN (NOx): Chemical compounds of nitrogen produced as a byproduct of combustion. They combine with hydrocarbons to produce smog.

OXYGEN SENSOR: Use with the feedback system to sense the presence of oxygen in the exhaust gas and signal the computer which can reference the voltage signal to an air/fuel ratio.

PINION: The smaller of two meshing gears.

PISTON RING: An open-ended ring with fits into a groove on the outer diameter of the piston. Its chief function is to form a seal between the piston and cylinder wall. Most automotive pistons have three rings: two for compression sealing; one for oil sealing.

PRELOAD: A predetermined load placed on a bearing during assembly or by adjustment.

PRIMARY CIRCUIT: the low voltage side of the ignition system which consists of the ignition switch, ballast resistor or resistance wire, bypass, coil, electronic control unit and pick-up coil as well as the connecting wires and harnesses.

PRESS FIT: The mating of two parts under pressure, due to the inner diameter of one being smaller than the outer diameter of the other, or vice versa; an interference fit.

RACE: The surface on the inner or outer ring of a bearing on which the balls, needles or rollers move.

REGULATOR: A device which maintains the amperage and/or voltage levels of a circuit at predetermined values.

RELAY: A switch which automatically opens and/or closes a circuit.

RESISTANCE: The opposition to the flow of current through a circuit or electrical device, and is measured in ohms. Resistance is equal to the voltage divided by the amperage.

RESISTOR: A device, usually made of wire, which offers a preset amount of resistance in an electrical circuit.

RING GEAR: The name given to a ring-shaped gear attached to a differential case, or affixed to a flywheel or as part of a planetary gear set.

ROLLER BEARING: A bearing made up of hardened inner and outer races between which hardened steel rollers move.

ROTOR: 1. The disc-shaped part of a disc brake assembly, upon which the brake pads bear; also called, brake disc. 2. The device mounted atop the distributor shaft, which passes current to the distributor cap tower contacts.

SECONDARY CIRCUIT: The high voltage side of the ignition system, usually above 20,000 volts. The secondary includes the ignition coil, coil wire, distributor cap and rotor, spark plug wires and spark plugs.

SENDING UNIT: A mechanical, electrical, hydraulic or electro-magnetic device which transmits information to a gauge.

SENSOR: Any device designed to measure engine operating conditions or ambient pressures and temperatures. Usually electronic in nature and designed to send a voltage signal to an on-board computer, some sensors may operate as a simple on/off switch or they may provide a variable voltage signal (like a potentiometer) as conditions or measured parameters change.

SHIM: Spacers of precise, predetermined thickness used between parts to establish a proper working relationship.

SLAVE CYLINDER: In automotive use, a device in the hydraulic clutch system which is activated by hydraulic force, disengaging the clutch.

SOLENOID: A coil used to produce a magnetic field, the effect of which is to produce work.

SPARK PLUG: A device screwed into the combustion chamber of a spark ignition engine. The basic construction is a conductive core inside of a ceramic insulator, mounted in an outer conductive base. An electrical charge from the spark plug wire travels along the conductive core and jumps a preset air gap to a grounding point or points at the end of the conductive base. The resultant spark ignites the fuel/air mixture in the combustion chamber.

SPLINES: Ridges machined or cast onto the outer diameter of a shaft or inner diameter of a bore to enable parts to mate without rotation.

TACHOMETER: A device used to measure the rotary speed of an engine, shaft, gear, etc., usually in rotations per minute.

THERMOSTAT: A valve, located in the cooling system of an engine, which is closed when cold and opens gradually in response to engine heating, controlling the temperature of the coolant and rate of coolant flow.

TOP DEAD CENTER (TDC): The point at which the piston reaches the top of its travel on the compression stroke.

TORQUE: The twisting force applied to an object.

TORQUE CONVERTER: A turbine used to transmit power from a driving member to a driven member via hydraulic action, providing changes in drive ratio and torque. In automotive use, it links the driveplate at the rear of the engine to the automatic transmission.

TRANSDUCER: A device used to change a force into an electrical signal.

TRANSISTOR: A semi-conductor component which can be actuated by a small voltage to perform an electrical switching function.

TUNE-UP: A regular maintenance function, usually associated with the replacement and adjustment of parts and components in the electrical and fuel systems of a vehicle for the purpose of attaining optimum performance.

TURBOCHARGER: An exhaust driven pump which compresses intake air and forces it into the combustion chambers at higher than atmospheric pressures. The increased air pressure allows more fuel to be burned and results in increased horsepower being produced.

VACUUM ADVANCE: A device which advances the ignition timing in response to increased engine vacuum.

VACUUM GAUGE: An instrument used to measure the presence of vacuum in a chamber.

VALVE: A device which control the pressure, direction of flow or rate of flow of a liquid or gas.

VALVE CLEARANCE: The measured gap between the end of the valve stem and the rocker arm, cam lobe or follower that activates the valve.

VISCOSITY: The rating of a liquid's internal resistance to flow.

VOLTMETER: An instrument used for measuring electrical force in units called volts. Voltmeters are always connected parallel with the circuit being tested.

WHEEL CYLINDER: Found in the automotive drum brake assembly, it is a device, actuated by hydraulic pressure, which, through internal pistons, pushes the brake shoes outward against the drums.

MASTER INDEX